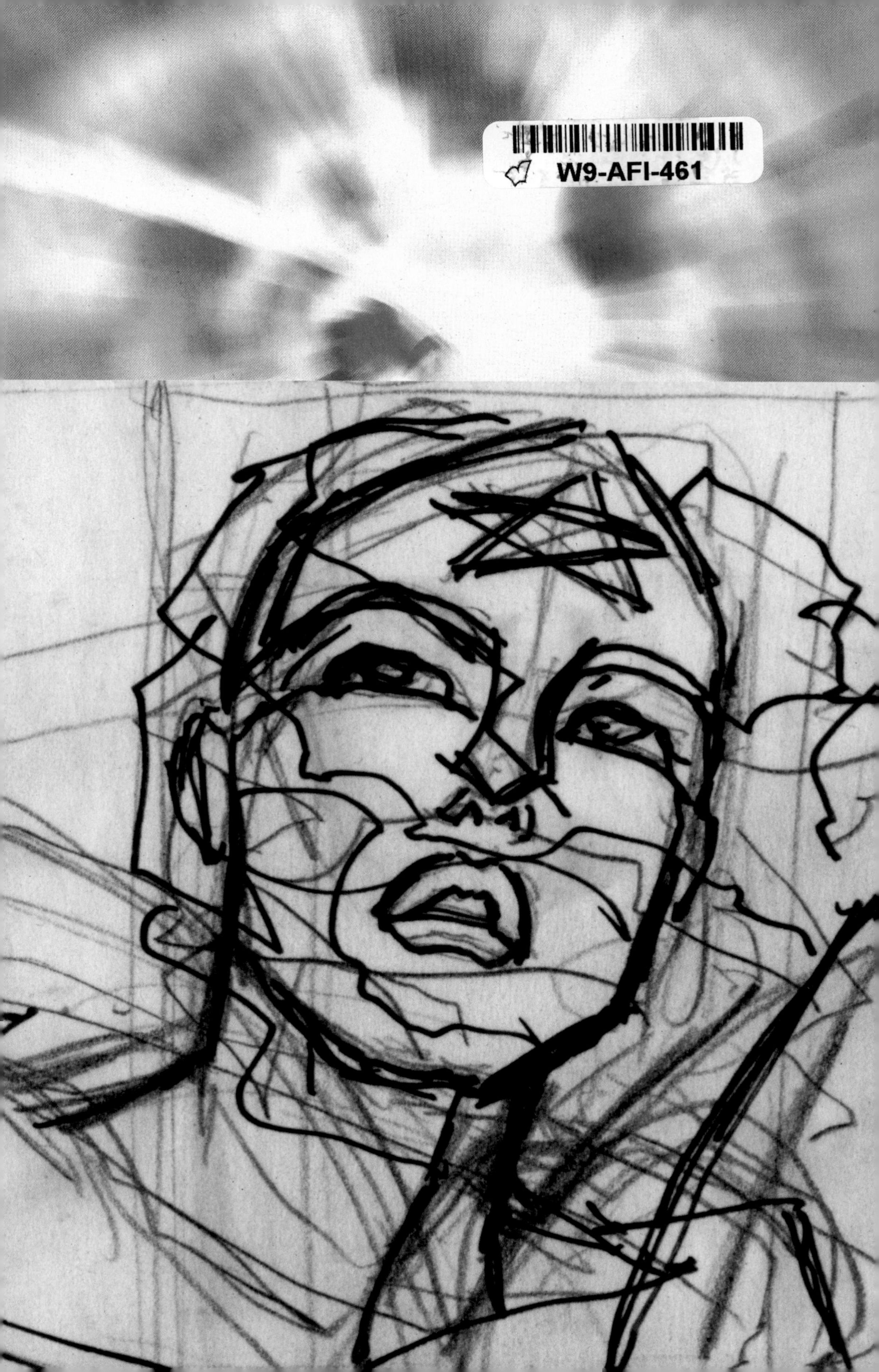

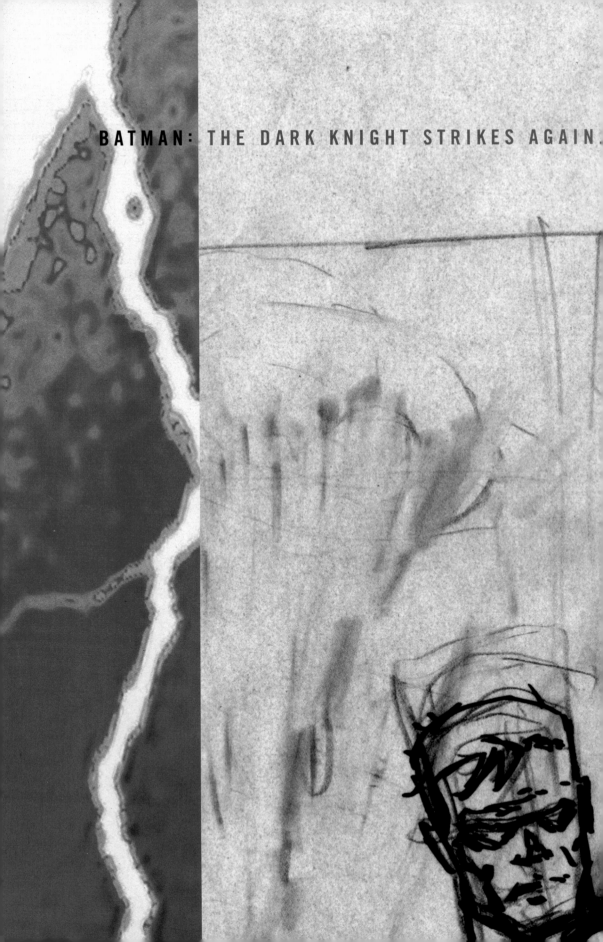

BATMAN: THE DARK KNIGHT STRIKES AGAIN.

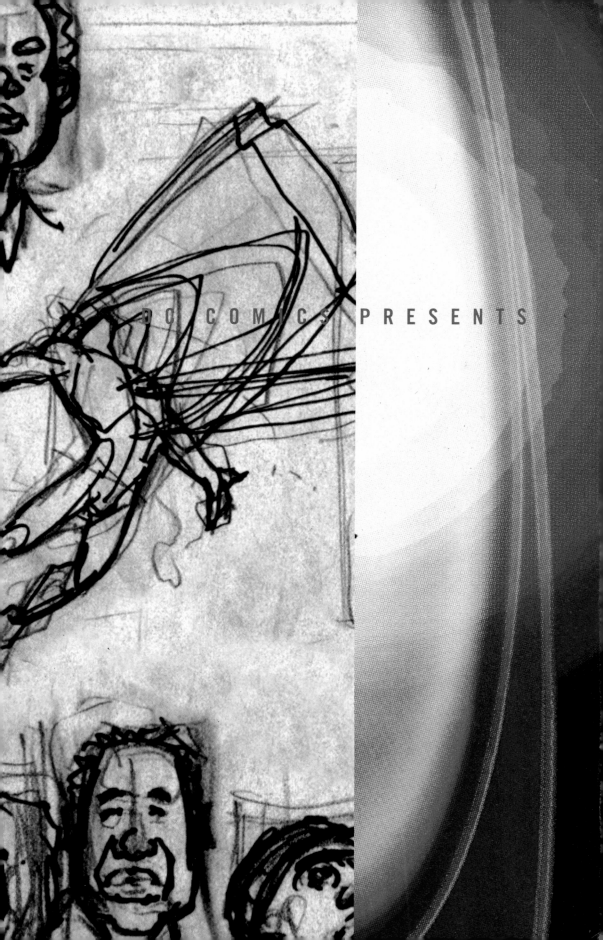

DC COMICS PRESENTS

FRANK MILLER · LYNN VARLEY

TODD KLEIN

Batman created by BOB KANE with BILL FINGER

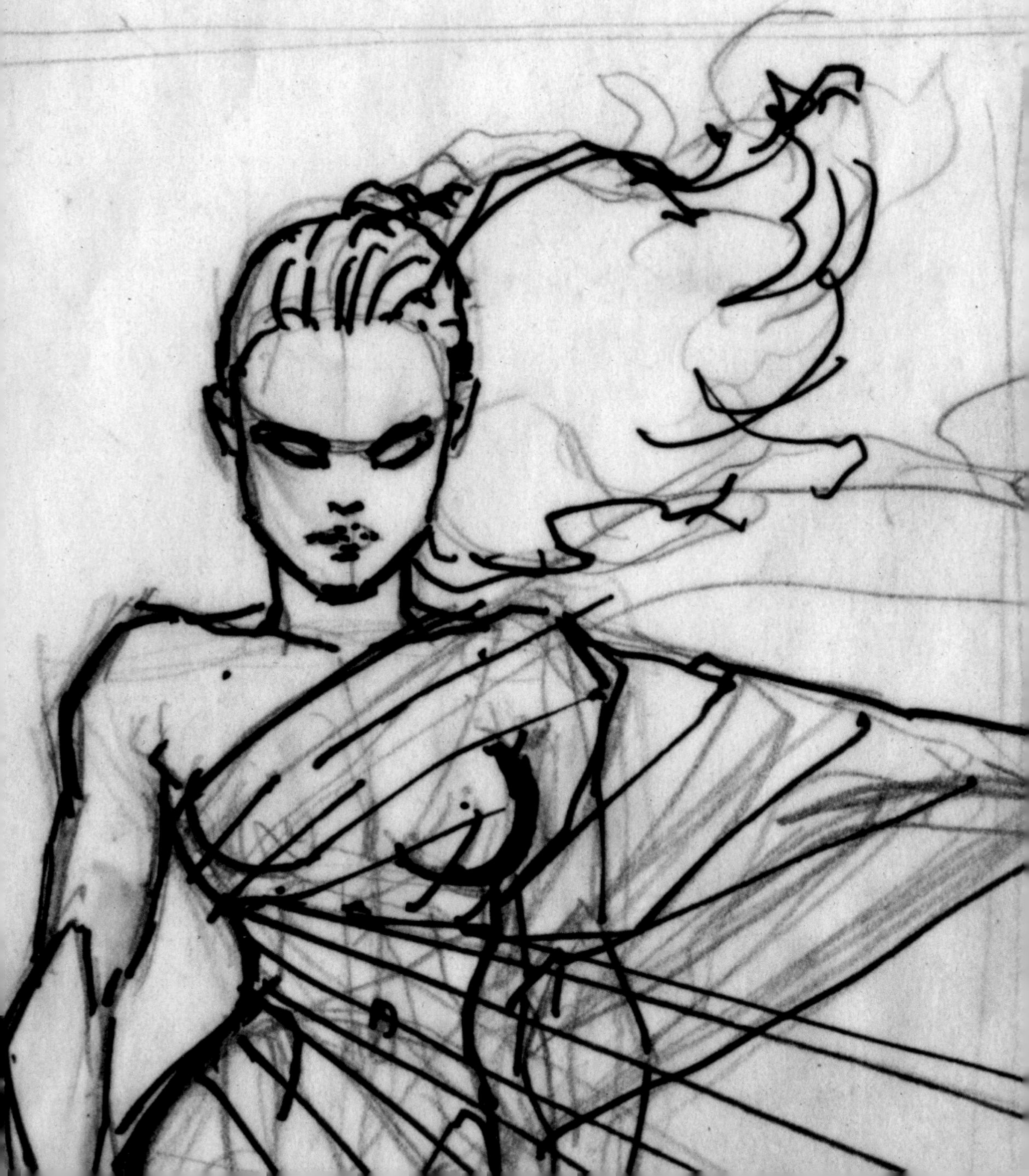

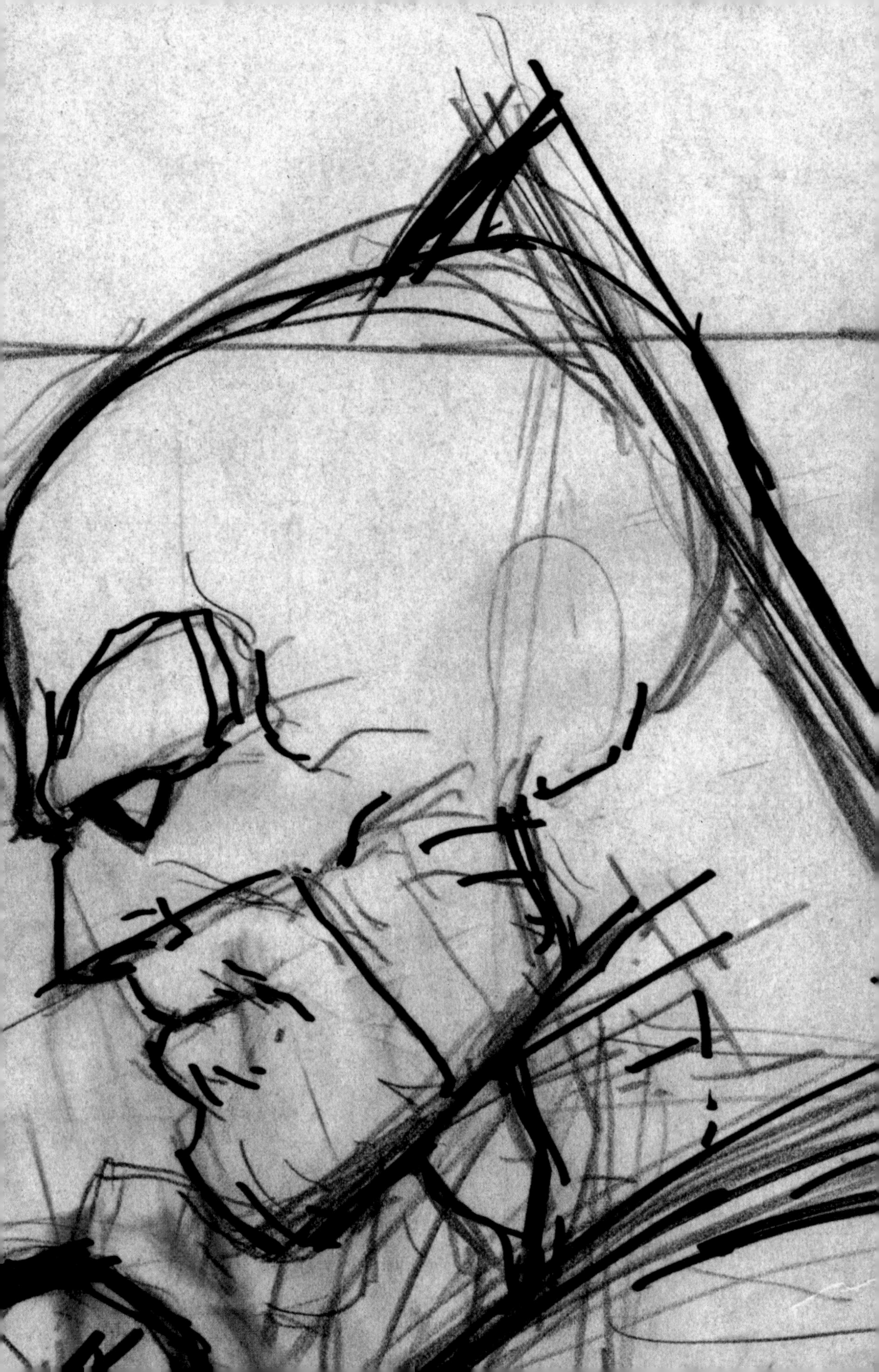

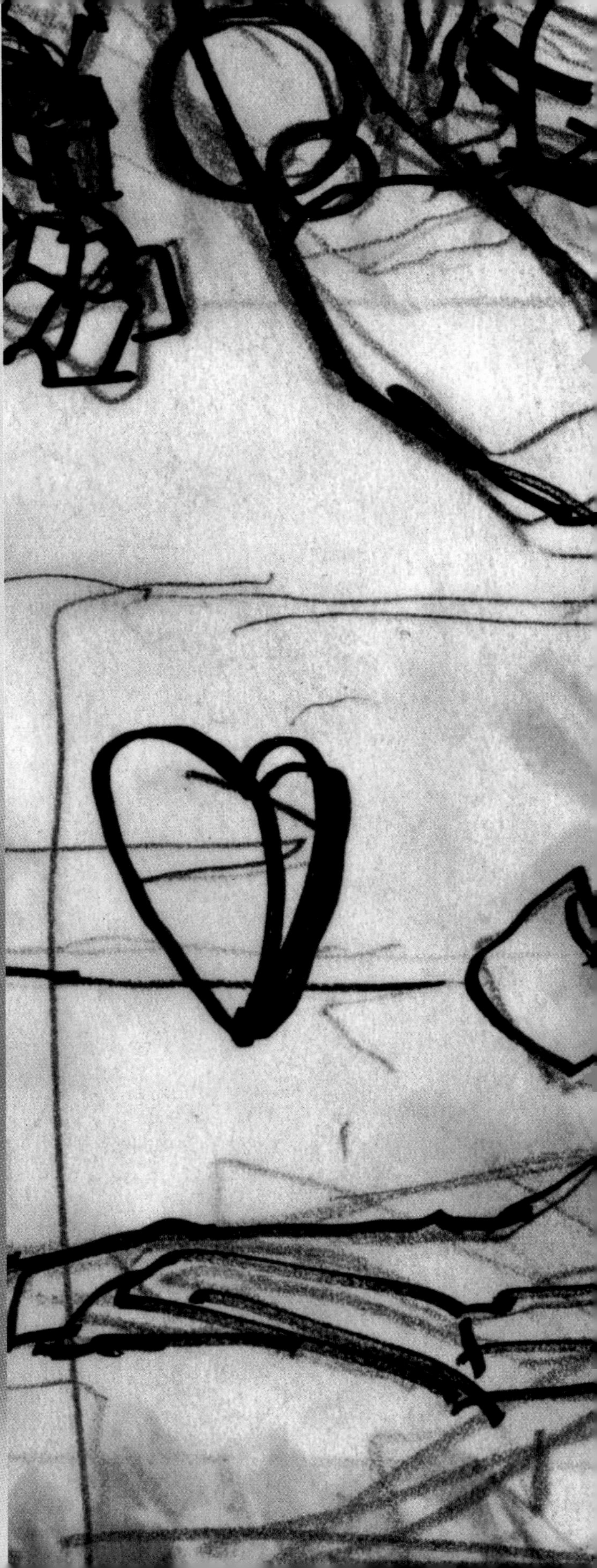

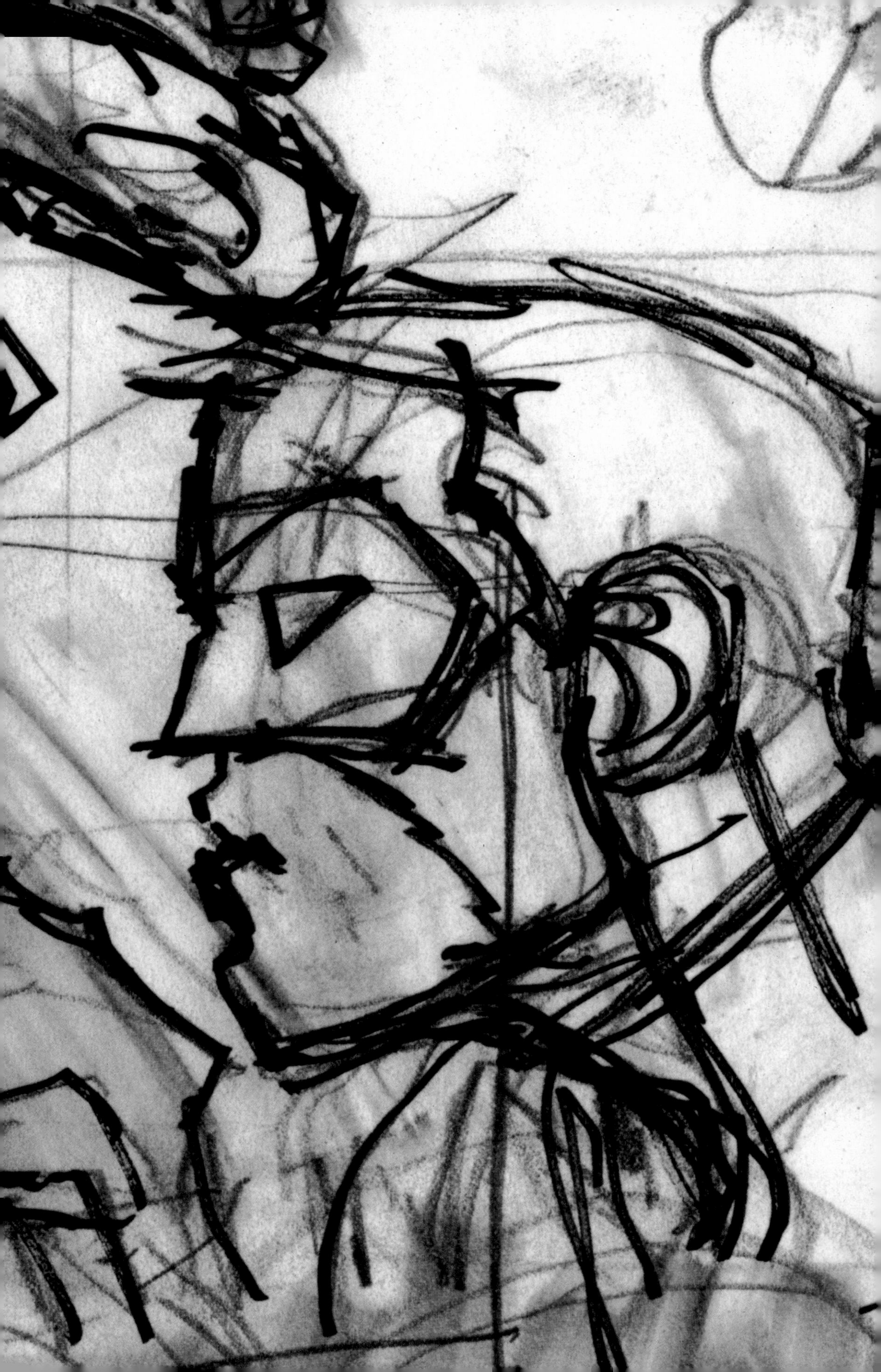

Cover illustration by Frank Miller & Lynn Varley.

BATMAN: THE DARK KNIGHT STRIKES AGAIN

Published by DC Comics. Cover, introduction and compilation Copyright © 2002 DC Comics.
Originally published in single magazine form as BATMAN: THE DARK KNIGHT STRIKES AGAIN 1-3.
Copyright © 2001, 2002 DC Comics. All Rights Reserved.
All characters, the distinctive likenesses thereof, and all related elements are trademarks of DC Comics.
The stories, characters and incidents featured in this publication are entirely fictional.
DC Comics does not read or accept unsolicited submissions of ideas, stories or artwork.

DC Comics 2900 W. Alameda Avenue, Burbank, CA 91505
Printed by Solisco Printers, Scott, QC, Canada. 1/8/16.
Ninth Printing.
ISBN: 978-1-5638-9929-4.

Library of Congress Cataloging-in-Publication Data.

Miller, Frank, 1957-
Batman : the dark knight strikes again / Frank Miller, Lynn Varley.
p. cm.
ISBN 978-1-5638-9929-4
"Originally published in single magazine form as Batman: The Dark Knight Strikes Again 1-3."
1. Graphic novels. I. Varley, Lynn. II. Title. III. Title: Dark Knight strikes again.
PN6728.B36M546 2012
741.5'973—dc23
2012038329

Special thanks to Kyle Baker, Lorenzo DiBonaventura, William Katz,
James Kochalka, Tony Millionaire, Jim Morrison,
Alex Sinclair, Jeff Smith, Paul Pope, Diana Schutz, Bill Sienkiewicz.

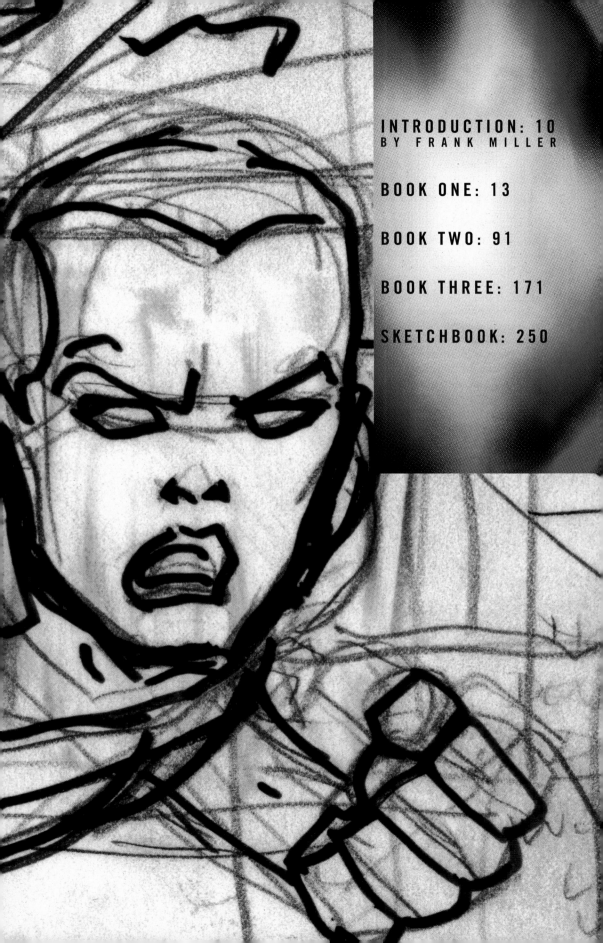

INTRODUCTION: 10
BY FRANK MILLER

BOOK ONE: 13

BOOK TWO: 91

BOOK THREE: 171

SKETCHBOOK: 250

TOP COP POPS

EXCLUSIVE

Vicky Vale

The Dish

You could've heard a pin drop. The kind that comes out of a hand grenade.

It was total social self-decapitation. Not to mention professional suicide. And at a funeral, no less.

It was at Bruce Wayne's funeral, an otherwise restrained affair, honoring Gotham City's most famous native son and the two lives he led, as bodacious billionaire businessman and burly, bad-guy-bashing Batman.

In case you were in another galaxy when it happened: The generationally-challenged Caped Crusader made with a comeback that was more splash than substance, only to drop stone dead from ticker shock when the feds closed in.

Or maybe they shot him. Who knows? They don't talk, not too often, those Fedsters, not these days. And if they do, they lie. Not to put too fine a point on it.

Whatever. The Masked Manhunter bought the farm. The Dark Knight croaked. Bruce Wayne was room temperature.

Somebody threw him a pricy funeral. And Jim Gordon made a flaming ass of himself.

It was quite the scene, even before Gordon discovered the joys of self-immolation. There was Clark Kent in the third row, looking like he hadn't slept in days. Selina Kyle, who used to turn 'em on and knock 'em dead - and I mean dead - as the Catwoman, in the first row, puffy, medicated, barely vertical. And there at the lectern was Jim Gordon, giving his reputation the maximum flush.

His reputation. James Gordon. Career cop. Carrying some old baggage, some sketchy business, from his early days in Chicago, sure. But a good cop. More than that, as it turned out. Jim Gordon was a goddamn hero.

He cleaned up Gotham City for a good long time. He went right at the old mafioso stooges who used to run our town. Busted them every chance he got. The Roman, he's still sitting in his cell, cursing Jim Gordon.

Lord only knows how crazy the Cowled Curmudgeon might've gotten if Gordon hadn't known how to play him. Old Wayne had a temper. He wasn't exactly what You'd call a bucket of mental health.

The man dressed up like a rodent, for goodness sake.

So there was Gordon, clearing his throat, looking over the audience. Glaring. We half-expected him to do the Miranda on the bunch of us.

"We murdered him," he growled. "We murdered Bruce Wayne, damn our souls to hell."

Looks shot across the room like thunderbolts. Over on the right side of the audience, there was Police Commissioner Ellen Yindel, who'd taken over Gordon's thankless job. She looked like she was working on swallowing a watermelon whole. For all their differences, she loves Jim Gordon. He was killing her, losing it like this.

And maybe he would've slowed down his pace a bit, Gordon might've, if it Hadn't been for Selina Kyle. Was she ever full of piss and vinegar. "Say it," she hissed, all of a sudden reminding us who Eartha Kitt was impersonating, way back when.

"Say it. Say it all," said Selina. Said Catwoman.

Yeah. Back in the old days, they called her Catwoman. And you gave that little cougar her propers, you did.

"SAY IT!", she hissed, Selina did. And it was a hiss that would've made Eartha proud, angry as it was. The old

See **Vale** Page 4

Vale

from Page 1

bat was positively feral. Hot stuff, baby.

You could've heard a pin drop.

And say it, Gordon did.

"We murdered Bruce Wayne. It was us. Whoever pulled the trigger, that doesn't matter. Whoever that killer was, he was just working for us.

"We couldn't live with a giant in our midst. So we murdered him."

Mayor Giordano looked like he was going to vapor-lock. Kent, like he was going to vomit.

Jimmy Olsen leaned forward, trembling with that scary fury of his, all of a sudden red-eyed.

Like he always does when anybody brings up the Tights.

"All the rest of the heroes spared us the trouble," sneered Gordon. "They went away. They knew we couldn't stand the sight of them, looming over us, saving our lives all over the place but who the hell cares about that, huh? They made us feel small.

"But at least the rest of them had the good manners to go away and let us forget about them. And so did Bruce Wayne. For ten years. Ten years we spent turning smaller and meaner.

"I was sitting across the table from my friend when he turned back into Batman. Not that he pulled the tights back on or anything. No. It was all in the jaw, that big damn jaw of his, the way he crooked it to the side. And the eyes. A saint's passion. An executioner's calm. I knew he was turning back into Batman before he did.

"And I knew we'd murder him.

"When Batman came back, we couldn't handle it. This time, he wouldn't let himself be deputized."

"Deputized." The career cop spat the word. Like it was obscene.

"He wouldn't apologize for what he was. So we murdered him."

Jim Gordon stopped talking. Took a breath. "Thank god," somebody nearby whispered. Wishful thinking, as it turned out.

In the audience, Perry White coughed. Loudly. Lois Lane squeezed his shoulder, as red-eyed as Olsen.

The Penguin burst into tears. Like he always does.

Gordon resumed. To just about everybody's utter horror.

"We murdered him for one very simple reason: there's no room in our wretched little world for a man who sees far and who sets wrongs right. We're chubby, coddled little things, content. Well-fed. Bruce Wayne - Batman - he wasn't so goddamn accommodating as we are. Bruce Wayne saw something wrong, he punched it out. He threw it through a window. He stomped its face in. He stopped it cold."

Right about then, District Attorney Robbins headed for the door. He'd heard enough. And he looked a little sick, to tell the truth.

And Gordon, he was just getting rolling. Really. It got worse.

"So we had to murder Bruce Wayne," ranted our former Commissioner of Police, our Hero Cop, our he-could've-been-on-the-ticket-as-a-vice-presidential-candidate-in-the-next-big-election-if-he-hadn't-lost-it-at-a-funeral Jim Gordon.

"We MURDERED him," he said, for what only felt like the billionth time.

Then he summed up everything he had to say about Batman in so few words it made me cry. And cry I did. Like a baby. So did everybody else.

"We're in trouble deep. We need him.

"We need Bruce Wayne."   ✳

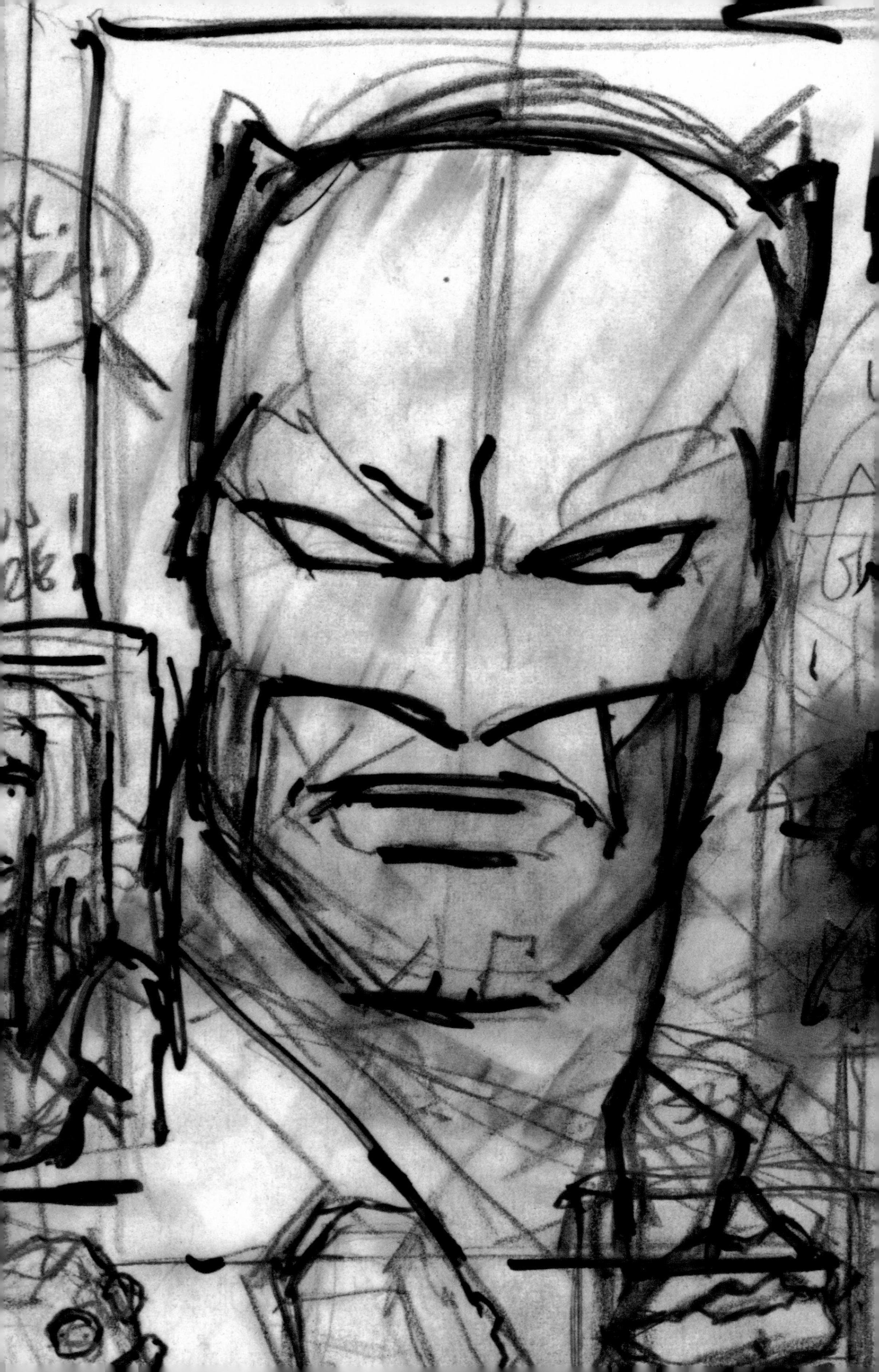

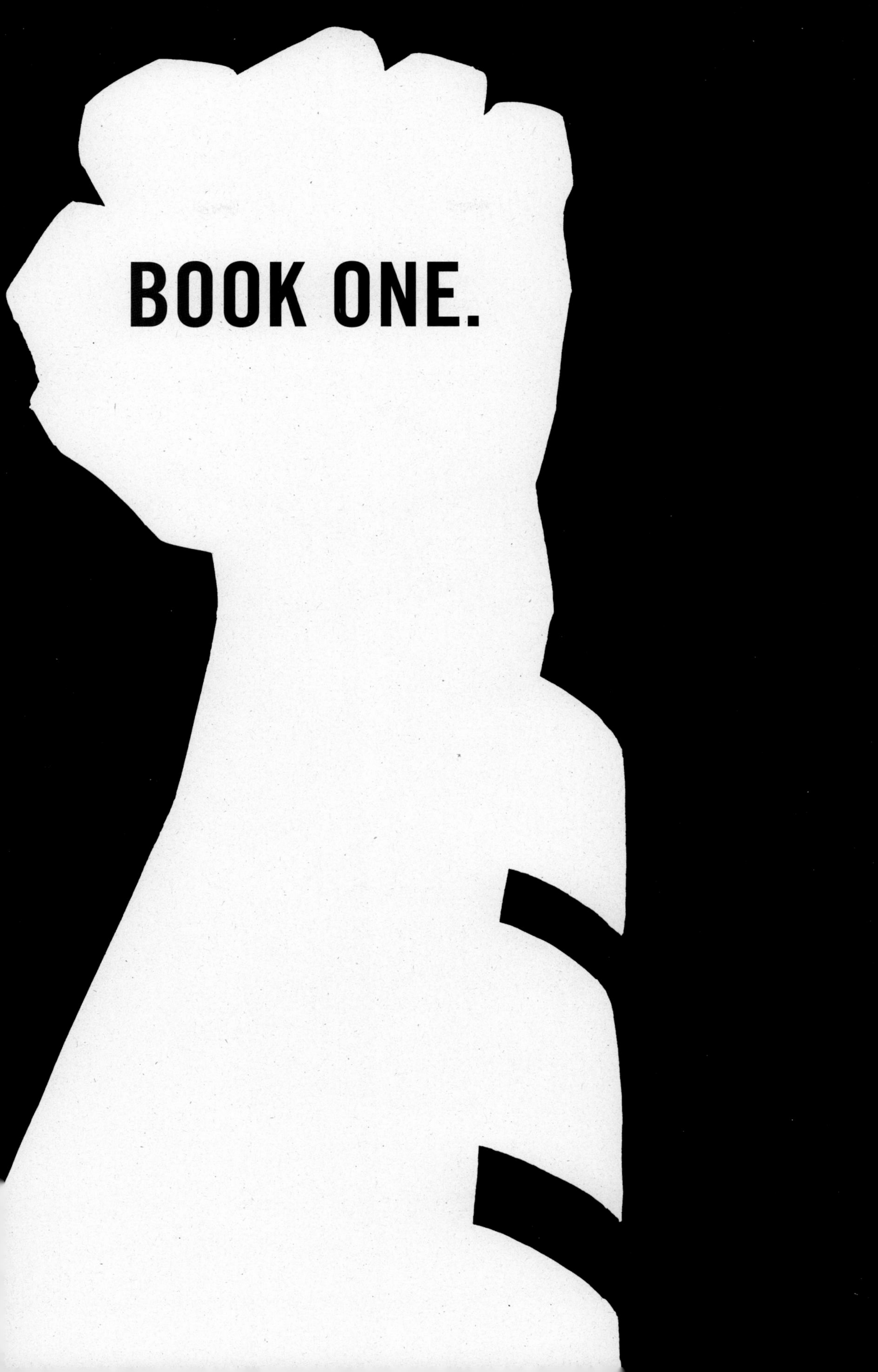
BOOK ONE.

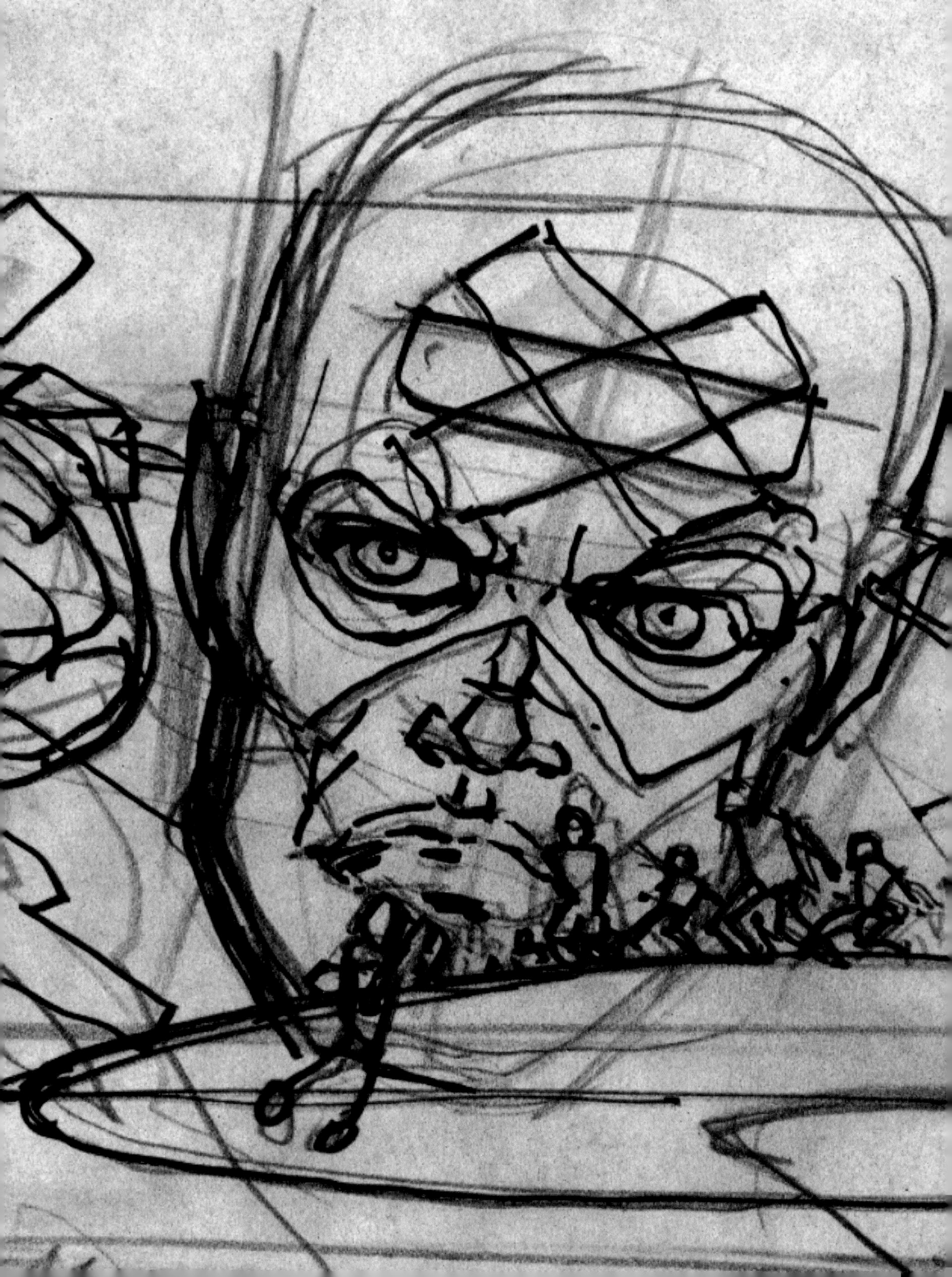

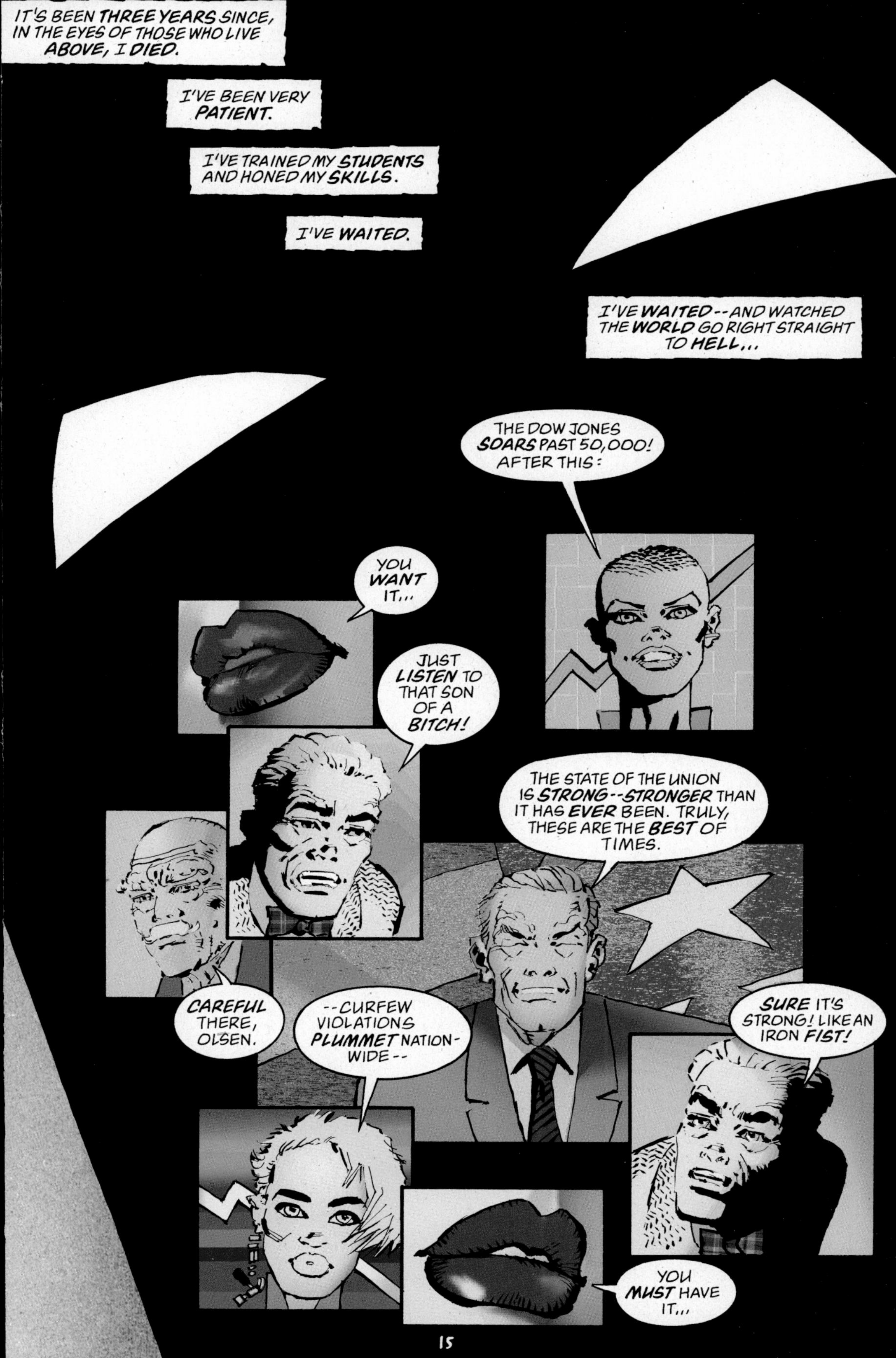
IT'S BEEN THREE YEARS SINCE, IN THE EYES OF THOSE WHO LIVE ABOVE, I DIED.
I'VE BEEN VERY PATIENT.
I'VE TRAINED MY STUDENTS AND HONED MY SKILLS.
I'VE WAITED.
I'VE WAITED--AND WATCHED THE WORLD GO RIGHT STRAIGHT TO HELL...
THE DOW JONES SOARS PAST 50,000! AFTER THIS:
YOU WANT IT...
JUST LISTEN TO THAT SON OF A BITCH!
THE STATE OF THE UNION IS STRONG--STRONGER THAN IT HAS EVER BEEN. TRULY, THESE ARE THE BEST OF TIMES.
CAREFUL THERE, OLSEN.
--CURFEW VIOLATIONS PLUMMET NATION-WIDE--
SURE IT'S STRONG! LIKE AN IRON FIST!
YOU MUST HAVE IT...

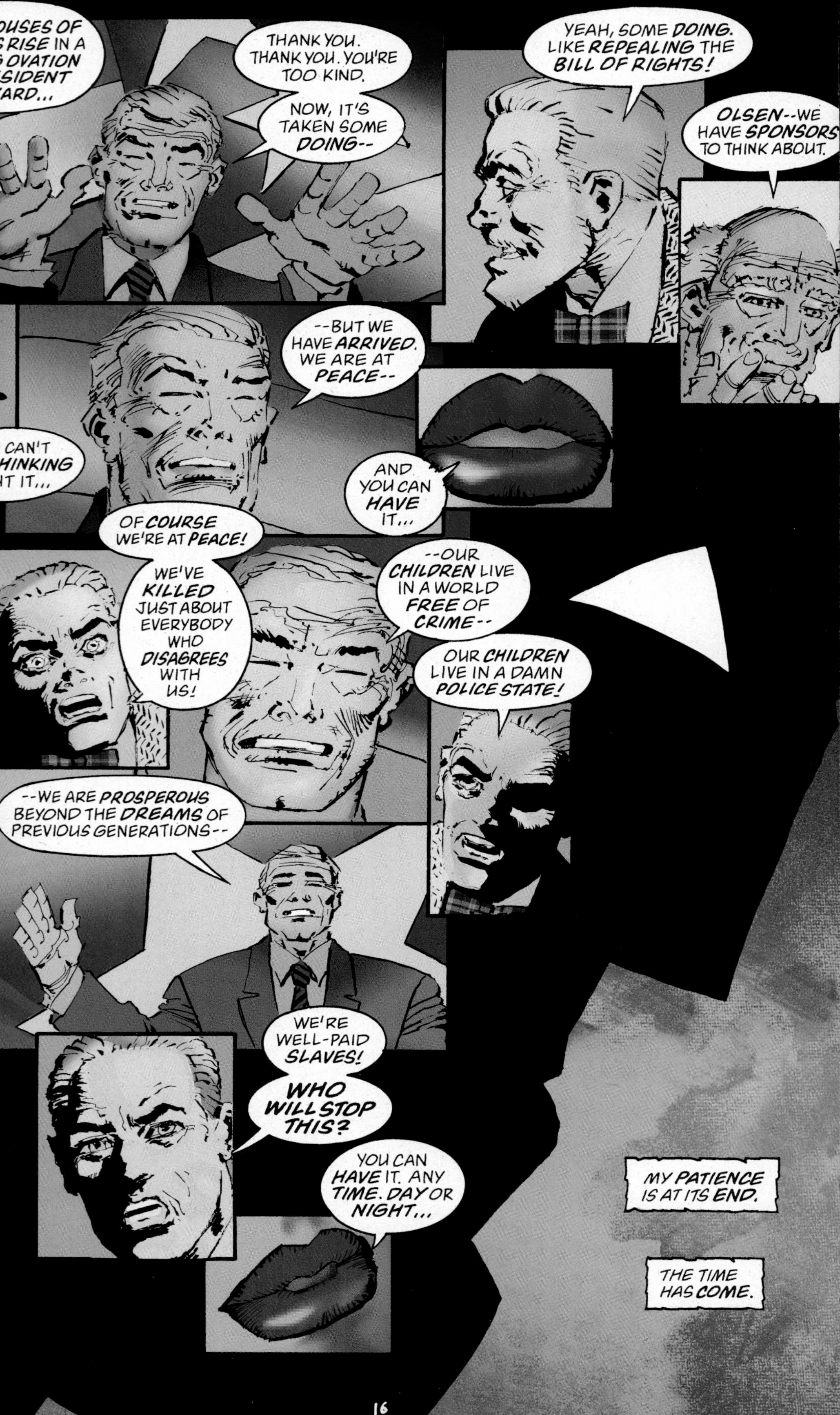

OUSES OF
S RISE IN A
G OVATION
SIDENT
ARD...
THANK YOU. THANK YOU. YOU'RE TOO KIND.
NOW, IT'S TAKEN SOME DOING--
YEAH, SOME DOING. LIKE REPEALING THE BILL OF RIGHTS!
OLSEN--WE HAVE SPONSORS TO THINK ABOUT.
--BUT WE HAVE ARRIVED. WE ARE AT PEACE--
CAN'T
HINKING
HT IT...
AND YOU CAN HAVE IT...
OF COURSE WE'RE AT PEACE!
WE'VE KILLED JUST ABOUT EVERYBODY WHO DISAGREES WITH US!
--OUR CHILDREN LIVE IN A WORLD FREE OF CRIME--
OUR CHILDREN LIVE IN A DAMN POLICE STATE!
--WE ARE PROSPEROUS BEYOND THE DREAMS OF PREVIOUS GENERATIONS--
WE'RE WELL-PAID SLAVES!
WHO WILL STOP THIS?
YOU CAN HAVE IT. ANY TIME. DAY OR NIGHT...
MY PATIENCE IS AT ITS END.
THE TIME HAS COME.

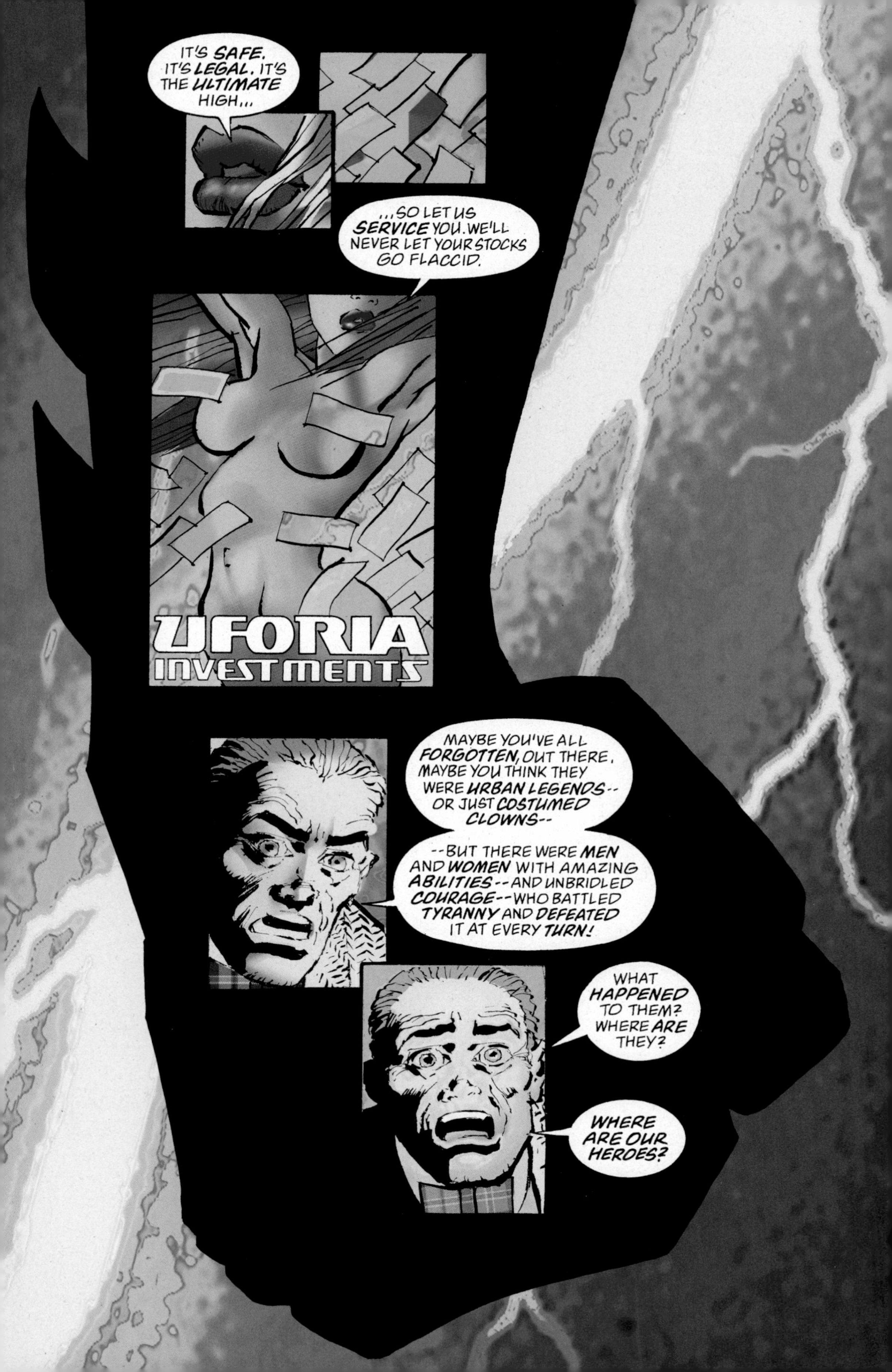
IT'S SAFE. IT'S LEGAL. IT'S THE ULTIMATE HIGH...
...SO LET US SERVICE YOU. WE'LL NEVER LET YOUR STOCKS GO FLACCID.
UFORIA INVESTMENTS
MAYBE YOU'VE ALL FORGOTTEN, OUT THERE. MAYBE YOU THINK THEY WERE URBAN LEGENDS-- OR JUST COSTUMED CLOWNS--
--BUT THERE WERE MEN AND WOMEN WITH AMAZING ABILITIES--AND UNBRIDLED COURAGE--WHO BATTLED TYRANNY AND DEFEATED IT AT EVERY TURN!
WHAT HAPPENED TO THEM? WHERE ARE THEY?
WHERE ARE OUR HEROES?

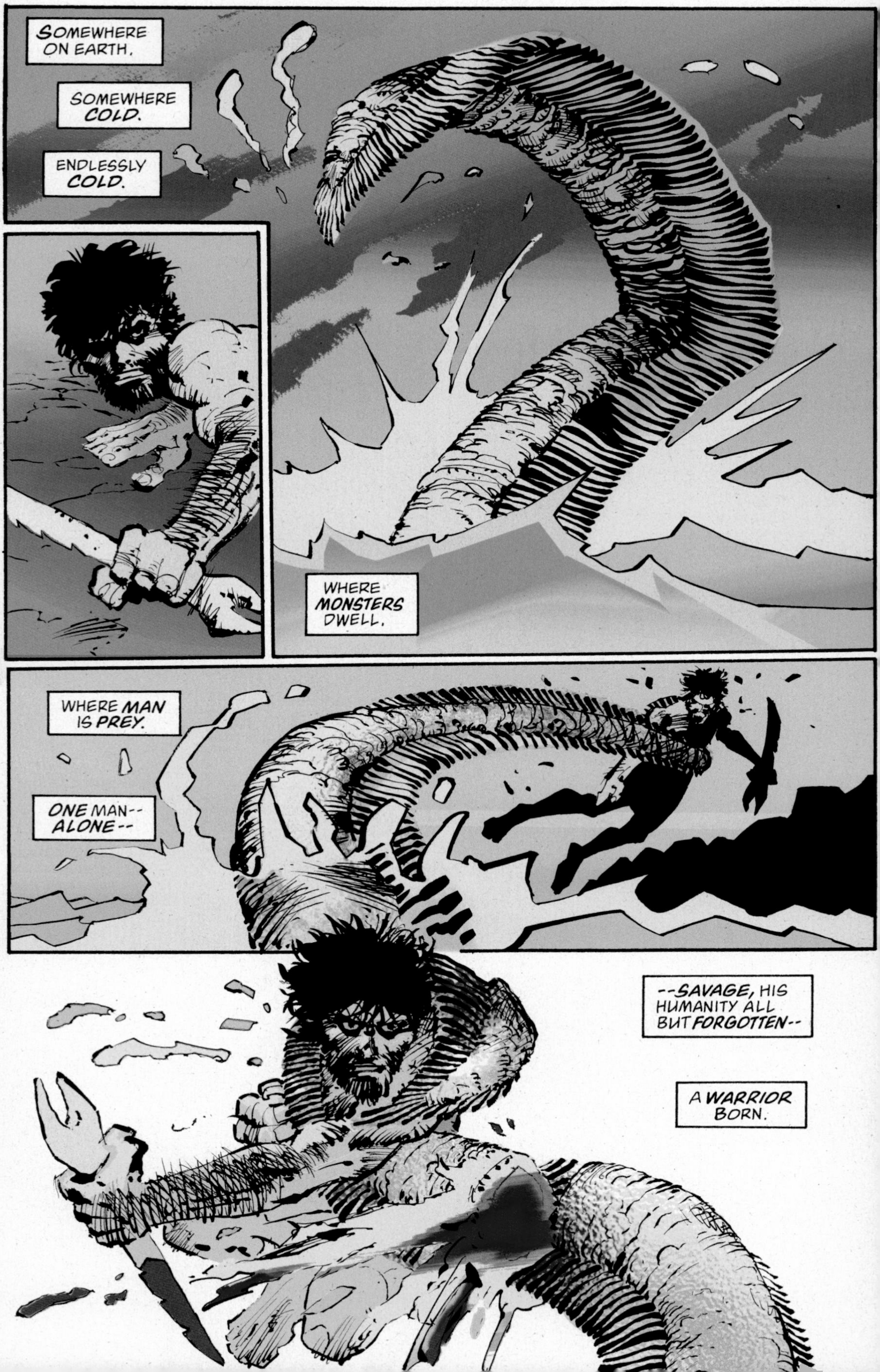
SOMEWHERE ON EARTH.
SOMEWHERE COLD.
ENDLESSLY COLD.
WHERE MONSTERS DWELL.
WHERE MAN IS PREY.
ONE MAN-- ALONE--
--SAVAGE, HIS HUMANITY ALL BUT FORGOTTEN--
A WARRIOR BORN.

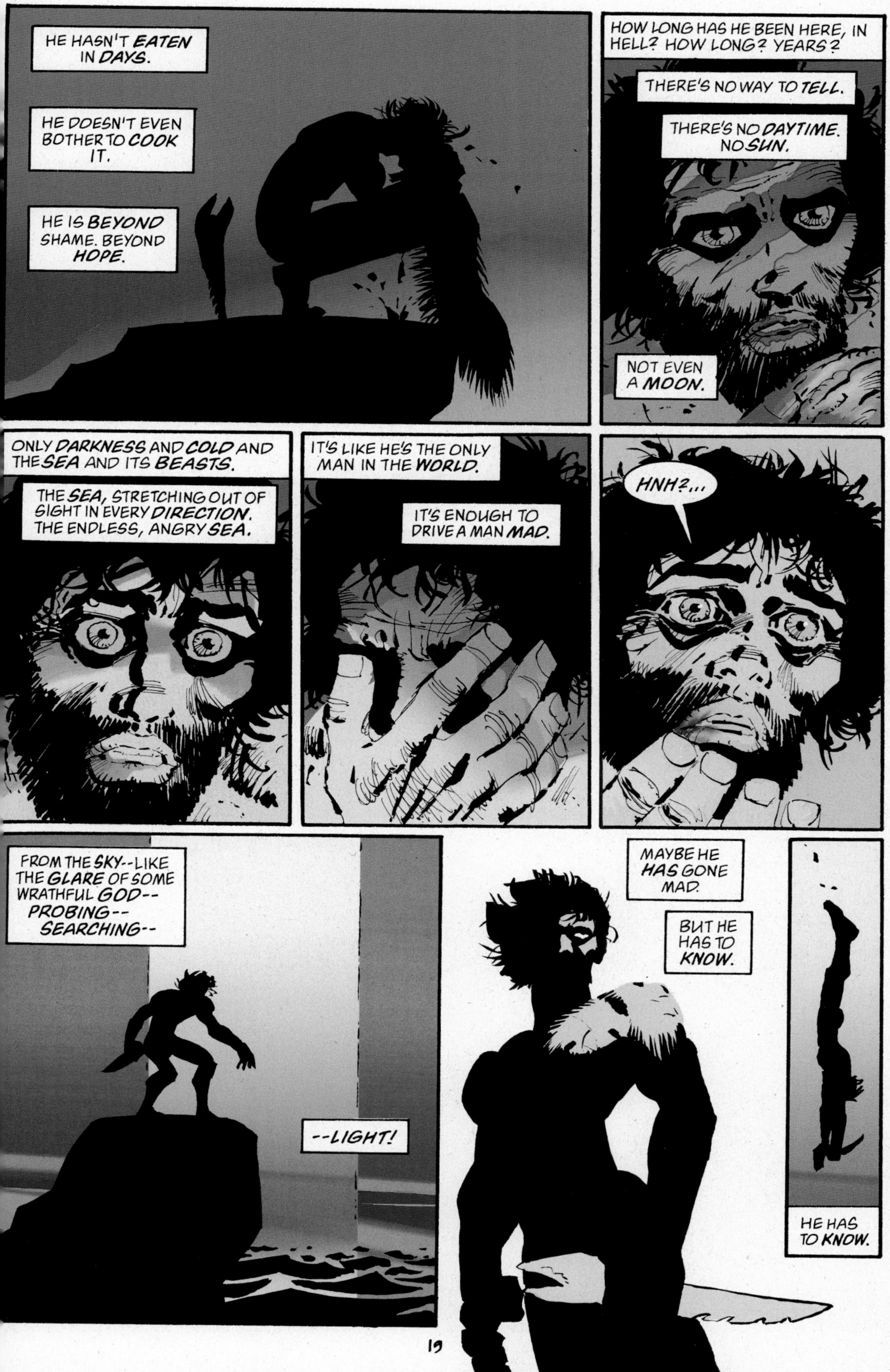
HE HASN'T EATEN IN DAYS.
HE DOESN'T EVEN BOTHER TO COOK IT.
HE IS BEYOND SHAME. BEYOND HOPE.
HOW LONG HAS HE BEEN HERE, IN HELL? HOW LONG? YEARS?
THERE'S NO WAY TO TELL.
THERE'S NO DAYTIME. NO SUN.
NOT EVEN A MOON.
ONLY DARKNESS AND COLD AND THE SEA AND ITS BEASTS.
THE SEA, STRETCHING OUT OF SIGHT IN EVERY DIRECTION. THE ENDLESS, ANGRY SEA.
IT'S LIKE HE'S THE ONLY MAN IN THE WORLD.
IT'S ENOUGH TO DRIVE A MAN MAD.
HNH?...
FROM THE SKY--LIKE THE GLARE OF SOME WRATHFUL GOD-- PROBING-- SEARCHING--
--LIGHT!
MAYBE HE HAS GONE MAD.
BUT HE HAS TO KNOW.
HE HAS TO KNOW.

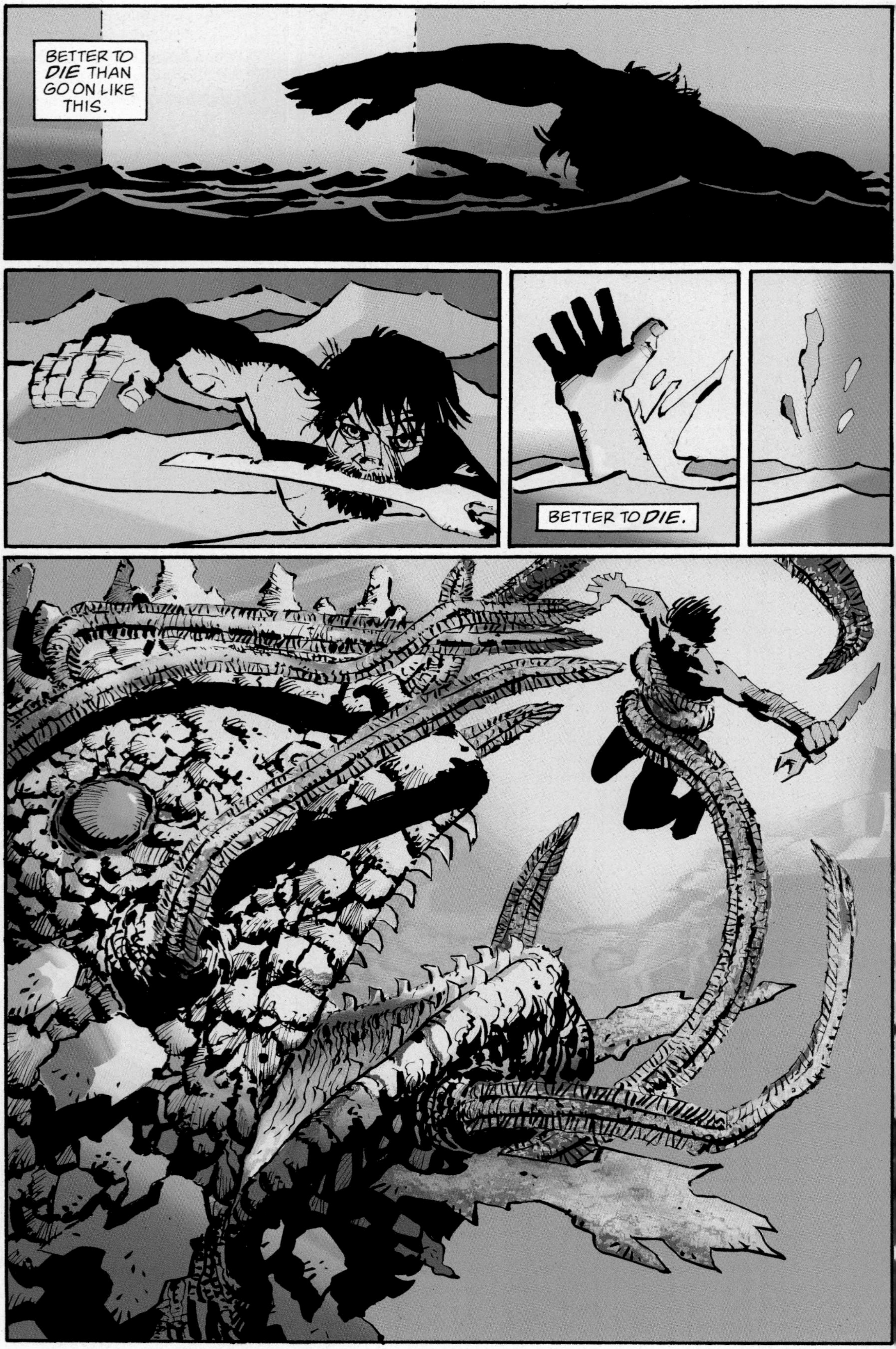
BETTER TO DIE THAN GO ON LIKE THIS.
BETTER TO DIE.

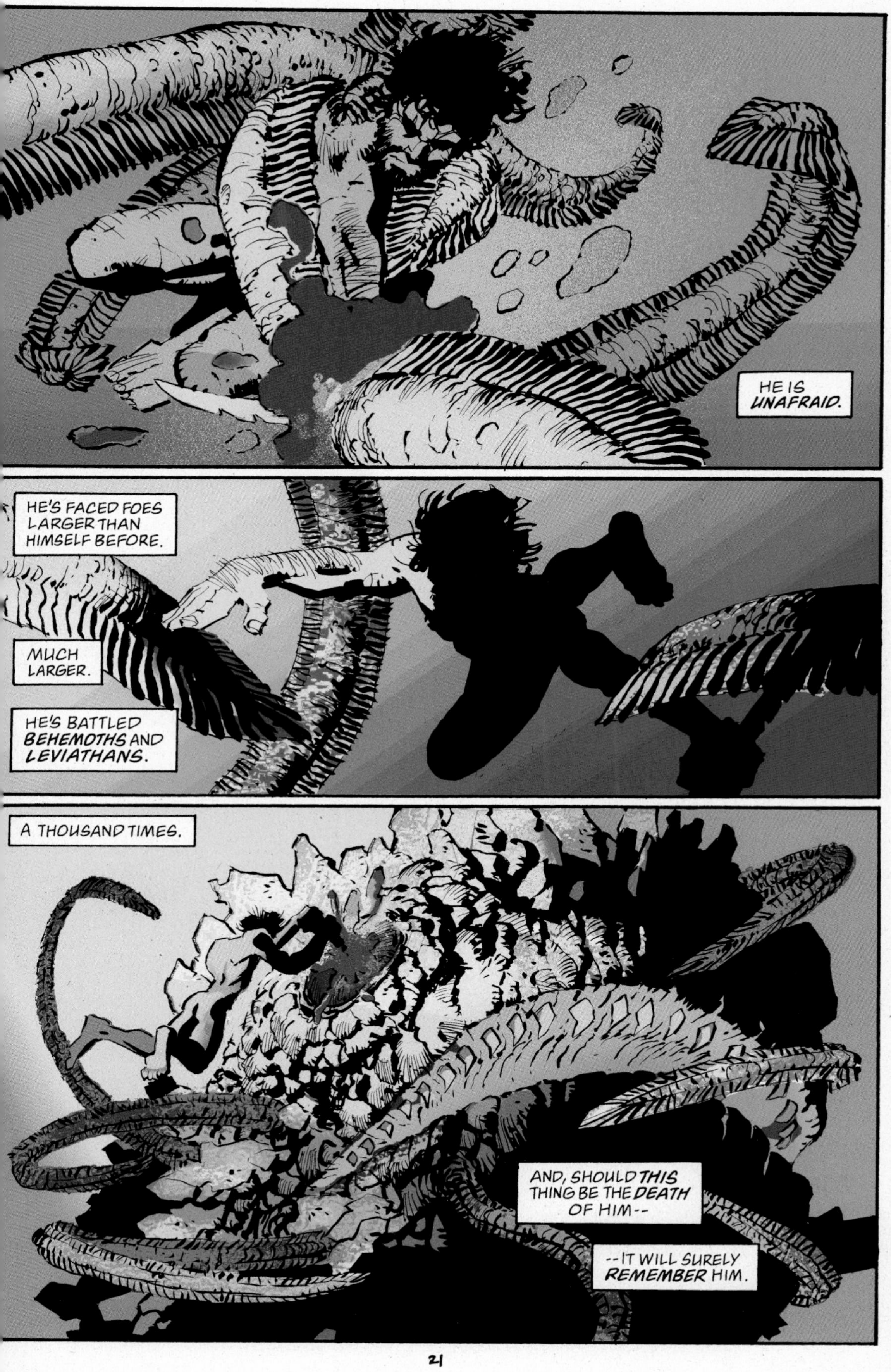
HE IS *UNAFRAID*.
HE'S FACED FOES LARGER THAN HIMSELF BEFORE.
MUCH LARGER.
HE'S BATTLED ***BEHEMOTHS*** AND ***LEVIATHANS***.
A THOUSAND TIMES.
AND, SHOULD *THIS* THING BE THE *DEATH* OF HIM--
--IT WILL SURELY *REMEMBER* HIM.

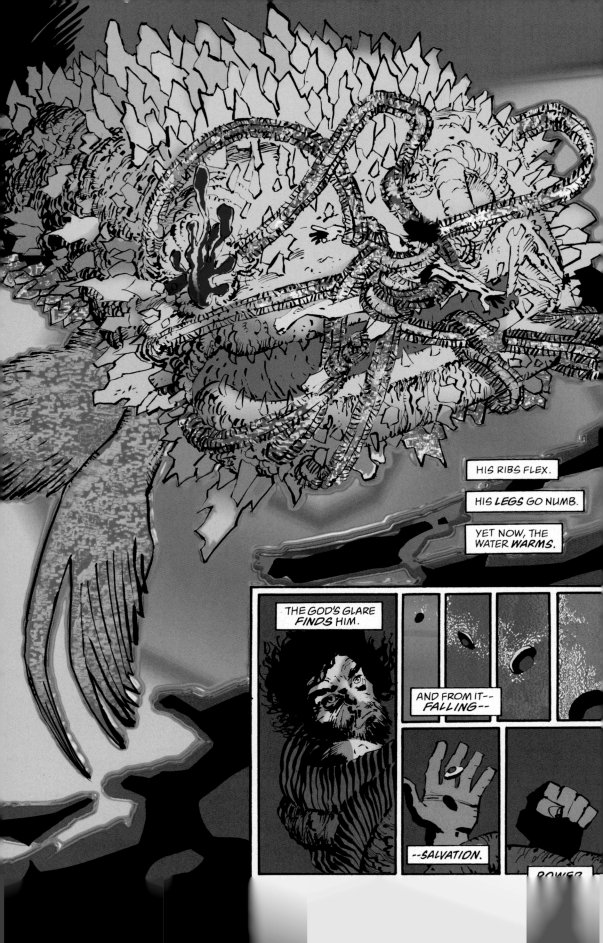

HIS RIBS FLEX.

HIS *LEGS* GO NUMB.

YET NOW, THE WATER *WARMS.*

THE GOD'S GLARE *FINDS* HIM.

AND FROM IT-- *FALLING*--

--SALVATION.

POWER

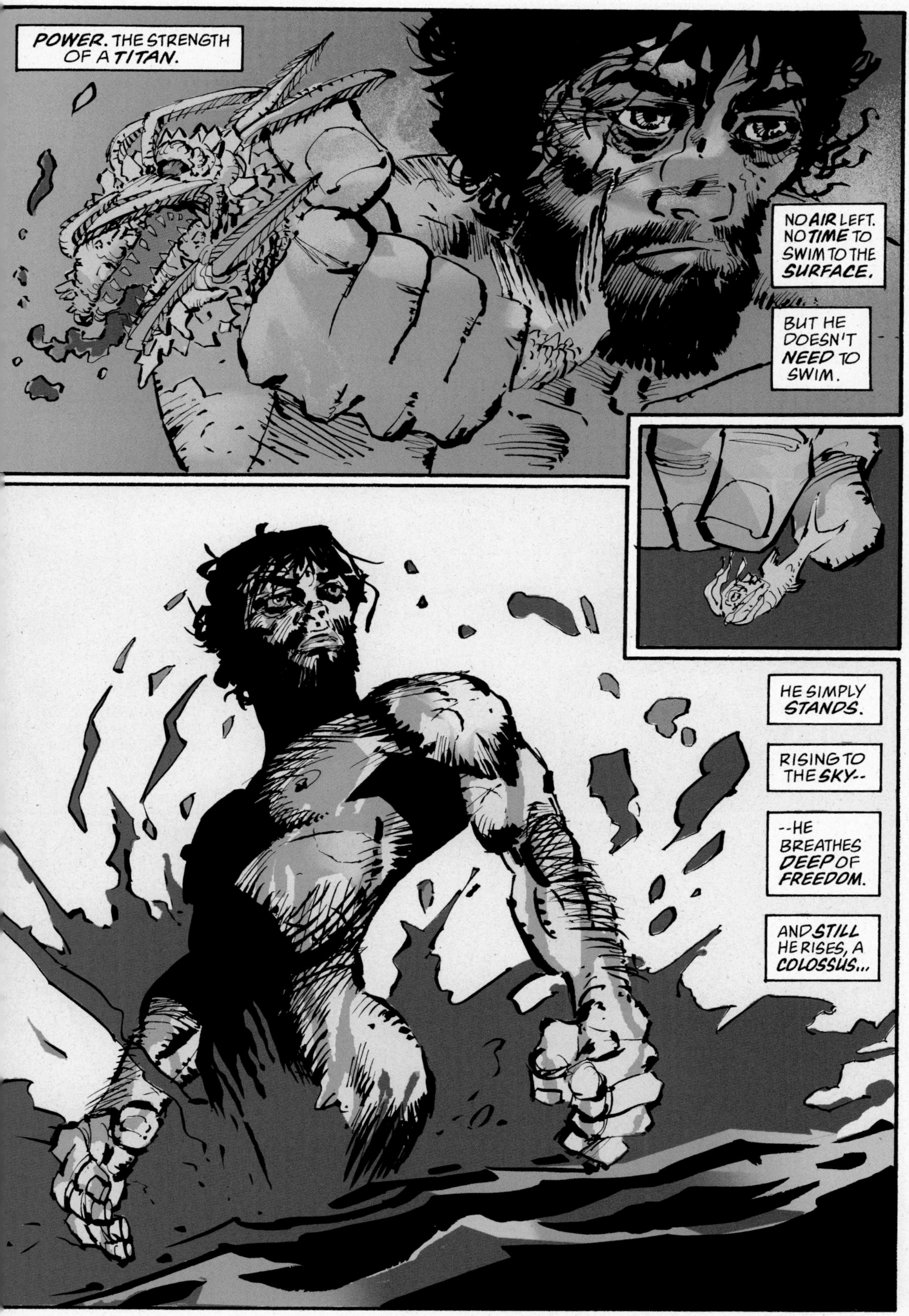
POWER. THE STRENGTH OF A TITAN.
NO AIR LEFT. NO TIME TO SWIM TO THE SURFACE.
BUT HE DOESN'T NEED TO SWIM.
HE SIMPLY STANDS.
RISING TO THE SKY--
--HE BREATHES DEEP OF FREEDOM.
AND STILL HE RISES, A COLOSSUS...

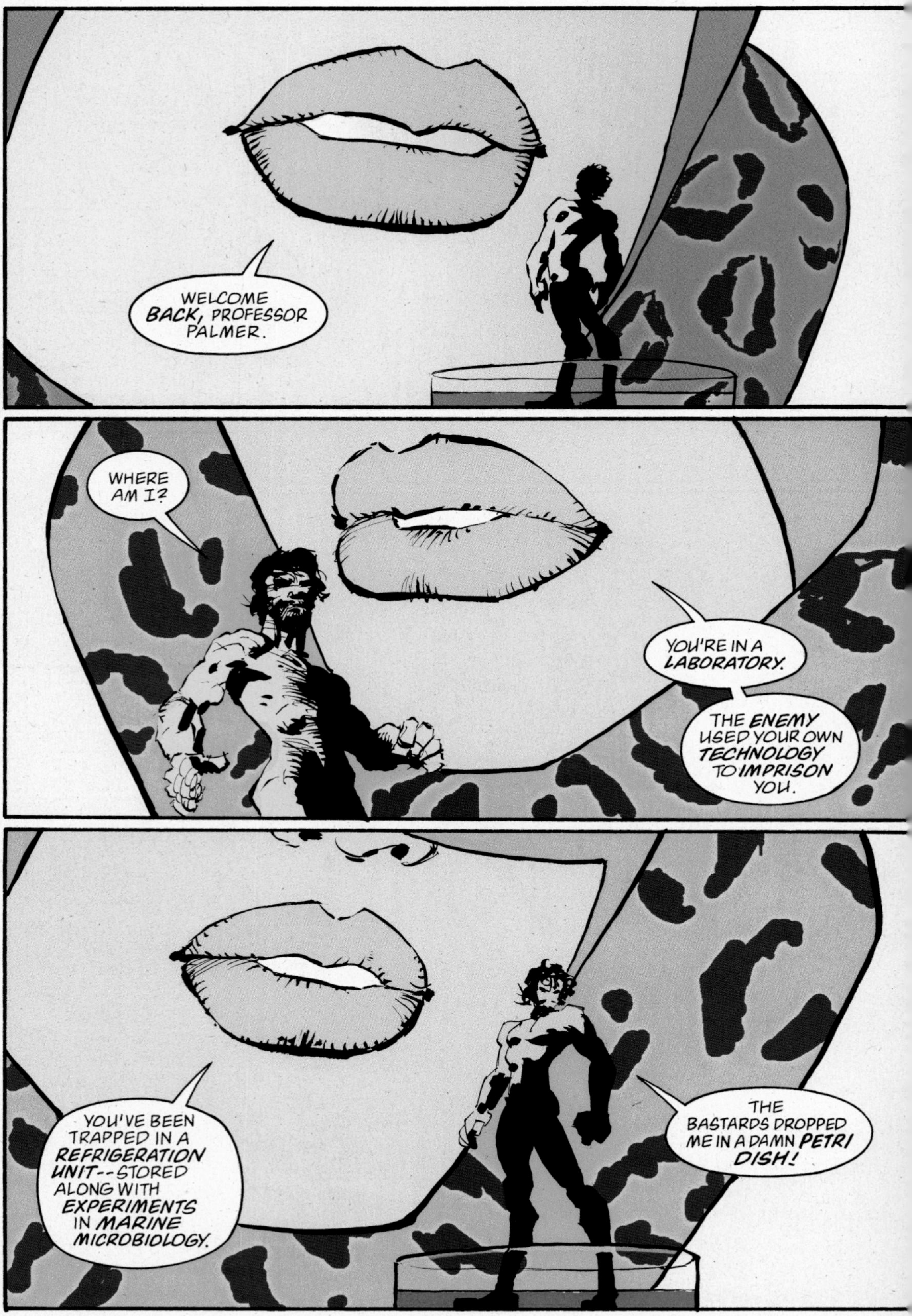
WELCOME BACK, PROFESSOR PALMER.
WHERE AM I?
YOU'RE IN A LABORATORY.
THE ENEMY USED YOUR OWN TECHNOLOGY TO IMPRISON YOU.
YOU'VE BEEN TRAPPED IN A REFRIGERATION UNIT--STORED ALONG WITH EXPERIMENTS IN MARINE MICROBIOLOGY.
THE BASTARDS DROPPED ME IN A DAMN PETRI DISH!

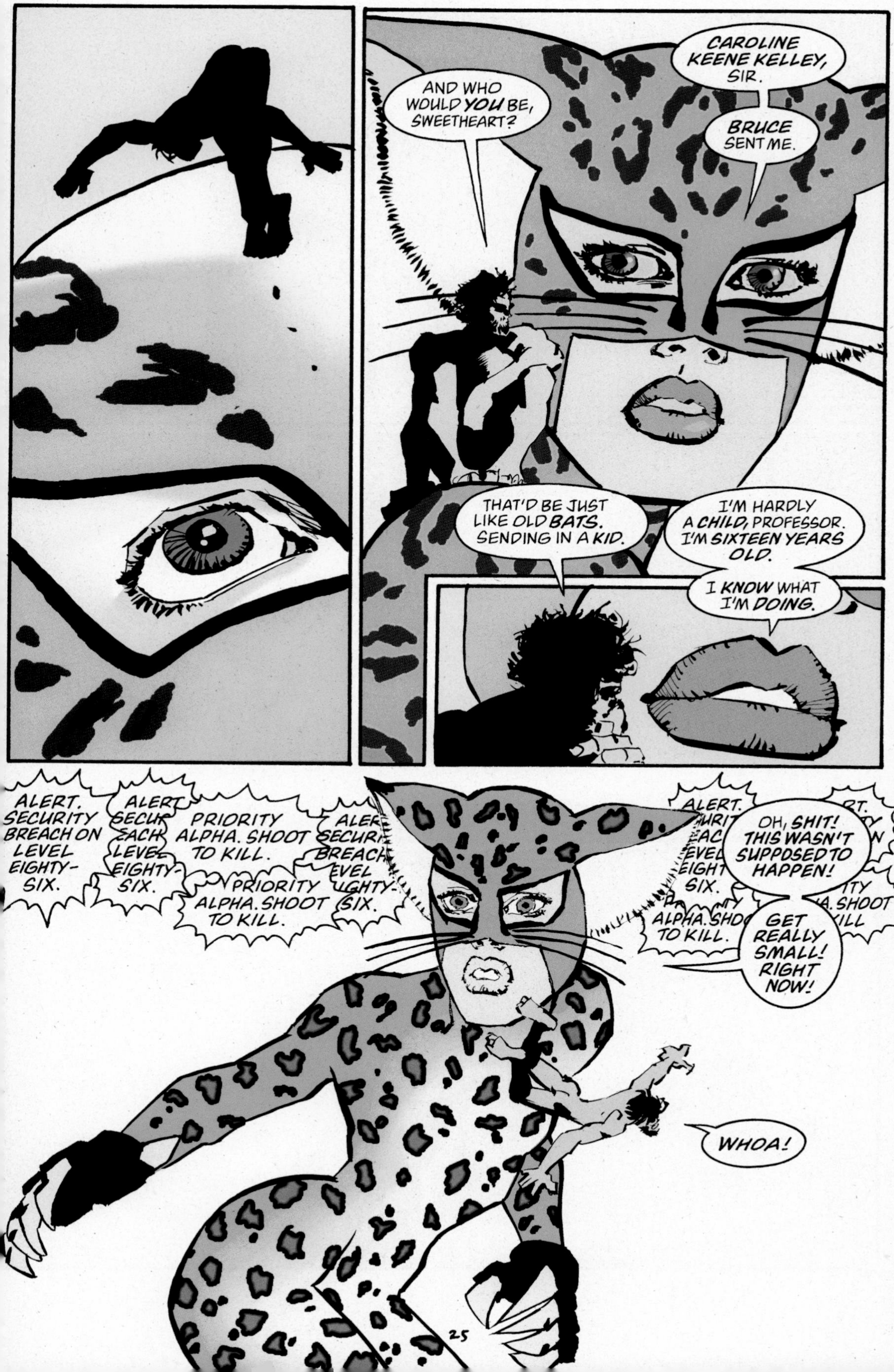
AND WHO WOULD YOU BE, SWEETHEART?
CAROLINE KEENE KELLEY, SIR.
BRUCE SENT ME.
THAT'D BE JUST LIKE OLD BATS. SENDING IN A KID.
I'M HARDLY A CHILD, PROFESSOR. I'M SIXTEEN YEARS OLD.
I KNOW WHAT I'M DOING.
ALERT. SECURITY BREACH ON LEVEL EIGHTY-SIX.
PRIORITY ALPHA. SHOOT TO KILL.
PRIORITY ALPHA. SHOOT TO KILL.
OH, SHIT! THIS WASN'T SUPPOSED TO HAPPEN!
GET REALLY SMALL! RIGHT NOW!
WHOA!

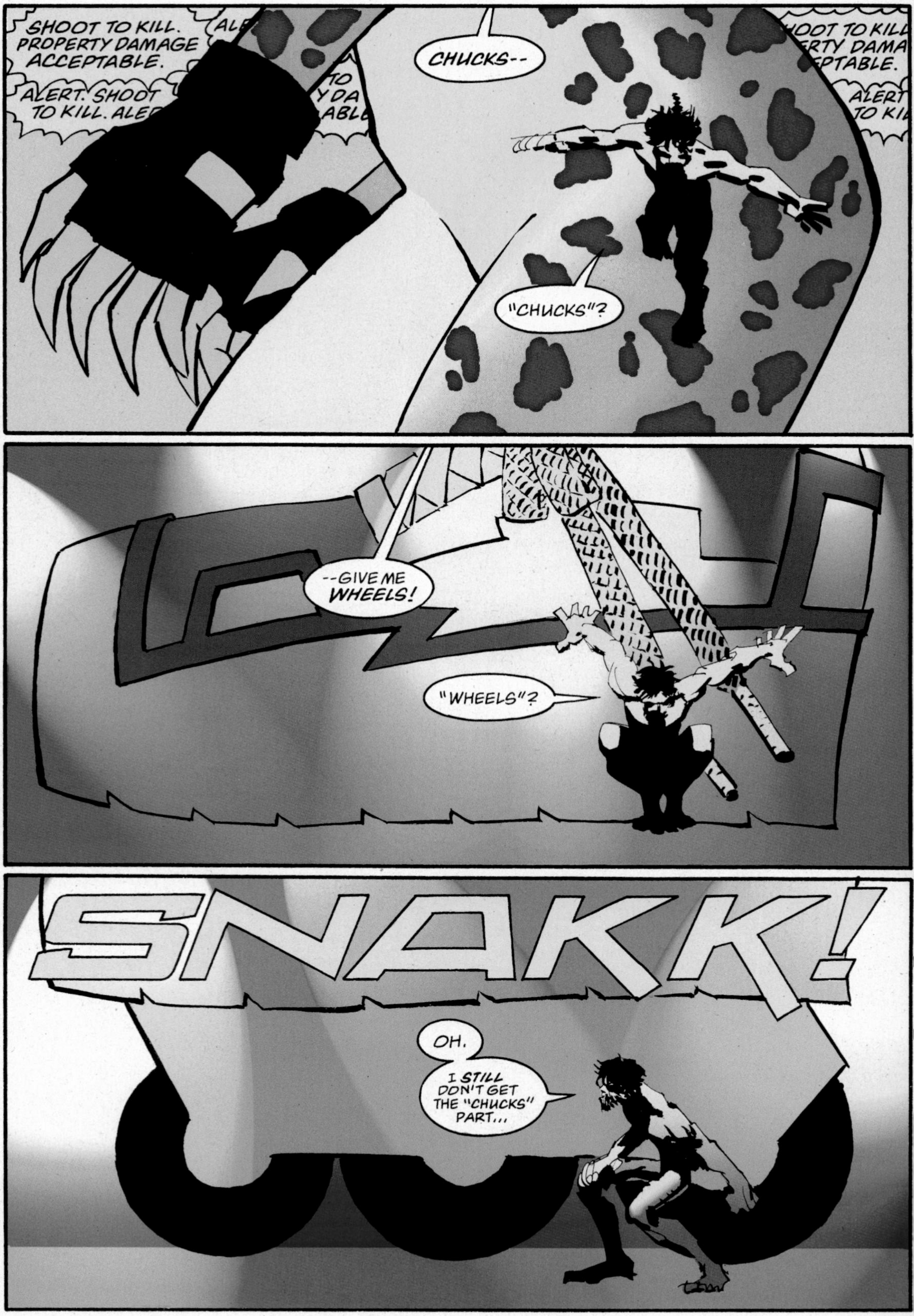
SHOOT TO KILL. PROPERTY DAMAGE ACCEPTABLE.
ALERT. SHOOT TO KILL.
CHUCKS--
"CHUCKS"?
--GIVE ME WHEELS!
"WHEELS"?
SNAKK!
OH.
I STILL DON'T GET THE "CHUCKS" PART...

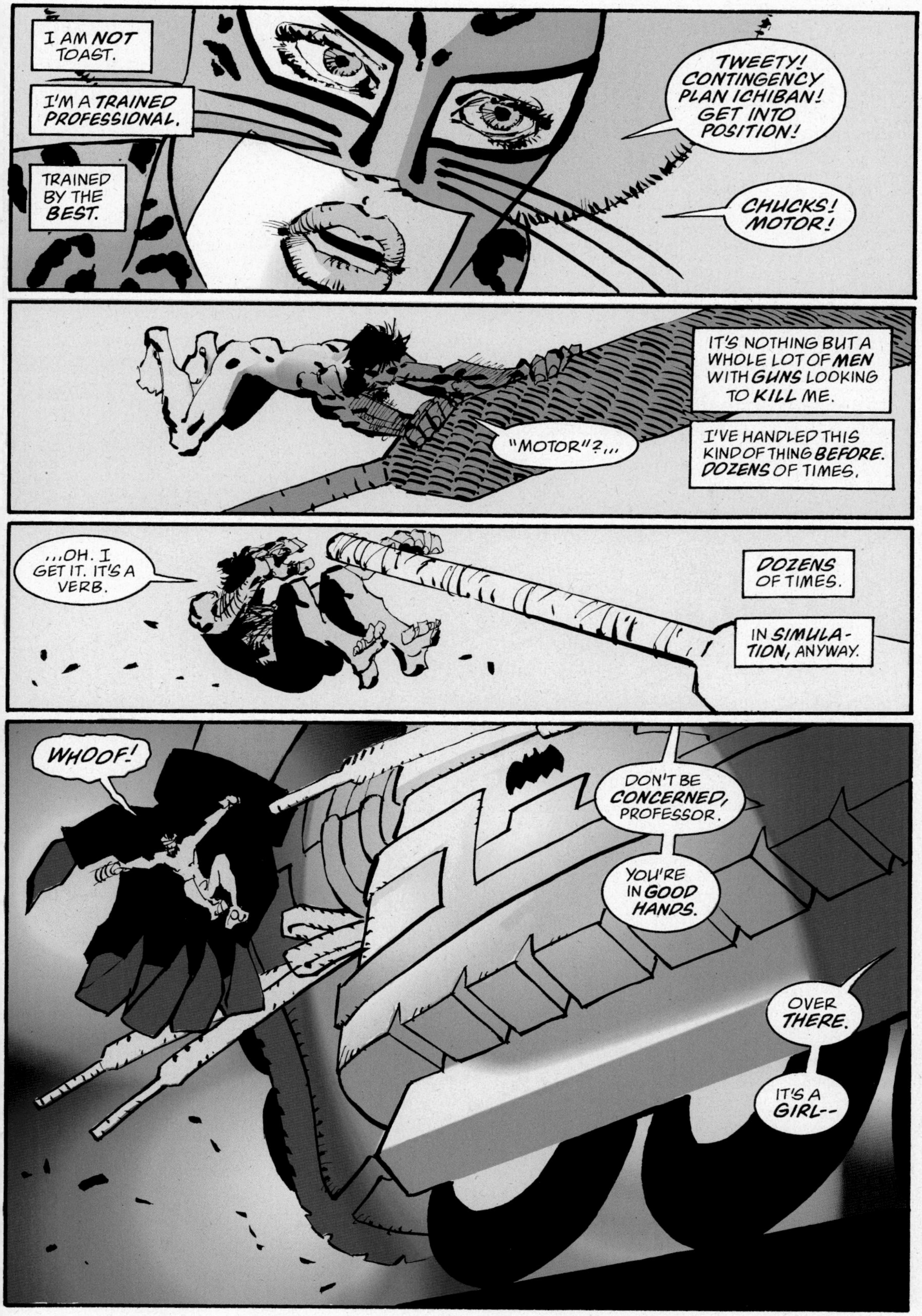
I AM NOT TOAST.
I'M A TRAINED PROFESSIONAL.
TRAINED BY THE BEST.
TWEETY! CONTINGENCY PLAN ICHIBAN! GET INTO POSITION!
CHUCKS! MOTOR!
IT'S NOTHING BUT A WHOLE LOT OF MEN WITH GUNS LOOKING TO KILL ME.
"MOTOR"?...
I'VE HANDLED THIS KIND OF THING BEFORE. DOZENS OF TIMES.
...OH. I GET IT. IT'S A VERB.
DOZENS OF TIMES.
IN SIMULATION, ANYWAY.
WHOOF!
DON'T BE CONCERNED, PROFESSOR.
YOU'RE IN GOOD HANDS.
OVER THERE.
IT'S A GIRL--

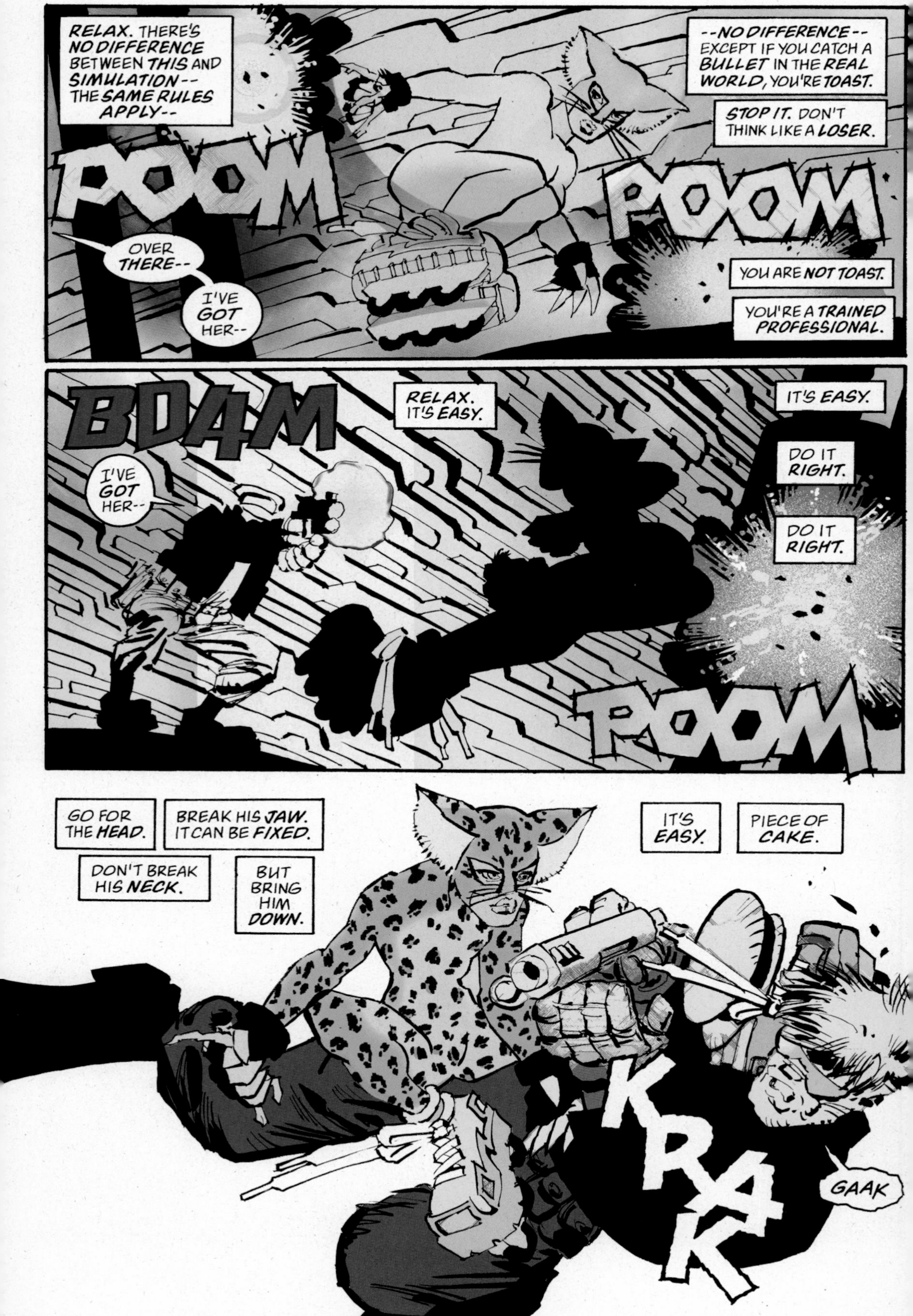
RELAX. THERE'S NO DIFFERENCE BETWEEN THIS AND SIMULATION-- THE SAME RULES APPLY--
--NO DIFFERENCE-- EXCEPT IF YOU CATCH A BULLET IN THE REAL WORLD, YOU'RE TOAST.
STOP IT. DON'T THINK LIKE A LOSER.
POOM
POOM
OVER THERE--
I'VE GOT HER--
YOU ARE NOT TOAST.
YOU'RE A TRAINED PROFESSIONAL.
BDAM
RELAX. IT'S EASY.
IT'S EASY.
I'VE GOT HER--
DO IT RIGHT.
DO IT RIGHT.
POOM
GO FOR THE HEAD.
BREAK HIS JAW. IT CAN BE FIXED.
DON'T BREAK HIS NECK.
BUT BRING HIM DOWN.
IT'S EASY.
PIECE OF CAKE.
KRAK
GAAK

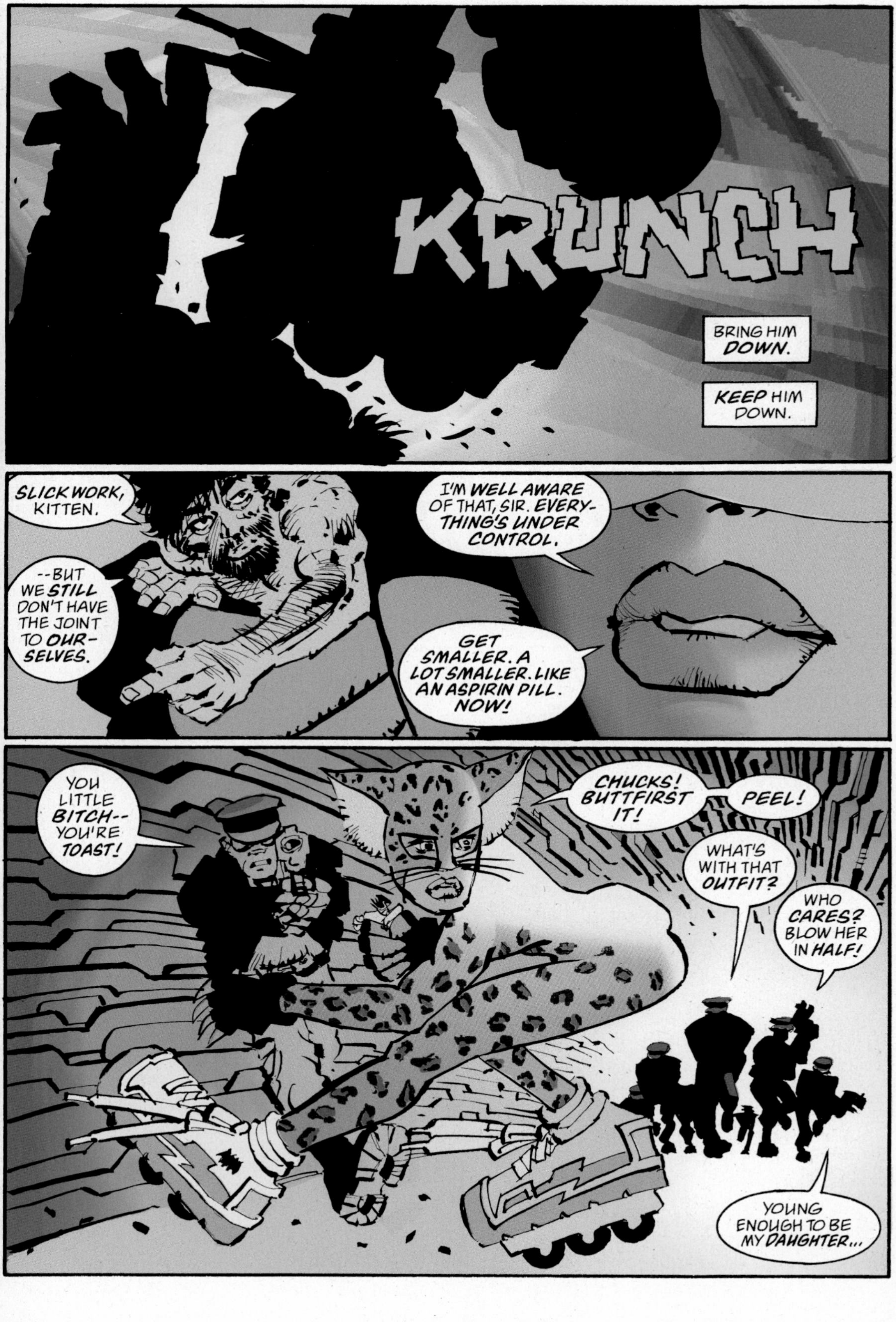
KRUNCH
BRING HIM DOWN.
KEEP HIM DOWN.
SLICK WORK, KITTEN.
I'M WELL AWARE OF THAT, SIR. EVERYTHING'S UNDER CONTROL.
--BUT WE STILL DON'T HAVE THE JOINT TO OURSELVES.
GET SMALLER. A LOT SMALLER. LIKE AN ASPIRIN PILL. NOW!
YOU LITTLE BITCH-- YOU'RE TOAST!
CHUCKS! BUTTFIRST IT!
PEEL!
WHAT'S WITH THAT OUTFIT?
WHO CARES? BLOW HER IN HALF!
YOUNG ENOUGH TO BE MY DAUGHTER...

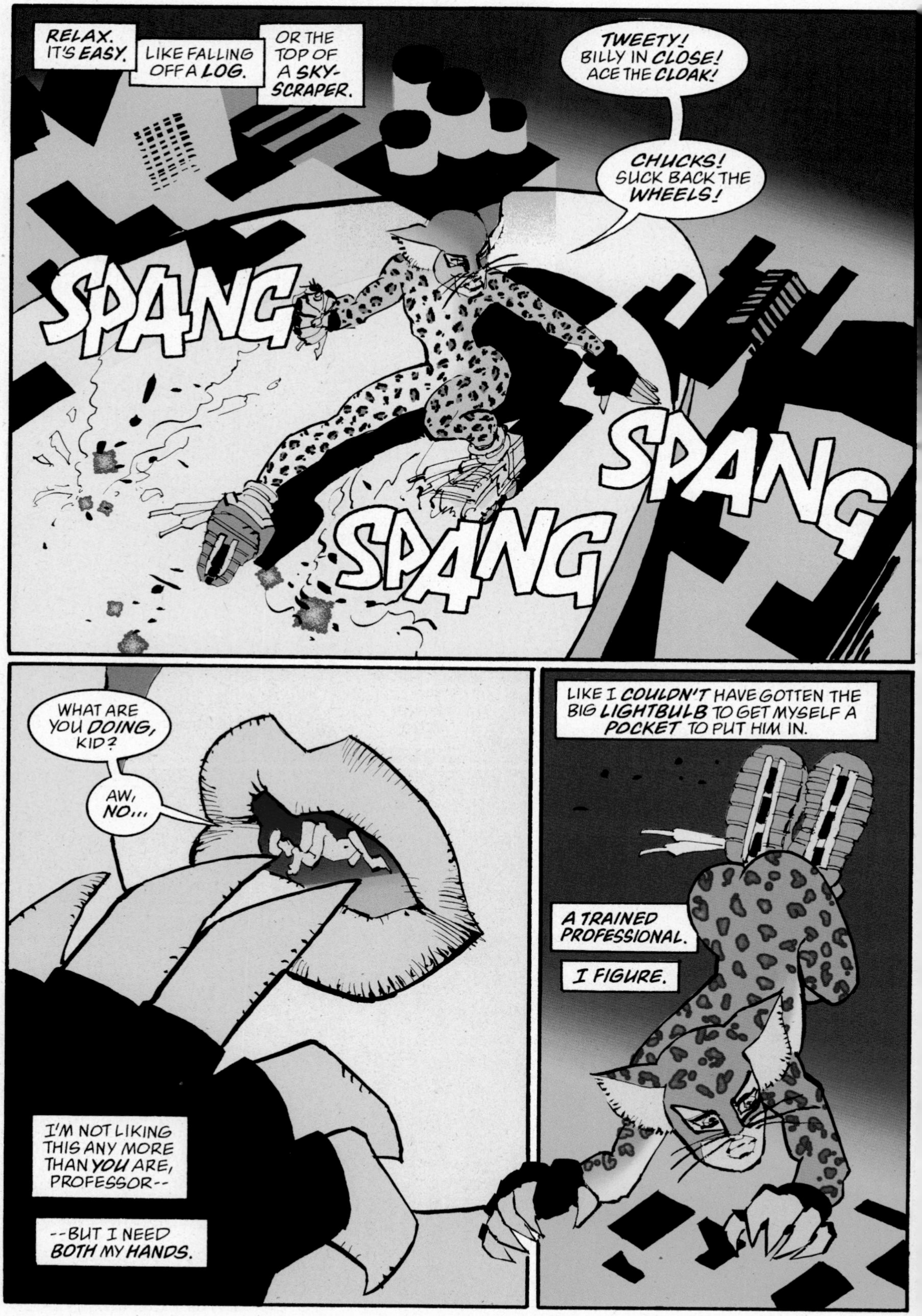
RELAX. IT'S EASY.
LIKE FALLING OFF A LOG.
OR THE TOP OF A SKY-SCRAPER.
TWEETY! BILLY IN CLOSE! ACE THE CLOAK!
CHUCKS! SUCK BACK THE WHEELS!
SPANG
SPANG
SPANG
WHAT ARE YOU DOING, KID?
AW, NO...
I'M NOT LIKING THIS ANY MORE THAN YOU ARE, PROFESSOR--
--BUT I NEED BOTH MY HANDS.
LIKE I COULDN'T HAVE GOTTEN THE BIG LIGHTBULB TO GET MYSELF A POCKET TO PUT HIM IN.
A TRAINED PROFESSIONAL.
I FIGURE.

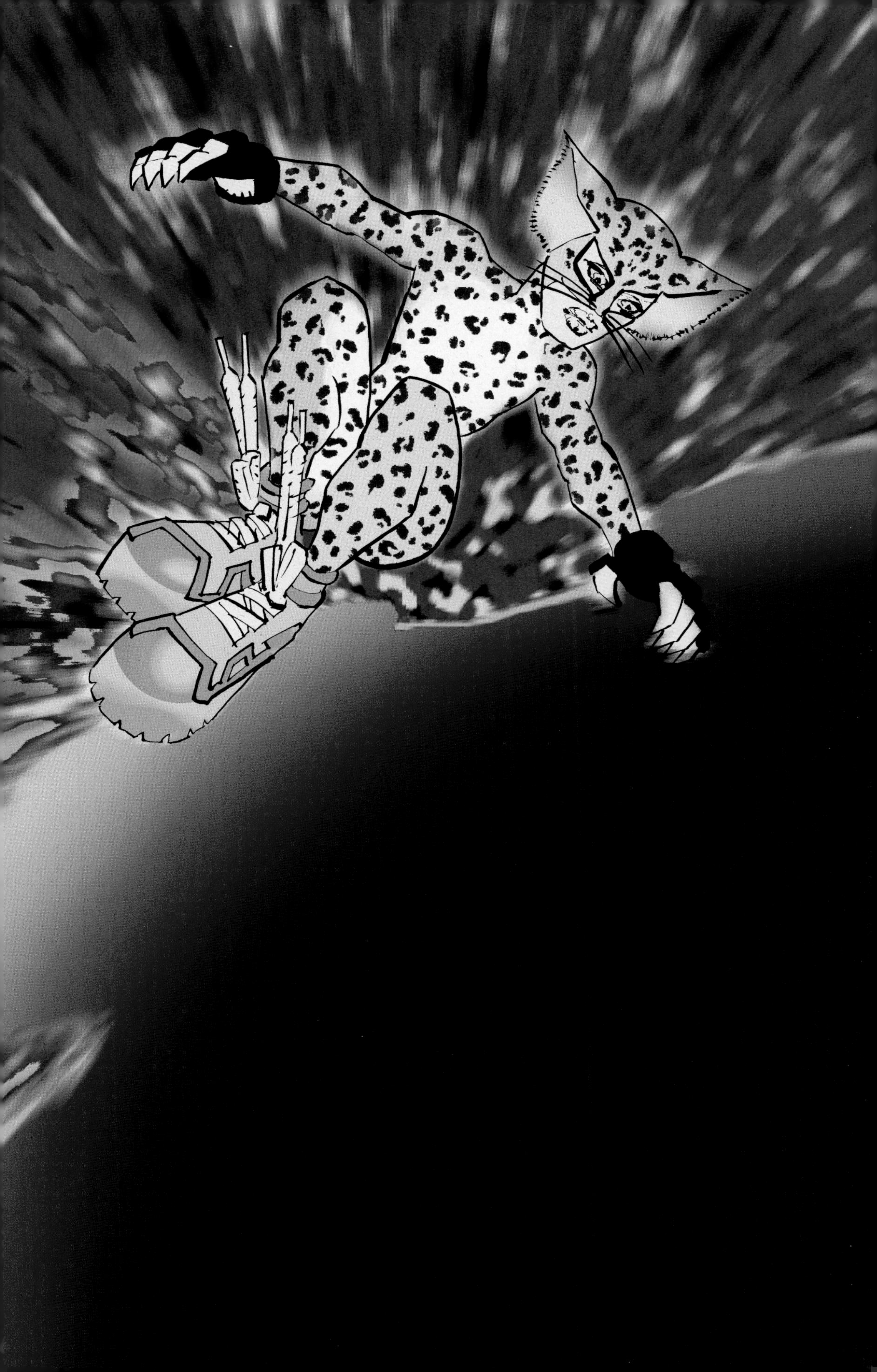

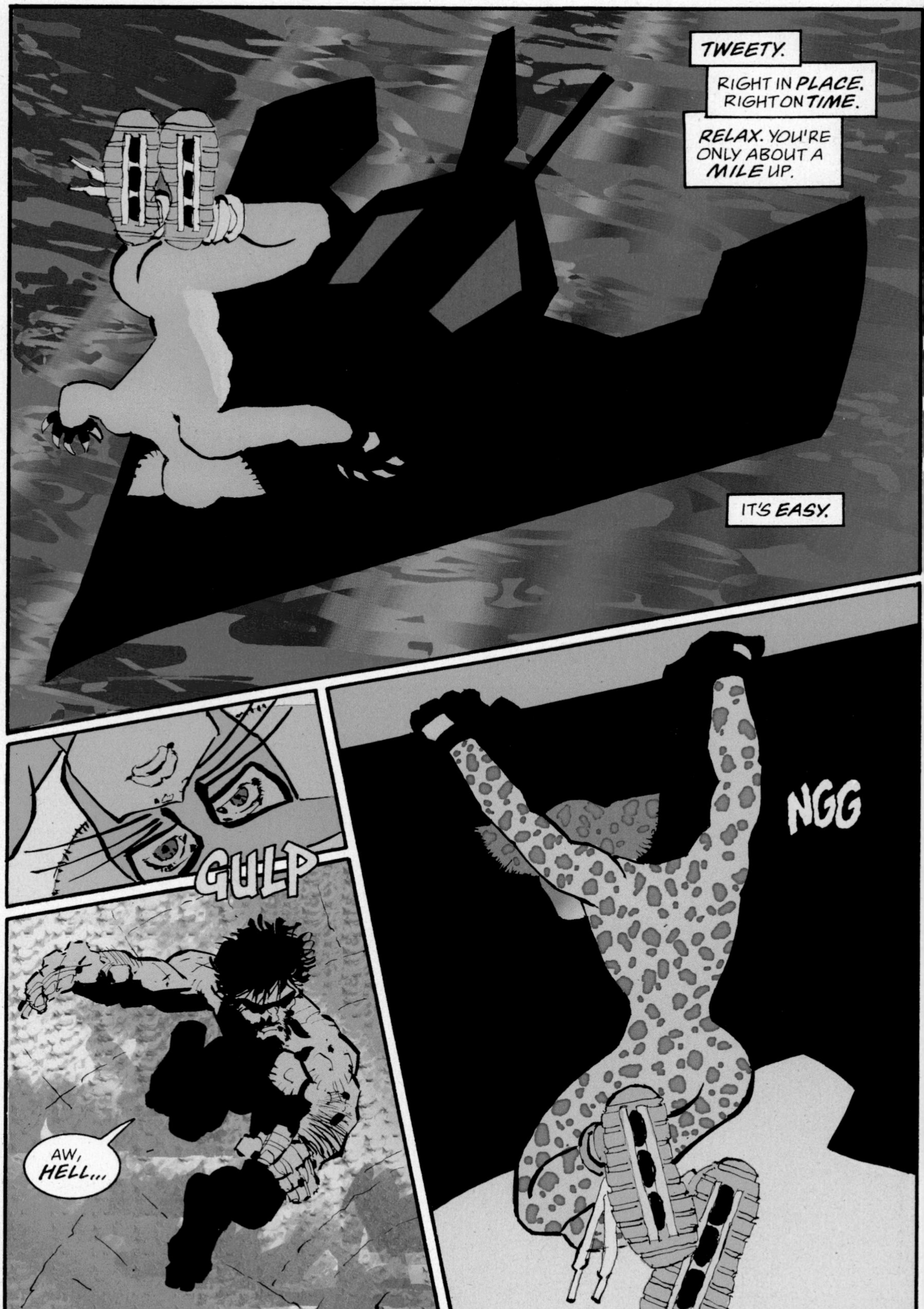
TWEETY.
RIGHT IN PLACE. RIGHT ON TIME.
RELAX. YOU'RE ONLY ABOUT A MILE UP.
IT'S EASY.
GULP
NGG
AW, HELL...

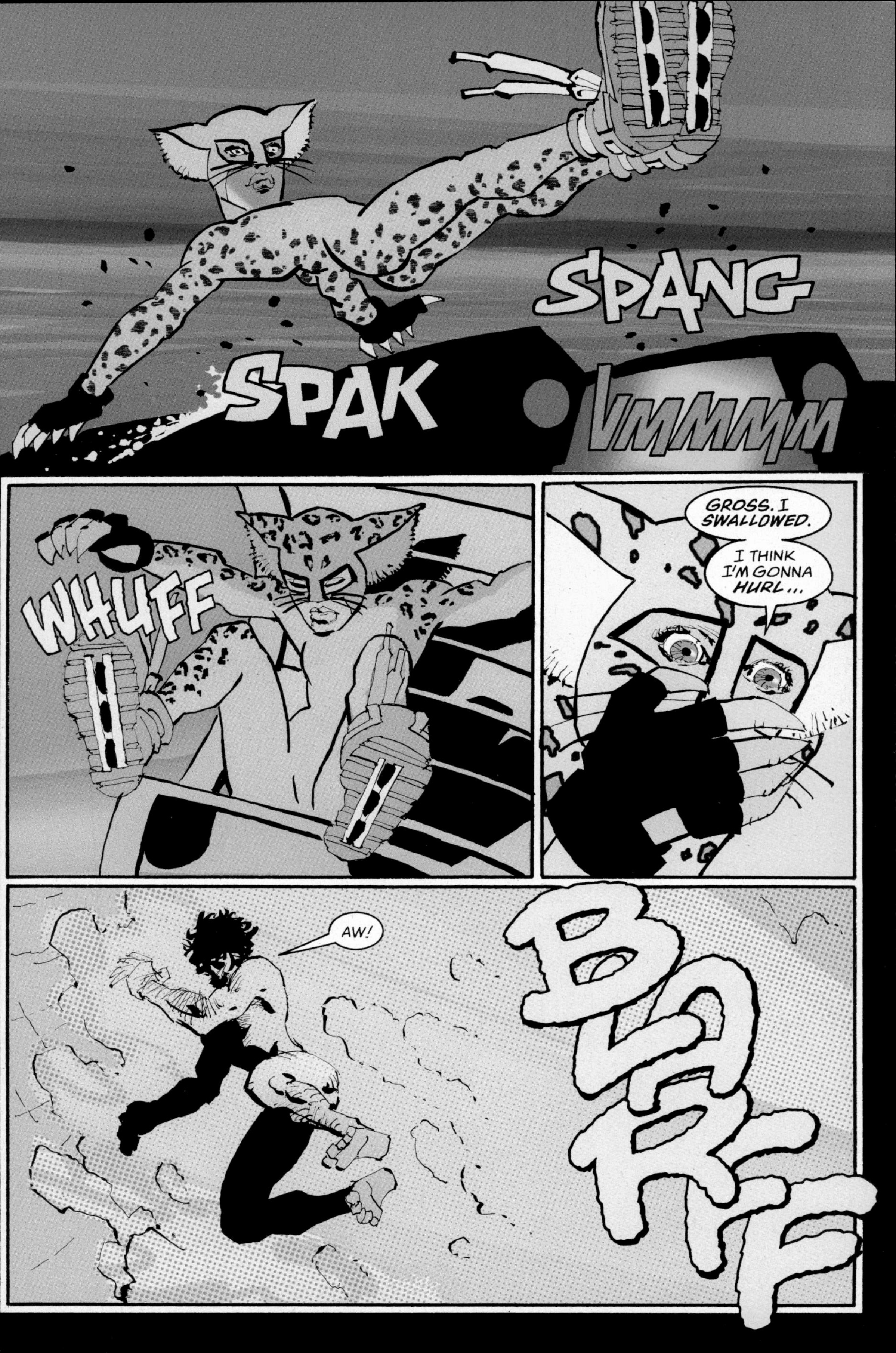
SPANG
SPAK
VMMMMM
WHUFF
GROSS. I SWALLOWED.
I THINK I'M GONNA HURL...
AW!
BUDFF

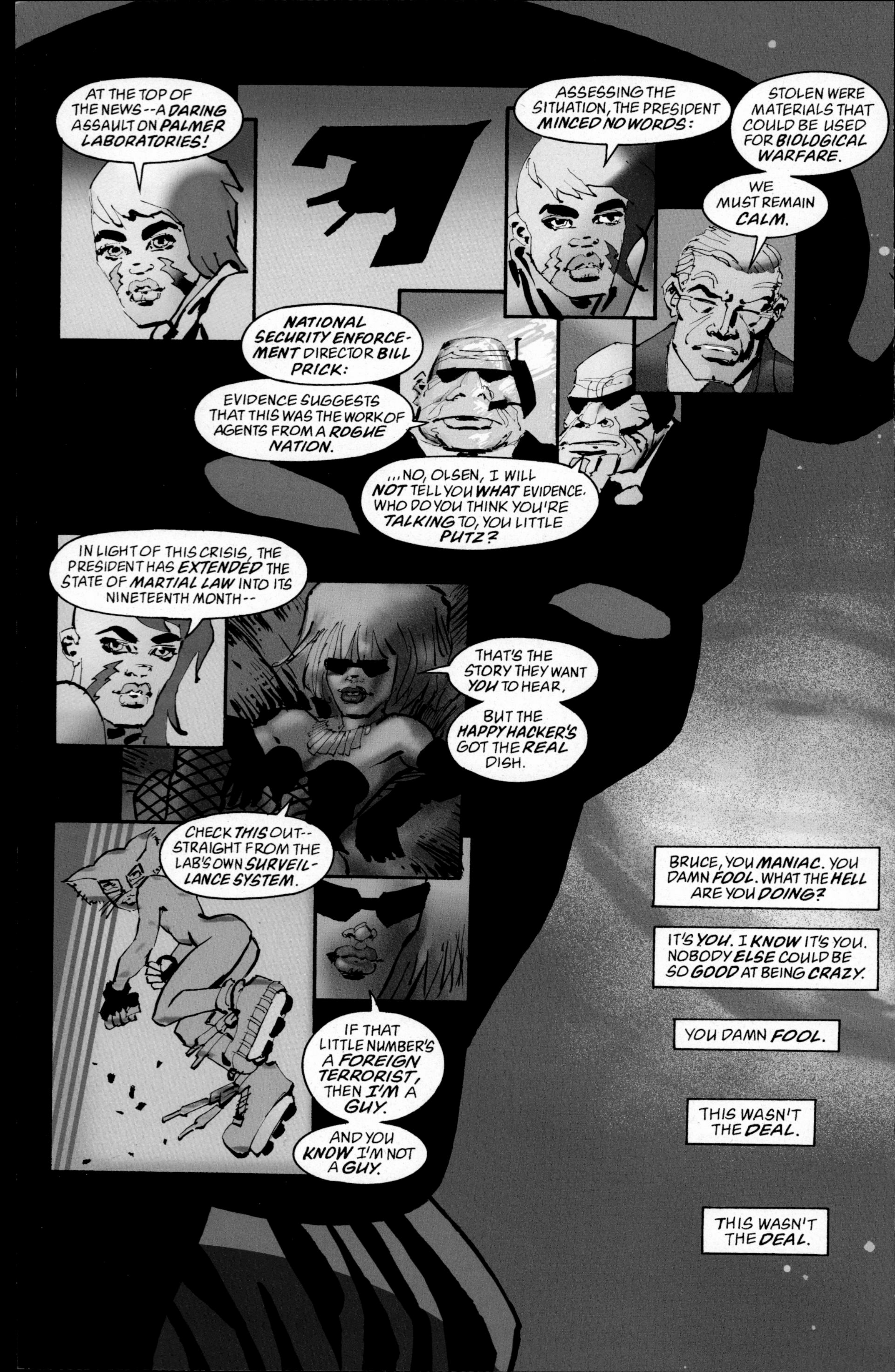
AT THE TOP OF THE NEWS--A DARING ASSAULT ON PALMER LABORATORIES!
ASSESSING THE SITUATION, THE PRESIDENT MINCED NO WORDS:
STOLEN WERE MATERIALS THAT COULD BE USED FOR BIOLOGICAL WARFARE.
WE MUST REMAIN CALM.
NATIONAL SECURITY ENFORCEMENT DIRECTOR BILL PRICK:
EVIDENCE SUGGESTS THAT THIS WAS THE WORK OF AGENTS FROM A ROGUE NATION.
...NO, OLSEN, I WILL NOT TELL YOU WHAT EVIDENCE. WHO DO YOU THINK YOU'RE TALKING TO, YOU LITTLE PUTZ?
IN LIGHT OF THIS CRISIS, THE PRESIDENT HAS EXTENDED THE STATE OF MARTIAL LAW INTO ITS NINETEENTH MONTH--
THAT'S THE STORY THEY WANT YOU TO HEAR,
BUT THE HAPPY HACKER'S GOT THE REAL DISH.
CHECK THIS OUT--STRAIGHT FROM THE LAB'S OWN SURVEILLANCE SYSTEM.
IF THAT LITTLE NUMBER'S A FOREIGN TERRORIST, THEN I'M A GUY.
AND YOU KNOW I'M NOT A GUY.
BRUCE, YOU MANIAC. YOU DAMN FOOL. WHAT THE HELL ARE YOU DOING?
IT'S YOU. I KNOW IT'S YOU. NOBODY ELSE COULD BE SO GOOD AT BEING CRAZY.
YOU DAMN FOOL.
THIS WASN'T THE DEAL.
THIS WASN'T THE DEAL.

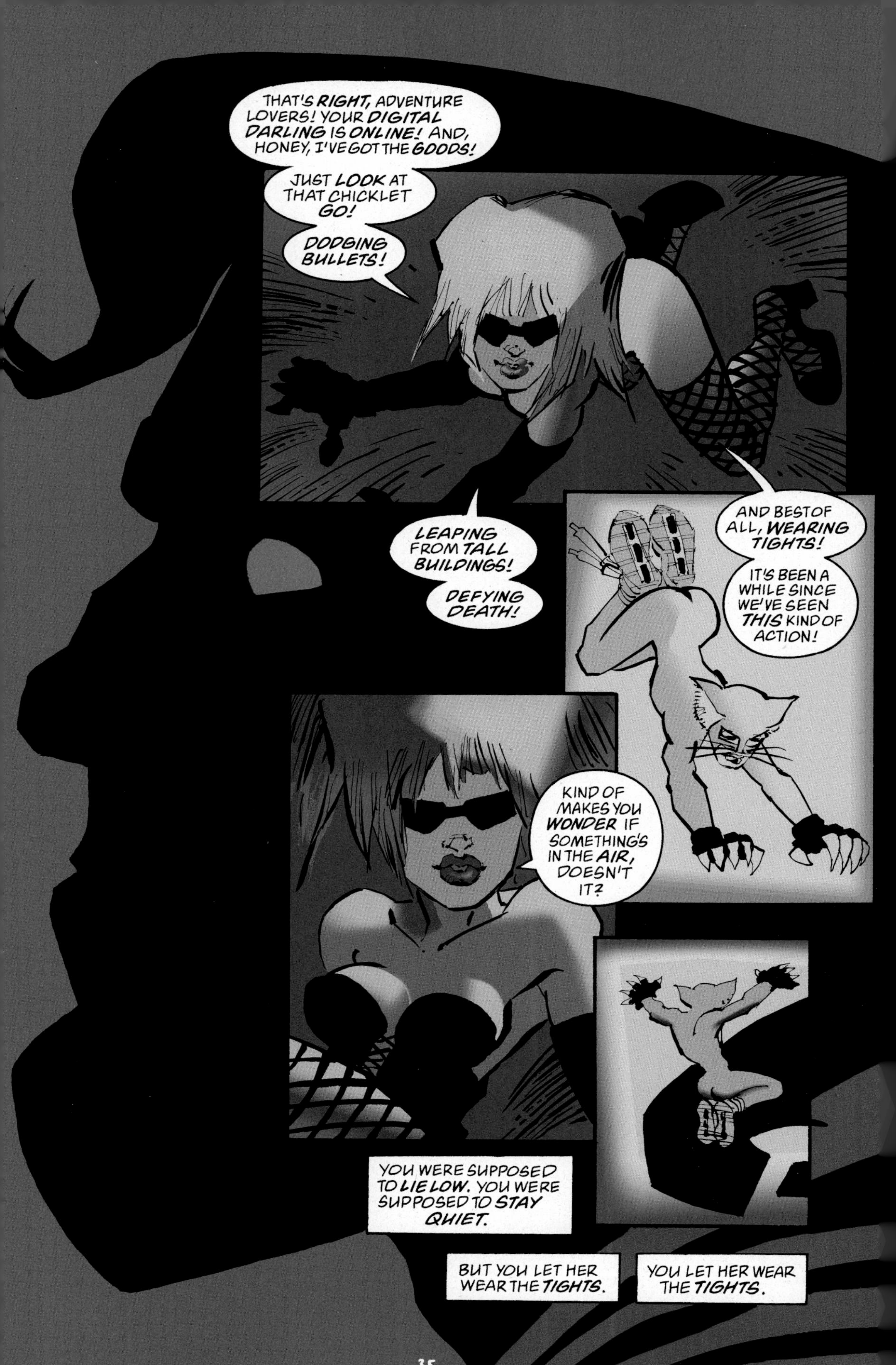
THAT'S RIGHT, ADVENTURE LOVERS! YOUR DIGITAL DARLING IS ONLINE! AND, HONEY, I'VE GOT THE GOODS!
JUST LOOK AT THAT CHICKLET GO!
DODGING BULLETS!
LEAPING FROM TALL BUILDINGS!
DEFYING DEATH!
AND BEST OF ALL, WEARING TIGHTS!
IT'S BEEN A WHILE SINCE WE'VE SEEN THIS KIND OF ACTION!
KIND OF MAKES YOU WONDER IF SOMETHING'S IN THE AIR, DOESN'T IT?
YOU WERE SUPPOSED TO LIE LOW. YOU WERE SUPPOSED TO STAY QUIET.
BUT YOU LET HER WEAR THE TIGHTS.
YOU LET HER WEAR THE TIGHTS.

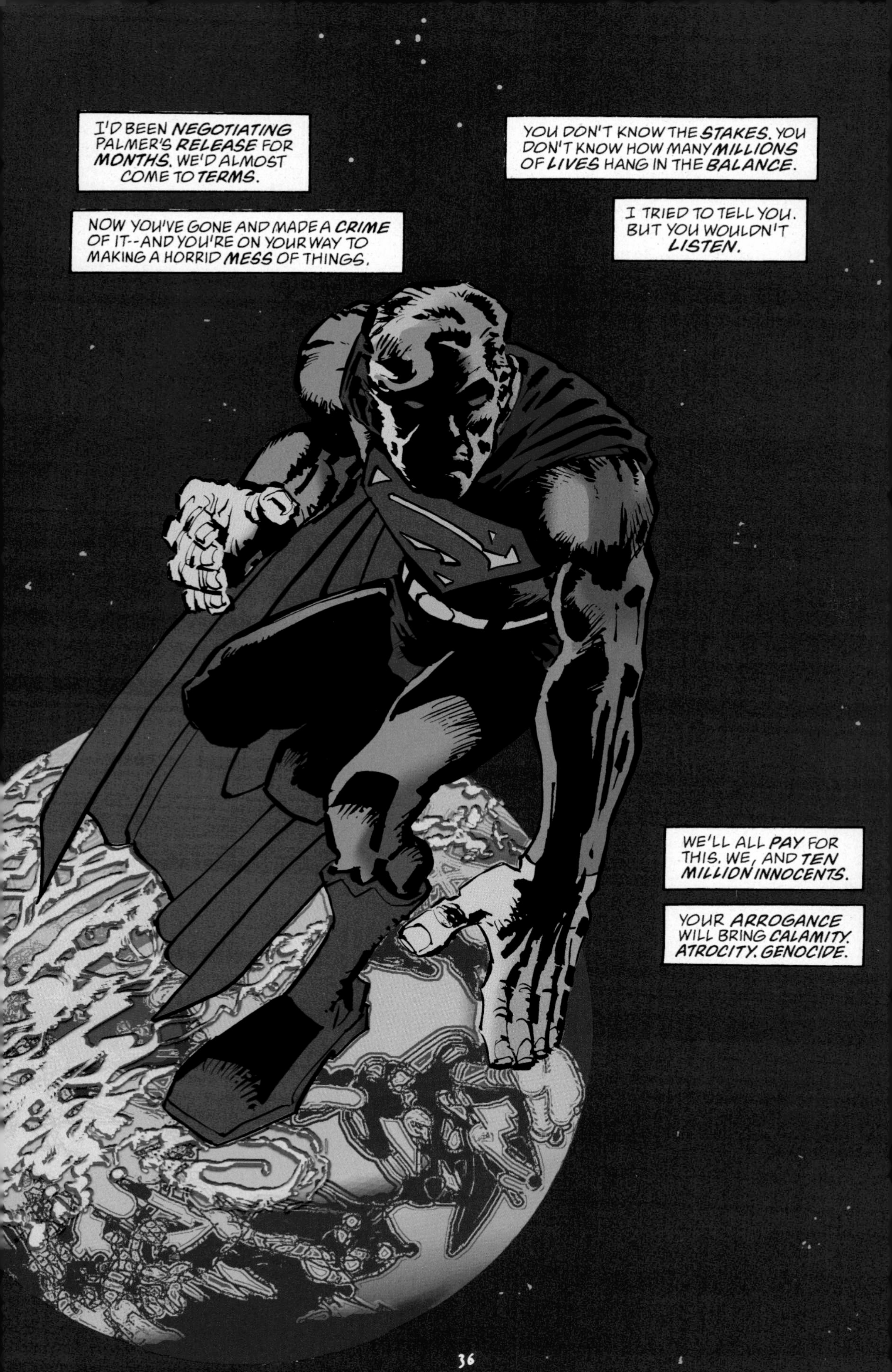
I'D BEEN NEGOTIATING PALMER'S RELEASE FOR MONTHS. WE'D ALMOST COME TO TERMS.
NOW YOU'VE GONE AND MADE A CRIME OF IT--AND YOU'RE ON YOUR WAY TO MAKING A HORRID MESS OF THINGS.
YOU DON'T KNOW THE STAKES. YOU DON'T KNOW HOW MANY MILLIONS OF LIVES HANG IN THE BALANCE.
I TRIED TO TELL YOU. BUT YOU WOULDN'T LISTEN.
WE'LL ALL PAY FOR THIS. WE, AND TEN MILLION INNOCENTS.
YOUR ARROGANCE WILL BRING CALAMITY. ATROCITY. GENOCIDE.

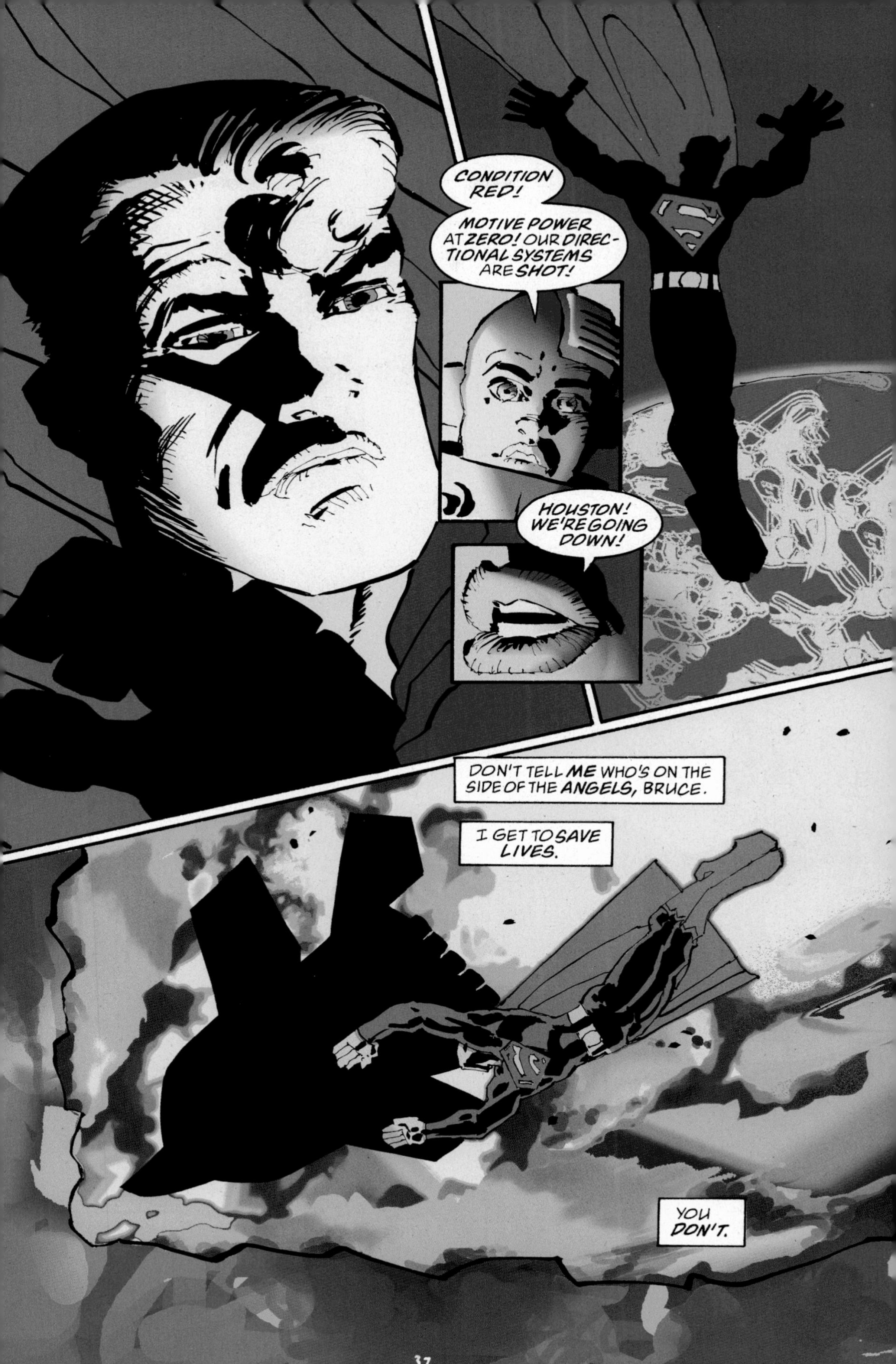
CONDITION RED!
MOTIVE POWER AT ZERO! OUR DIRECTIONAL SYSTEMS ARE SHOT!
HOUSTON! WE'RE GOING DOWN!
DON'T TELL ME WHO'S ON THE SIDE OF THE ANGELS, BRUCE.
I GET TO SAVE LIVES.
YOU DON'T.

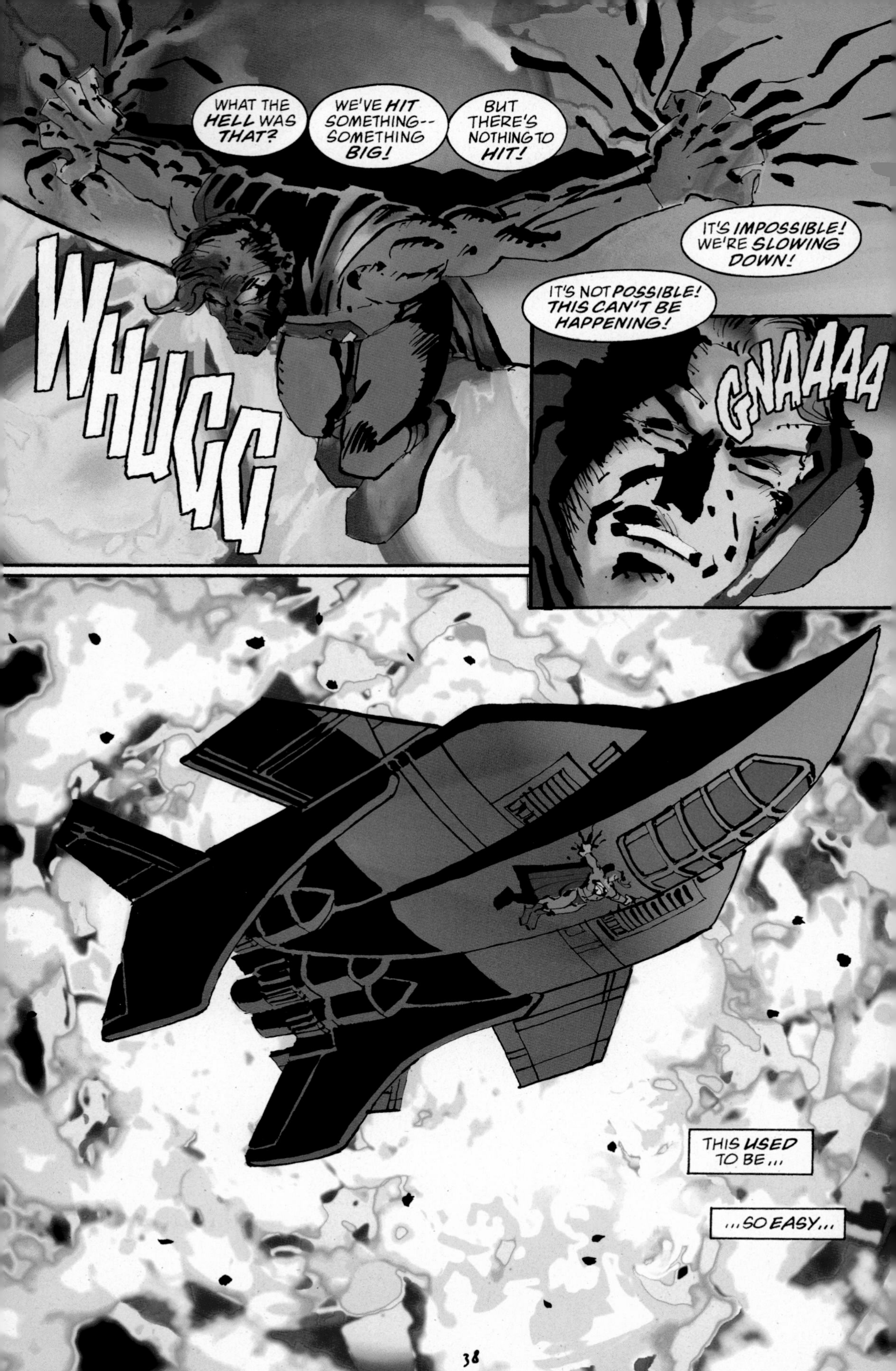
WHAT THE HELL WAS THAT?
WE'VE HIT SOMETHING-- SOMETHING BIG!
BUT THERE'S NOTHING TO HIT!
WHUGG
IT'S IMPOSSIBLE! WE'RE SLOWING DOWN!
IT'S NOT POSSIBLE! THIS CAN'T BE HAPPENING!
GNAAAA
THIS USED TO BE...
...SO EASY...

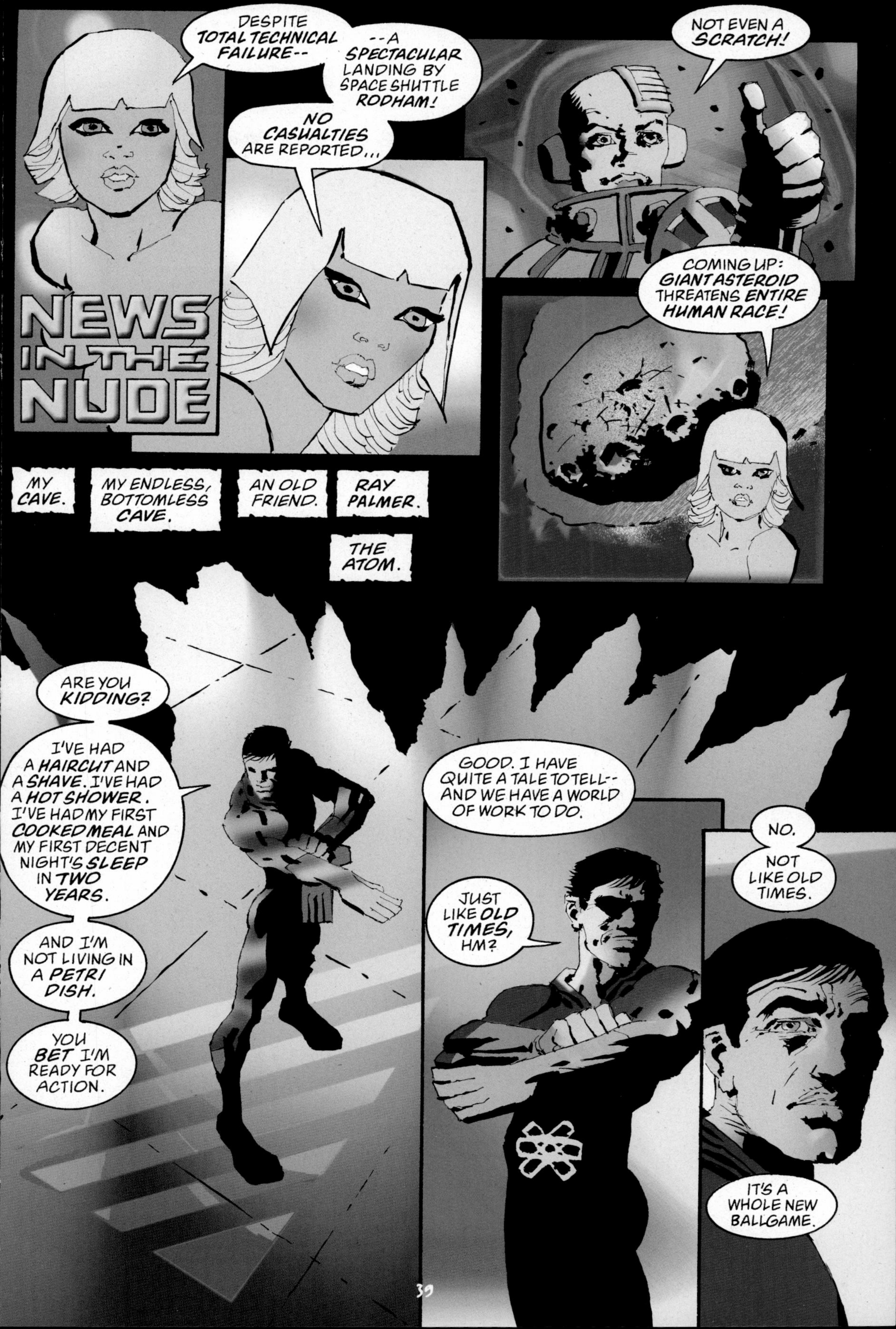
DESPITE TOTAL TECHNICAL FAILURE--
--A SPECTACULAR LANDING BY SPACE SHUTTLE RODHAM!
NO CASUALTIES ARE REPORTED...
NEWS IN THE NUDE
NOT EVEN A SCRATCH!
COMING UP: GIANT ASTEROID THREATENS ENTIRE HUMAN RACE!
MY CAVE.
MY ENDLESS, BOTTOMLESS CAVE.
AN OLD FRIEND.
RAY PALMER.
THE ATOM.
ARE YOU KIDDING?
I'VE HAD A HAIRCUT AND A SHAVE. I'VE HAD A HOT SHOWER. I'VE HAD MY FIRST COOKED MEAL AND MY FIRST DECENT NIGHT'S SLEEP IN TWO YEARS.
AND I'M NOT LIVING IN A PETRI DISH.
YOU BET I'M READY FOR ACTION.
GOOD. I HAVE QUITE A TALE TO TELL-- AND WE HAVE A WORLD OF WORK TO DO.
JUST LIKE OLD TIMES, HM?
NO.
NOT LIKE OLD TIMES.
IT'S A WHOLE NEW BALLGAME.

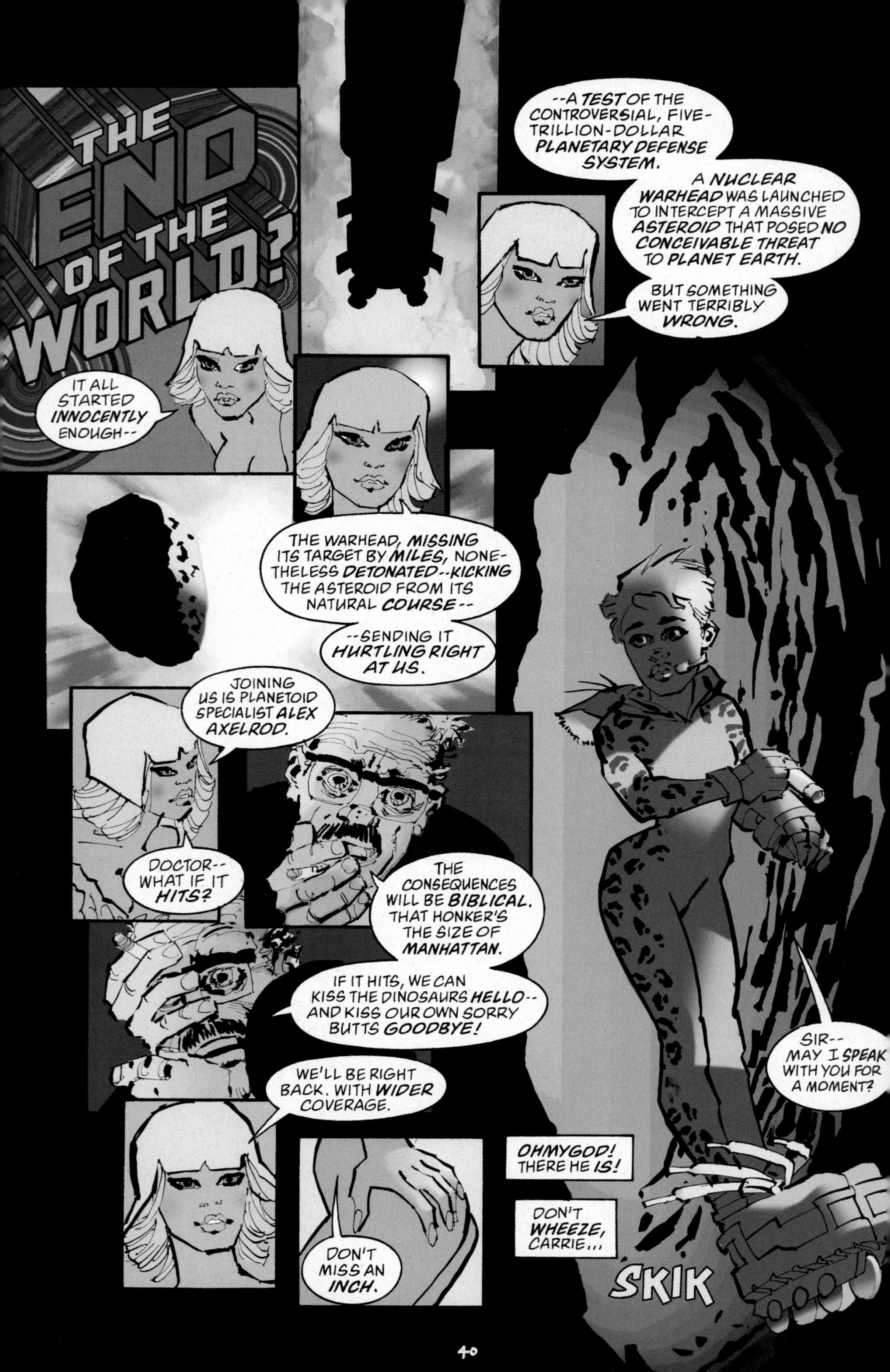
THE END OF THE WORLD?
IT ALL STARTED INNOCENTLY ENOUGH--
--A TEST OF THE CONTROVERSIAL, FIVE-TRILLION-DOLLAR PLANETARY DEFENSE SYSTEM.
A NUCLEAR WARHEAD WAS LAUNCHED TO INTERCEPT A MASSIVE ASTEROID THAT POSED NO CONCEIVABLE THREAT TO PLANET EARTH.
BUT SOMETHING WENT TERRIBLY WRONG.
THE WARHEAD, MISSING ITS TARGET BY MILES, NONETHELESS DETONATED--KICKING THE ASTEROID FROM ITS NATURAL COURSE--
--SENDING IT HURTLING RIGHT AT US.
JOINING US IS PLANETOID SPECIALIST ALEX AXELROD.
DOCTOR--WHAT IF IT HITS?
THE CONSEQUENCES WILL BE BIBLICAL. THAT HONKER'S THE SIZE OF MANHATTAN.
IF IT HITS, WE CAN KISS THE DINOSAURS HELLO--AND KISS OUR OWN SORRY BUTTS GOODBYE!
WE'LL BE RIGHT BACK. WITH WIDER COVERAGE.
DON'T MISS AN INCH.
SIR--MAY I SPEAK WITH YOU FOR A MOMENT?
OHMYGOD! THERE HE IS!
DON'T WHEEZE, CARRIE...
SKIK

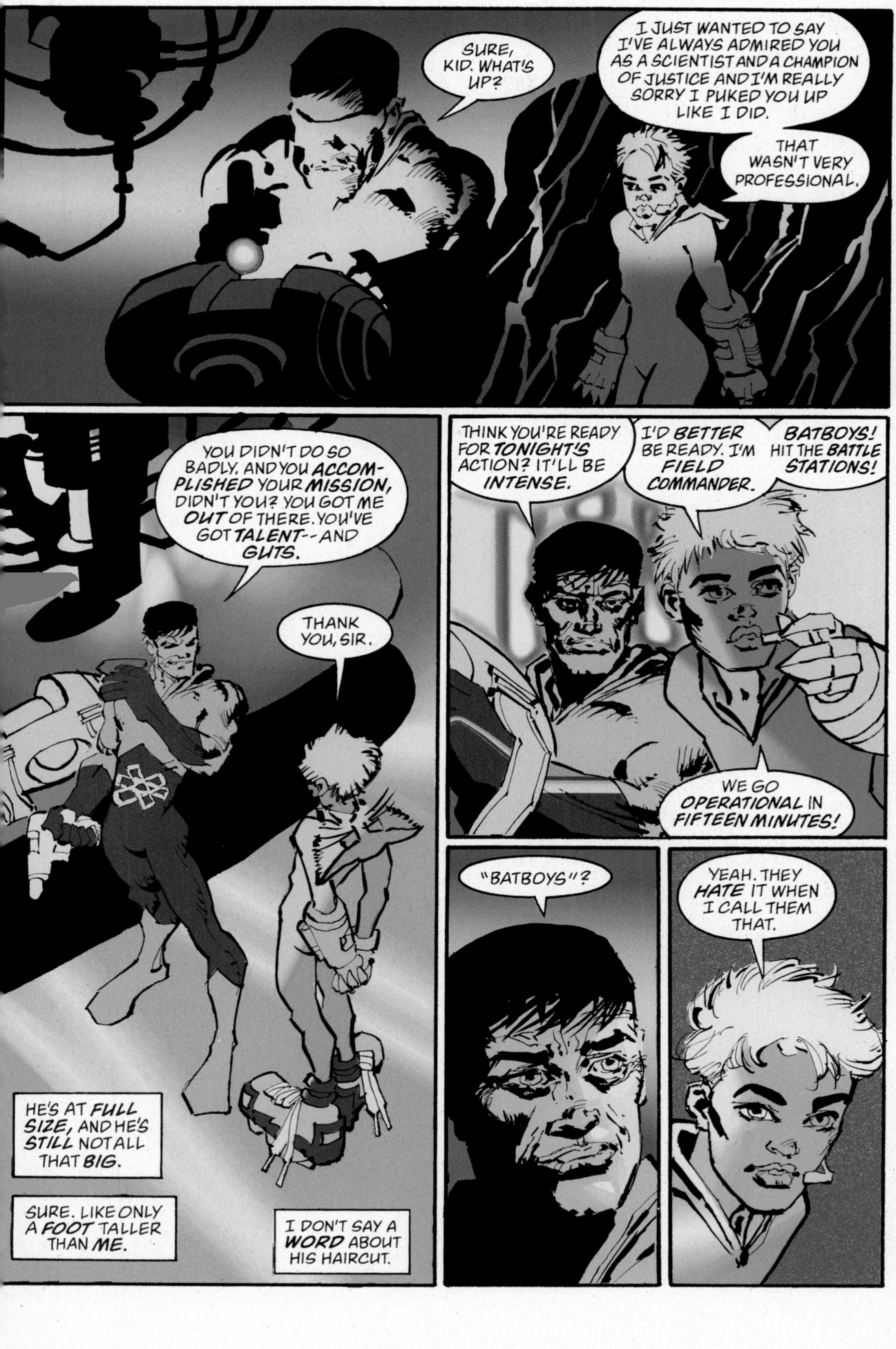
SURE, KID. WHAT'S UP?
I JUST WANTED TO SAY I'VE ALWAYS ADMIRED YOU AS A SCIENTIST AND A CHAMPION OF JUSTICE AND I'M REALLY SORRY I PUKED YOU UP LIKE I DID.
THAT WASN'T VERY PROFESSIONAL.
YOU DIDN'T DO SO BADLY. AND YOU ACCOMPLISHED YOUR MISSION, DIDN'T YOU? YOU GOT ME OUT OF THERE. YOU'VE GOT TALENT-- AND GUTS.
THANK YOU, SIR.
HE'S AT FULL SIZE, AND HE'S STILL NOT ALL THAT BIG.
SURE. LIKE ONLY A FOOT TALLER THAN ME.
I DON'T SAY A WORD ABOUT HIS HAIRCUT.
THINK YOU'RE READY FOR TONIGHT'S ACTION? IT'LL BE INTENSE.
I'D BETTER BE READY. I'M FIELD COMMANDER.
BATBOYS! HIT THE BATTLE STATIONS!
WE GO OPERATIONAL IN FIFTEEN MINUTES!
"BATBOYS"?
YEAH. THEY HATE IT WHEN I CALL THEM THAT.

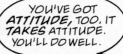

YOU'VE GOT *ATTITUDE*, TOO. IT *TAKES* ATTITUDE. YOU'LL DO WELL.

I'VE GOT *ONE* REQUEST-- IF YOU *WOULD*, OUT OF RESPECT FOR YOUR *ELDERS*--

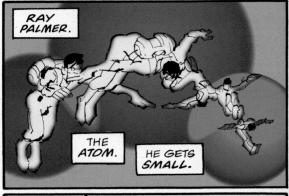

RAY PALMER.

THE *ATOM*.

HE GETS *SMALL*.

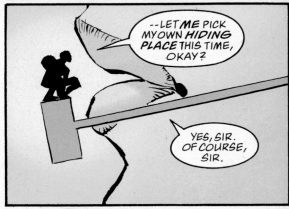

--LET *ME* PICK MY OWN *HIDING PLACE* THIS TIME, OKAY?

YES, SIR. OF COURSE, SIR.

BACK TO THAT *KILLER ASTEROID*.

SPEAKING TO *REPORTERS*, THE *PRESIDENT* EXUDED AN *UNNATURAL* LEVEL OF *CONFIDENCE*...

NEWS IN THE NUDE

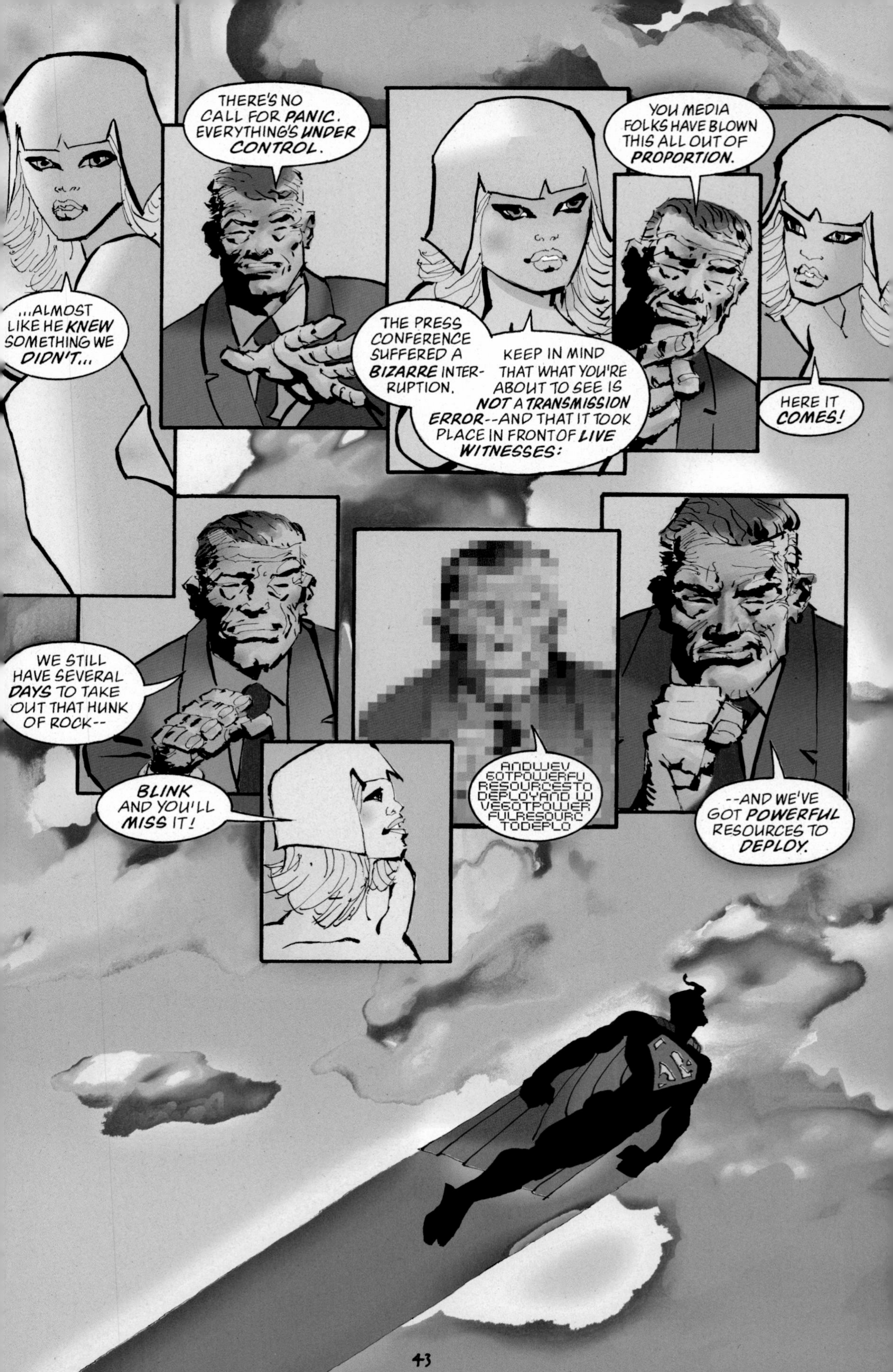
...ALMOST LIKE HE KNEW SOMETHING WE DIDN'T...
THERE'S NO CALL FOR PANIC. EVERYTHING'S UNDER CONTROL.
THE PRESS CONFERENCE SUFFERED A BIZARRE INTER-RUPTION.
KEEP IN MIND THAT WHAT YOU'RE ABOUT TO SEE IS NOT A TRANSMISSION ERROR--AND THAT IT TOOK PLACE IN FRONT OF LIVE WITNESSES:
YOU MEDIA FOLKS HAVE BLOWN THIS ALL OUT OF PROPORTION.
HERE IT COMES!
WE STILL HAVE SEVERAL DAYS TO TAKE OUT THAT HUNK OF ROCK--
BLINK AND YOU'LL MISS IT!
ANDWEV GOTPOWERFU RESOURCESTO DEPLOYAND W VEGOTPOWER FULRESOURC TODEPLO
--AND WE'VE GOT POWERFUL RESOURCES TO DEPLOY.

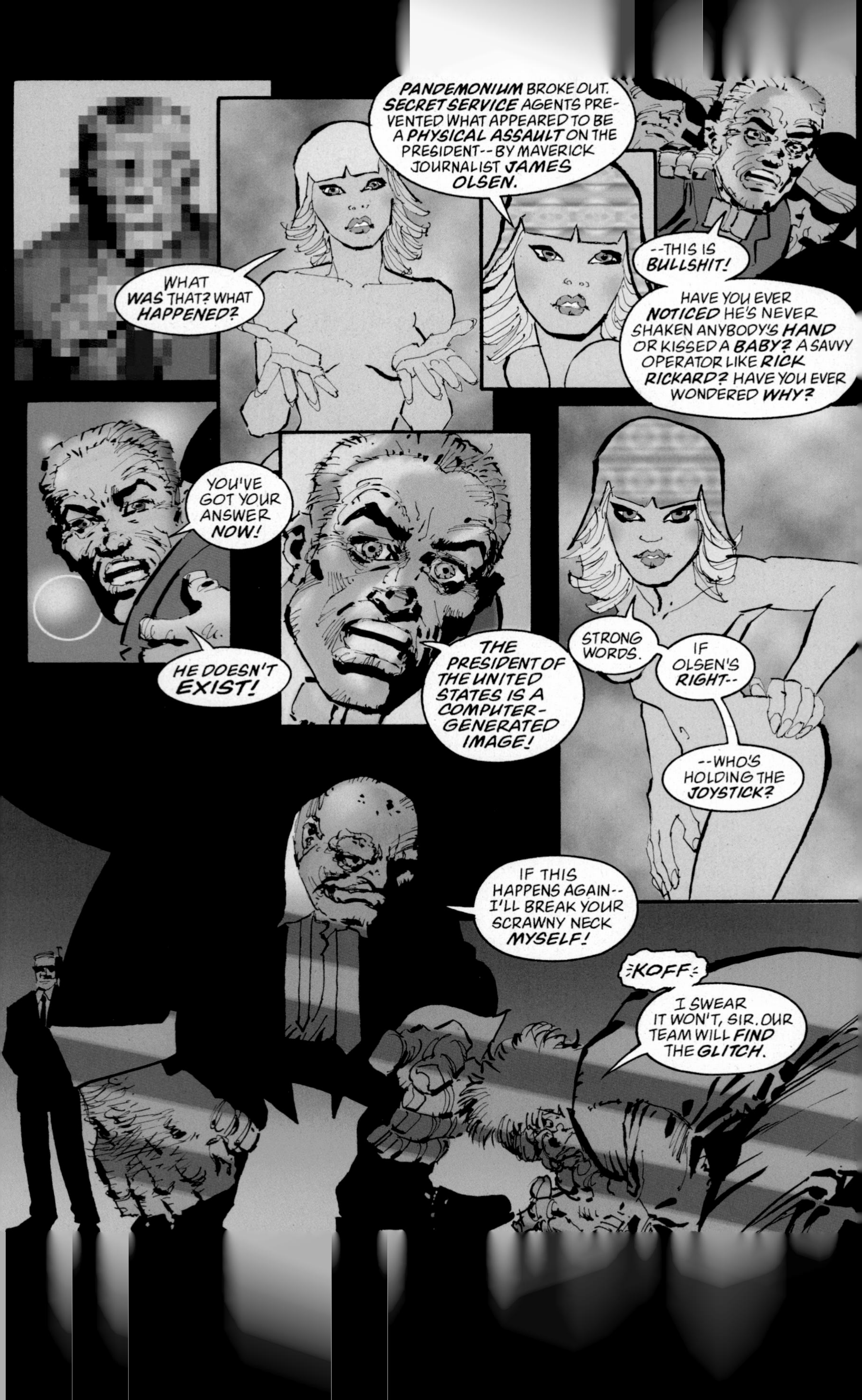
WHAT WAS THAT? WHAT HAPPENED?
PANDEMONIUM BROKE OUT. SECRET SERVICE AGENTS PREVENTED WHAT APPEARED TO BE A PHYSICAL ASSAULT ON THE PRESIDENT--BY MAVERICK JOURNALIST JAMES OLSEN.
--THIS IS BULLSHIT!
HAVE YOU EVER NOTICED HE'S NEVER SHAKEN ANYBODY'S HAND OR KISSED A BABY? A SAVVY OPERATOR LIKE RICK RICKARD? HAVE YOU EVER WONDERED WHY?
YOU'VE GOT YOUR ANSWER NOW!
HE DOESN'T EXIST!
THE PRESIDENT OF THE UNITED STATES IS A COMPUTER-GENERATED IMAGE!
STRONG WORDS.
IF OLSEN'S RIGHT--
--WHO'S HOLDING THE JOYSTICK?
IF THIS HAPPENS AGAIN--I'LL BREAK YOUR SCRAWNY NECK MYSELF!
KOFF
I SWEAR IT WON'T, SIR. OUR TEAM WILL FIND THE GLITCH.

THAT'S NOT GOOD ENOUGH. HE NEEDS A WHOLE NEW PROGRAM.

REFORMAT THE PRESIDENT--AND WHILE YOU'RE AT IT, SPIKE UP HIS COMPASSION LEVELS. HE'S COMING ACROSS A LITTLE COLD. NOW GET OUT OF MY SIGHT.

SIR-- WHAT ABOUT OLSEN?

WE'VE GOT HIM ON A FELONY.

RELEASE HIM.

FREEDOM OF SPEECH IS A WONDERFUL THING-- SO LONG AS NOBODY'S LISTENING.

--SO LONG AS NOBODY'S LISTENING.

The world spins MAD.

The PEOPLE are so INTOXICATED by LUXURY they have FORGOTTEN everything that makes us more than HOUSE PETS.

REASON. TRUTH. JUSTICE.

FREEDOM.

The HUMAN SPIRIT is a shattered pane of GLASS-- wrapped in soft VELVET and soaked in sugary POISON.

EVIL has SEDUCED mankind. And MANKIND has shown all the CHASTITY of a three-dollar WHORE.

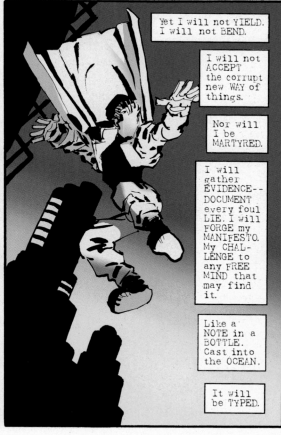

Yet I will not YIELD. I will not BEND.

I will not ACCEPT the corrupt new WAY of things.

Nor will I be MARTYRED.

I will gather EVIDENCE-- DOCUMENT every foul LIE. I will FORGE my MANIFESTO. My CHALLENGE to any FREE MIND that may find it.

Like a NOTE in a BOTTLE. Cast into the OCEAN.

It will be TYPED.

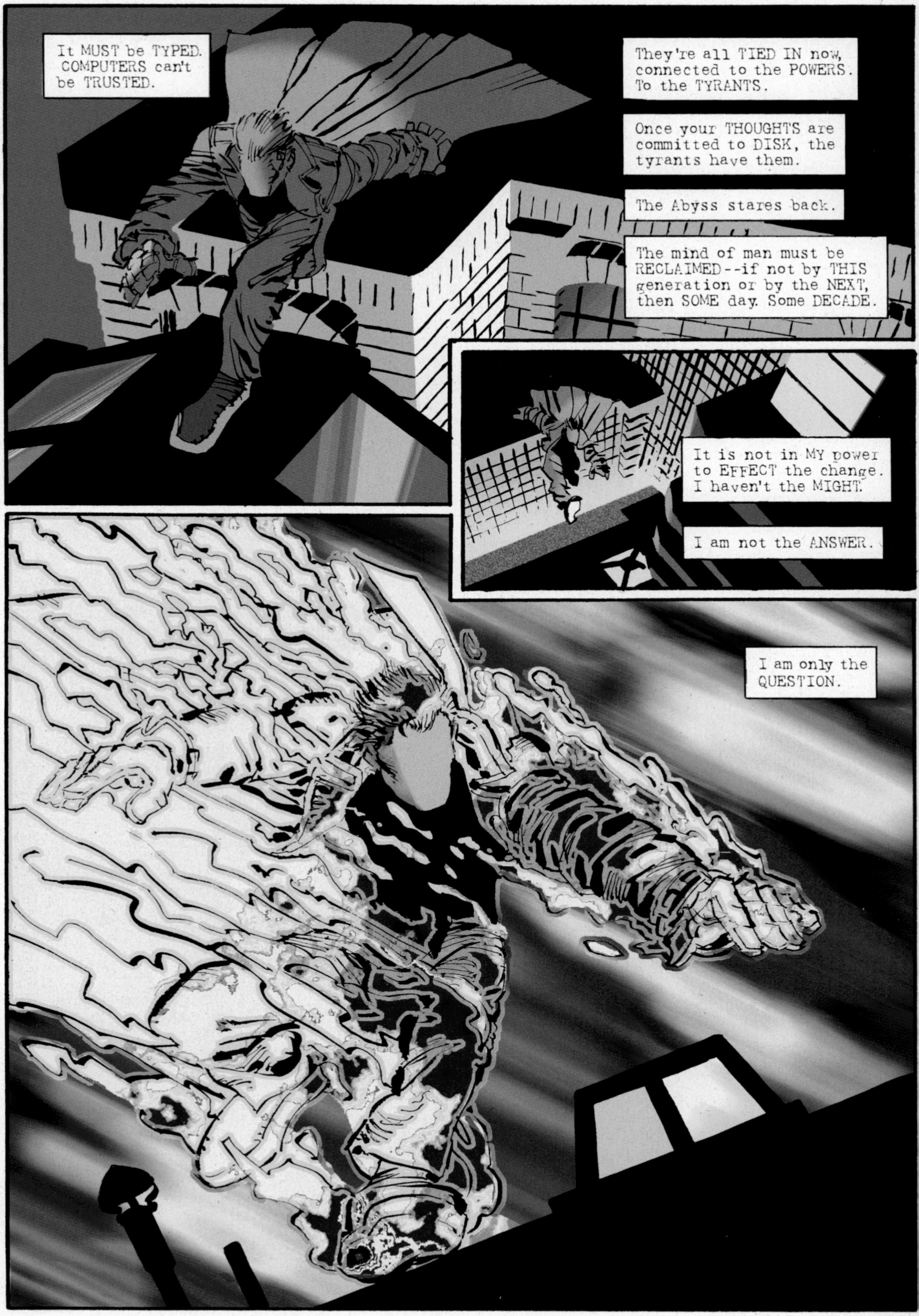
It MUST be TYPED. COMPUTERS can't be TRUSTED.
They're all TIED IN now, connected to the POWERS. To the TYRANTS.
Once your THOUGHTS are committed to DISK, the tyrants have them.
The Abyss stares back.
The mind of man must be RECLAIMED--if not by THIS generation or by the NEXT, then SOME day. Some DECADE.
It is not in MY power to EFFECT the change. I haven't the MIGHT.
I am not the ANSWER.
I am only the QUESTION.

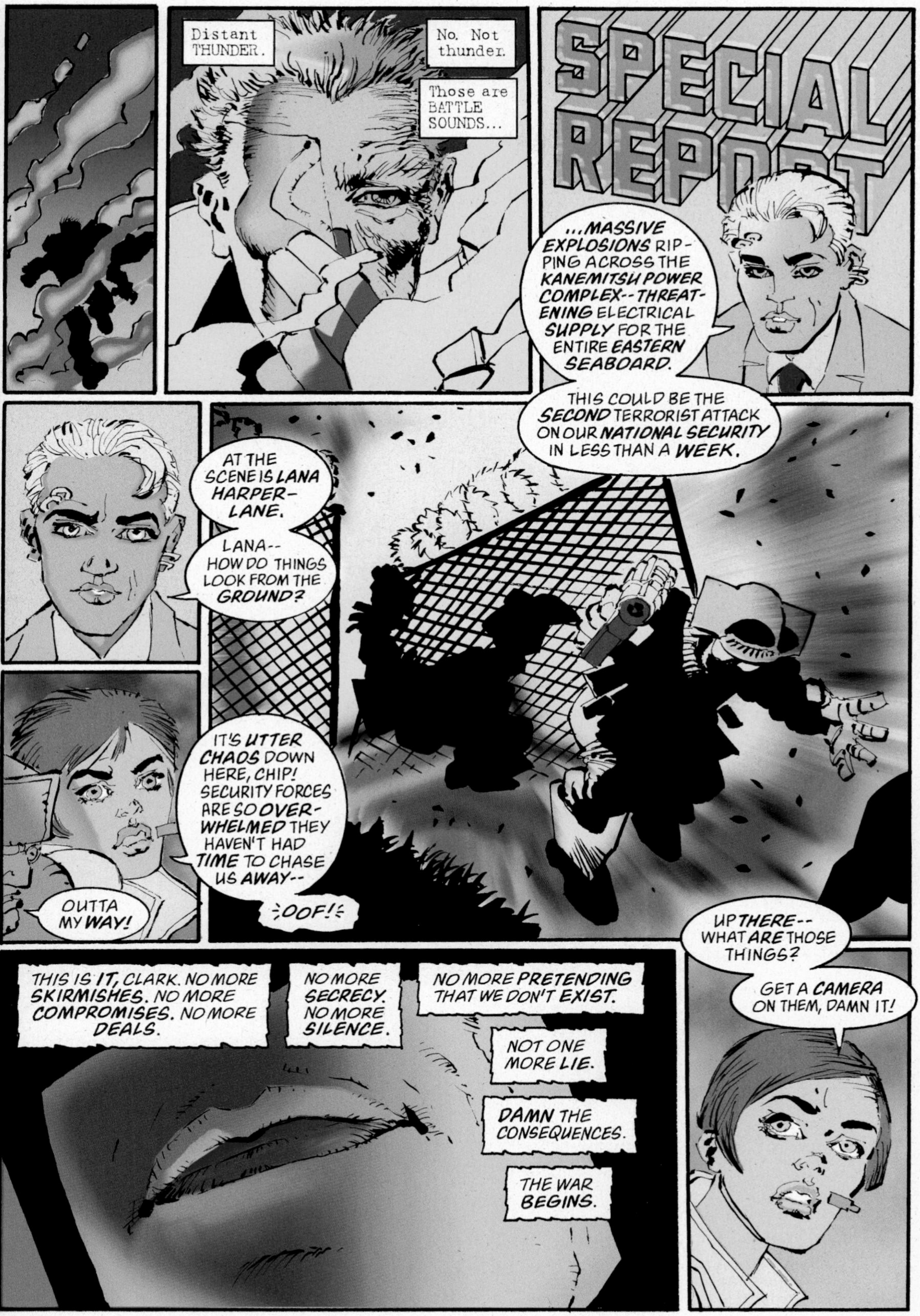

Distant THUNDER.
No. Not thunder.
Those are BATTLE SOUNDS...
SPECIAL REPORT
...MASSIVE EXPLOSIONS RIPPING ACROSS THE KANEMITSU POWER COMPLEX--THREATENING ELECTRICAL SUPPLY FOR THE ENTIRE EASTERN SEABOARD.
THIS COULD BE THE SECOND TERRORIST ATTACK ON OUR NATIONAL SECURITY IN LESS THAN A WEEK.
AT THE SCENE IS LANA HARPER-LANE.
LANA--HOW DO THINGS LOOK FROM THE GROUND?
IT'S UTTER CHAOS DOWN HERE, CHIP! SECURITY FORCES ARE SO OVERWHELMED THEY HAVEN'T HAD TIME TO CHASE US AWAY--
OUTTA MY WAY!
OOF!
THIS IS IT, CLARK. NO MORE SKIRMISHES. NO MORE COMPROMISES. NO MORE DEALS.
NO MORE SECRECY. NO MORE SILENCE.
NO MORE PRETENDING THAT WE DON'T EXIST.
NOT ONE MORE LIE.
DAMN THE CONSEQUENCES.
THE WAR BEGINS.
UP THERE--WHAT ARE THOSE THINGS?
GET A CAMERA ON THEM, DAMN IT!

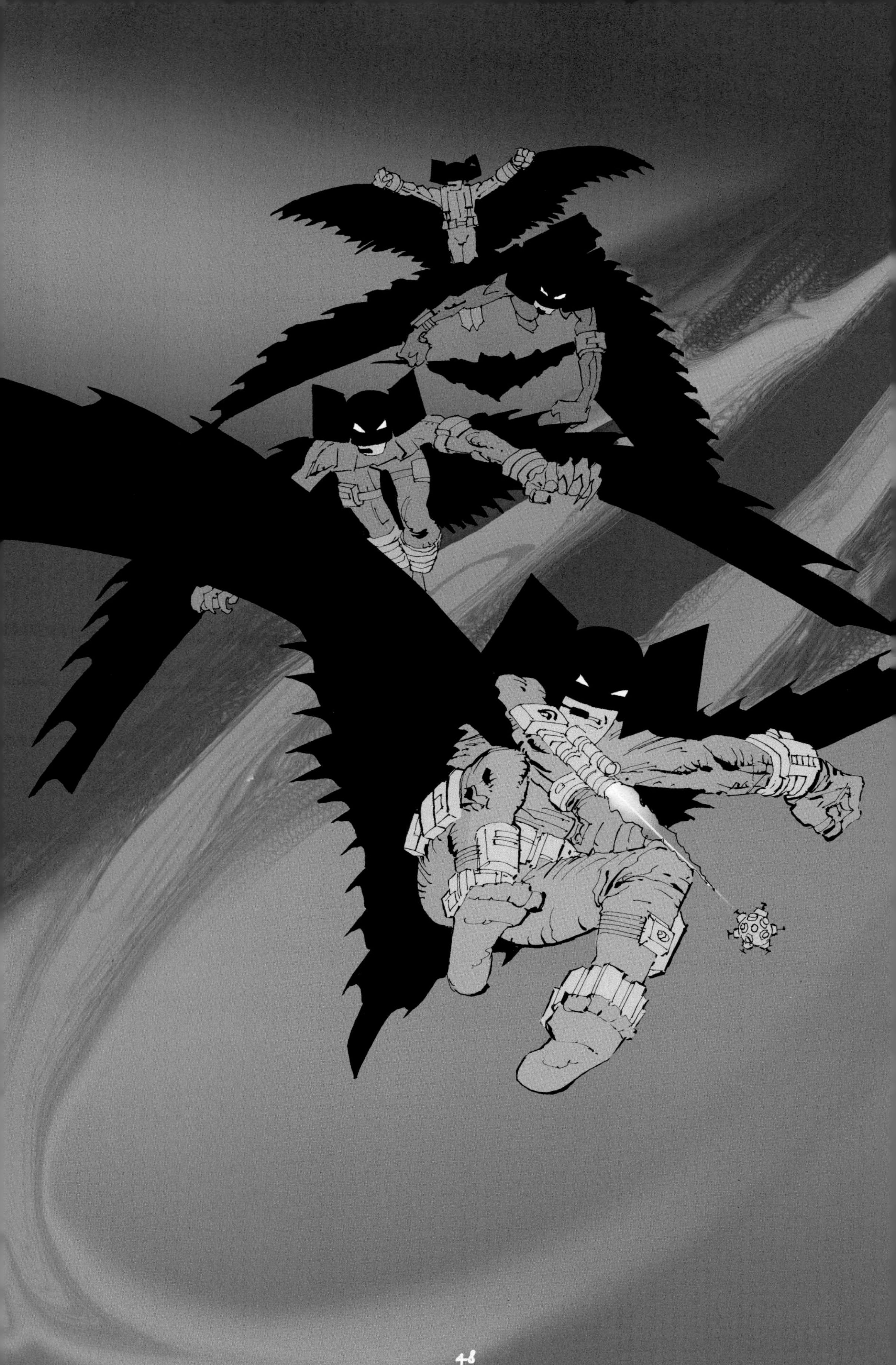

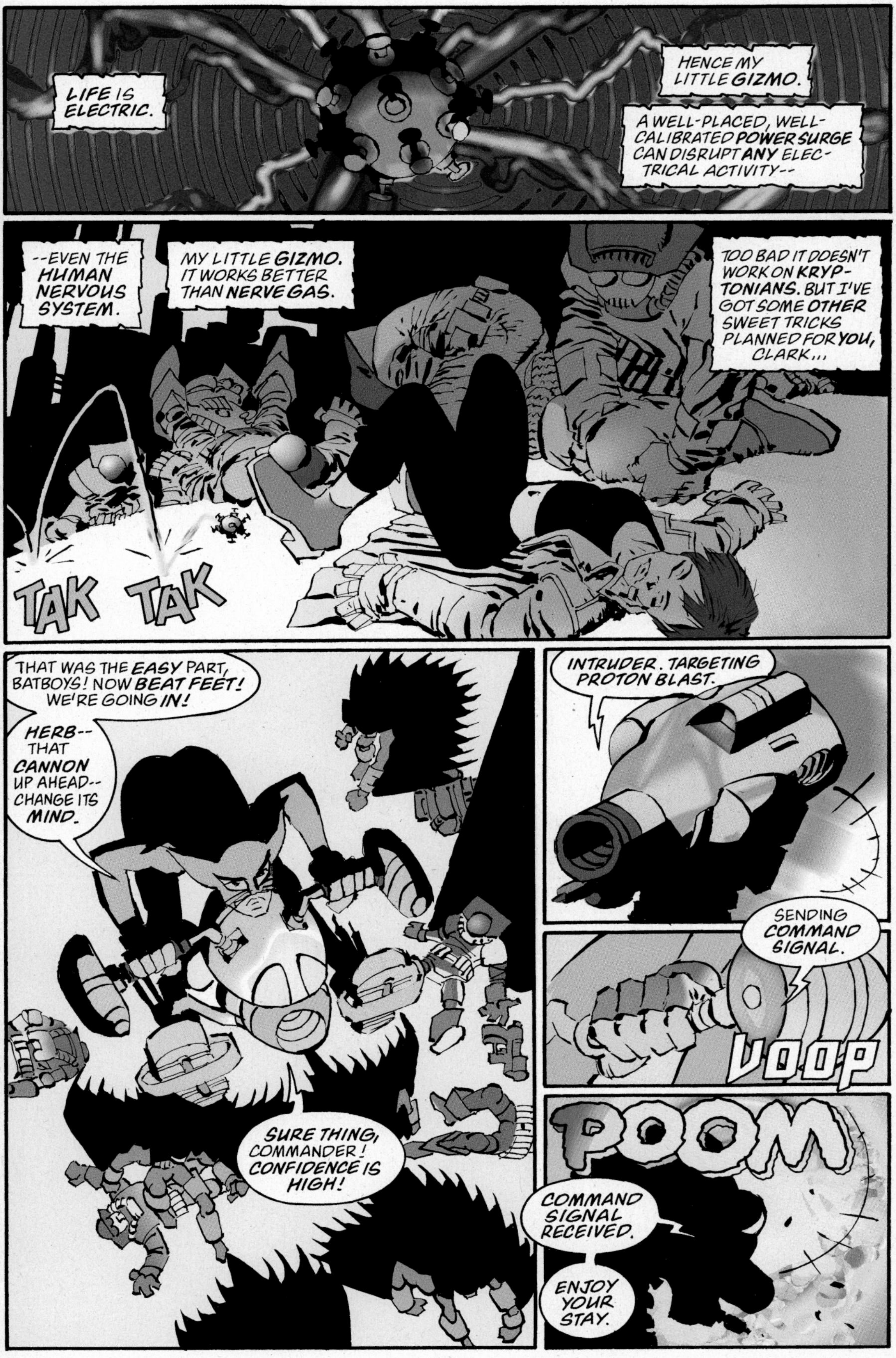
LIFE IS ELECTRIC.
HENCE MY LITTLE GIZMO.
A WELL-PLACED, WELL-CALIBRATED POWER SURGE CAN DISRUPT ANY ELECTRICAL ACTIVITY--
--EVEN THE HUMAN NERVOUS SYSTEM.
MY LITTLE GIZMO. IT WORKS BETTER THAN NERVE GAS.
TOO BAD IT DOESN'T WORK ON KRYPTONIANS. BUT I'VE GOT SOME OTHER SWEET TRICKS PLANNED FOR YOU, CLARK...
TAK TAK
THAT WAS THE EASY PART, BATBOYS! NOW BEAT FEET! WE'RE GOING IN!
HERB--THAT CANNON UP AHEAD--CHANGE ITS MIND.
SURE THING, COMMANDER! CONFIDENCE IS HIGH!
INTRUDER. TARGETING PROTON BLAST.
SENDING COMMAND SIGNAL.
VOOP
POOM
COMMAND SIGNAL RECEIVED.
ENJOY YOUR STAY.

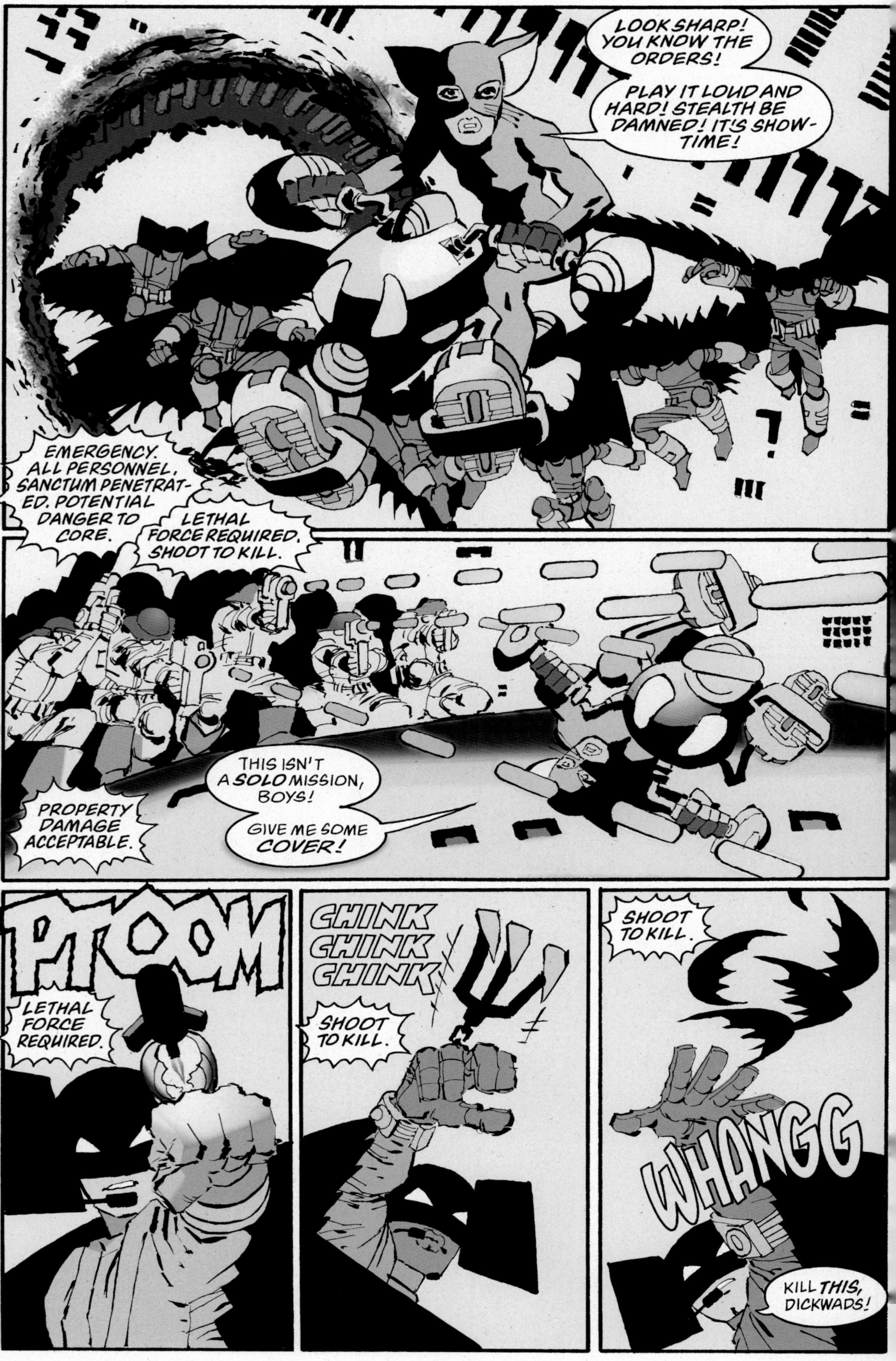

LOOK SHARP! YOU KNOW THE ORDERS!
PLAY IT LOUD AND HARD! STEALTH BE DAMNED! IT'S SHOW-TIME!
EMERGENCY. ALL PERSONNEL. SANCTUM PENETRATED. POTENTIAL DANGER TO CORE.
LETHAL FORCE REQUIRED. SHOOT TO KILL.
PROPERTY DAMAGE ACCEPTABLE.
THIS ISN'T A SOLO MISSION, BOYS!
GIVE ME SOME COVER!
PTOOM
LETHAL FORCE REQUIRED.
CHINK CHINK CHINK
SHOOT TO KILL.
SHOOT TO KILL.
WHANGG
KILL THIS, DICKWADS!

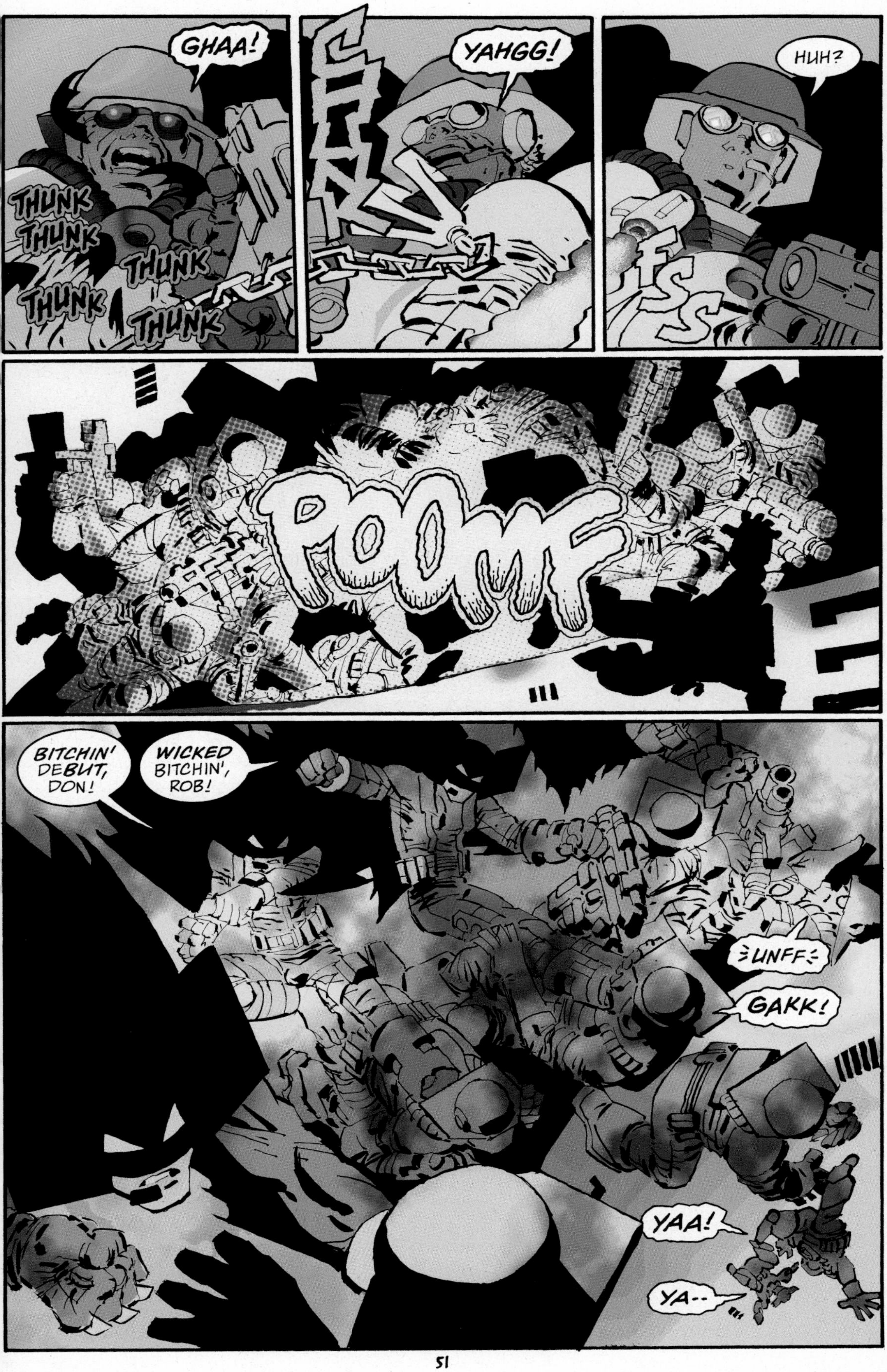
GHAA!
THUNK
THUNK
THUNK
THUNK
THUNK
YAHGG!
HUH?
FSS
POOMF
BITCHIN' DEBUT, DON!
WICKED BITCHIN', ROB!
UNFF
GAKK!
YAA!
YA--

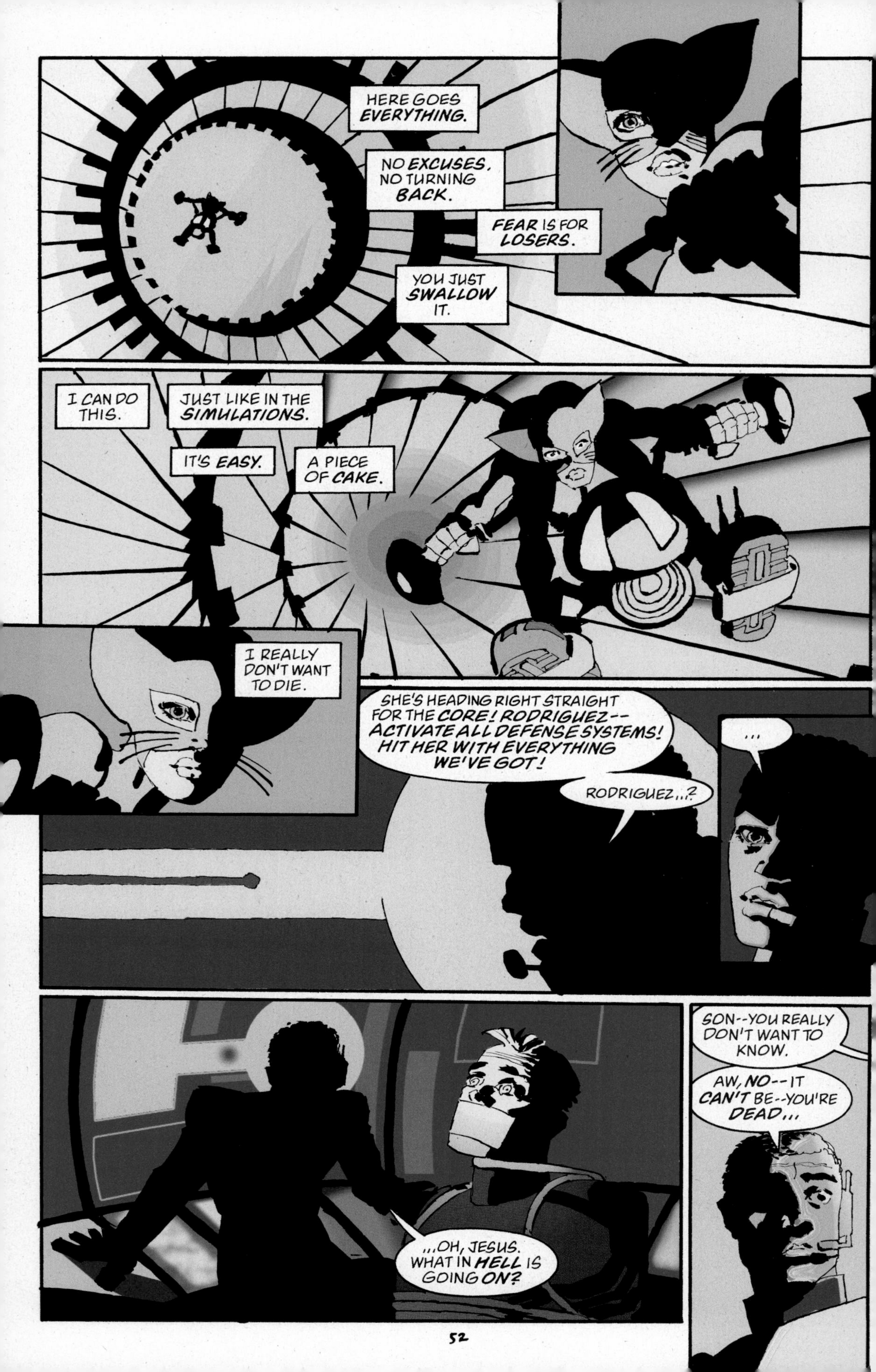
HERE GOES EVERYTHING.
NO EXCUSES. NO TURNING BACK.
FEAR IS FOR LOSERS.
YOU JUST SWALLOW IT.
I CAN DO THIS.
JUST LIKE IN THE SIMULATIONS.
IT'S EASY.
A PIECE OF CAKE.
I REALLY DON'T WANT TO DIE.
SHE'S HEADING RIGHT STRAIGHT FOR THE CORE! RODRIGUEZ-- ACTIVATE ALL DEFENSE SYSTEMS! HIT HER WITH EVERYTHING WE'VE GOT!
...
RODRIGUEZ...?
...OH, JESUS. WHAT IN HELL IS GOING ON?
SON--YOU REALLY DON'T WANT TO KNOW.
AW, NO--IT CAN'T BE--YOU'RE DEAD...

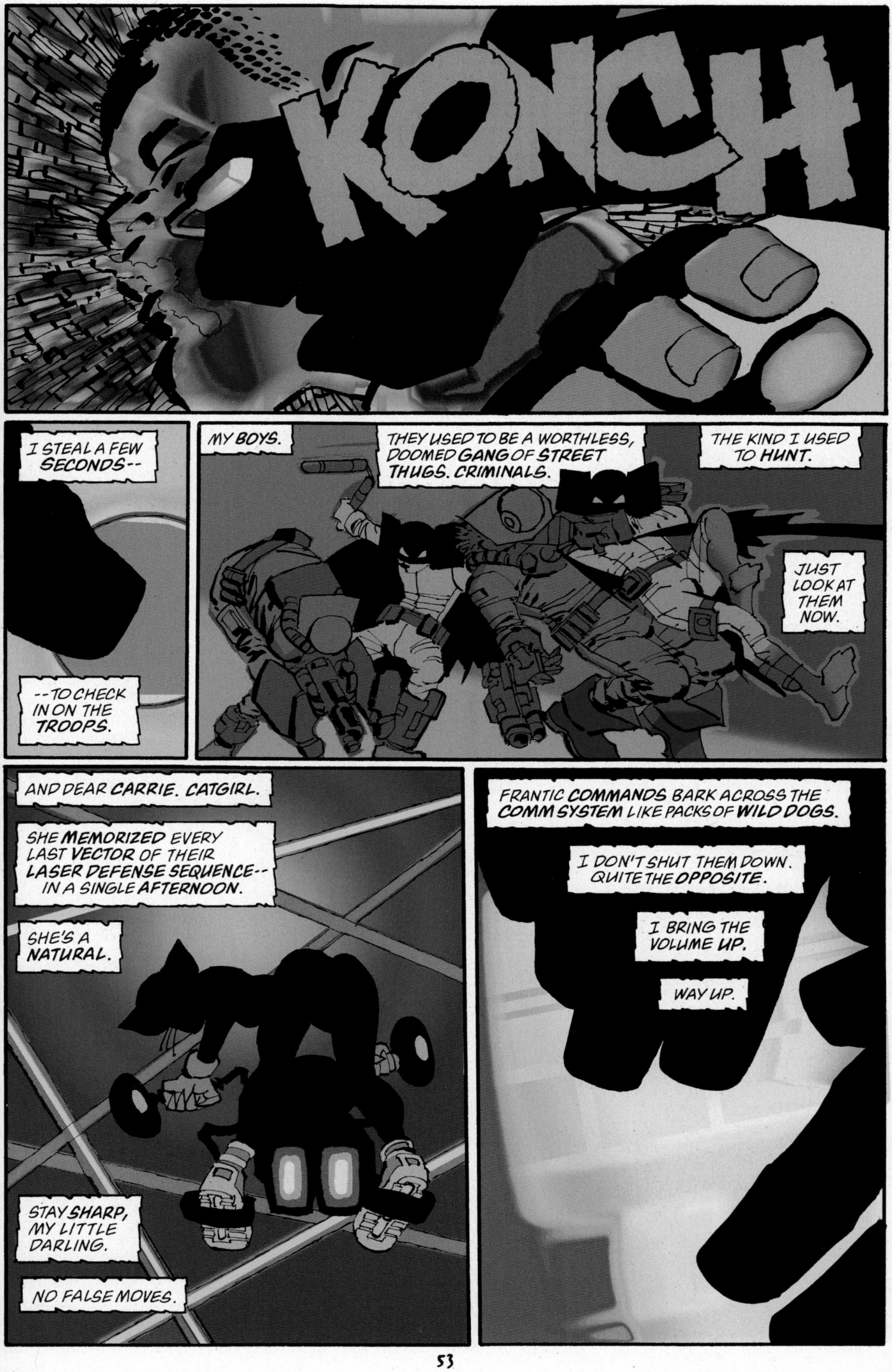
KONCH
I STEAL A FEW SECONDS--
--TO CHECK IN ON THE TROOPS.
MY BOYS.
THEY USED TO BE A WORTHLESS, DOOMED GANG OF STREET THUGS. CRIMINALS.
THE KIND I USED TO HUNT.
JUST LOOK AT THEM NOW.
AND DEAR CARRIE. CATGIRL.
SHE MEMORIZED EVERY LAST VECTOR OF THEIR LASER DEFENSE SEQUENCE-- IN A SINGLE AFTERNOON.
SHE'S A NATURAL.
STAY SHARP, MY LITTLE DARLING.
NO FALSE MOVES.
FRANTIC COMMANDS BARK ACROSS THE COMM SYSTEM LIKE PACKS OF WILD DOGS.
I DON'T SHUT THEM DOWN. QUITE THE OPPOSITE.
I BRING THE VOLUME UP.
WAY UP.

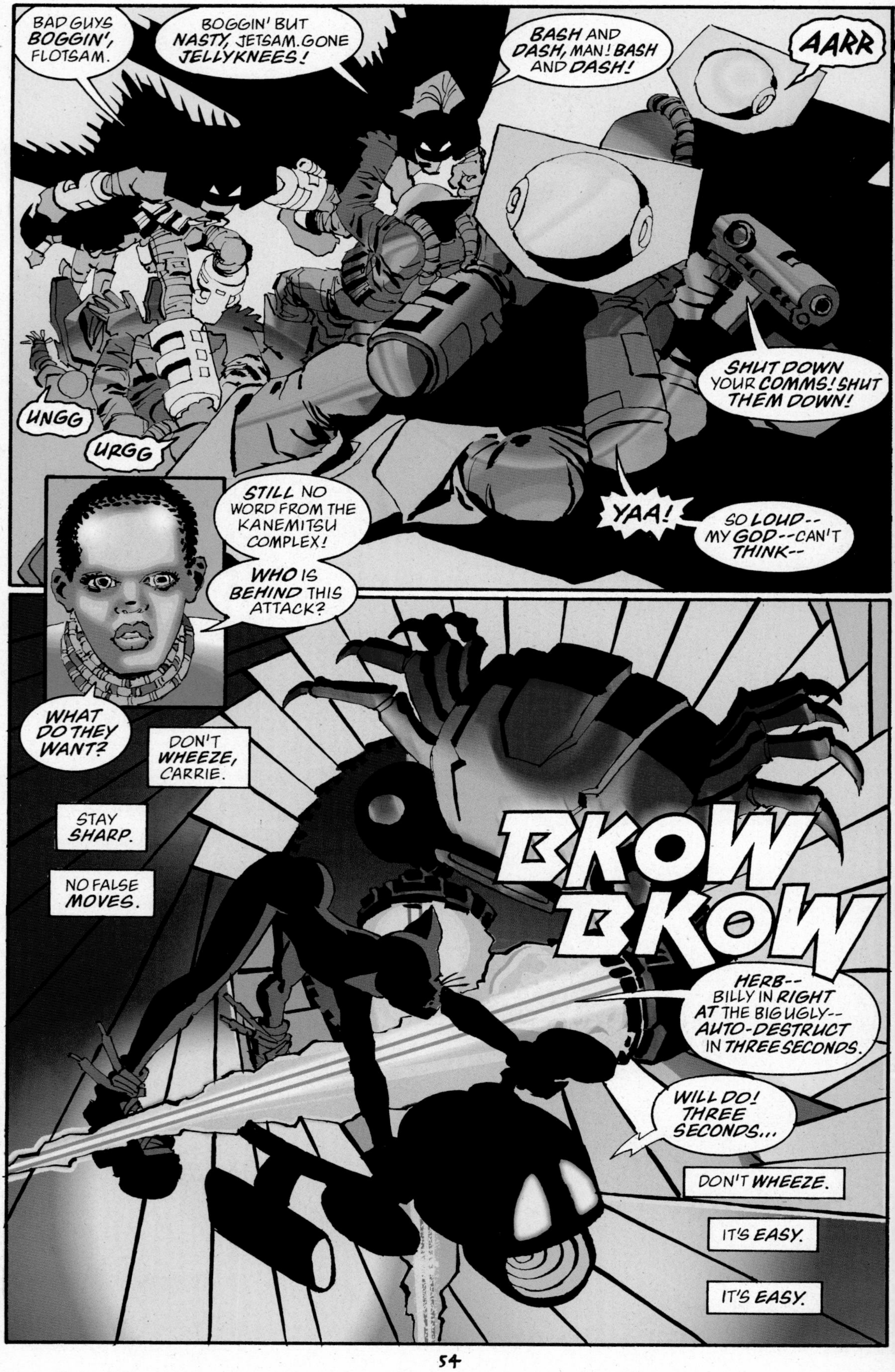
BAD GUYS BOGGIN', FLOTSAM.
BOGGIN' BUT NASTY, JETSAM. GONE JELLYKNEES!
BASH AND DASH, MAN! BASH AND DASH!
AARR
UNGG
URGG
SHUT DOWN YOUR COMMS! SHUT THEM DOWN!
STILL NO WORD FROM THE KANEMITSU COMPLEX!
WHO IS BEHIND THIS ATTACK?
YAA!
SO LOUD-- MY GOD--CAN'T THINK--
WHAT DO THEY WANT?
DON'T WHEEZE, CARRIE.
STAY SHARP.
NO FALSE MOVES.
BKOW BKOW
HERB-- BILLY IN RIGHT AT THE BIG UGLY-- AUTO-DESTRUCT IN THREE SECONDS.
WILL DO! THREE SECONDS...
DON'T WHEEZE.
IT'S EASY.
IT'S EASY.

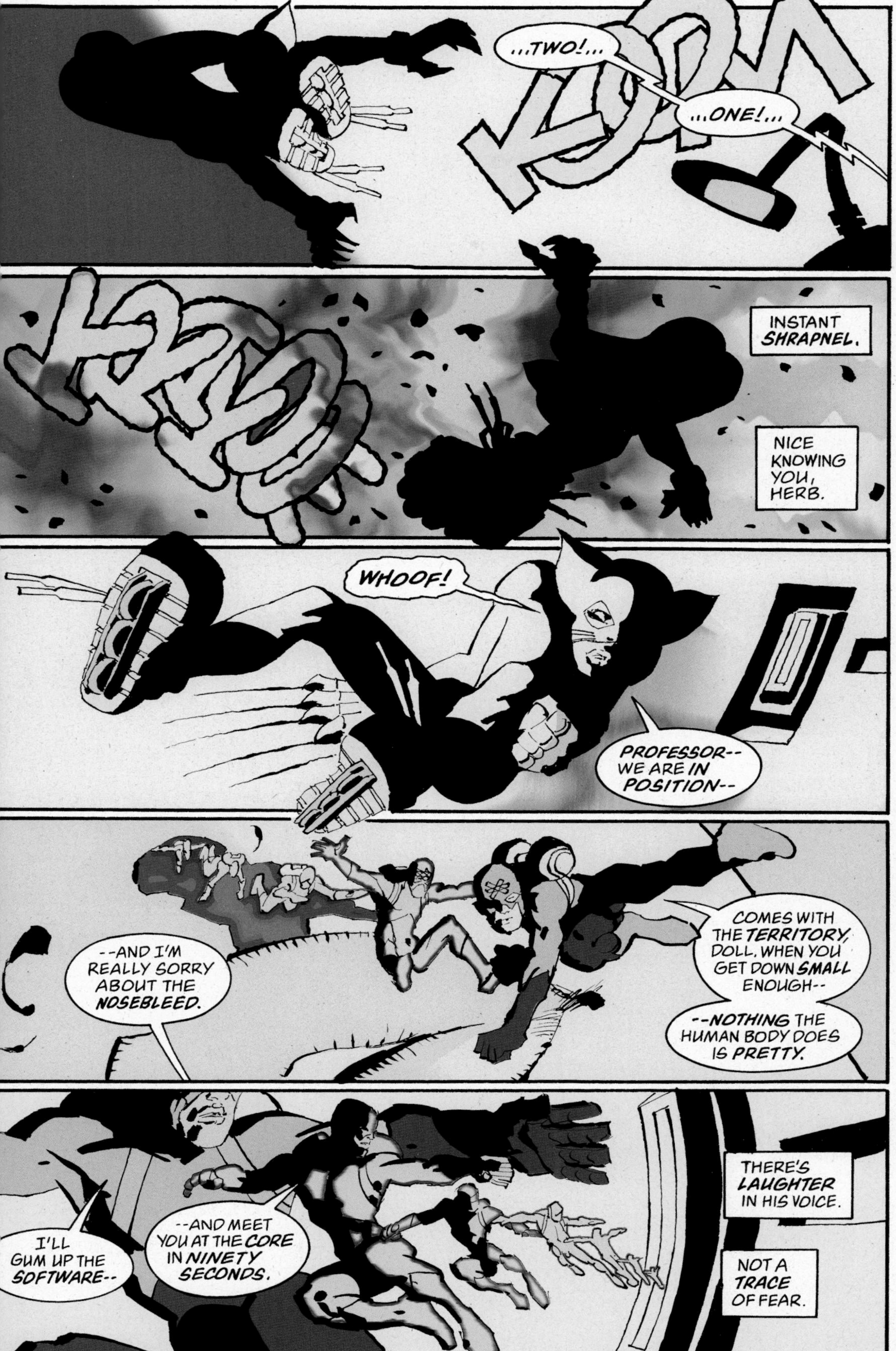
KOOM
...TWO!...
...ONE!...
KROOM
INSTANT SHRAPNEL.
NICE KNOWING YOU, HERB.
WHOOF!
PROFESSOR-- WE ARE IN POSITION--
--AND I'M REALLY SORRY ABOUT THE NOSEBLEED.
COMES WITH THE TERRITORY, DOLL, WHEN YOU GET DOWN SMALL ENOUGH--
--NOTHING THE HUMAN BODY DOES IS PRETTY.
I'LL GUM UP THE SOFTWARE--
--AND MEET YOU AT THE CORE IN NINETY SECONDS.
THERE'S LAUGHTER IN HIS VOICE.
NOT A TRACE OF FEAR.

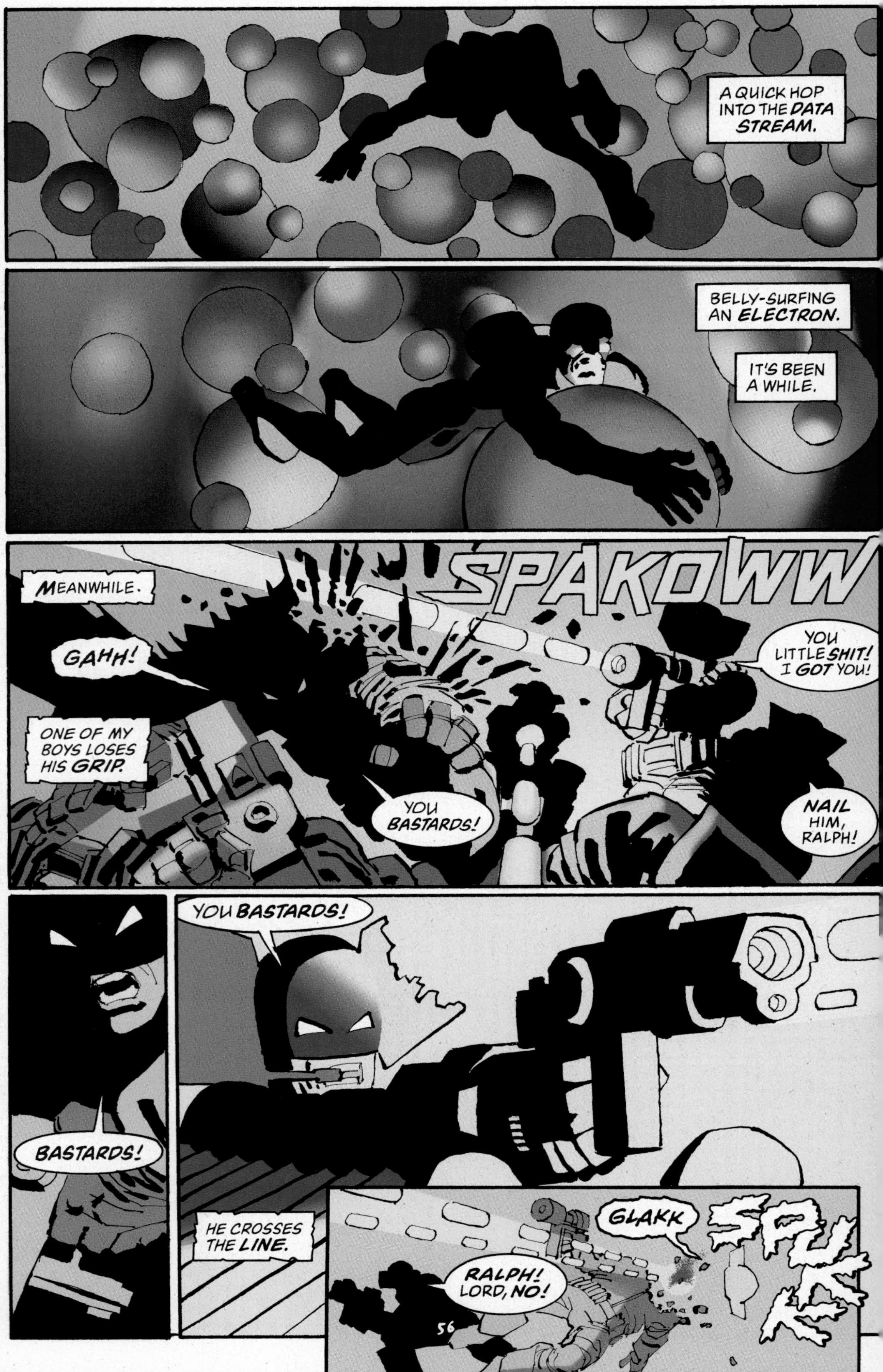

A QUICK HOP INTO THE DATA STREAM.
BELLY-SURFING AN ELECTRON.
IT'S BEEN A WHILE.
SPAKOWW
MEANWHILE.
GAHH!
YOU LITTLE SHIT! I GOT YOU!
ONE OF MY BOYS LOSES HIS GRIP.
YOU BASTARDS!
NAIL HIM, RALPH!
BASTARDS!
YOU BASTARDS!
HE CROSSES THE LINE.
GLAKK
SPUK
RALPH! LORD, NO!

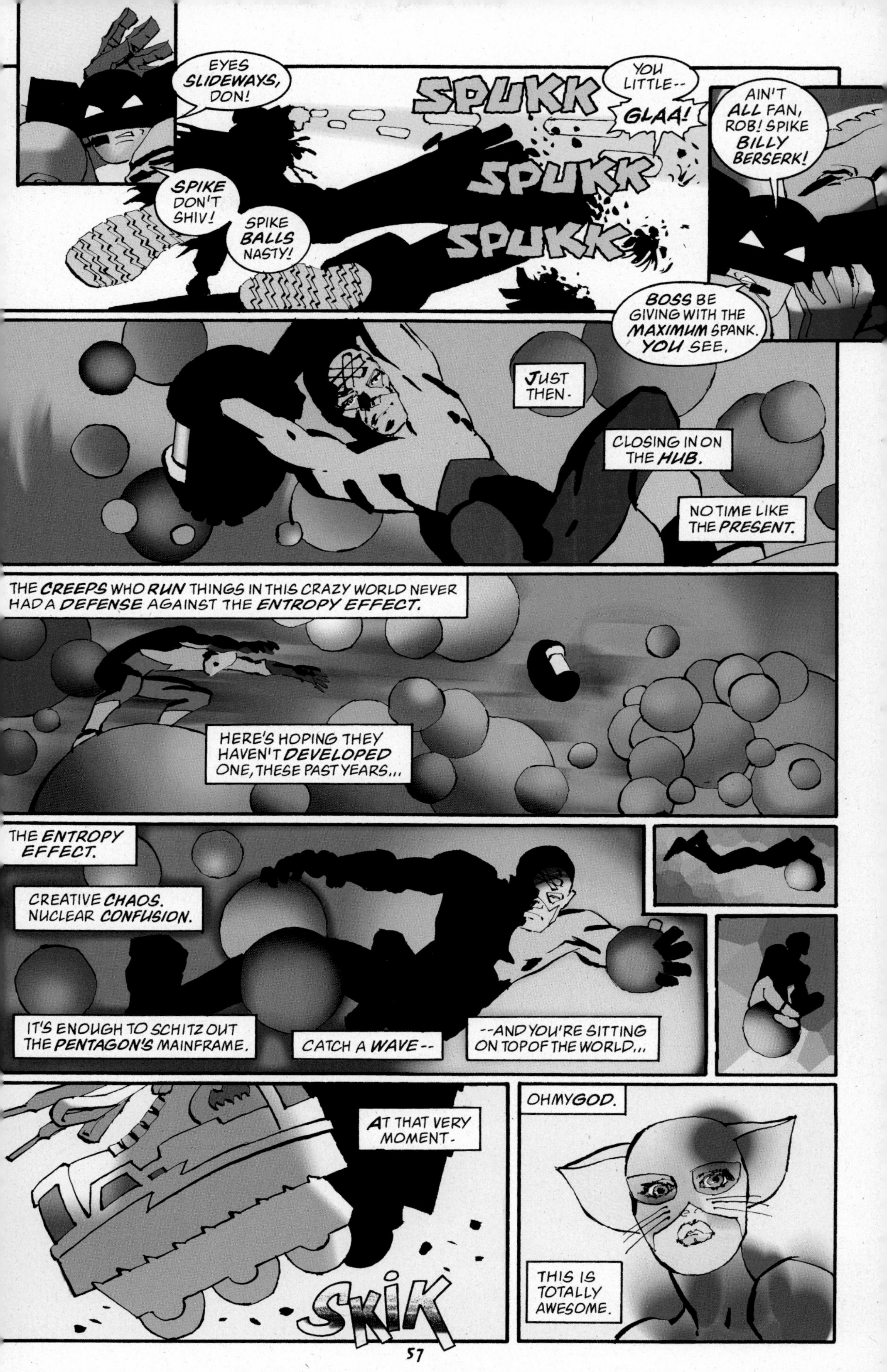
EYES SLIDEWAYS, DON!
SPUKK
YOU LITTLE-- GLAA!
SPUKK
SPUKK
SPIKE DON'T SHIV!
SPIKE BALLS NASTY!
AIN'T ALL FAN, ROB! SPIKE BILLY BERSERK!
BOSS BE GIVING WITH THE MAXIMUM SPANK. YOU SEE.
JUST THEN-
CLOSING IN ON THE HUB.
NO TIME LIKE THE PRESENT.
THE CREEPS WHO RUN THINGS IN THIS CRAZY WORLD NEVER HAD A DEFENSE AGAINST THE ENTROPY EFFECT.
HERE'S HOPING THEY HAVEN'T DEVELOPED ONE, THESE PAST YEARS...
THE ENTROPY EFFECT.
CREATIVE CHAOS. NUCLEAR CONFUSION.
IT'S ENOUGH TO SCHITZ OUT THE PENTAGON'S MAINFRAME.
CATCH A WAVE--
--AND YOU'RE SITTING ON TOP OF THE WORLD...
AT THAT VERY MOMENT-
SKIK
OHMYGOD.
THIS IS TOTALLY AWESOME.

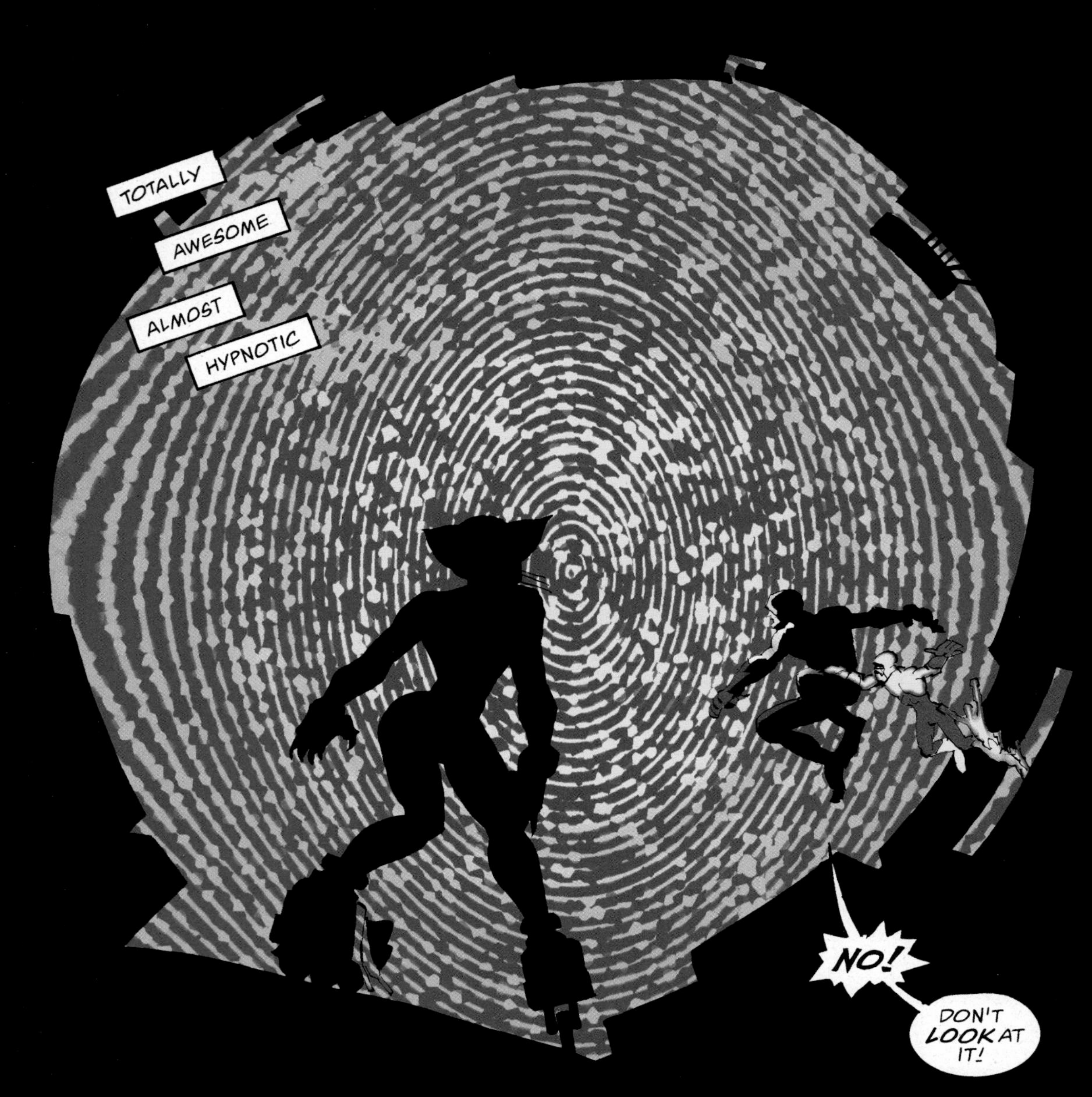
TOTALLY
AWESOME
ALMOST
HYPNOTIC
NO!
DON'T LOOK AT IT!

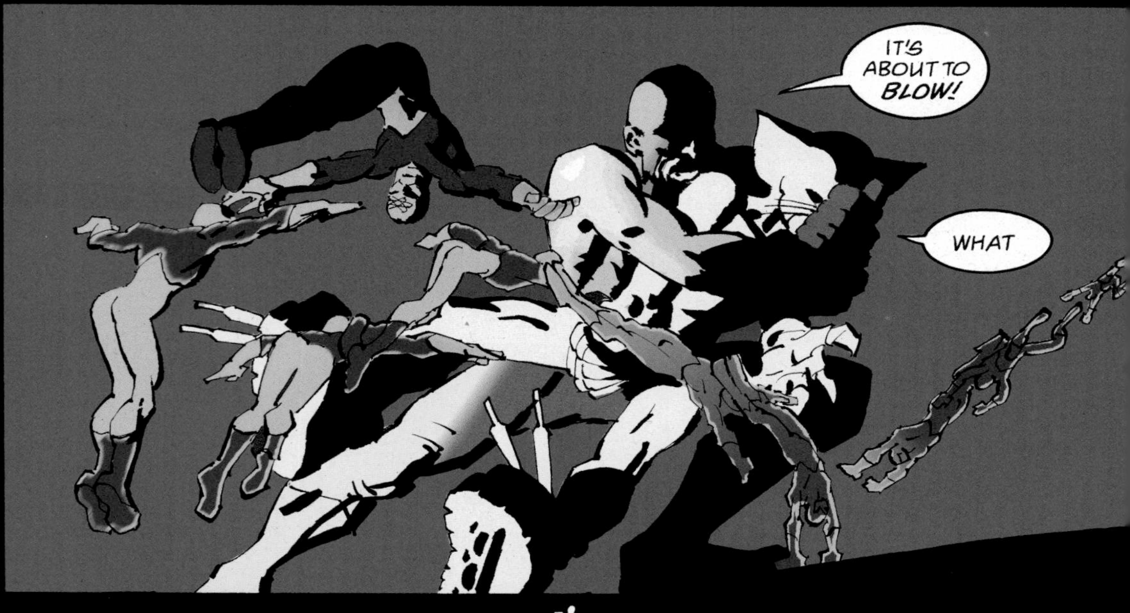
IT'S ABOUT TO BLOW!
WHAT

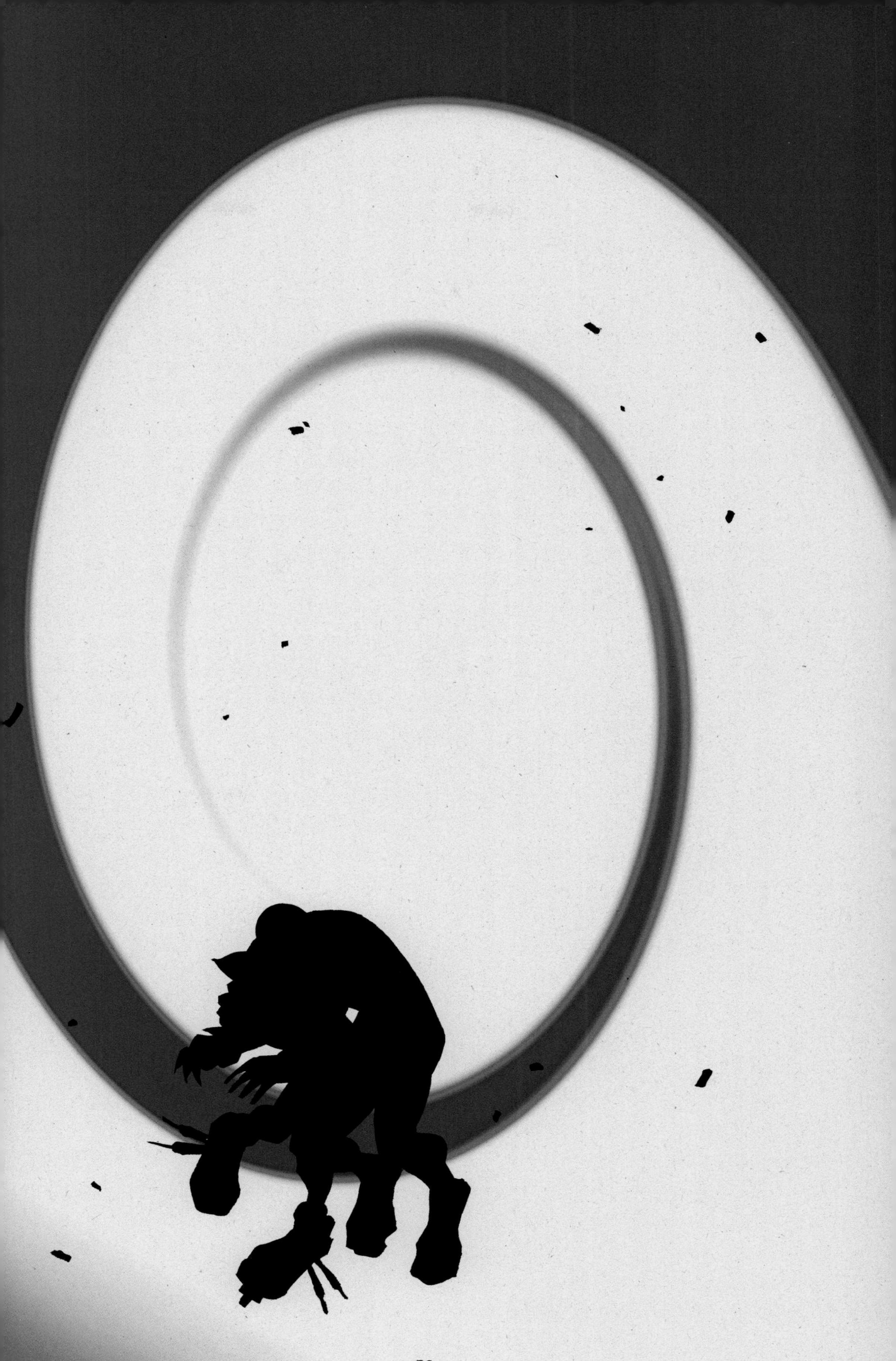

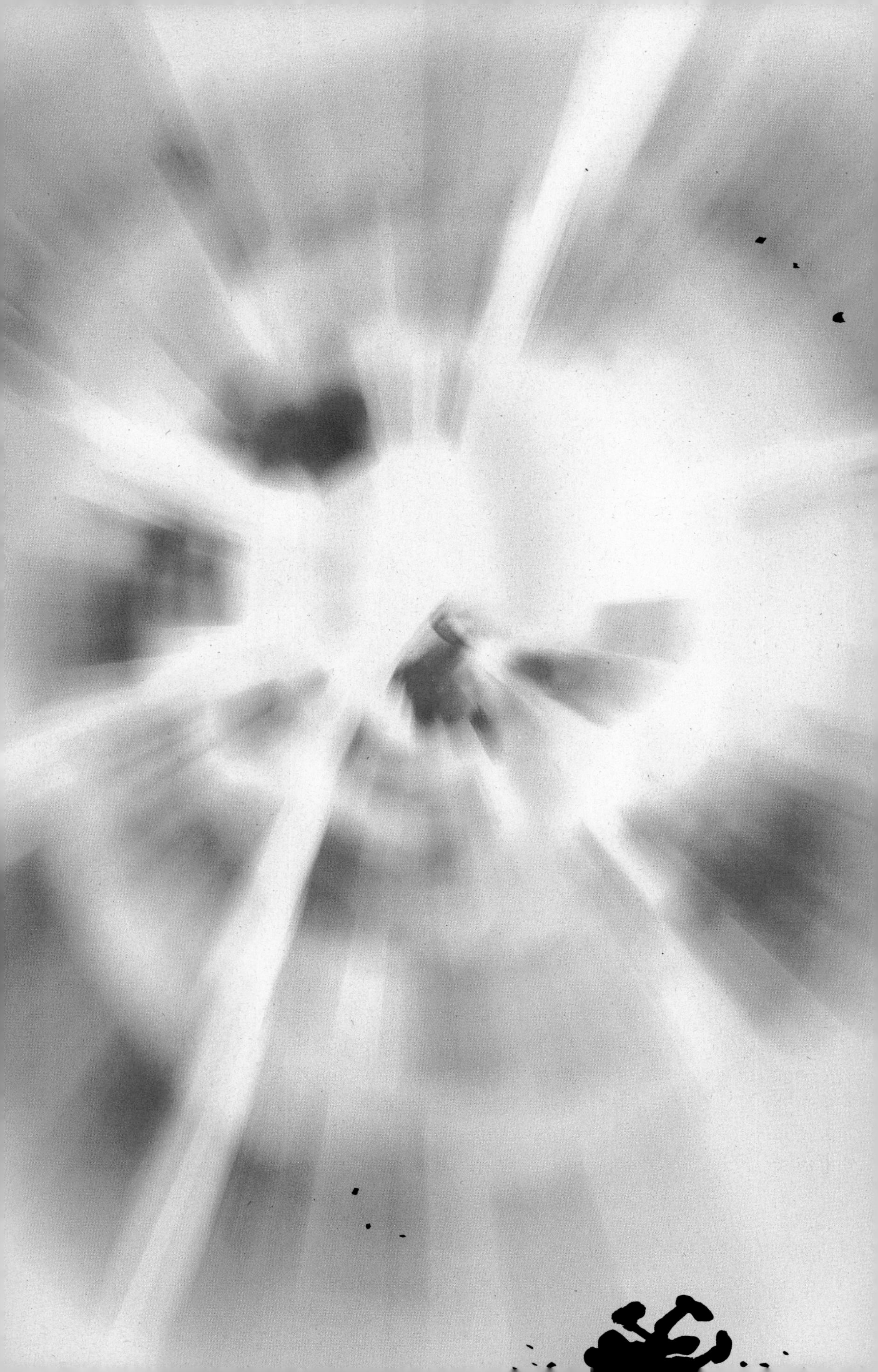

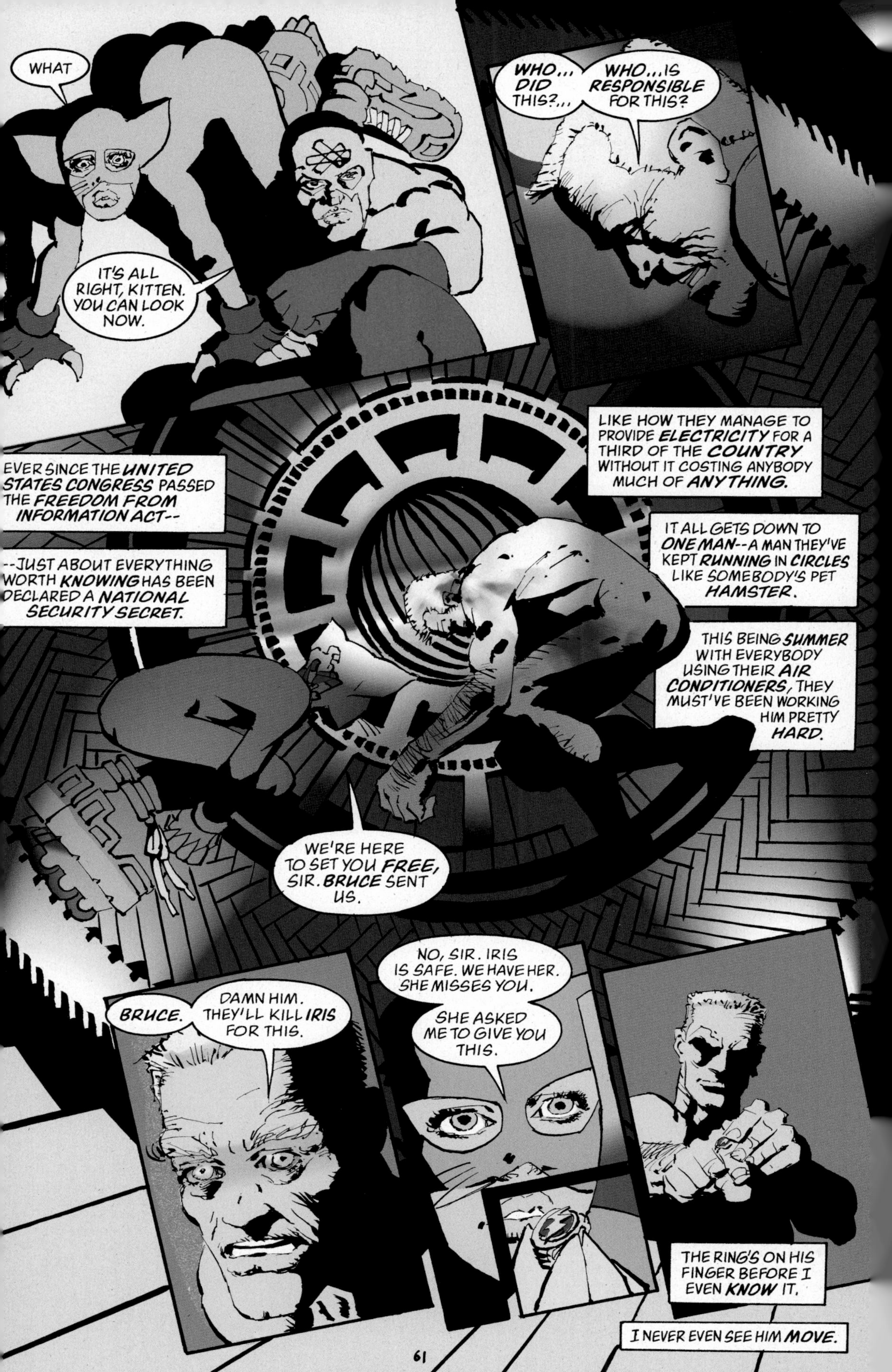
WHAT
IT'S ALL RIGHT, KITTEN. YOU CAN LOOK NOW.
WHO... DID THIS?...
WHO... IS RESPONSIBLE FOR THIS?
EVER SINCE THE UNITED STATES CONGRESS PASSED THE FREEDOM FROM INFORMATION ACT--
--JUST ABOUT EVERYTHING WORTH KNOWING HAS BEEN DECLARED A NATIONAL SECURITY SECRET.
LIKE HOW THEY MANAGE TO PROVIDE ELECTRICITY FOR A THIRD OF THE COUNTRY WITHOUT IT COSTING ANYBODY MUCH OF ANYTHING.
IT ALL GETS DOWN TO ONE MAN--A MAN THEY'VE KEPT RUNNING IN CIRCLES LIKE SOMEBODY'S PET HAMSTER.
THIS BEING SUMMER WITH EVERYBODY USING THEIR AIR CONDITIONERS, THEY MUST'VE BEEN WORKING HIM PRETTY HARD.
WE'RE HERE TO SET YOU FREE, SIR. BRUCE SENT US.
BRUCE.
DAMN HIM. THEY'LL KILL IRIS FOR THIS.
NO, SIR. IRIS IS SAFE. WE HAVE HER. SHE MISSES YOU.
SHE ASKED ME TO GIVE YOU THIS.
THE RING'S ON HIS FINGER BEFORE I EVEN KNOW IT.
I NEVER EVEN SEE HIM MOVE.

YOU CHANGED MY OUTFIT.

HUH?

...UH, YEAH. THE OLD DESIGN WAS REALLY... OLD.

KIDS, THESE DAYS. CAN'T TELL THE DIFFERENCE BETWEEN JUST PLAIN OLD AND CLASSIC.

I ASSUME BRUCE GAVE YOU AN EXIT STRATEGY?

HUH?...RIGHT. EXIT STRATEGY. YEAH. YOU.

FAIR ENOUGH. HOLD YOUR BREATH.

PALMER-- YOU COMING ALONG FOR THE RIDE?

I'LL FIND MY OWN WAY, THANKS.

I'M GETTING WHIPLASH JUST WATCHING YOU.

HIS COSTUME EXPANDS ON CONTACT WITH AIR. DON'T ASK ME HOW.

ASK HIM.

BARRY ALLEN.

THE FLASH.

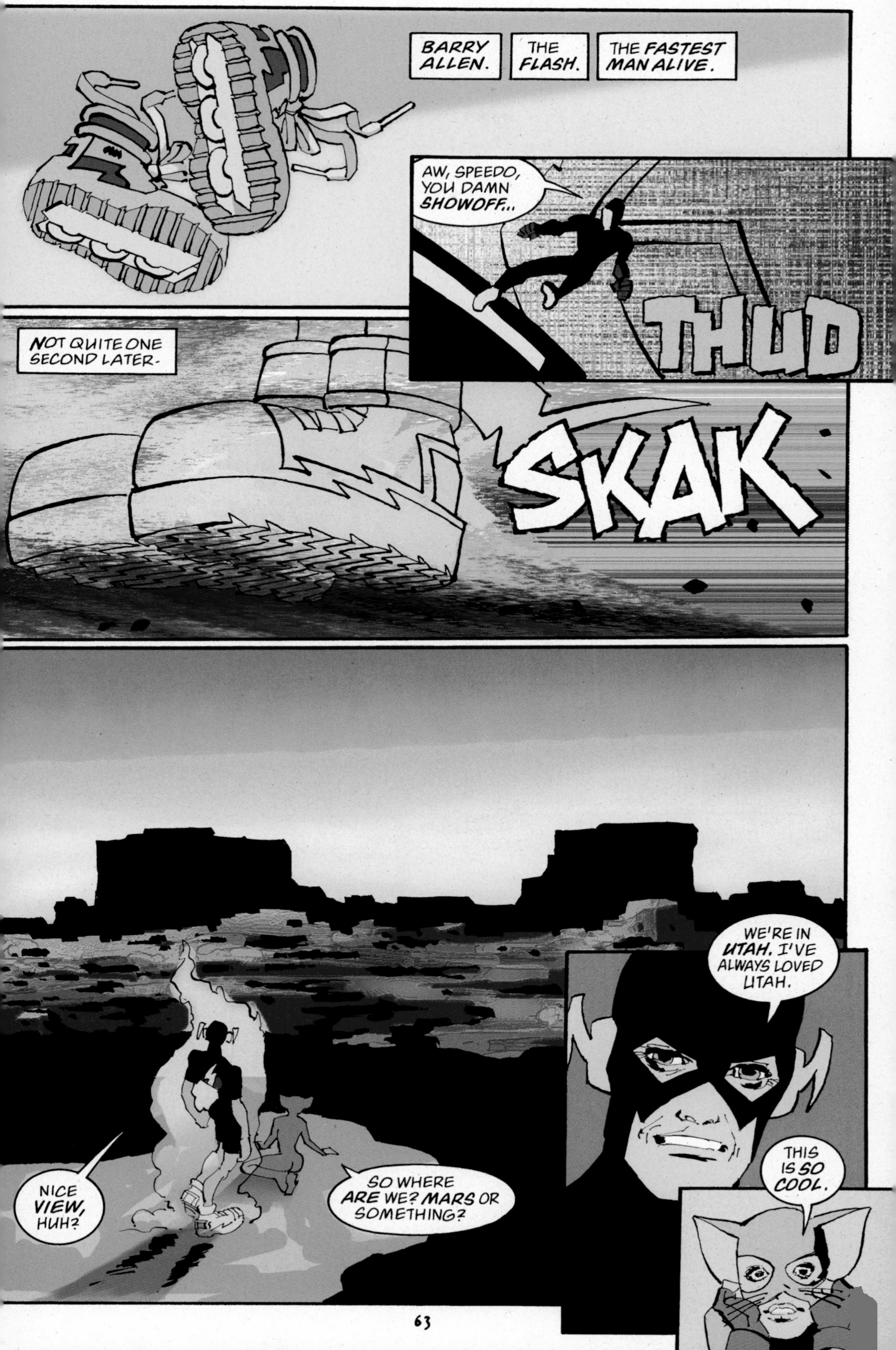
BARRY ALLEN.
THE FLASH.
THE FASTEST MAN ALIVE.
AW, SPEEDO, YOU DAMN SHOWOFF...
THUD
NOT QUITE ONE SECOND LATER-
SKAK
NICE VIEW, HUH?
SO WHERE ARE WE? MARS OR SOMETHING?
WE'RE IN UTAH. I'VE ALWAYS LOVED UTAH.
THIS IS SO COOL.

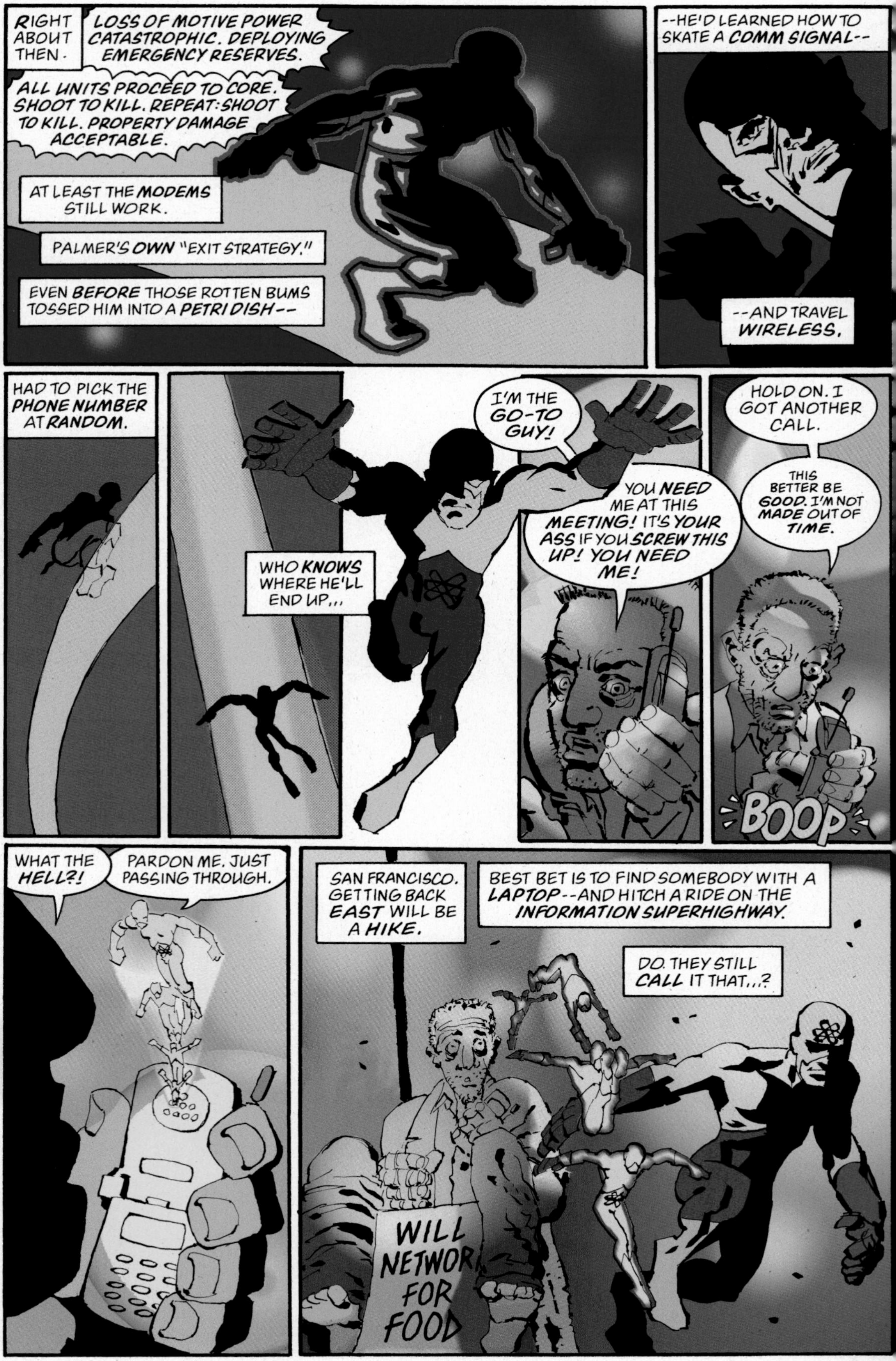
RIGHT ABOUT THEN.
LOSS OF MOTIVE POWER CATASTROPHIC. DEPLOYING EMERGENCY RESERVES.
ALL UNITS PROCEED TO CORE. SHOOT TO KILL. REPEAT: SHOOT TO KILL. PROPERTY DAMAGE ACCEPTABLE.
AT LEAST THE MODEMS STILL WORK.
PALMER'S OWN "EXIT STRATEGY."
EVEN BEFORE THOSE ROTTEN BUMS TOSSED HIM INTO A PETRI DISH--
--HE'D LEARNED HOW TO SKATE A COMM SIGNAL--
--AND TRAVEL WIRELESS.
HAD TO PICK THE PHONE NUMBER AT RANDOM.
WHO KNOWS WHERE HE'LL END UP...
I'M THE GO-TO GUY!
YOU NEED ME AT THIS MEETING! IT'S YOUR ASS IF YOU SCREW THIS UP! YOU NEED ME!
HOLD ON. I GOT ANOTHER CALL.
THIS BETTER BE GOOD. I'M NOT MADE OUT OF TIME.
BOOP
WHAT THE HELL?!
PARDON ME. JUST PASSING THROUGH.
SAN FRANCISCO. GETTING BACK EAST WILL BE A HIKE.
BEST BET IS TO FIND SOMEBODY WITH A LAPTOP--AND HITCH A RIDE ON THE INFORMATION SUPERHIGHWAY.
DO. THEY STILL CALL IT THAT...?
WILL NETWOR FOR FOOD

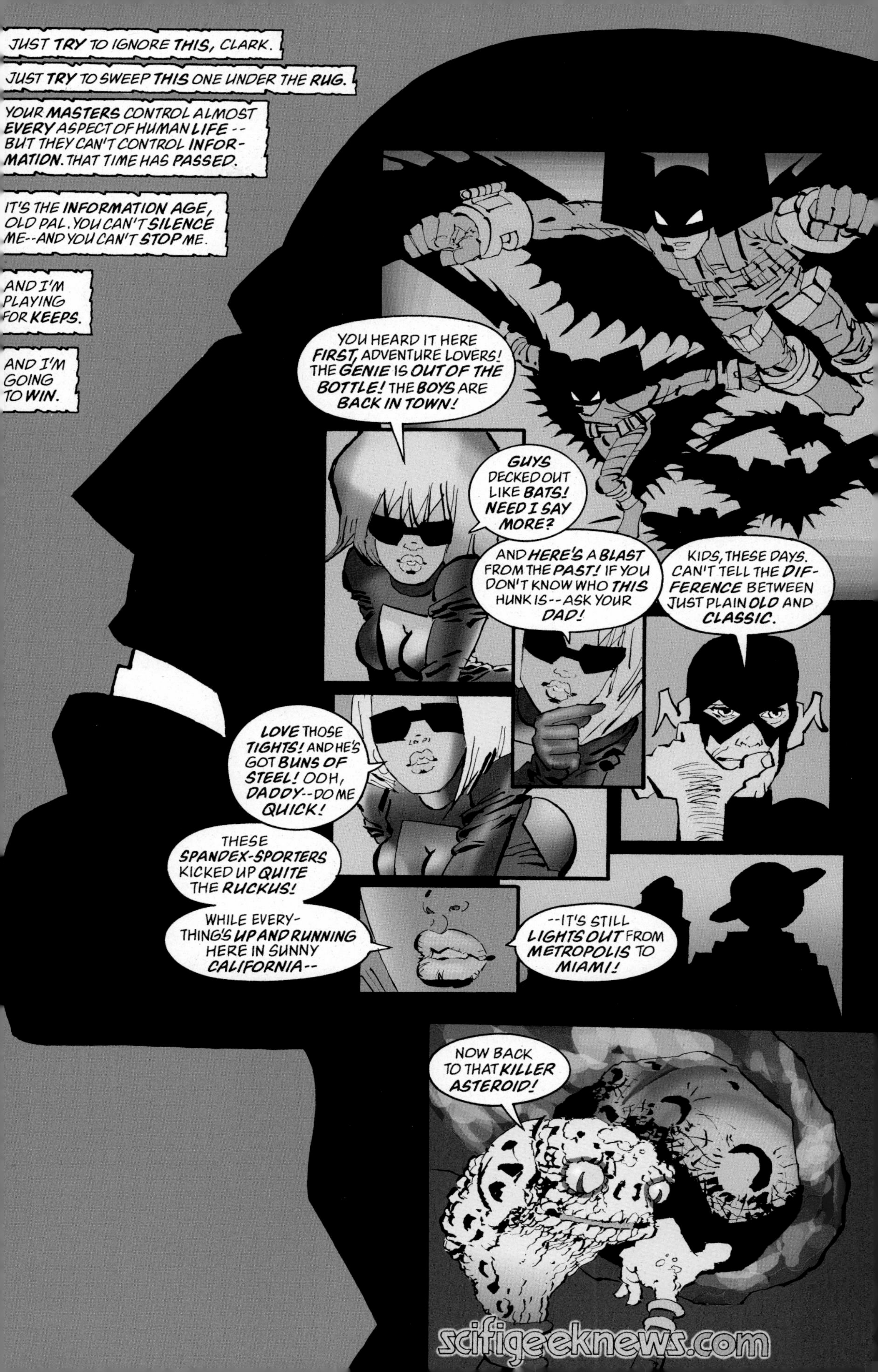
JUST TRY TO IGNORE THIS, CLARK.
JUST TRY TO SWEEP THIS ONE UNDER THE RUG.
YOUR MASTERS CONTROL ALMOST EVERY ASPECT OF HUMAN LIFE -- BUT THEY CAN'T CONTROL INFORMATION. THAT TIME HAS PASSED.
IT'S THE INFORMATION AGE, OLD PAL. YOU CAN'T SILENCE ME--AND YOU CAN'T STOP ME.
AND I'M PLAYING FOR KEEPS.
AND I'M GOING TO WIN.
YOU HEARD IT HERE FIRST, ADVENTURE LOVERS! THE GENIE IS OUT OF THE BOTTLE! THE BOYS ARE BACK IN TOWN!
GUYS DECKED OUT LIKE BATS! NEED I SAY MORE?
AND HERE'S A BLAST FROM THE PAST! IF YOU DON'T KNOW WHO THIS HUNK IS--ASK YOUR DAD!
KIDS, THESE DAYS. CAN'T TELL THE DIFFERENCE BETWEEN JUST PLAIN OLD AND CLASSIC.
LOVE THOSE TIGHTS! AND HE'S GOT BUNS OF STEEL! OOH, DADDY--DO ME QUICK!
THESE SPANDEX-SPORTERS KICKED UP QUITE THE RUCKUS!
WHILE EVERYTHING'S UP AND RUNNING HERE IN SUNNY CALIFORNIA--
--IT'S STILL LIGHTS OUT FROM METROPOLIS TO MIAMI!
NOW BACK TO THAT KILLER ASTEROID!
scifigeeknews.com

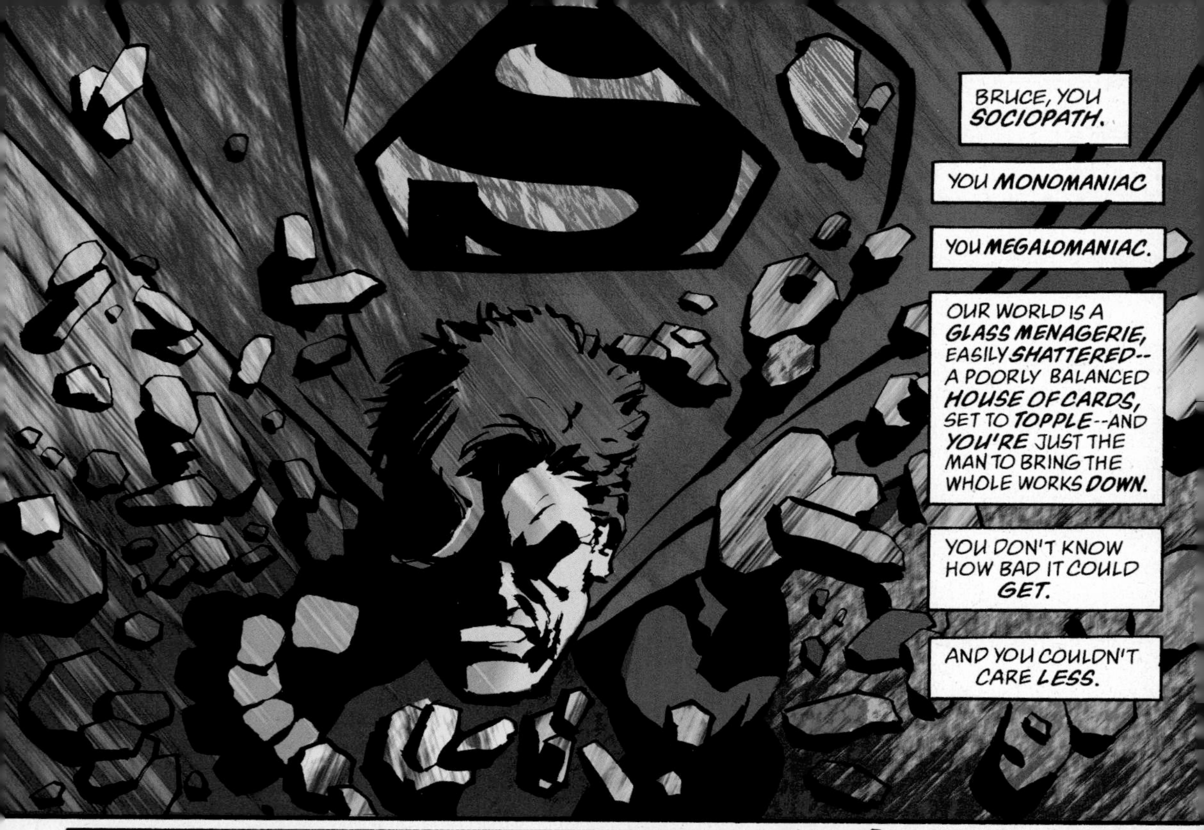
BRUCE, YOU SOCIOPATH.
YOU MONOMANIAC
YOU MEGALOMANIAC.
OUR WORLD IS A GLASS MENAGERIE, EASILY SHATTERED-- A POORLY BALANCED HOUSE OF CARDS, SET TO TOPPLE--AND YOU'RE JUST THE MAN TO BRING THE WHOLE WORKS DOWN.
YOU DON'T KNOW HOW BAD IT COULD GET.
AND YOU COULDN'T CARE LESS.

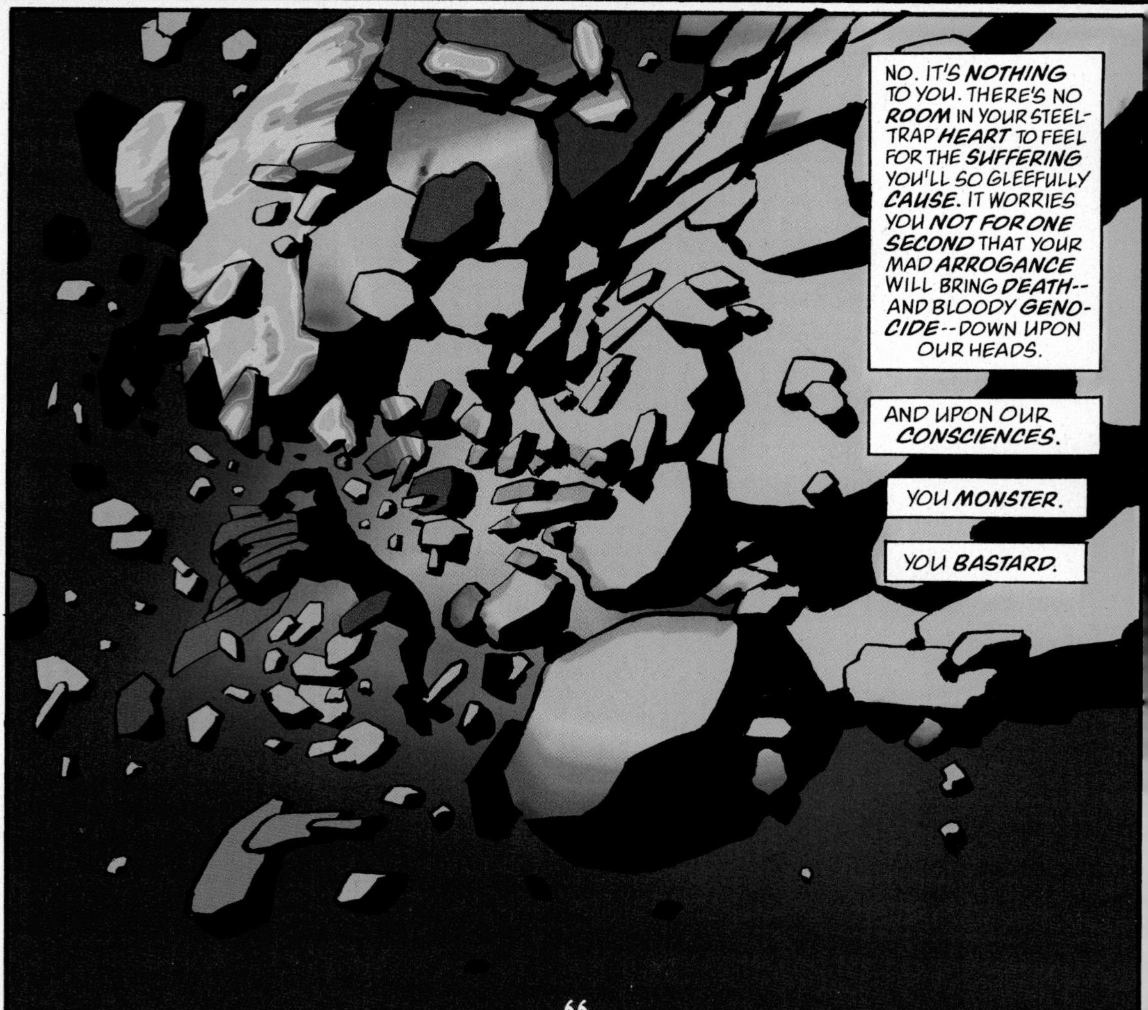
NO. IT'S NOTHING TO YOU. THERE'S NO ROOM IN YOUR STEEL-TRAP HEART TO FEEL FOR THE SUFFERING YOU'LL SO GLEEFULLY CAUSE. IT WORRIES YOU NOT FOR ONE SECOND THAT YOUR MAD ARROGANCE WILL BRING DEATH-- AND BLOODY GENOCIDE--DOWN UPON OUR HEADS.
AND UPON OUR CONSCIENCES.
YOU MONSTER.
YOU BASTARD.

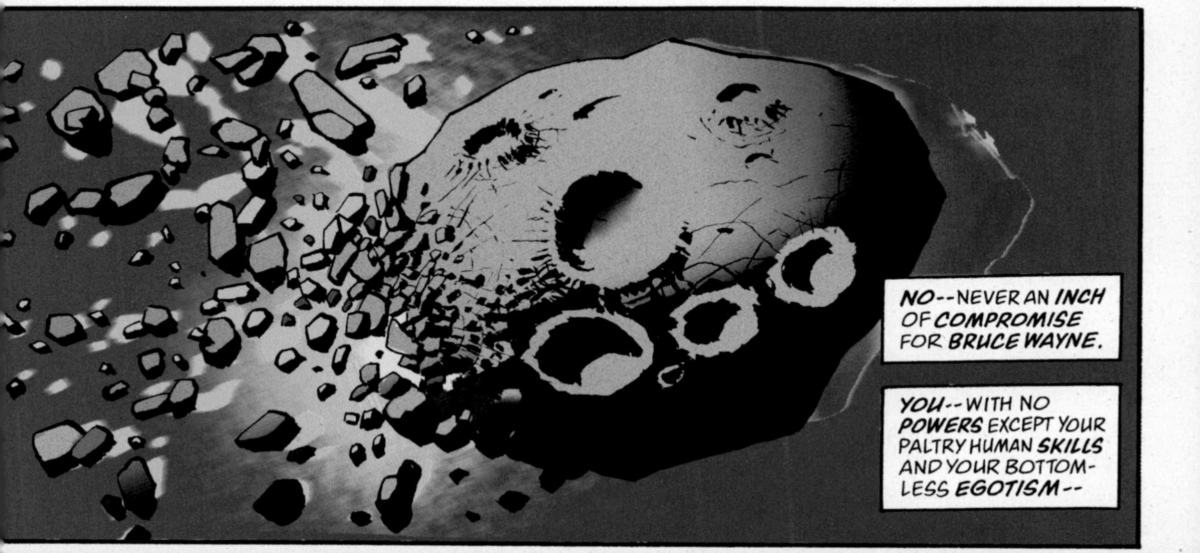
NO--NEVER AN INCH OF COMPROMISE FOR BRUCE WAYNE.
YOU--WITH NO POWERS EXCEPT YOUR PALTRY HUMAN SKILLS AND YOUR BOTTOM-LESS EGOTISM--

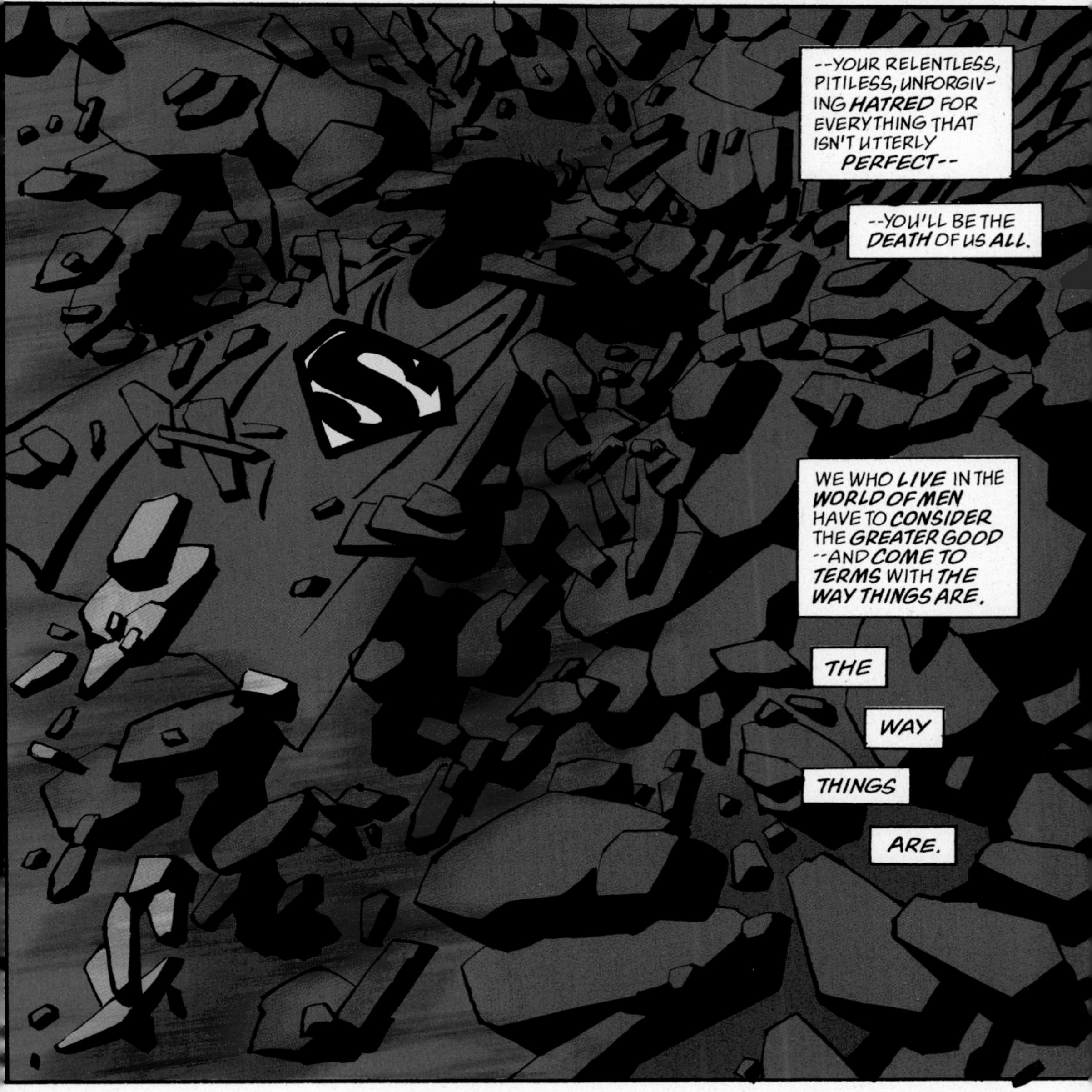
--YOUR RELENTLESS, PITILESS, UNFORGIV-ING HATRED FOR EVERYTHING THAT ISN'T UTTERLY PERFECT--
--YOU'LL BE THE DEATH OF US ALL.
WE WHO LIVE IN THE WORLD OF MEN HAVE TO CONSIDER THE GREATER GOOD --AND COME TO TERMS WITH THE WAY THINGS ARE.
THE
WAY
THINGS
ARE.

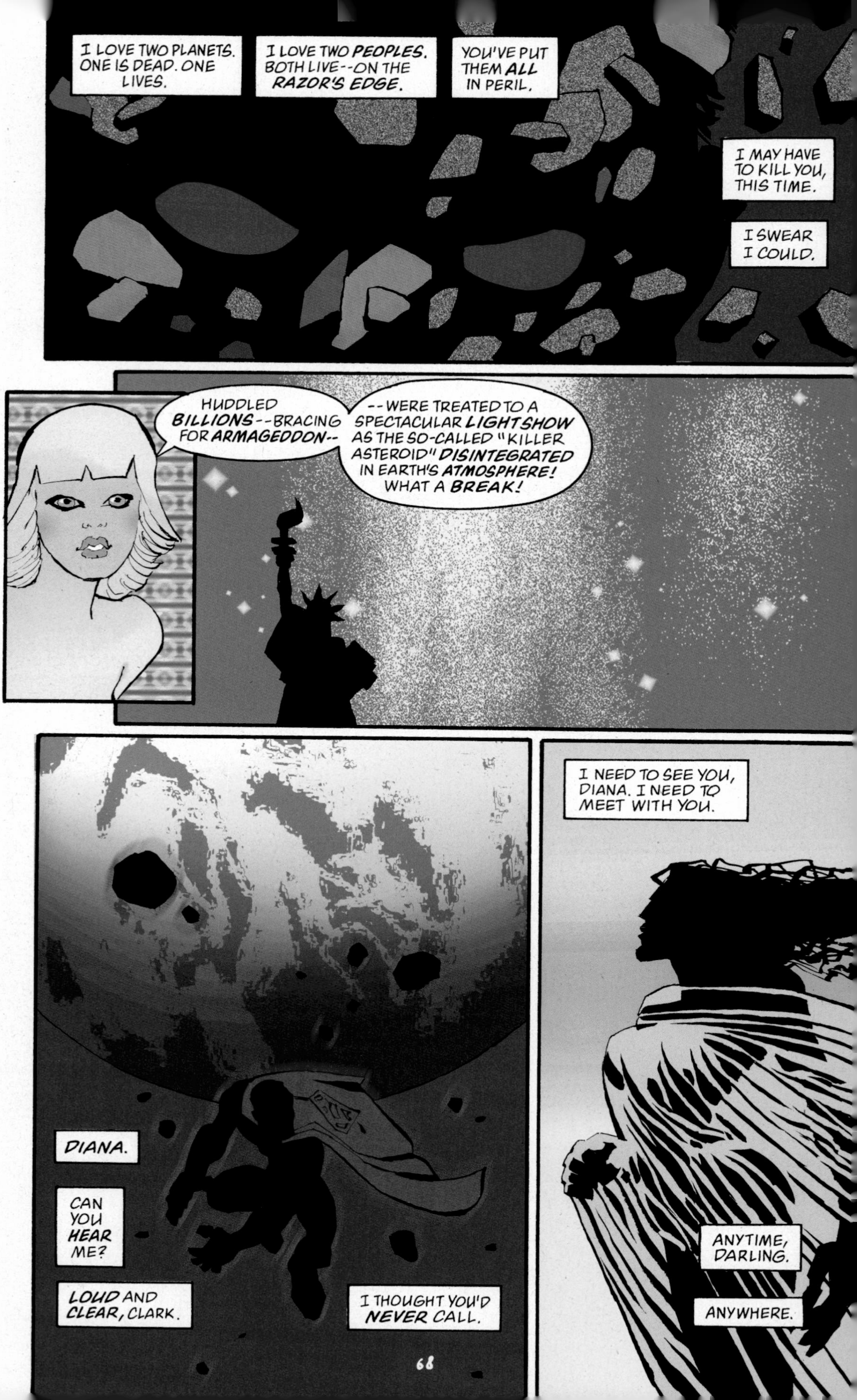

I LOVE TWO PLANETS. ONE IS DEAD. ONE LIVES.
I LOVE TWO PEOPLES. BOTH LIVE--ON THE RAZOR'S EDGE.
YOU'VE PUT THEM ALL IN PERIL.
I MAY HAVE TO KILL YOU, THIS TIME.
I SWEAR I COULD.
HUDDLED BILLIONS--BRACING FOR ARMAGEDDON--
--WERE TREATED TO A SPECTACULAR LIGHT SHOW AS THE SO-CALLED "KILLER ASTEROID" DISINTEGRATED IN EARTH'S ATMOSPHERE! WHAT A BREAK!
DIANA.
CAN YOU HEAR ME?
LOUD AND CLEAR, CLARK.
I THOUGHT YOU'D NEVER CALL.
I NEED TO SEE YOU, DIANA. I NEED TO MEET WITH YOU.
ANYTIME, DARLING.
ANYWHERE.

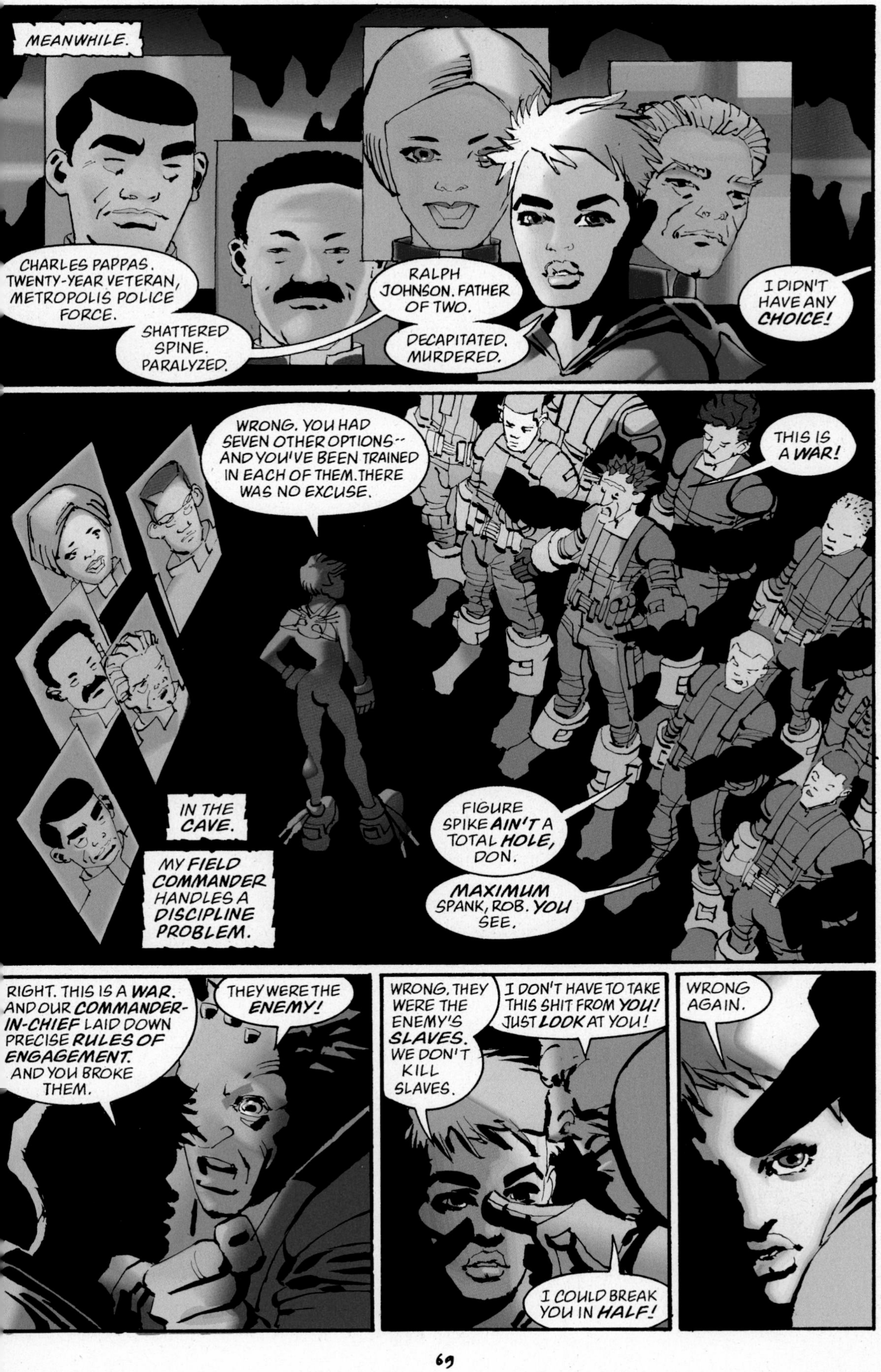
MEANWHILE.
CHARLES PAPPAS. TWENTY-YEAR VETERAN, METROPOLIS POLICE FORCE.
SHATTERED SPINE. PARALYZED.
RALPH JOHNSON. FATHER OF TWO.
DECAPITATED. MURDERED.
I DIDN'T HAVE ANY CHOICE!
WRONG. YOU HAD SEVEN OTHER OPTIONS-- AND YOU'VE BEEN TRAINED IN EACH OF THEM. THERE WAS NO EXCUSE.
THIS IS A WAR!
IN THE CAVE.
MY FIELD COMMANDER HANDLES A DISCIPLINE PROBLEM.
FIGURE SPIKE AIN'T A TOTAL HOLE, DON.
MAXIMUM SPANK, ROB. YOU SEE.
RIGHT. THIS IS A WAR. AND OUR COMMANDER-IN-CHIEF LAID DOWN PRECISE RULES OF ENGAGEMENT. AND YOU BROKE THEM.
THEY WERE THE ENEMY!
WRONG. THEY WERE THE ENEMY'S SLAVES. WE DON'T KILL SLAVES.
I DON'T HAVE TO TAKE THIS SHIT FROM YOU! JUST LOOK AT YOU!
I COULD BREAK YOU IN HALF!
WRONG AGAIN.

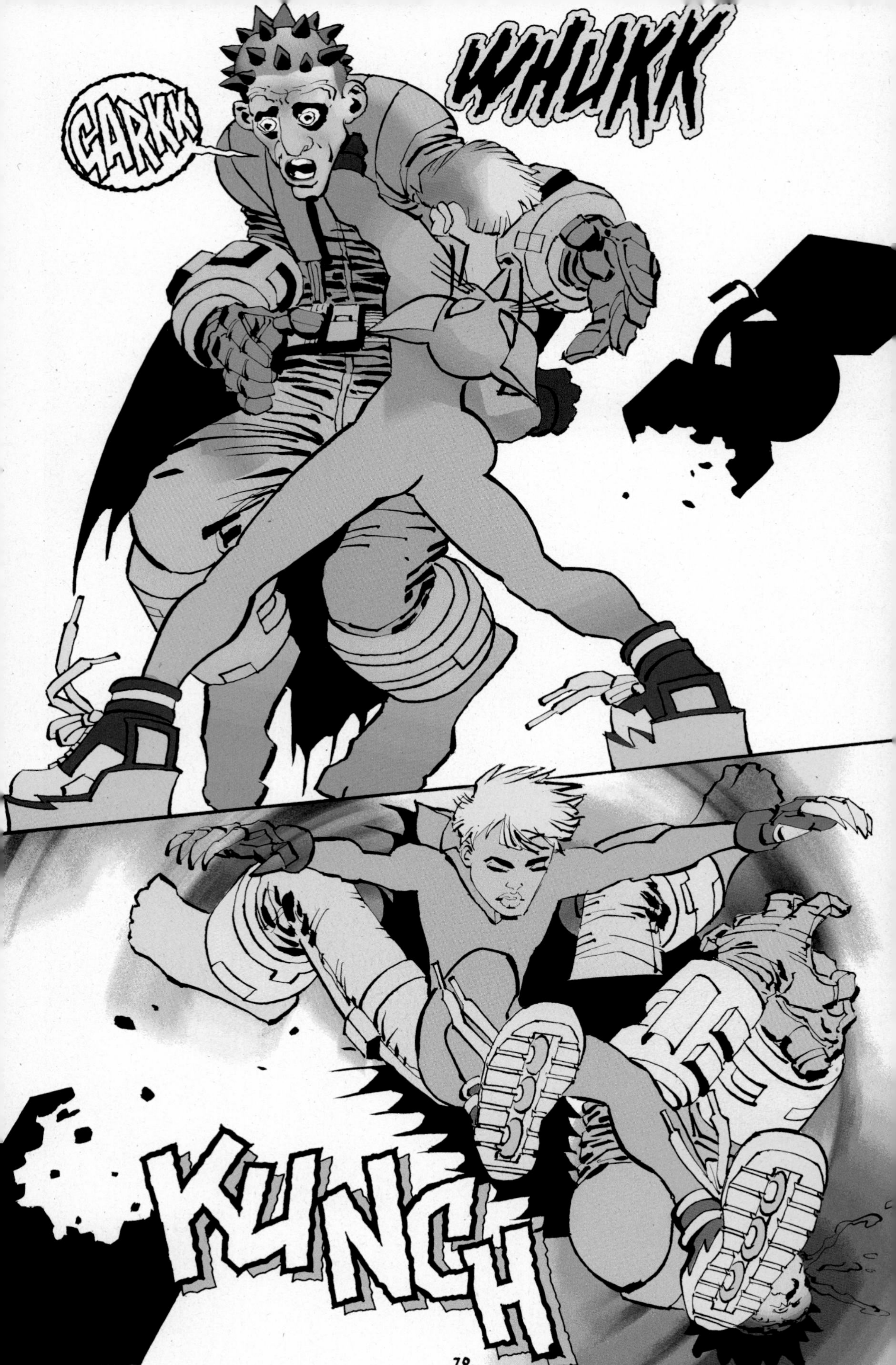
GARKK
WHUKK
KUNCH

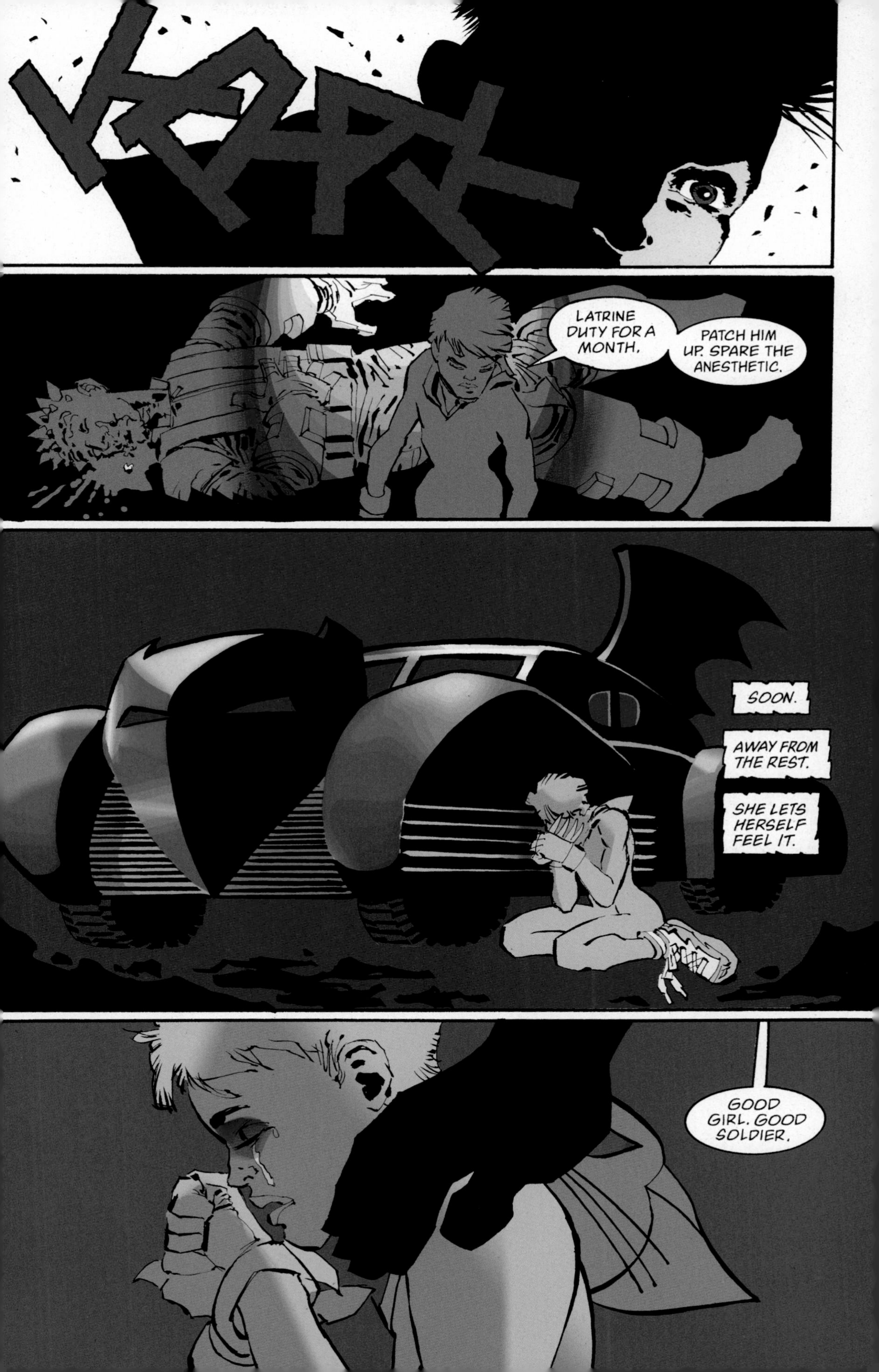
KRAK
LATRINE DUTY FOR A MONTH.
PATCH HIM UP. SPARE THE ANESTHETIC.
SOON.
AWAY FROM THE REST.
SHE LETS HERSELF FEEL IT.
GOOD GIRL. GOOD SOLDIER.

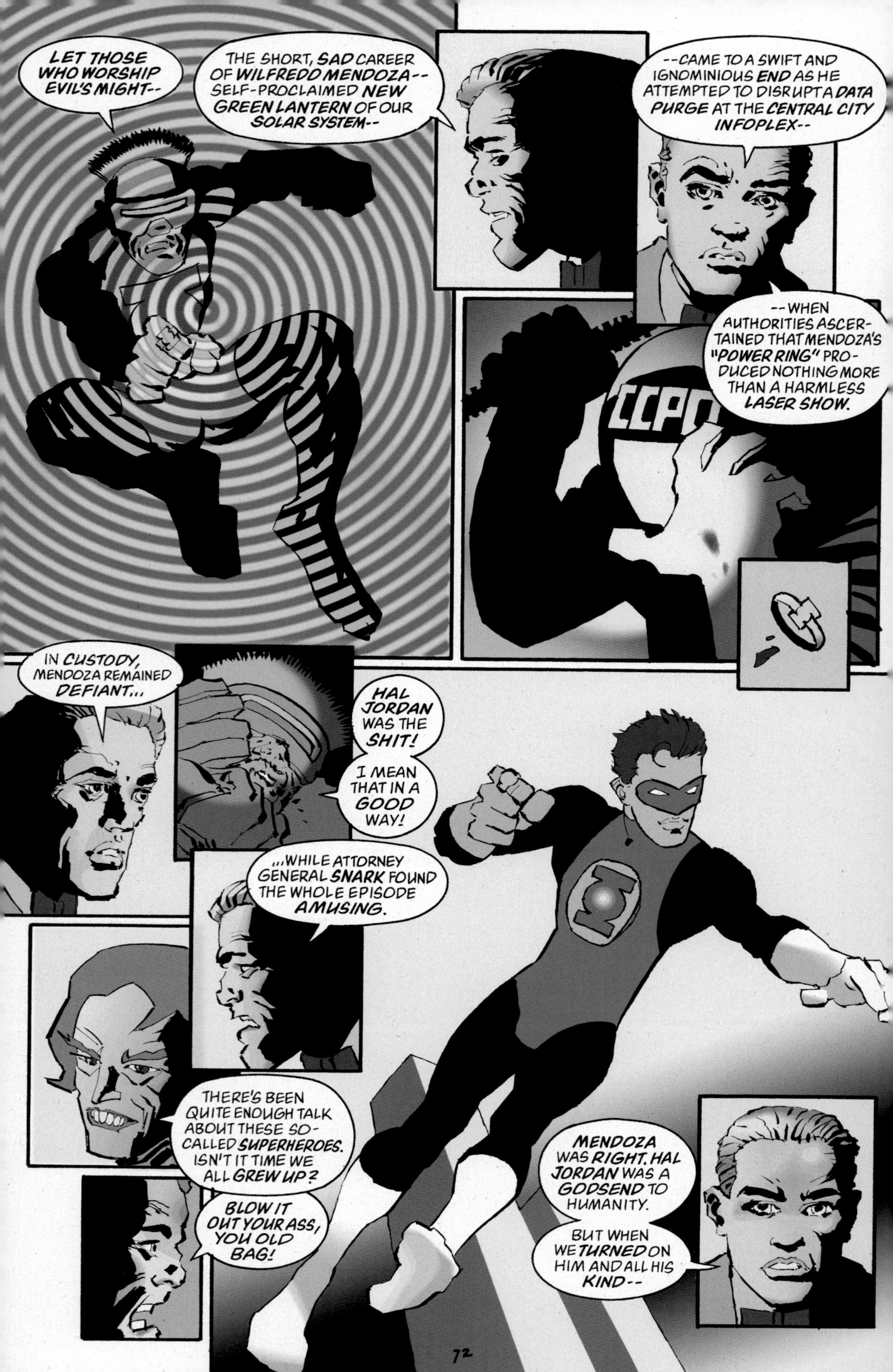

LET THOSE WHO WORSHIP EVIL'S MIGHT--
THE SHORT, SAD CAREER OF WILFREDD MENDOZA-- SELF-PROCLAIMED NEW GREEN LANTERN OF OUR SOLAR SYSTEM--
--CAME TO A SWIFT AND IGNOMINIOUS END AS HE ATTEMPTED TO DISRUPT A DATA PURGE AT THE CENTRAL CITY INFOPLEX--
--WHEN AUTHORITIES ASCERTAINED THAT MENDOZA'S "POWER RING" PRODUCED NOTHING MORE THAN A HARMLESS LASER SHOW.
CCPD
IN CUSTODY, MENDOZA REMAINED DEFIANT...
HAL JORDAN WAS THE SHIT!
I MEAN THAT IN A GOOD WAY!
...WHILE ATTORNEY GENERAL SNARK FOUND THE WHOLE EPISODE AMUSING.
THERE'S BEEN QUITE ENOUGH TALK ABOUT THESE SO-CALLED SUPERHEROES. ISN'T IT TIME WE ALL GREW UP?
BLOW IT OUT YOUR ASS, YOU OLD BAG!
MENDOZA WAS RIGHT. HAL JORDAN WAS A GODSEND TO HUMANITY.
BUT WHEN WE TURNED ON HIM AND ALL HIS KIND--

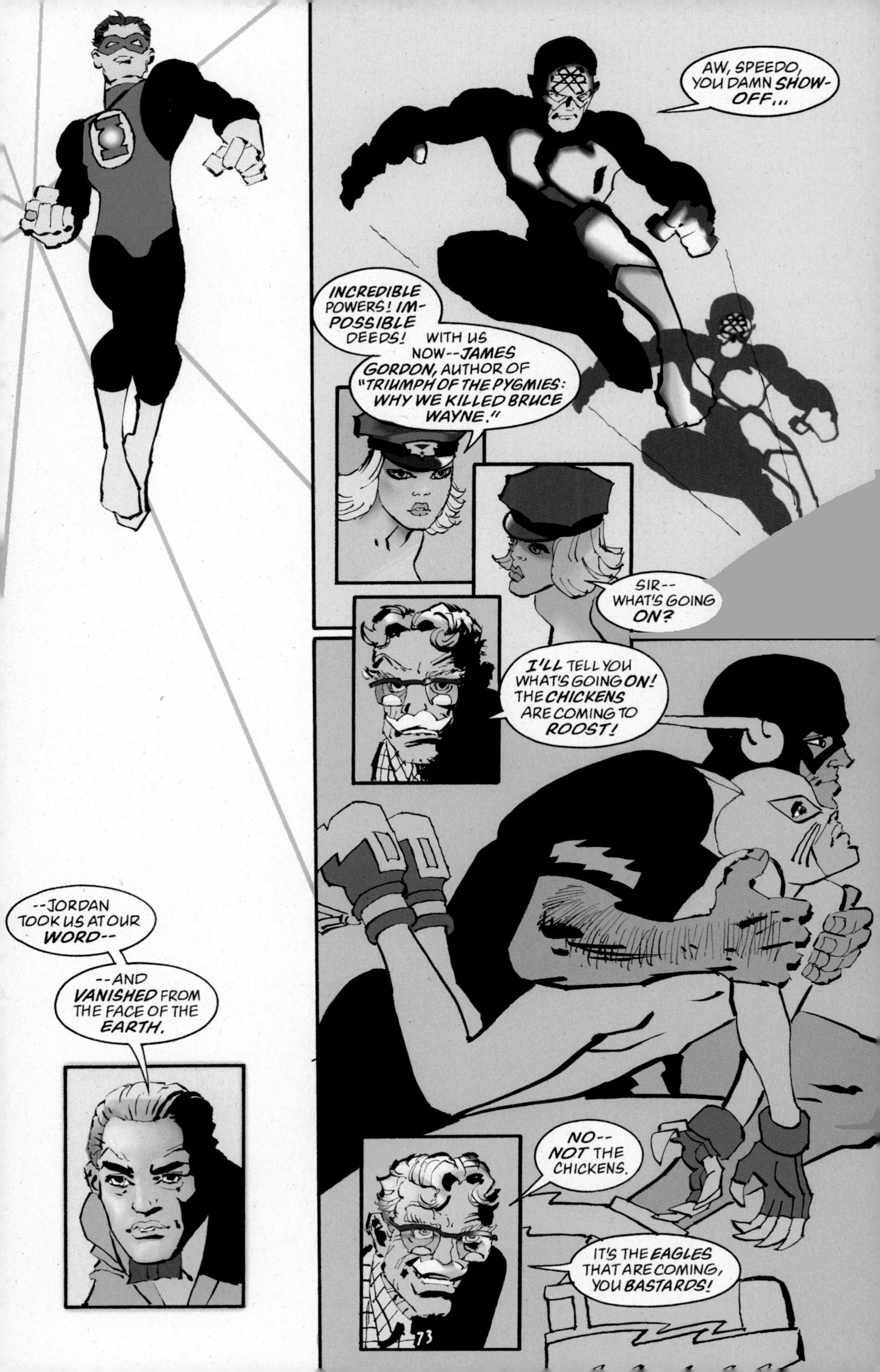
AW, SPEEDO, YOU DAMN SHOW-OFF...
INCREDIBLE POWERS! IMPOSSIBLE DEEDS! WITH US NOW--JAMES GORDON, AUTHOR OF "TRIUMPH OF THE PYGMIES: WHY WE KILLED BRUCE WAYNE."
SIR-- WHAT'S GOING ON?
I'LL TELL YOU WHAT'S GOING ON! THE CHICKENS ARE COMING TO ROOST!
NO-- NOT THE CHICKENS.
IT'S THE EAGLES THAT ARE COMING, YOU BASTARDS!
--JORDAN TOOK US AT OUR WORD--
--AND VANISHED FROM THE FACE OF THE EARTH.
73

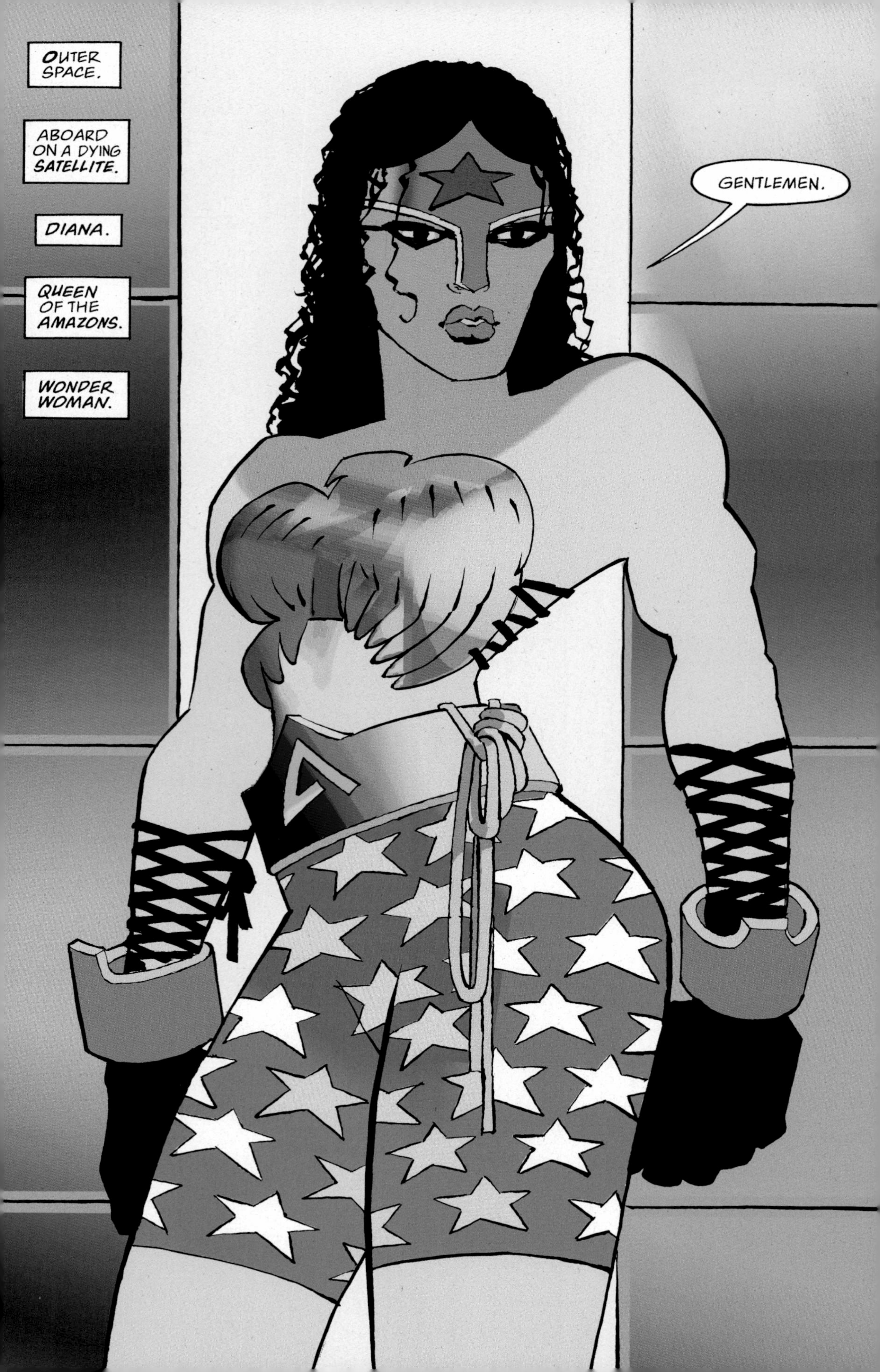
OUTER SPACE.
ABOARD ON A DYING SATELLITE.
DIANA.
QUEEN OF THE AMAZONS.
WONDER WOMAN.
GENTLEMEN.

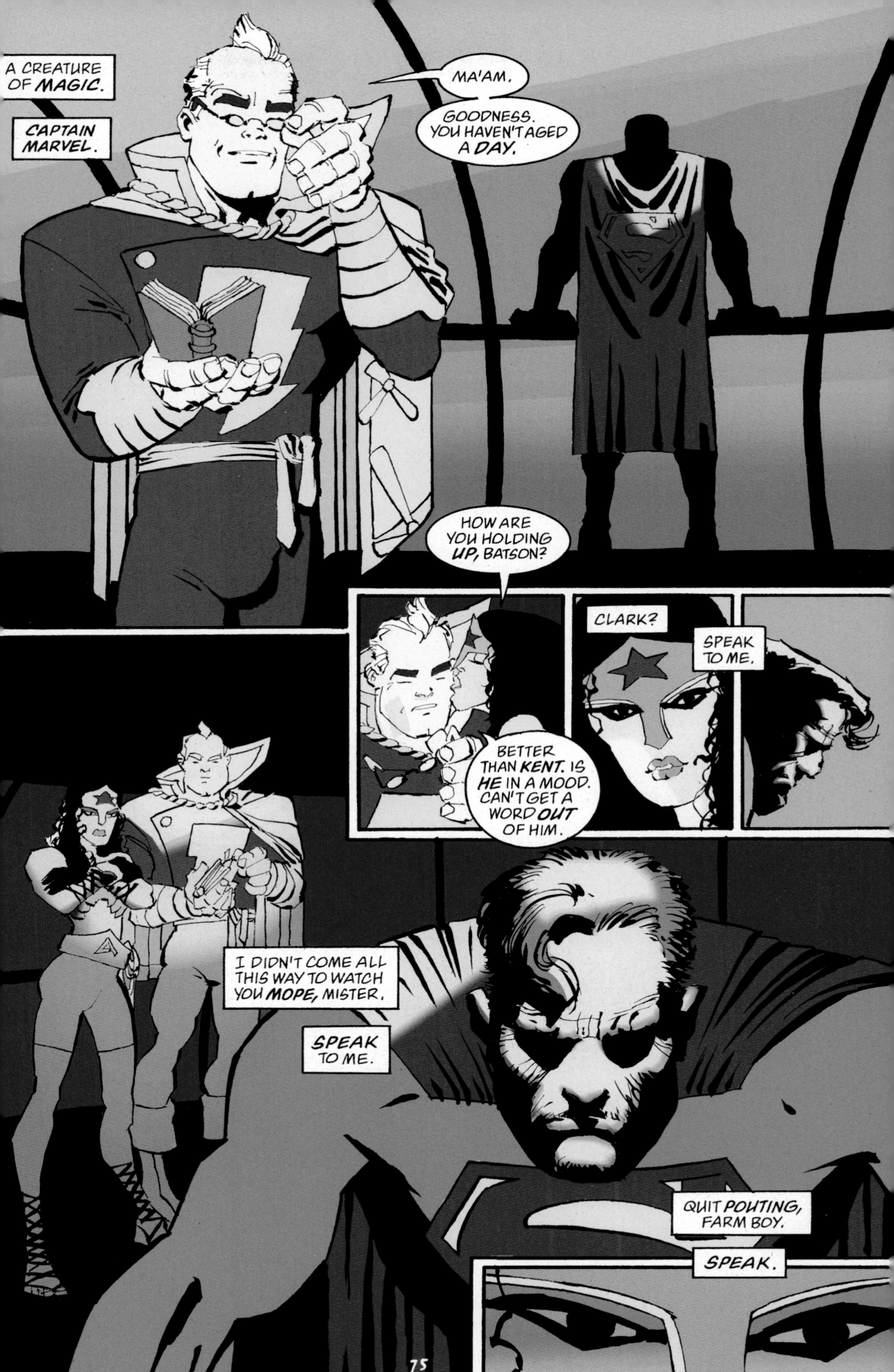
A CREATURE OF MAGIC.
CAPTAIN MARVEL.
MA'AM.
GOODNESS. YOU HAVEN'T AGED A DAY.
HOW ARE YOU HOLDING UP, BATSON?
BETTER THAN KENT. IS HE IN A MOOD. CAN'T GET A WORD OUT OF HIM.
CLARK?
SPEAK TO ME.
I DIDN'T COME ALL THIS WAY TO WATCH YOU MOPE, MISTER.
SPEAK TO ME.
QUIT POUTING, FARM BOY.
SPEAK.

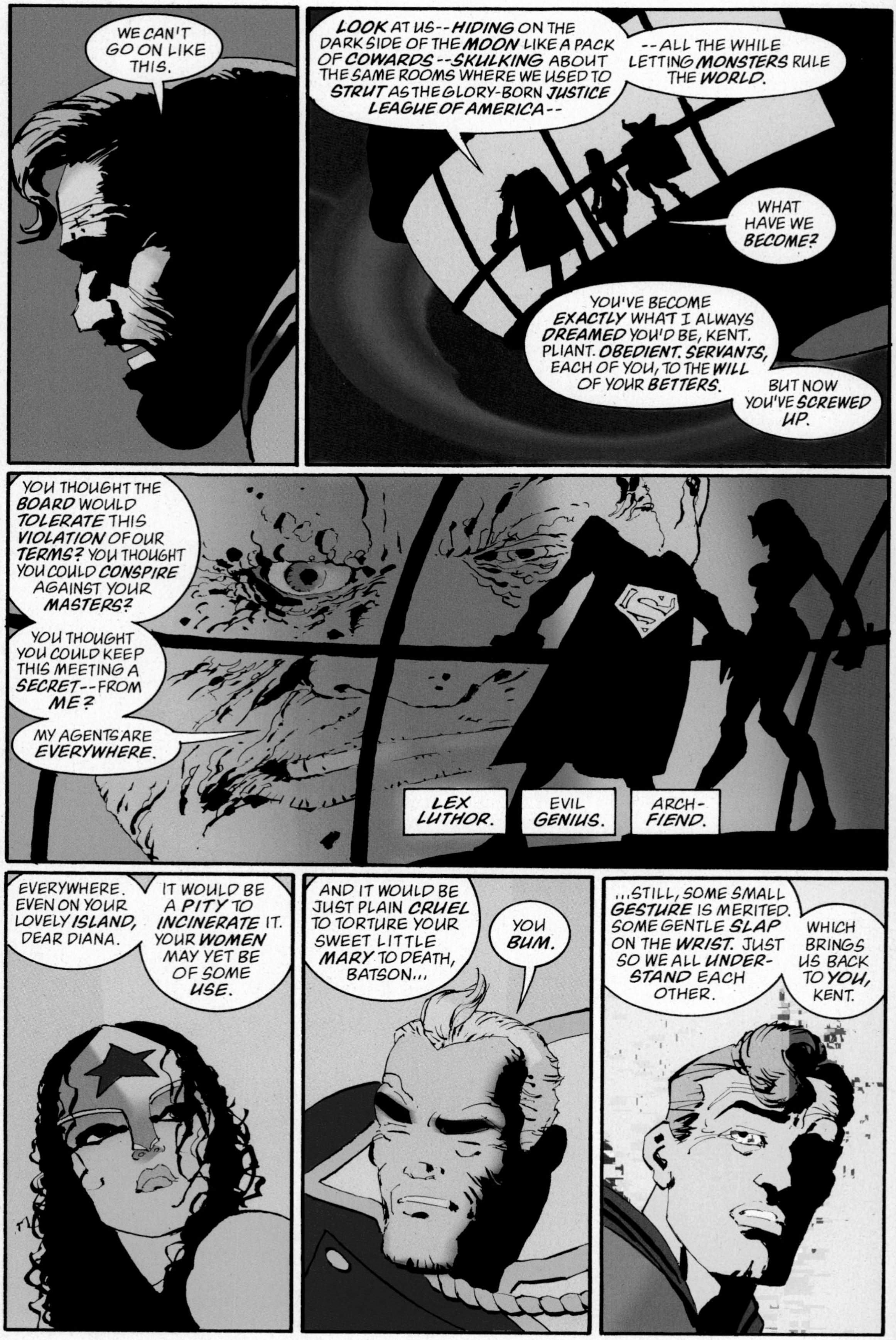
WE CAN'T GO ON LIKE THIS.
LOOK AT US--HIDING ON THE DARK SIDE OF THE MOON LIKE A PACK OF COWARDS--SKULKING ABOUT THE SAME ROOMS WHERE WE USED TO STRUT AS THE GLORY-BORN JUSTICE LEAGUE OF AMERICA--
--ALL THE WHILE LETTING MONSTERS RULE THE WORLD.
WHAT HAVE WE BECOME?
YOU'VE BECOME EXACTLY WHAT I ALWAYS DREAMED YOU'D BE, KENT. PLIANT. OBEDIENT. SERVANTS, EACH OF YOU, TO THE WILL OF YOUR BETTERS.
BUT NOW YOU'VE SCREWED UP.
YOU THOUGHT THE BOARD WOULD TOLERATE THIS VIOLATION OF OUR TERMS? YOU THOUGHT YOU COULD CONSPIRE AGAINST YOUR MASTERS?
YOU THOUGHT YOU COULD KEEP THIS MEETING A SECRET--FROM ME?
MY AGENTS ARE EVERYWHERE.
LEX LUTHOR.
EVIL GENIUS.
ARCH-FIEND.
EVERYWHERE. EVEN ON YOUR LOVELY ISLAND, DEAR DIANA.
IT WOULD BE A PITY TO INCINERATE IT. YOUR WOMEN MAY YET BE OF SOME USE.
AND IT WOULD BE JUST PLAIN CRUEL TO TORTURE YOUR SWEET LITTLE MARY TO DEATH, BATSON...
YOU BUM.
...STILL, SOME SMALL GESTURE IS MERITED. SOME GENTLE SLAP ON THE WRIST. JUST SO WE ALL UNDERSTAND EACH OTHER.
WHICH BRINGS US BACK TO YOU, KENT.

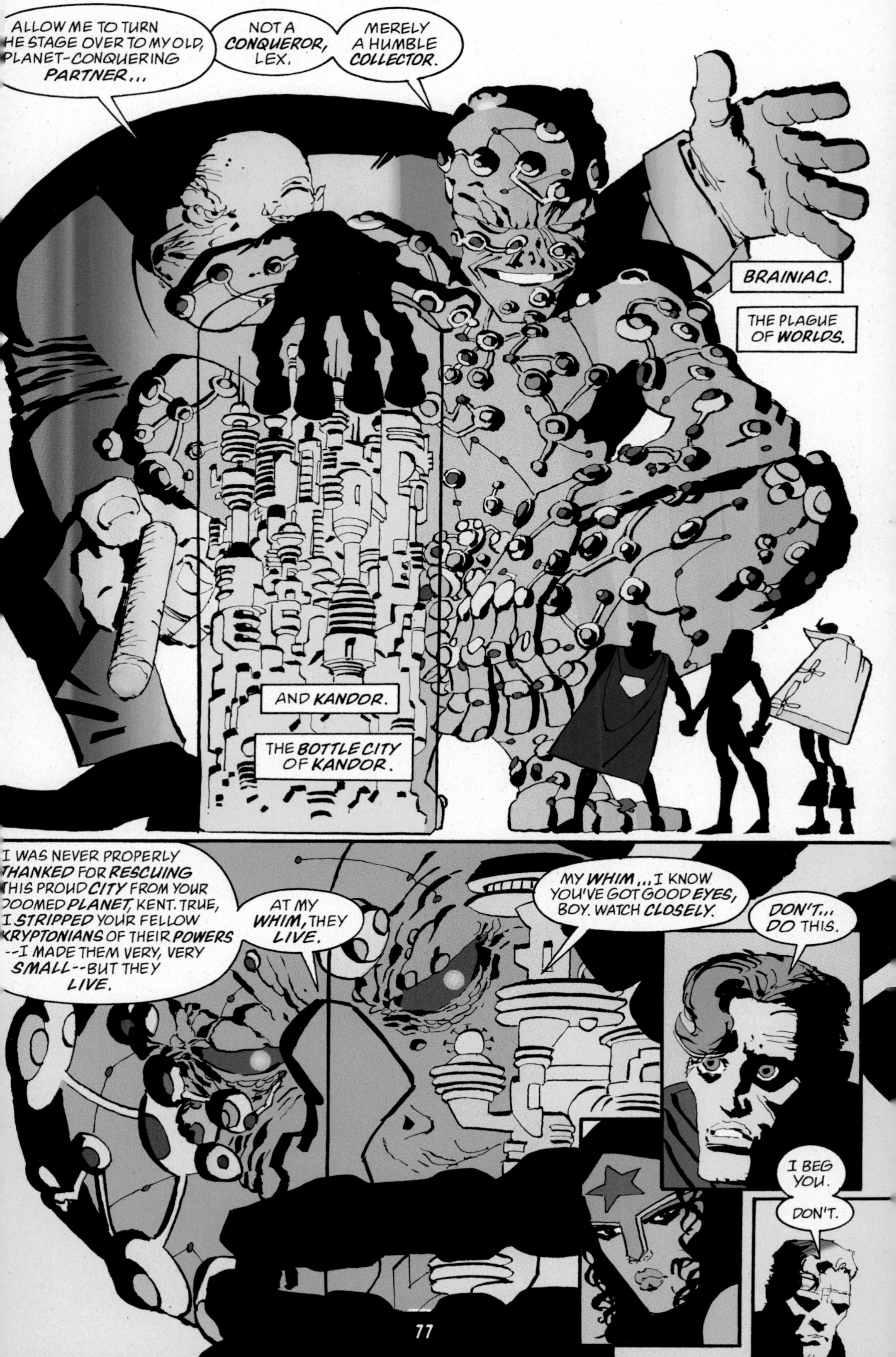
ALLOW ME TO TURN THE STAGE OVER TO MY OLD, PLANET-CONQUERING PARTNER...
NOT A CONQUEROR, LEX.
MERELY A HUMBLE COLLECTOR.
BRAINIAC.
THE PLAGUE OF WORLDS.
AND KANDOR.
THE BOTTLE CITY OF KANDOR.
I WAS NEVER PROPERLY THANKED FOR RESCUING THIS PROUD CITY FROM YOUR DOOMED PLANET, KENT. TRUE, I STRIPPED YOUR FELLOW KRYPTONIANS OF THEIR POWERS --I MADE THEM VERY, VERY SMALL--BUT THEY LIVE.
AT MY WHIM, THEY LIVE.
MY WHIM... I KNOW YOU'VE GOT GOOD EYES, BOY. WATCH CLOSELY.
DON'T... DO THIS.
I BEG YOU.
DON'T.

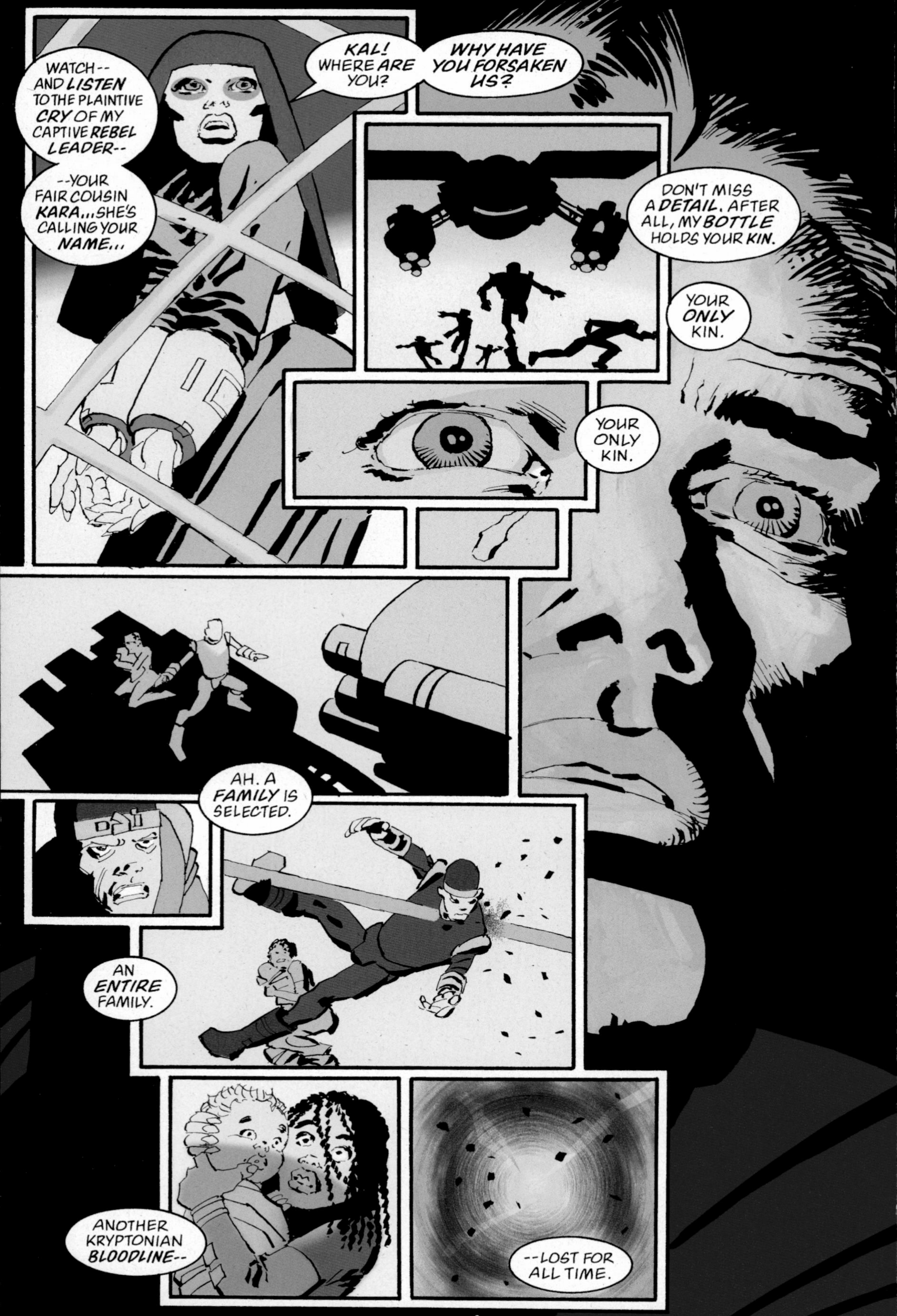
WATCH-- AND LISTEN TO THE PLAINTIVE CRY OF MY CAPTIVE REBEL LEADER--
--YOUR FAIR COUSIN KARA... SHE'S CALLING YOUR NAME...
KAL! WHERE ARE YOU?
WHY HAVE YOU FORSAKEN US?
DON'T MISS A DETAIL. AFTER ALL, MY BOTTLE HOLDS YOUR KIN.
YOUR ONLY KIN.
YOUR ONLY KIN.
AH. A FAMILY IS SELECTED.
AN ENTIRE FAMILY.
ANOTHER KRYPTONIAN BLOODLINE--
--LOST FOR ALL TIME.

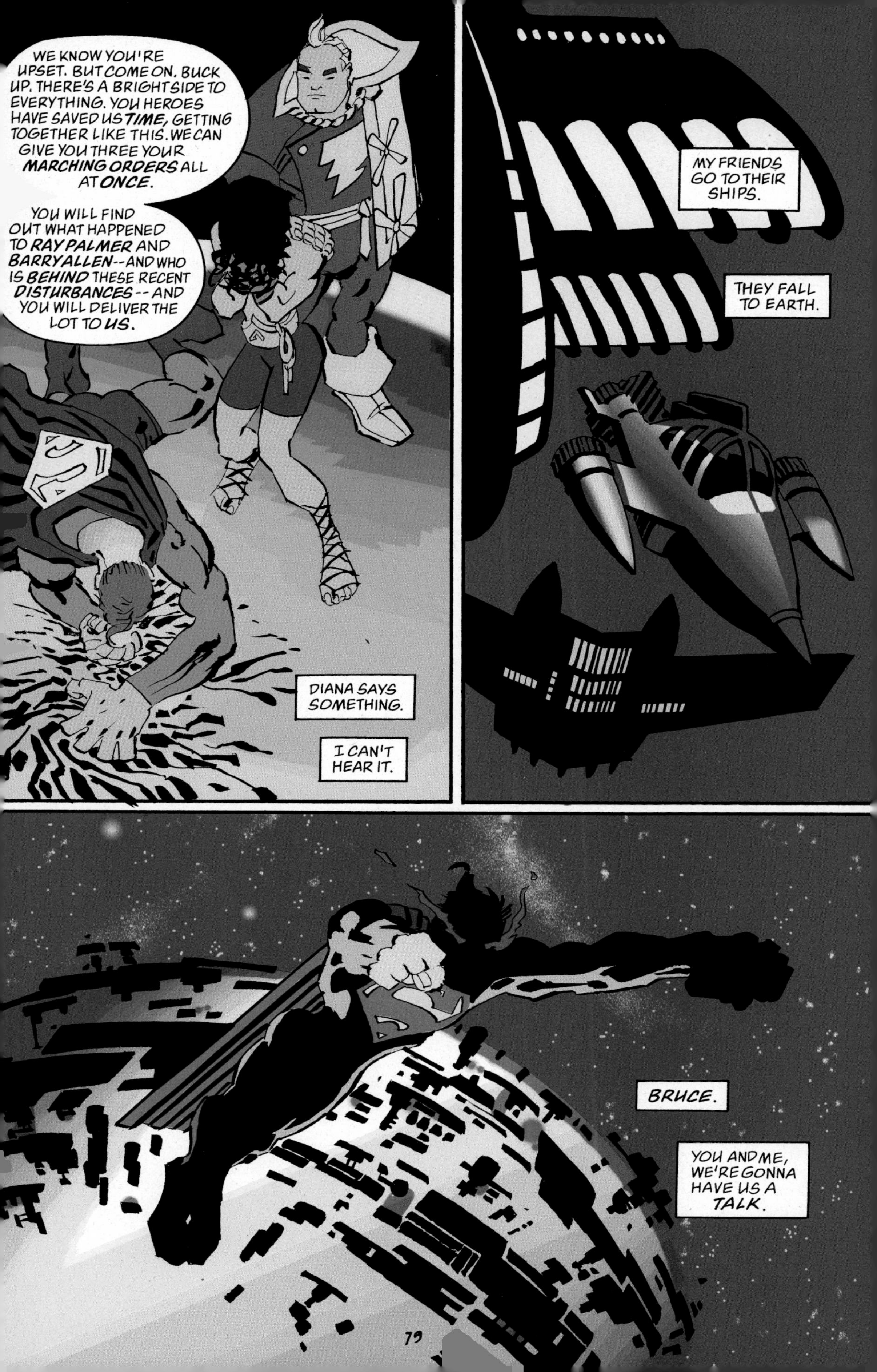
WE KNOW YOU'RE UPSET. BUT COME ON. BUCK UP. THERE'S A BRIGHT SIDE TO EVERYTHING. YOU HEROES HAVE SAVED US *TIME*, GETTING TOGETHER LIKE THIS. WE CAN GIVE YOU THREE YOUR *MARCHING ORDERS* ALL AT *ONCE*.
YOU WILL FIND OUT WHAT HAPPENED TO *RAY PALMER* AND *BARRY ALLEN*--AND WHO IS *BEHIND* THESE RECENT *DISTURBANCES*-- AND YOU WILL DELIVER THE LOT TO *US*.
DIANA SAYS SOMETHING.
I CAN'T HEAR IT.
MY FRIENDS GO TO THEIR SHIPS.
THEY FALL TO EARTH.
BRUCE.
YOU AND ME, WE'RE GONNA HAVE US A *TALK*.

LOOK. UP IN THE SKY.

GOSH, WE'RE ALL *IMPRESSED*, DOWN HERE.

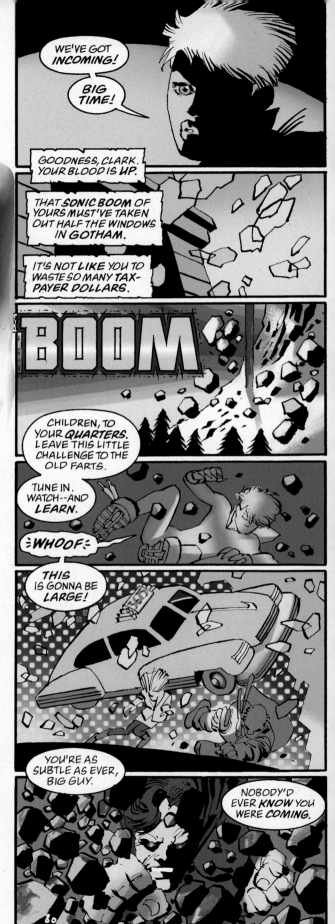

WE'VE GOT *INCOMING!*

BIG TIME!

GOODNESS, CLARK. YOUR BLOOD IS *UP.*

THAT *SONIC BOOM* OF YOURS MUST'VE TAKEN OUT HALF THE WINDOWS IN *GOTHAM.*

IT'S NOT *LIKE* YOU TO WASTE SO MANY TAX-PAYER DOLLARS.

BOOM

CHILDREN, TO YOUR *QUARTERS.* LEAVE THIS LITTLE CHALLENGE TO THE OLD FARTS.

TUNE IN. WATCH--AND *LEARN.*

≡WHOOF≡

THIS IS GONNA BE *LARGE!*

YOU'RE AS SUBTLE AS EVER, BIG GUY.

NOBODY'D EVER *KNOW* YOU WERE *COMING.*

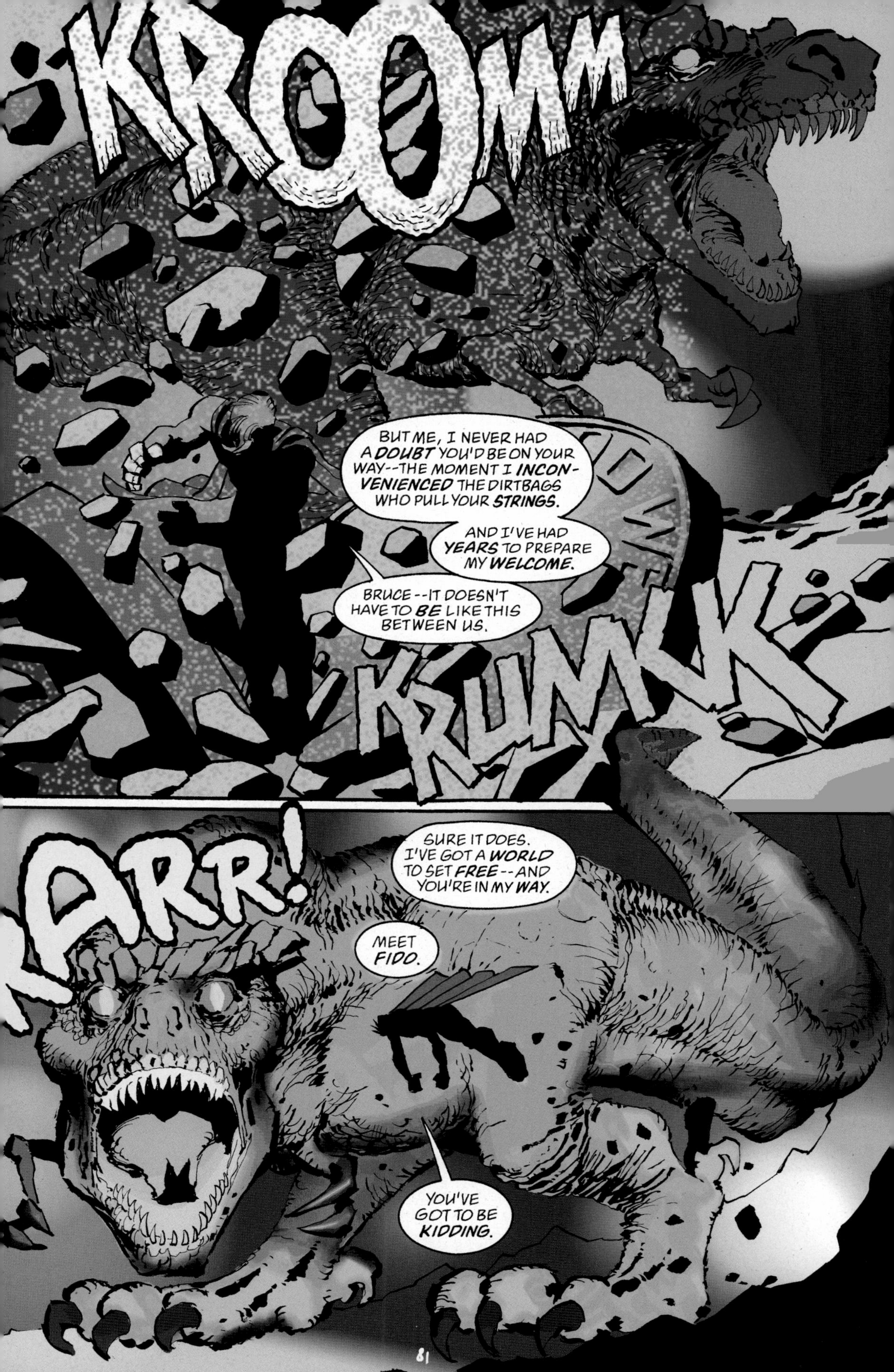
KROOM
BUT ME, I NEVER HAD A DOUBT YOU'D BE ON YOUR WAY--THE MOMENT I INCONVENIENCED THE DIRTBAGS WHO PULL YOUR STRINGS.
AND I'VE HAD YEARS TO PREPARE MY WELCOME.
BRUCE--IT DOESN'T HAVE TO BE LIKE THIS BETWEEN US.
KRUNK
ARR!
SURE IT DOES. I'VE GOT A WORLD TO SET FREE--AND YOU'RE IN MY WAY.
MEET FIDO.
YOU'VE GOT TO BE KIDDING.

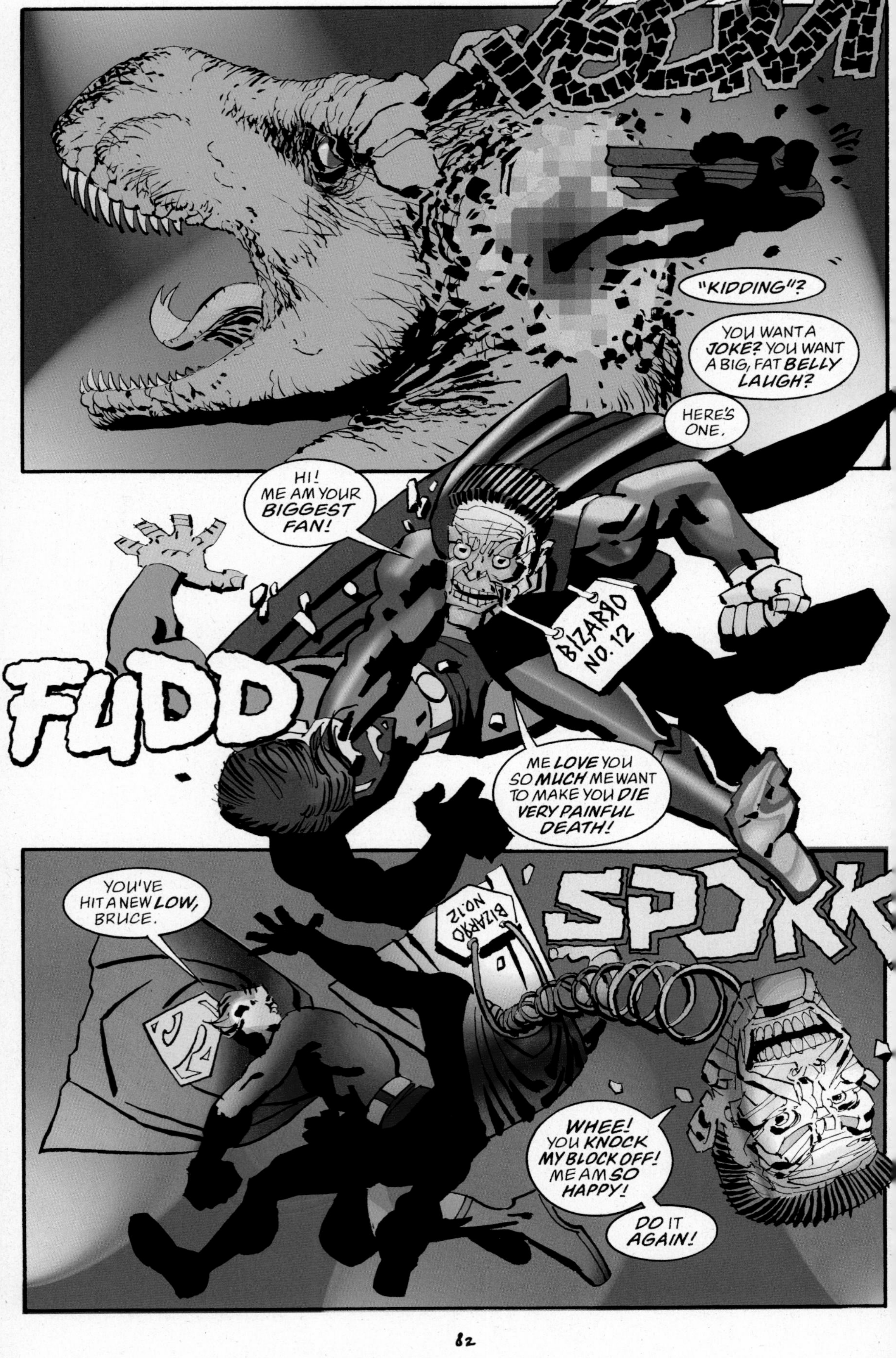
KRAKOOM
"KIDDING"?
YOU WANT A JOKE? YOU WANT A BIG, FAT BELLY LAUGH?
HERE'S ONE.
HI! ME AM YOUR BIGGEST FAN!
BIZARRO NO. 12
FUDD
ME LOVE YOU SO MUCH ME WANT TO MAKE YOU DIE VERY PAINFUL DEATH!
YOU'VE HIT A NEW LOW, BRUCE.
BIZARRO NO. 12
SPOKK
WHEE! YOU KNOCK MY BLOCK OFF! ME AM SO HAPPY!
DO IT AGAIN!

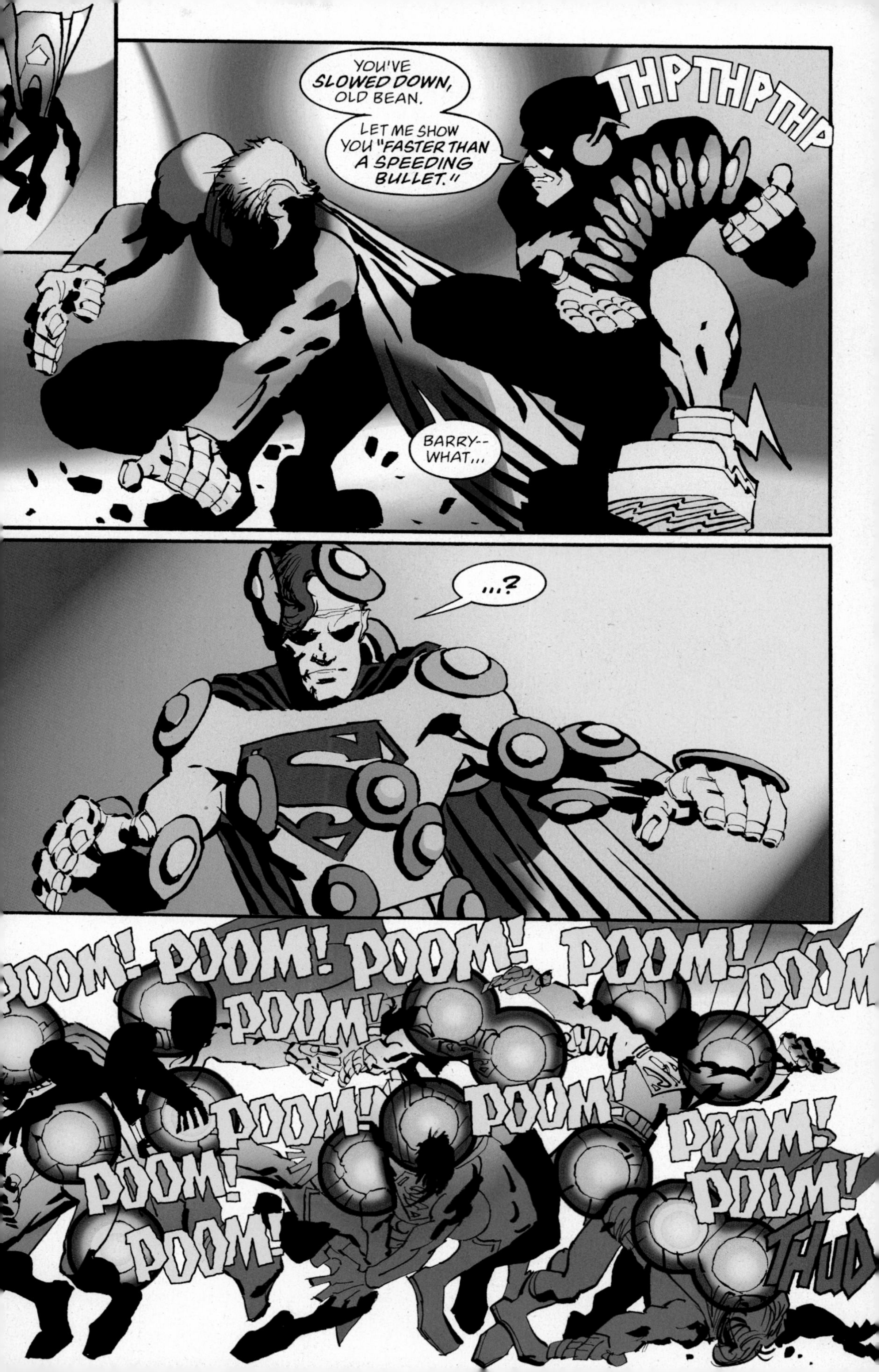
YOU'VE SLOWED DOWN, OLD BEAN.
LET ME SHOW YOU "FASTER THAN A SPEEDING BULLET."
THPTHPTHP
BARRY-- WHAT...
...?
POOM! POOM! POOM! POOM! POOM!
POOM!
POOM! POOM!
POOM! POOM! POOM!
POOM!
THUD

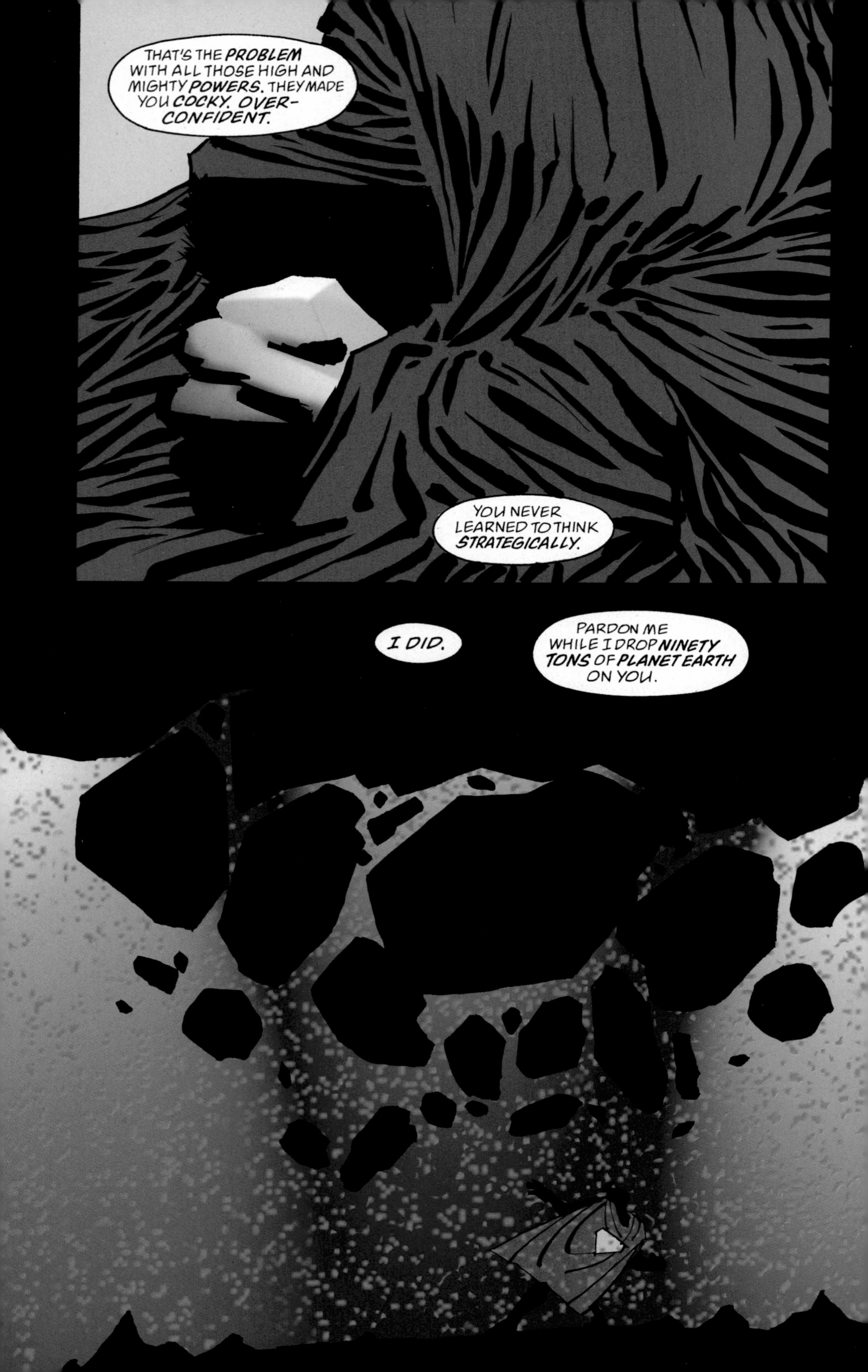
THAT'S THE PROBLEM WITH ALL THOSE HIGH AND MIGHTY POWERS. THEY MADE YOU COCKY. OVER-CONFIDENT.
YOU NEVER LEARNED TO THINK STRATEGICALLY.
I DID.
PARDON ME WHILE I DROP NINETY TONS OF PLANET EARTH ON YOU.

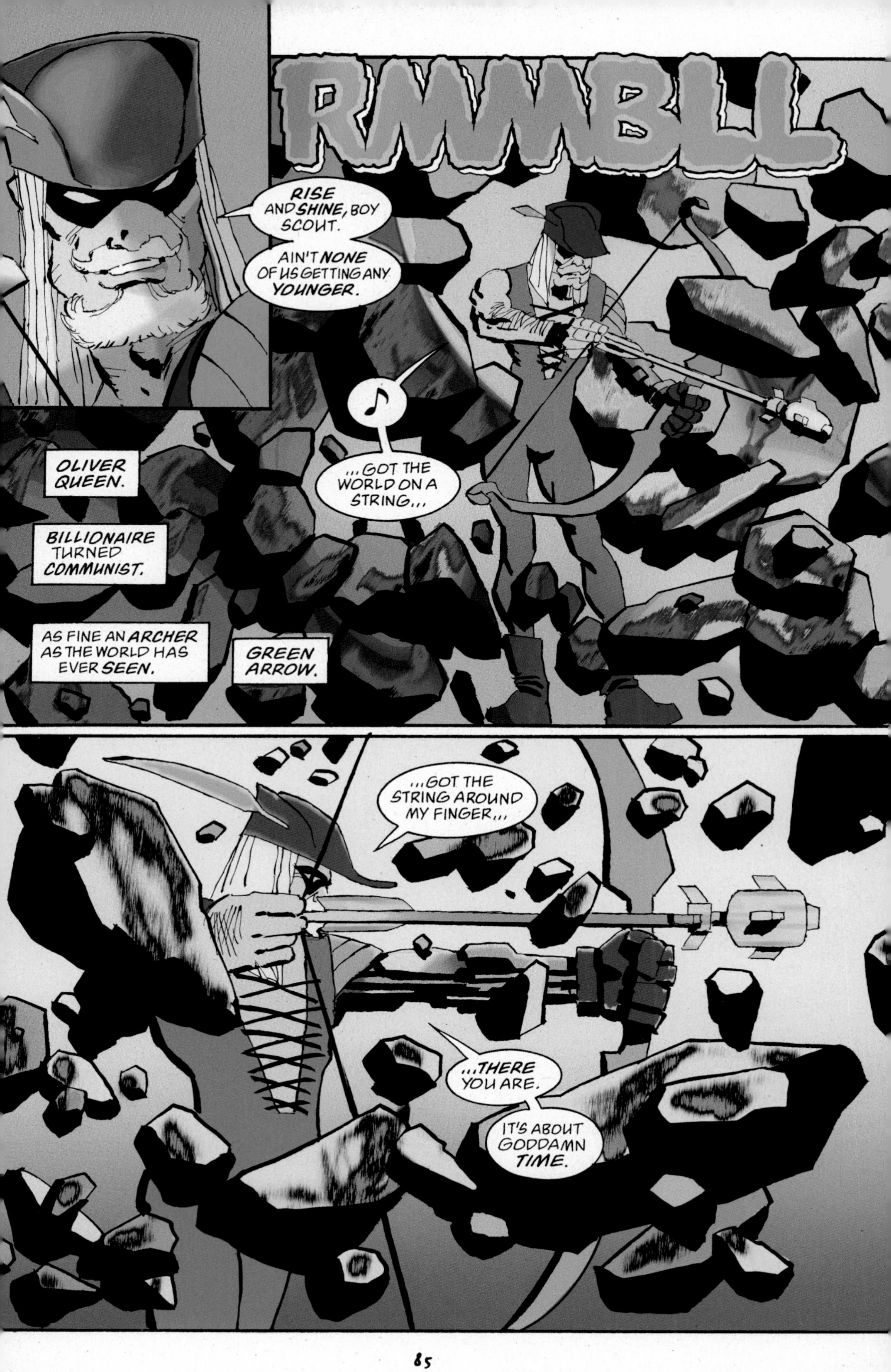
RWWBLL
RISE AND SHINE, BOY SCOUT.
AIN'T NONE OF US GETTING ANY YOUNGER.
♪
...GOT THE WORLD ON A STRING...
OLIVER QUEEN.
BILLIONAIRE TURNED COMMUNIST.
AS FINE AN ARCHER AS THE WORLD HAS EVER SEEN.
GREEN ARROW.
...GOT THE STRING AROUND MY FINGER...
...THERE YOU ARE.
IT'S ABOUT GODDAMN TIME.

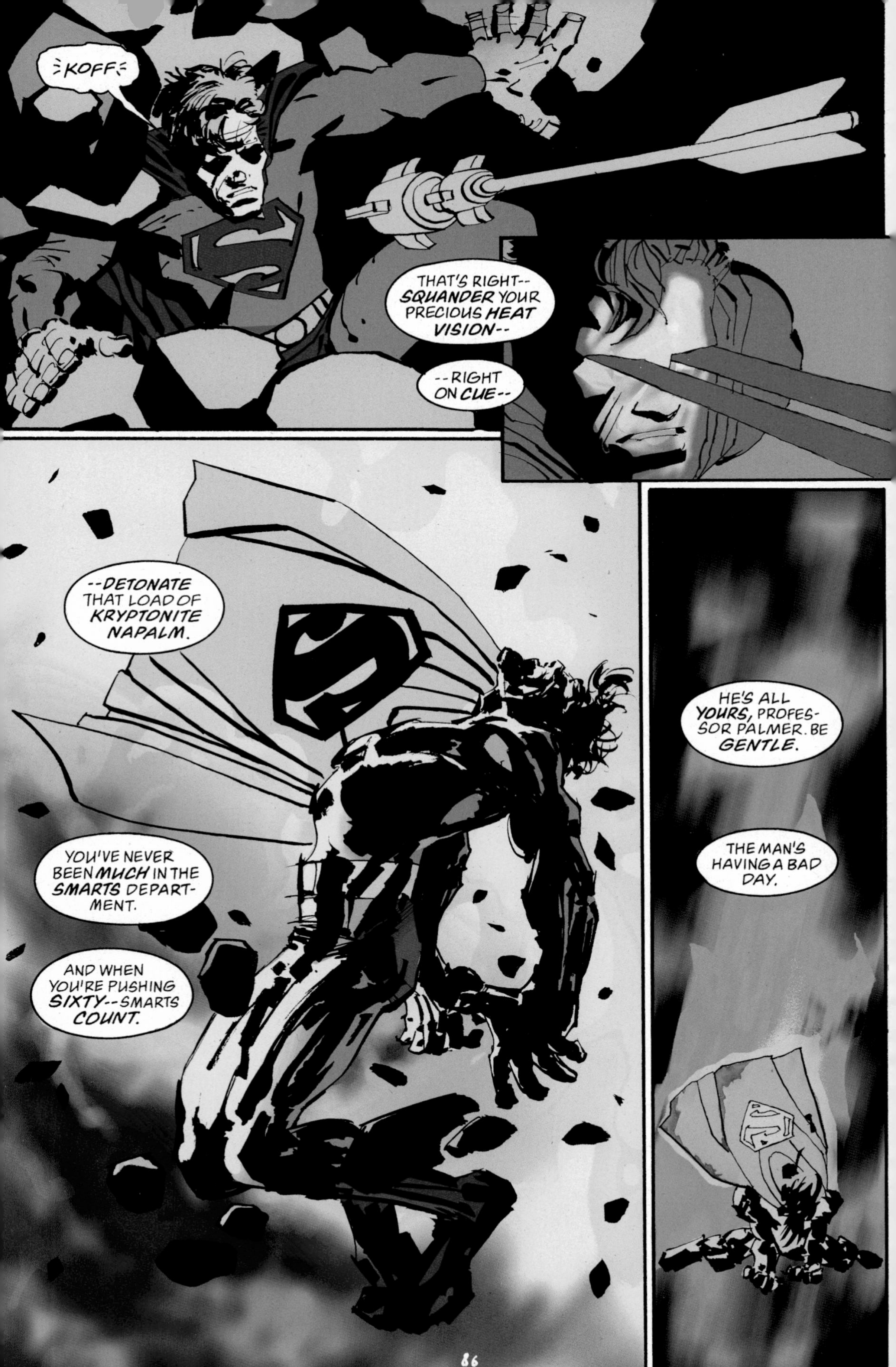
KOFF
THAT'S RIGHT-- SQUANDER YOUR PRECIOUS HEAT VISION--
--RIGHT ON CUE--
--DETONATE THAT LOAD OF KRYPTONITE NAPALM.
YOU'VE NEVER BEEN MUCH IN THE SMARTS DEPARTMENT.
AND WHEN YOU'RE PUSHING SIXTY--SMARTS COUNT.
HE'S ALL YOURS, PROFESSOR PALMER. BE GENTLE.
THE MAN'S HAVING A BAD DAY.

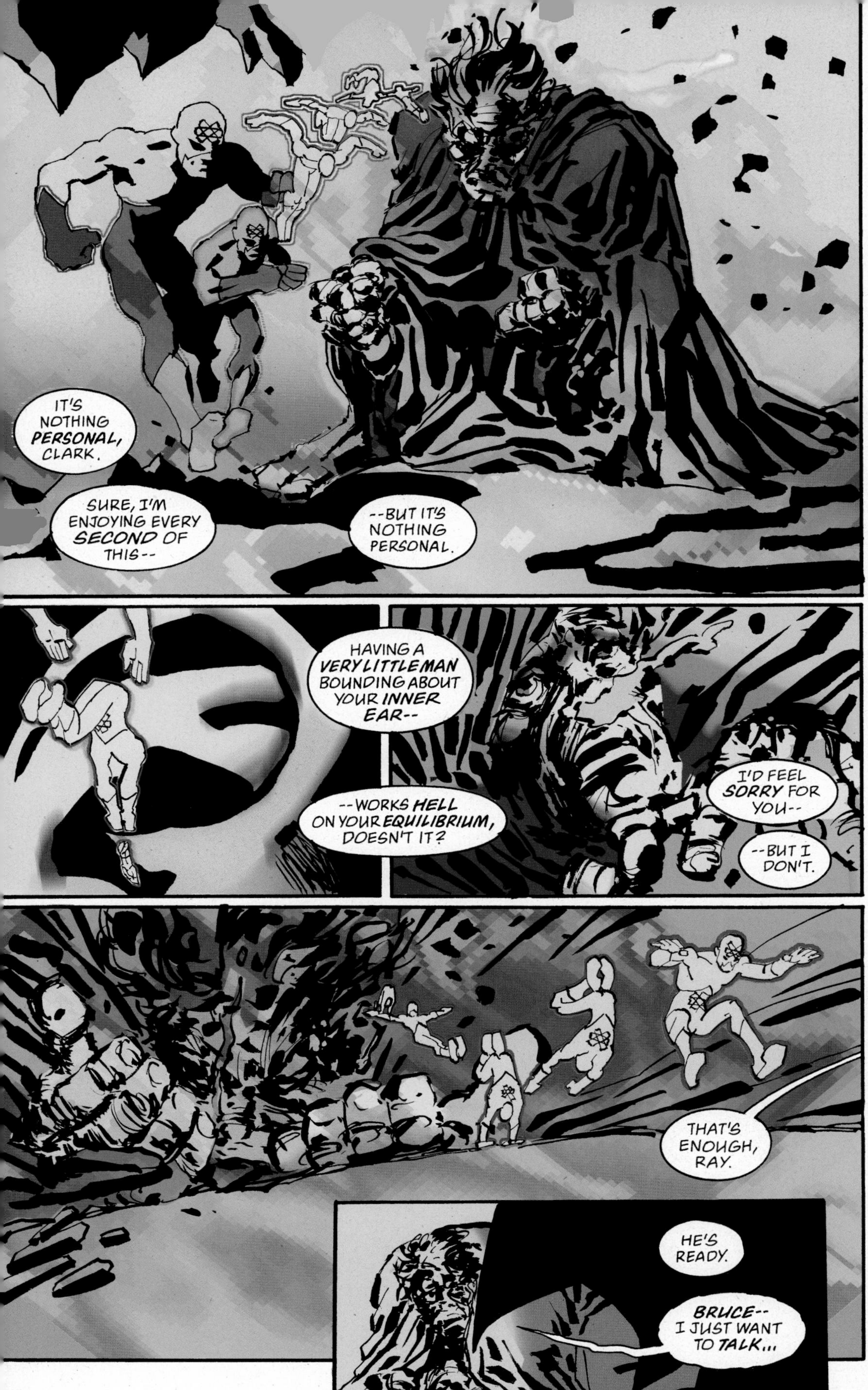
IT'S NOTHING PERSONAL, CLARK.
SURE, I'M ENJOYING EVERY SECOND OF THIS--
--BUT IT'S NOTHING PERSONAL.
HAVING A VERY LITTLE MAN BOUNDING ABOUT YOUR INNER EAR--
--WORKS HELL ON YOUR EQUILIBRIUM, DOESN'T IT?
I'D FEEL SORRY FOR YOU--
--BUT I DON'T.
THAT'S ENOUGH, RAY.
HE'S READY.
BRUCE-- I JUST WANT TO TALK...

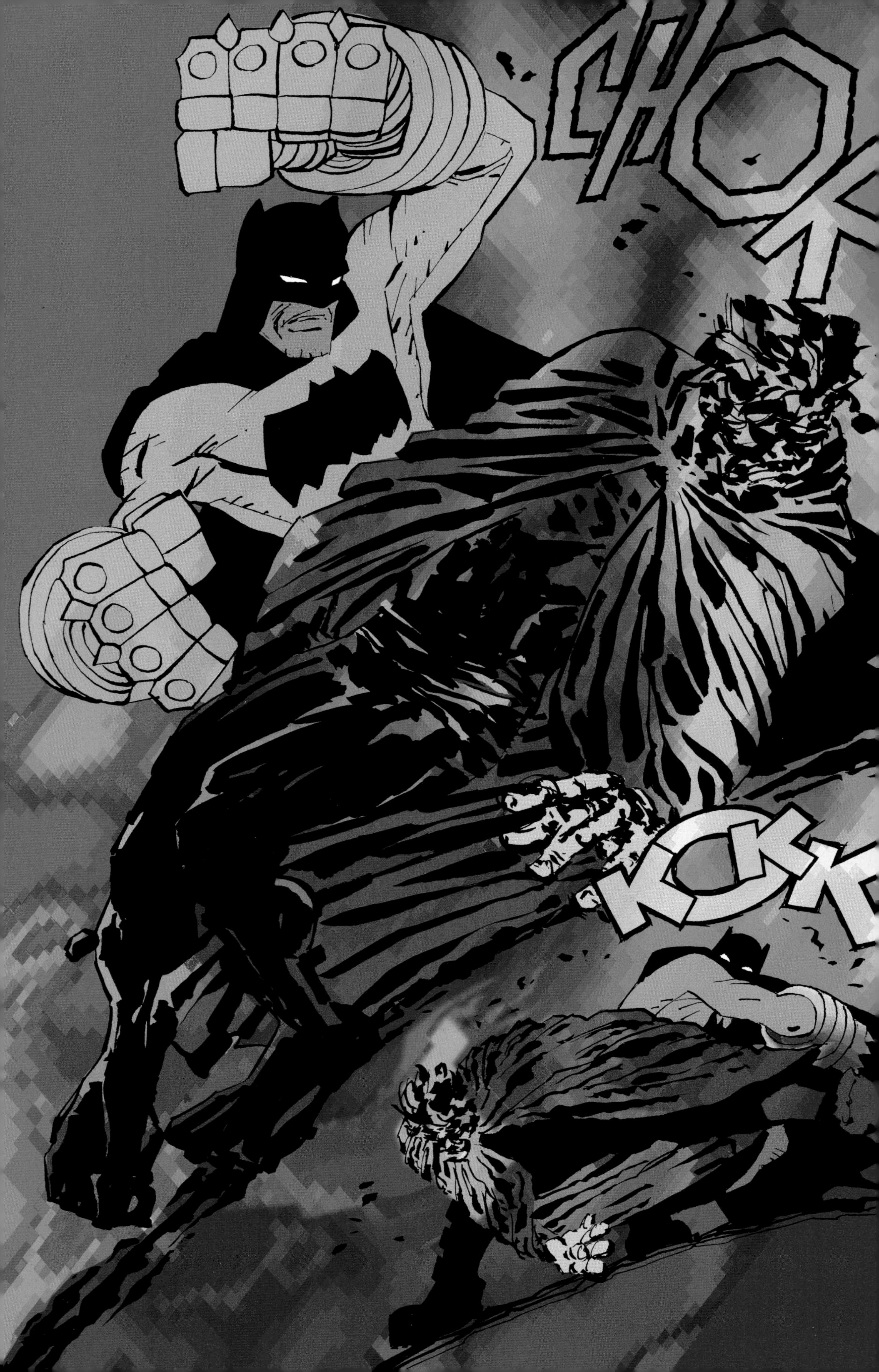
CHOK
KCK

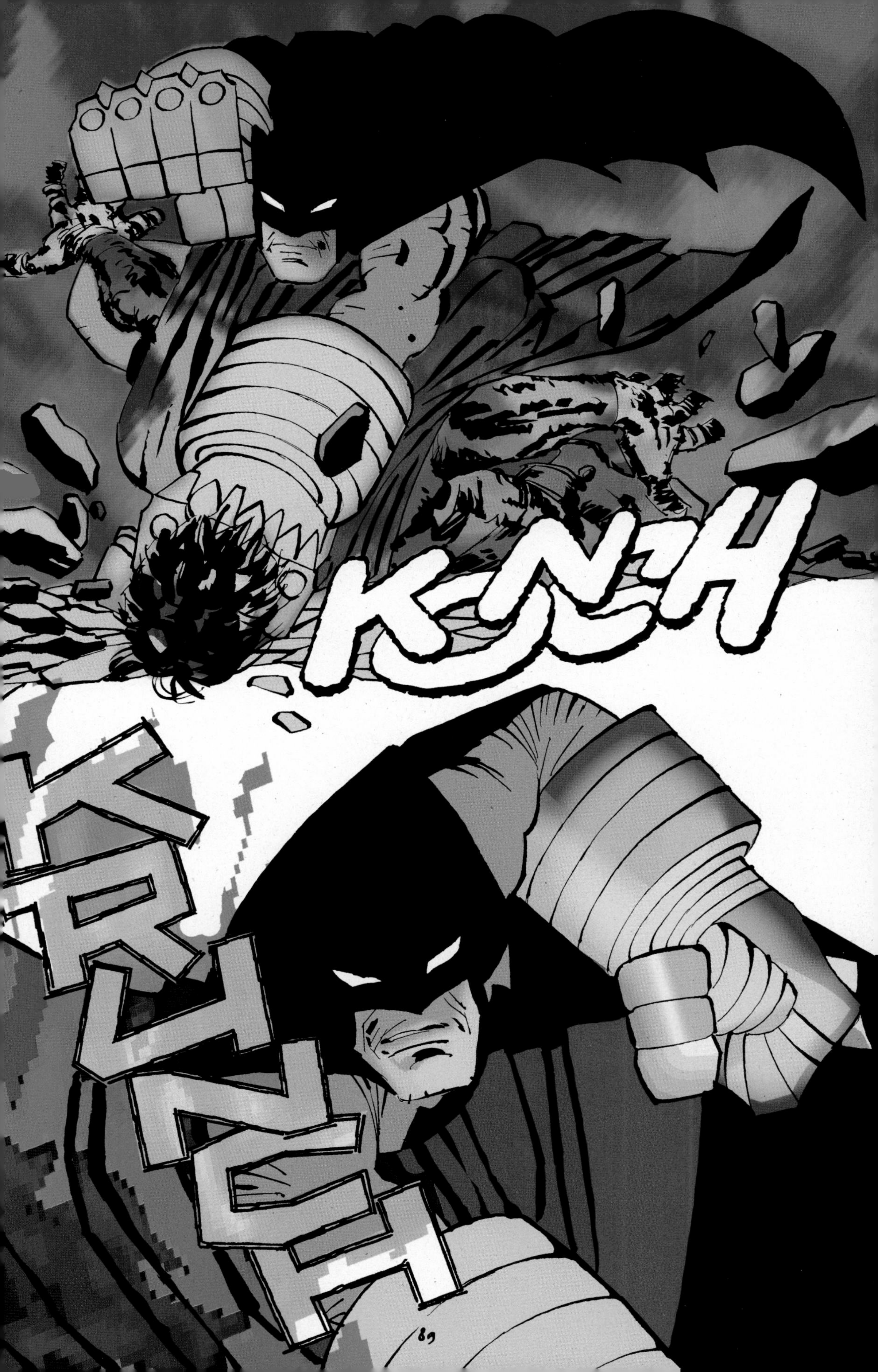
KNCH
KRUNCH

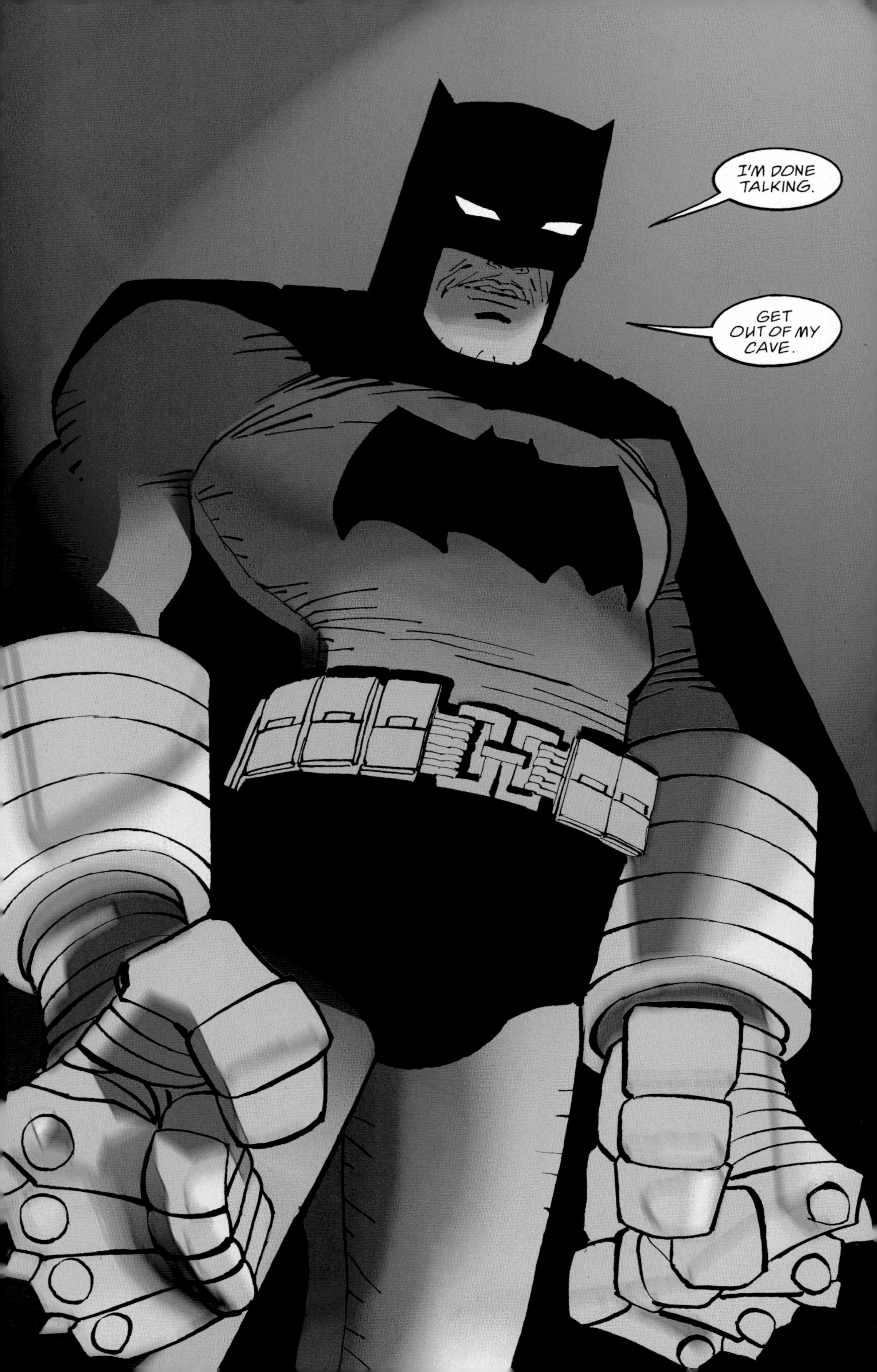
I'M DONE TALKING.
GET OUT OF MY CAVE.

BOOK TWO.

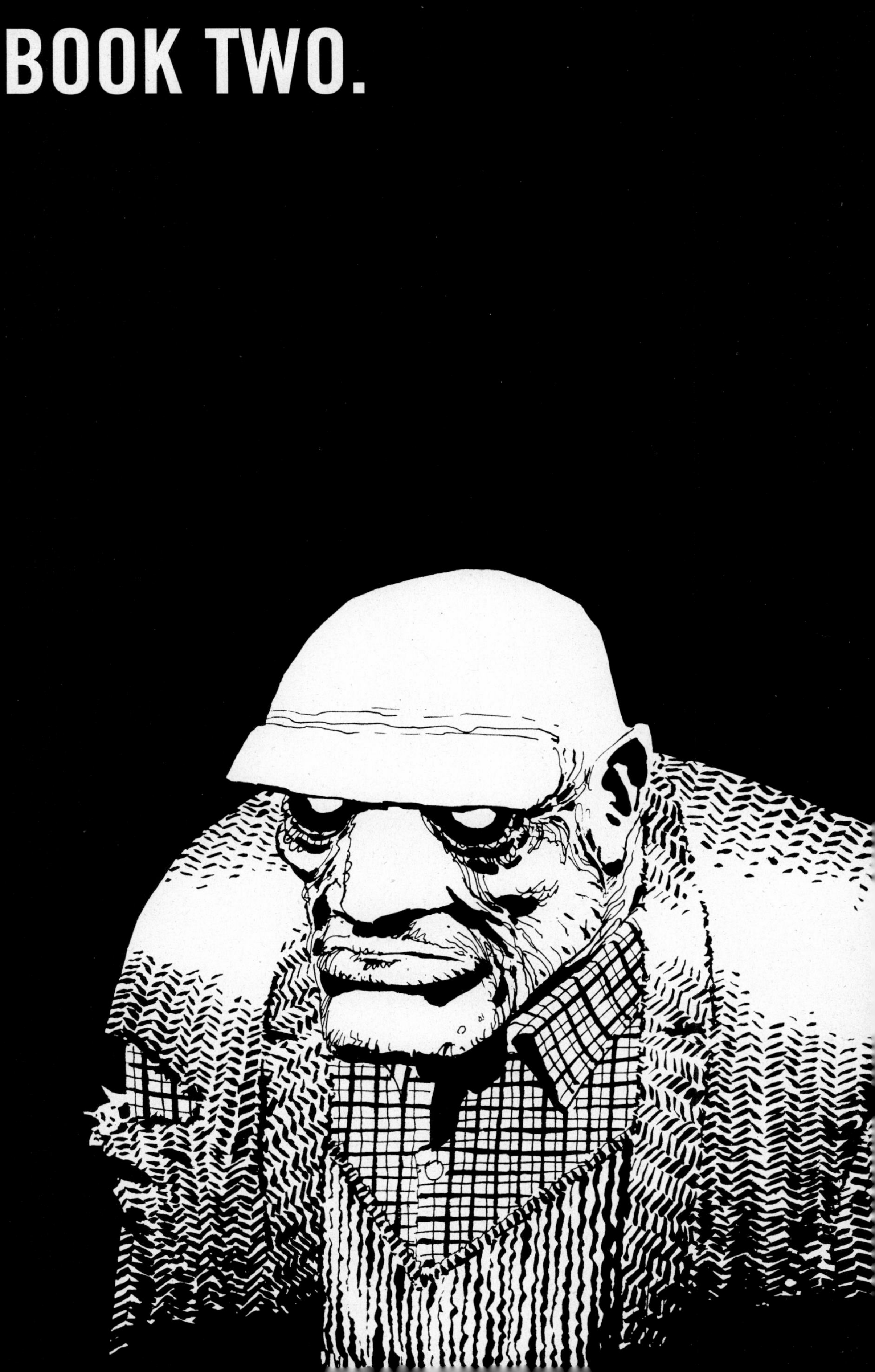

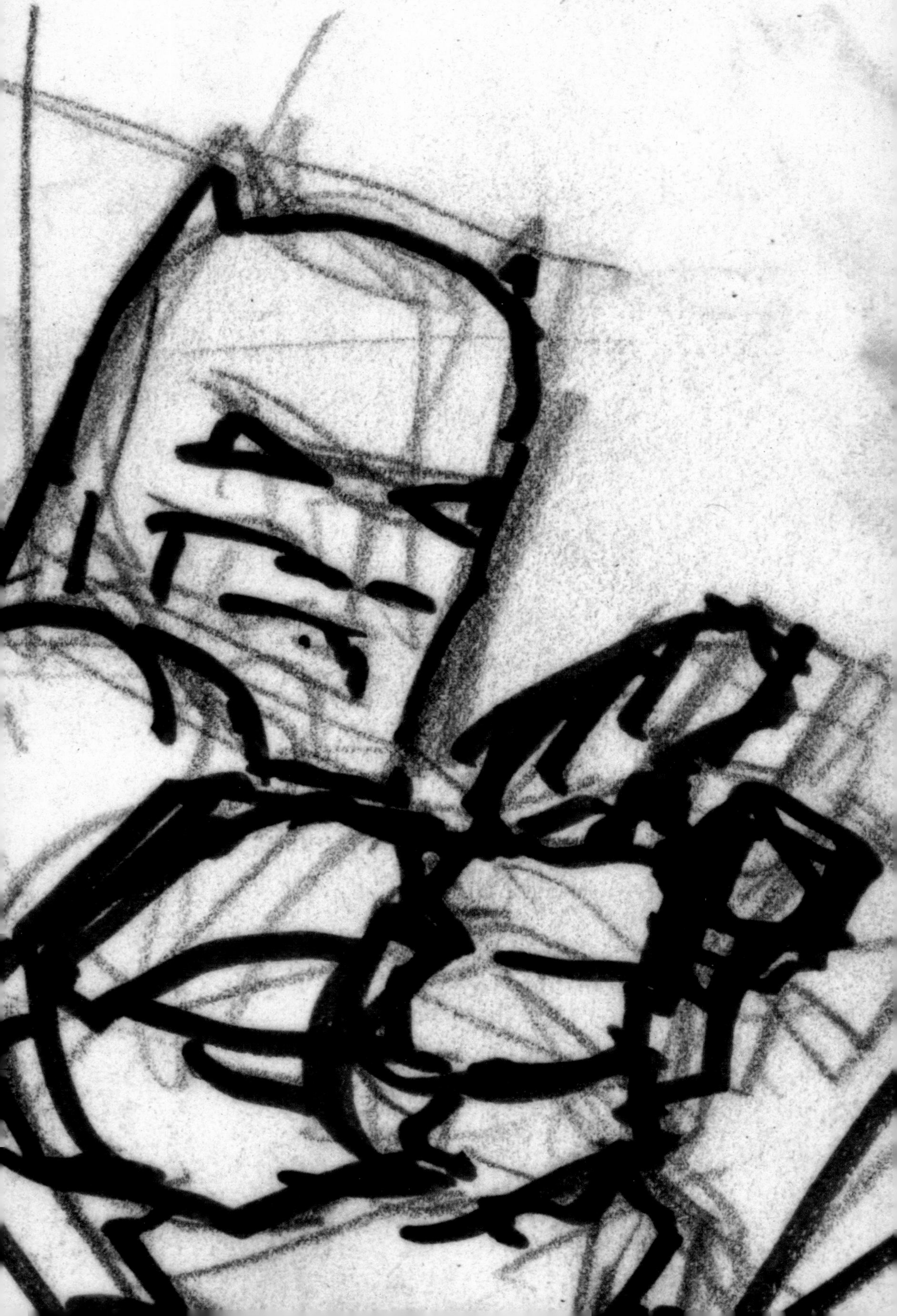

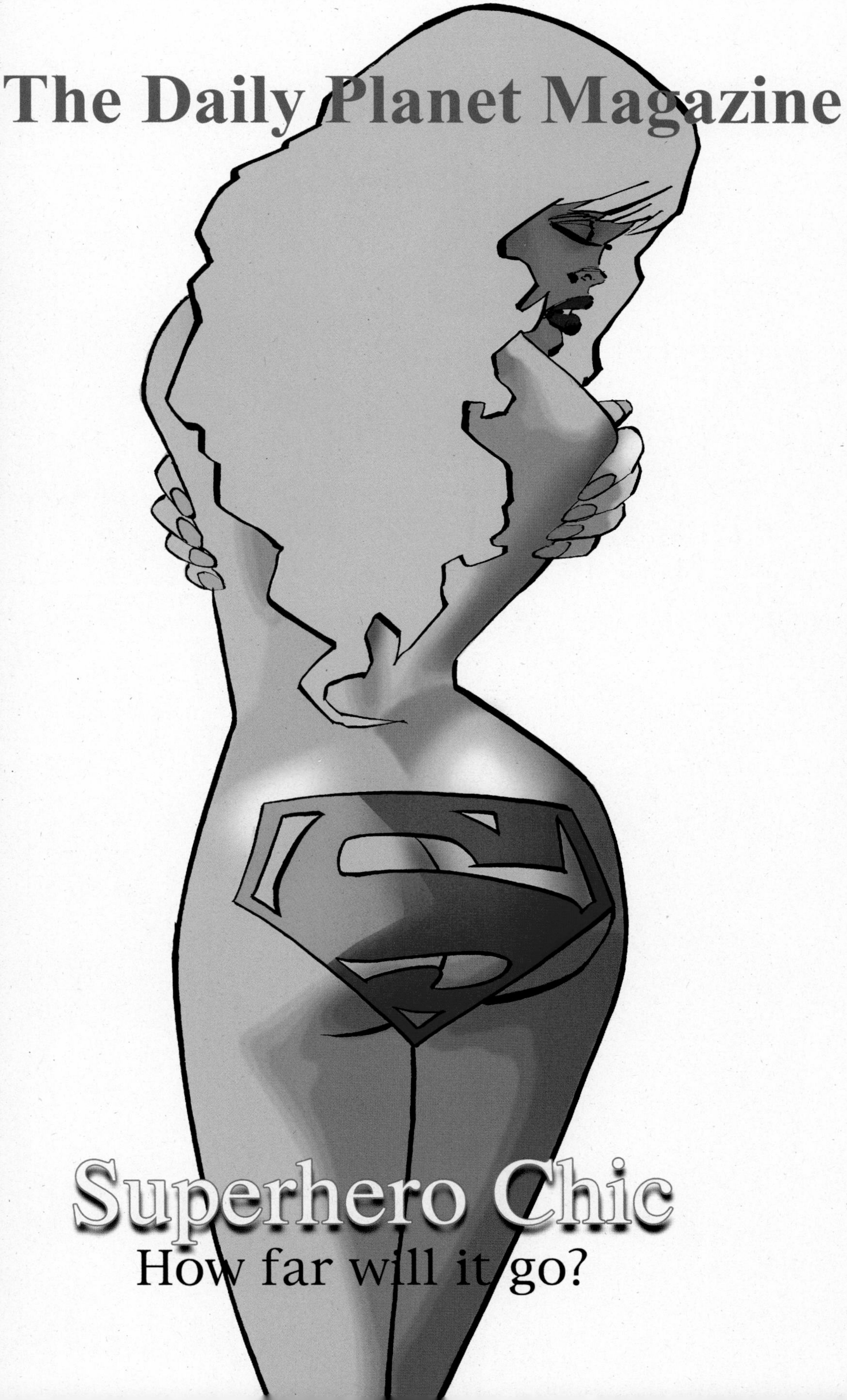
The Daily Planet Magazine
Superhero Chic
How far will it go?

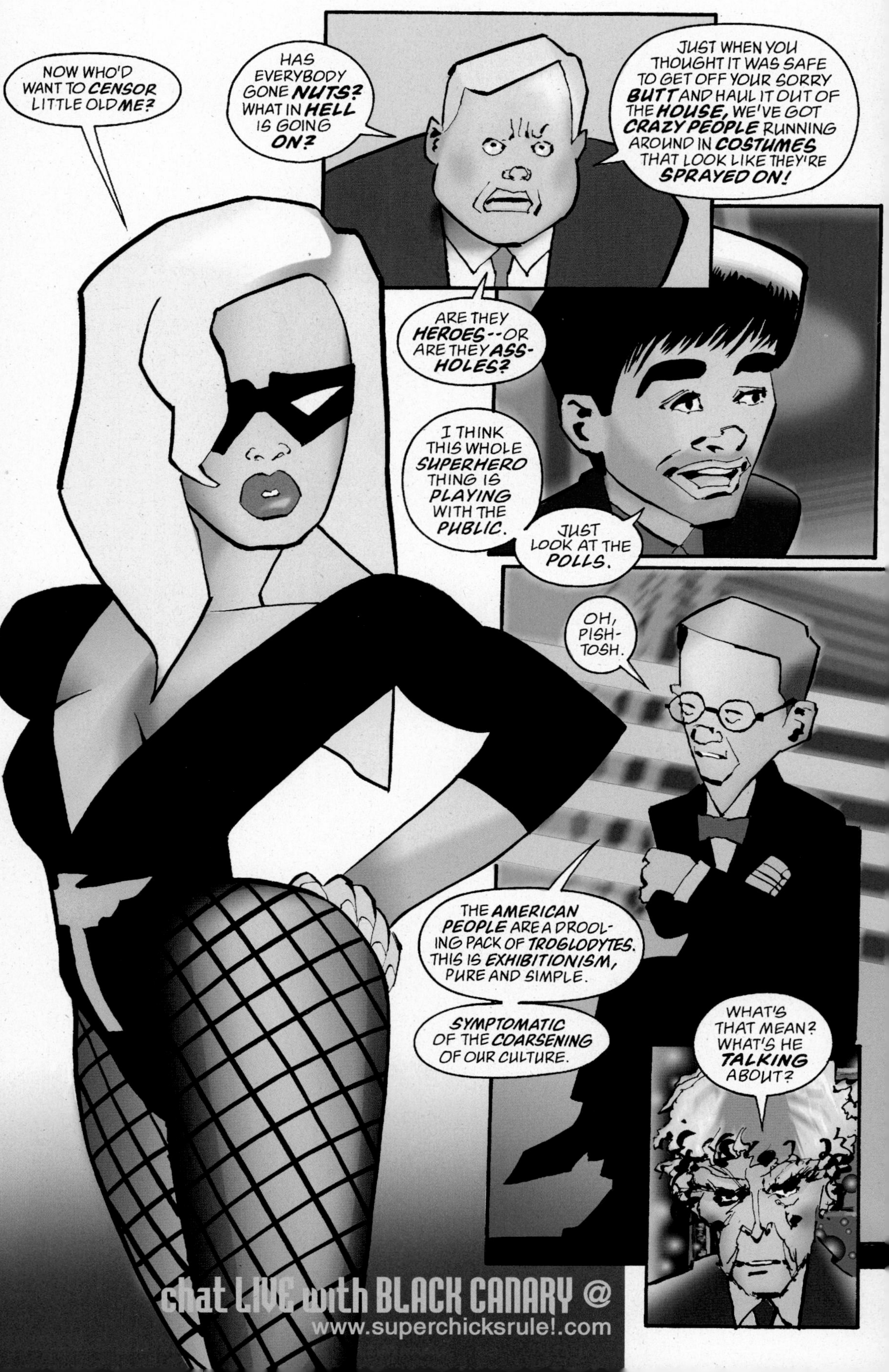

NOW WHO'D WANT TO CENSOR LITTLE OLD ME?
HAS EVERYBODY GONE NUTS? WHAT IN HELL IS GOING ON?
JUST WHEN YOU THOUGHT IT WAS SAFE TO GET OFF YOUR SORRY BUTT AND HAUL IT OUT OF THE HOUSE, WE'VE GOT CRAZY PEOPLE RUNNING AROUND IN COSTUMES THAT LOOK LIKE THEY'RE SPRAYED ON!
ARE THEY HEROES--OR ARE THEY ASS-HOLES?
I THINK THIS WHOLE SUPERHERO THING IS PLAYING WITH THE PUBLIC.
JUST LOOK AT THE POLLS.
OH, PISH-TOSH.
THE AMERICAN PEOPLE ARE A DROOL-ING PACK OF TROGLODYTES. THIS IS EXHIBITIONISM, PURE AND SIMPLE.
SYMPTOMATIC OF THE COARSENING OF OUR CULTURE.
WHAT'S THAT MEAN? WHAT'S HE TALKING ABOUT?
chat LIVE with BLACK CANARY @
www.superchicksrule!.com

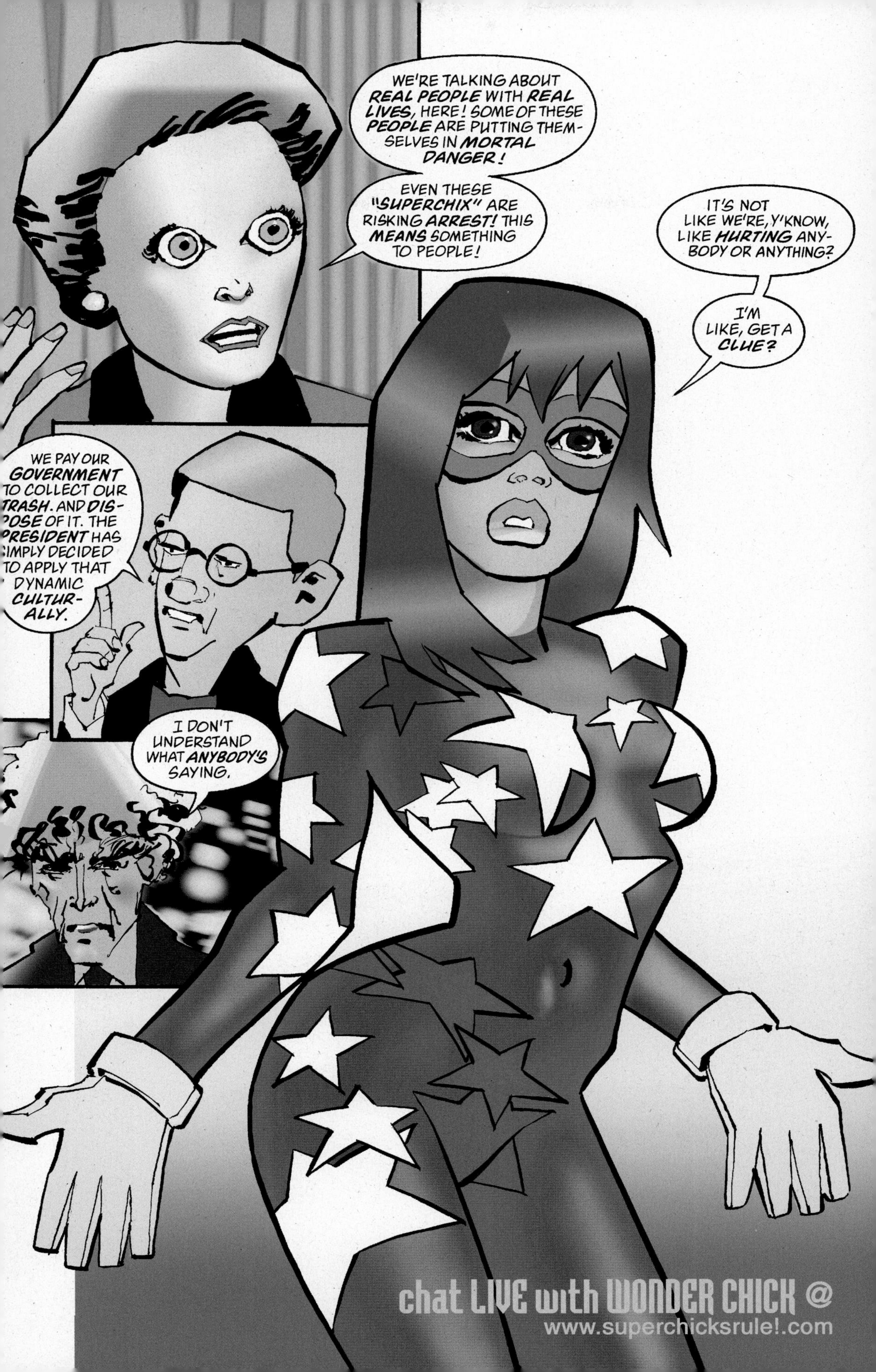
WE'RE TALKING ABOUT REAL PEOPLE WITH REAL LIVES, HERE! SOME OF THESE PEOPLE ARE PUTTING THEMSELVES IN MORTAL DANGER!
EVEN THESE "SUPERCHIX" ARE RISKING ARREST! THIS MEANS SOMETHING TO PEOPLE!
IT'S NOT LIKE WE'RE, Y'KNOW, LIKE HURTING ANYBODY OR ANYTHING?
I'M LIKE, GET A CLUE?
WE PAY OUR GOVERNMENT TO COLLECT OUR TRASH. AND DISPOSE OF IT. THE PRESIDENT HAS SIMPLY DECIDED TO APPLY THAT DYNAMIC CULTURALLY.
I DON'T UNDERSTAND WHAT ANYBODY'S SAYING.
chat LIVE with WONDER CHICK @
www.superchicksrule!.com

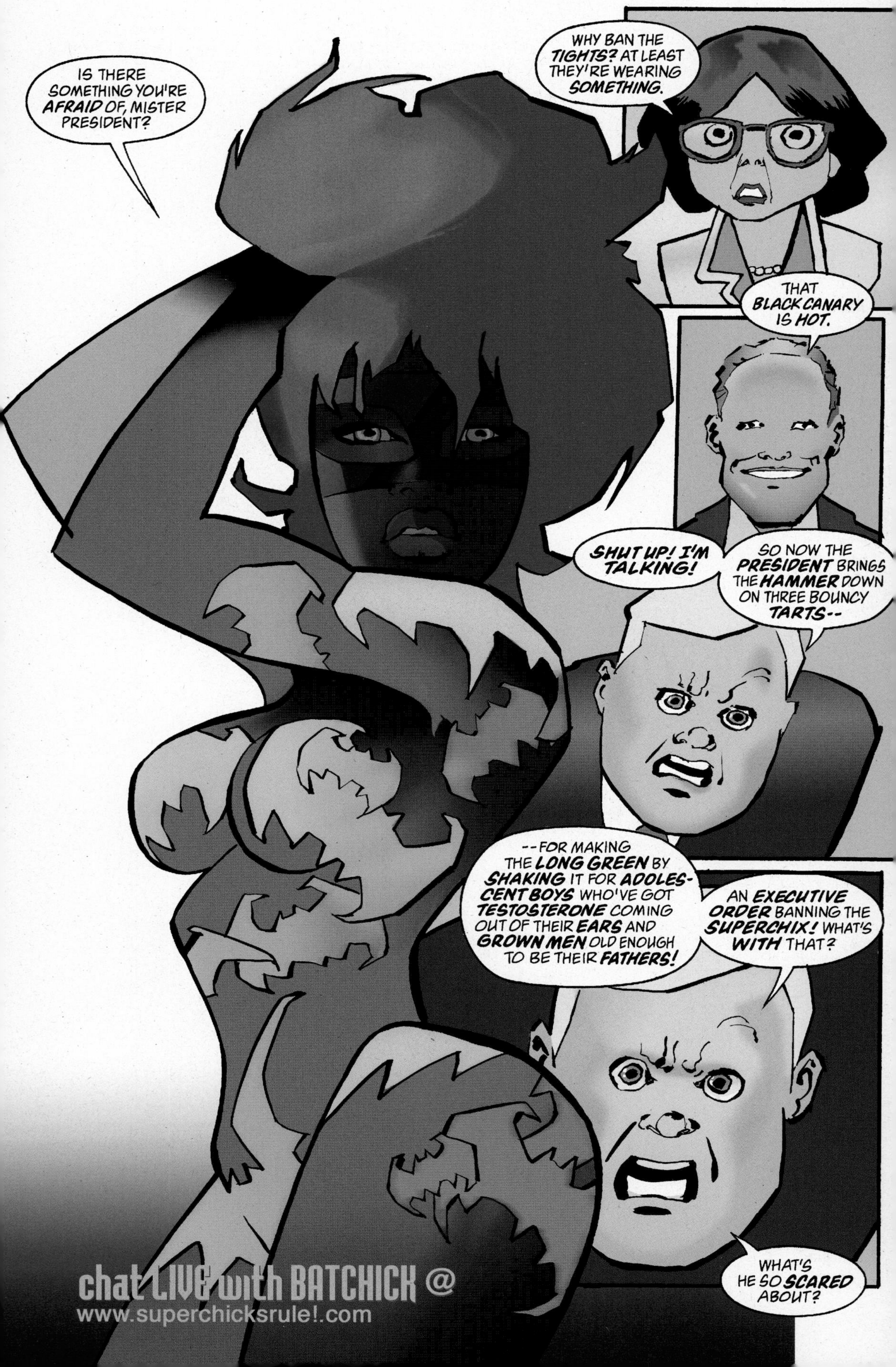
IS THERE SOMETHING YOU'RE AFRAID OF, MISTER PRESIDENT?
WHY BAN THE TIGHTS? AT LEAST THEY'RE WEARING SOMETHING.
THAT BLACK CANARY IS HOT.
SHUT UP! I'M TALKING!
SO NOW THE PRESIDENT BRINGS THE HAMMER DOWN ON THREE BOUNCY TARTS--
--FOR MAKING THE LONG GREEN BY SHAKING IT FOR ADOLES-CENT BOYS WHO'VE GOT TESTOSTERONE COMING OUT OF THEIR EARS AND GROWN MEN OLD ENOUGH TO BE THEIR FATHERS!
AN EXECUTIVE ORDER BANNING THE SUPERCHIX! WHAT'S WITH THAT?
WHAT'S HE SO SCARED ABOUT?
chat LIVE with BATCHICK @
www.superchicksrule!.com

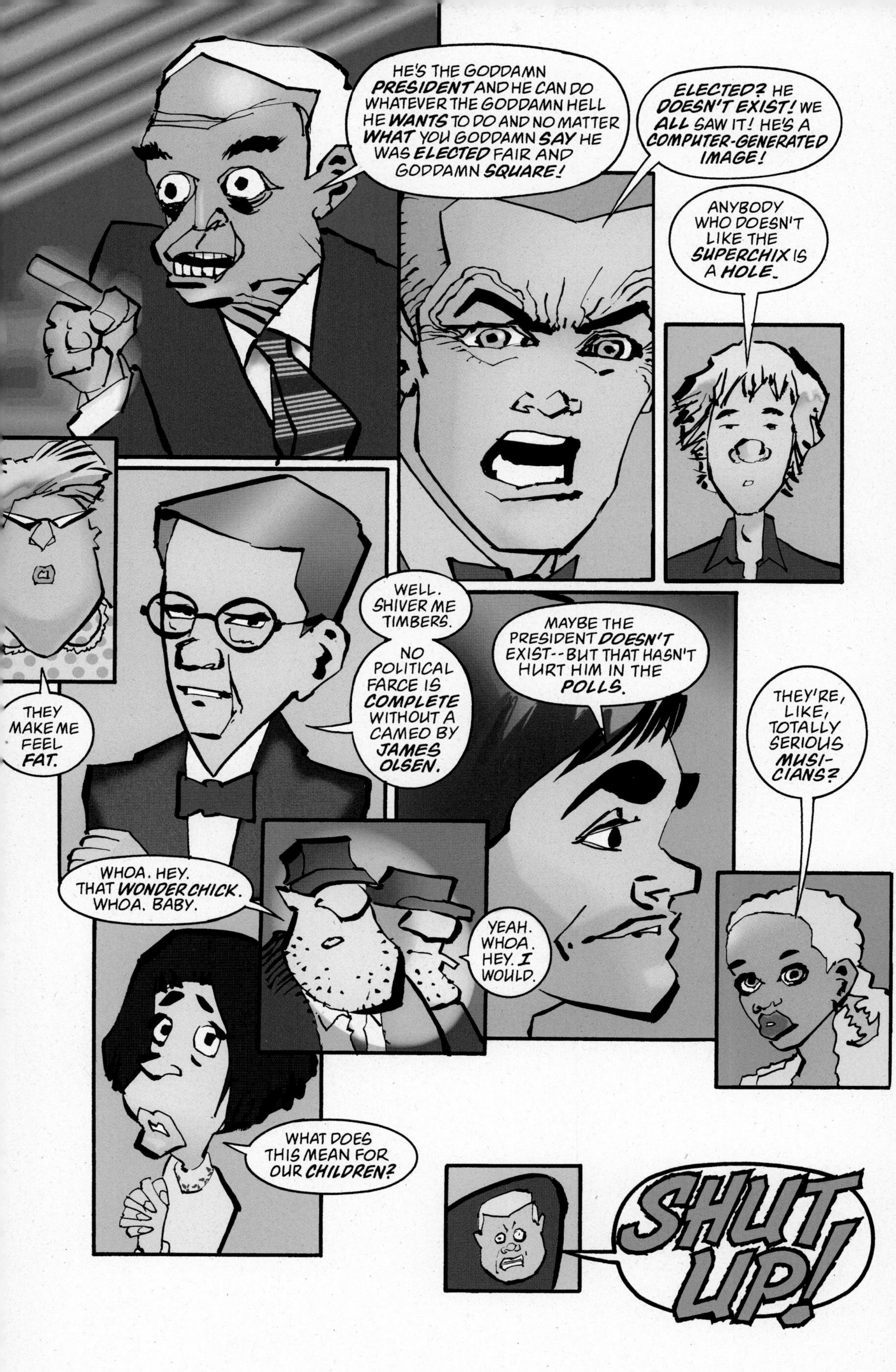
HE'S THE GODDAMN PRESIDENT AND HE CAN DO WHATEVER THE GODDAMN HELL HE WANTS TO DO AND NO MATTER WHAT YOU GODDAMN SAY HE WAS ELECTED FAIR AND GODDAMN SQUARE!
ELECTED? HE DOESN'T EXIST! WE ALL SAW IT! HE'S A COMPUTER-GENERATED IMAGE!
ANYBODY WHO DOESN'T LIKE THE SUPERCHIX IS A HOLE.
THEY MAKE ME FEEL FAT.
WELL. SHIVER ME TIMBERS.
NO POLITICAL FARCE IS COMPLETE WITHOUT A CAMEO BY JAMES OLSEN.
MAYBE THE PRESIDENT DOESN'T EXIST--BUT THAT HASN'T HURT HIM IN THE POLLS.
THEY'RE, LIKE, TOTALLY SERIOUS MUSI-CIANS?
WHOA. HEY. THAT WONDER CHICK. WHOA. BABY.
YEAH. WHOA. HEY. I WOULD.
WHAT DOES THIS MEAN FOR OUR CHILDREN?
SHUT UP!

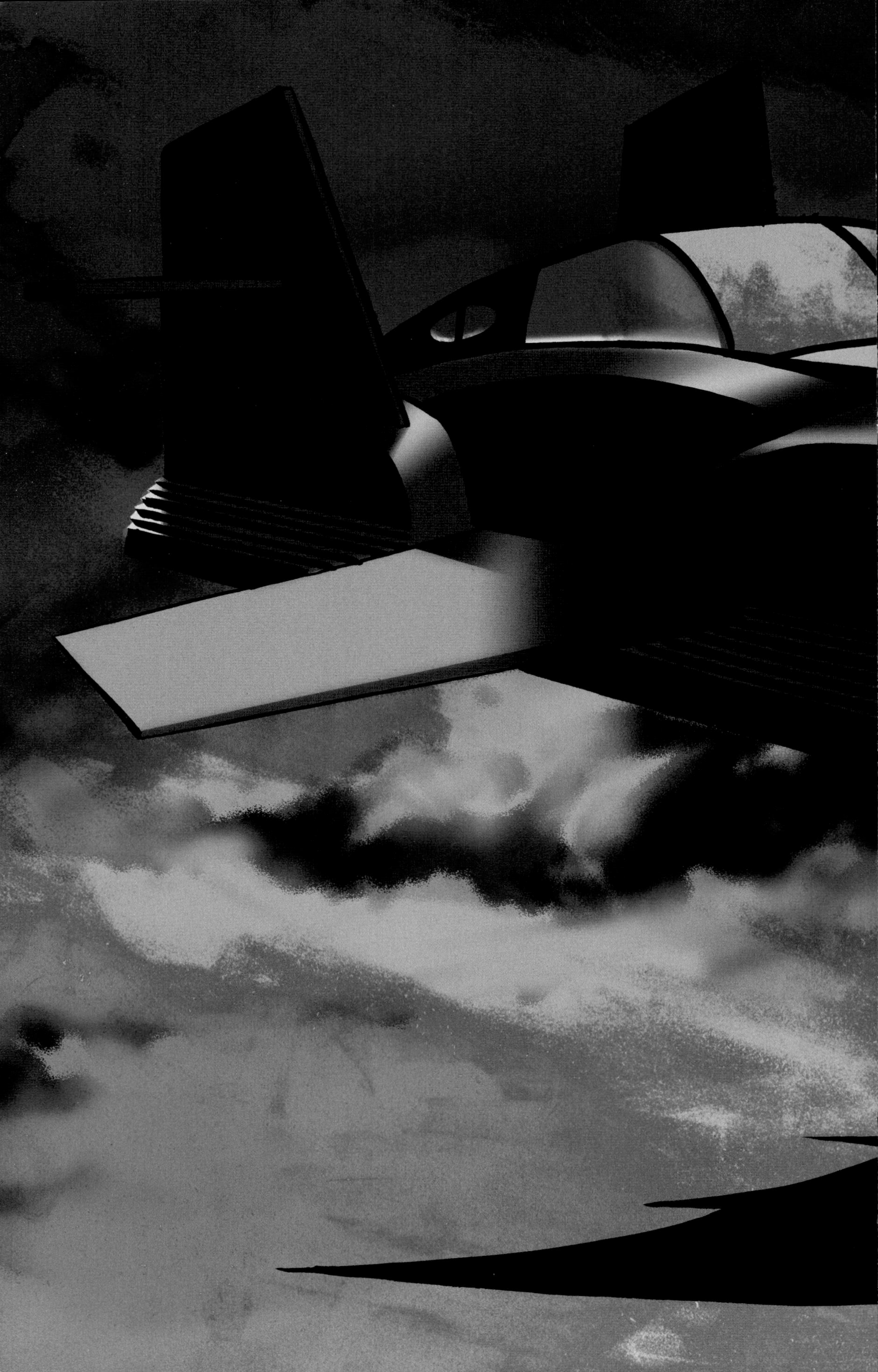

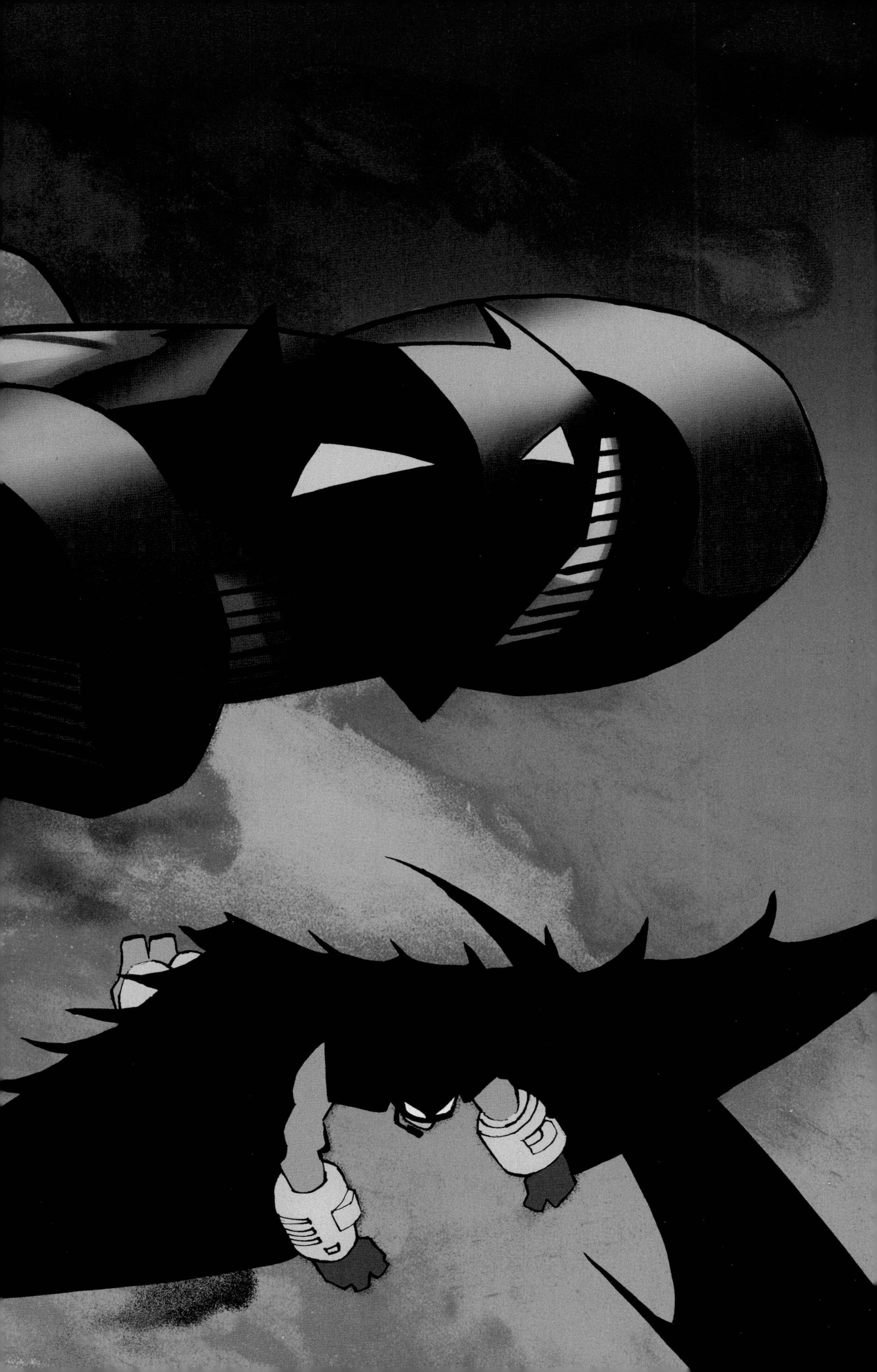

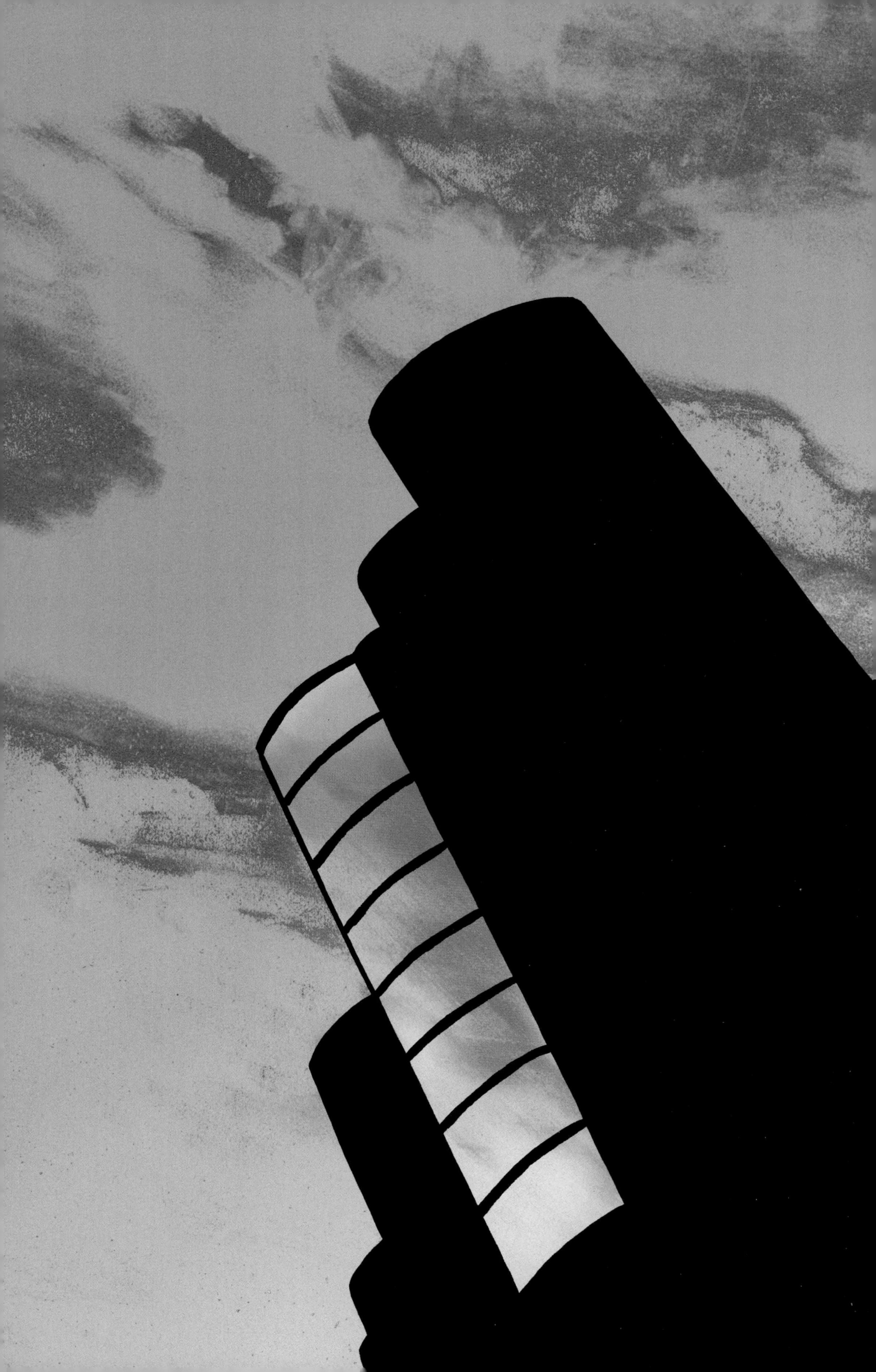

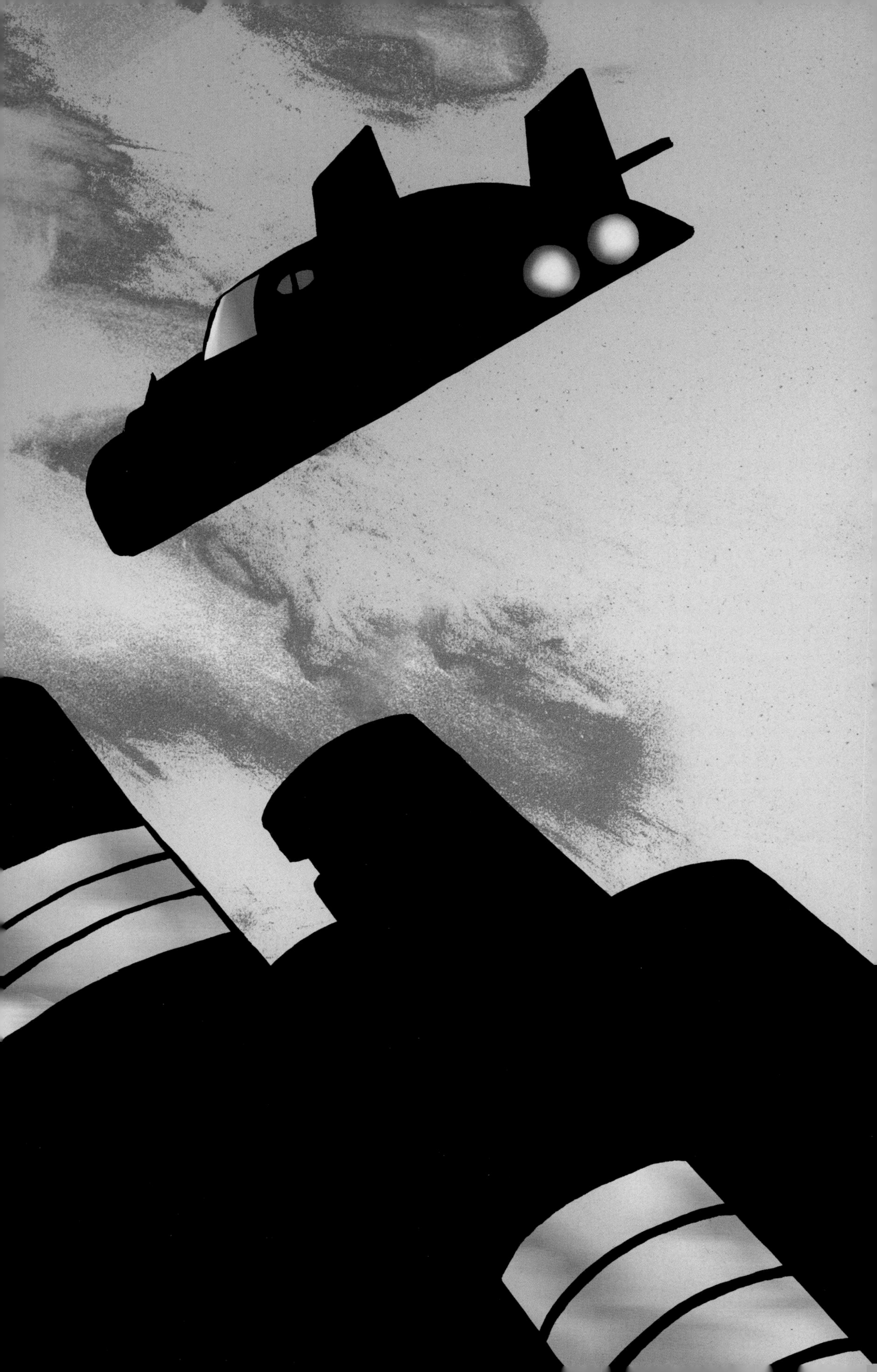

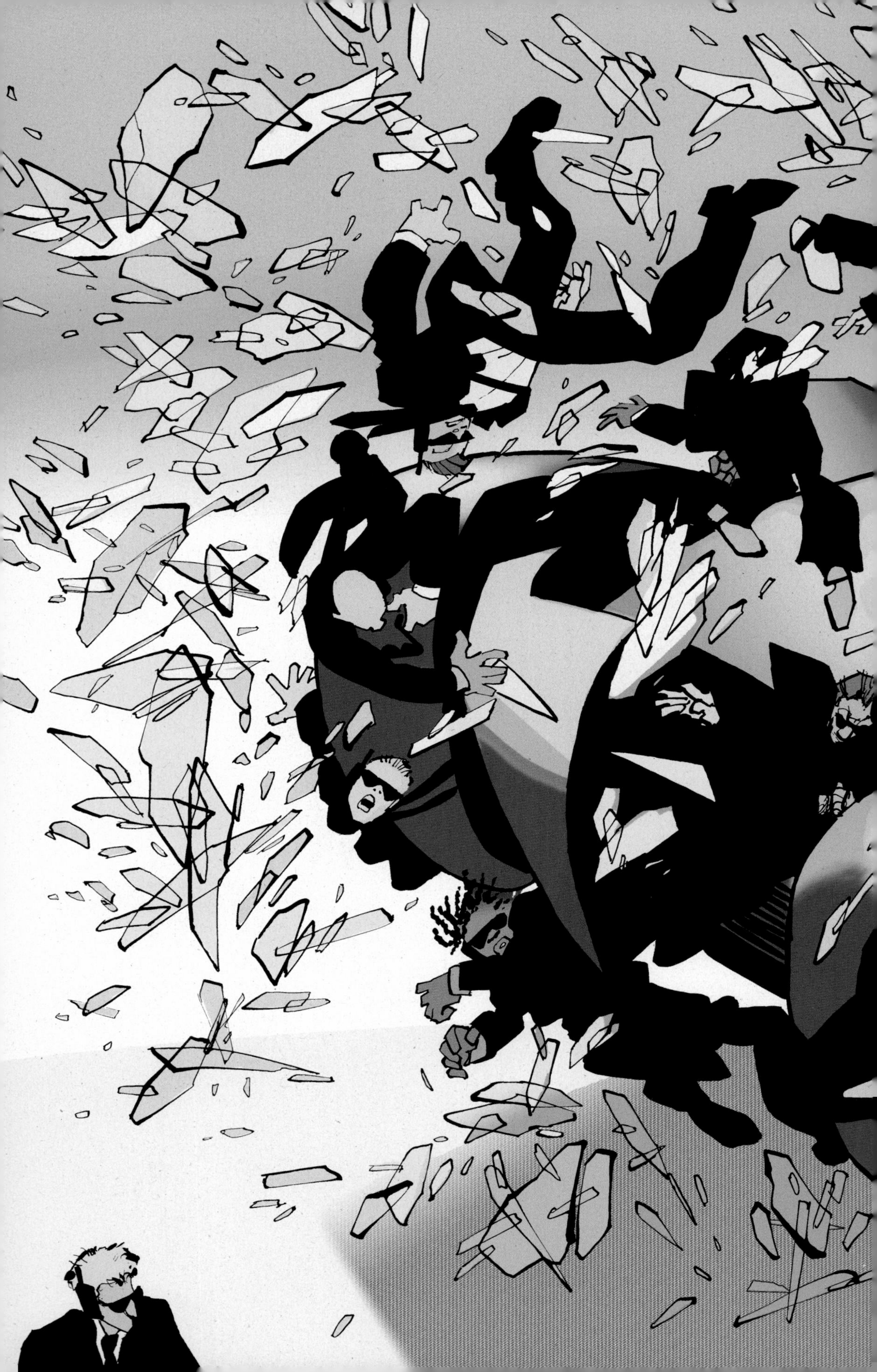

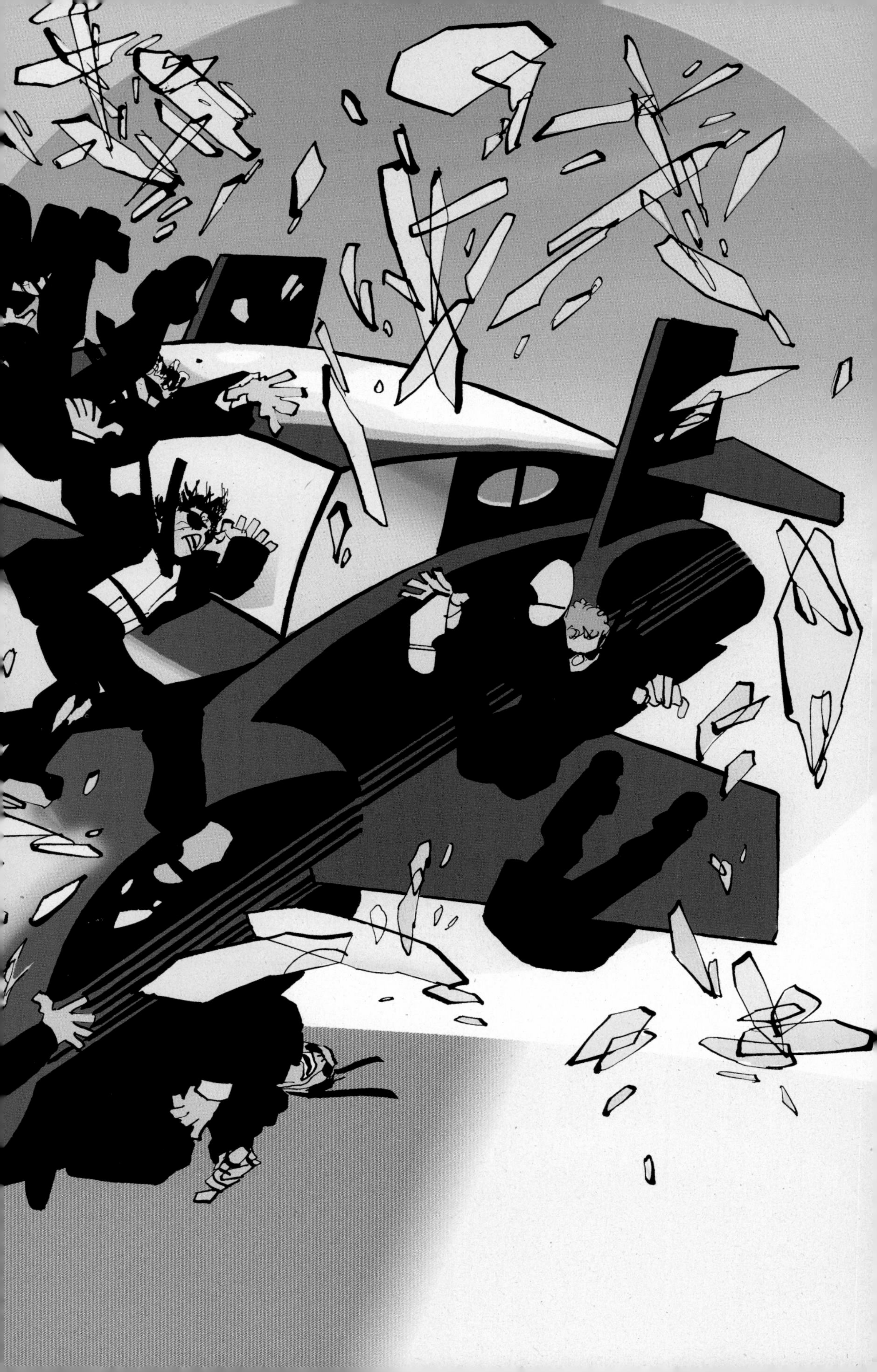

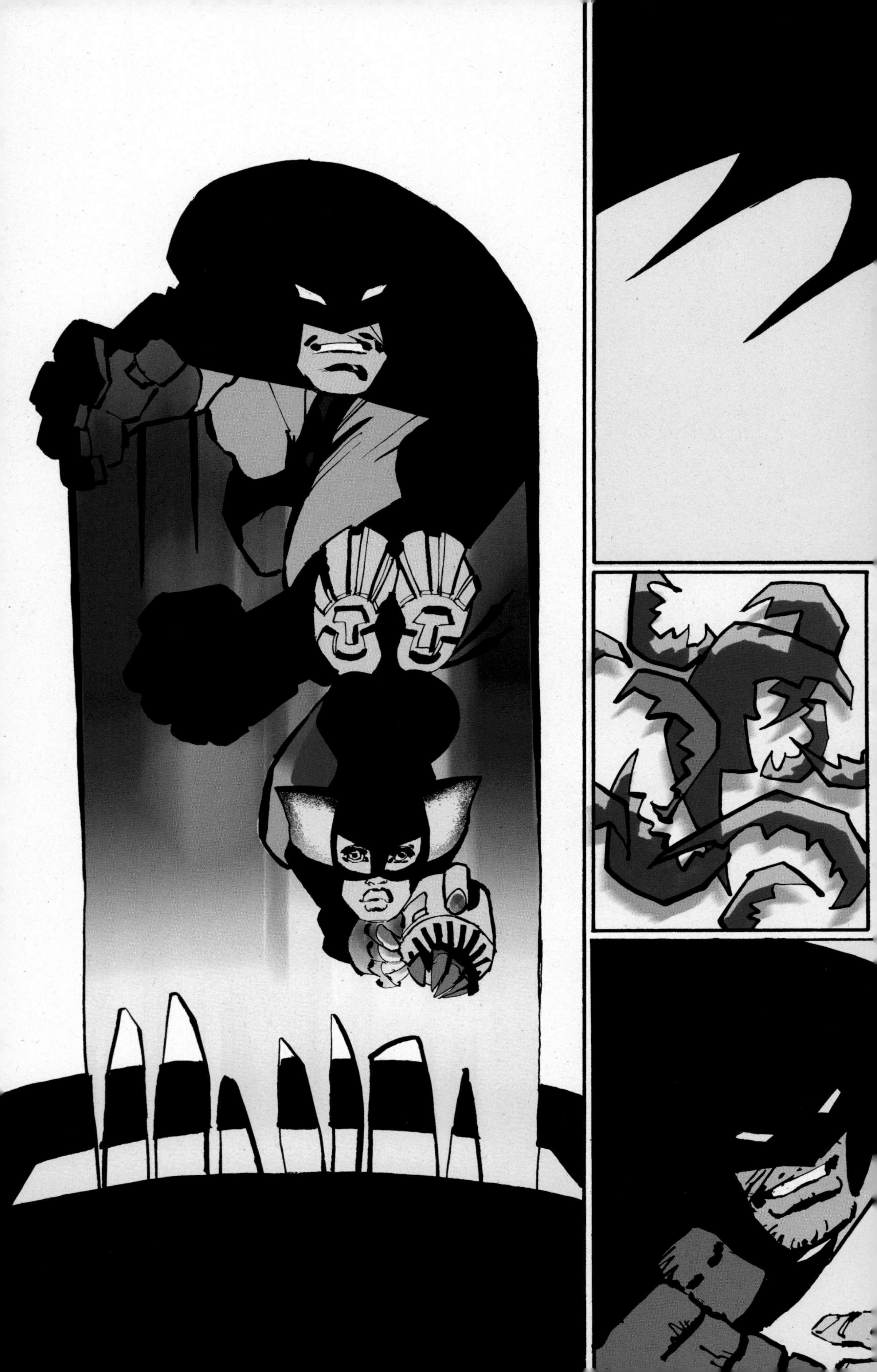

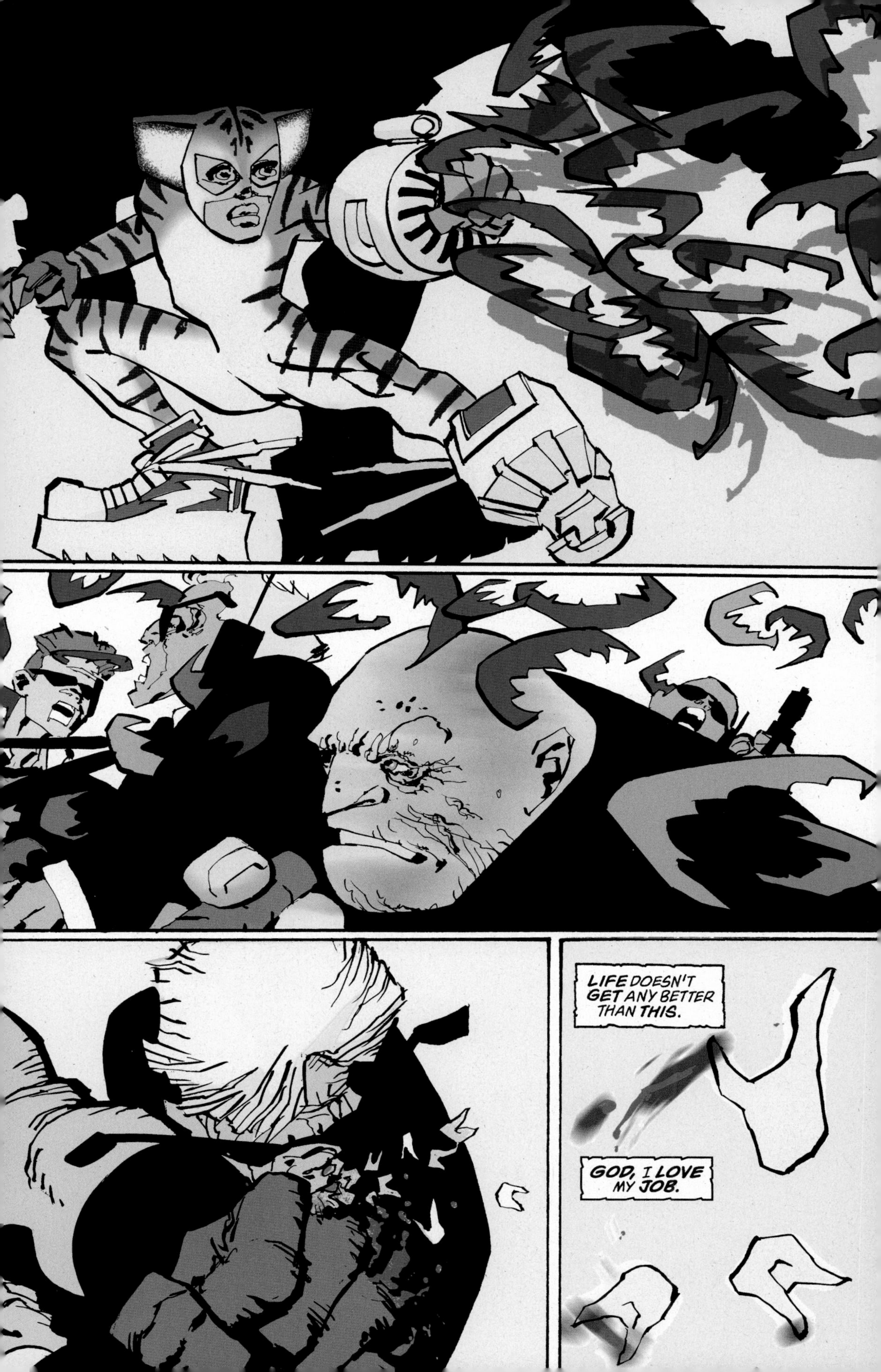
LIFE DOESN'T GET ANY BETTER THAN THIS.
GOD, I LOVE MY JOB.

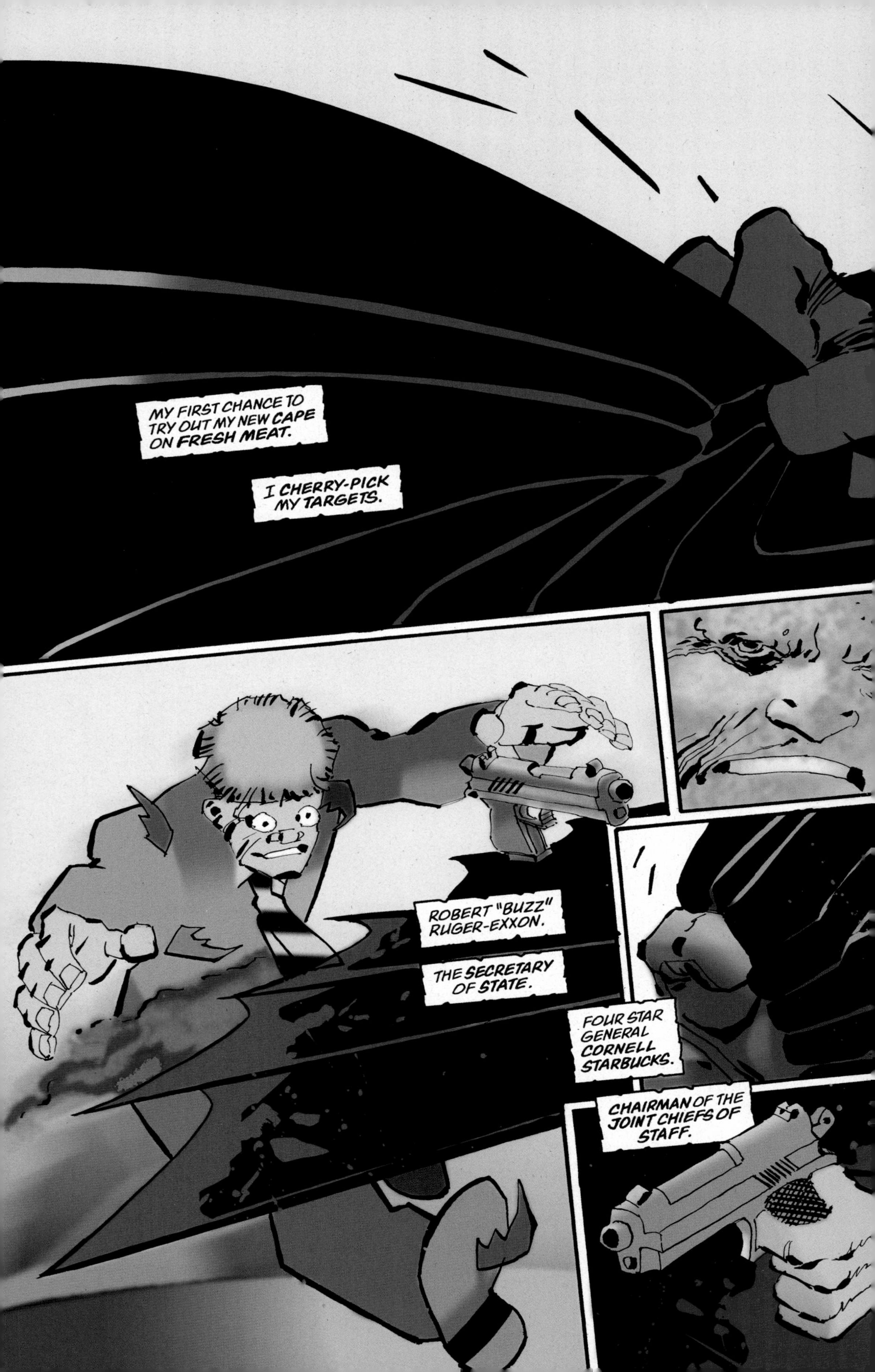
MY FIRST CHANCE TO TRY OUT MY NEW CAPE ON FRESH MEAT.
I CHERRY-PICK MY TARGETS.
ROBERT "BUZZ" RUGER-EXXON.
THE SECRETARY OF STATE.
FOUR STAR GENERAL CORNELL STARBUCKS.
CHAIRMAN OF THE JOINT CHIEFS OF STAFF.

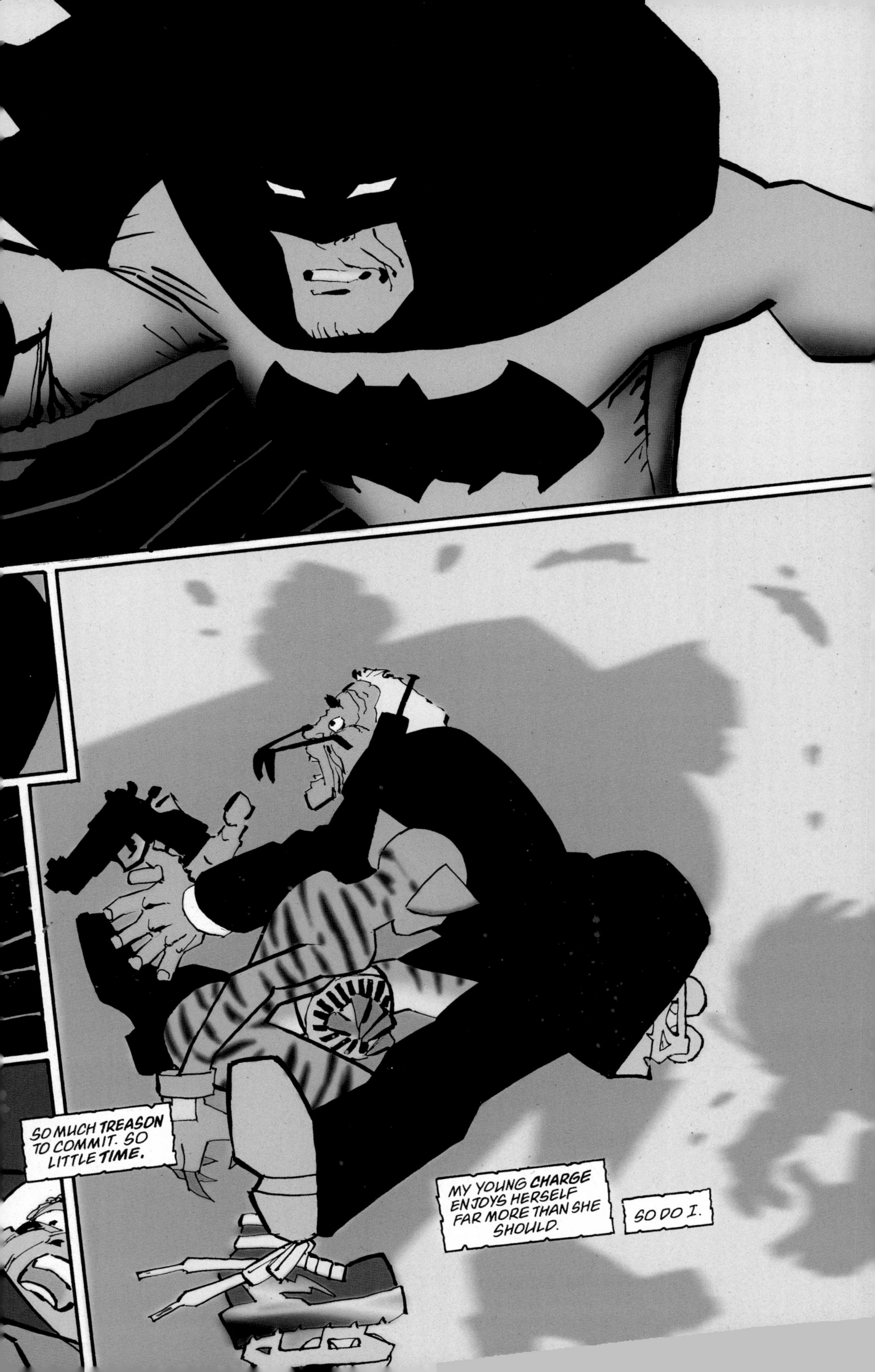
SO MUCH TREASON TO COMMIT. SO LITTLE TIME.
MY YOUNG CHARGE ENJOYS HERSELF FAR MORE THAN SHE SHOULD.
SO DO I.

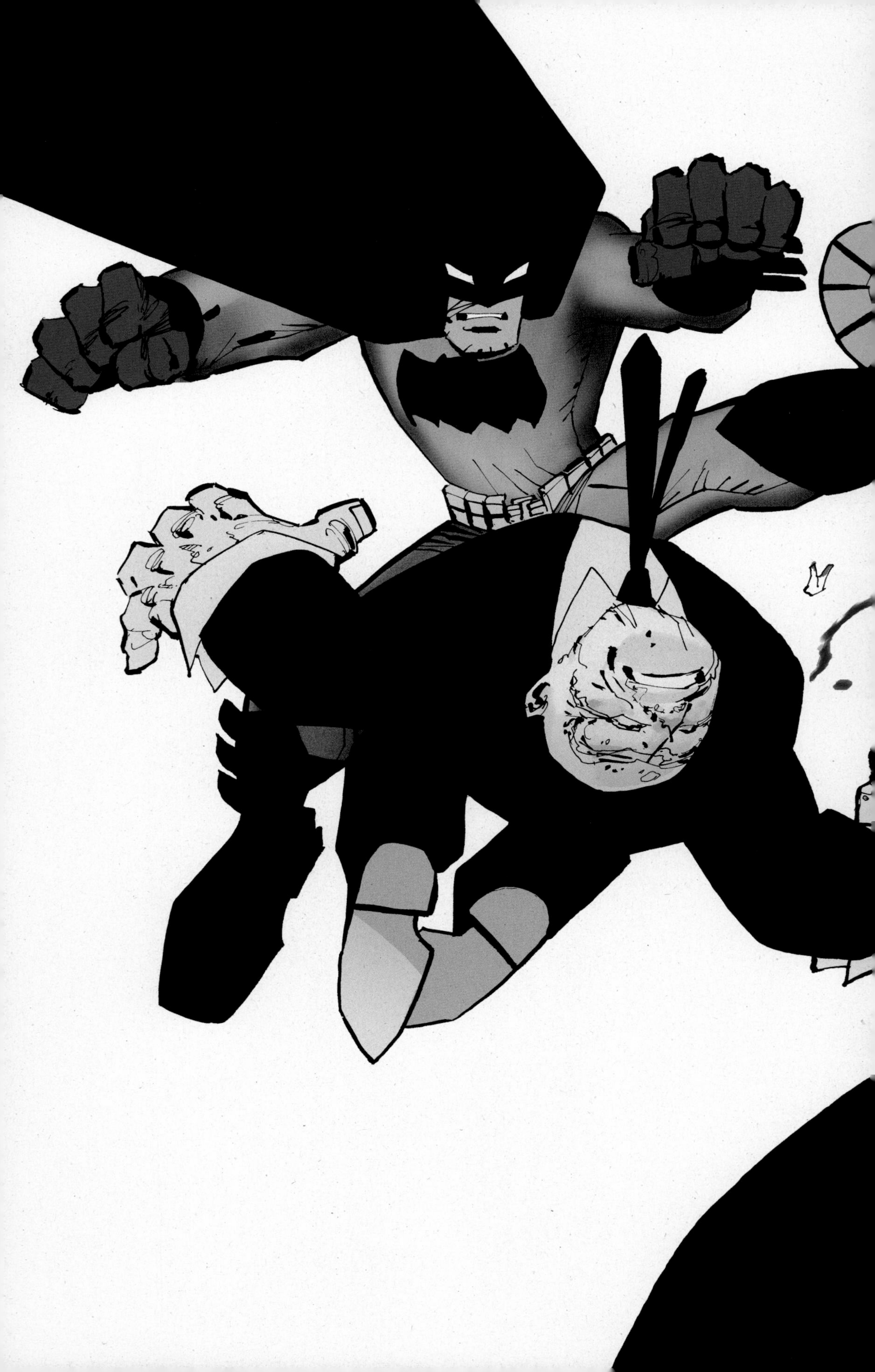

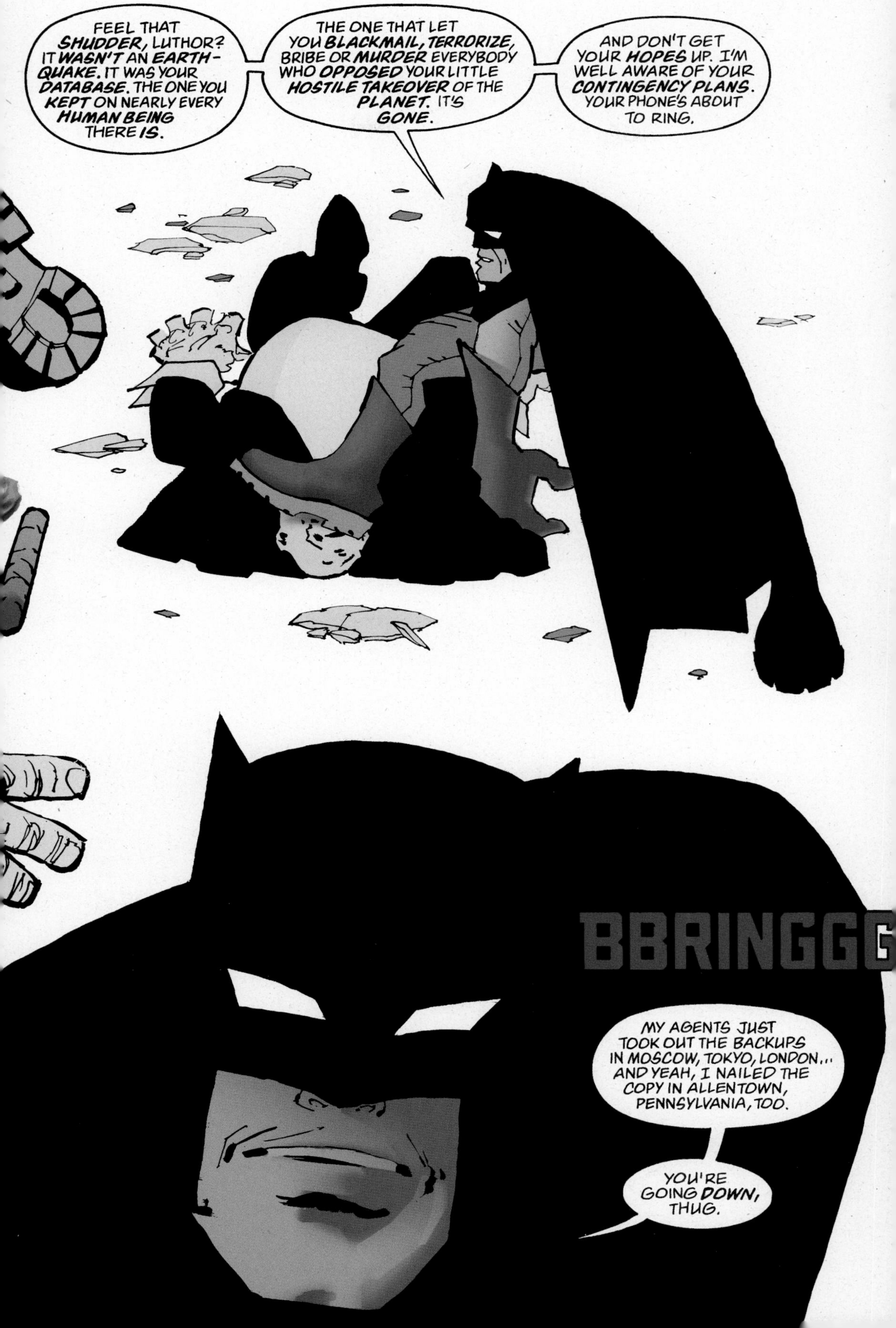
FEEL THAT SHUDDER, LUTHOR? IT WASN'T AN EARTH-QUAKE. IT WAS YOUR DATABASE. THE ONE YOU KEPT ON NEARLY EVERY HUMAN BEING THERE IS.
THE ONE THAT LET YOU BLACKMAIL, TERRORIZE, BRIBE OR MURDER EVERYBODY WHO OPPOSED YOUR LITTLE HOSTILE TAKEOVER OF THE PLANET. IT'S GONE.
AND DON'T GET YOUR HOPES UP. I'M WELL AWARE OF YOUR CONTINGENCY PLANS. YOUR PHONE'S ABOUT TO RING.
BBRINGGG
MY AGENTS JUST TOOK OUT THE BACKUPS IN MOSCOW, TOKYO, LONDON... AND YEAH, I NAILED THE COPY IN ALLENTOWN, PENNSYLVANIA, TOO.
YOU'RE GOING DOWN, THUG.

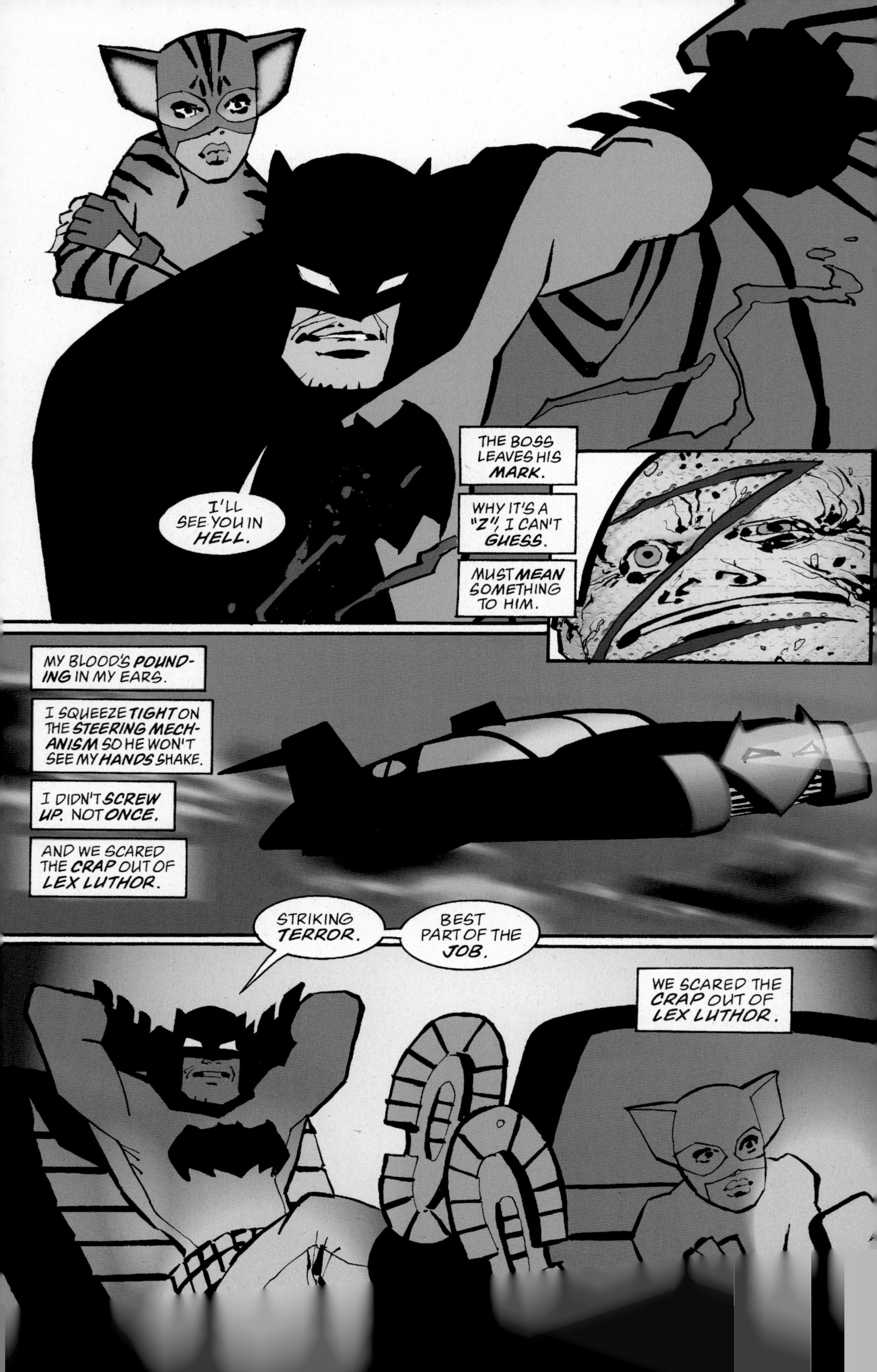
I'LL SEE YOU IN HELL.
THE BOSS LEAVES HIS MARK.
WHY IT'S A "Z", I CAN'T GUESS.
MUST MEAN SOMETHING TO HIM.
MY BLOOD'S POUNDING IN MY EARS.
I SQUEEZE TIGHT ON THE STEERING MECHANISM SO HE WON'T SEE MY HANDS SHAKE.
I DIDN'T SCREW UP. NOT ONCE.
AND WE SCARED THE CRAP OUT OF LEX LUTHOR.
STRIKING TERROR.
BEST PART OF THE JOB.
WE SCARED THE CRAP OUT OF LEX LUTHOR.

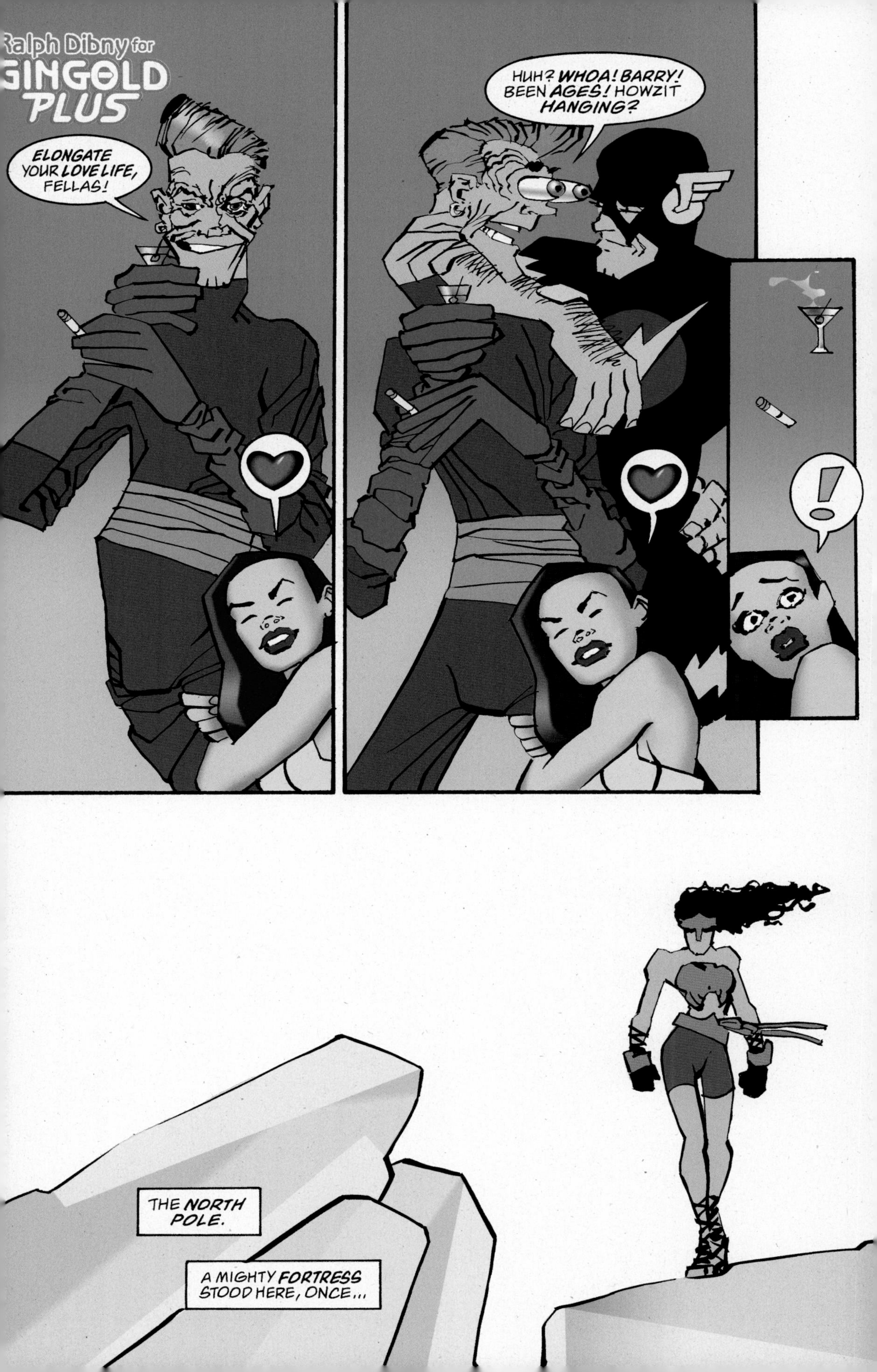

Ralph Dibny for
GINGOLD PLUS
ELONGATE YOUR LOVE LIFE, FELLAS!
HUH? WHOA! BARRY! BEEN AGES! HOWZIT HANGING?
!
THE NORTH POLE.
A MIGHTY FORTRESS STOOD HERE, ONCE...

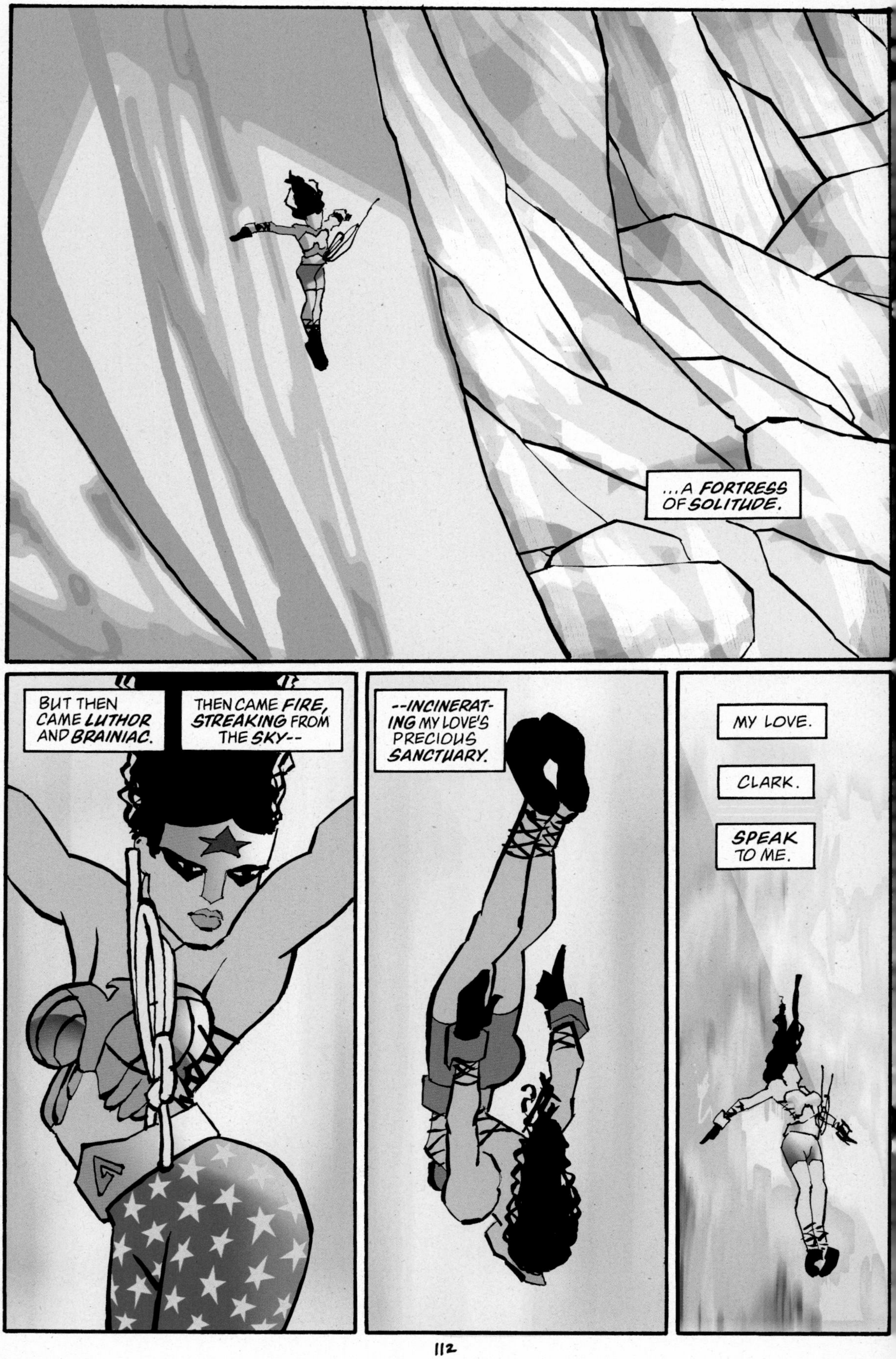
...A FORTRESS OF SOLITUDE.
BUT THEN CAME LUTHOR AND BRAINIAC.
THEN CAME FIRE, STREAKING FROM THE SKY--
--INCINERATING MY LOVE'S PRECIOUS SANCTUARY.
MY LOVE.
CLARK.
SPEAK TO ME.

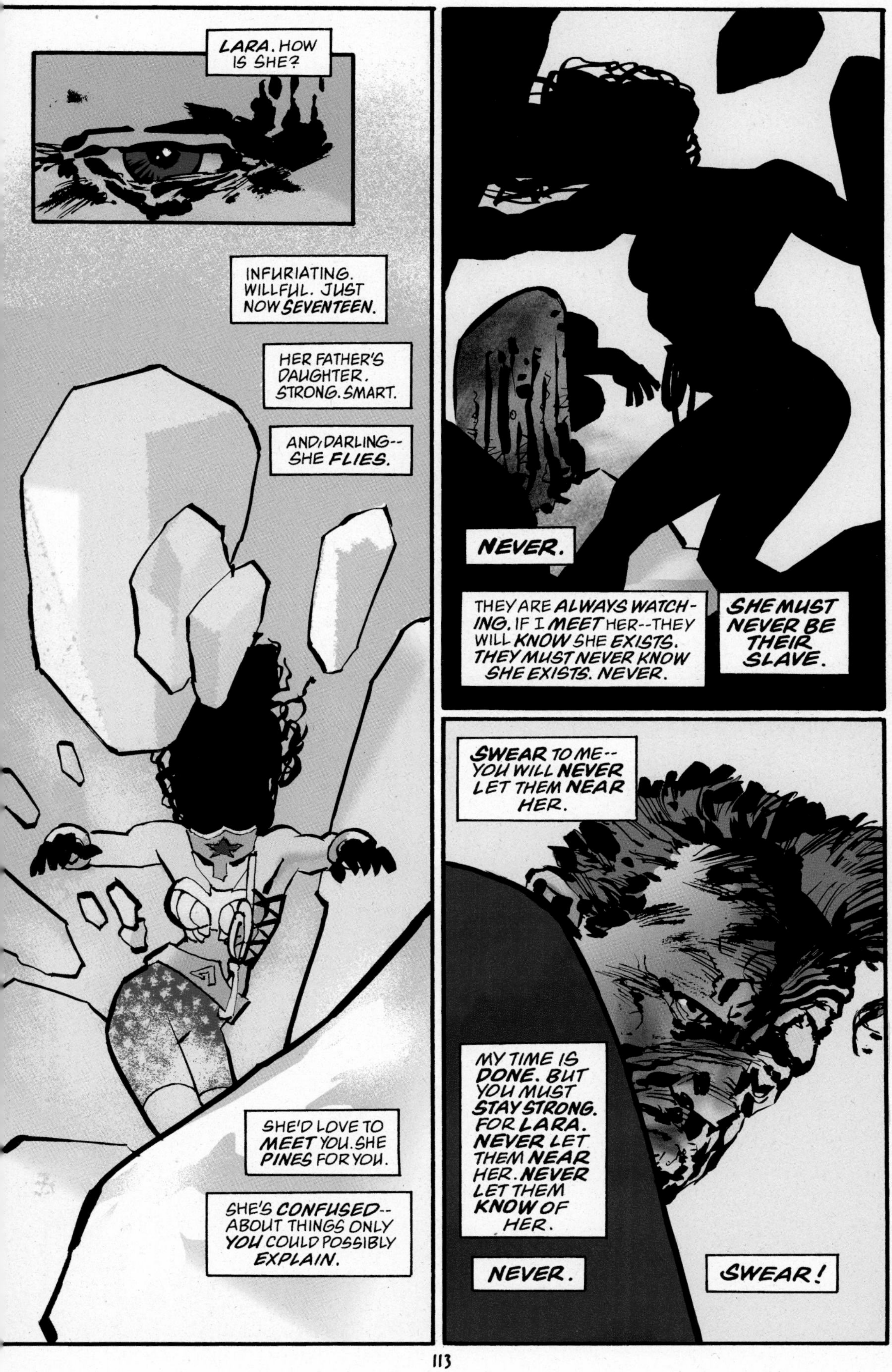

LARA. HOW IS SHE?
INFURIATING. WILLFUL. JUST NOW SEVENTEEN.
HER FATHER'S DAUGHTER. STRONG. SMART.
AND, DARLING-- SHE FLIES.
SHE'D LOVE TO MEET YOU. SHE PINES FOR YOU.
SHE'S CONFUSED-- ABOUT THINGS ONLY YOU COULD POSSIBLY EXPLAIN.
NEVER.
THEY ARE ALWAYS WATCHING. IF I MEET HER--THEY WILL KNOW SHE EXISTS. THEY MUST NEVER KNOW SHE EXISTS. NEVER.
SHE MUST NEVER BE THEIR SLAVE.
SWEAR TO ME-- YOU WILL NEVER LET THEM NEAR HER.
MY TIME IS DONE. BUT YOU MUST STAY STRONG. FOR LARA. NEVER LET THEM NEAR HER. NEVER LET THEM KNOW OF HER.
NEVER.
SWEAR!

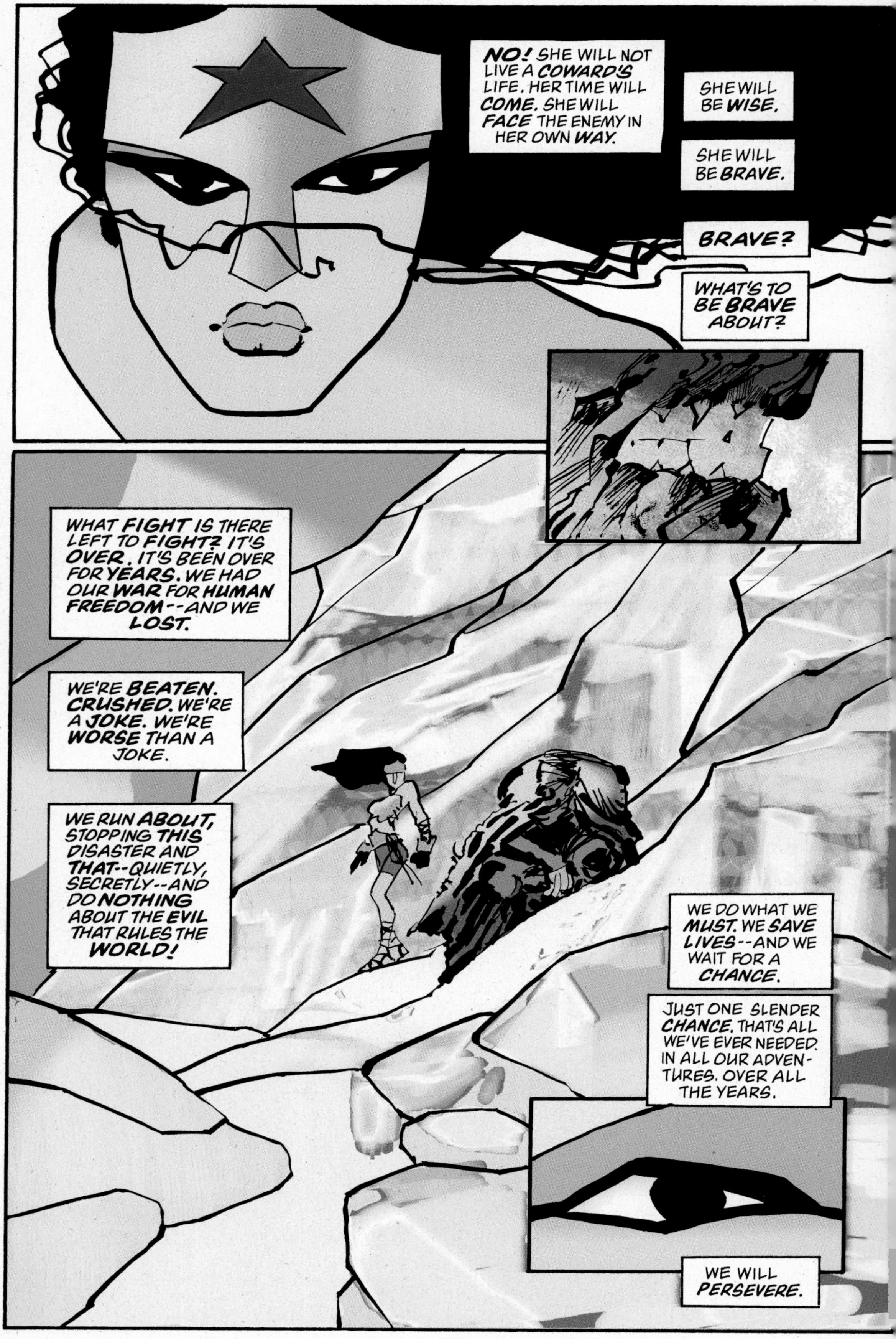
NO! SHE WILL NOT LIVE A COWARD'S LIFE. HER TIME WILL COME. SHE WILL FACE THE ENEMY IN HER OWN WAY.
SHE WILL BE WISE.
SHE WILL BE BRAVE.
BRAVE?
WHAT'S TO BE BRAVE ABOUT?
WHAT FIGHT IS THERE LEFT TO FIGHT? IT'S OVER. IT'S BEEN OVER FOR YEARS. WE HAD OUR WAR FOR HUMAN FREEDOM--AND WE LOST.
WE'RE BEATEN. CRUSHED. WE'RE A JOKE. WE'RE WORSE THAN A JOKE.
WE RUN ABOUT, STOPPING THIS DISASTER AND THAT--QUIETLY, SECRETLY--AND DO NOTHING ABOUT THE EVIL THAT RULES THE WORLD!
WE DO WHAT WE MUST. WE SAVE LIVES--AND WE WAIT FOR A CHANCE.
JUST ONE SLENDER CHANCE. THAT'S ALL WE'VE EVER NEEDED. IN ALL OUR ADVENTURES. OVER ALL THE YEARS.
WE WILL PERSEVERE.

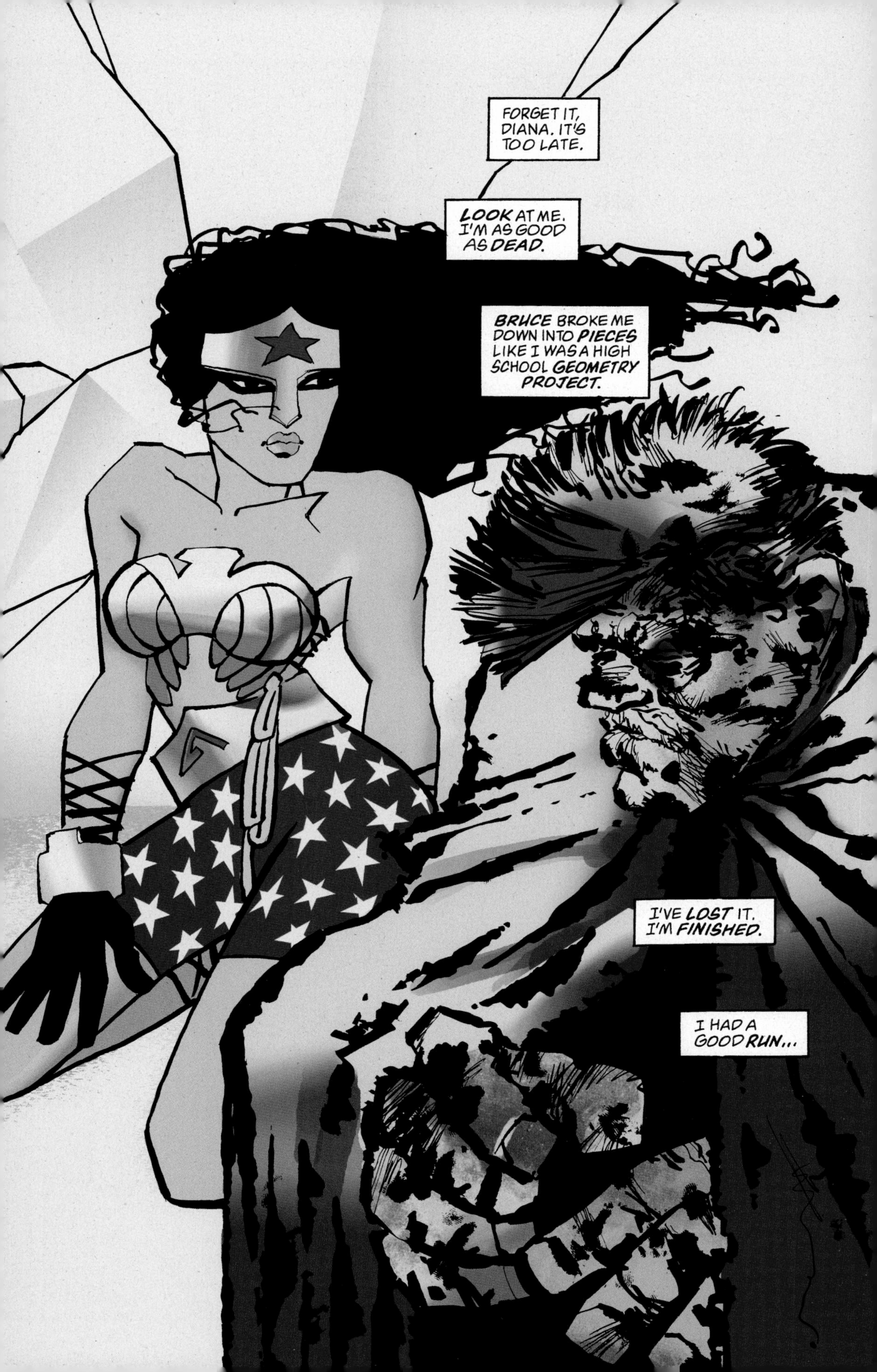
FORGET IT, DIANA. IT'S TOO LATE.
LOOK AT ME. I'M AS GOOD AS DEAD.
BRUCE BROKE ME DOWN INTO PIECES LIKE I WAS A HIGH SCHOOL GEOMETRY PROJECT.
I'VE LOST IT. I'M FINISHED.
I HAD A GOOD RUN...

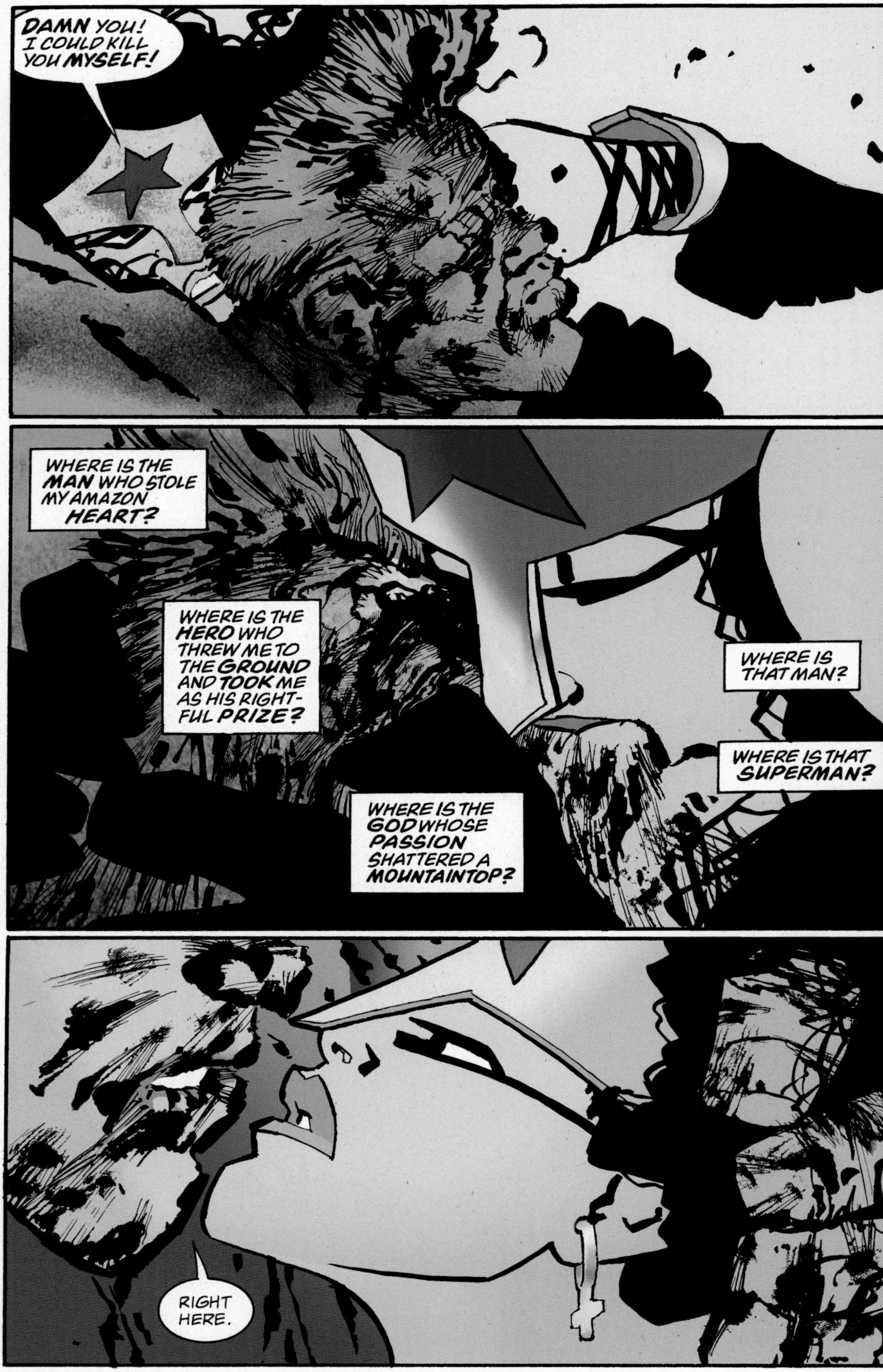
DAMN YOU! I COULD KILL YOU MYSELF!
WHERE IS THE MAN WHO STOLE MY AMAZON HEART?
WHERE IS THE HERO WHO THREW ME TO THE GROUND AND TOOK ME AS HIS RIGHT-FUL PRIZE?
WHERE IS THE GOD WHOSE PASSION SHATTERED A MOUNTAINTOP?
WHERE IS THAT MAN?
WHERE IS THAT SUPERMAN?
RIGHT HERE.

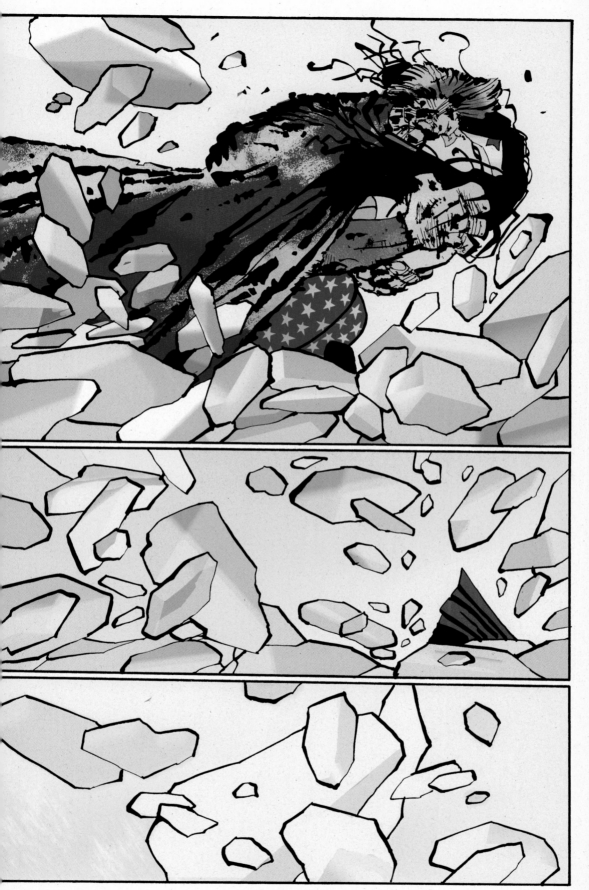

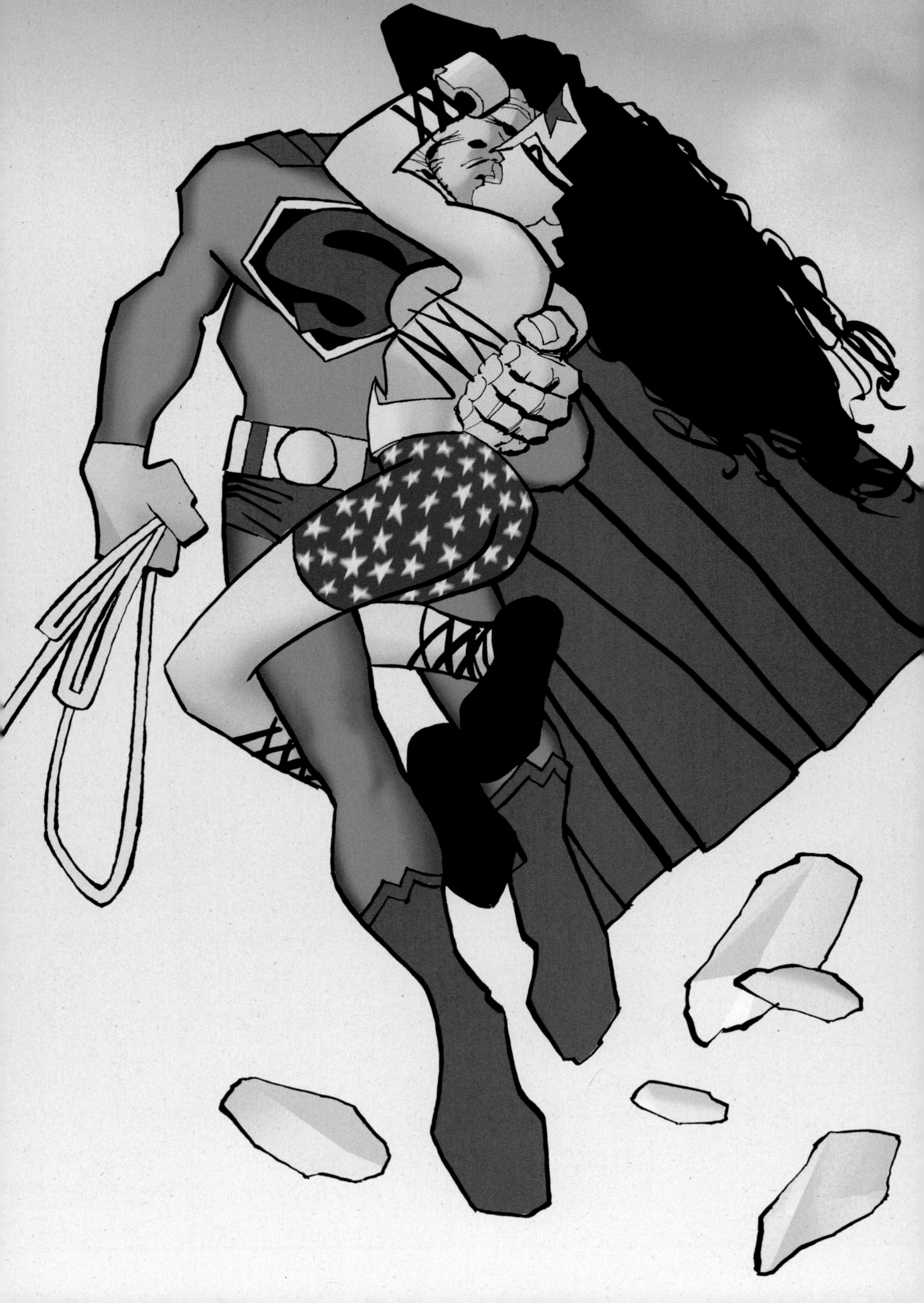

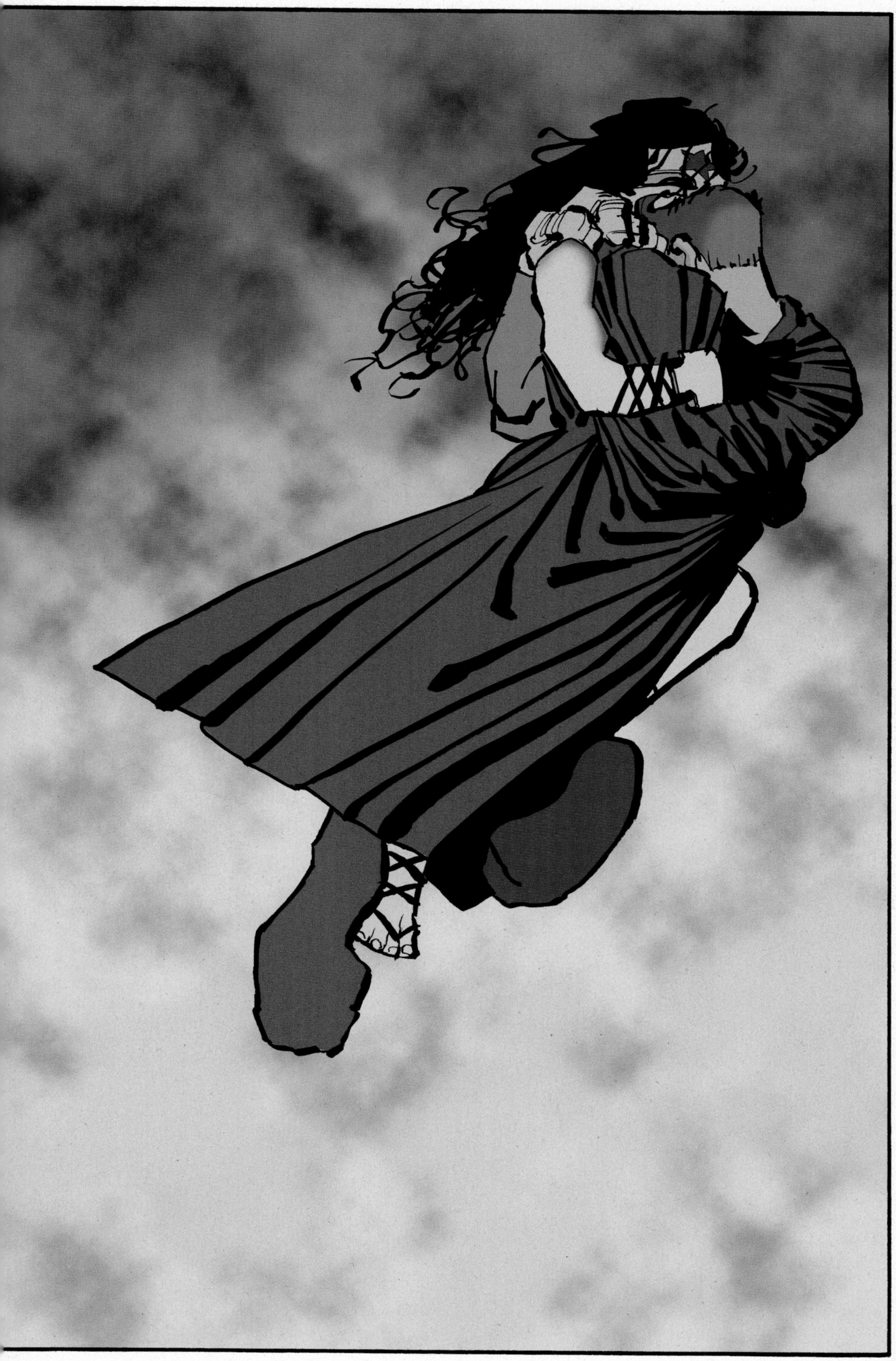

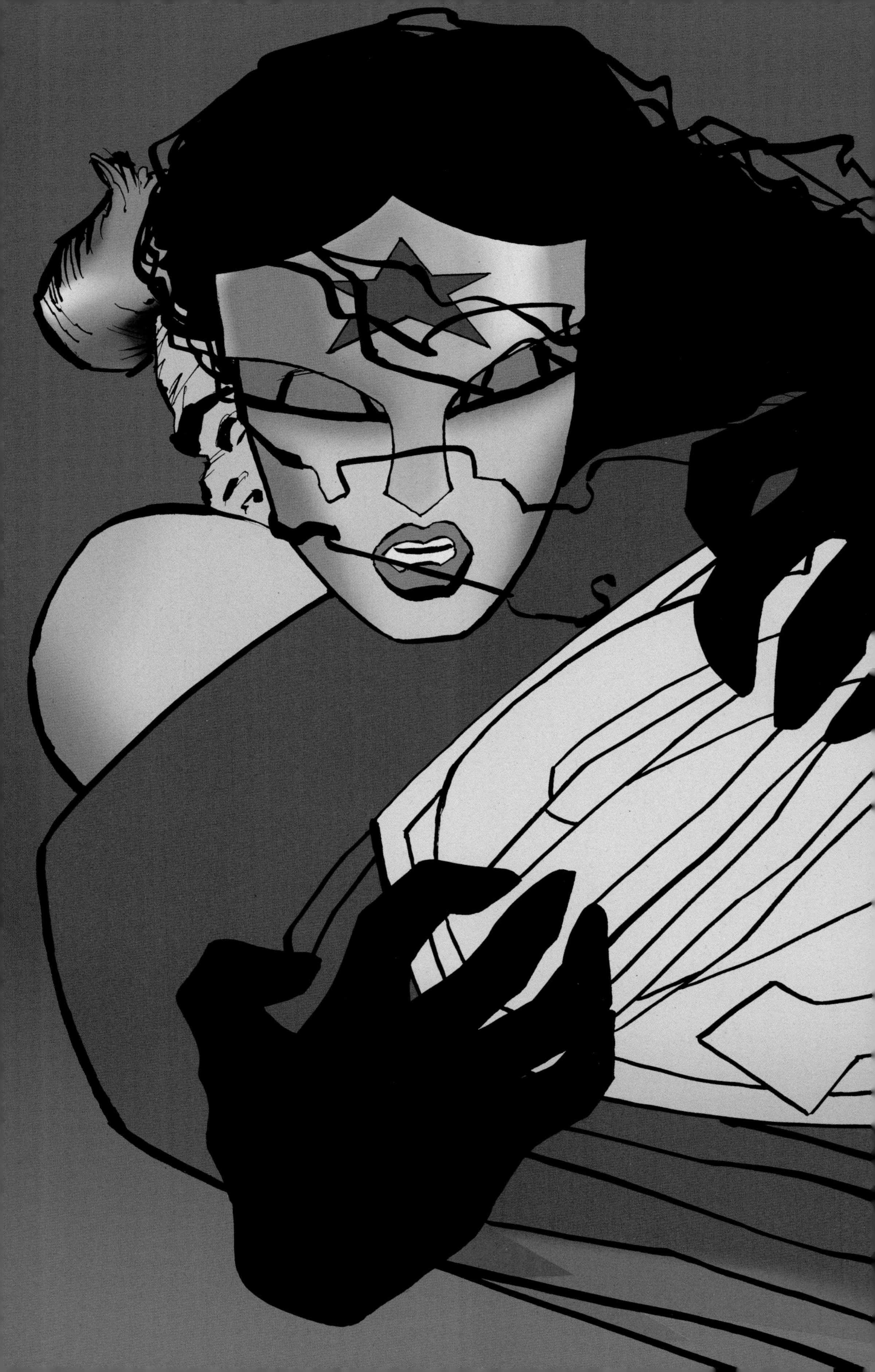

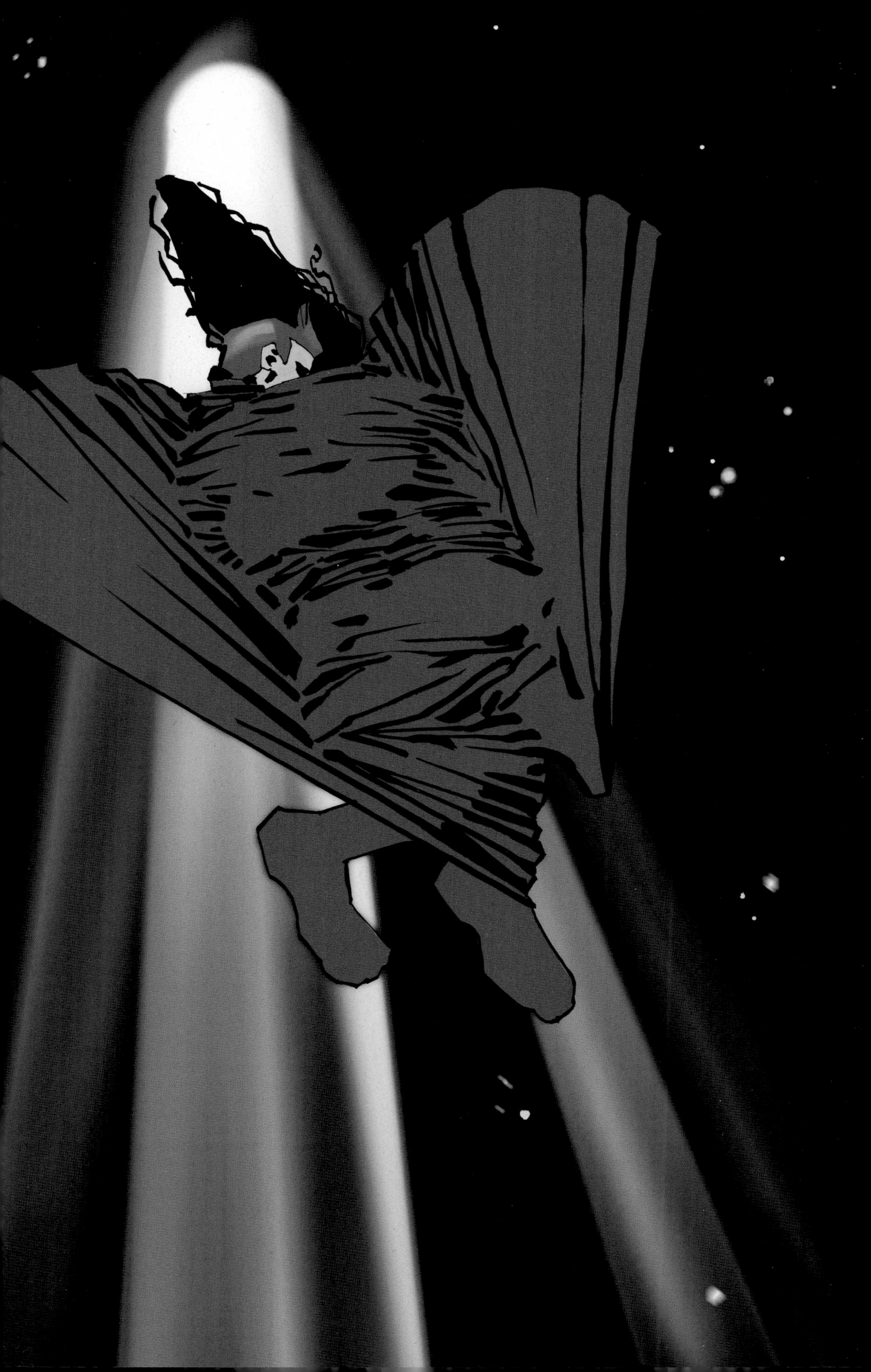

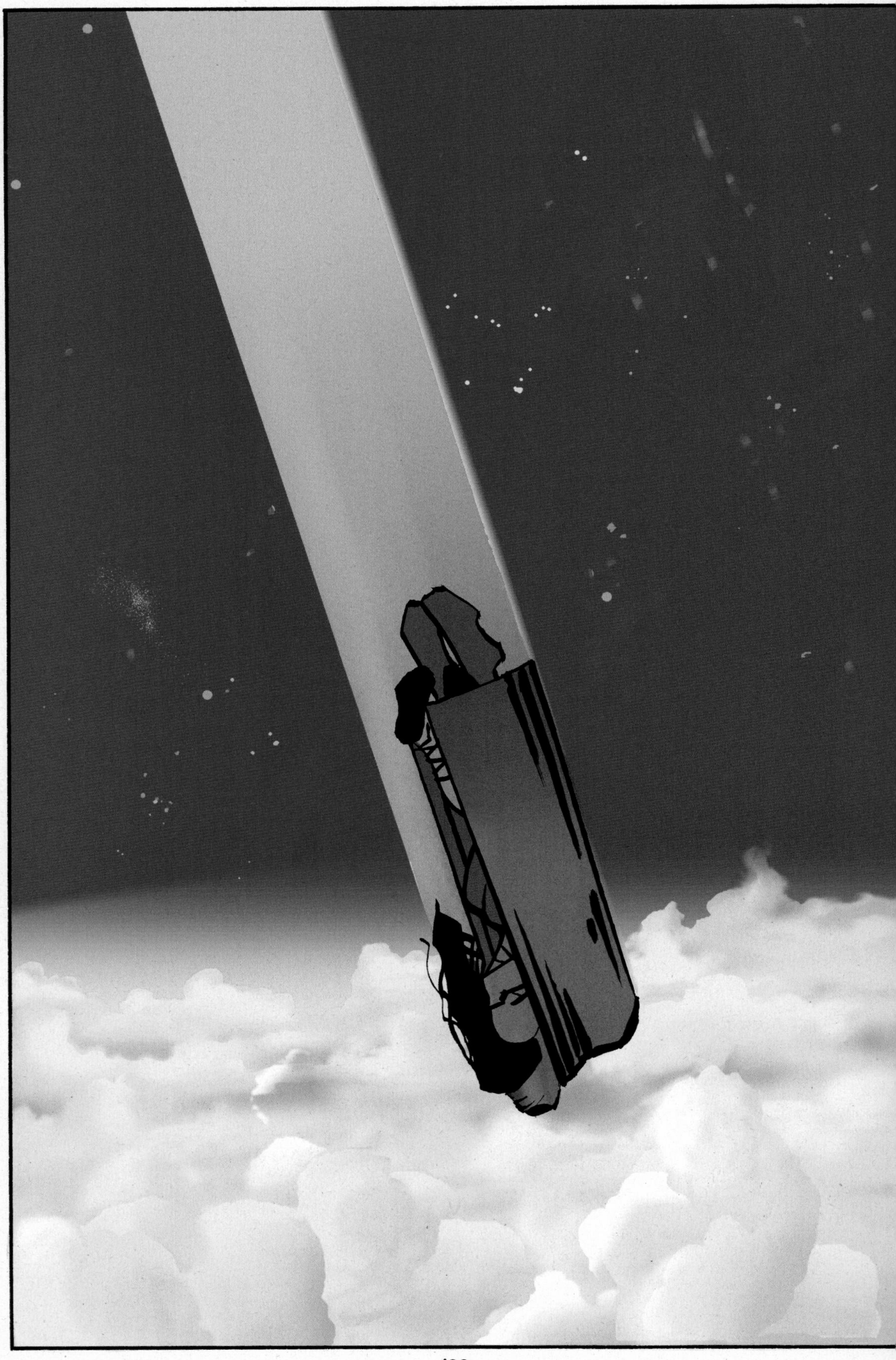

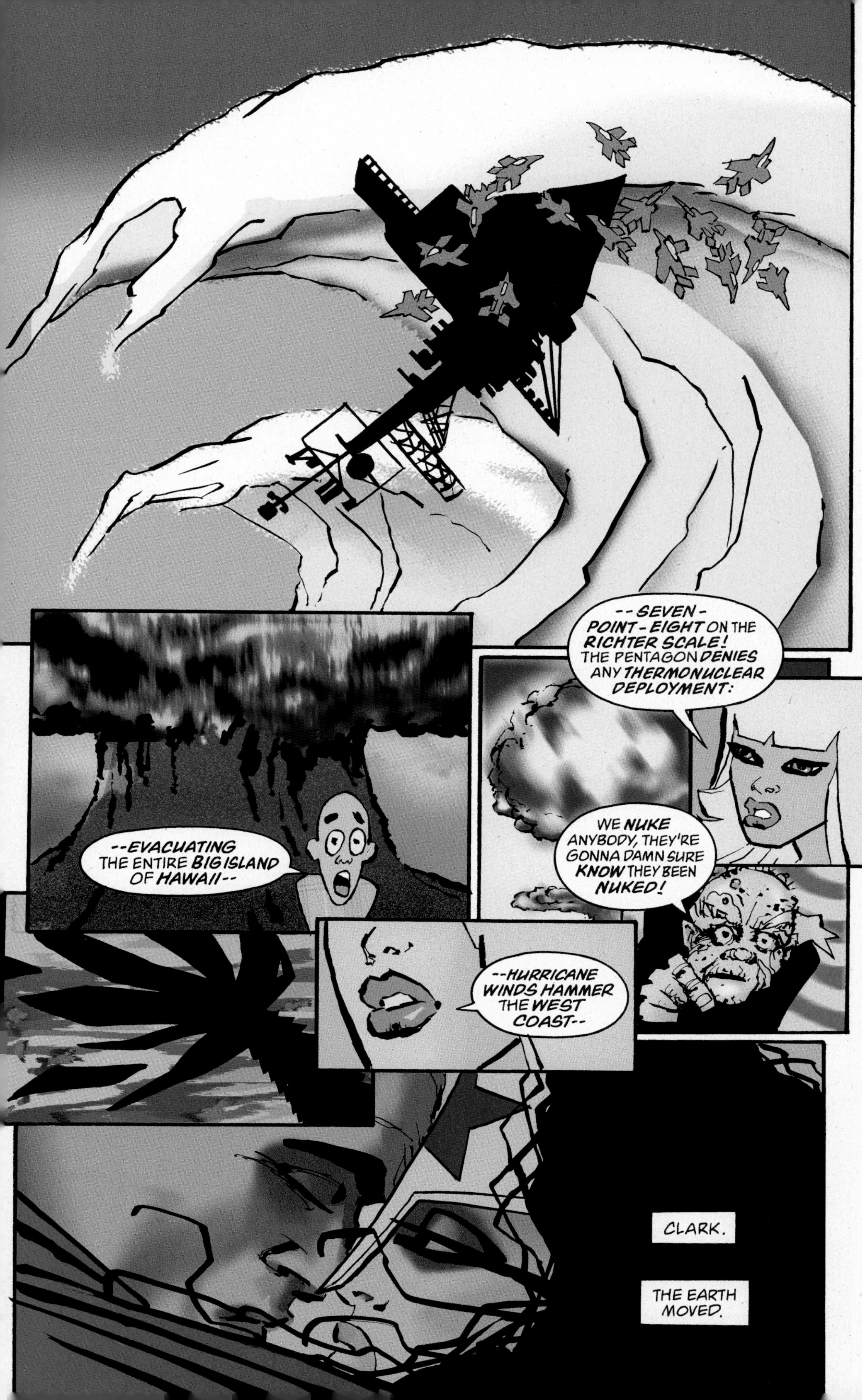
--SEVEN-POINT-EIGHT ON THE RICHTER SCALE! THE PENTAGON DENIES ANY THERMONUCLEAR DEPLOYMENT:
--EVACUATING THE ENTIRE BIG ISLAND OF HAWAII--
WE NUKE ANYBODY, THEY'RE GONNA DAMN SURE KNOW THEY BEEN NUKED!
--HURRICANE WINDS HAMMER THE WEST COAST--
CLARK.
THE EARTH MOVED.

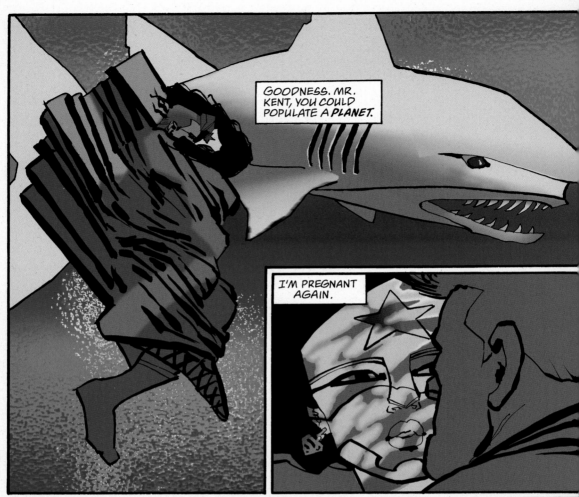

GOODNESS, MR. KENT, YOU COULD POPULATE A *PLANET.*

I'M PREGNANT AGAIN.

AND I'M HUNGRY AS A *BEAR.* HOW ABOUT *DINNER?* I KNOW A *GREAT* PLACE.

IN *ATHENS.*

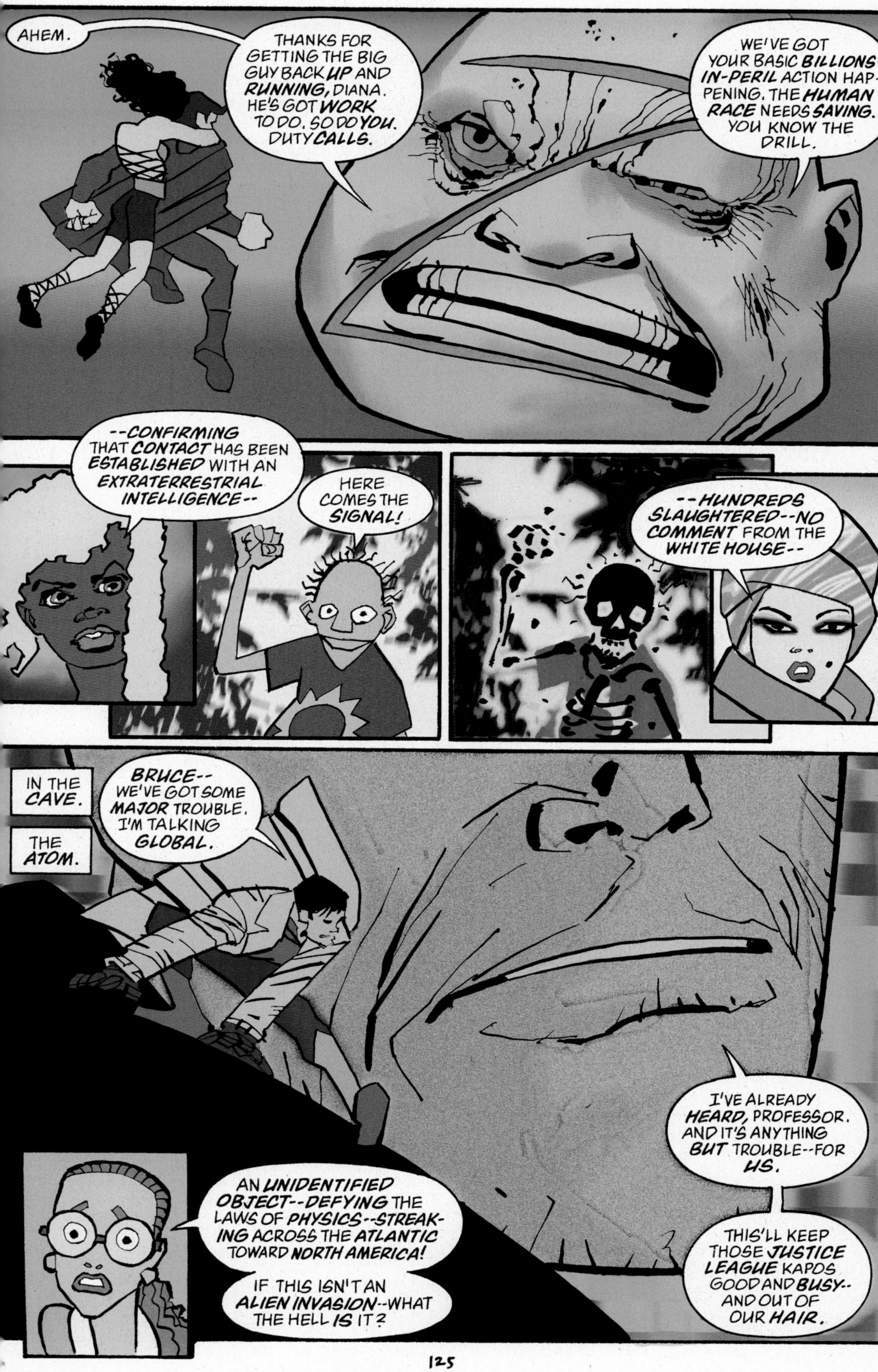
AHEM.
THANKS FOR GETTING THE BIG GUY BACK UP AND RUNNING, DIANA. HE'S GOT WORK TO DO. SO DO YOU. DUTY CALLS.
WE'VE GOT YOUR BASIC BILLIONS-IN-PERIL ACTION HAPPENING. THE HUMAN RACE NEEDS SAVING. YOU KNOW THE DRILL.
--CONFIRMING THAT CONTACT HAS BEEN ESTABLISHED WITH AN EXTRATERRESTRIAL INTELLIGENCE--
HERE COMES THE SIGNAL!
--HUNDREDS SLAUGHTERED--NO COMMENT FROM THE WHITE HOUSE--
IN THE CAVE.
THE ATOM.
BRUCE-- WE'VE GOT SOME MAJOR TROUBLE. I'M TALKING GLOBAL.
AN UNIDENTIFIED OBJECT--DEFYING THE LAWS OF PHYSICS--STREAKING ACROSS THE ATLANTIC TOWARD NORTH AMERICA!
IF THIS ISN'T AN ALIEN INVASION--WHAT THE HELL IS IT?
I'VE ALREADY HEARD, PROFESSOR. AND IT'S ANYTHING BUT TROUBLE--FOR US.
THIS'LL KEEP THOSE JUSTICE LEAGUE KAPOS GOOD AND BUSY--AND OUT OF OUR HAIR.

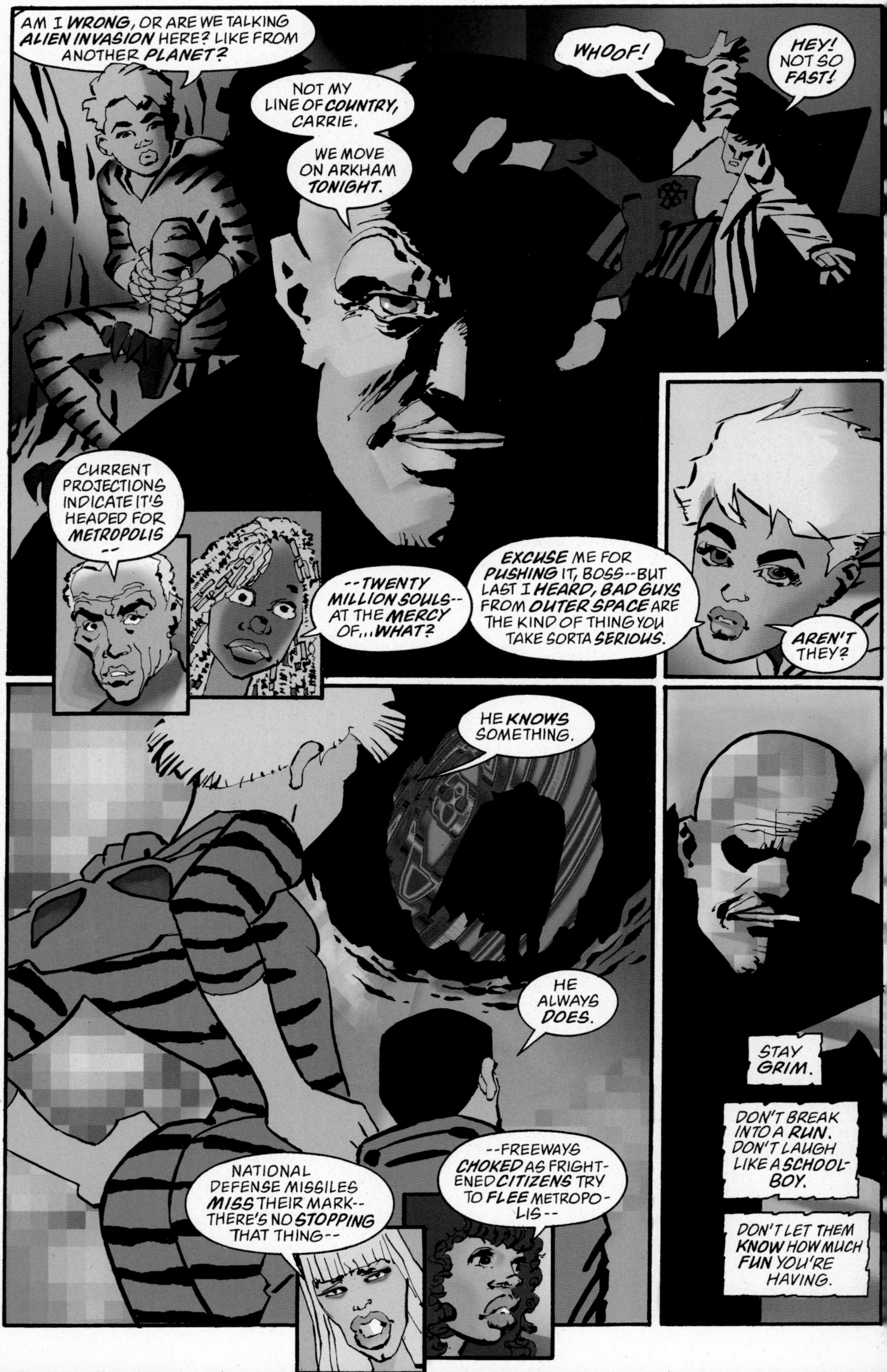
AM I WRONG, OR ARE WE TALKING ALIEN INVASION HERE? LIKE FROM ANOTHER PLANET?
NOT MY LINE OF COUNTRY, CARRIE.
WE MOVE ON ARKHAM TONIGHT.
WHOOF!
HEY! NOT SO FAST!
CURRENT PROJECTIONS INDICATE IT'S HEADED FOR METROPOLIS --
--TWENTY MILLION SOULS-- AT THE MERCY OF...WHAT?
EXCUSE ME FOR PUSHING IT, BOSS--BUT LAST I HEARD, BAD GUYS FROM OUTER SPACE ARE THE KIND OF THING YOU TAKE SORTA SERIOUS.
AREN'T THEY?
HE KNOWS SOMETHING.
HE ALWAYS DOES.
STAY GRIM.
DON'T BREAK INTO A RUN. DON'T LAUGH LIKE A SCHOOL-BOY.
DON'T LET THEM KNOW HOW MUCH FUN YOU'RE HAVING.
NATIONAL DEFENSE MISSILES MISS THEIR MARK-- THERE'S NO STOPPING THAT THING--
--FREEWAYS CHOKED AS FRIGHT-ENED CITIZENS TRY TO FLEE METROPO-LIS--

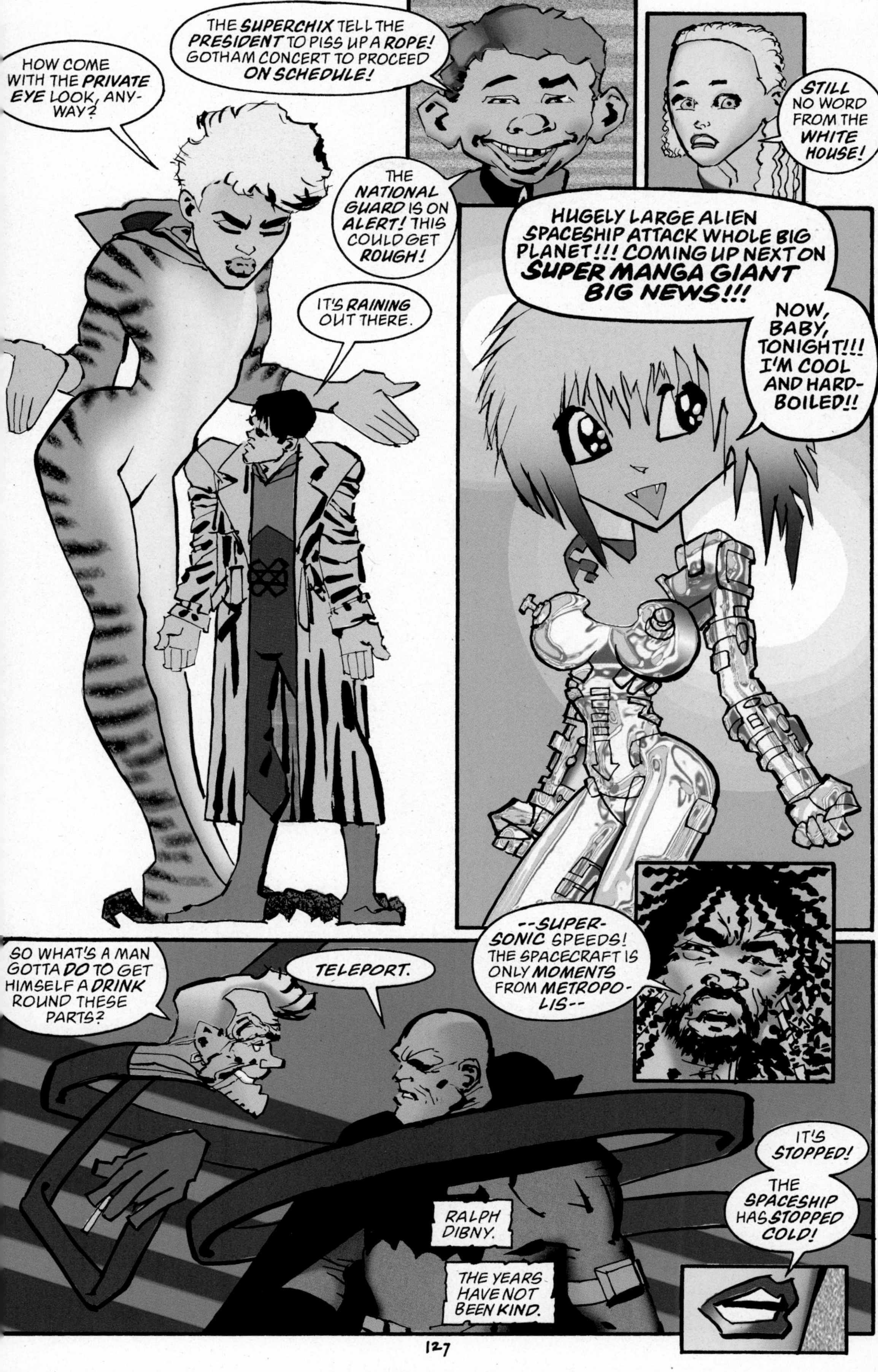
HOW COME WITH THE PRIVATE EYE LOOK, ANY-WAY?
THE SUPERCHIX TELL THE PRESIDENT TO PISS UP A ROPE! GOTHAM CONCERT TO PROCEED ON SCHEDULE!
STILL NO WORD FROM THE WHITE HOUSE!
THE NATIONAL GUARD IS ON ALERT! THIS COULD GET ROUGH!
IT'S RAINING OUT THERE.
HUGELY LARGE ALIEN SPACESHIP ATTACK WHOLE BIG PLANET!!! COMING UP NEXT ON SUPER MANGA GIANT BIG NEWS!!!
NOW, BABY, TONIGHT!!! I'M COOL AND HARD-BOILED!!
SO WHAT'S A MAN GOTTA DO TO GET HIMSELF A DRINK ROUND THESE PARTS?
TELEPORT.
--SUPER-SONIC SPEEDS! THE SPACECRAFT IS ONLY MOMENTS FROM METROPO-LIS--
RALPH DIBNY.
THE YEARS HAVE NOT BEEN KIND.
IT'S STOPPED!
THE SPACESHIP HAS STOPPED COLD!

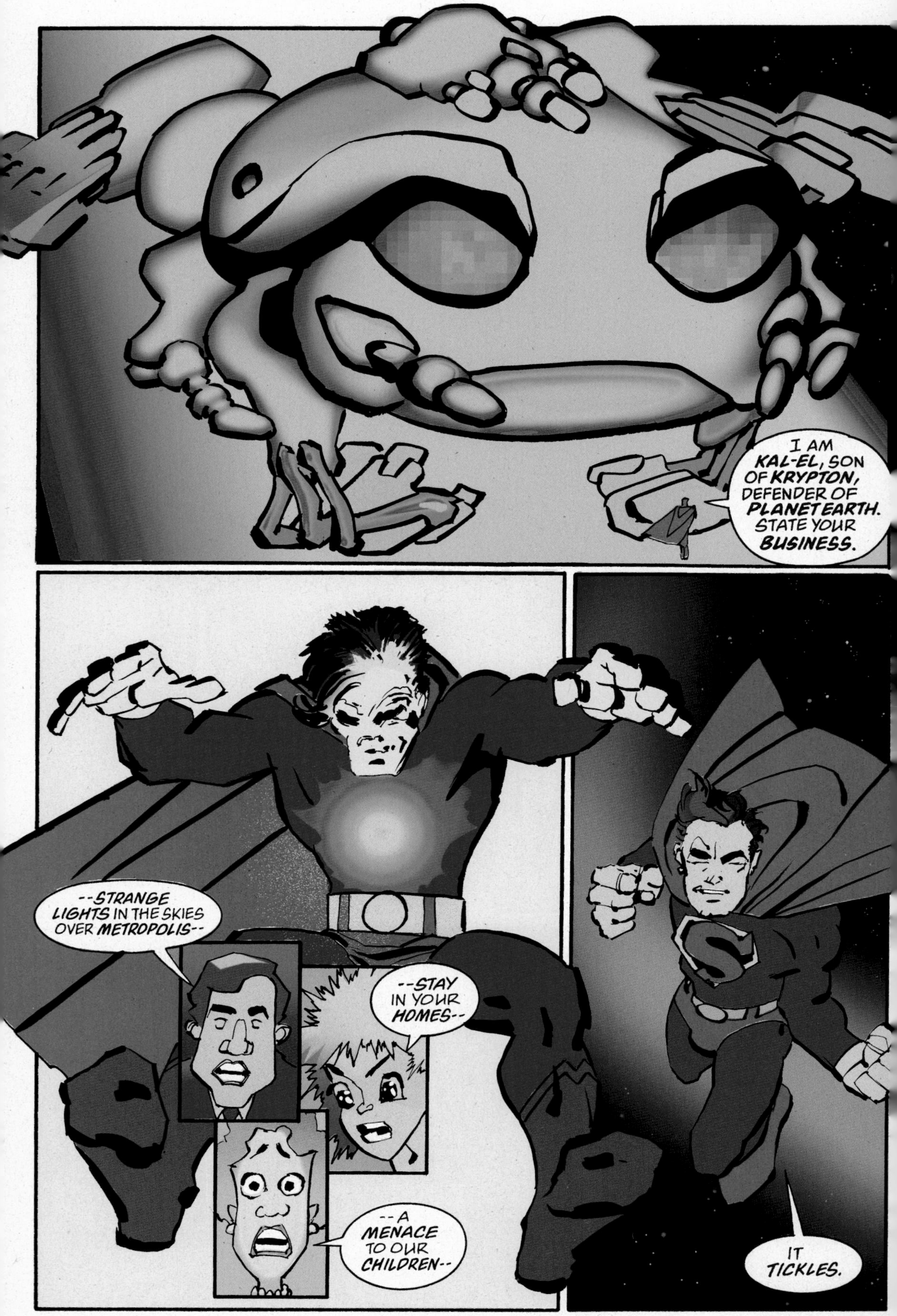
I AM KAL-EL, SON OF KRYPTON, DEFENDER OF PLANET EARTH. STATE YOUR BUSINESS.
--STRANGE LIGHTS IN THE SKIES OVER METROPOLIS--
--STAY IN YOUR HOMES--
--A MENACE TO OUR CHILDREN--
IT TICKLES.

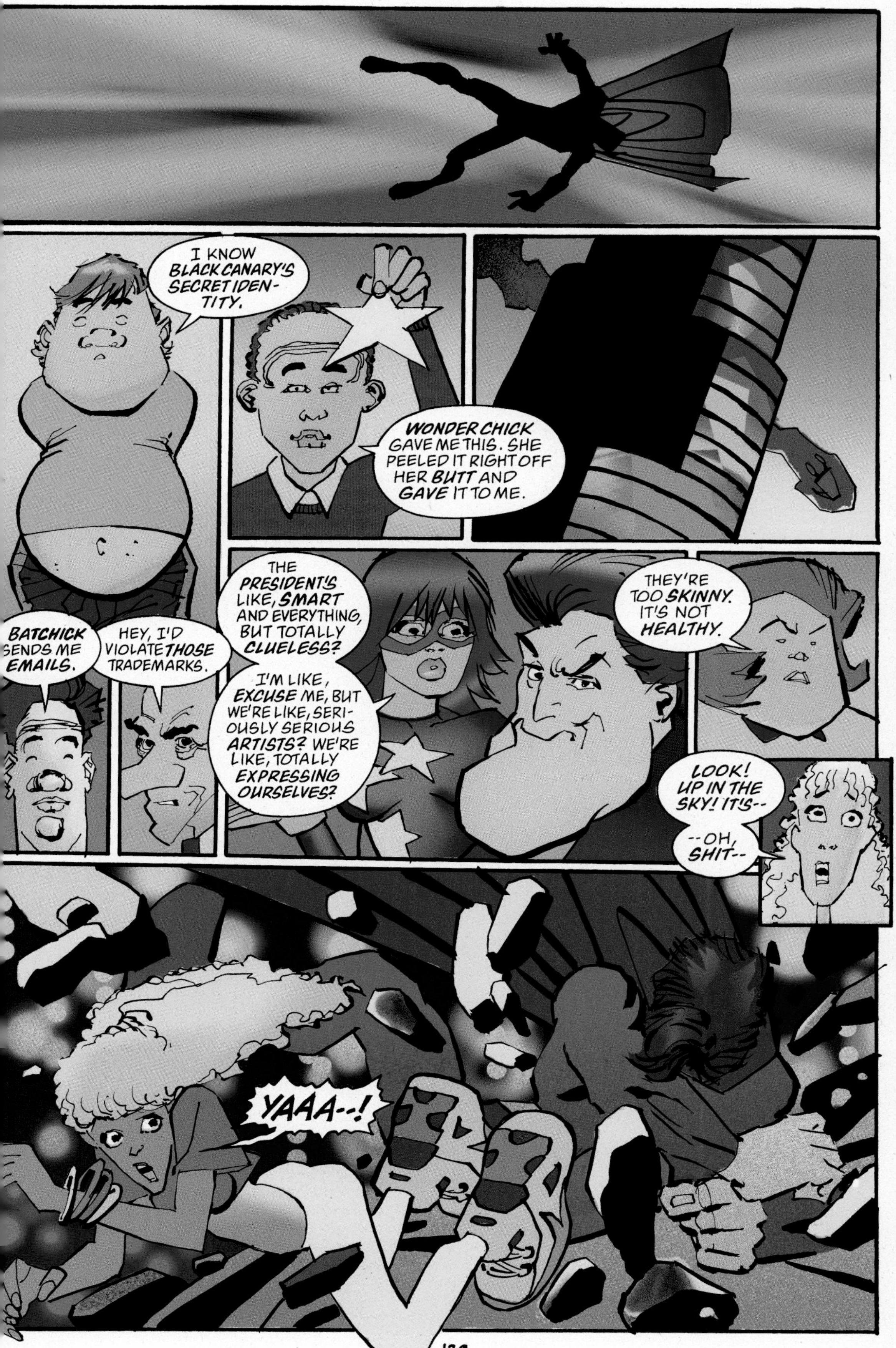

I KNOW BLACK CANARY'S SECRET IDEN-TITY.
WONDER CHICK GAVE ME THIS. SHE PEELED IT RIGHT OFF HER BUTT AND GAVE IT TO ME.
BATCHICK SENDS ME EMAILS.
HEY, I'D VIOLATE THOSE TRADEMARKS.
THE PRESIDENT'S LIKE, SMART AND EVERYTHING, BUT TOTALLY CLUELESS?
I'M LIKE, EXCUSE ME, BUT WE'RE LIKE, SERI-OUSLY SERIOUS ARTISTS? WE'RE LIKE, TOTALLY EXPRESSING OURSELVES?
THEY'RE TOO SKINNY. IT'S NOT HEALTHY.
LOOK! UP IN THE SKY! IT'S--
--OH, SHIT--
YAAA--!

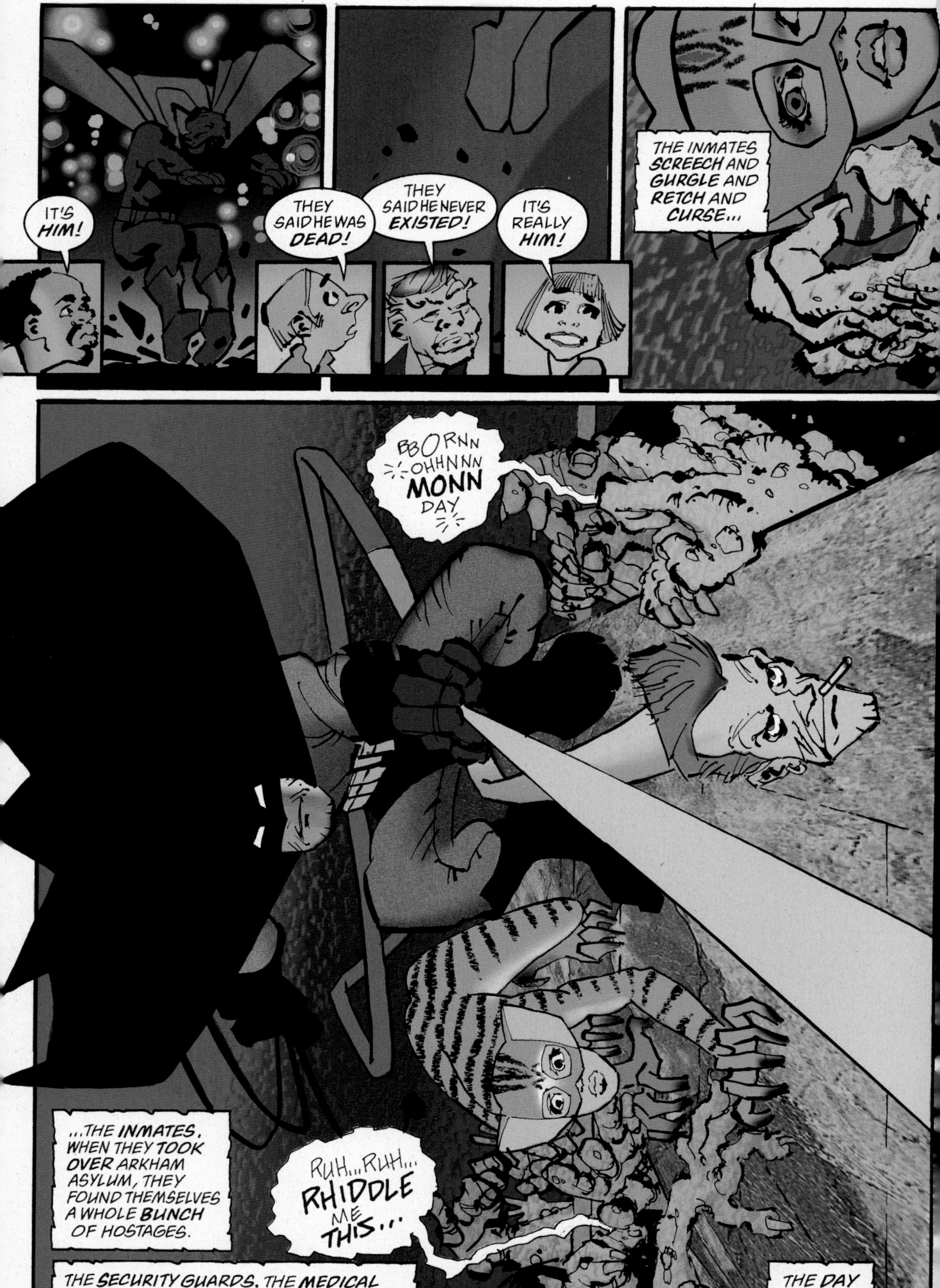

IT'S HIM!
THEY SAID HE WAS DEAD!
THEY SAID HE NEVER EXISTED!
IT'S REALLY HIM!
THE INMATES SCREECH AND GURGLE AND RETCH AND CURSE...
BBORNN OHHNNN MONN DAY
...THE INMATES. WHEN THEY TOOK OVER ARKHAM ASYLUM, THEY FOUND THEMSELVES A WHOLE BUNCH OF HOSTAGES.
RUH... RUH... RHIDDLE ME THIS...
THE SECURITY GUARDS. THE MEDICAL STAFF. A VISITING CLASS OF SOCIOLOGY STUDENTS.
THE DAY CARE CENTER.

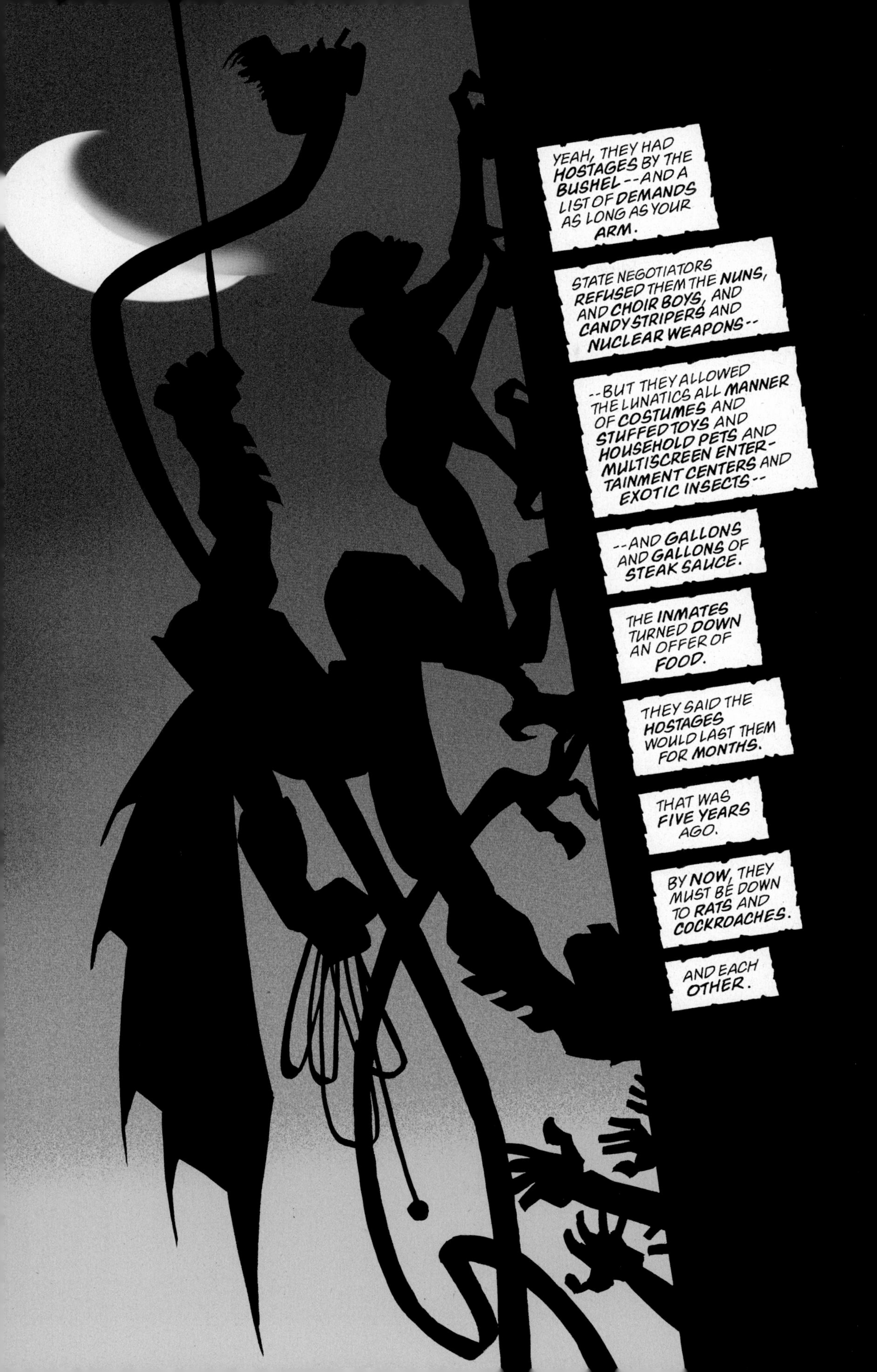
YEAH, THEY HAD HOSTAGES BY THE BUSHEL--AND A LIST OF DEMANDS AS LONG AS YOUR ARM.
STATE NEGOTIATORS REFUSED THEM THE NUNS, AND CHOIR BOYS, AND CANDY STRIPERS AND NUCLEAR WEAPONS--
--BUT THEY ALLOWED THE LUNATICS ALL MANNER OF COSTUMES AND STUFFED TOYS AND HOUSEHOLD PETS AND MULTISCREEN ENTER-TAINMENT CENTERS AND EXOTIC INSECTS--
--AND GALLONS AND GALLONS OF STEAK SAUCE.
THE INMATES TURNED DOWN AN OFFER OF FOOD.
THEY SAID THE HOSTAGES WOULD LAST THEM FOR MONTHS.
THAT WAS FIVE YEARS AGO.
BY NOW, THEY MUST BE DOWN TO RATS AND COCKROACHES.
AND EACH OTHER.

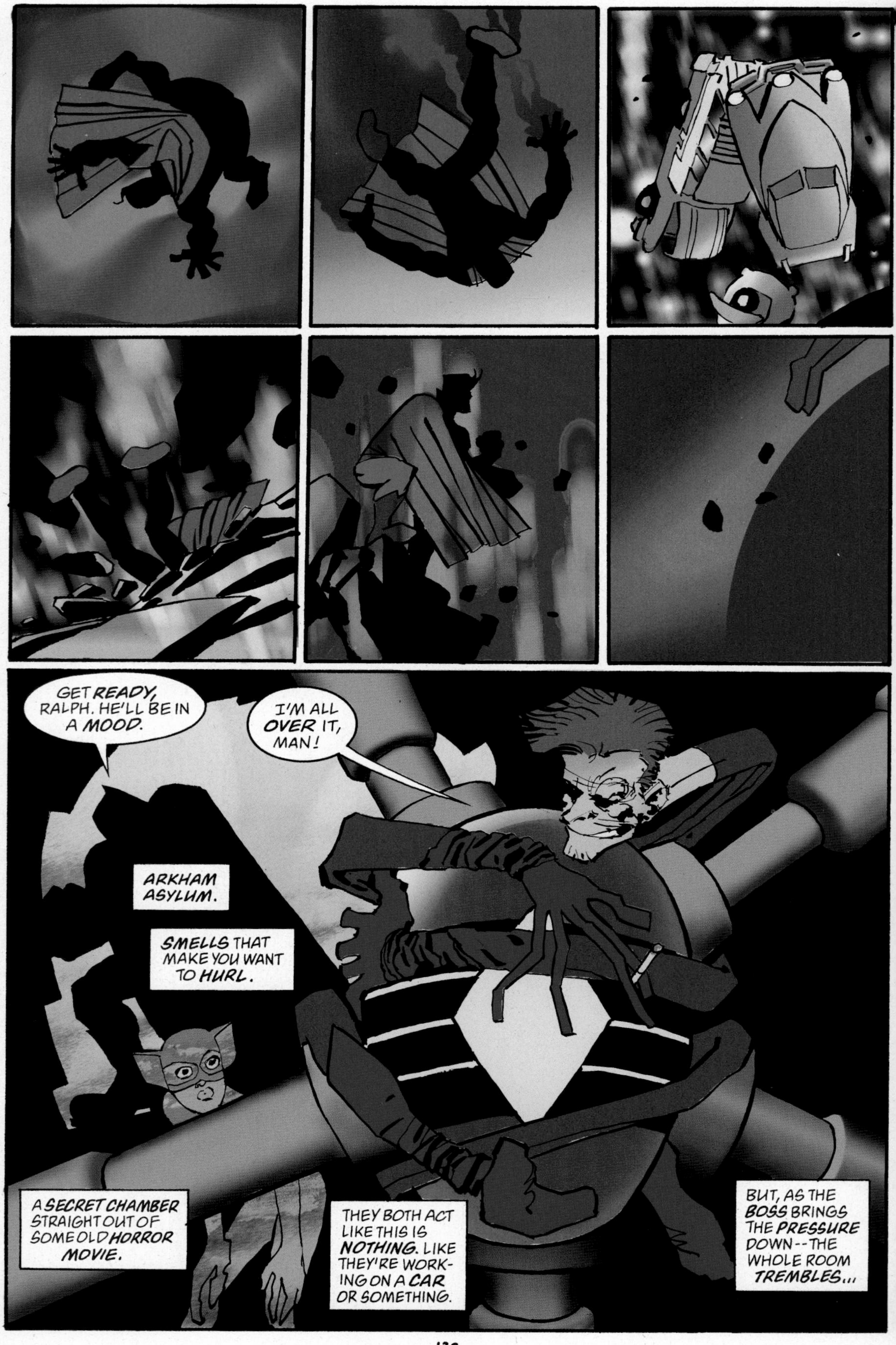
GET READY, RALPH. HE'LL BE IN A MOOD.
I'M ALL OVER IT, MAN!
ARKHAM ASYLUM.
SMELLS THAT MAKE YOU WANT TO HURL.
A SECRET CHAMBER STRAIGHT OUT OF SOME OLD HORROR MOVIE.
THEY BOTH ACT LIKE THIS IS NOTHING. LIKE THEY'RE WORKING ON A CAR OR SOMETHING.
BUT, AS THE BOSS BRINGS THE PRESSURE DOWN--THE WHOLE ROOM TREMBLES...

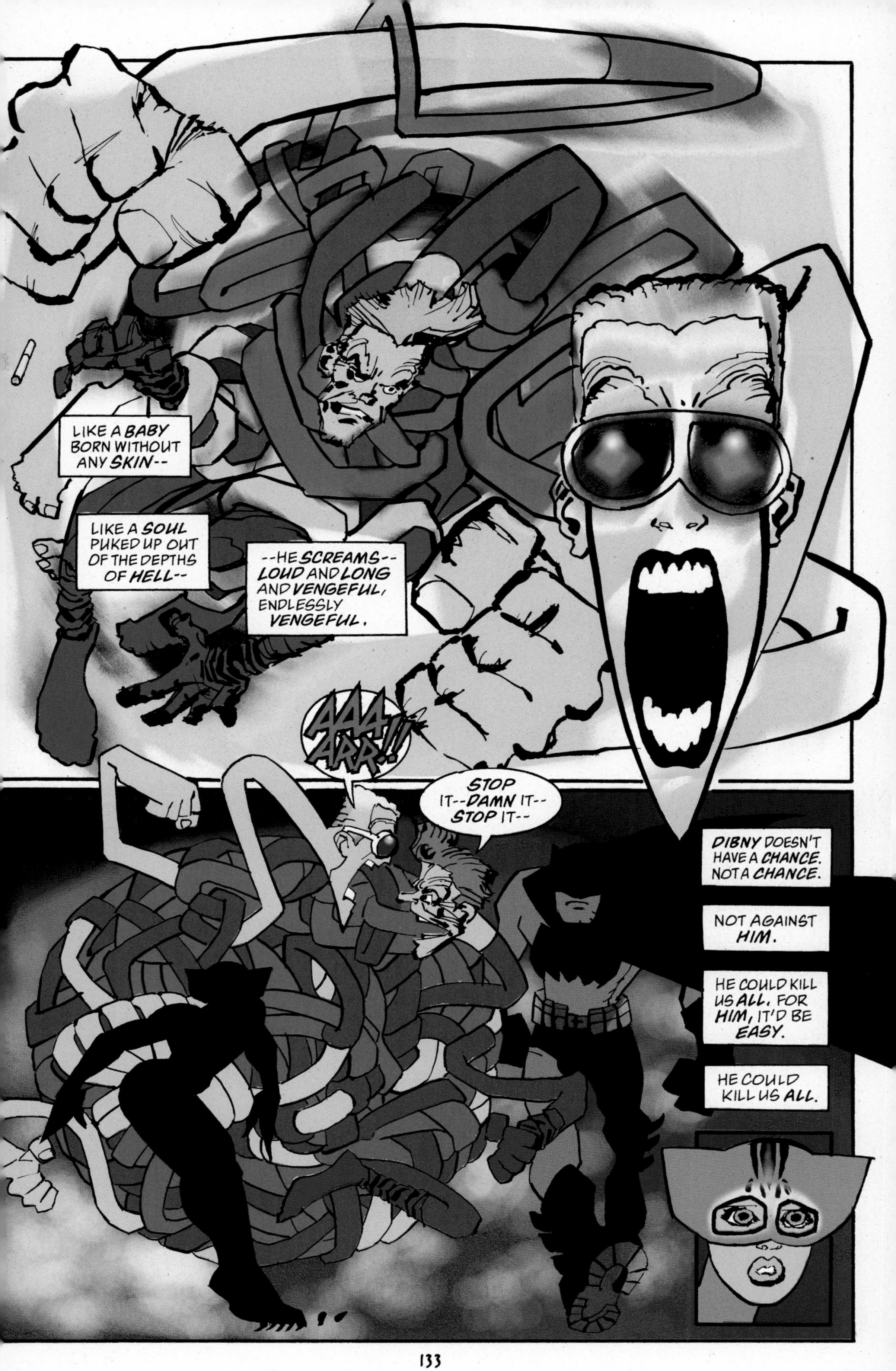

LIKE A BABY BORN WITHOUT ANY SKIN--
LIKE A SOUL PUKED UP OUT OF THE DEPTHS OF HELL--
--HE SCREAMS-- LOUD AND LONG AND VENGEFUL, ENDLESSLY VENGEFUL.
AAAARR!!
STOP IT--DAMN IT-- STOP IT--
DIBNY DOESN'T HAVE A CHANCE. NOT A CHANCE.
NOT AGAINST HIM.
HE COULD KILL US ALL. FOR HIM, IT'D BE EASY.
HE COULD KILL US ALL.

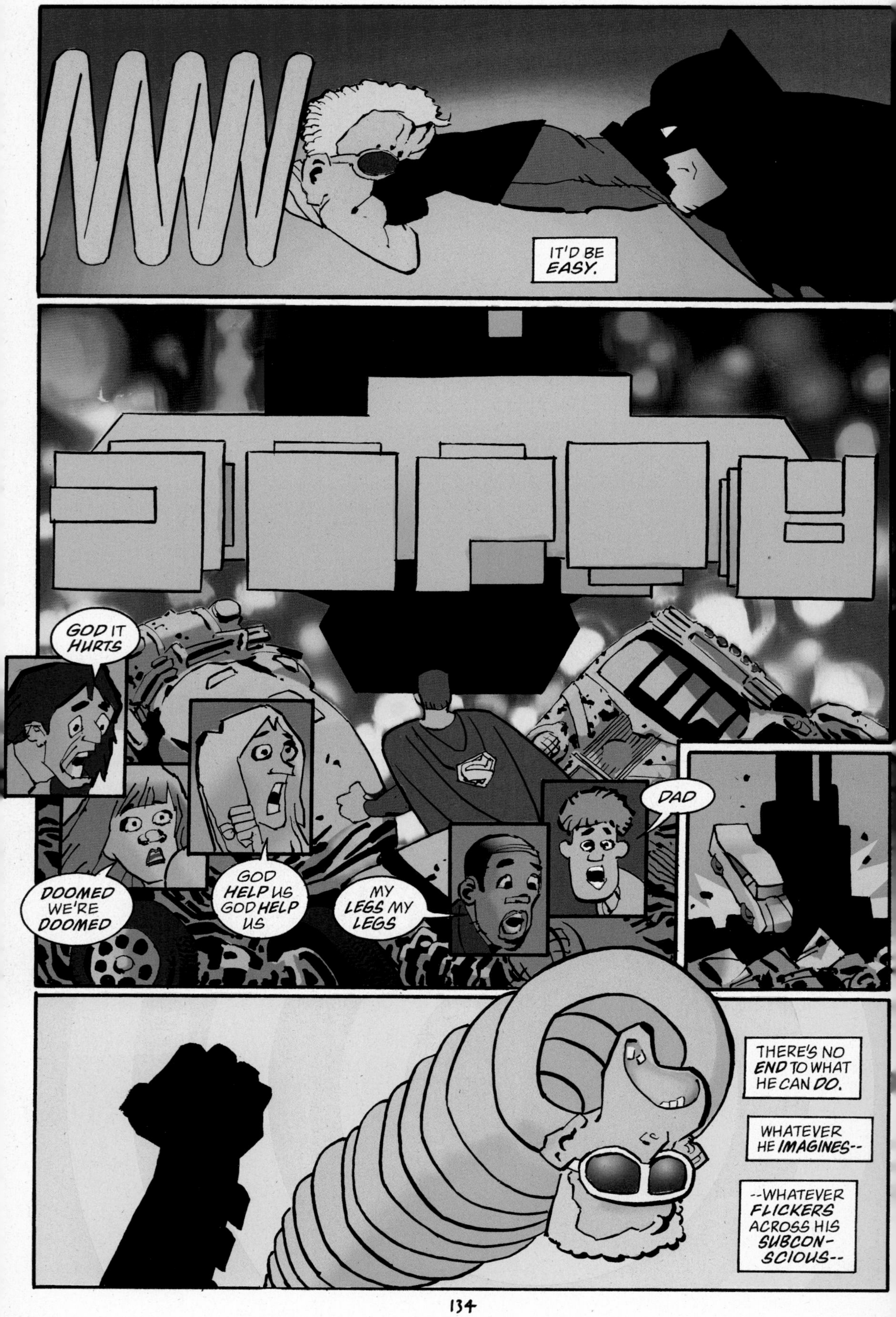

IT'D BE EASY.
GOD IT HURTS
DOOMED WE'RE DOOMED
GOD HELP US GOD HELP US
MY LEGS MY LEGS
DAD
THERE'S NO END TO WHAT HE CAN DO.
WHATEVER HE IMAGINES--
--WHATEVER FLICKERS ACROSS HIS SUBCON-SCIOUS--

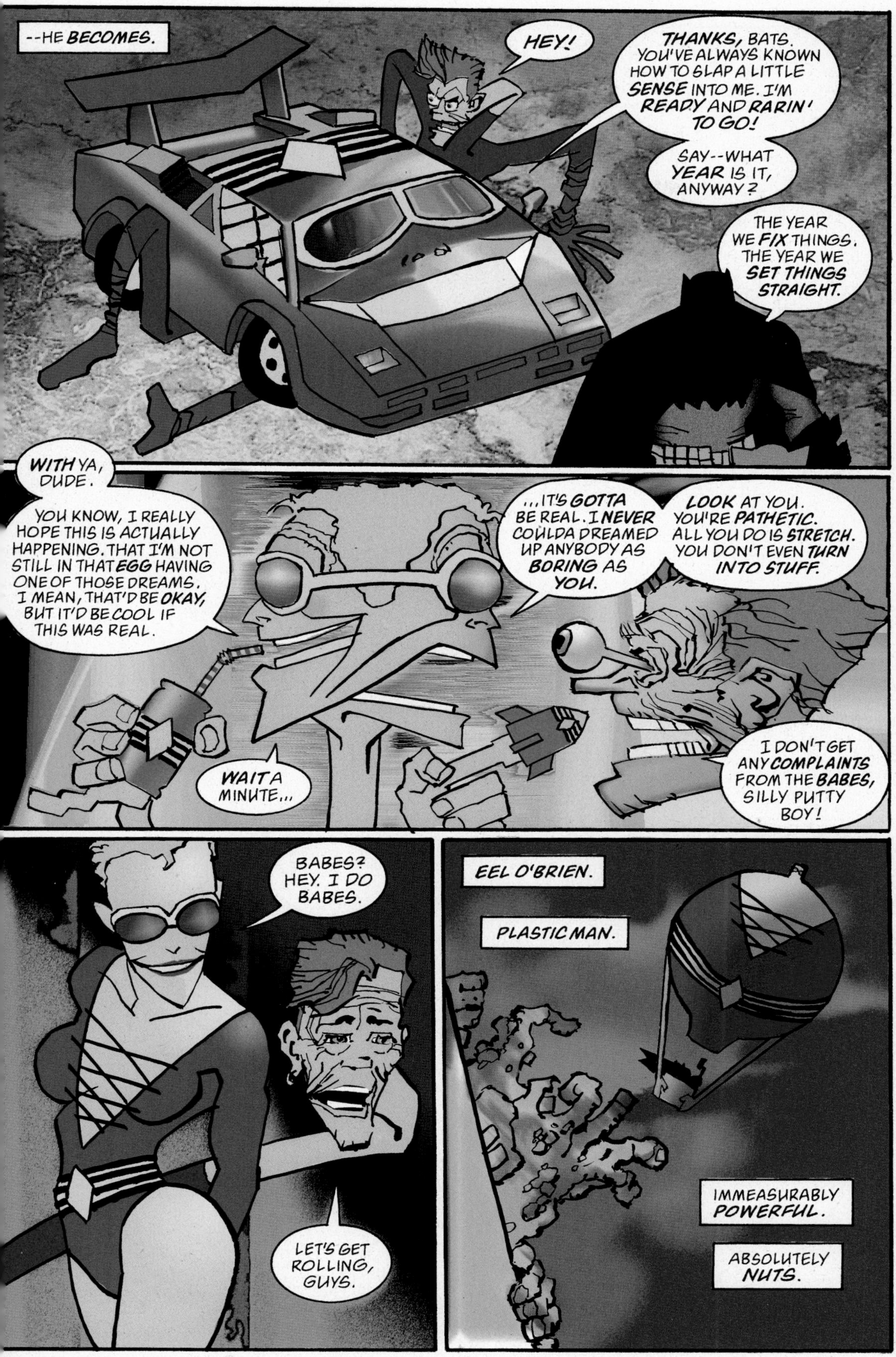
--HE BECOMES.
HEY!
THANKS, BATS. YOU'VE ALWAYS KNOWN HOW TO SLAP A LITTLE SENSE INTO ME. I'M READY AND RARIN' TO GO!
SAY--WHAT YEAR IS IT, ANYWAY?
THE YEAR WE FIX THINGS. THE YEAR WE SET THINGS STRAIGHT.
WITH YA, DUDE.
YOU KNOW, I REALLY HOPE THIS IS ACTUALLY HAPPENING. THAT I'M NOT STILL IN THAT EGG HAVING ONE OF THOSE DREAMS. I MEAN, THAT'D BE OKAY, BUT IT'D BE COOL IF THIS WAS REAL.
WAIT A MINUTE...
...IT'S GOTTA BE REAL. I NEVER COULDA DREAMED UP ANYBODY AS BORING AS YOU.
LOOK AT YOU. YOU'RE PATHETIC. ALL YOU DO IS STRETCH. YOU DON'T EVEN TURN INTO STUFF.
I DON'T GET ANY COMPLAINTS FROM THE BABES, SILLY PUTTY BOY!
BABES? HEY. I DO BABES.
LET'S GET ROLLING, GUYS.
EEL O'BRIEN.
PLASTIC MAN.
IMMEASURABLY POWERFUL.
ABSOLUTELY NUTS.

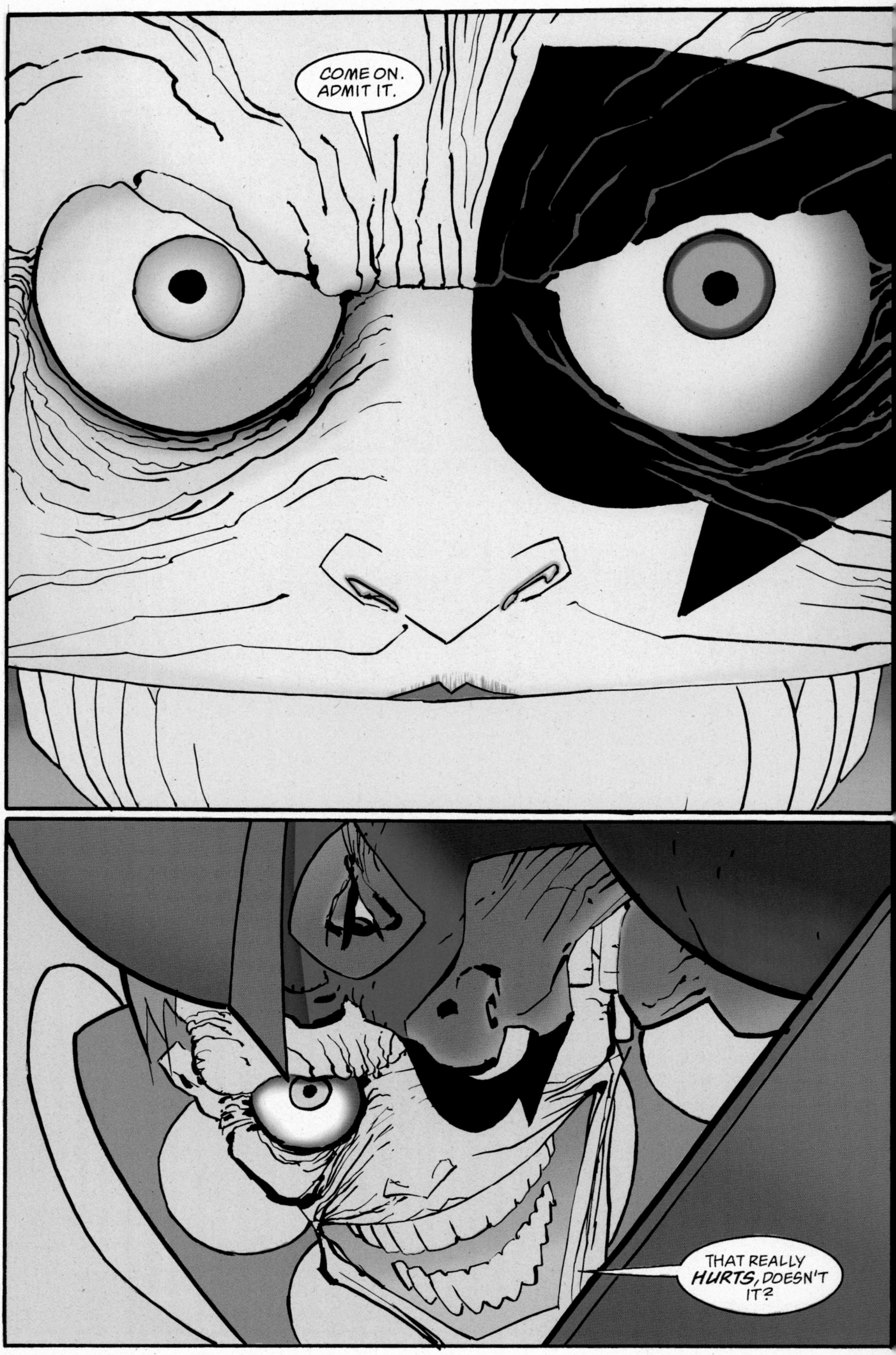
COME ON. ADMIT IT.
THAT REALLY HURTS, DOESN'T IT?

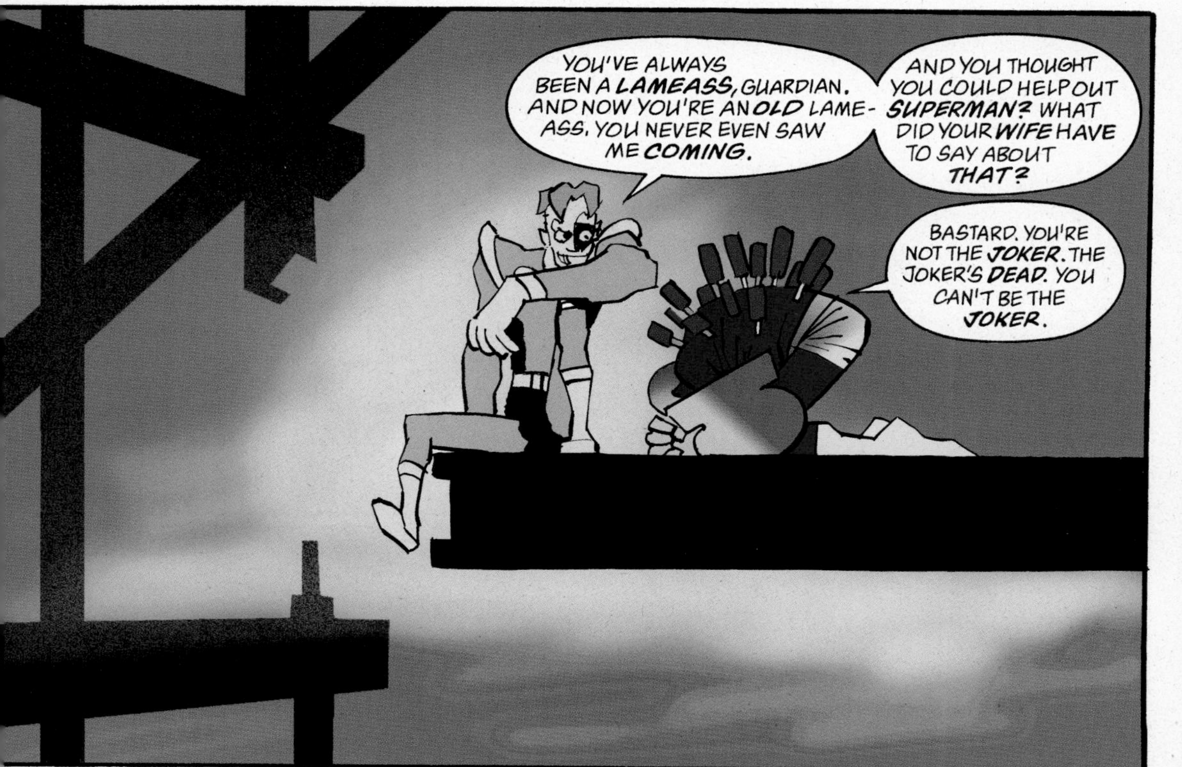
YOU'VE ALWAYS BEEN A LAMEASS, GUARDIAN. AND NOW YOU'RE AN OLD LAME-ASS. YOU NEVER EVEN SAW ME COMING.
AND YOU THOUGHT YOU COULD HELP OUT SUPERMAN? WHAT DID YOUR WIFE HAVE TO SAY ABOUT THAT?
BASTARD. YOU'RE NOT THE JOKER. THE JOKER'S DEAD. YOU CAN'T BE THE JOKER.

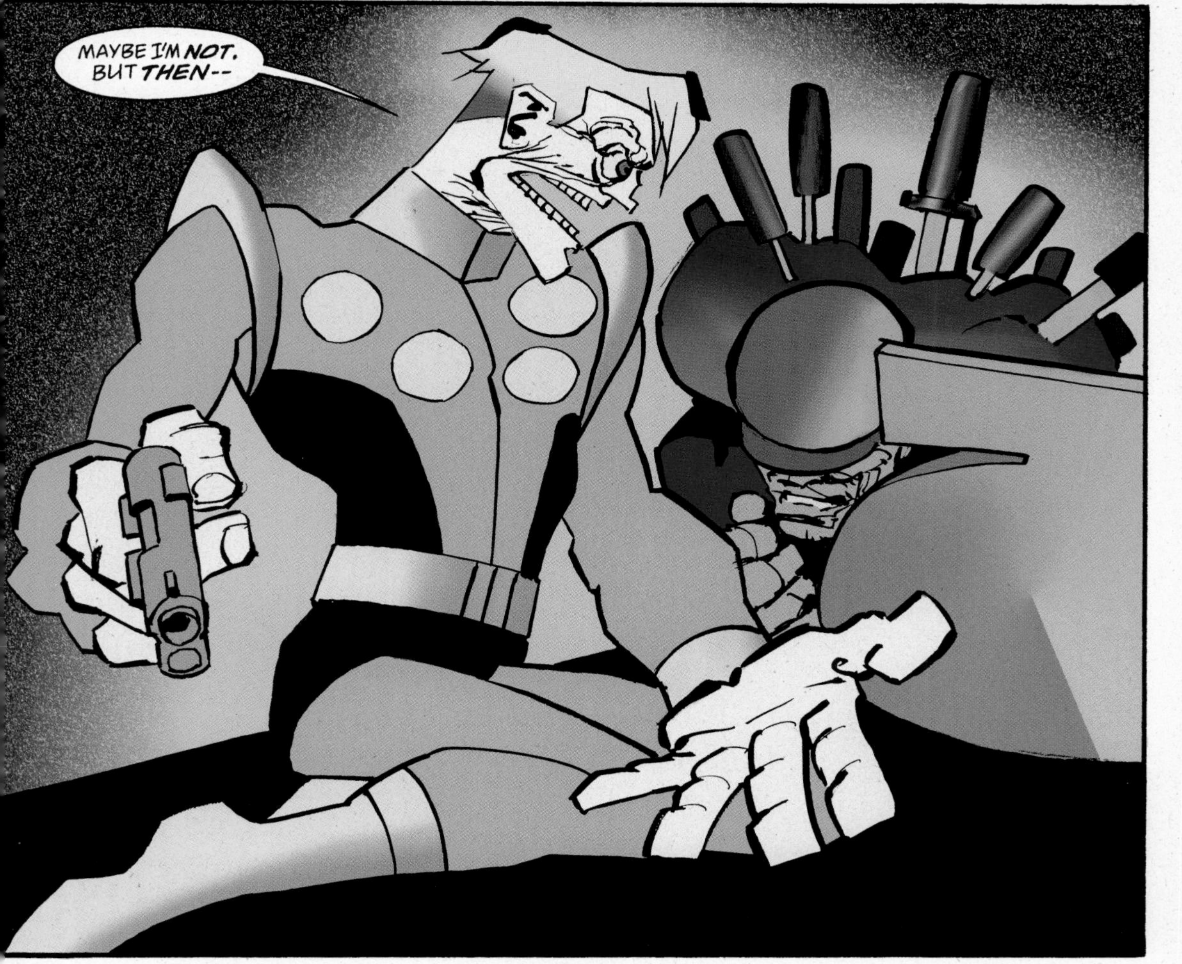
MAYBE I'M NOT. BUT THEN--

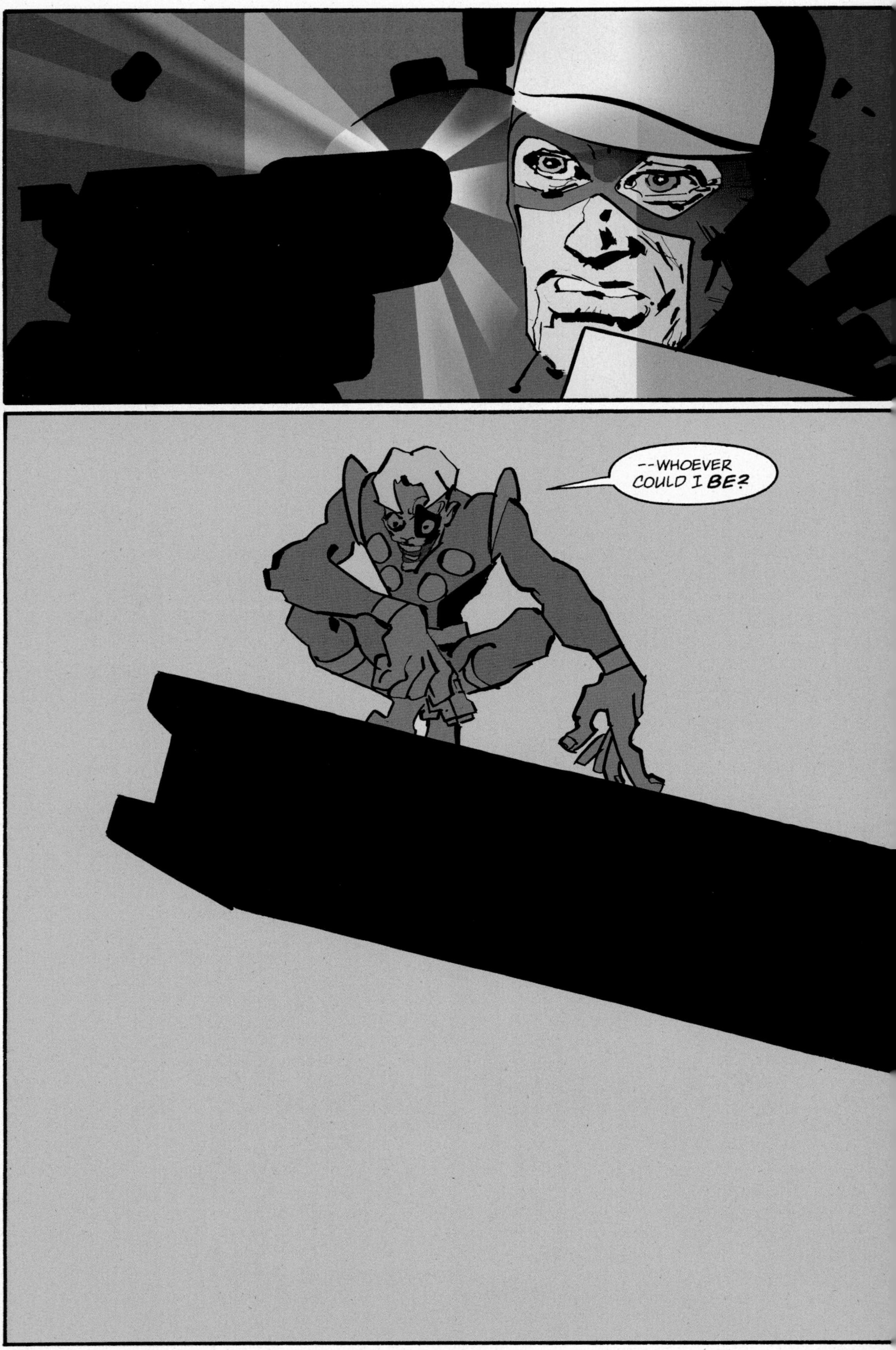
--WHOEVER COULD I BE?

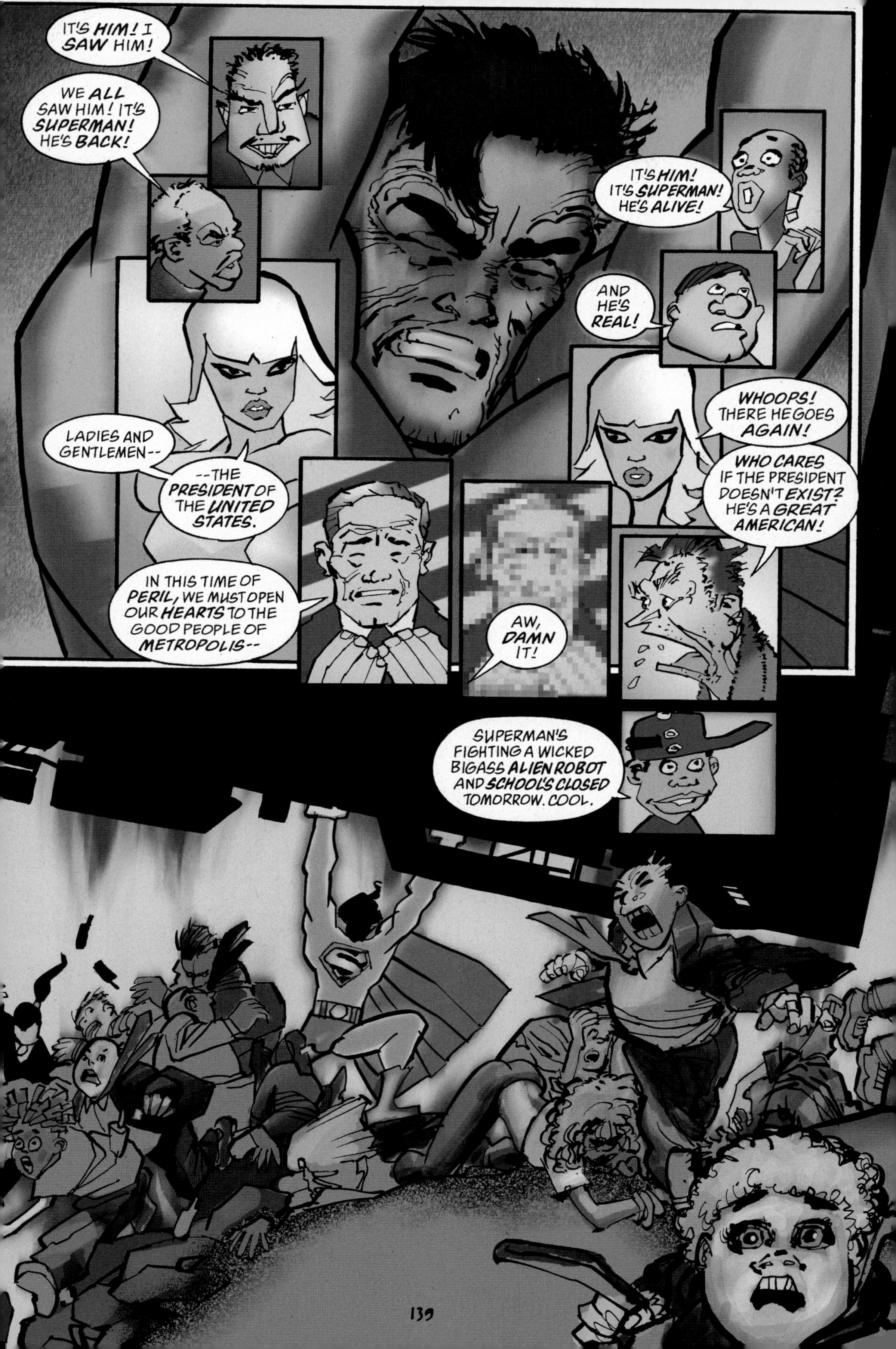
IT'S HIM! I SAW HIM!
WE ALL SAW HIM! IT'S SUPERMAN! HE'S BACK!
IT'S HIM! IT'S SUPERMAN! HE'S ALIVE!
AND HE'S REAL!
WHOOPS! THERE HE GOES AGAIN!
LADIES AND GENTLEMEN--
--THE PRESIDENT OF THE UNITED STATES.
WHO CARES IF THE PRESIDENT DOESN'T EXIST? HE'S A GREAT AMERICAN!
IN THIS TIME OF PERIL, WE MUST OPEN OUR HEARTS TO THE GOOD PEOPLE OF METROPOLIS--
AW, DAMN IT!
SUPERMAN'S FIGHTING A WICKED BIGASS ALIEN ROBOT AND SCHOOL'S CLOSED TOMORROW. COOL.

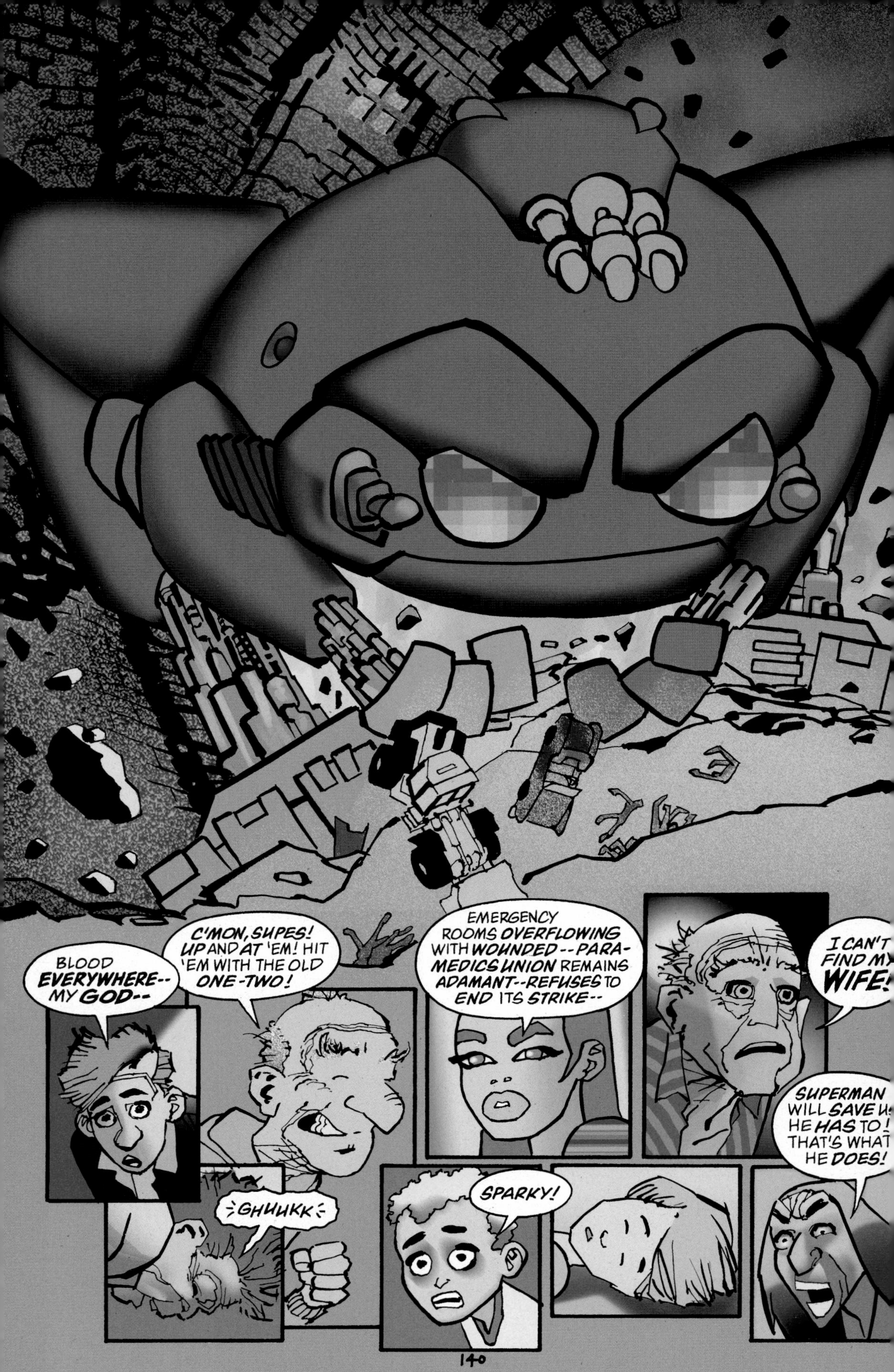
BLOOD EVERYWHERE-- MY GOD--
C'MON, SUPES! UP AND AT 'EM! HIT 'EM WITH THE OLD ONE-TWO!
EMERGENCY ROOMS OVERFLOWING WITH WOUNDED--PARA-MEDICS UNION REMAINS ADAMANT--REFUSES TO END ITS STRIKE--
I CAN'T FIND MY WIFE!
SUPERMAN WILL SAVE US! HE HAS TO! THAT'S WHAT HE DOES!
GHUUKK
SPARKY!

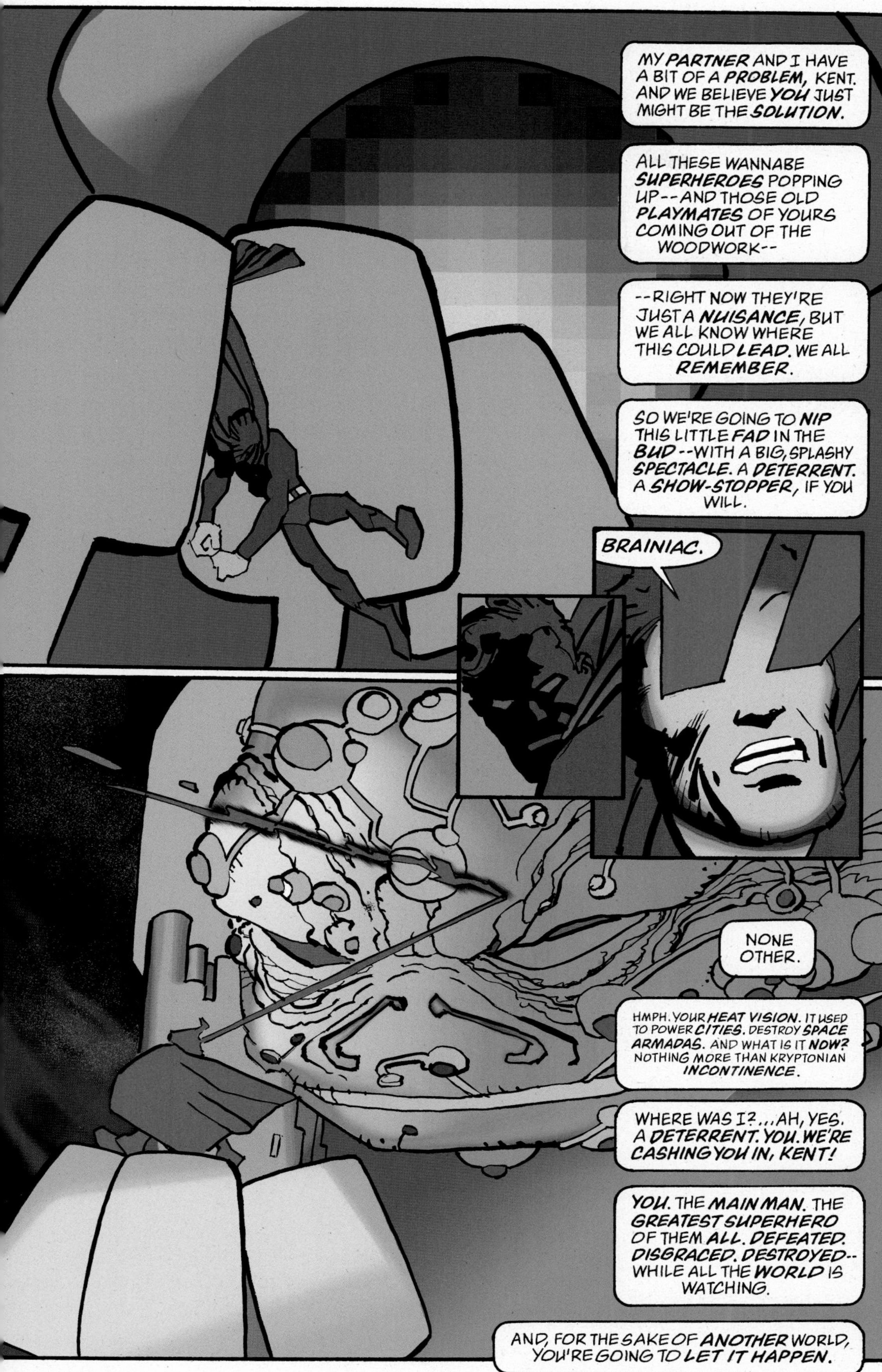
MY PARTNER AND I HAVE A BIT OF A PROBLEM, KENT. AND WE BELIEVE YOU JUST MIGHT BE THE SOLUTION.
ALL THESE WANNABE SUPERHEROES POPPING UP--AND THOSE OLD PLAYMATES OF YOURS COMING OUT OF THE WOODWORK--
--RIGHT NOW THEY'RE JUST A NUISANCE, BUT WE ALL KNOW WHERE THIS COULD LEAD. WE ALL REMEMBER.
SO WE'RE GOING TO NIP THIS LITTLE FAD IN THE BUD--WITH A BIG, SPLASHY SPECTACLE. A DETERRENT. A SHOW-STOPPER, IF YOU WILL.
BRAINIAC.
NONE OTHER.
HMPH. YOUR HEAT VISION. IT USED TO POWER CITIES. DESTROY SPACE ARMADAS. AND WHAT IS IT NOW? NOTHING MORE THAN KRYPTONIAN INCONTINENCE.
WHERE WAS I?...AH, YES. A DETERRENT. YOU. WE'RE CASHING YOU IN, KENT!
YOU. THE MAIN MAN. THE GREATEST SUPERHERO OF THEM ALL. DEFEATED. DISGRACED. DESTROYED--WHILE ALL THE WORLD IS WATCHING.
AND, FOR THE SAKE OF ANOTHER WORLD, YOU'RE GOING TO LET IT HAPPEN.

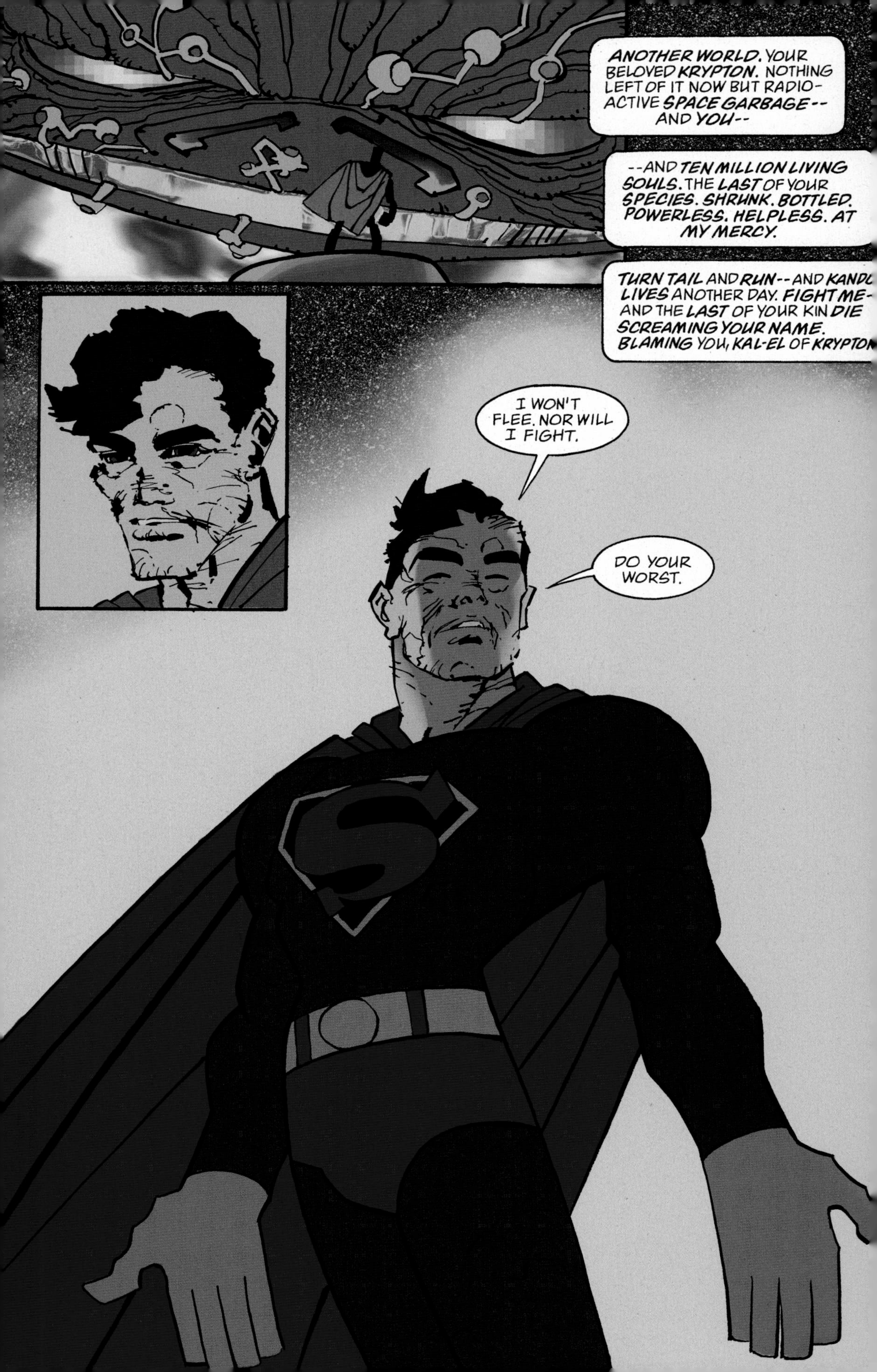
ANOTHER WORLD. YOUR BELOVED KRYPTON. NOTHING LEFT OF IT NOW BUT RADIO-ACTIVE SPACE GARBAGE-- AND YOU--
--AND TEN MILLION LIVING SOULS. THE LAST OF YOUR SPECIES. SHRUNK. BOTTLED. POWERLESS. HELPLESS. AT MY MERCY.
TURN TAIL AND RUN--AND KANDO LIVES ANOTHER DAY. FIGHT ME-AND THE LAST OF YOUR KIN DIE SCREAMING YOUR NAME. BLAMING YOU, KAL-EL OF KRYPTON
I WON'T FLEE. NOR WILL I FIGHT.
DO YOUR WORST.

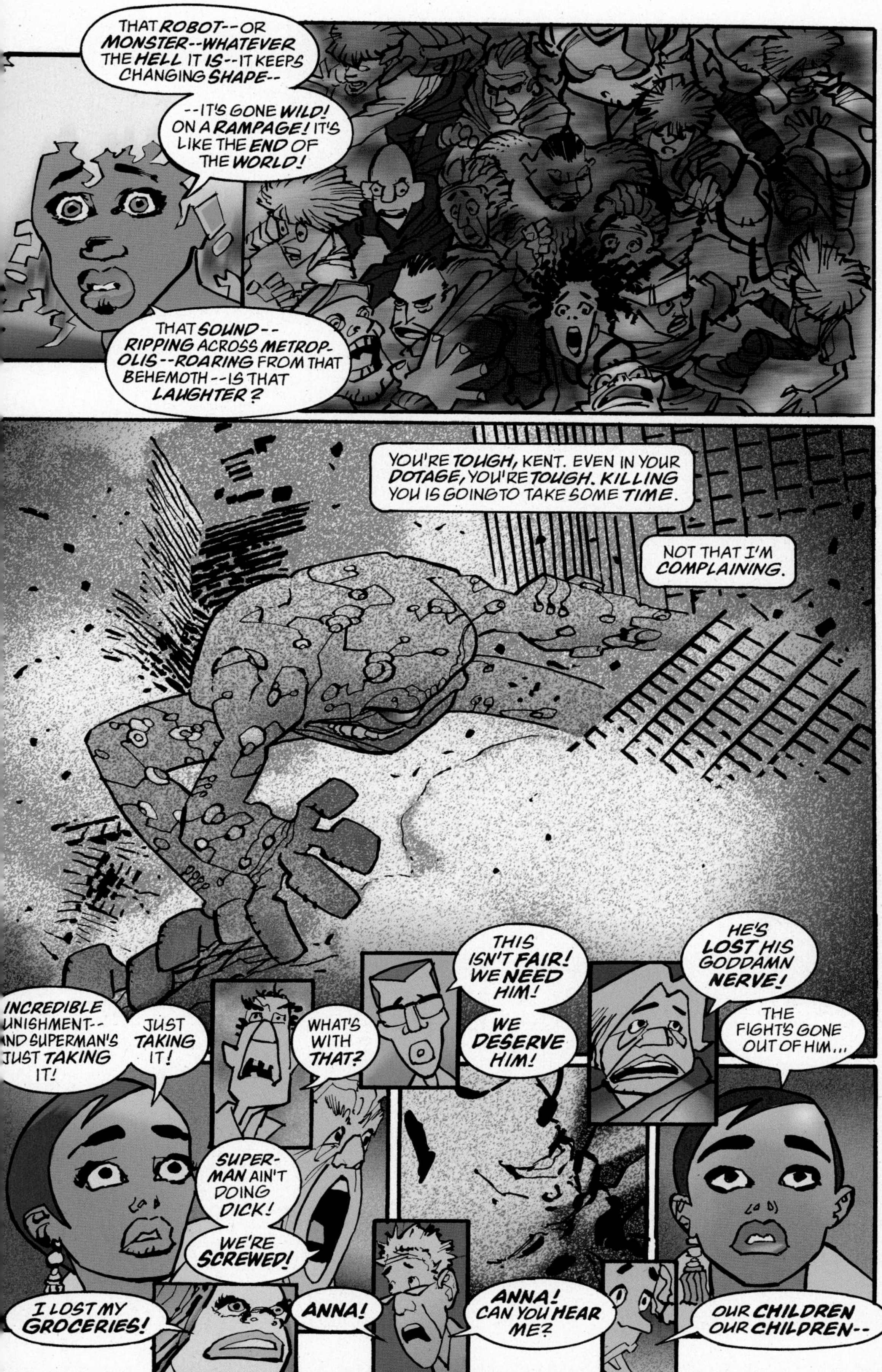
THAT ROBOT--OR MONSTER--WHATEVER THE HELL IT IS--IT KEEPS CHANGING SHAPE--
--IT'S GONE WILD! ON A RAMPAGE! IT'S LIKE THE END OF THE WORLD!
THAT SOUND--RIPPING ACROSS METROPOLIS--ROARING FROM THAT BEHEMOTH--IS THAT LAUGHTER?
YOU'RE TOUGH, KENT. EVEN IN YOUR DOTAGE, YOU'RE TOUGH. KILLING YOU IS GOING TO TAKE SOME TIME.
NOT THAT I'M COMPLAINING.
INCREDIBLE UNISHMENT--AND SUPERMAN'S JUST TAKING IT!
JUST TAKING IT!
WHAT'S WITH THAT?
THIS ISN'T FAIR! WE NEED HIM!
WE DESERVE HIM!
HE'S LOST HIS GODDAMN NERVE!
THE FIGHT'S GONE OUT OF HIM...
SUPERMAN AIN'T DOING DICK!
WE'RE SCREWED!
I LOST MY GROCERIES!
ANNA!
ANNA! CAN YOU HEAR ME?
OUR CHILDREN OUR CHILDREN--

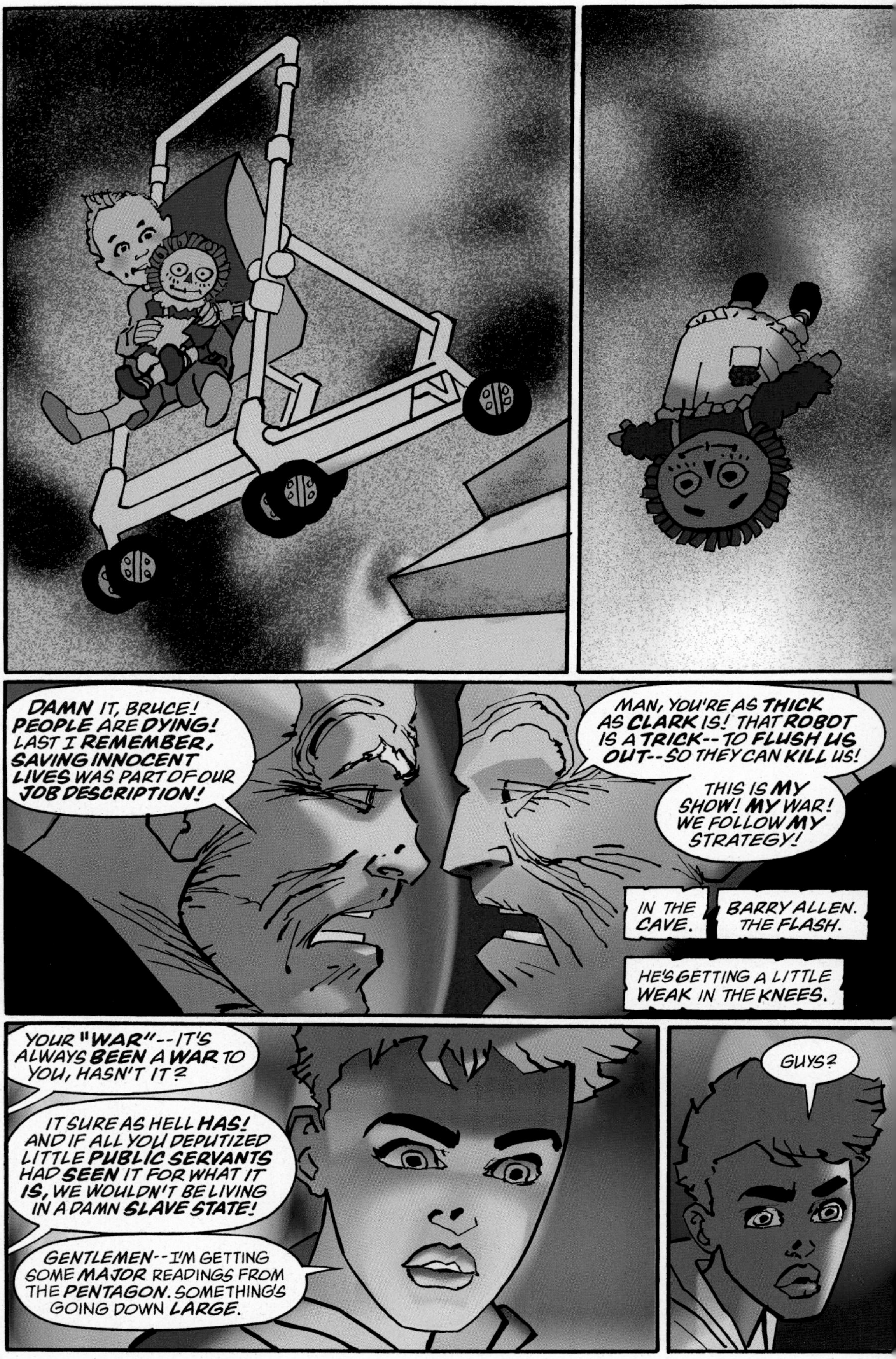
DAMN IT, BRUCE! PEOPLE ARE DYING! LAST I REMEMBER, SAVING INNOCENT LIVES WAS PART OF OUR JOB DESCRIPTION!
MAN, YOU'RE AS THICK AS CLARK IS! THAT ROBOT IS A TRICK-- TO FLUSH US OUT-- SO THEY CAN KILL US!
THIS IS MY SHOW! MY WAR! WE FOLLOW MY STRATEGY!
IN THE CAVE.
BARRY ALLEN. THE FLASH.
HE'S GETTING A LITTLE WEAK IN THE KNEES.
YOUR "WAR"-- IT'S ALWAYS BEEN A WAR TO YOU, HASN'T IT?
IT SURE AS HELL HAS! AND IF ALL YOU DEPUTIZED LITTLE PUBLIC SERVANTS HAD SEEN IT FOR WHAT IT IS, WE WOULDN'T BE LIVING IN A DAMN SLAVE STATE!
GENTLEMEN-- I'M GETTING SOME MAJOR READINGS FROM THE PENTAGON. SOMETHING'S GOING DOWN LARGE.
GUYS?

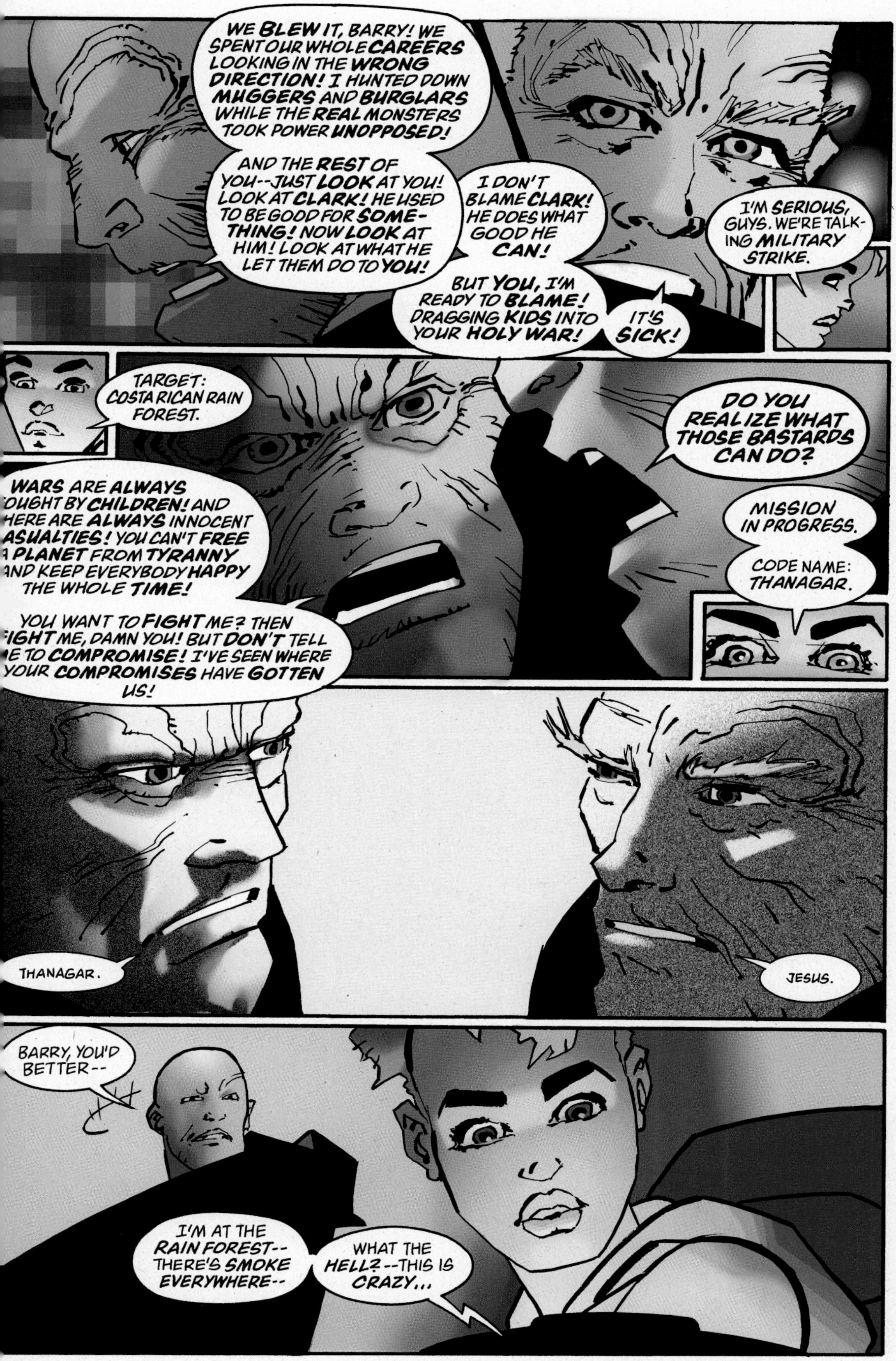

WE BLEW IT, BARRY! WE SPENT OUR WHOLE CAREERS LOOKING IN THE WRONG DIRECTION! I HUNTED DOWN MUGGERS AND BURGLARS WHILE THE REAL MONSTERS TOOK POWER UNOPPOSED!
AND THE REST OF YOU--JUST LOOK AT YOU! LOOK AT CLARK! HE USED TO BE GOOD FOR SOME-THING! NOW LOOK AT HIM! LOOK AT WHAT HE LET THEM DO TO YOU!
I DON'T BLAME CLARK! HE DOES WHAT GOOD HE CAN!
BUT YOU, I'M READY TO BLAME! DRAGGING KIDS INTO YOUR HOLY WAR!
IT'S SICK!
I'M SERIOUS, GUYS. WE'RE TALK-ING MILITARY STRIKE.
TARGET: COSTA RICAN RAIN FOREST.
DO YOU REALIZE WHAT THOSE BASTARDS CAN DO?
WARS ARE ALWAYS FOUGHT BY CHILDREN! AND THERE ARE ALWAYS INNOCENT CASUALTIES! YOU CAN'T FREE A PLANET FROM TYRANNY AND KEEP EVERYBODY HAPPY THE WHOLE TIME!
YOU WANT TO FIGHT ME? THEN FIGHT ME, DAMN YOU! BUT DON'T TELL ME TO COMPROMISE! I'VE SEEN WHERE YOUR COMPROMISES HAVE GOTTEN US!
MISSION IN PROGRESS.
CODE NAME: THANAGAR.
THANAGAR.
JESUS.
BARRY, YOU'D BETTER--
I'M AT THE RAIN FOREST-- THERE'S SMOKE EVERYWHERE--
WHAT THE HELL? --THIS IS CRAZY...

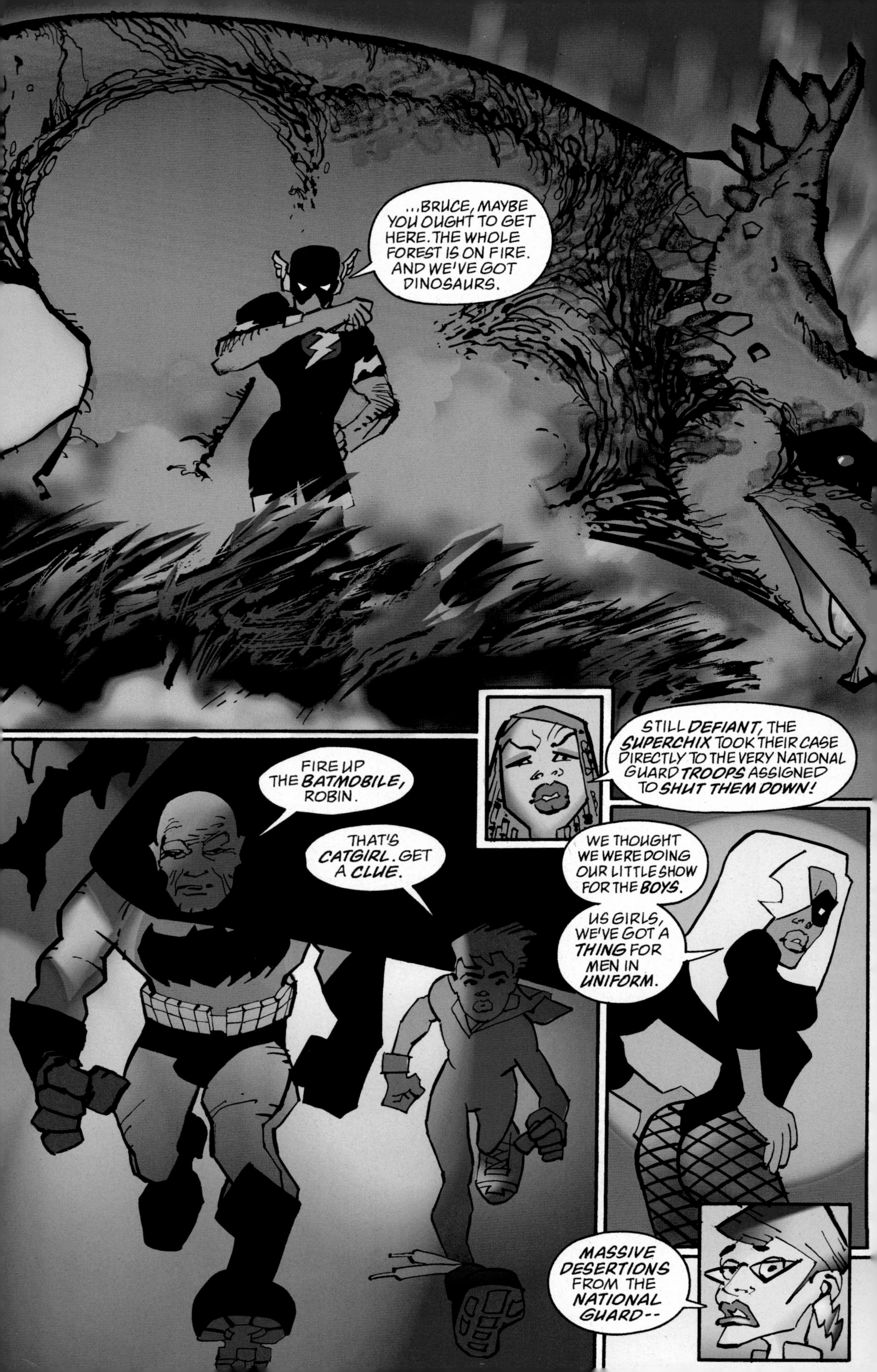
...BRUCE, MAYBE YOU OUGHT TO GET HERE. THE WHOLE FOREST IS ON FIRE. AND WE'VE GOT DINOSAURS.
FIRE UP THE BATMOBILE, ROBIN.
THAT'S CATGIRL. GET A CLUE.
STILL DEFIANT, THE SUPERCHIX TOOK THEIR CASE DIRECTLY TO THE VERY NATIONAL GUARD TROOPS ASSIGNED TO SHUT THEM DOWN!
WE THOUGHT WE WERE DOING OUR LITTLE SHOW FOR THE BOYS.
US GIRLS, WE'VE GOT A THING FOR MEN IN UNIFORM.
MASSIVE DESERTIONS FROM THE NATIONAL GUARD--

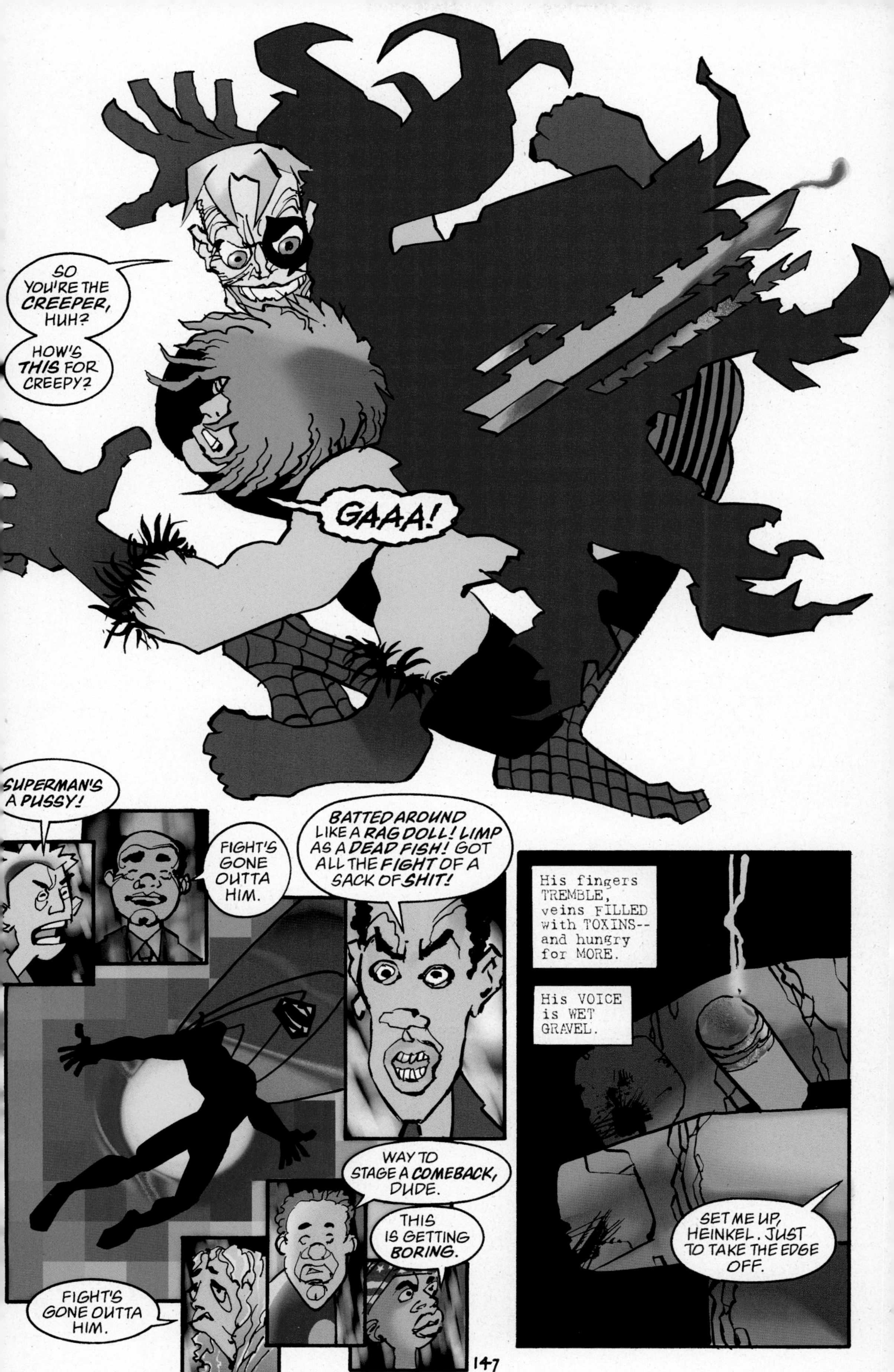

SO YOU'RE THE CREEPER, HUH?
HOW'S THIS FOR CREEPY?
GAAA!
SUPERMAN'S A PUSSY!
FIGHT'S GONE OUTTA HIM.
BATTED AROUND LIKE A RAG DOLL! LIMP AS A DEAD FISH! GOT ALL THE FIGHT OF A SACK OF SHIT!
WAY TO STAGE A COMEBACK, DUDE.
THIS IS GETTING BORING.
FIGHT'S GONE OUTTA HIM.
His fingers TREMBLE, veins FILLED with TOXINS-- and hungry for MORE.
His VOICE is WET GRAVEL.
SET ME UP, HEINKEL. JUST TO TAKE THE EDGE OFF.

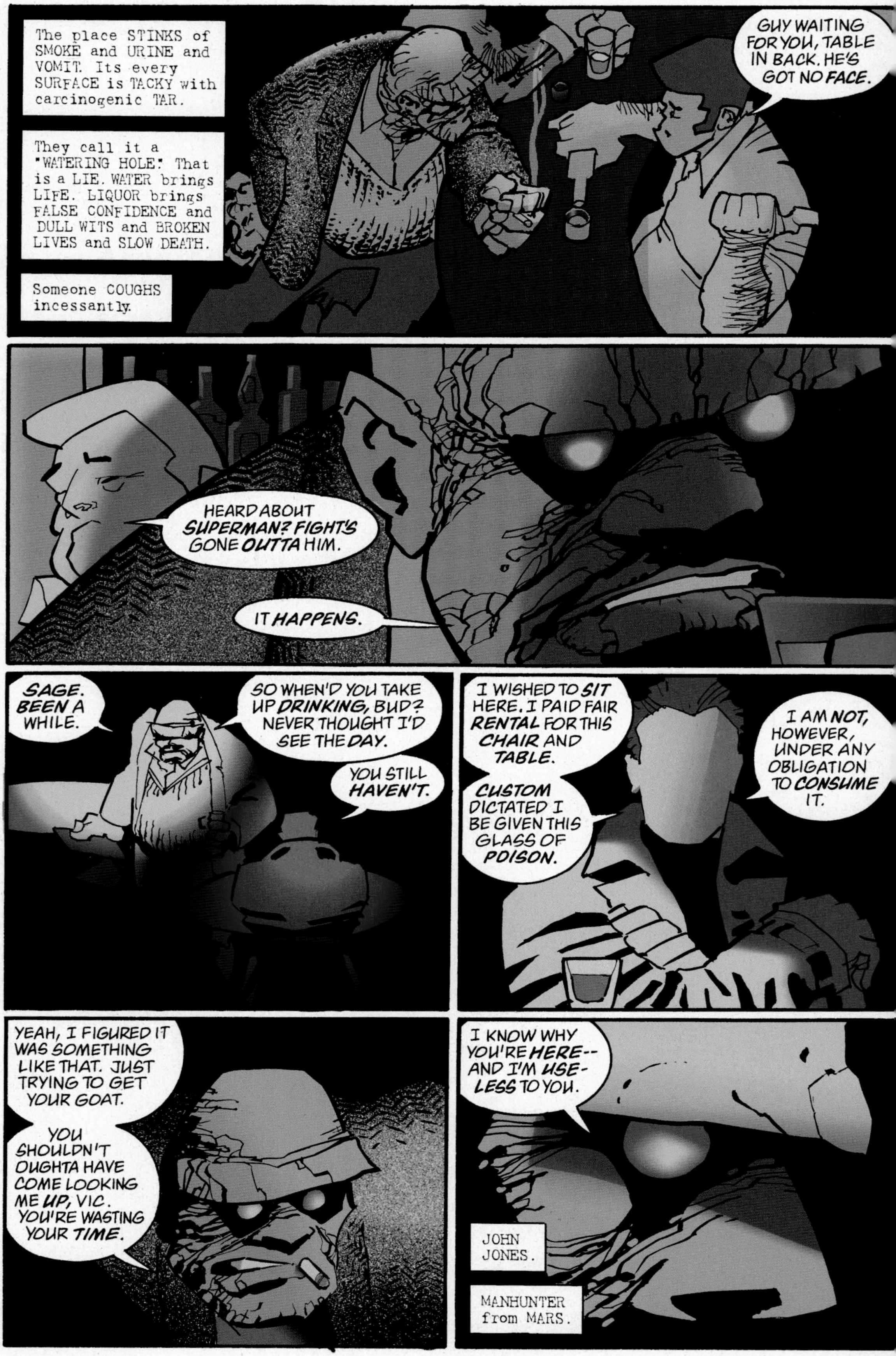
The place STINKS of SMOKE and URINE and VOMIT. Its every SURFACE is TACKY with carcinogenic TAR.
They call it a "WATERING HOLE." That is a LIE. WATER brings LIFE. LIQUOR brings FALSE CONFIDENCE and DULL WITS and BROKEN LIVES and SLOW DEATH.
Someone COUGHS incessantly.
GUY WAITING FOR YOU, TABLE IN BACK. HE'S GOT NO FACE.
HEARD ABOUT SUPERMAN? FIGHT'S GONE OUTTA HIM.
IT HAPPENS.
SAGE. BEEN A WHILE.
SO WHEN'D YOU TAKE UP DRINKING, BUD? NEVER THOUGHT I'D SEE THE DAY.
YOU STILL HAVEN'T.
I WISHED TO SIT HERE. I PAID FAIR RENTAL FOR THIS CHAIR AND TABLE.
CUSTOM DICTATED I BE GIVEN THIS GLASS OF POISON.
I AM NOT, HOWEVER, UNDER ANY OBLIGATION TO CONSUME IT.
YEAH, I FIGURED IT WAS SOMETHING LIKE THAT. JUST TRYING TO GET YOUR GOAT.
YOU SHOULDN'T OUGHTA HAVE COME LOOKING ME UP, VIC. YOU'RE WASTING YOUR TIME.
I KNOW WHY YOU'RE HERE-- AND I'M USELESS TO YOU.
JOHN JONES.
MANHUNTER from MARS.

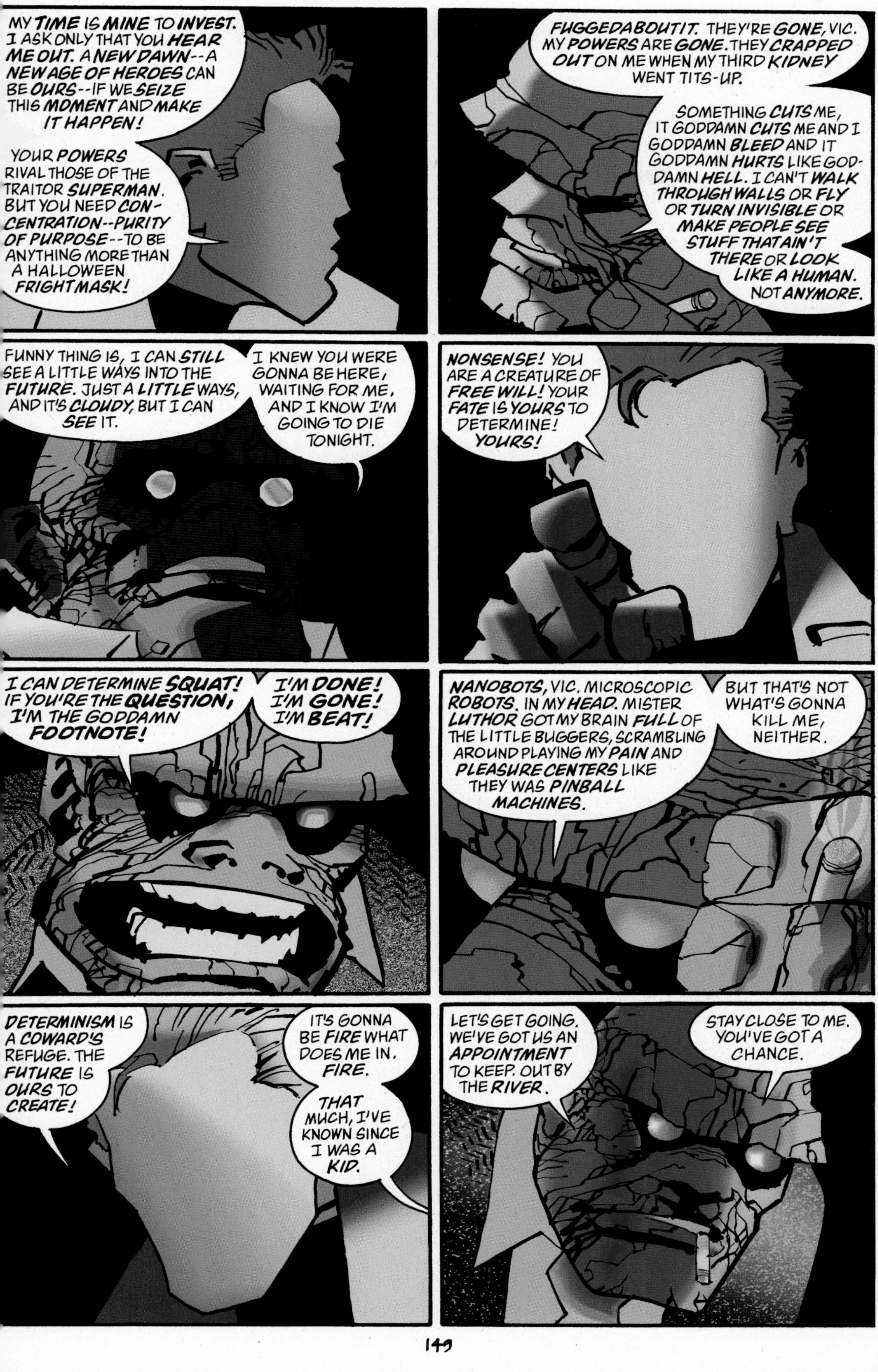
MY TIME IS MINE TO INVEST. I ASK ONLY THAT YOU HEAR ME OUT. A NEW DAWN--A NEW AGE OF HEROES CAN BE OURS--IF WE SEIZE THIS MOMENT AND MAKE IT HAPPEN!
YOUR POWERS RIVAL THOSE OF THE TRAITOR SUPERMAN. BUT YOU NEED CONCENTRATION--PURITY OF PURPOSE--TO BE ANYTHING MORE THAN A HALLOWEEN FRIGHT MASK!
FUGGEDABOUTIT. THEY'RE GONE, VIC. MY POWERS ARE GONE. THEY CRAPPED OUT ON ME WHEN MY THIRD KIDNEY WENT TITS-UP.
SOMETHING CUTS ME, IT GODDAMN CUTS ME AND I GODDAMN BLEED AND IT GODDAMN HURTS LIKE GODDAMN HELL. I CAN'T WALK THROUGH WALLS OR FLY OR TURN INVISIBLE OR MAKE PEOPLE SEE STUFF THAT AIN'T THERE OR LOOK LIKE A HUMAN. NOT ANYMORE.
FUNNY THING IS, I CAN STILL SEE A LITTLE WAYS INTO THE FUTURE. JUST A LITTLE WAYS, AND IT'S CLOUDY, BUT I CAN SEE IT.
I KNEW YOU WERE GONNA BE HERE, WAITING FOR ME, AND I KNOW I'M GOING TO DIE TONIGHT.
NONSENSE! YOU ARE A CREATURE OF FREE WILL! YOUR FATE IS YOURS TO DETERMINE! YOURS!
I CAN DETERMINE SQUAT! IF YOU'RE THE QUESTION, I'M THE GODDAMN FOOTNOTE!
I'M DONE! I'M GONE! I'M BEAT!
NANOBOTS, VIC. MICROSCOPIC ROBOTS. IN MY HEAD. MISTER LUTHOR GOT MY BRAIN FULL OF THE LITTLE BUGGERS, SCRAMBLING AROUND PLAYING MY PAIN AND PLEASURE CENTERS LIKE THEY WAS PINBALL MACHINES.
BUT THAT'S NOT WHAT'S GONNA KILL ME, NEITHER.
DETERMINISM IS A COWARD'S REFUGE. THE FUTURE IS OURS TO CREATE!
IT'S GONNA BE FIRE WHAT DOES ME IN. FIRE.
THAT MUCH, I'VE KNOWN SINCE I WAS A KID.
LET'S GET GOING. WE'VE GOT US AN APPOINTMENT TO KEEP. OUT BY THE RIVER.
STAY CLOSE TO ME. YOU'VE GOT A CHANCE.

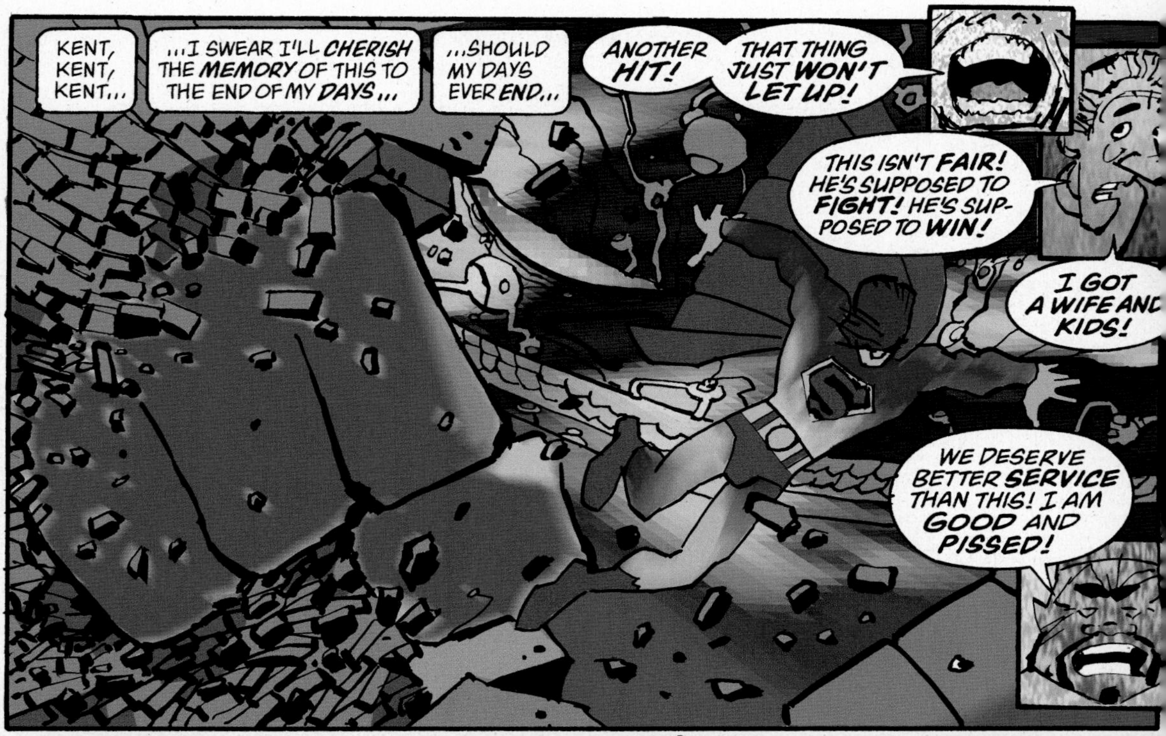
KENT, KENT, KENT...
...I SWEAR I'LL CHERISH THE MEMORY OF THIS TO THE END OF MY DAYS...
...SHOULD MY DAYS EVER END...
ANOTHER HIT!
THAT THING JUST WON'T LET UP!
THIS ISN'T FAIR! HE'S SUPPOSED TO FIGHT! HE'S SUPPOSED TO WIN!
I GOT A WIFE AND KIDS!
WE DESERVE BETTER SERVICE THAN THIS! I AM GOOD AND PISSED!

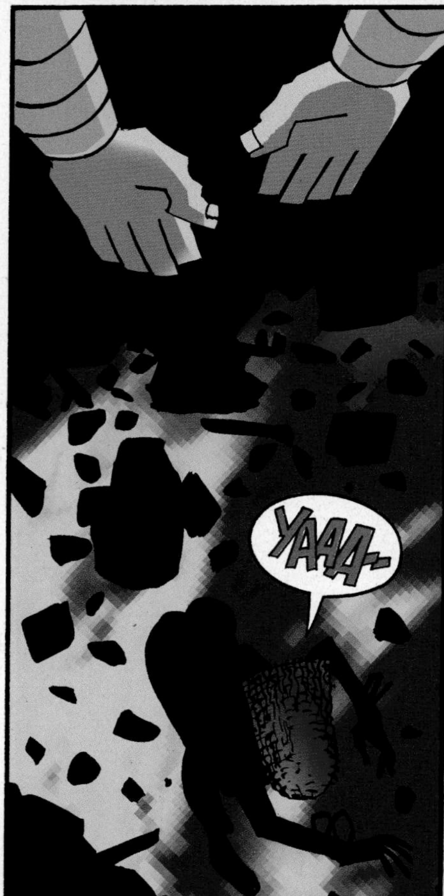
YAAA-

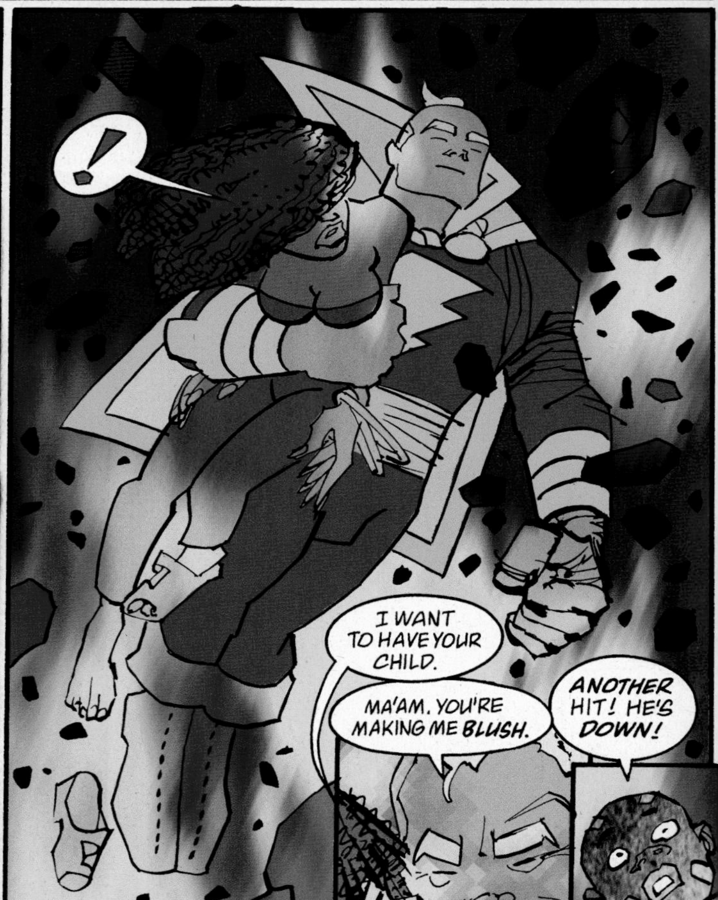
!
I WANT TO HAVE YOUR CHILD.
MA'AM. YOU'RE MAKING ME BLUSH.
ANOTHER HIT! HE'S DOWN!

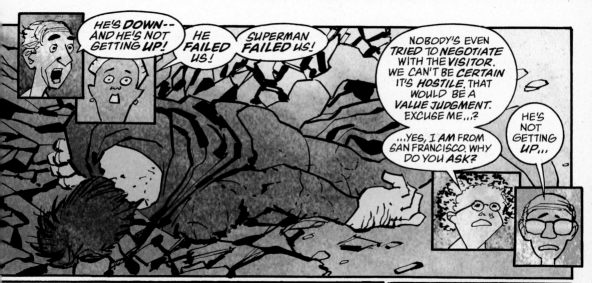

HE'S DOWN-- AND HE'S NOT GETTING UP!

HE FAILED US!

SUPERMAN FAILED US!

NOBODY'S EVEN TRIED TO NEGOTIATE WITH THE VISITOR. WE CAN'T BE CERTAIN IT'S HOSTILE. THAT WOULD BE A VALUE JUDGMENT. EXCUSE ME...?

...YES, I AM FROM SAN FRANCISCO. WHY DO YOU ASK?

HE'S NOT GETTING UP...

MOTHER.

HE NEEDS ME.

NO. NOT YET.

NOT YET.

I AM TRAINED. I AM READY.

I HAVE THE POWER.

WAIT. LET ME SHOW YOU WHAT YOUR DEAR OLD MOMMA CAN DO--

--WITH A LITTLE HELP FROM ZEUS.

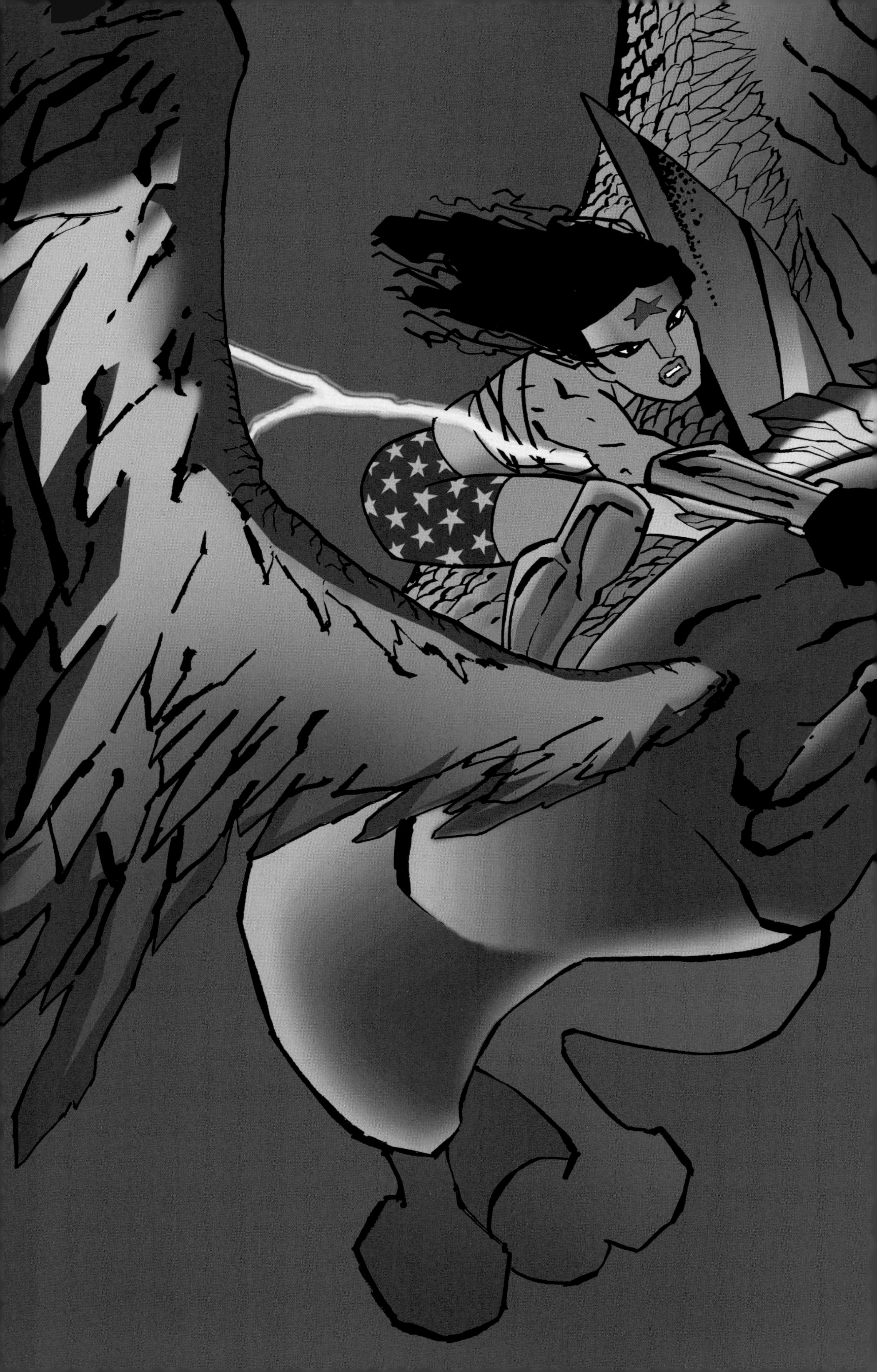

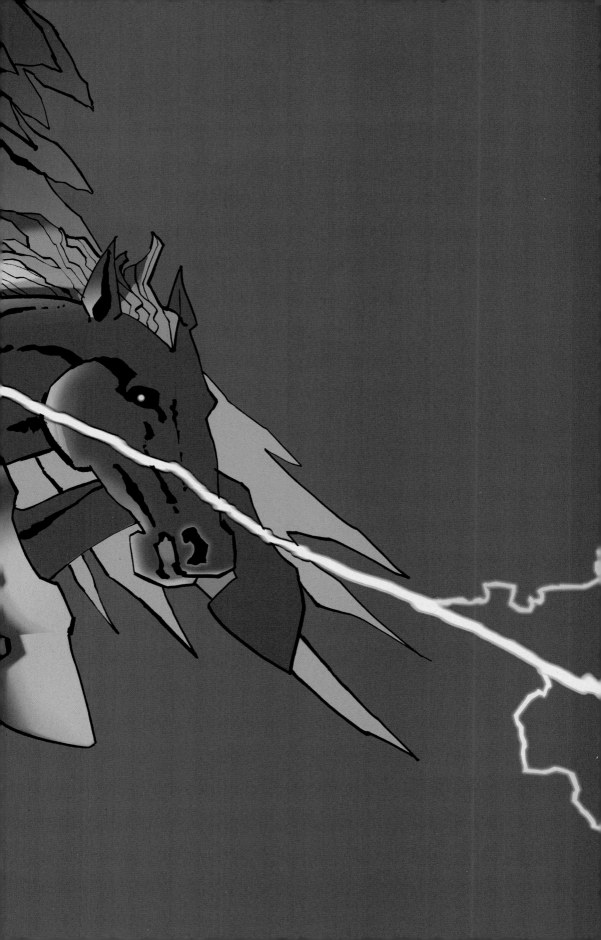

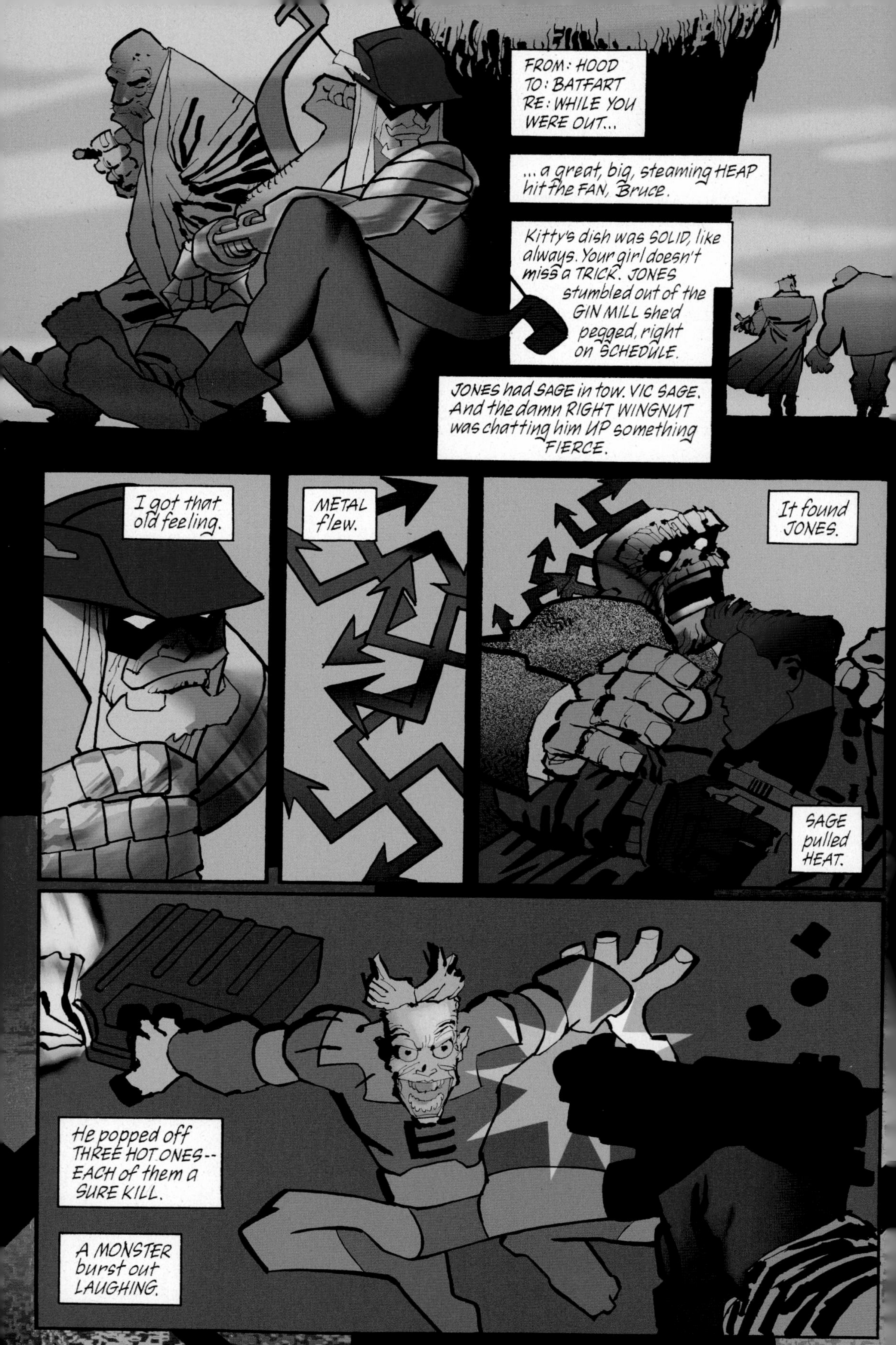

FROM: HOOD
TO: BATFART
RE: WHILE YOU WERE OUT...
... a great, big, steaming HEAP hit the FAN, Bruce.
Kitty's dish was SOLID, like always. Your girl doesn't miss a TRICK. JONES stumbled out of the GIN MILL she'd pegged, right on SCHEDULE.
JONES had SAGE in tow. VIC SAGE. And the damn RIGHT WINGNUT was chatting him UP something FIERCE.
I got that old feeling.
METAL flew.
It found JONES.
SAGE pulled HEAT.
He popped off THREE HOT ONES-- EACH of them a SURE KILL.
A MONSTER burst out LAUGHING.

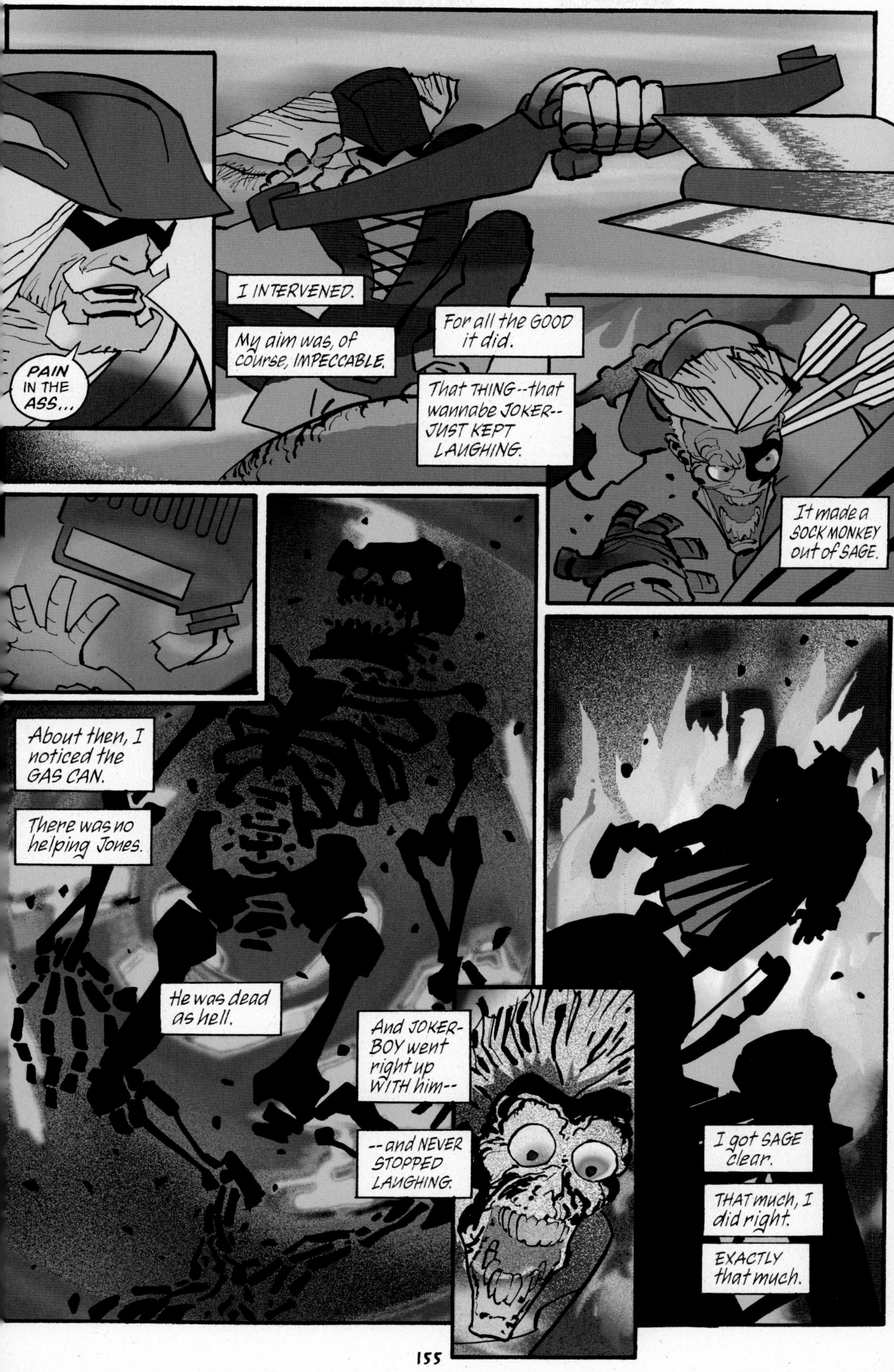
PAIN IN THE ASS...
I INTERVENED.
My aim was, of course, IMPECCABLE.
For all the GOOD it did.
That THING--that wannabe JOKER--JUST KEPT LAUGHING.
It made a SOCK MONKEY out of SAGE.
About then, I noticed the GAS CAN.
There was no helping Jones.
He was dead as hell.
And JOKER-BOY went right up WITH him--
--and NEVER STOPPED LAUGHING.
I got SAGE clear.
THAT much, I did right.
EXACTLY that much.

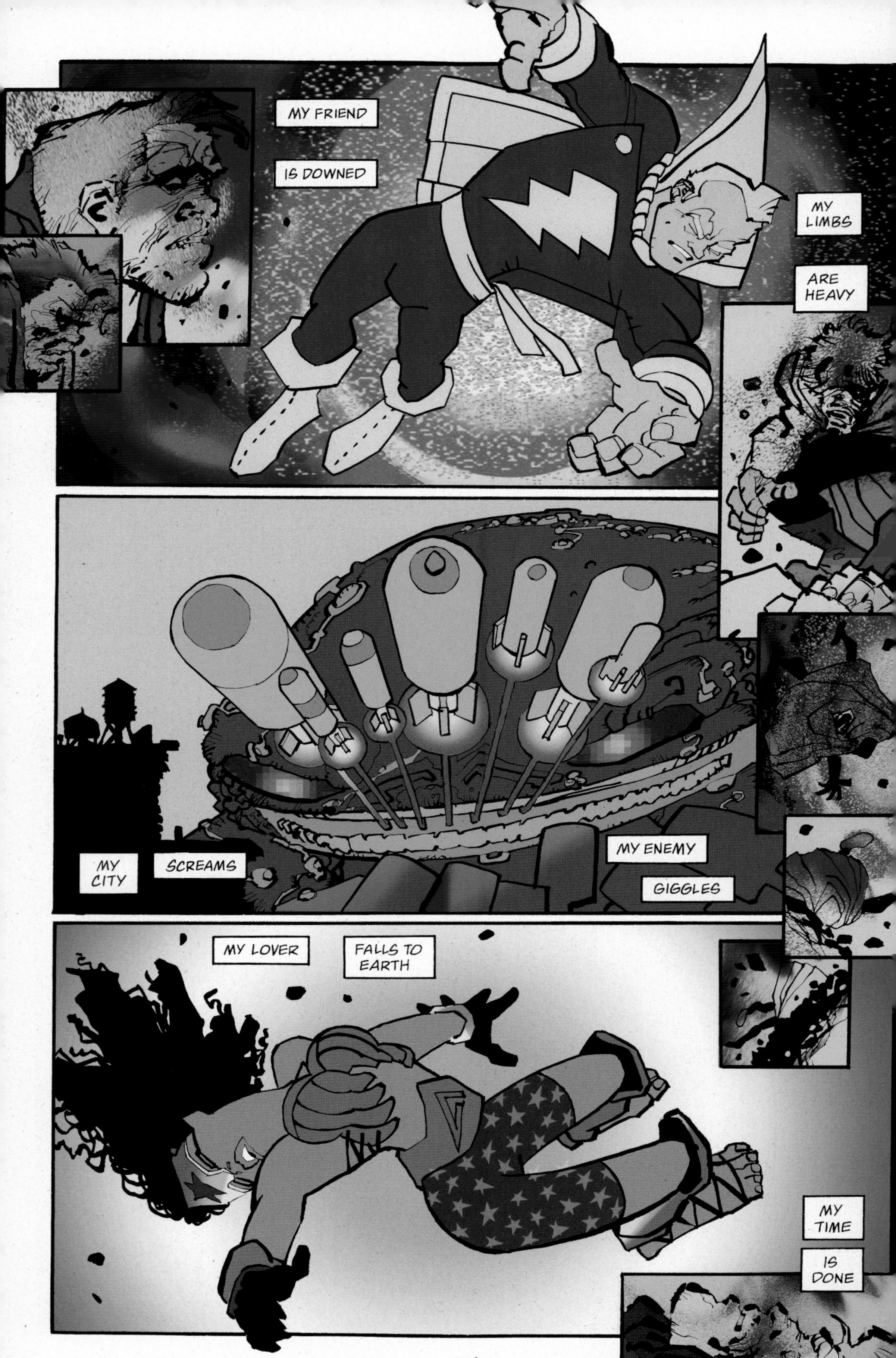
MY FRIEND
IS DOWNED
MY LIMBS
ARE HEAVY
MY CITY
SCREAMS
MY ENEMY
GIGGLES
MY LOVER
FALLS TO EARTH
MY TIME
IS DONE

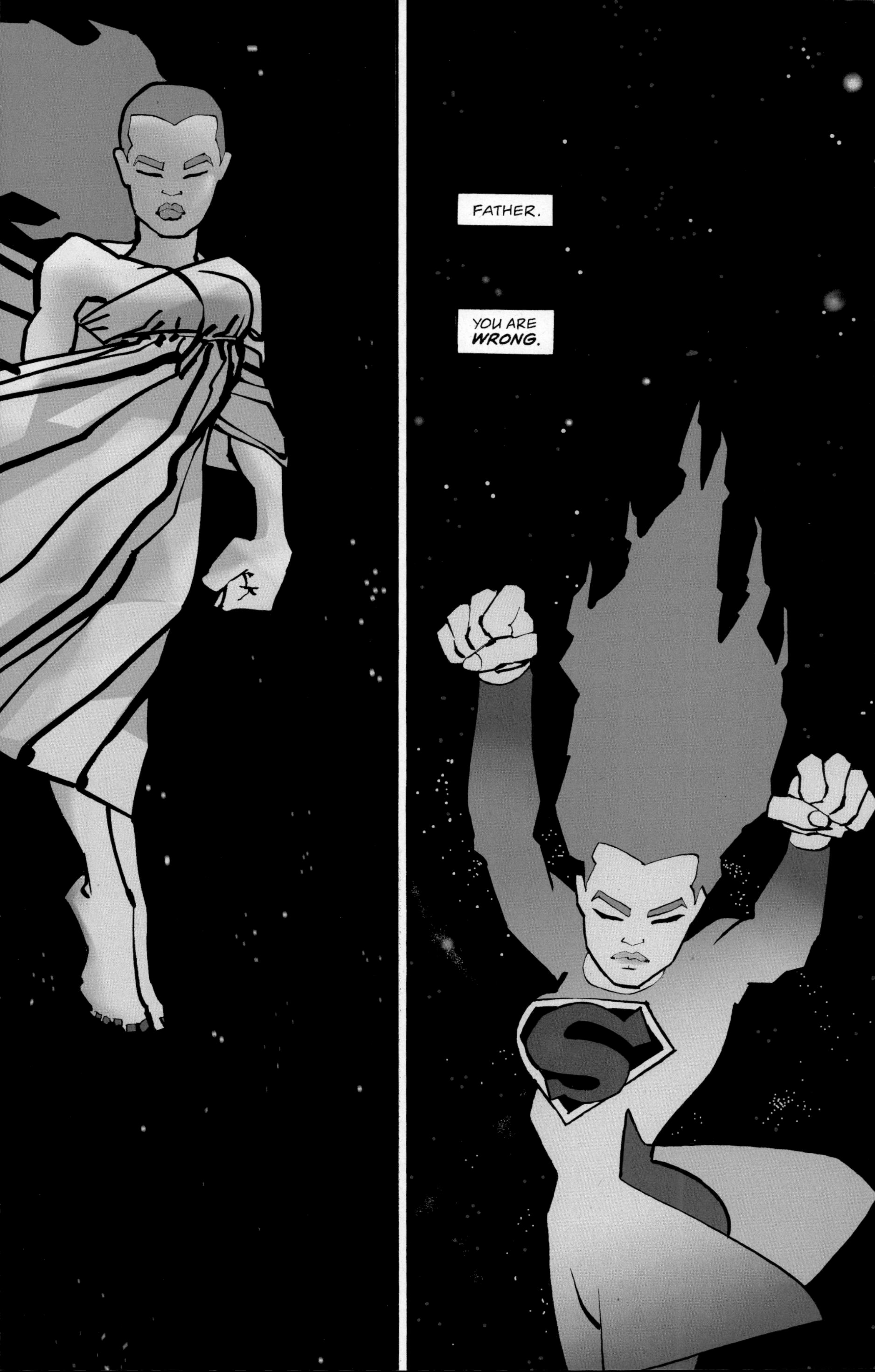

FATHER.
YOU ARE **WRONG.**

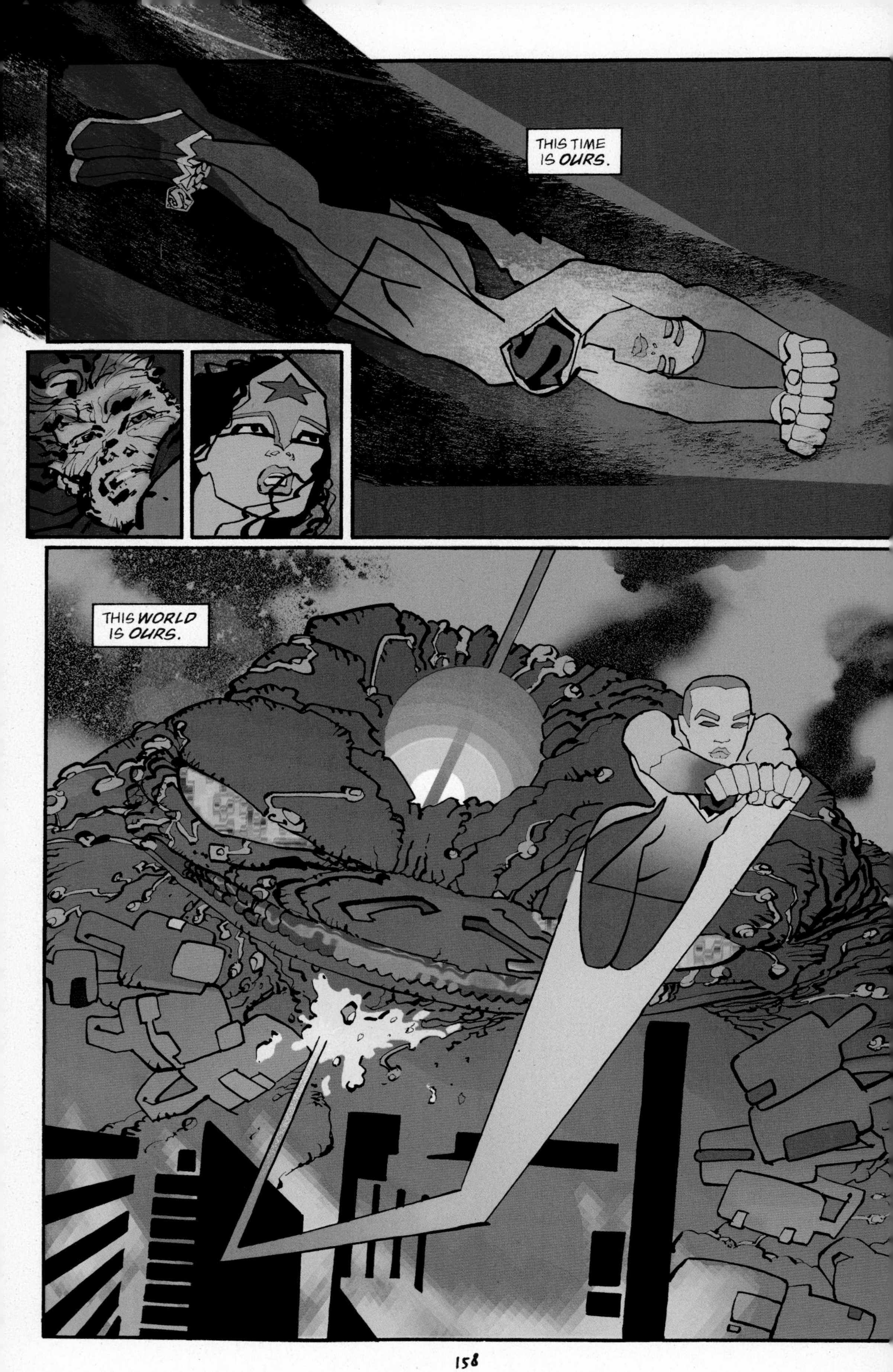
THIS TIME IS OURS.
THIS WORLD IS OURS.

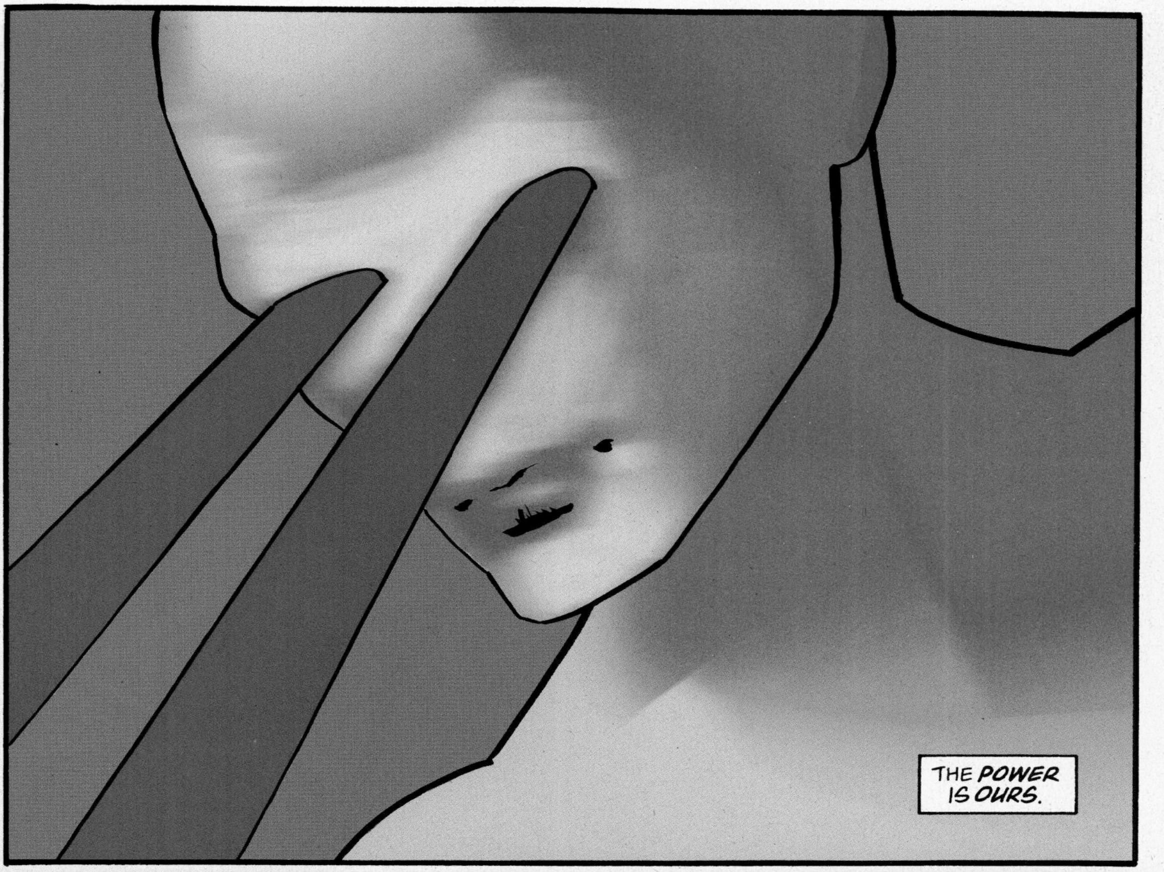
THE POWER IS OURS.

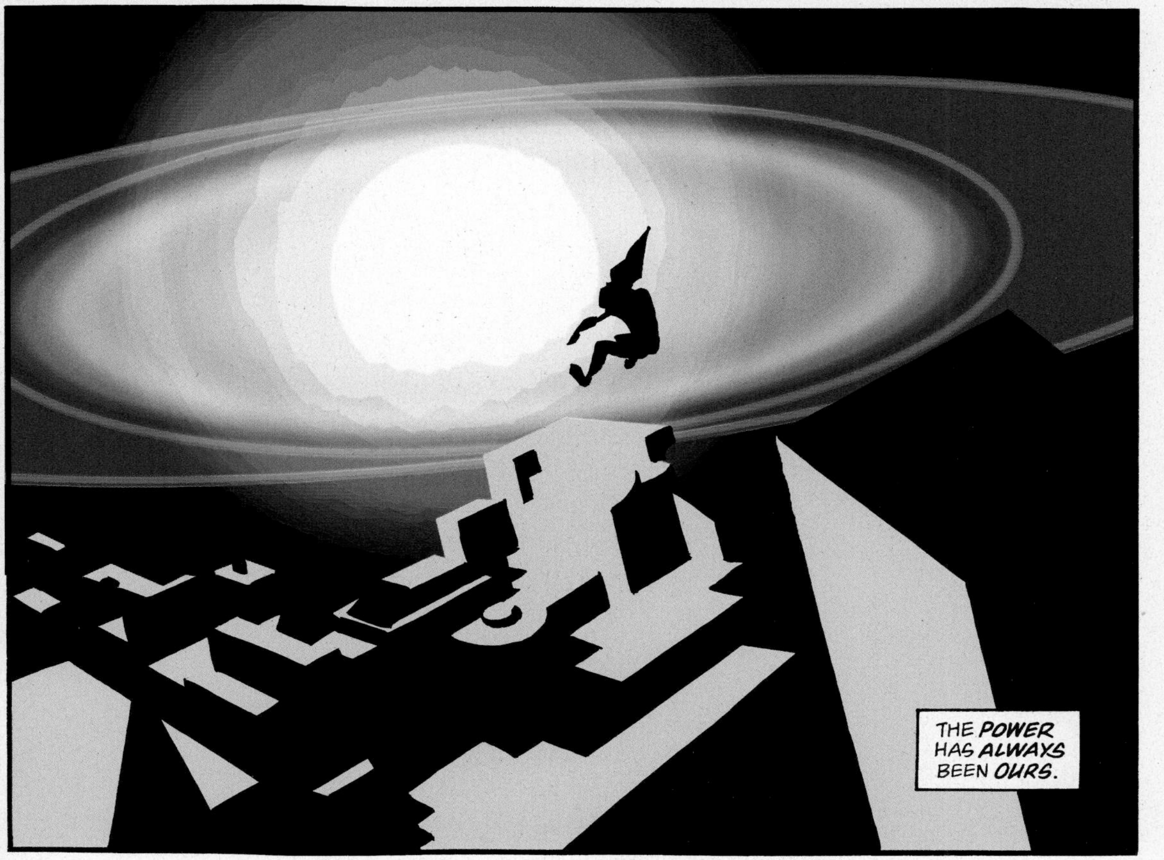
THE POWER HAS ALWAYS BEEN OURS.

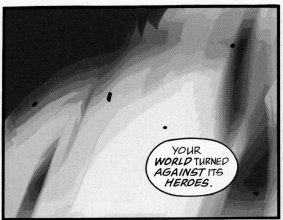

YOUR *WORLD* TURNED *AGAINST* ITS HEROES.

MOTHER AND *FATHER* TRIED TO TAKE US *AWAY* FROM YOUR PLANET-- TO *RETURN* TO OUR HOMEWORLD *THANAGAR.*

WE WERE *BLASTED* FROM THE *SKY.*

WE CRASHED *HERE.* IN THIS *FOREST.*

THOUGH IN *EXILE*, WE *THRIVED.*

FATHER BUILT OUR *HOME.*

MOTHER USED THANAGARIAN *SCIENCE* AND HER OWN FERTILE *WITS* TO BRING ANCIENT *SPECIES* BACK TO LIFE.

MY *SISTER* AND I EARNED OUR *WINGS.*

THIS WAS A *HAPPY* PLACE.

THEN CAME THE *FIRE.*

FROM THE *SKY.*

MOTHER ORDERED US *HERE.* INTO THIS *CAVE.*

AND SHE *FLEW.*

SHE CALLED FOR HER HUSBAND.

HE FOUND HER.

THERE WAS NOWHERE TO RUN.

LOVERS, THEY DIED.

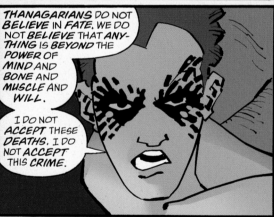

THANAGARIANS DO NOT *BELIEVE* IN *FATE*. WE DO NOT *BELIEVE* THAT *ANYTHING* IS *BEYOND* THE *POWER* OF *MIND* AND *BONE* AND *MUSCLE* AND *WILL*.

I DO NOT *ACCEPT* THESE *DEATHS*. I DO NOT *ACCEPT* THIS *CRIME*.

YOU'RE GOING TO GET WHAT I NEVER GOT.

RETRIBUTION.

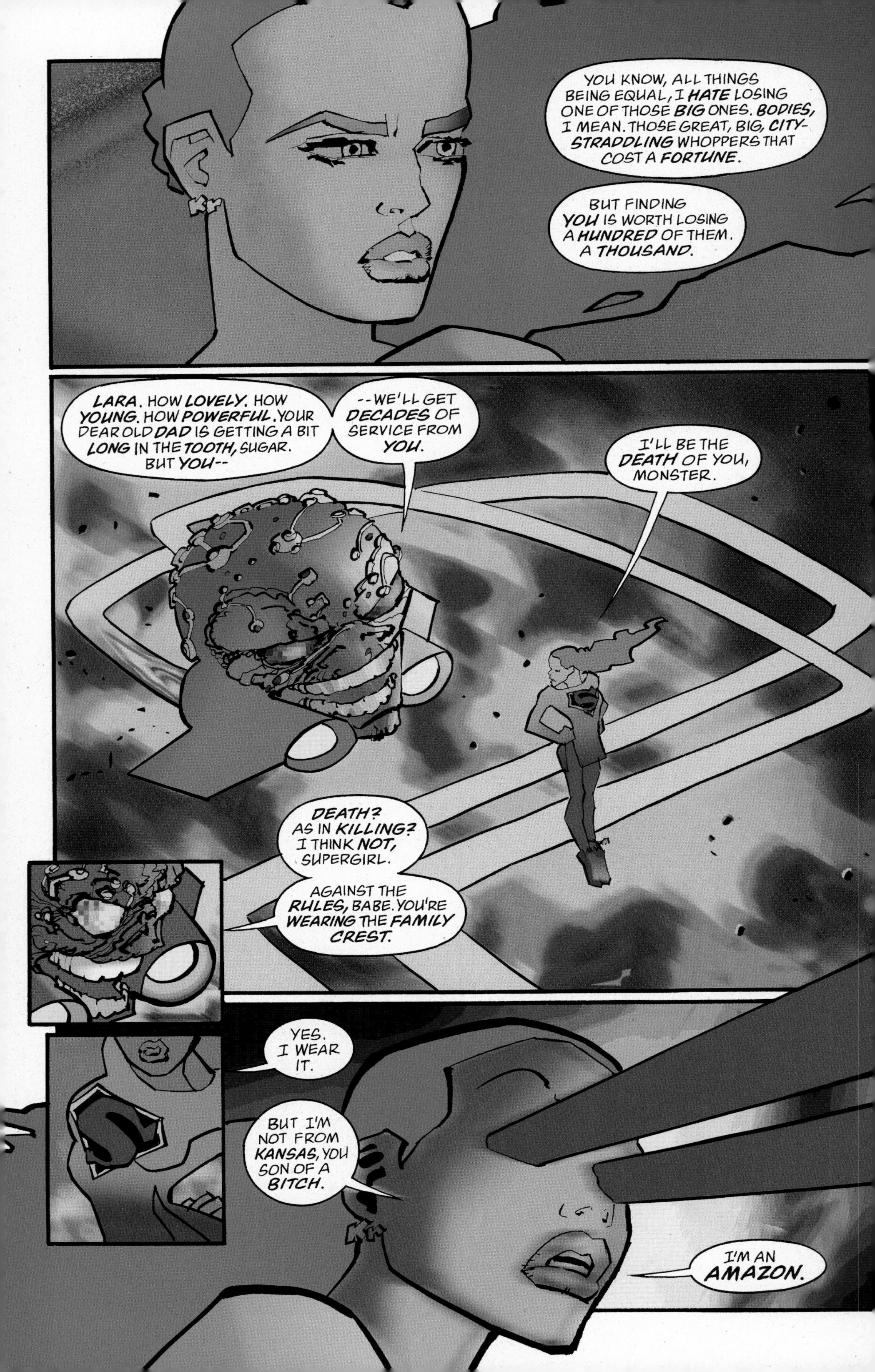
YOU KNOW, ALL THINGS BEING EQUAL, I HATE LOSING ONE OF THOSE BIG ONES. BODIES, I MEAN. THOSE GREAT, BIG, CITY-STRADDLING WHOPPERS THAT COST A FORTUNE.
BUT FINDING YOU IS WORTH LOSING A HUNDRED OF THEM. A THOUSAND.
LARA. HOW LOVELY. HOW YOUNG. HOW POWERFUL. YOUR DEAR OLD DAD IS GETTING A BIT LONG IN THE TOOTH, SUGAR. BUT YOU--
--WE'LL GET DECADES OF SERVICE FROM YOU.
I'LL BE THE DEATH OF YOU, MONSTER.
DEATH? AS IN KILLING? I THINK NOT, SUPERGIRL.
AGAINST THE RULES, BABE. YOU'RE WEARING THE FAMILY CREST.
YES. I WEAR IT.
BUT I'M NOT FROM KANSAS, YOU SON OF A BITCH.
I'M AN AMAZON.

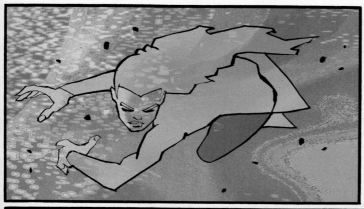

IT'S HARD TO *CONTROL*, ISN'T IT?

THE *HEAT VISION.* OF ALL THE *POWERS*, IT TAKES THE *LONGEST* TO MASTER. WHEN I WAS A *BABY*, I ALMOST BURNED DOWN MY PARENTS' *HOUSE.*

IT *DID* COST THEM A *SHED.* PA WAS *FURIOUS...*

LARA, WHAT SORT OF WORLD HAVE I GIVEN YOU?

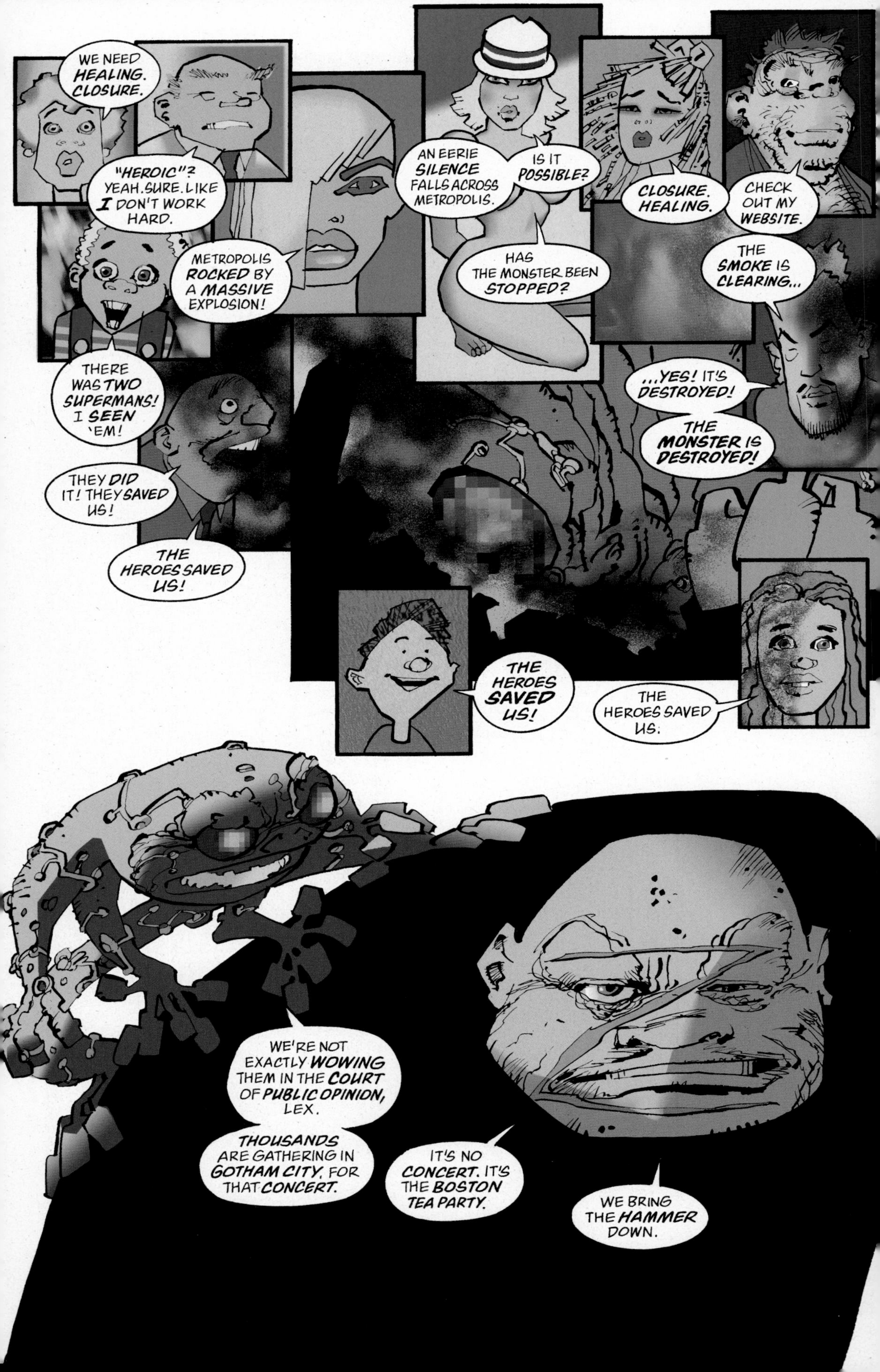

WE NEED HEALING. CLOSURE.
"HEROIC"? YEAH. SURE. LIKE I DON'T WORK HARD.
METROPOLIS ROCKED BY A MASSIVE EXPLOSION!
AN EERIE SILENCE FALLS ACROSS METROPOLIS.
IS IT POSSIBLE?
HAS THE MONSTER BEEN STOPPED?
CLOSURE. HEALING.
CHECK OUT MY WEBSITE.
THE SMOKE IS CLEARING...
THERE WAS TWO SUPERMANS! I SEEN 'EM!
THEY DID IT! THEY SAVED US!
THE HEROES SAVED US!
...YES! IT'S DESTROYED!
THE MONSTER IS DESTROYED!
THE HEROES SAVED US!
THE HEROES SAVED US.
WE'RE NOT EXACTLY WOWING THEM IN THE COURT OF PUBLIC OPINION, LEX.
THOUSANDS ARE GATHERING IN GOTHAM CITY, FOR THAT CONCERT.
IT'S NO CONCERT. IT'S THE BOSTON TEA PARTY.
WE BRING THE HAMMER DOWN.

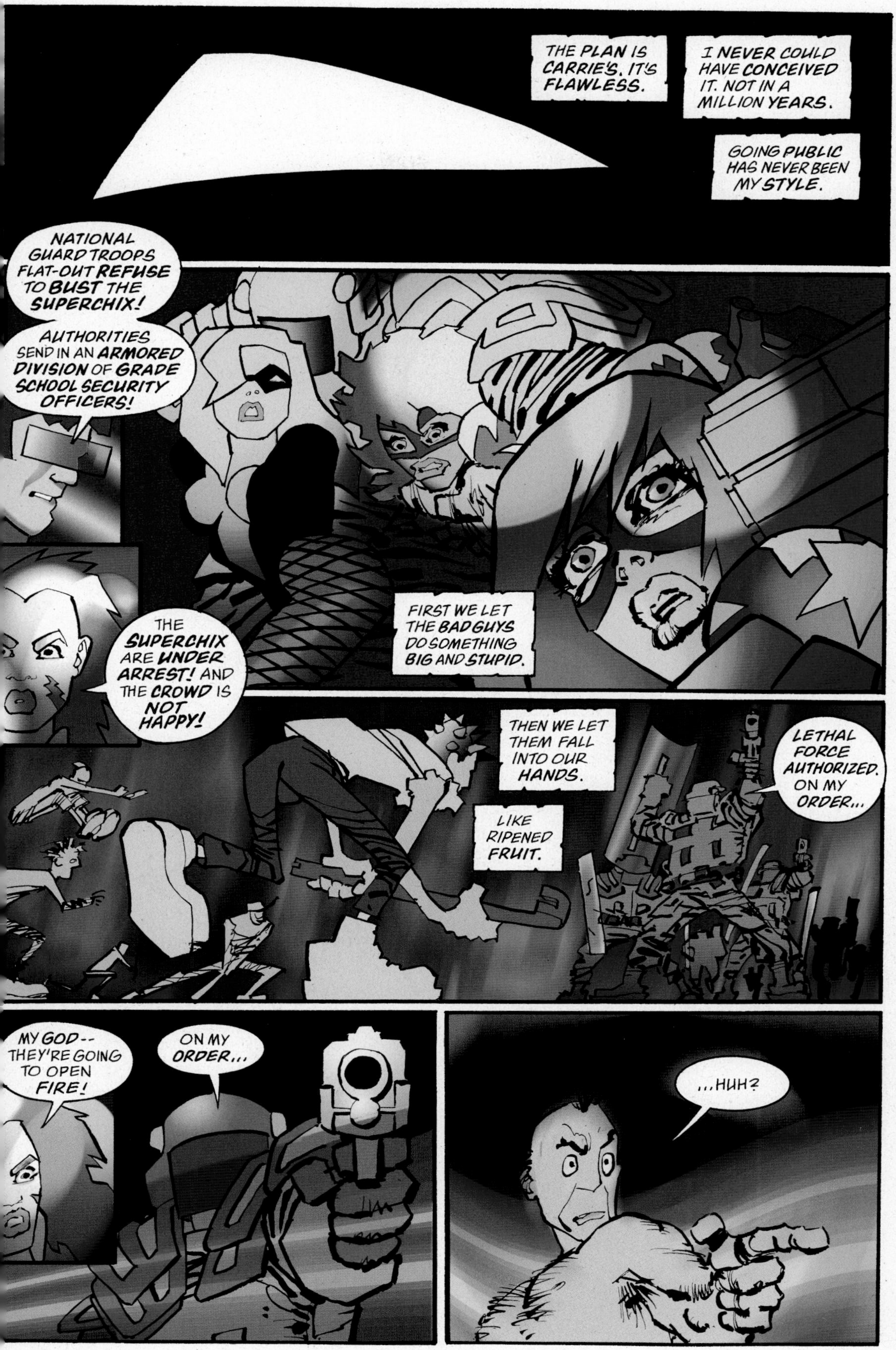
THE PLAN IS CARRIE'S. IT'S FLAWLESS.
I NEVER COULD HAVE CONCEIVED IT. NOT IN A MILLION YEARS.
GOING PUBLIC HAS NEVER BEEN MY STYLE.
NATIONAL GUARD TROOPS FLAT-OUT REFUSE TO BUST THE SUPERCHIX!
AUTHORITIES SEND IN AN ARMORED DIVISION OF GRADE SCHOOL SECURITY OFFICERS!
THE SUPERCHIX ARE UNDER ARREST! AND THE CROWD IS NOT HAPPY!
FIRST WE LET THE BAD GUYS DO SOMETHING BIG AND STUPID.
THEN WE LET THEM FALL INTO OUR HANDS.
LIKE RIPENED FRUIT.
LETHAL FORCE AUTHORIZED. ON MY ORDER...
MY GOD -- THEY'RE GOING TO OPEN FIRE!
ON MY ORDER...
...HUH?

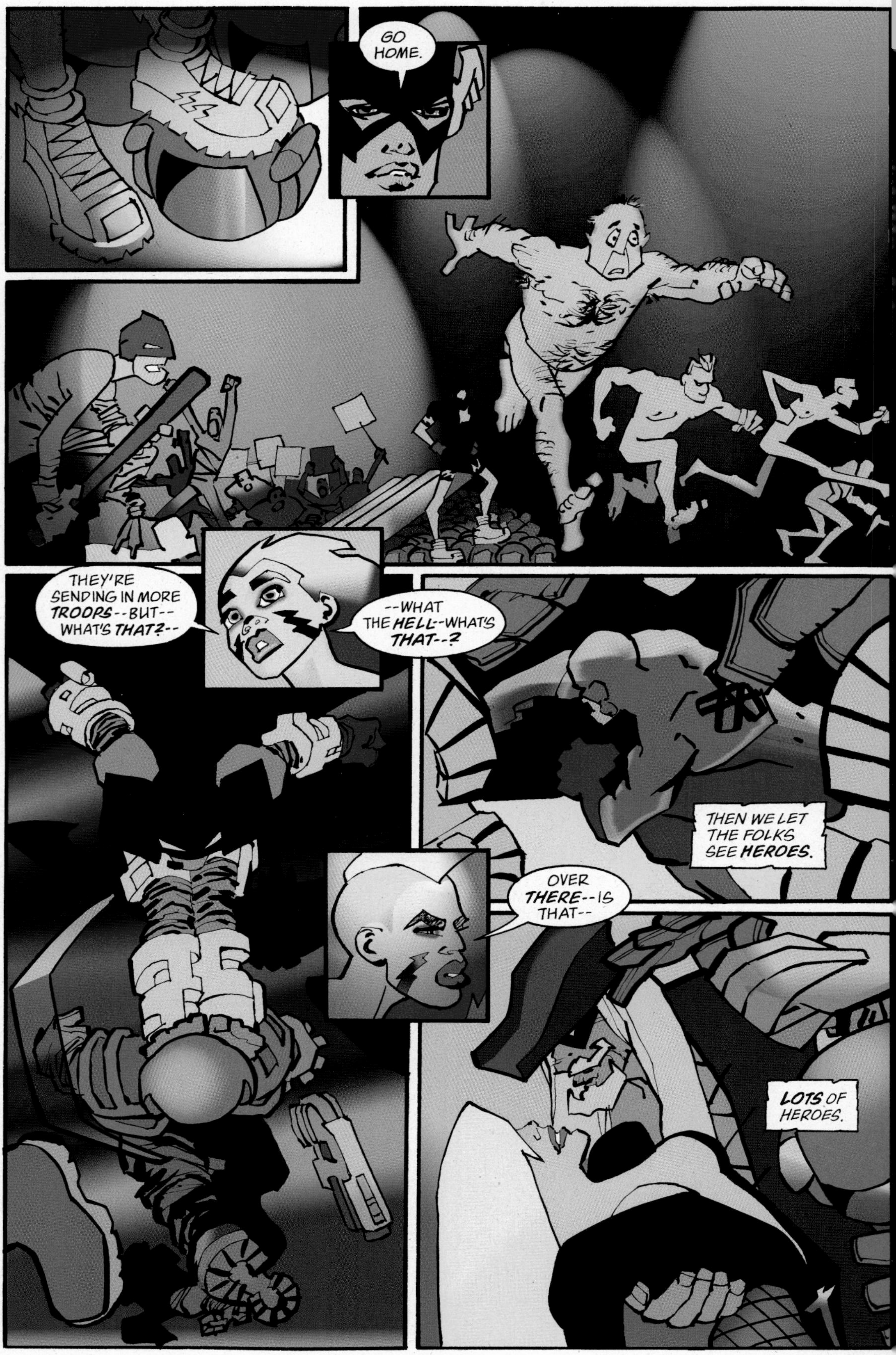
GO HOME.
THEY'RE SENDING IN MORE TROOPS--BUT--WHAT'S THAT?--
--WHAT THE HELL--WHAT'S THAT--?
THEN WE LET THE FOLKS SEE HEROES.
OVER THERE--IS THAT--
LOTS OF HEROES.

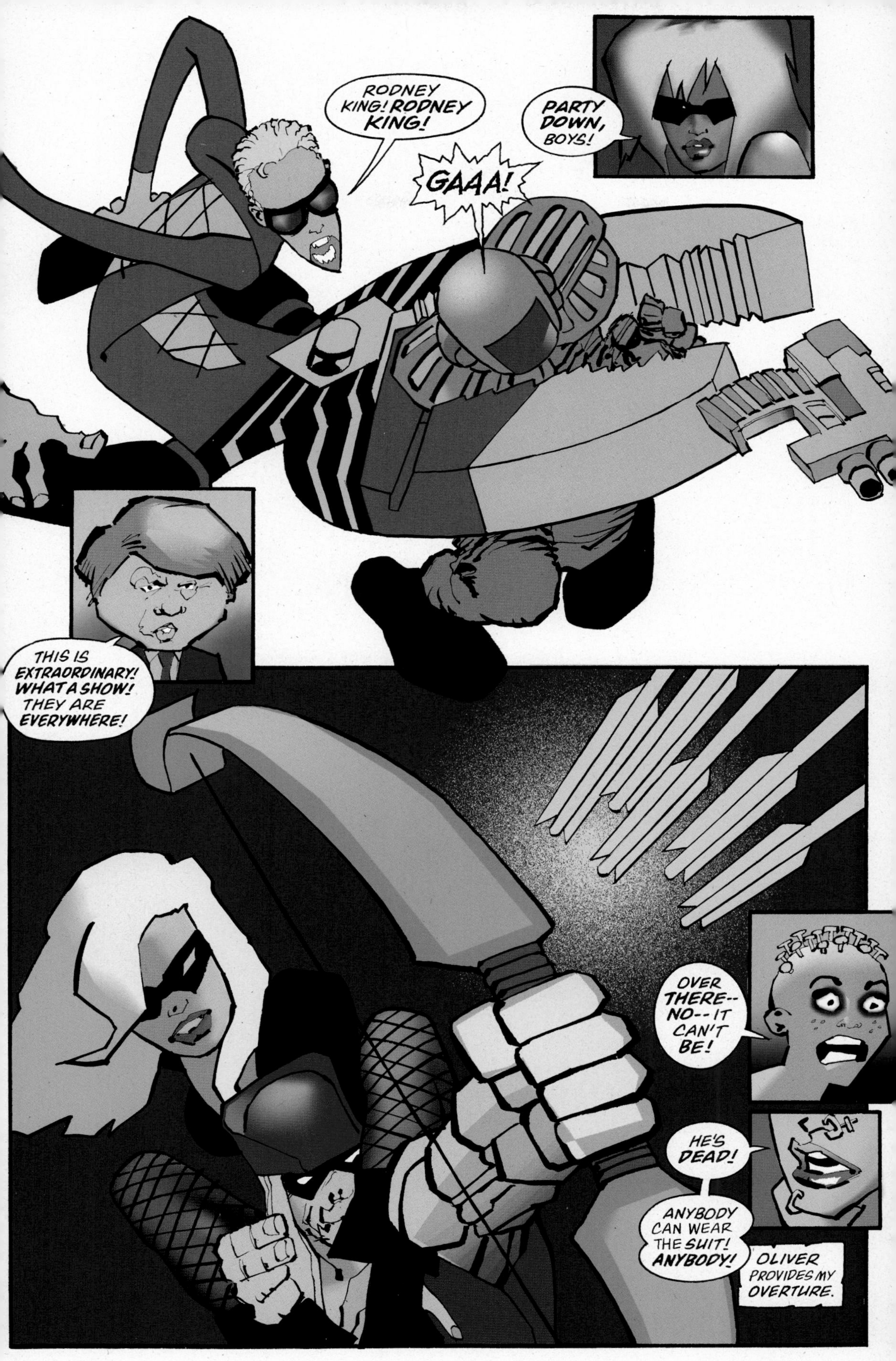
RODNEY KING! RODNEY KING!
PARTY DOWN, BOYS!
GAAA!
THIS IS EXTRAORDINARY! WHAT A SHOW! THEY ARE EVERYWHERE!
OVER THERE-- NO-- IT CAN'T BE!
HE'S DEAD!
ANYBODY CAN WEAR THE SUIT! ANYBODY!
OLIVER PROVIDES MY OVERTURE.

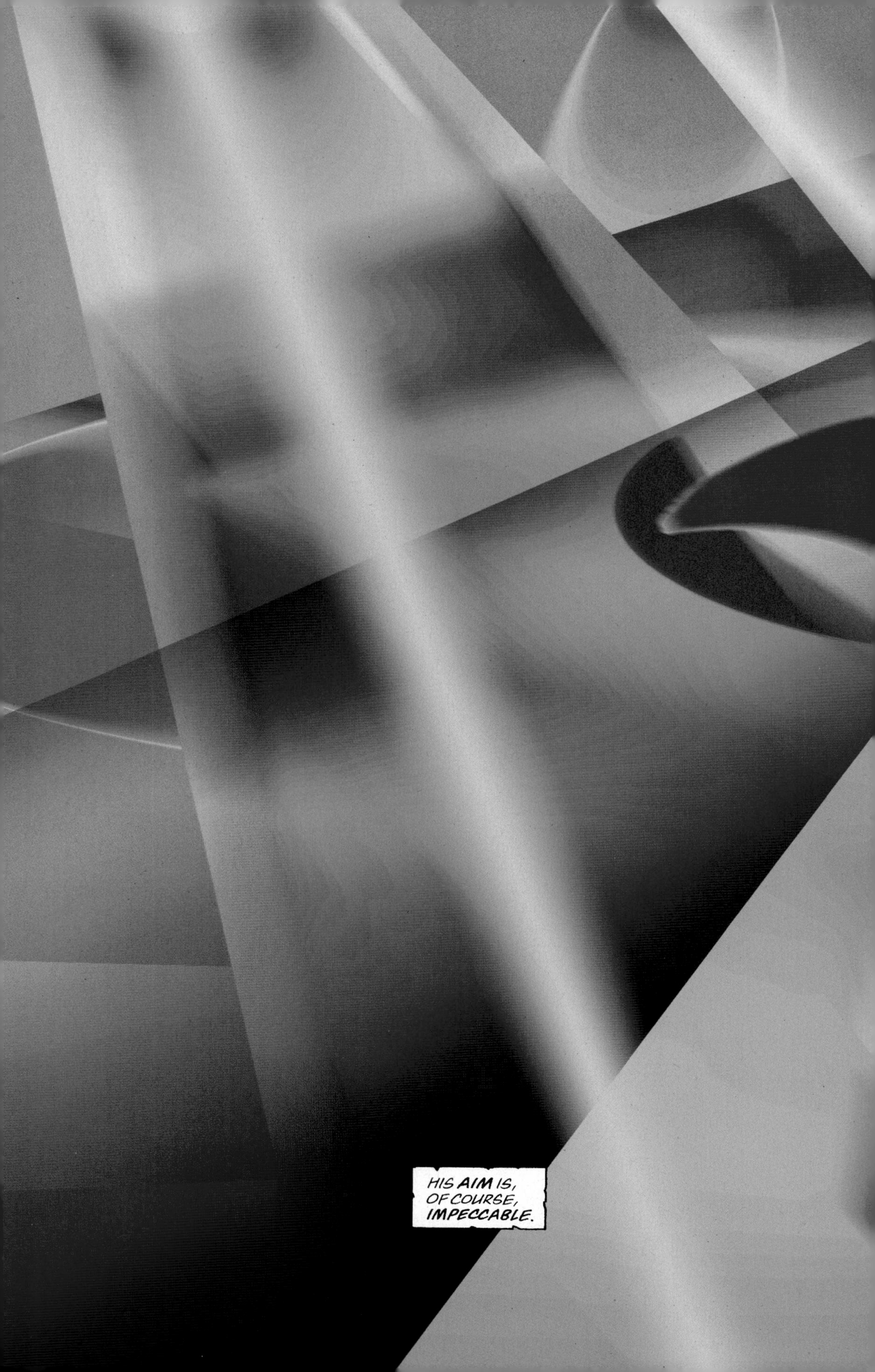
HIS **AIM** IS, OF COURSE, **IMPECCABLE**.

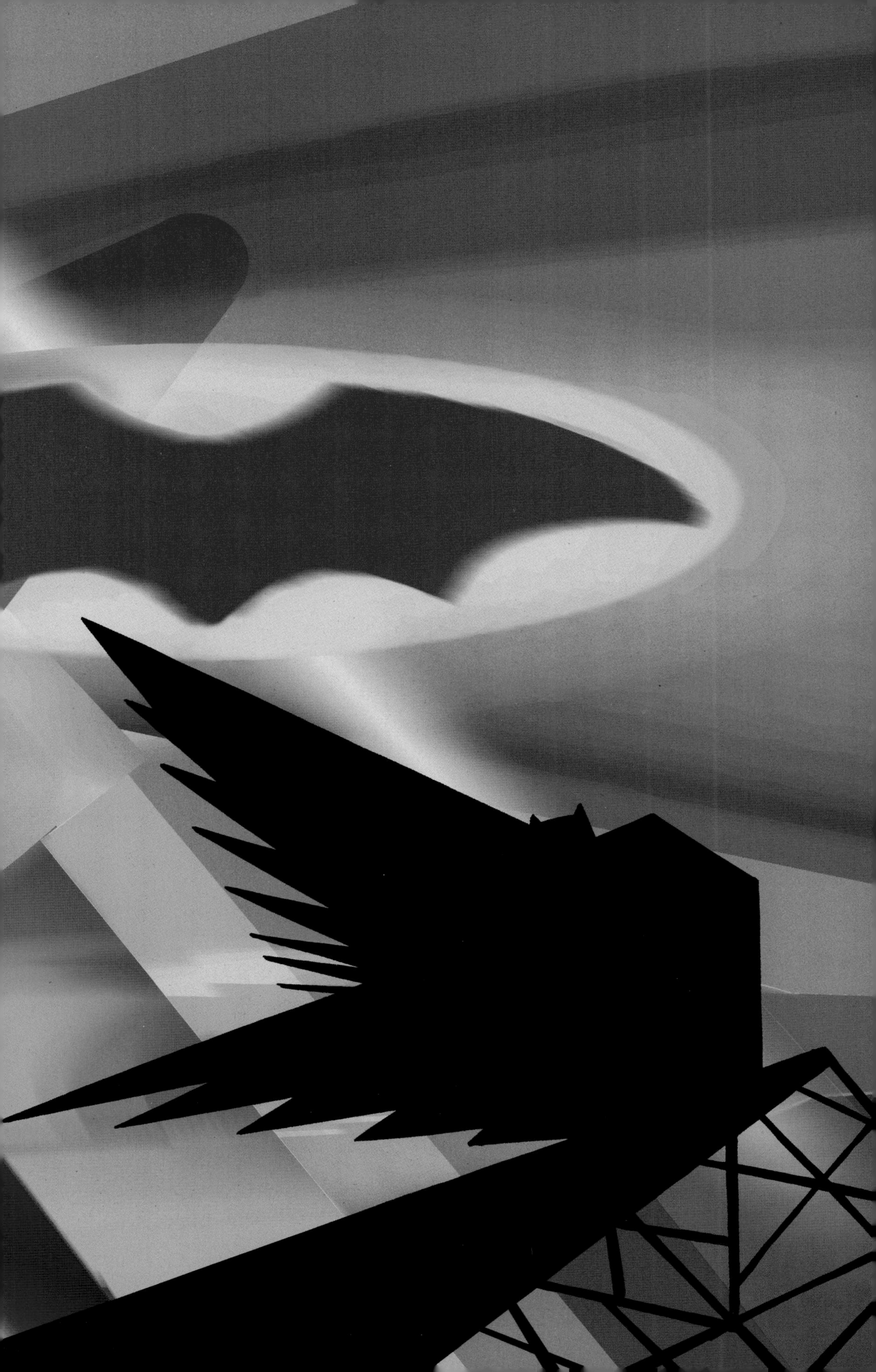

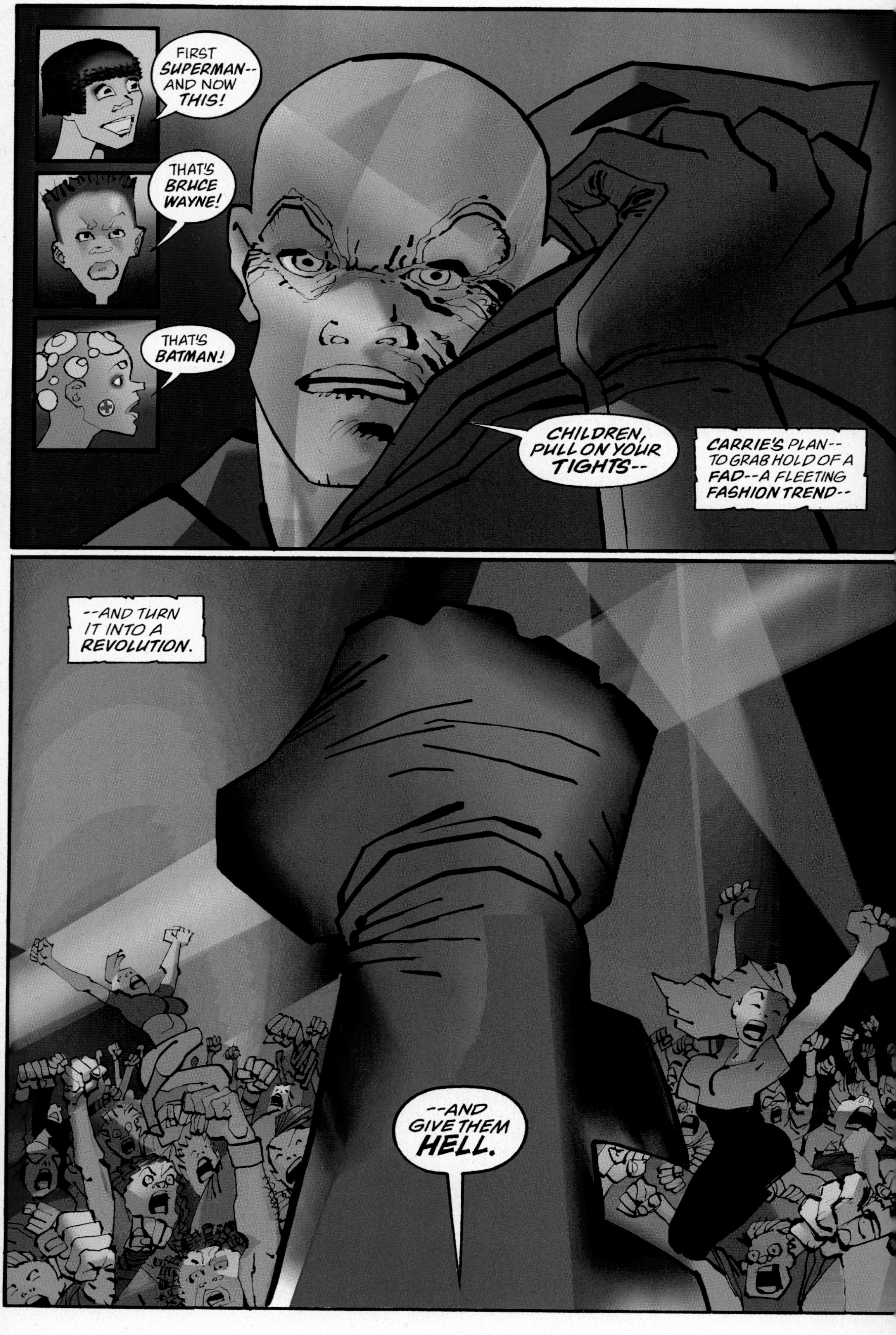
FIRST SUPERMAN-- AND NOW THIS!
THAT'S BRUCE WAYNE!
THAT'S BATMAN!
CHILDREN, PULL ON YOUR TIGHTS--
CARRIE'S PLAN-- TO GRAB HOLD OF A FAD--A FLEETING FASHION TREND--
--AND TURN IT INTO A REVOLUTION.
--AND GIVE THEM HELL.

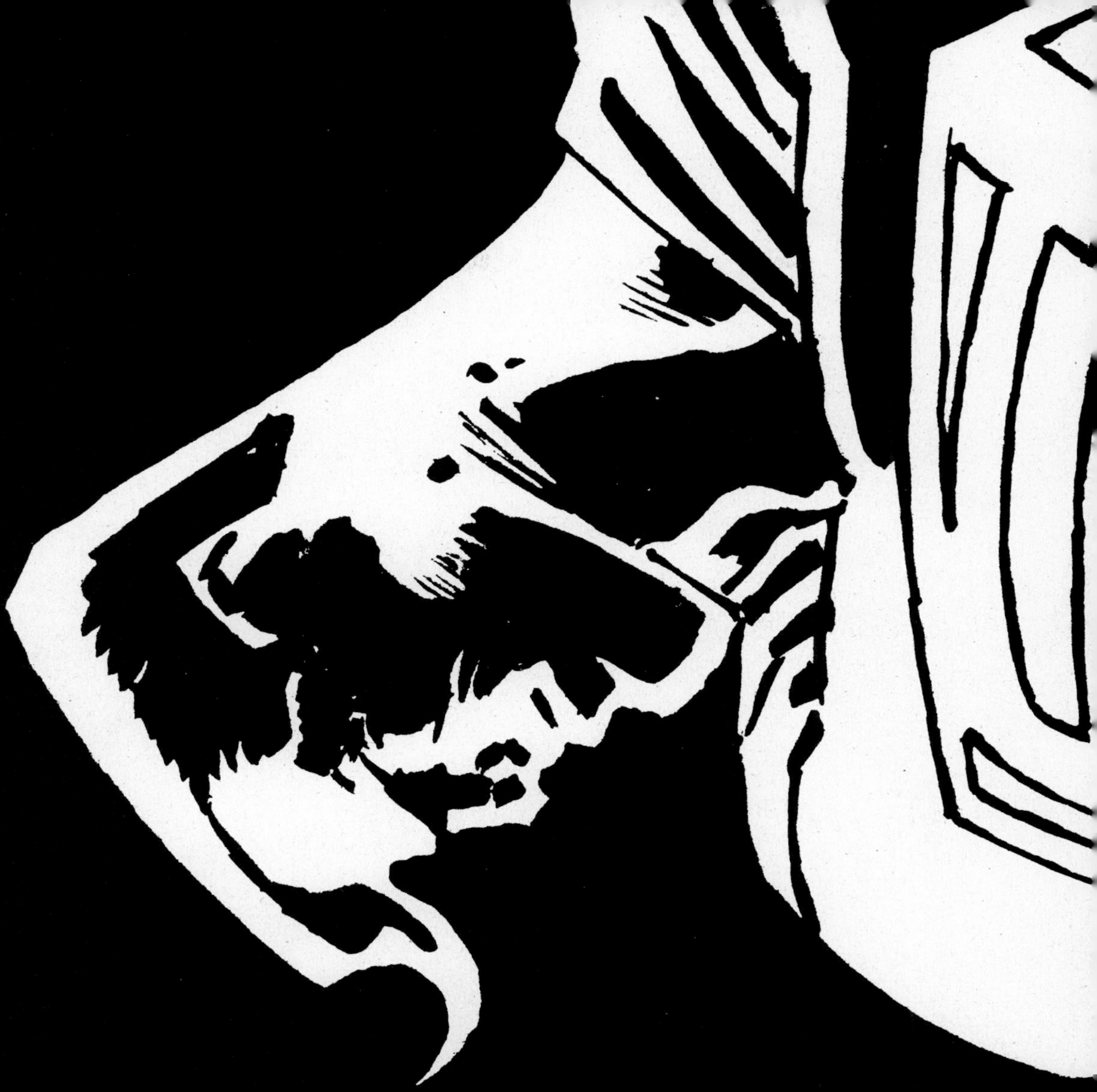

BOOK THREE.

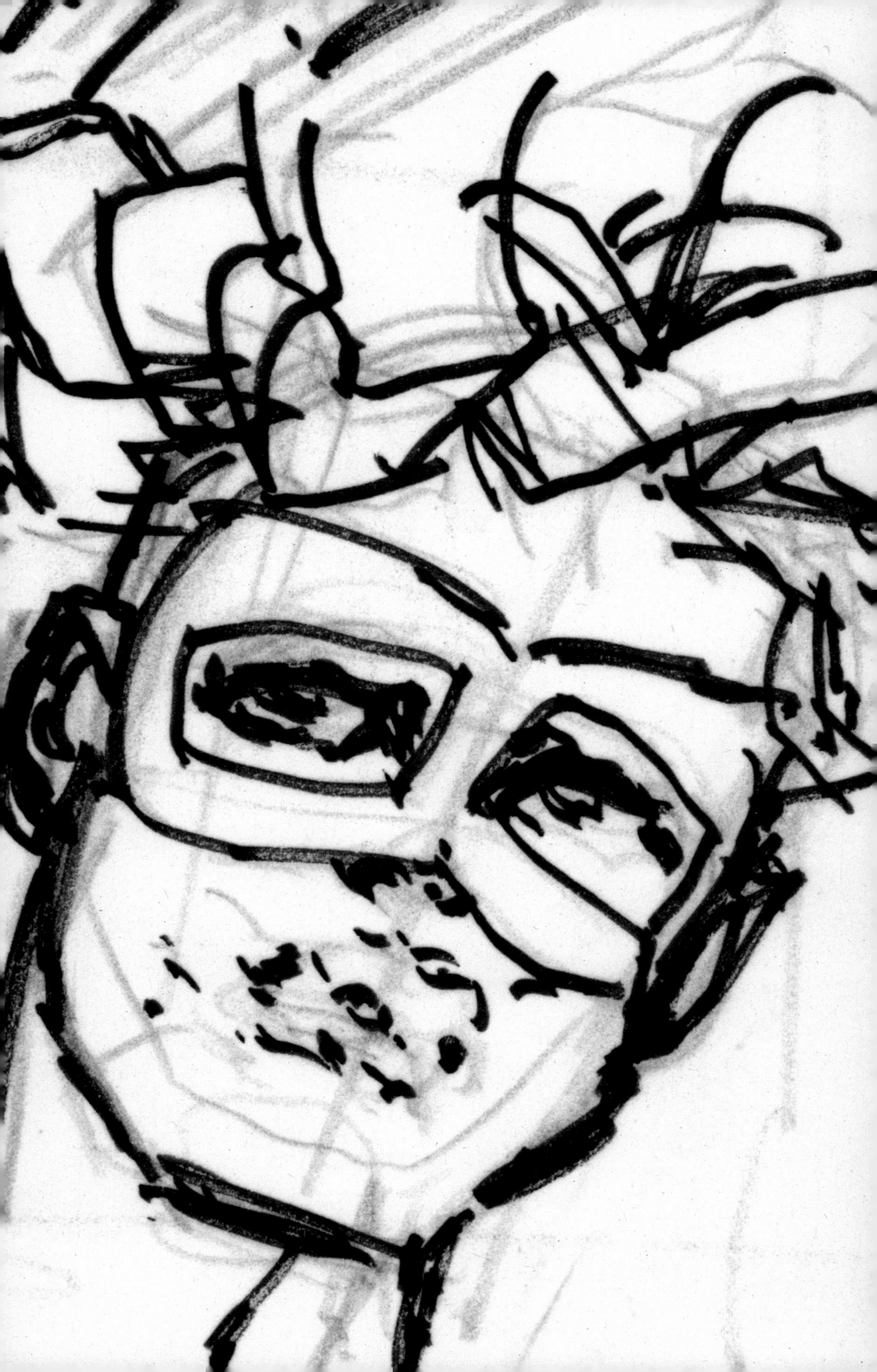

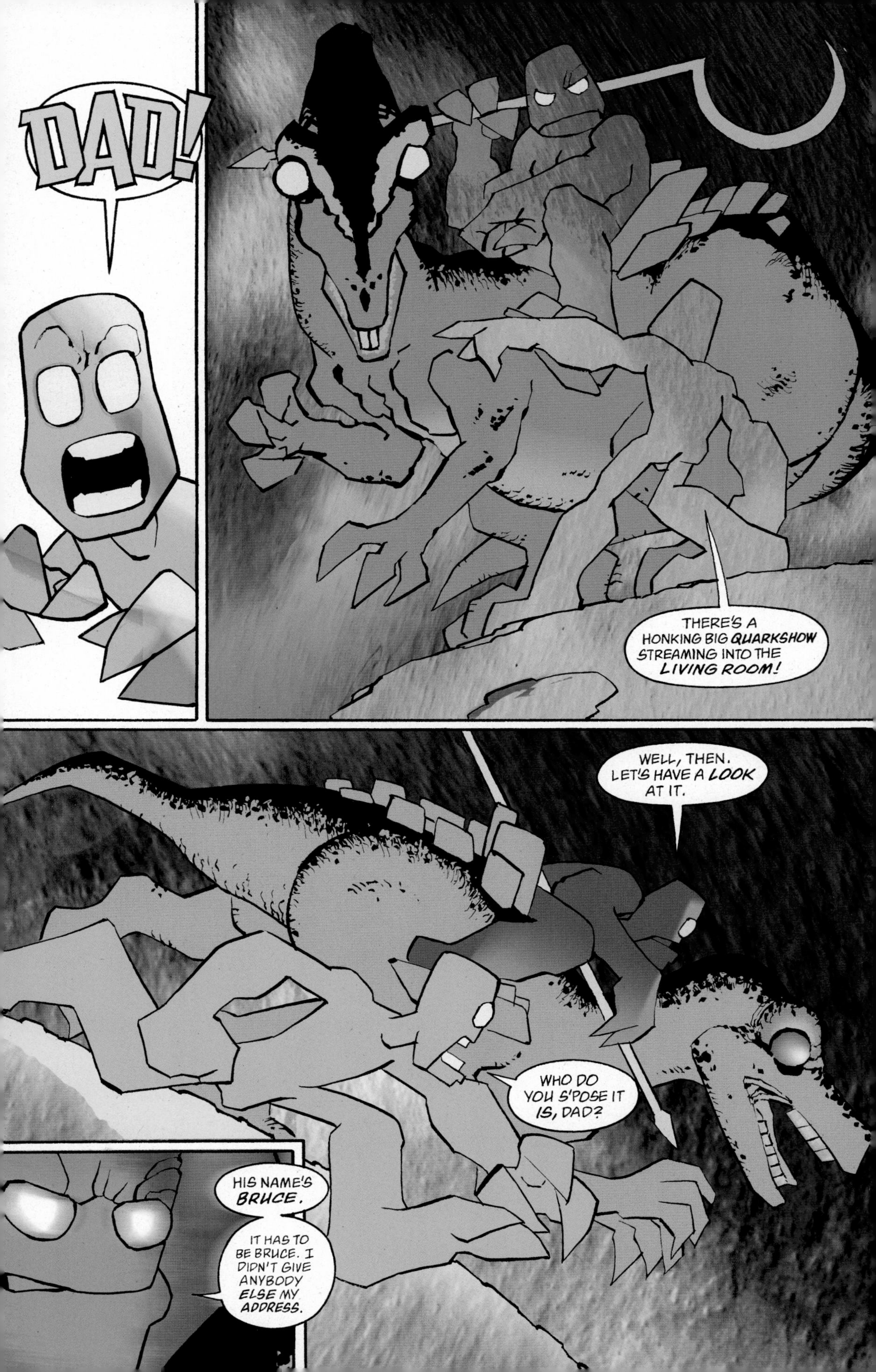
DAD!
THERE'S A HONKING BIG QUARKSHOW STREAMING INTO THE LIVING ROOM!
WELL, THEN. LET'S HAVE A LOOK AT IT.
WHO DO YOU S'POSE IT IS, DAD?
HIS NAME'S BRUCE.
IT HAS TO BE BRUCE. I DIDN'T GIVE ANYBODY ELSE MY ADDRESS.

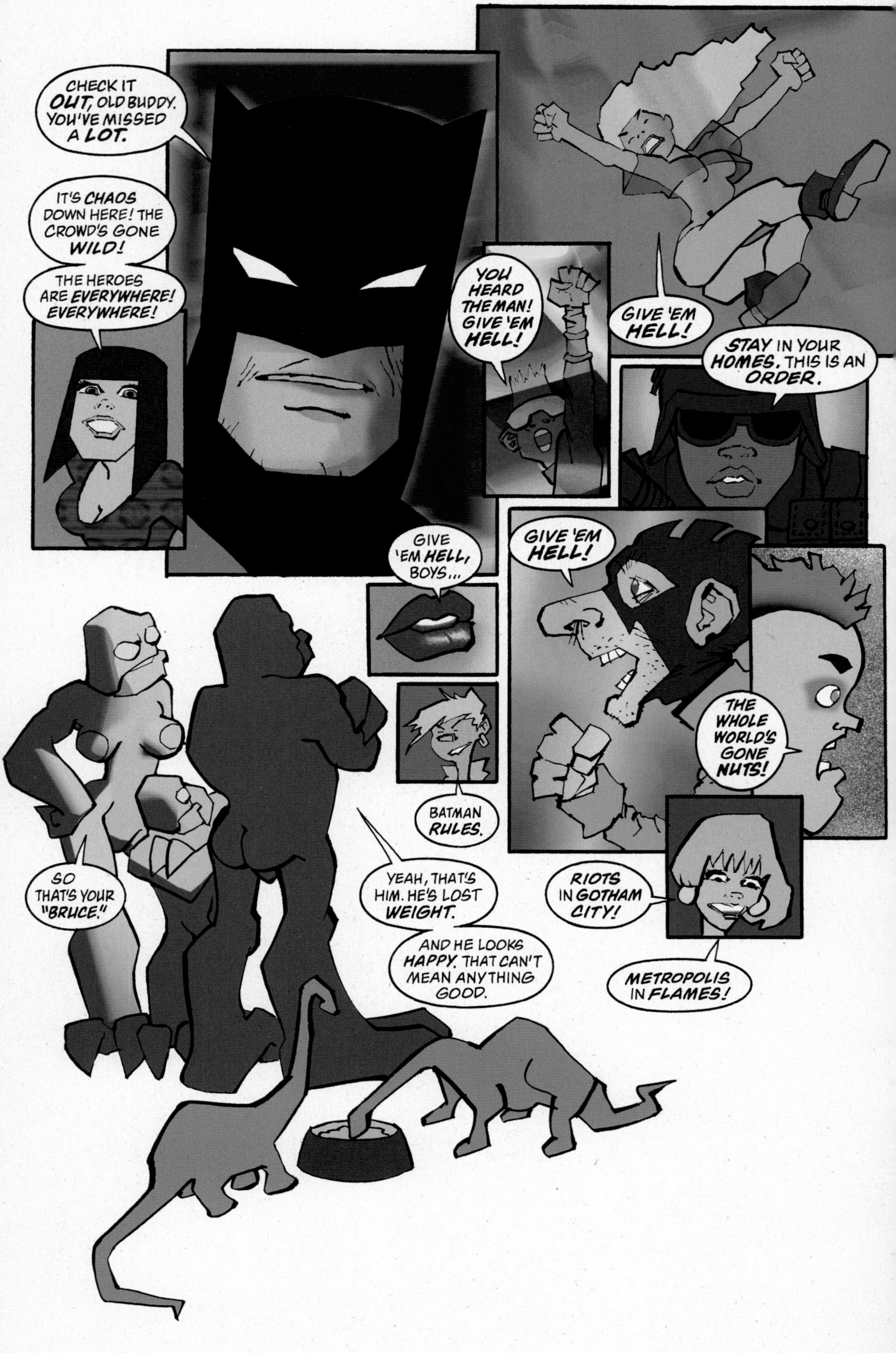
CHECK IT OUT, OLD BUDDY. YOU'VE MISSED A LOT.
IT'S CHAOS DOWN HERE! THE CROWD'S GONE WILD!
THE HEROES ARE EVERYWHERE! EVERYWHERE!
YOU HEARD THE MAN! GIVE 'EM HELL!
GIVE 'EM HELL!
STAY IN YOUR HOMES. THIS IS AN ORDER.
GIVE 'EM HELL, BOYS...
GIVE 'EM HELL!
BATMAN RULES.
THE WHOLE WORLD'S GONE NUTS!
SO THAT'S YOUR "BRUCE."
YEAH, THAT'S HIM. HE'S LOST WEIGHT.
AND HE LOOKS HAPPY. THAT CAN'T MEAN ANYTHING GOOD.
RIOTS IN GOTHAM CITY!
METROPOLIS IN FLAMES!

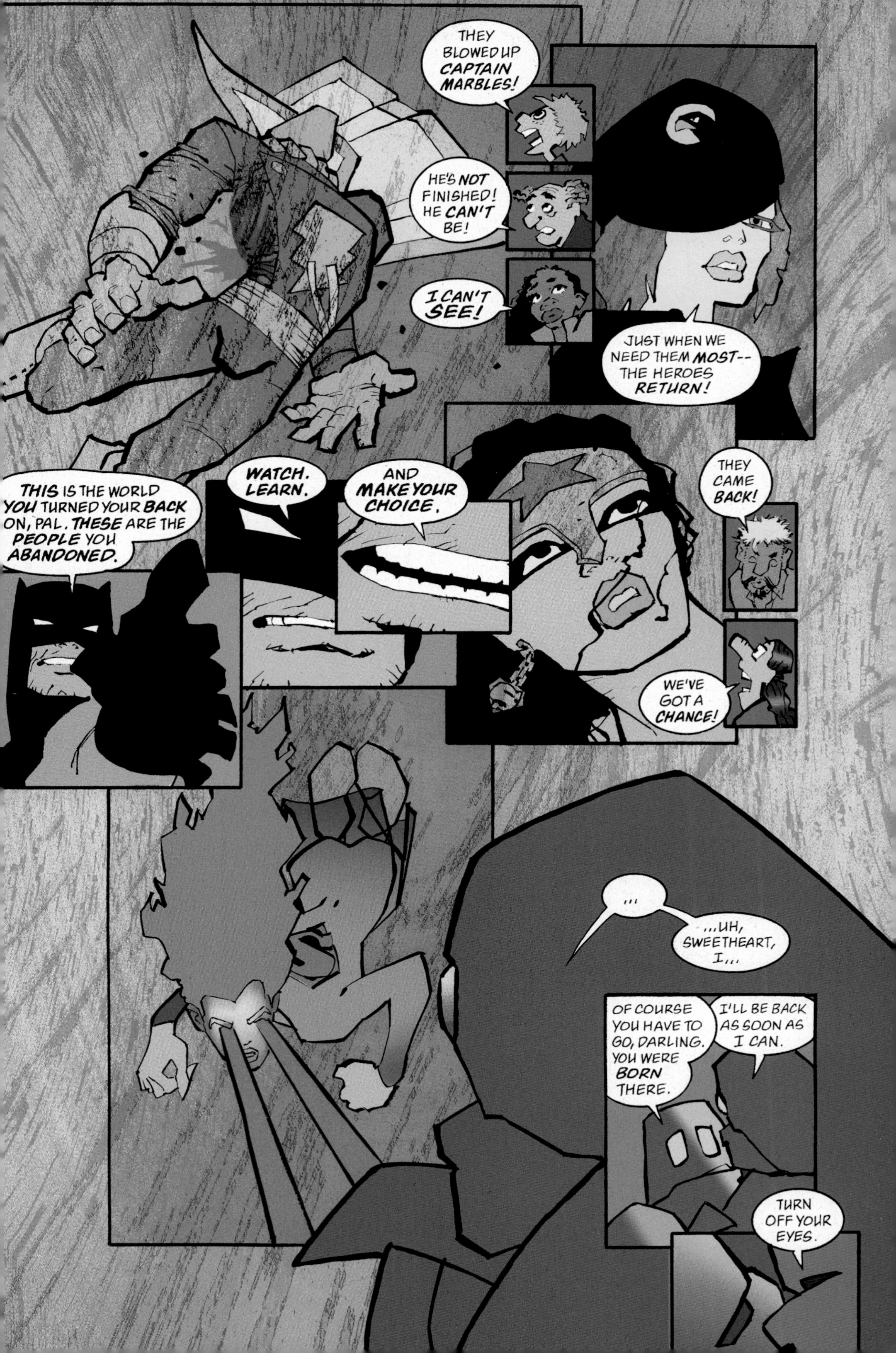
THEY BLOWED UP CAPTAIN MARBLES!
HE'S NOT FINISHED! HE CAN'T BE!
I CAN'T SEE!
JUST WHEN WE NEED THEM MOST-- THE HEROES RETURN!
THIS IS THE WORLD YOU TURNED YOUR BACK ON, PAL. THESE ARE THE PEOPLE YOU ABANDONED.
WATCH. LEARN.
AND MAKE YOUR CHOICE.
THEY CAME BACK!
WE'VE GOT A CHANCE!
...
...UH, SWEETHEART, I...
OF COURSE YOU HAVE TO GO, DARLING. YOU WERE BORN THERE.
I'LL BE BACK AS SOON AS I CAN.
TURN OFF YOUR EYES.

HE USED TO NEED A *RING*.

HE USED TO NEED A *LANTERN*.

NOW HE *IS* ONE.

HE IS PURE *WILL*. SHEER *POWER*.

HAL JORDAN.

GREEN LANTERN.

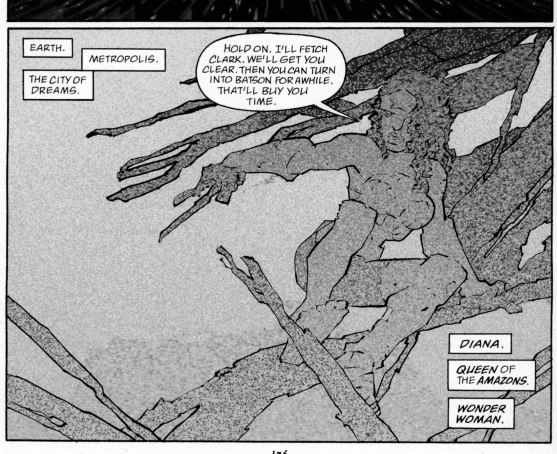

EARTH.

METROPOLIS.

THE CITY OF DREAMS.

HOLD ON. I'LL FETCH CLARK. WE'LL GET YOU CLEAR. THEN YOU CAN TURN INTO BATSON FOR AWHILE. THAT'LL BUY YOU TIME.

DIANA.

QUEEN OF THE *AMAZONS*.

WONDER WOMAN.

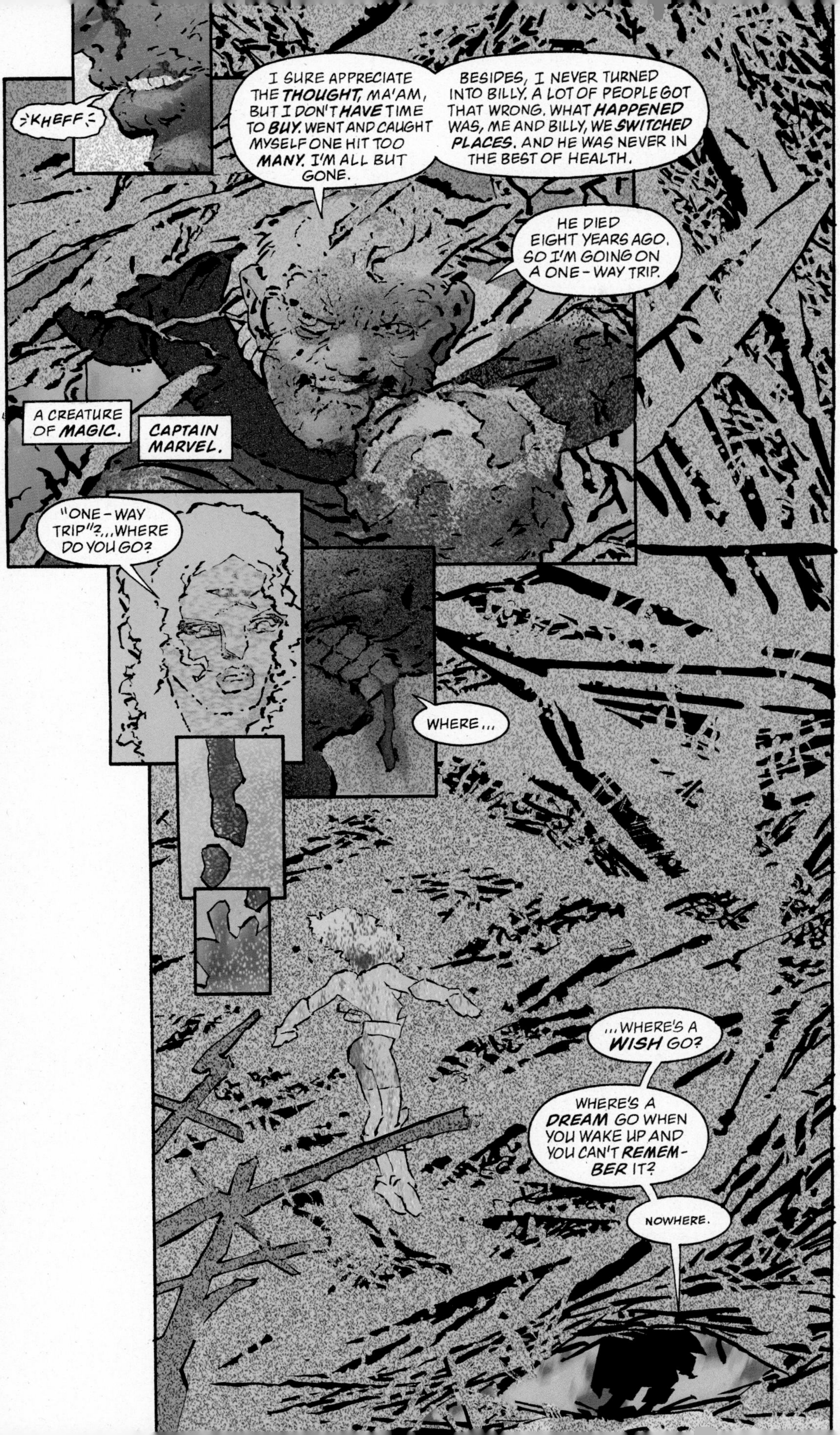
KHEFF
I SURE APPRECIATE THE THOUGHT, MA'AM, BUT I DON'T HAVE TIME TO BUY. WENT AND CAUGHT MYSELF ONE HIT TOO MANY. I'M ALL BUT GONE.
BESIDES, I NEVER TURNED INTO BILLY. A LOT OF PEOPLE GOT THAT WRONG. WHAT HAPPENED WAS, ME AND BILLY, WE SWITCHED PLACES. AND HE WAS NEVER IN THE BEST OF HEALTH.
HE DIED EIGHT YEARS AGO. SO I'M GOING ON A ONE-WAY TRIP.
A CREATURE OF MAGIC.
CAPTAIN MARVEL.
"ONE-WAY TRIP"?...WHERE DO YOU GO?
WHERE...
...WHERE'S A WISH GO?
WHERE'S A DREAM GO WHEN YOU WAKE UP AND YOU CAN'T REMEMBER IT?
NOWHERE.

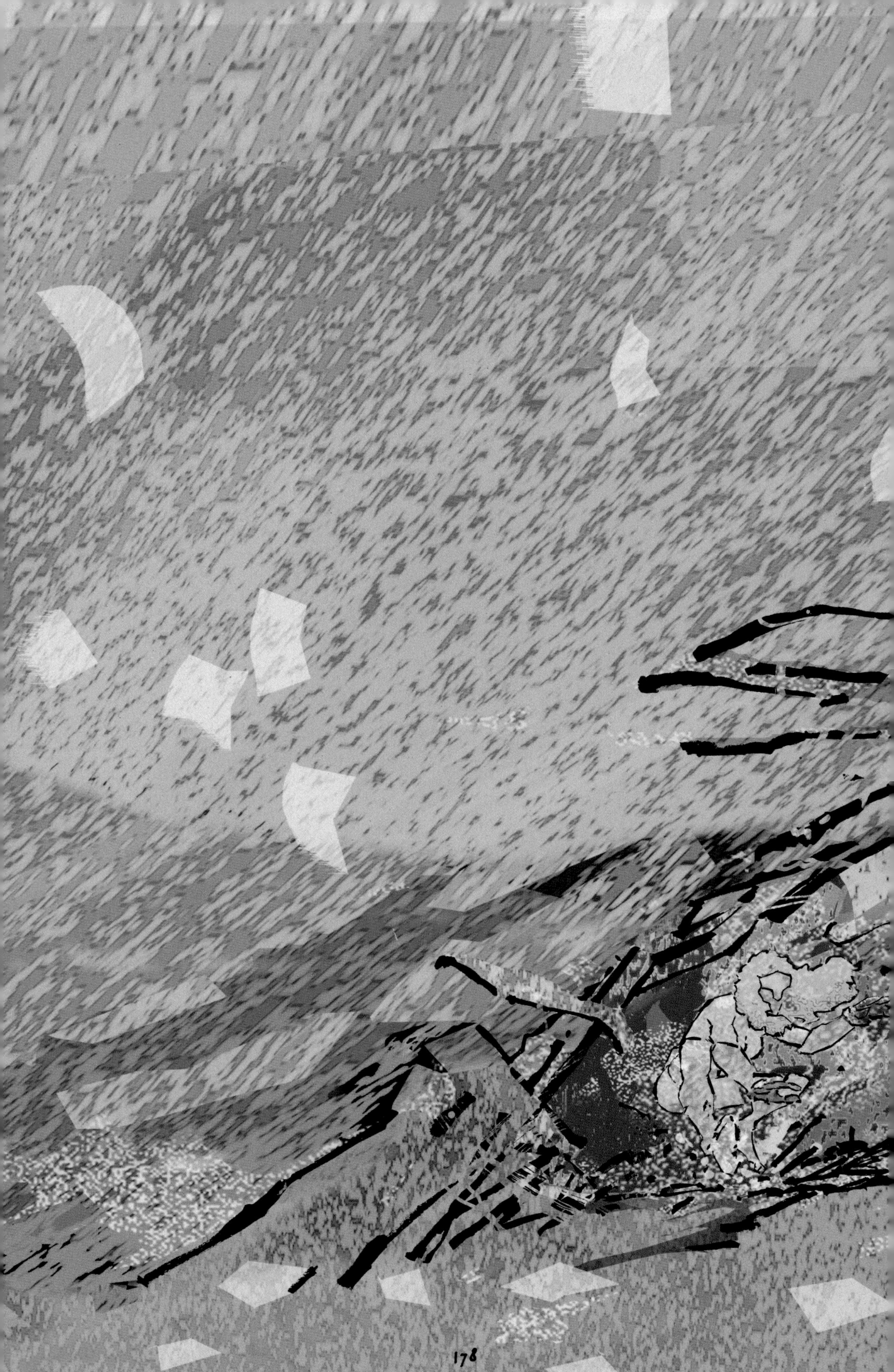

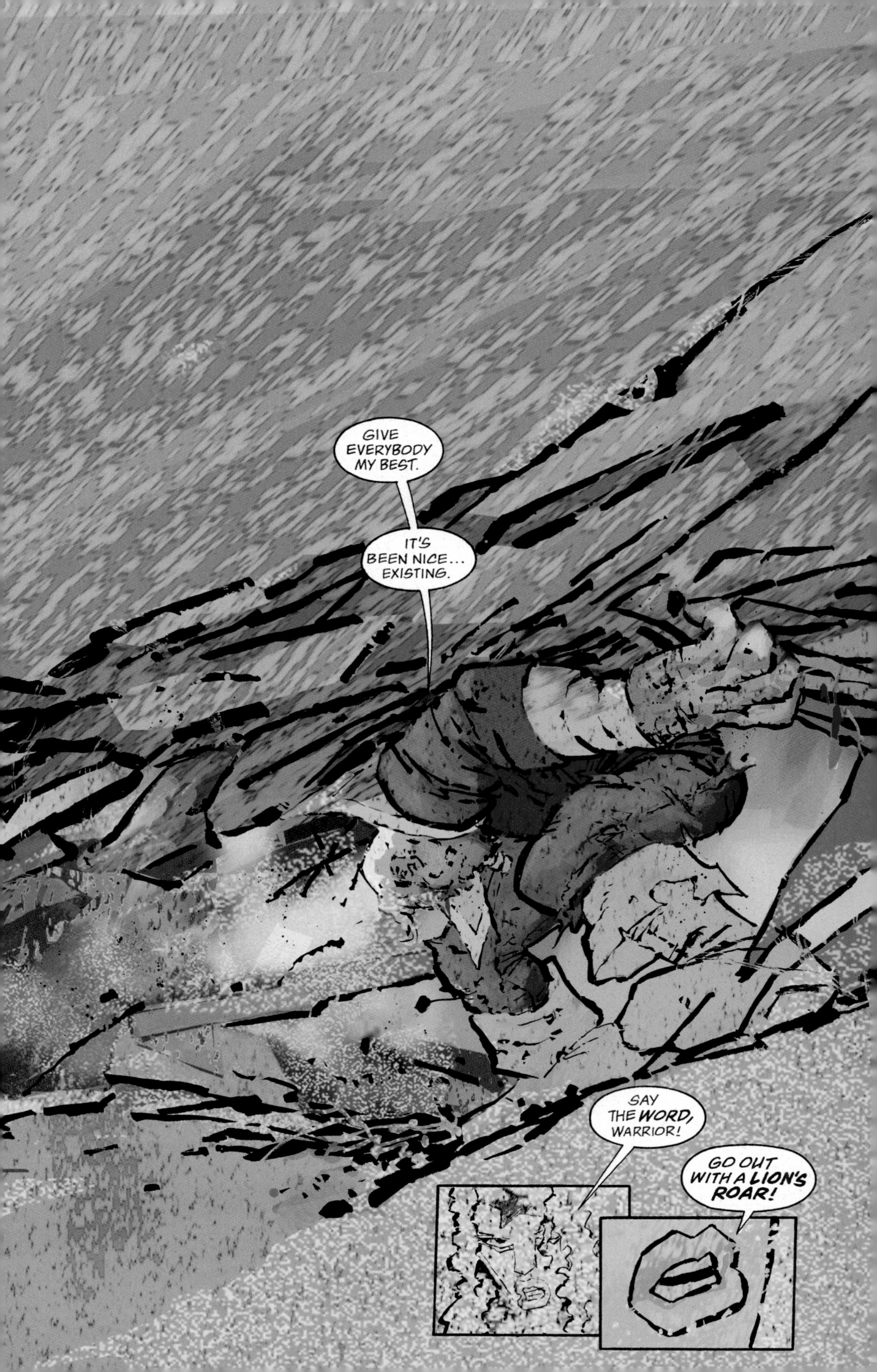
GIVE EVERYBODY MY BEST.
IT'S BEEN NICE... EXISTING.
SAY THE WORD, WARRIOR!
GO OUT WITH A LION'S ROAR!

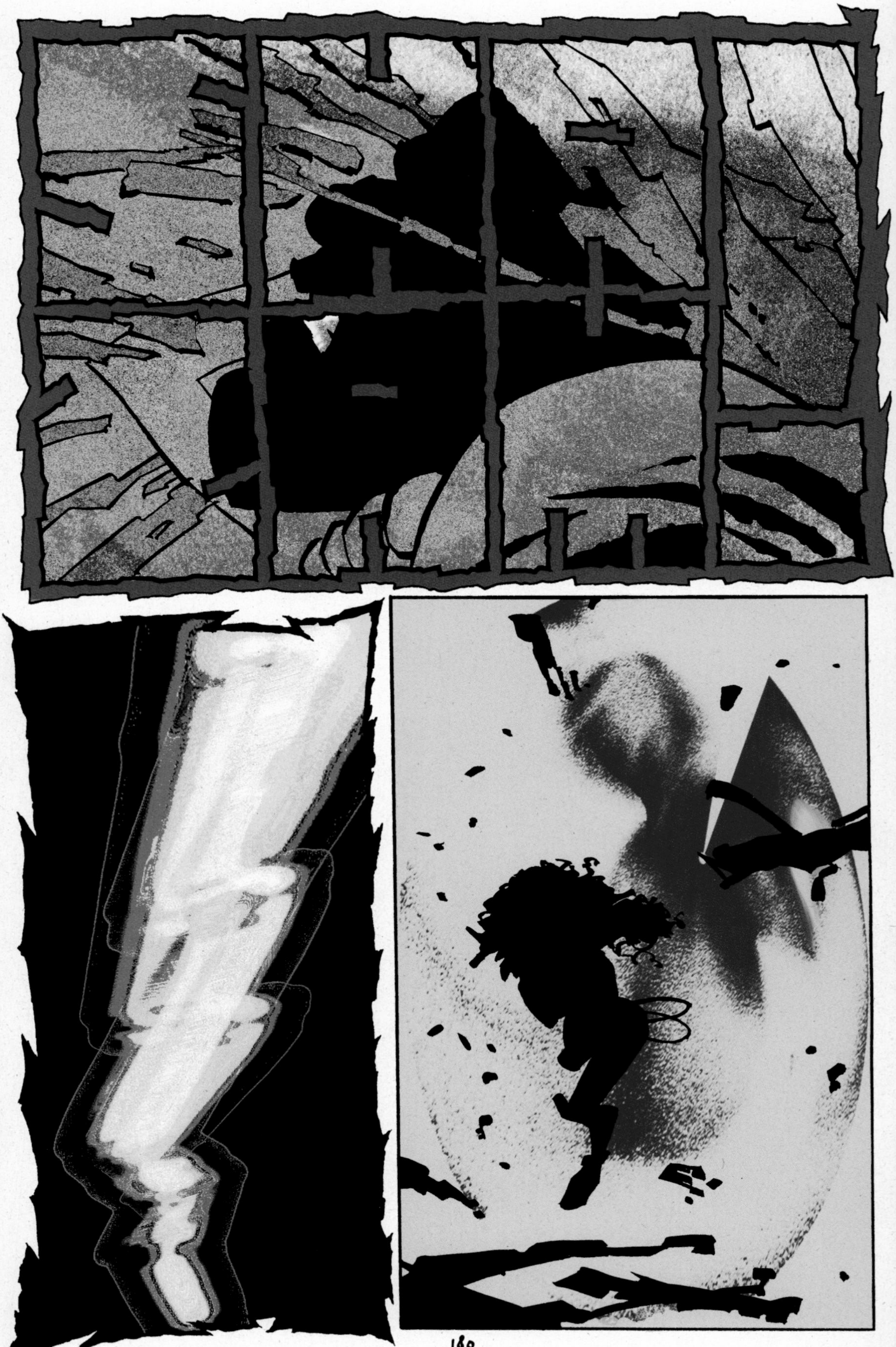

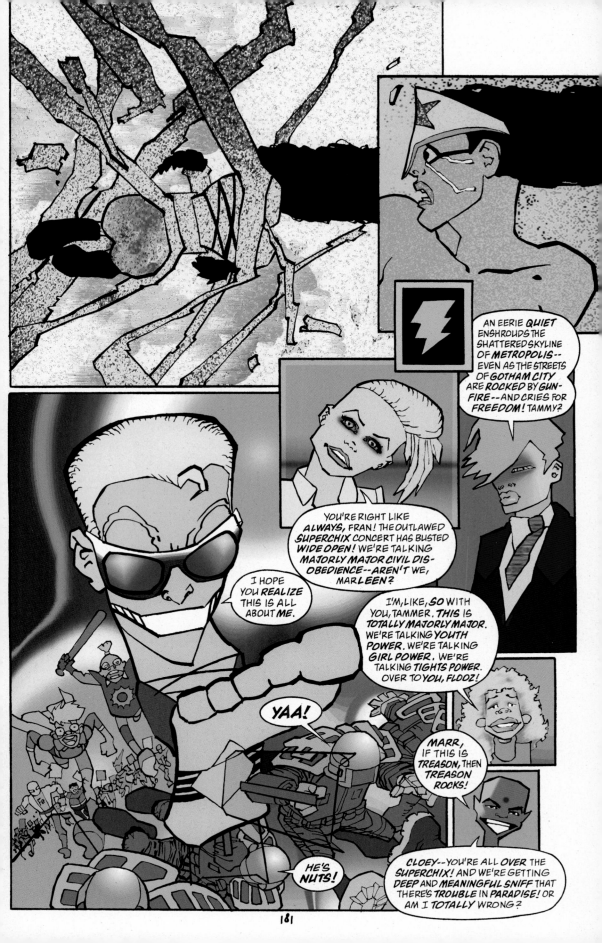

AN EERIE **QUIET** ENSHROUDS THE SHATTERED SKYLINE OF **METROPOLIS**-- EVEN AS THE STREETS OF **GOTHAM CITY** ARE **ROCKED** BY **GUN-FIRE**--AND CRIES FOR **FREEDOM**! TAMMY?

YOU'RE RIGHT LIKE **ALWAYS**, FRAN! THE OUTLAWED **SUPERCHIX** CONCERT HAS BUSTED **WIDE OPEN**! WE'RE TALKING **MAJORLY MAJOR** CIVIL DIS-OBEDIENCE--AREN'T WE, **MARLEEN**?

I HOPE YOU **REALIZE** THIS IS ALL ABOUT **ME**.

I'M, LIKE, **SO** WITH YOU, TAMMER. **THIS IS TOTALLY MAJORLY MAJOR.** WE'RE TALKING **YOUTH POWER.** WE'RE TALKING **GIRL POWER.** WE'RE TALKING **TIGHTS POWER.** OVER TO **YOU**, FLOOZ!

YAA!

MARR, IF THIS IS **TREASON**, THEN **TREASON ROCKS**!

HE'S **NUTS**!

CLOEY--YOU'RE ALL **OVER** THE **SUPERCHIX**! AND WE'RE GETTING **DEEP** AND **MEANINGFUL** SNIFF THAT THERE'S **TROUBLE** IN **PARADISE**! OR AM I **TOTALLY** WRONG?

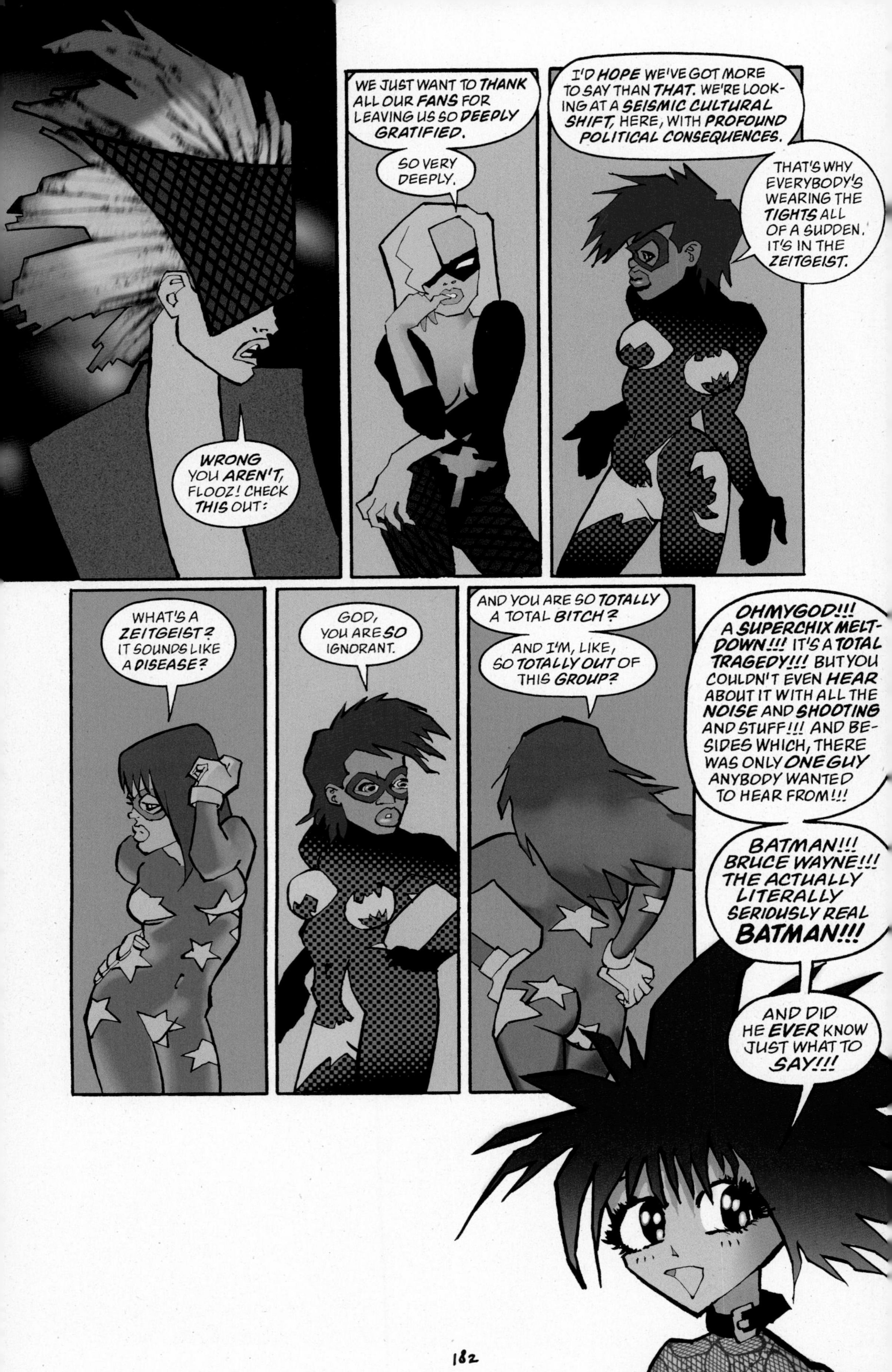
WRONG YOU AREN'T, FLOOZ! CHECK THIS OUT:
WE JUST WANT TO THANK ALL OUR FANS FOR LEAVING US SO DEEPLY GRATIFIED.
SO VERY DEEPLY.
I'D HOPE WE'VE GOT MORE TO SAY THAN THAT. WE'RE LOOKING AT A SEISMIC CULTURAL SHIFT, HERE, WITH PROFOUND POLITICAL CONSEQUENCES.
THAT'S WHY EVERYBODY'S WEARING THE TIGHTS ALL OF A SUDDEN. IT'S IN THE ZEITGEIST.
WHAT'S A ZEITGEIST? IT SOUNDS LIKE A DISEASE?
GOD, YOU ARE SO IGNORANT.
AND YOU ARE SO TOTALLY A TOTAL BITCH?
AND I'M, LIKE, SO TOTALLY OUT OF THIS GROUP?
OHMYGOD!!! A SUPERCHIX MELT-DOWN!!! IT'S A TOTAL TRAGEDY!!! BUT YOU COULDN'T EVEN HEAR ABOUT IT WITH ALL THE NOISE AND SHOOTING AND STUFF!!! AND BESIDES WHICH, THERE WAS ONLY ONE GUY ANYBODY WANTED TO HEAR FROM!!!
BATMAN!!! BRUCE WAYNE!!! THE ACTUALLY LITERALLY SERIOUSLY REAL BATMAN!!!
AND DID HE EVER KNOW JUST WHAT TO SAY!!!

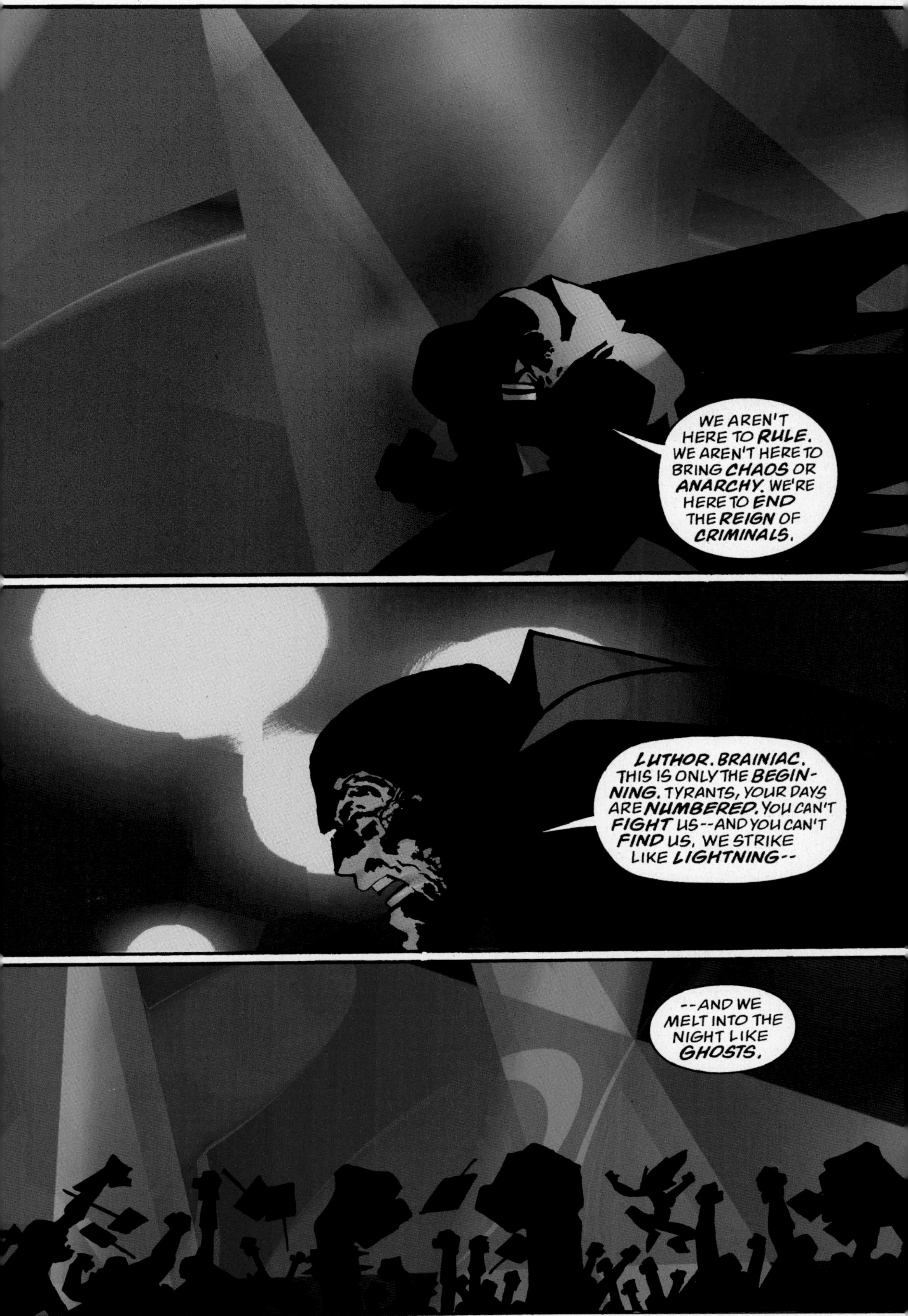
WE AREN'T HERE TO RULE. WE AREN'T HERE TO BRING CHAOS OR ANARCHY. WE'RE HERE TO END THE REIGN OF CRIMINALS.
LUTHOR. BRAINIAC. THIS IS ONLY THE BEGIN-NING. TYRANTS, YOUR DAYS ARE NUMBERED. YOU CAN'T FIGHT US--AND YOU CAN'T FIND US. WE STRIKE LIKE LIGHTNING--
--AND WE MELT INTO THE NIGHT LIKE GHOSTS.

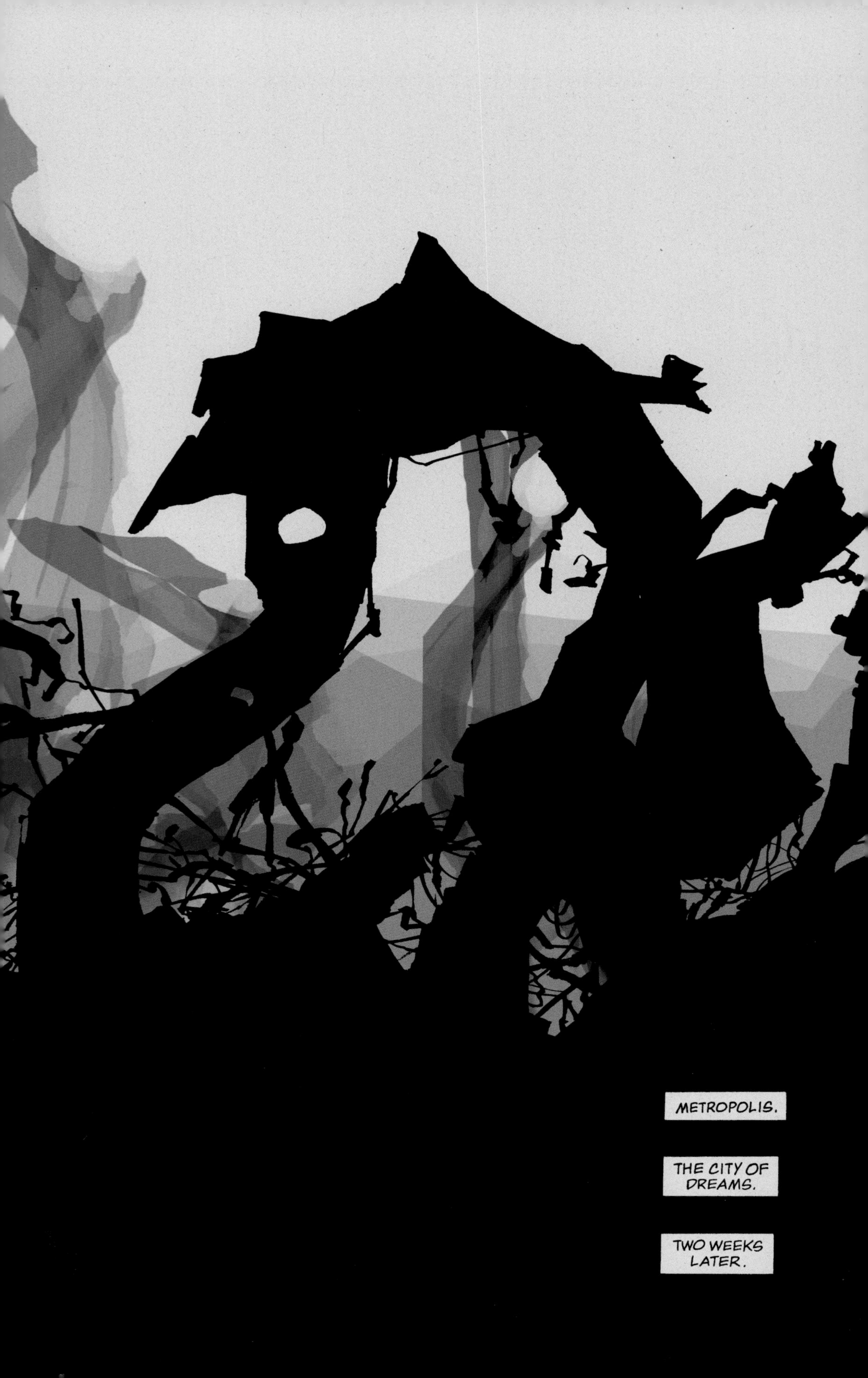
METROPOLIS.
THE CITY OF DREAMS.
TWO WEEKS LATER.

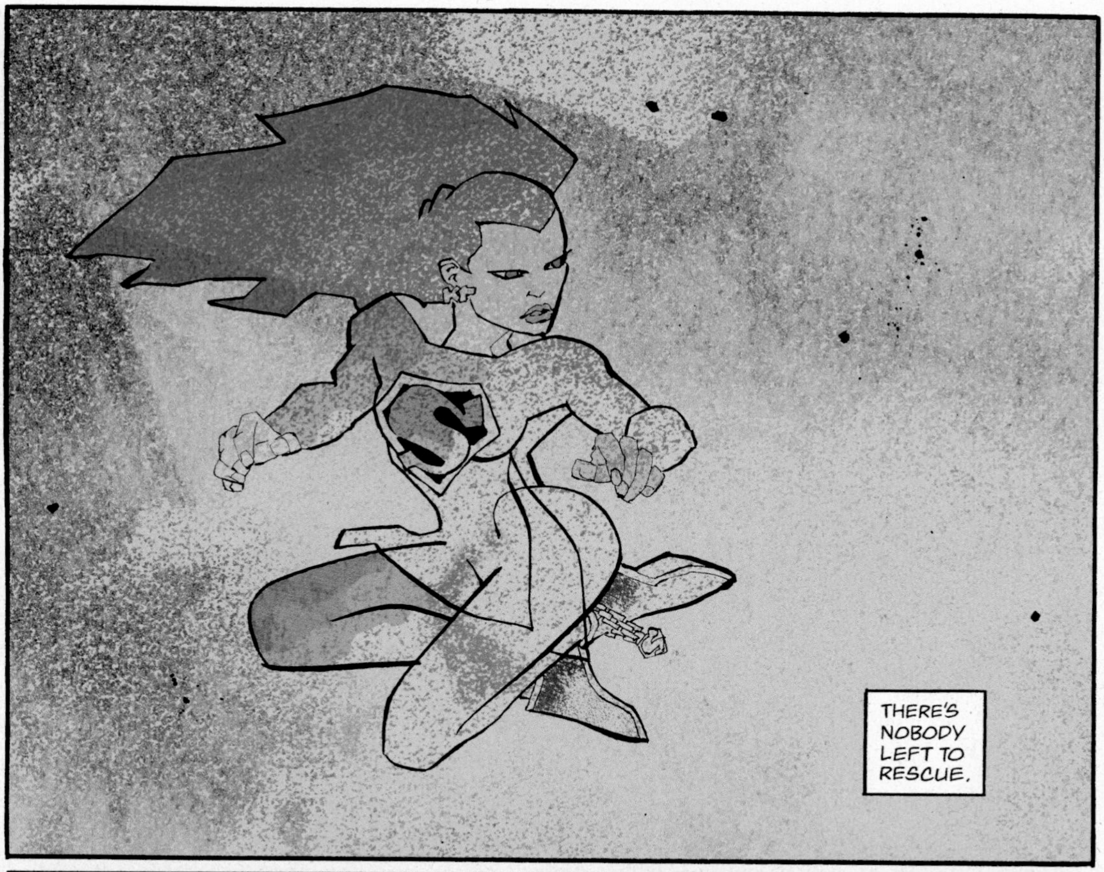
THERE'S NOBODY LEFT TO RESCUE.

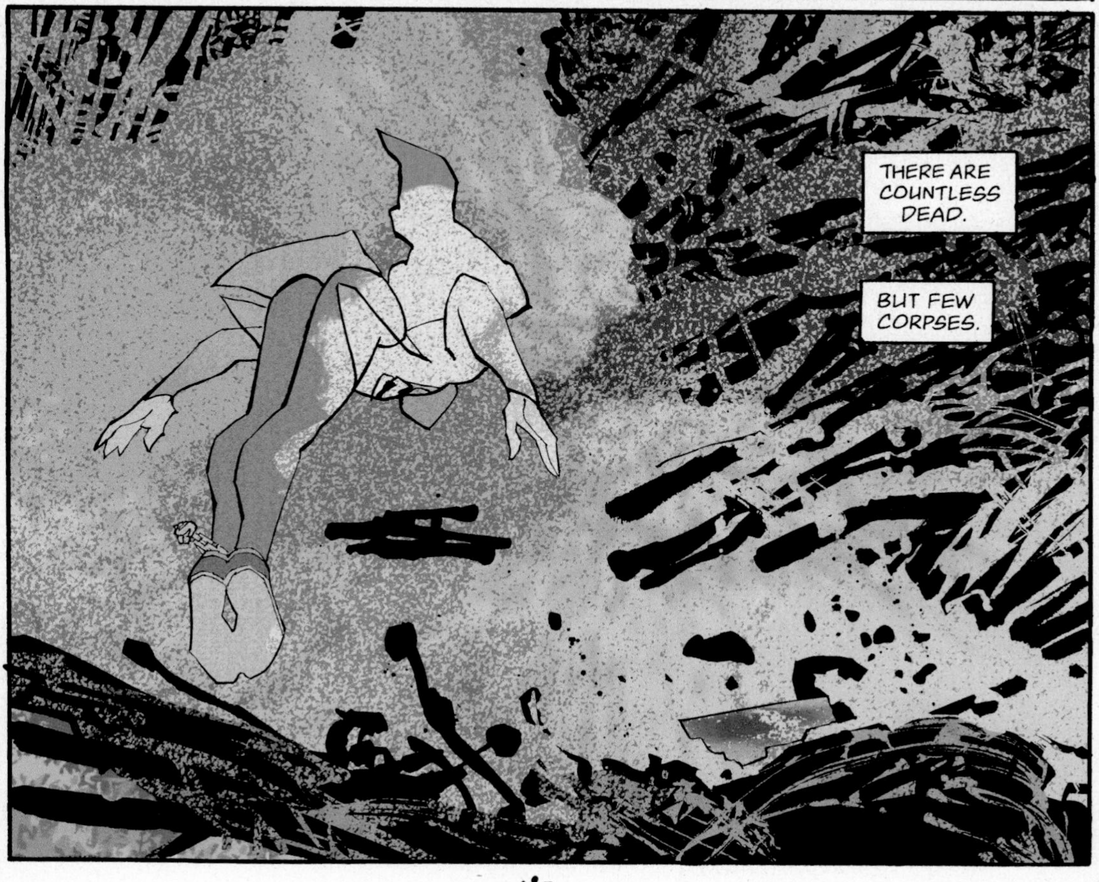
THERE ARE COUNTLESS DEAD.
BUT FEW CORPSES.

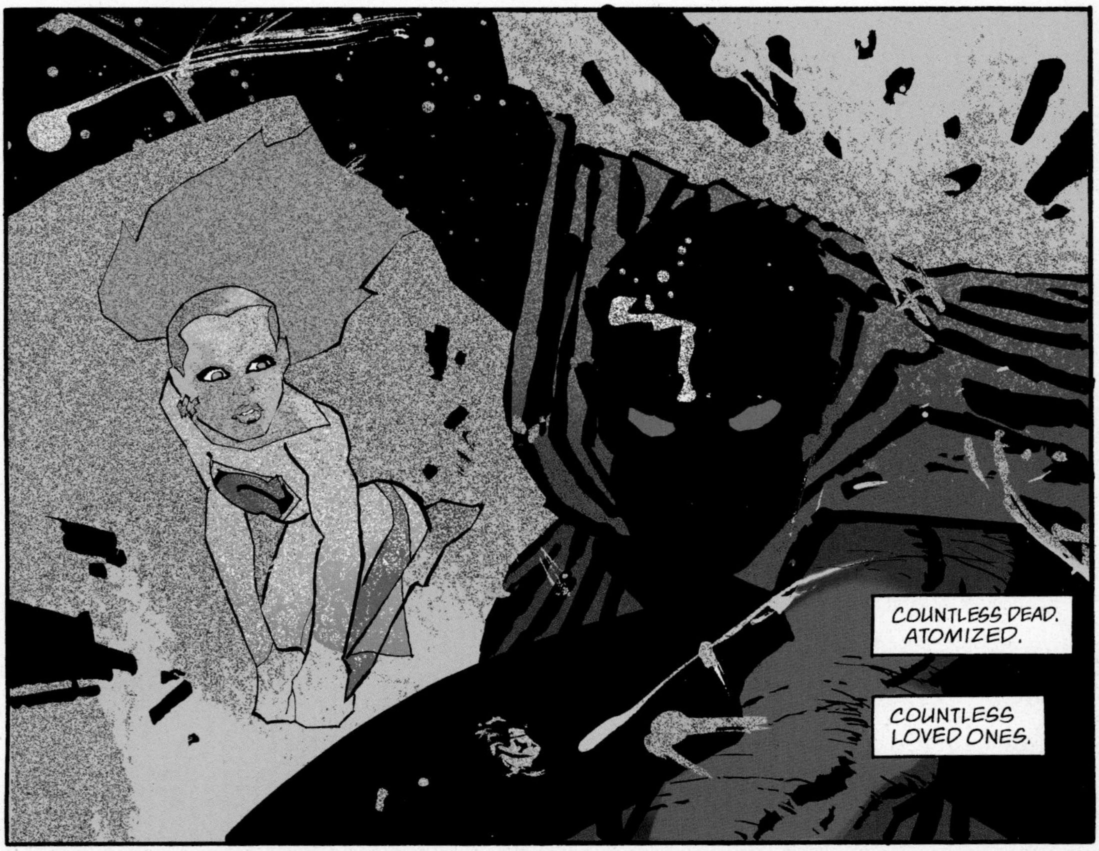
COUNTLESS DEAD.
ATOMIZED.
COUNTLESS
LOVED ONES.

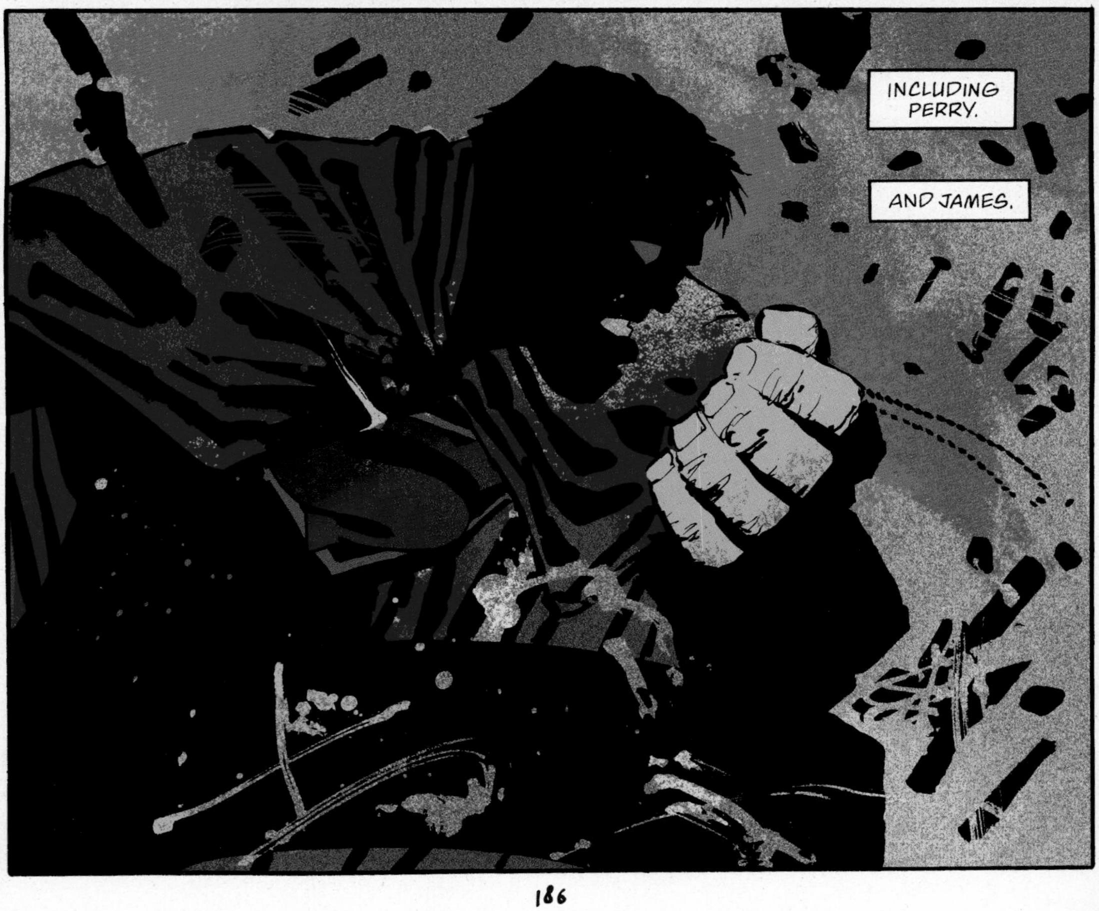
INCLUDING
PERRY.
AND JAMES.

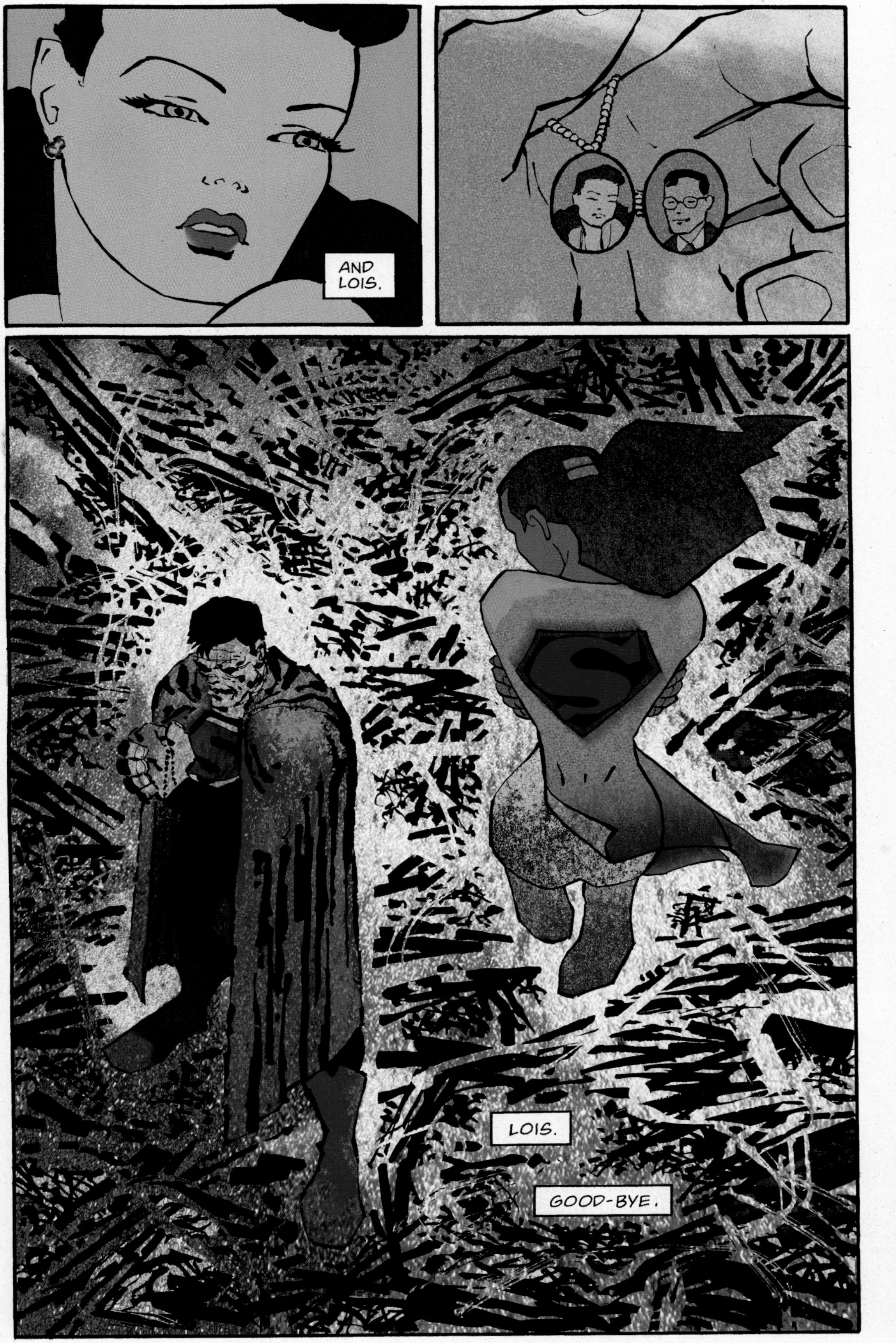
AND LOIS.
LOIS.
GOOD-BYE.

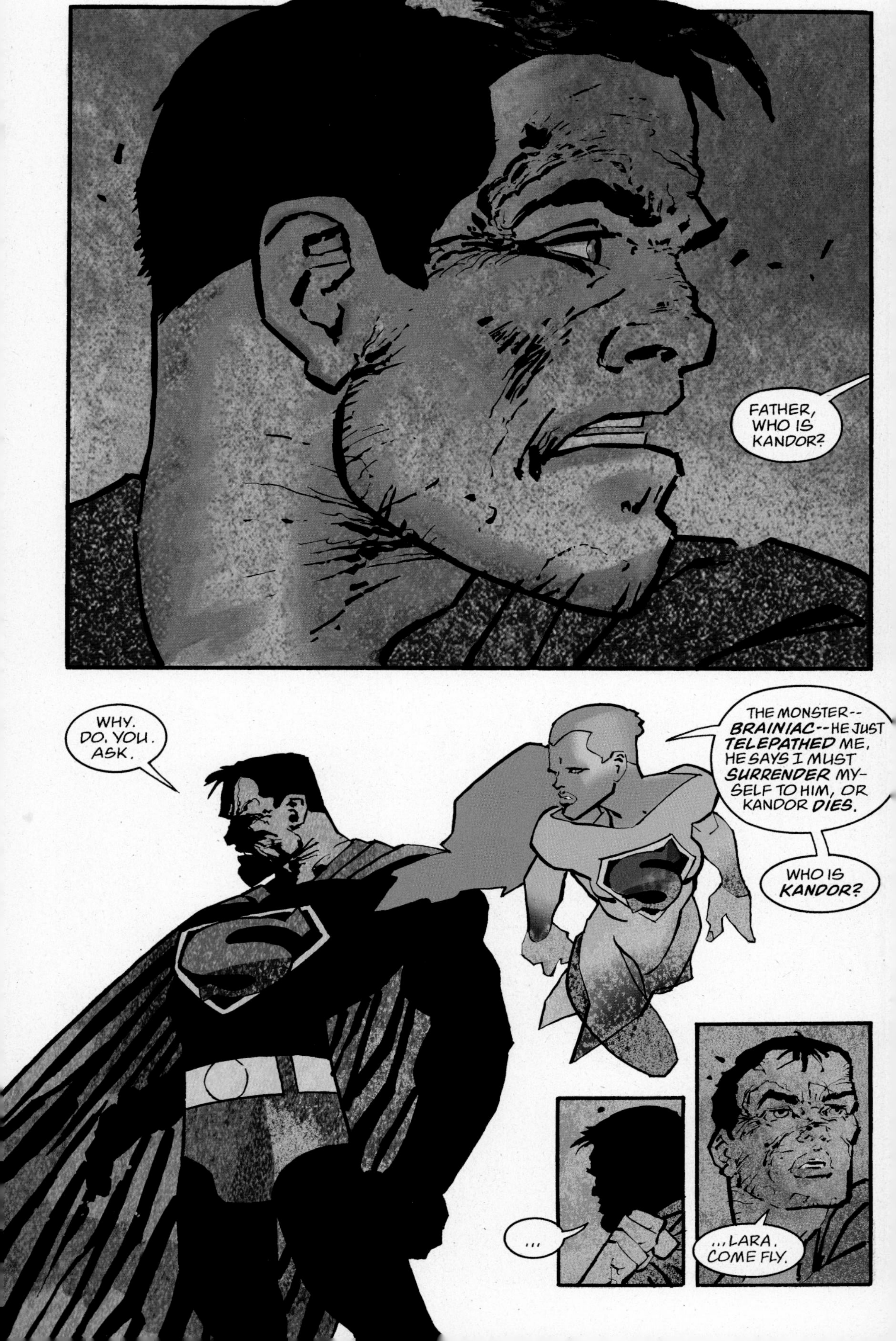
FATHER, WHO IS KANDOR?
WHY. DO. YOU. ASK.
THE MONSTER-- BRAINIAC--HE JUST TELEPATHED ME. HE SAYS I MUST SURRENDER MYSELF TO HIM, OR KANDOR DIES.
WHO IS KANDOR?
...
...LARA. COME FLY.

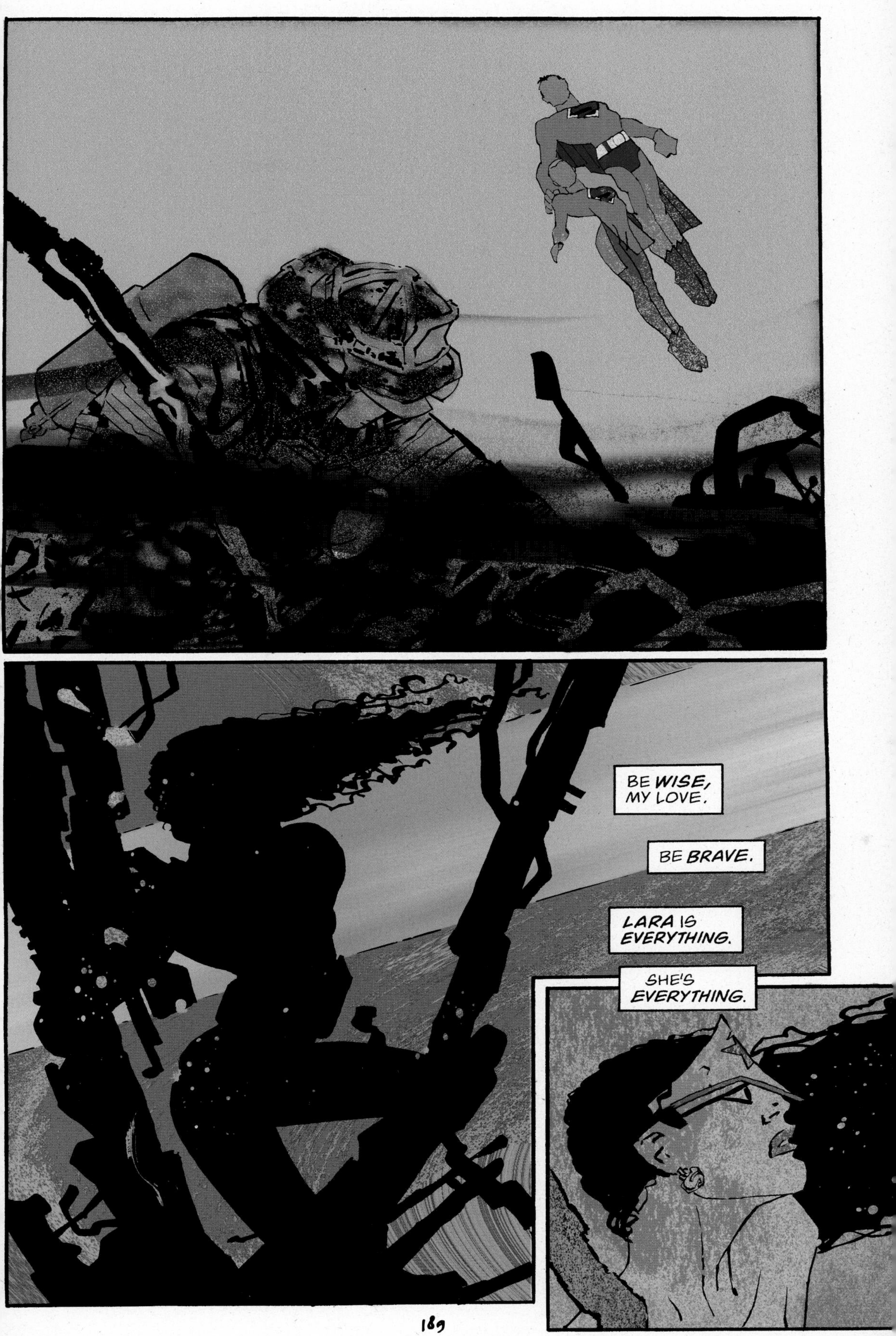
BE WISE, MY LOVE.
BE BRAVE.
LARA IS EVERYTHING.
SHE'S EVERYTHING.

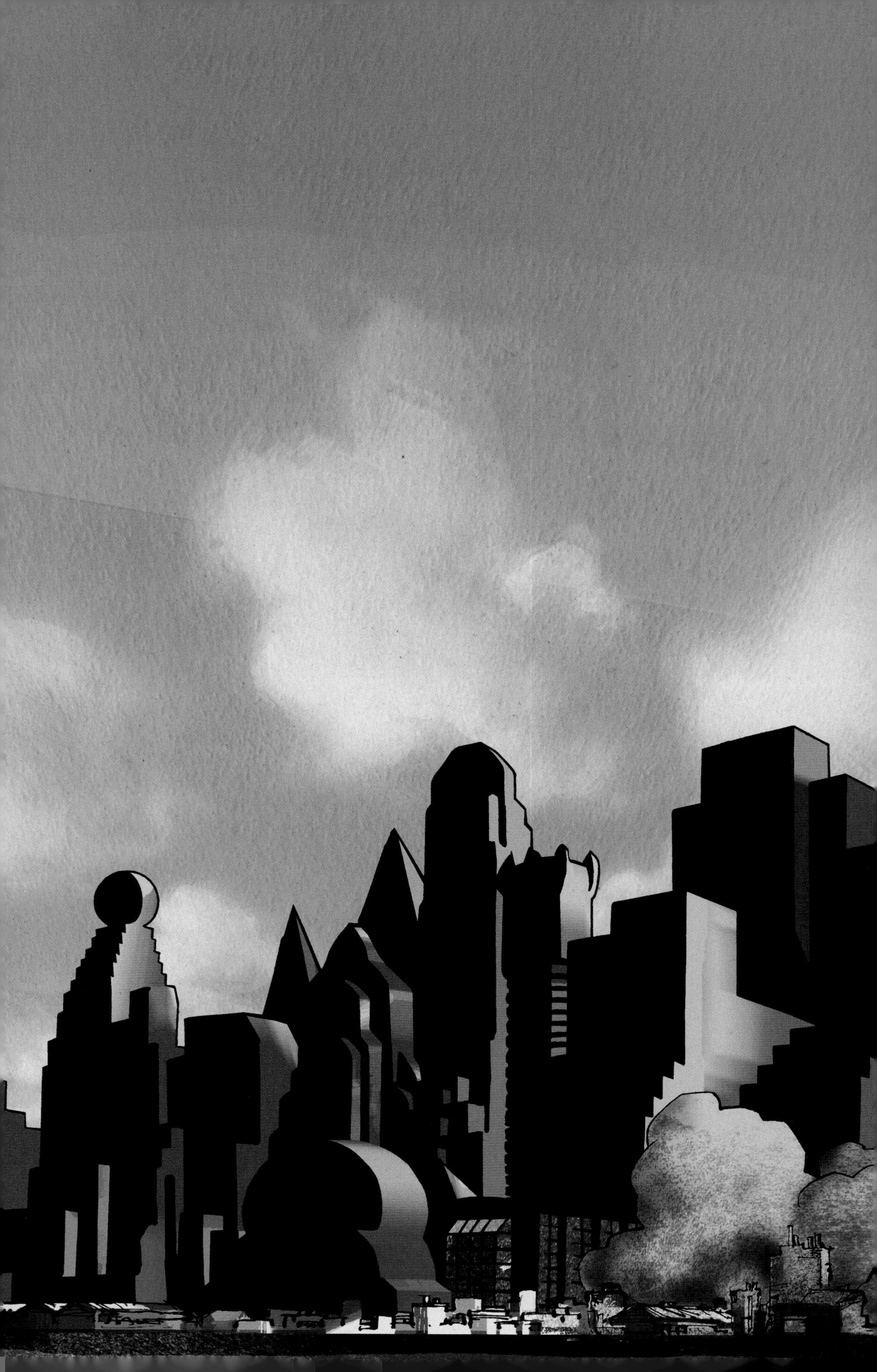

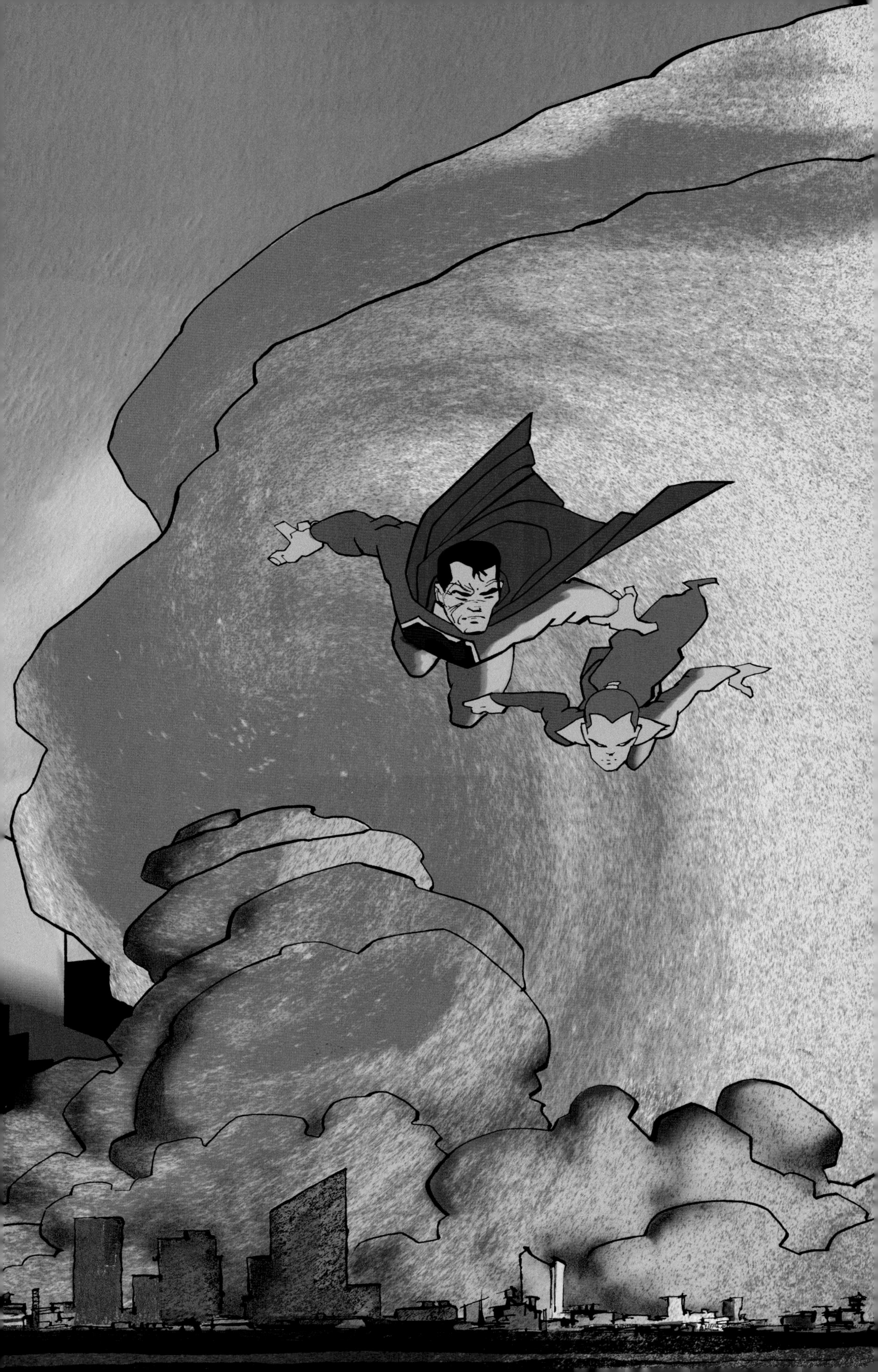

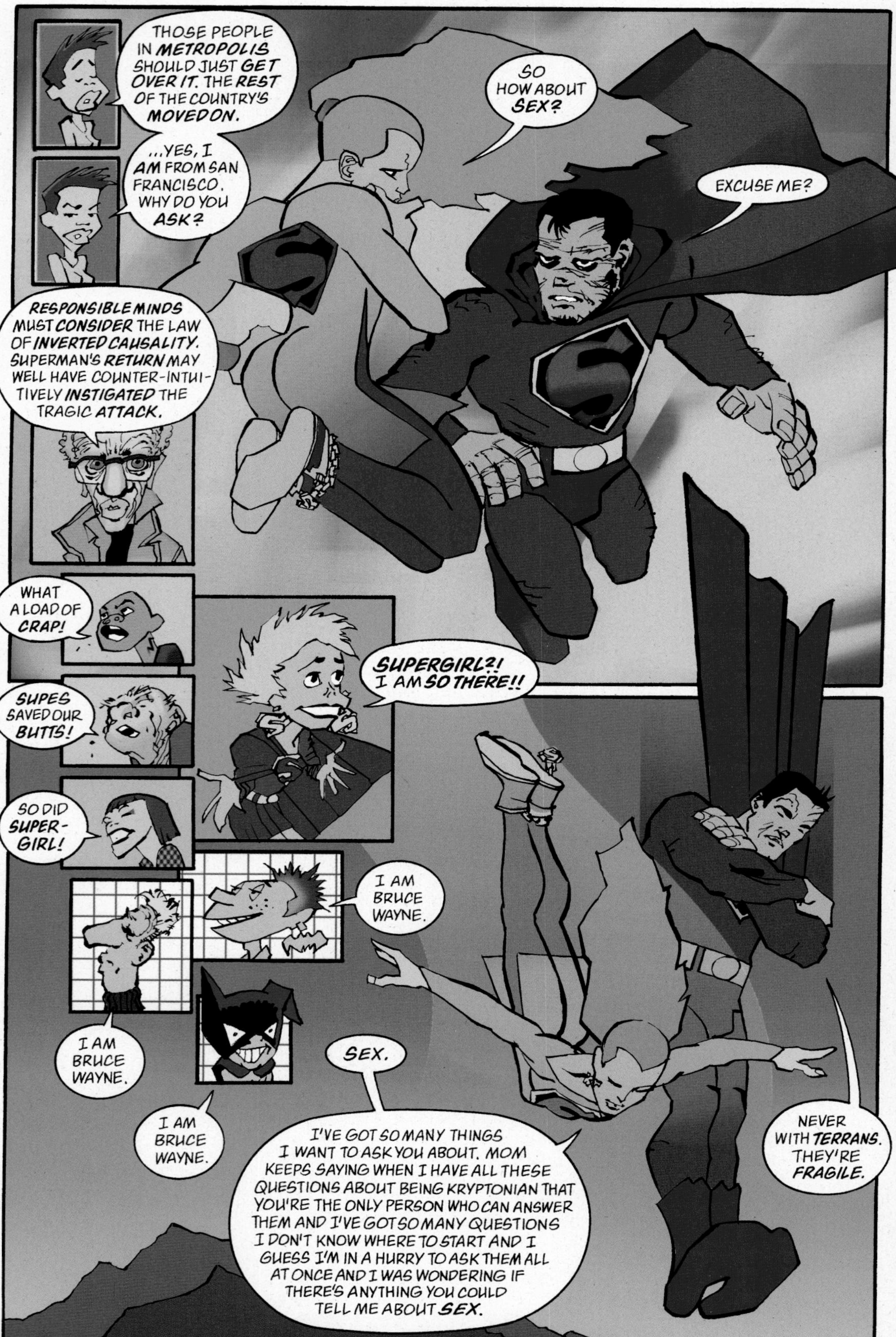
THOSE PEOPLE IN METROPOLIS SHOULD JUST GET OVER IT. THE REST OF THE COUNTRY'S MOVED ON.
...YES, I AM FROM SAN FRANCISCO. WHY DO YOU ASK?
SO HOW ABOUT SEX?
EXCUSE ME?
RESPONSIBLE MINDS MUST CONSIDER THE LAW OF INVERTED CAUSALITY. SUPERMAN'S RETURN MAY WELL HAVE COUNTER-INTUITIVELY INSTIGATED THE TRAGIC ATTACK.
WHAT A LOAD OF CRAP!
SUPES SAVED OUR BUTTS!
SO DID SUPER-GIRL!
SUPERGIRL?! I AM SO THERE!!
I AM BRUCE WAYNE.
I AM BRUCE WAYNE.
I AM BRUCE WAYNE.
SEX.
I'VE GOT SO MANY THINGS I WANT TO ASK YOU ABOUT. MOM KEEPS SAYING WHEN I HAVE ALL THESE QUESTIONS ABOUT BEING KRYPTONIAN THAT YOU'RE THE ONLY PERSON WHO CAN ANSWER THEM AND I'VE GOT SO MANY QUESTIONS I DON'T KNOW WHERE TO START AND I GUESS I'M IN A HURRY TO ASK THEM ALL AT ONCE AND I WAS WONDERING IF THERE'S ANYTHING YOU COULD TELL ME ABOUT SEX.
NEVER WITH TERRANS. THEY'RE FRAGILE.

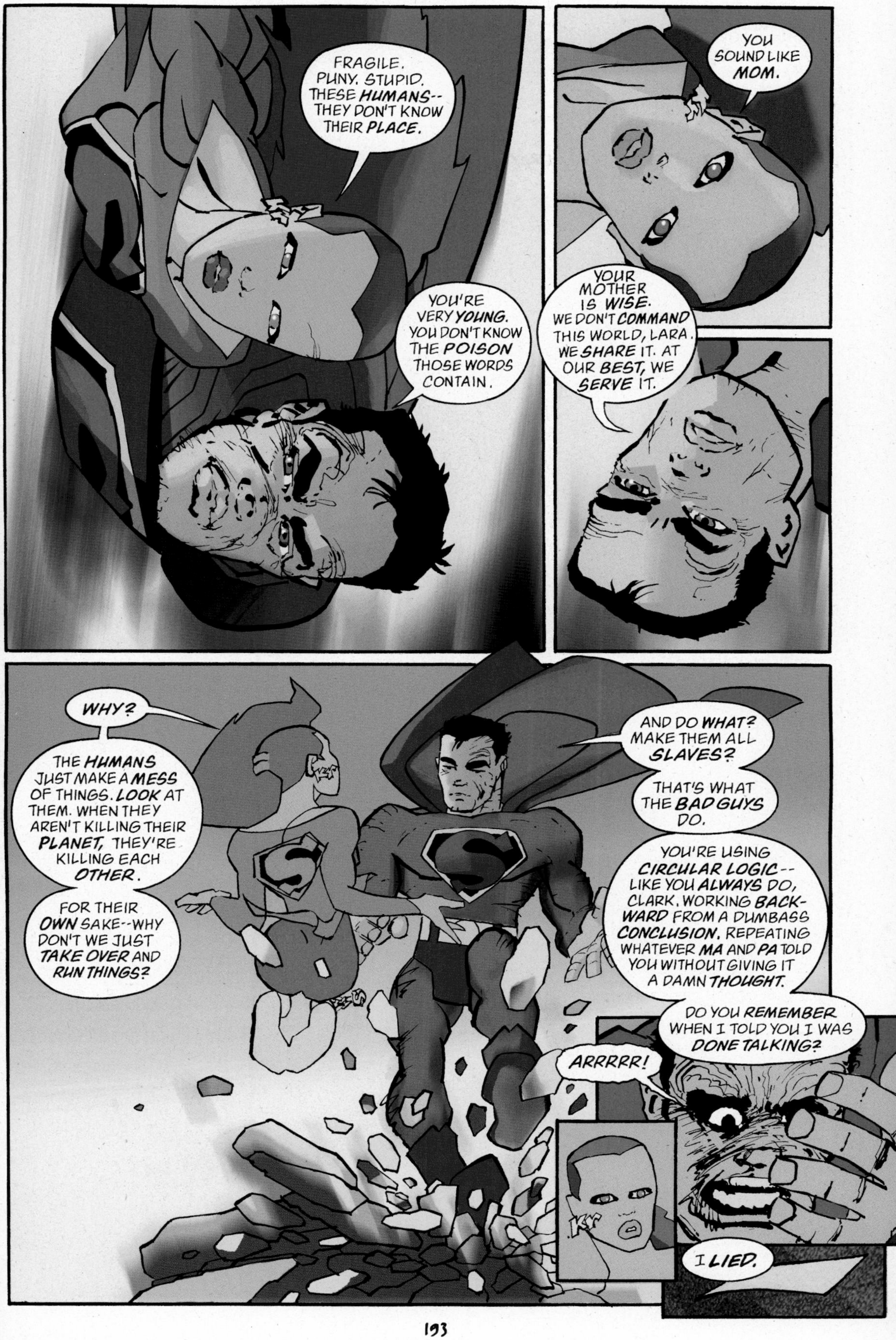
FRAGILE. PUNY. STUPID. THESE HUMANS-- THEY DON'T KNOW THEIR PLACE.
YOU SOUND LIKE MOM.
YOU'RE VERY YOUNG. YOU DON'T KNOW THE POISON THOSE WORDS CONTAIN.
YOUR MOTHER IS WISE. WE DON'T COMMAND THIS WORLD, LARA. WE SHARE IT. AT OUR BEST, WE SERVE IT.
WHY?
THE HUMANS JUST MAKE A MESS OF THINGS. LOOK AT THEM. WHEN THEY AREN'T KILLING THEIR PLANET, THEY'RE KILLING EACH OTHER.
FOR THEIR OWN SAKE--WHY DON'T WE JUST TAKE OVER AND RUN THINGS?
AND DO WHAT? MAKE THEM ALL SLAVES?
THAT'S WHAT THE BAD GUYS DO.
YOU'RE USING CIRCULAR LOGIC-- LIKE YOU ALWAYS DO, CLARK, WORKING BACK-WARD FROM A DUMBASS CONCLUSION. REPEATING WHATEVER MA AND PA TOLD YOU WITHOUT GIVING IT A DAMN THOUGHT.
DO YOU REMEMBER WHEN I TOLD YOU I WAS DONE TALKING?
ARRRRR!
I LIED.

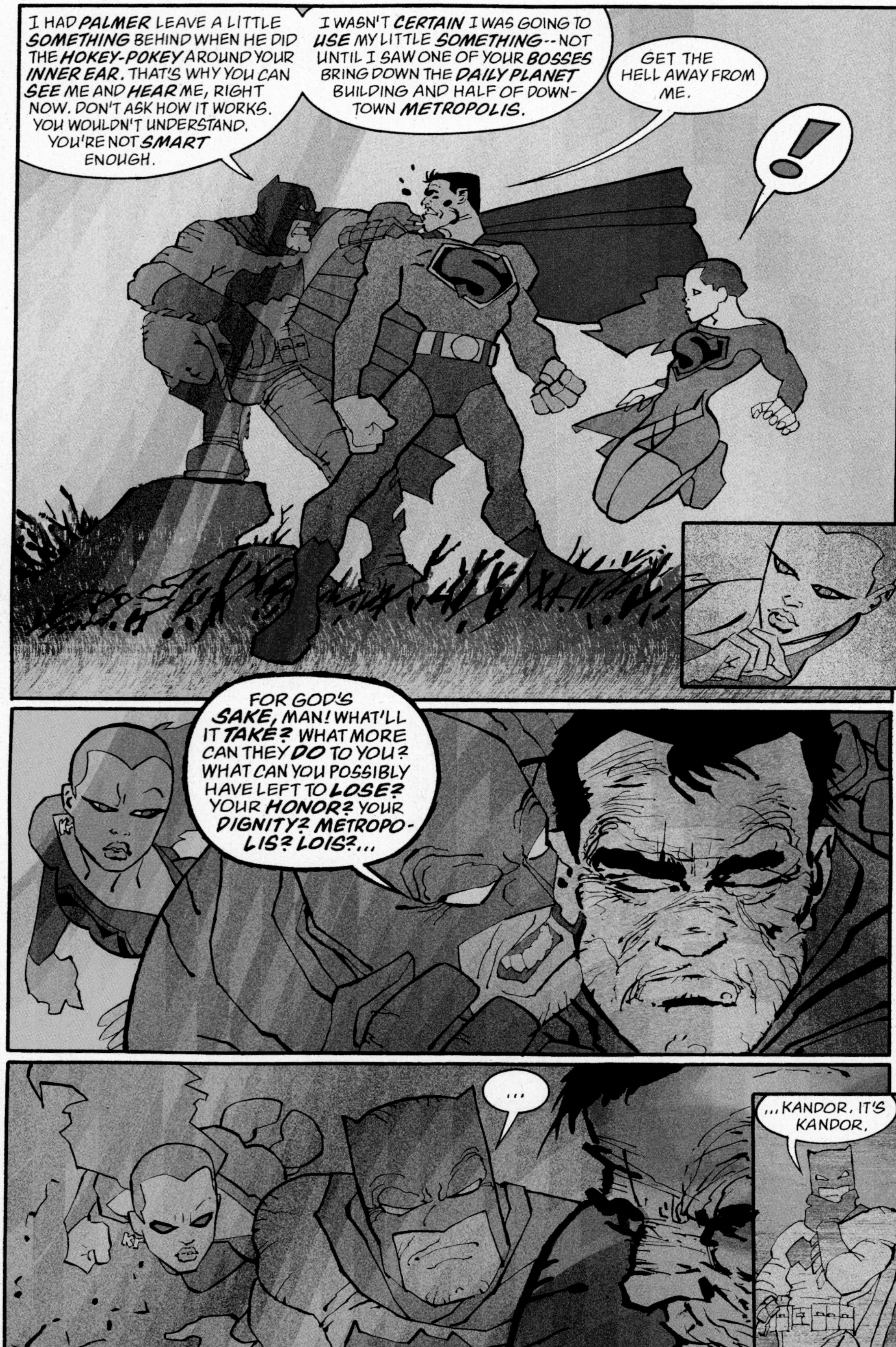

I HAD PALMER LEAVE A LITTLE SOMETHING BEHIND WHEN HE DID THE HOKEY-POKEY AROUND YOUR INNER EAR. THAT'S WHY YOU CAN SEE ME AND HEAR ME, RIGHT NOW. DON'T ASK HOW IT WORKS. YOU WOULDN'T UNDERSTAND. YOU'RE NOT SMART ENOUGH.
I WASN'T CERTAIN I WAS GOING TO USE MY LITTLE SOMETHING--NOT UNTIL I SAW ONE OF YOUR BOSSES BRING DOWN THE DAILY PLANET BUILDING AND HALF OF DOWN-TOWN METROPOLIS.
GET THE HELL AWAY FROM ME.
!
FOR GOD'S SAKE, MAN! WHAT'LL IT TAKE? WHAT MORE CAN THEY DO TO YOU? WHAT CAN YOU POSSIBLY HAVE LEFT TO LOSE? YOUR HONOR? YOUR DIGNITY? METROPO-LIS? LOIS?...
...
...KANDOR. IT'S KANDOR.

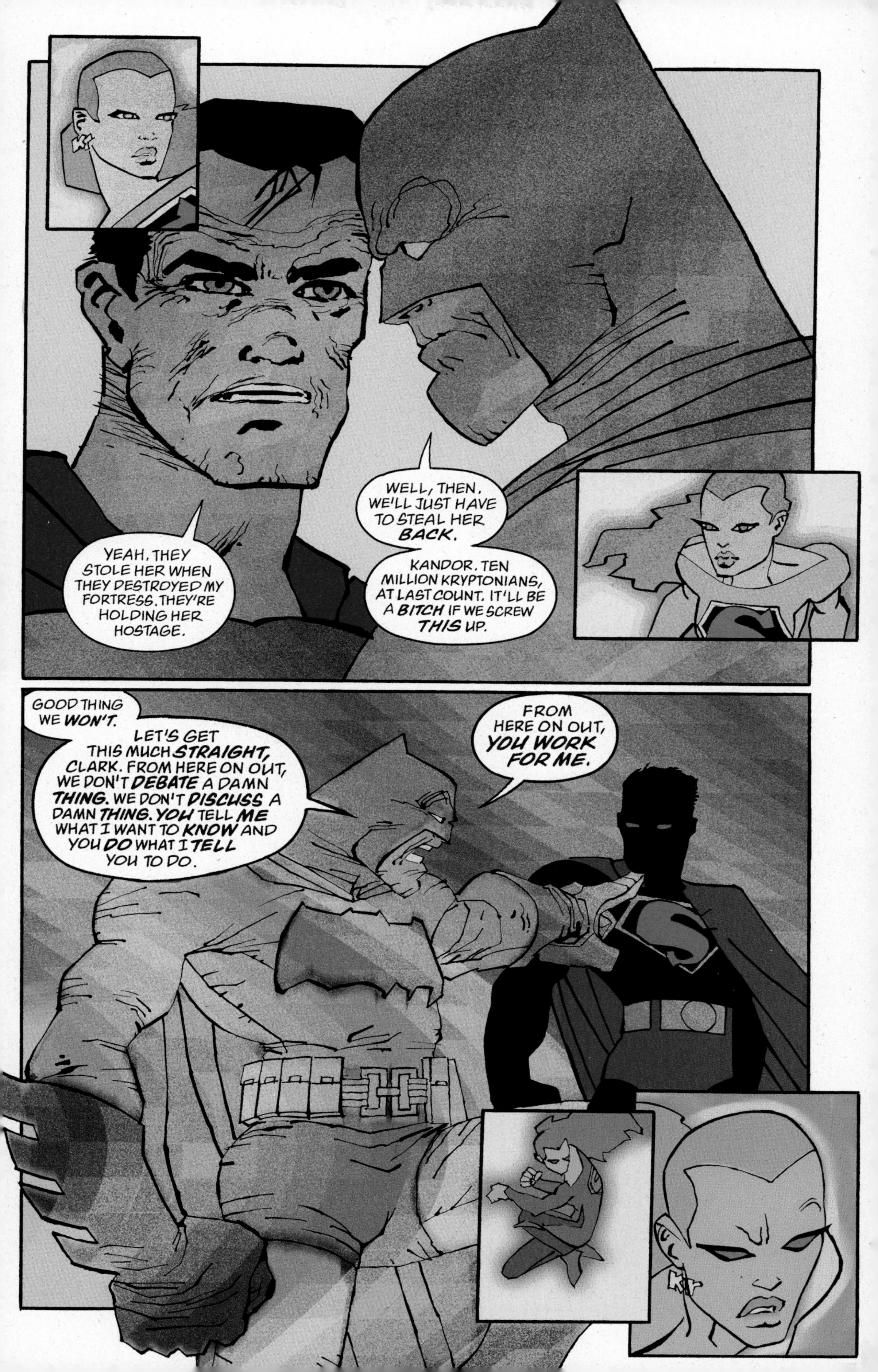
YEAH. THEY STOLE HER WHEN THEY DESTROYED MY FORTRESS. THEY'RE HOLDING HER HOSTAGE.
WELL, THEN, WE'LL JUST HAVE TO STEAL HER BACK.
KANDOR. TEN MILLION KRYPTONIANS, AT LAST COUNT. IT'LL BE A BITCH IF WE SCREW THIS UP.
GOOD THING WE WON'T.
LET'S GET THIS MUCH STRAIGHT, CLARK. FROM HERE ON OUT, WE DON'T DEBATE A DAMN THING. WE DON'T DISCUSS A DAMN THING. YOU TELL ME WHAT I WANT TO KNOW AND YOU DO WHAT I TELL YOU TO DO.
FROM HERE ON OUT, YOU WORK FOR ME.

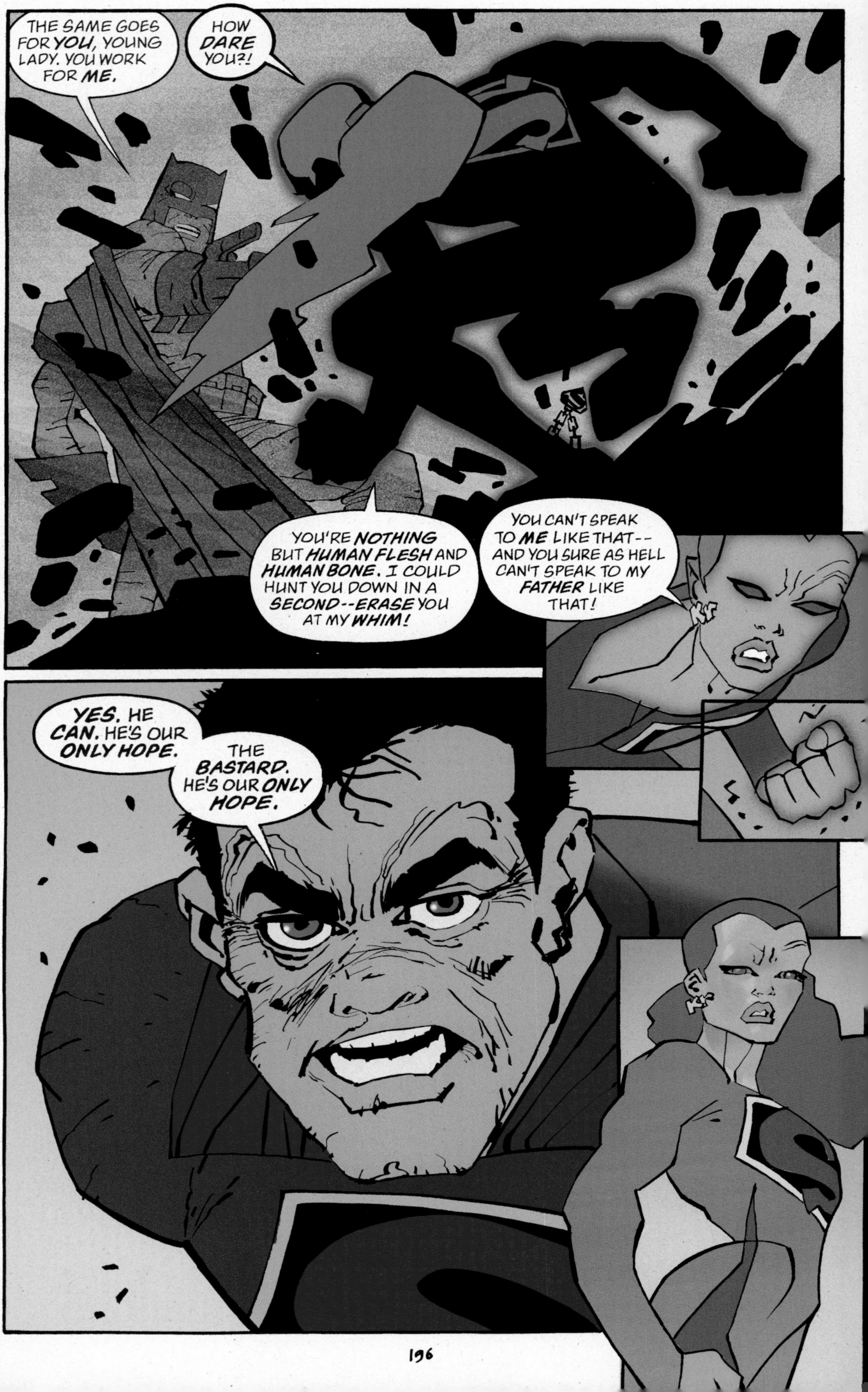
THE SAME GOES FOR **YOU**, YOUNG LADY. YOU WORK FOR **ME**.
HOW **DARE** YOU?!
YOU'RE **NOTHING** BUT **HUMAN FLESH** AND **HUMAN BONE**. I COULD HUNT YOU DOWN IN A **SECOND--ERASE** YOU AT MY **WHIM**!
YOU CAN'T SPEAK TO **ME** LIKE THAT-- AND YOU SURE AS HELL CAN'T SPEAK TO MY **FATHER** LIKE THAT!
YES. HE **CAN.** HE'S OUR **ONLY HOPE.**
THE **BASTARD.** HE'S OUR **ONLY HOPE.**

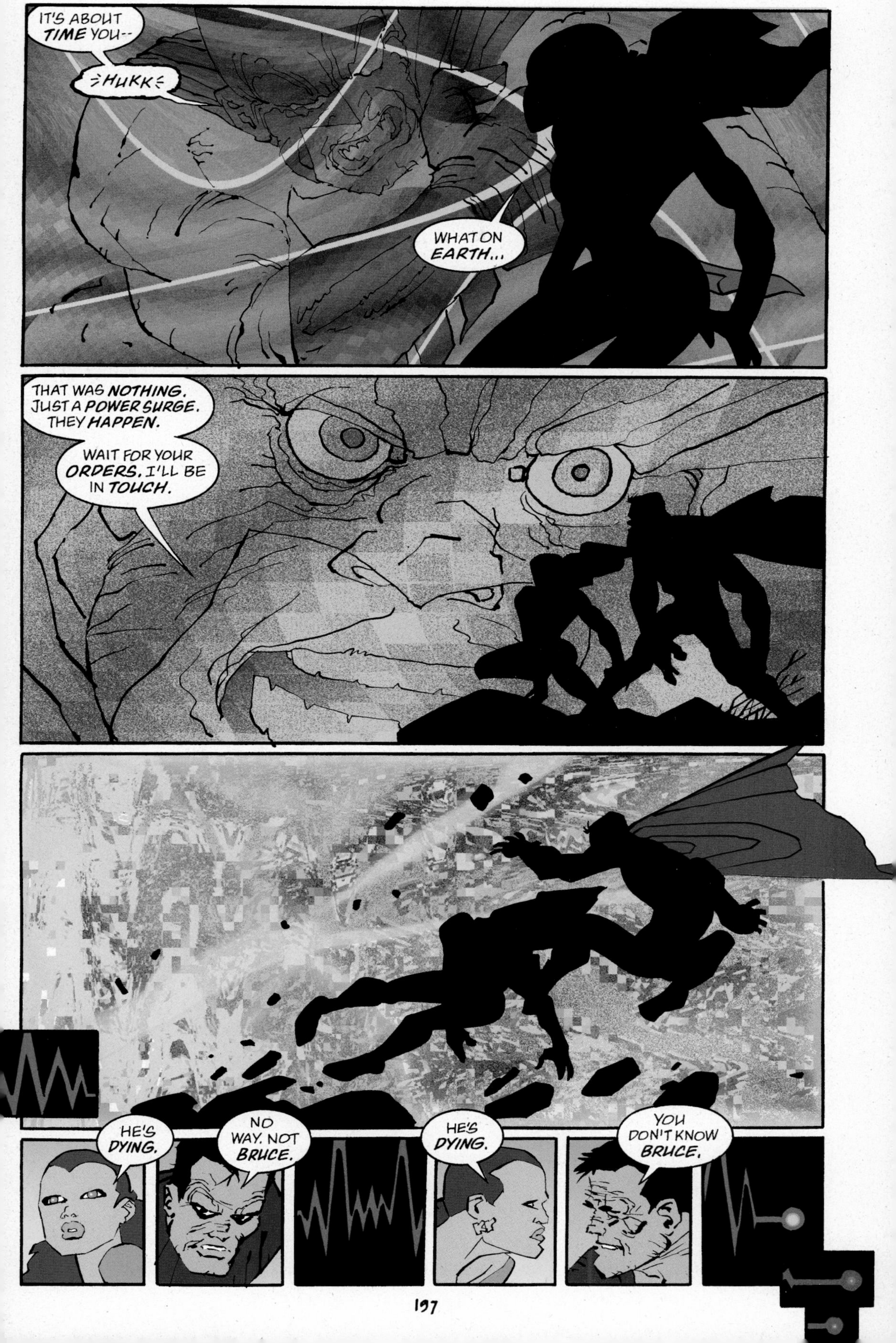
IT'S ABOUT TIME YOU--
HUKK
WHAT ON EARTH...
THAT WAS NOTHING. JUST A POWER SURGE. THEY HAPPEN.
WAIT FOR YOUR ORDERS. I'LL BE IN TOUCH.
HE'S DYING.
NO WAY. NOT BRUCE.
HE'S DYING.
YOU DON'T KNOW BRUCE.

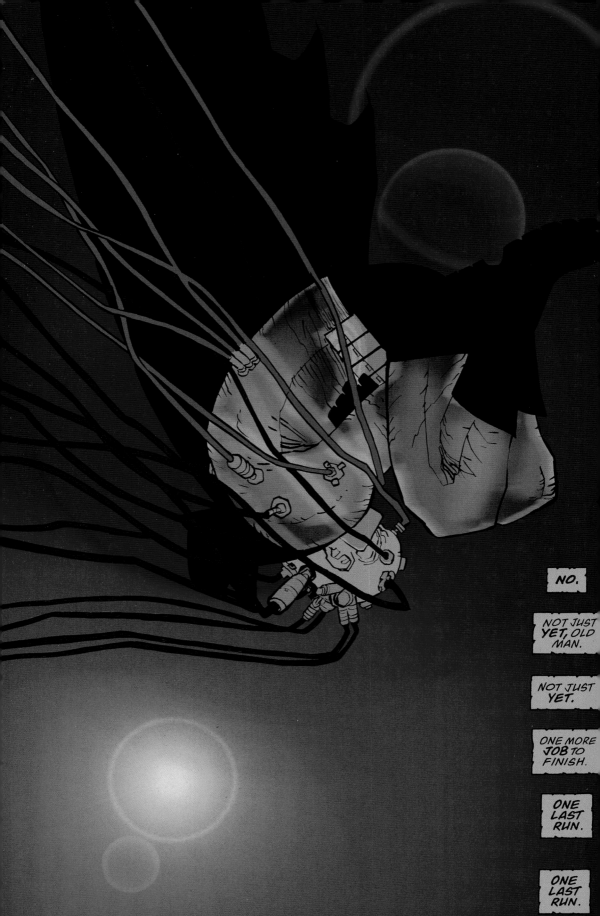

NO.

NOT JUST YET, OLD MAN.

NOT JUST YET.

ONE MORE JOB TO FINISH.

ONE LAST RUN.

ONE LAST RUN.

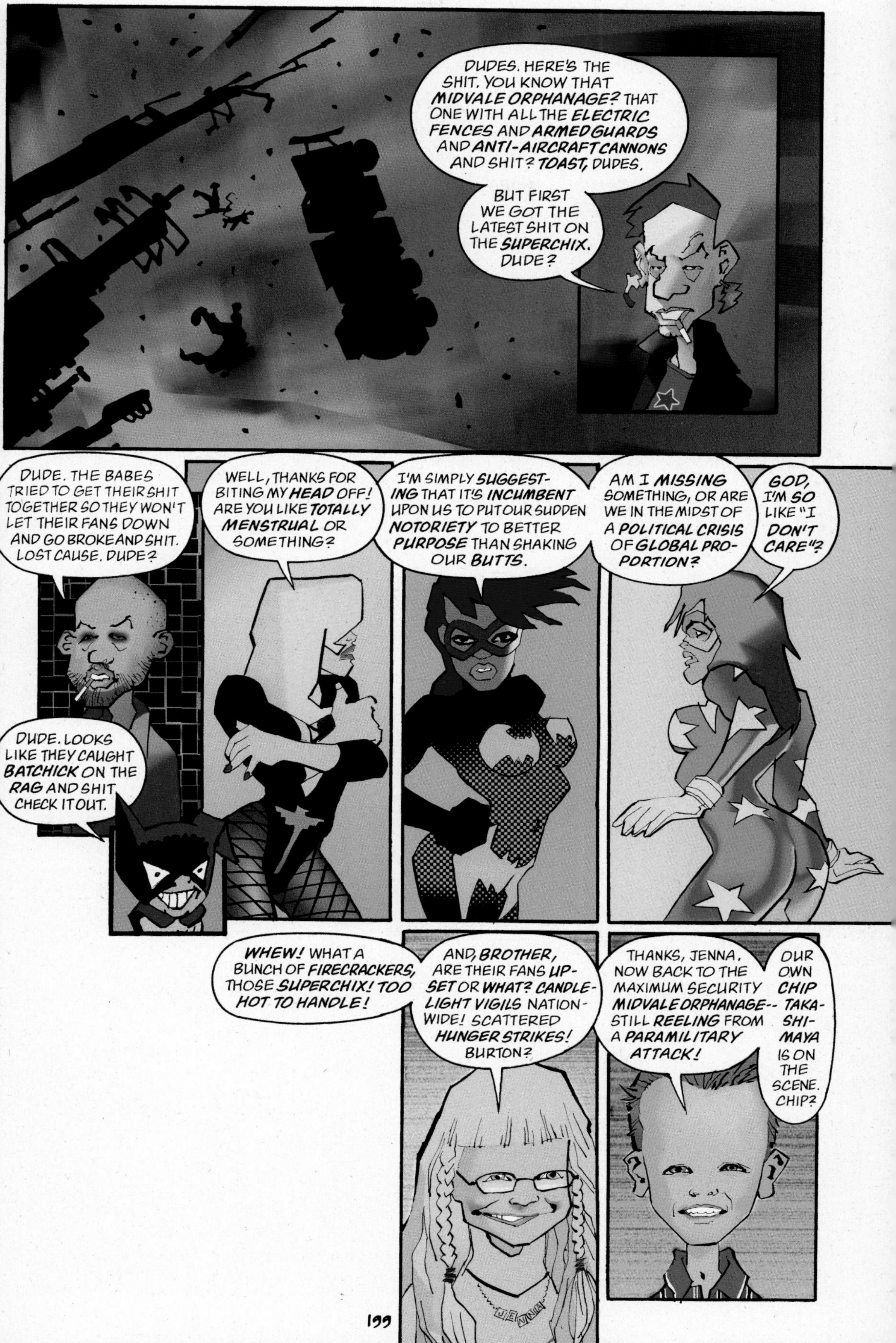
DUDES. HERE'S THE SHIT. YOU KNOW THAT MIDVALE ORPHANAGE? THAT ONE WITH ALL THE ELECTRIC FENCES AND ARMED GUARDS AND ANTI-AIRCRAFT CANNONS AND SHIT? TOAST, DUDES.
BUT FIRST WE GOT THE LATEST SHIT ON THE SUPERCHIX. DUDE?
DUDE. THE BABES TRIED TO GET THEIR SHIT TOGETHER SO THEY WON'T LET THEIR FANS DOWN AND GO BROKE AND SHIT. LOST CAUSE. DUDE?
DUDE. LOOKS LIKE THEY CAUGHT BATCHICK ON THE RAG AND SHIT. CHECK IT OUT.
WELL, THANKS FOR BITING MY HEAD OFF! ARE YOU LIKE TOTALLY MENSTRUAL OR SOMETHING?
I'M SIMPLY SUGGESTING THAT IT'S INCUMBENT UPON US TO PUT OUR SUDDEN NOTORIETY TO BETTER PURPOSE THAN SHAKING OUR BUTTS.
AM I MISSING SOMETHING, OR ARE WE IN THE MIDST OF A POLITICAL CRISIS OF GLOBAL PROPORTION?
GOD, I'M SO LIKE "I DON'T CARE"?
WHEW! WHAT A BUNCH OF FIRECRACKERS, THOSE SUPERCHIX! TOO HOT TO HANDLE!
AND, BROTHER, ARE THEIR FANS UPSET OR WHAT? CANDLELIGHT VIGILS NATIONWIDE! SCATTERED HUNGER STRIKES! BURTON?
THANKS, JENNA. NOW BACK TO THE MAXIMUM SECURITY MIDVALE ORPHANAGE-- STILL REELING FROM A PARAMILITARY ATTACK!
OUR OWN CHIP TAKASHIMAYA IS ON THE SCENE. CHIP?
JENNA

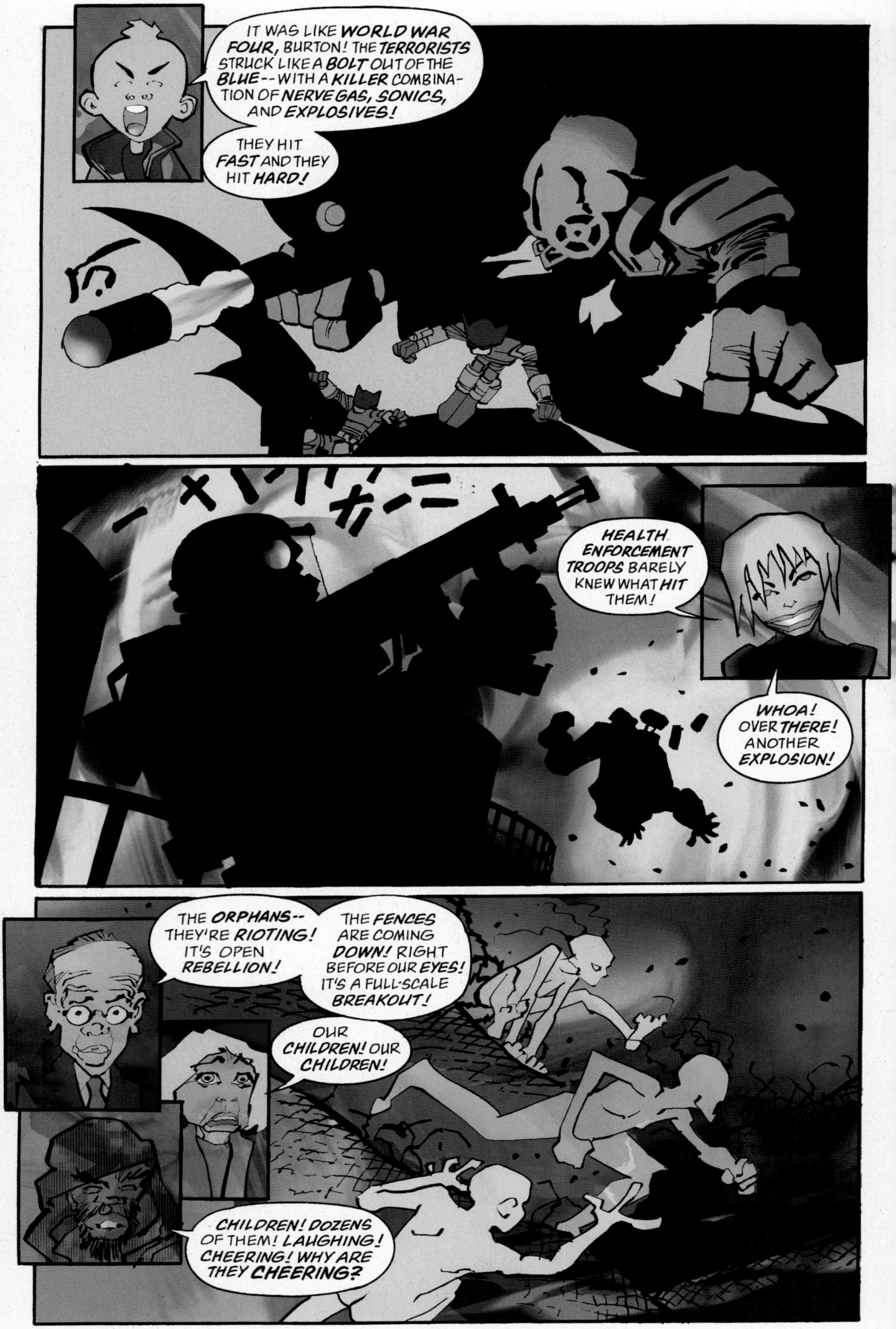
IT WAS LIKE WORLD WAR FOUR, BURTON! THE TERRORISTS STRUCK LIKE A BOLT OUT OF THE BLUE--WITH A KILLER COMBINATION OF NERVE GAS, SONICS, AND EXPLOSIVES!
THEY HIT FAST AND THEY HIT HARD!
HEALTH ENFORCEMENT TROOPS BARELY KNEW WHAT HIT THEM!
WHOA! OVER THERE! ANOTHER EXPLOSION!
THE ORPHANS-- THEY'RE RIOTING! IT'S OPEN REBELLION!
THE FENCES ARE COMING DOWN! RIGHT BEFORE OUR EYES! IT'S A FULL-SCALE BREAKOUT!
OUR CHILDREN! OUR CHILDREN!
CHILDREN! DOZENS OF THEM! LAUGHING! CHEERING! WHY ARE THEY CHEERING?

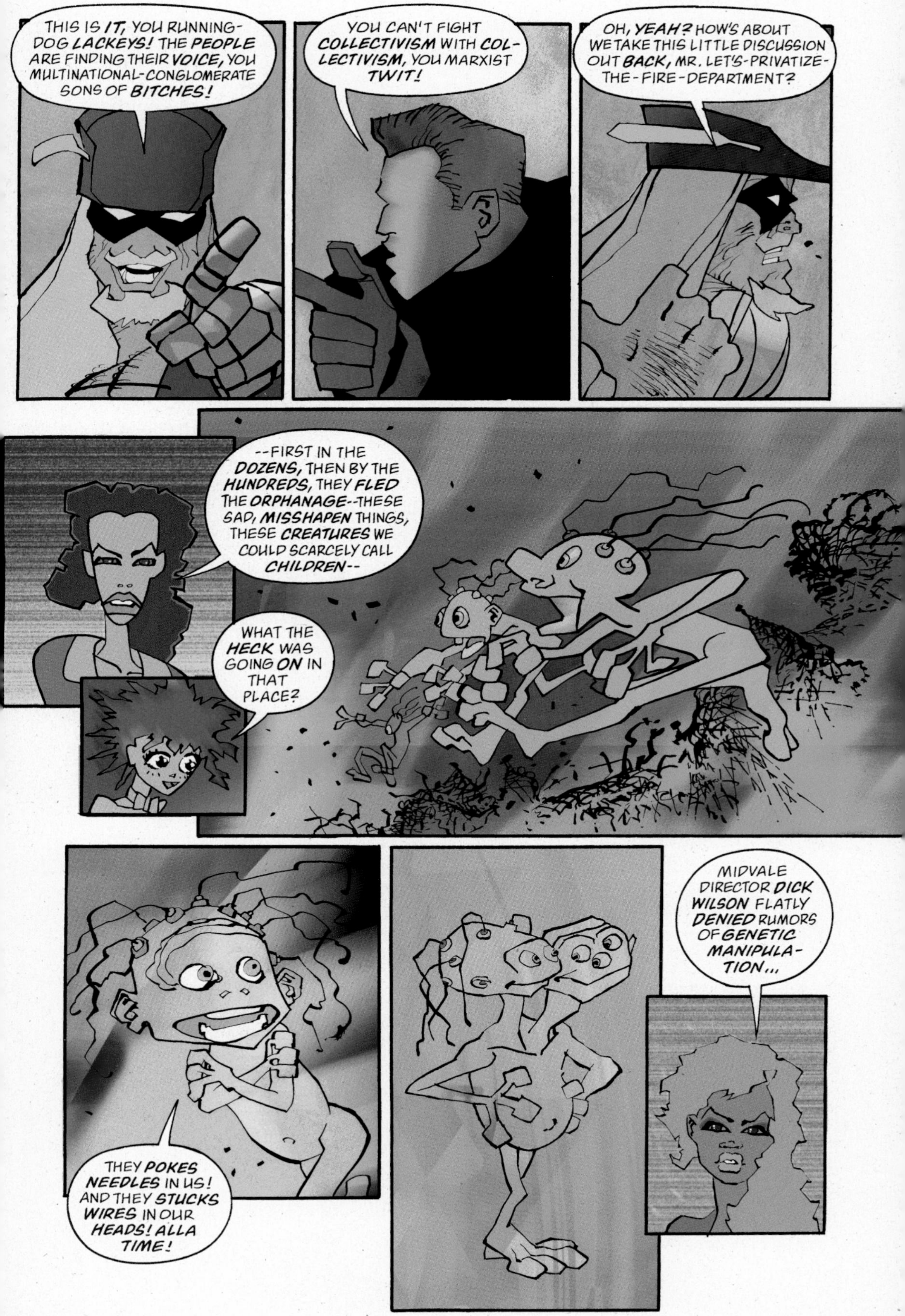
THIS IS IT, YOU RUNNING-DOG LACKEYS! THE PEOPLE ARE FINDING THEIR VOICE, YOU MULTINATIONAL-CONGLOMERATE SONS OF BITCHES!
YOU CAN'T FIGHT COLLECTIVISM WITH COLLECTIVISM, YOU MARXIST TWIT!
OH, YEAH? HOW'S ABOUT WE TAKE THIS LITTLE DISCUSSION OUT BACK, MR. LET'S-PRIVATIZE-THE-FIRE-DEPARTMENT?
--FIRST IN THE DOZENS, THEN BY THE HUNDREDS, THEY FLED THE ORPHANAGE--THESE SAD, MISSHAPEN THINGS, THESE CREATURES WE COULD SCARCELY CALL CHILDREN--
WHAT THE HECK WAS GOING ON IN THAT PLACE?
THEY POKES NEEDLES IN US! AND THEY STUCKS WIRES IN OUR HEADS! ALLA TIME!
MIDVALE DIRECTOR DICK WILSON FLATLY DENIED RUMORS OF GENETIC MANIPULATION...

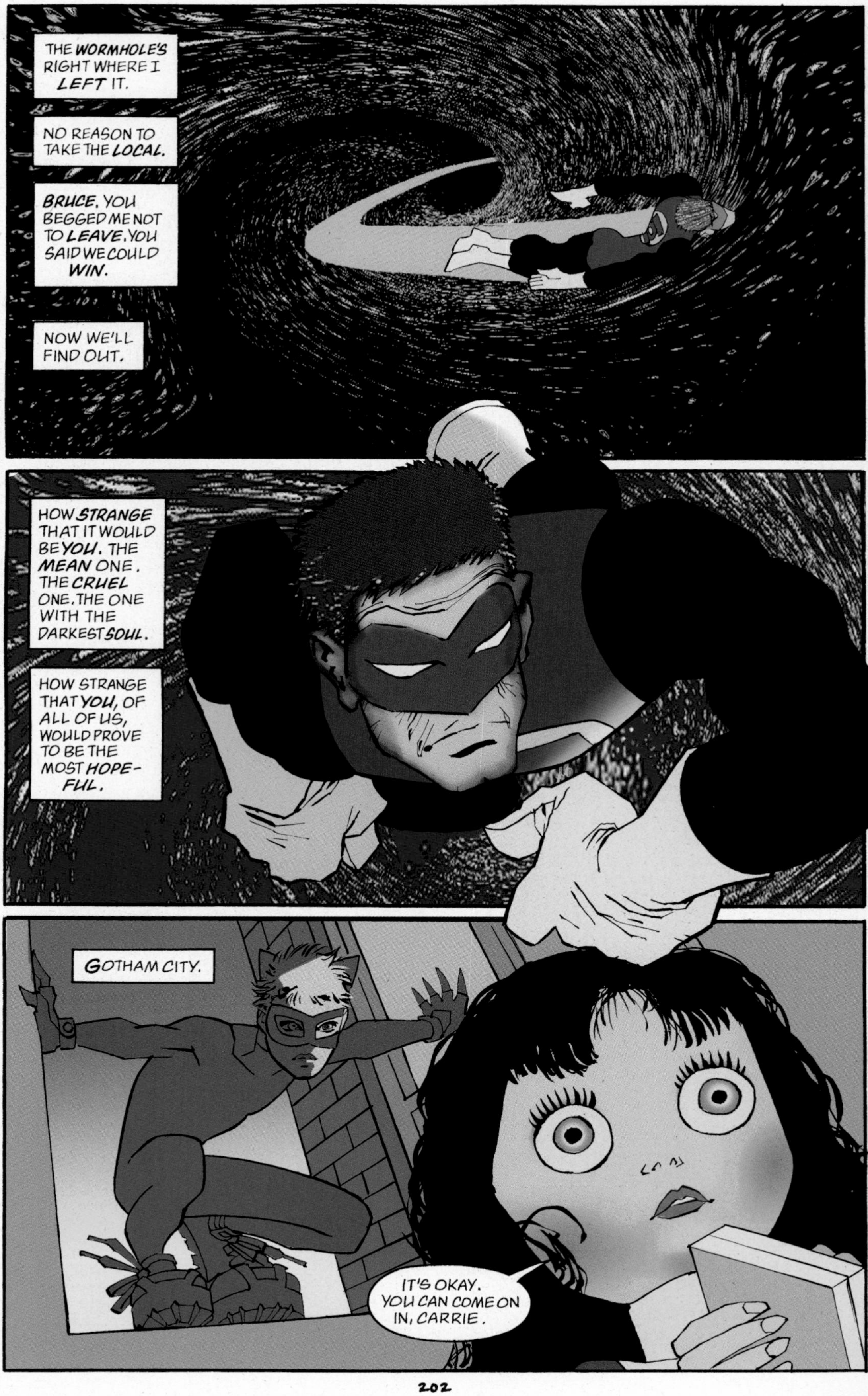
THE WORMHOLE'S RIGHT WHERE I LEFT IT.
NO REASON TO TAKE THE LOCAL.
BRUCE. YOU BEGGED ME NOT TO LEAVE. YOU SAID WE COULD WIN.
NOW WE'LL FIND OUT.
HOW STRANGE THAT IT WOULD BE YOU. THE MEAN ONE. THE CRUEL ONE. THE ONE WITH THE DARKEST SOUL.
HOW STRANGE THAT YOU, OF ALL OF US, WOULD PROVE TO BE THE MOST HOPE-FUL.
GOTHAM CITY.
IT'S OKAY. YOU CAN COME ON IN, CARRIE.

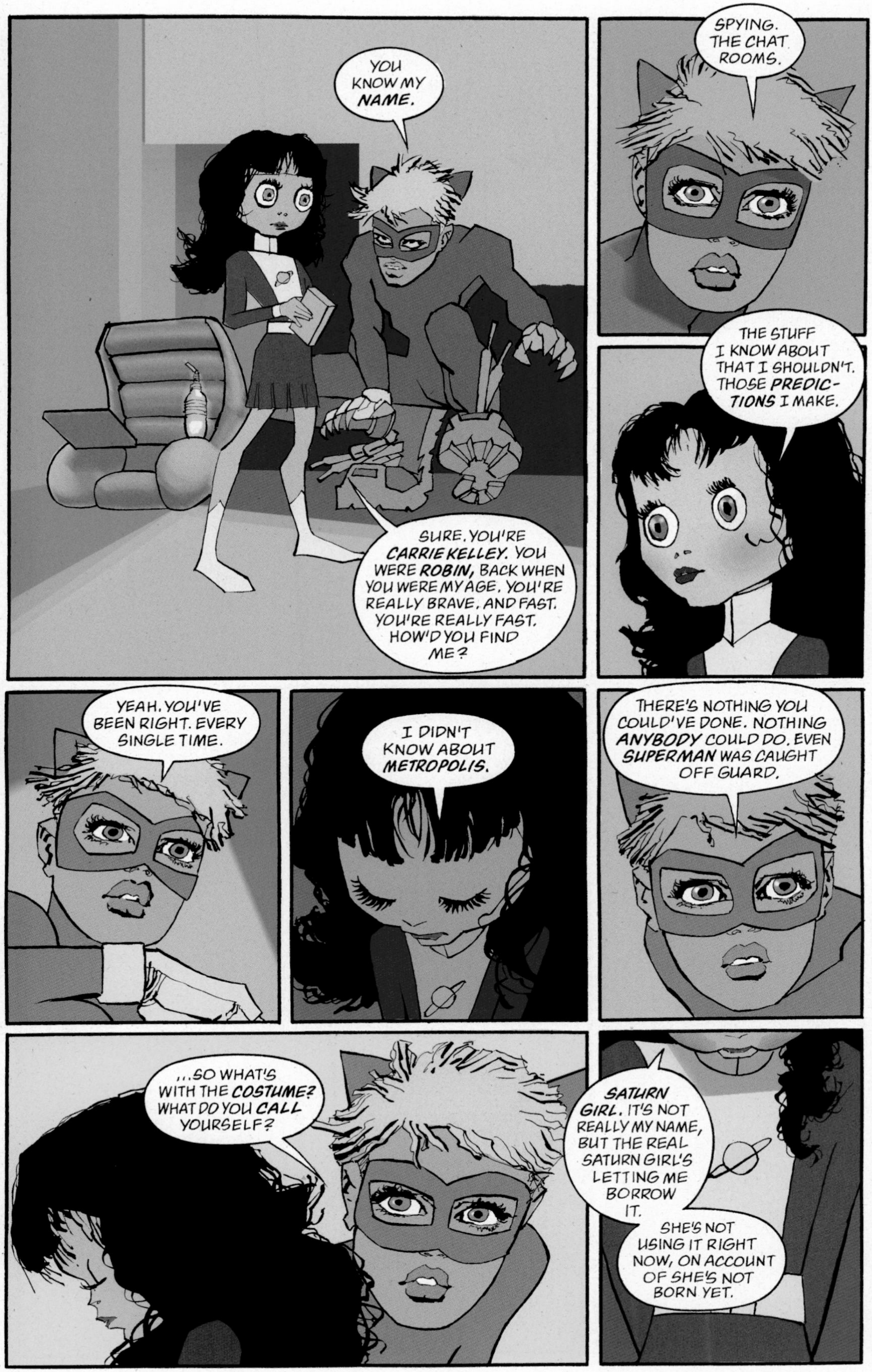
YOU KNOW MY NAME.
SURE. YOU'RE CARRIE KELLEY. YOU WERE ROBIN, BACK WHEN YOU WERE MY AGE. YOU'RE REALLY BRAVE, AND FAST. YOU'RE REALLY FAST. HOW'D YOU FIND ME?
SPYING. THE CHAT ROOMS.
THE STUFF I KNOW ABOUT THAT I SHOULDN'T. THOSE PREDIC-TIONS I MAKE.
YEAH. YOU'VE BEEN RIGHT. EVERY SINGLE TIME.
I DIDN'T KNOW ABOUT METROPOLIS.
THERE'S NOTHING YOU COULD'VE DONE. NOTHING ANYBODY COULD DO. EVEN SUPERMAN WAS CAUGHT OFF GUARD.
...SO WHAT'S WITH THE COSTUME? WHAT DO YOU CALL YOURSELF?
SATURN GIRL. IT'S NOT REALLY MY NAME, BUT THE REAL SATURN GIRL'S LETTING ME BORROW IT.
SHE'S NOT USING IT RIGHT NOW, ON ACCOUNT OF SHE'S NOT BORN YET.

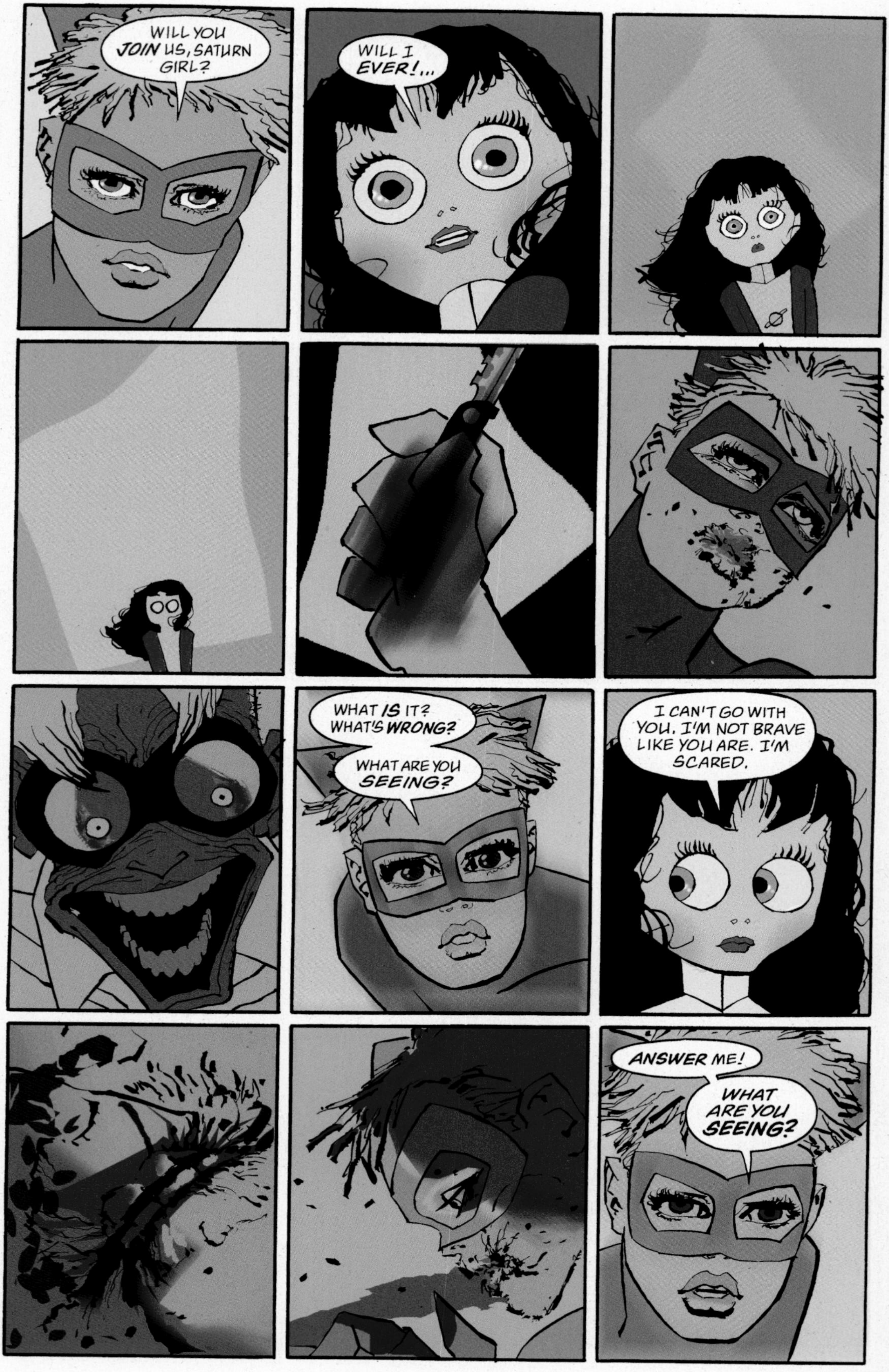

WILL YOU JOIN US, SATURN GIRL?
WILL I EVER!...
WHAT IS IT? WHAT'S WRONG?
WHAT ARE YOU SEEING?
I CAN'T GO WITH YOU. I'M NOT BRAVE LIKE YOU ARE. I'M SCARED.
ANSWER ME!
WHAT ARE YOU SEEING?

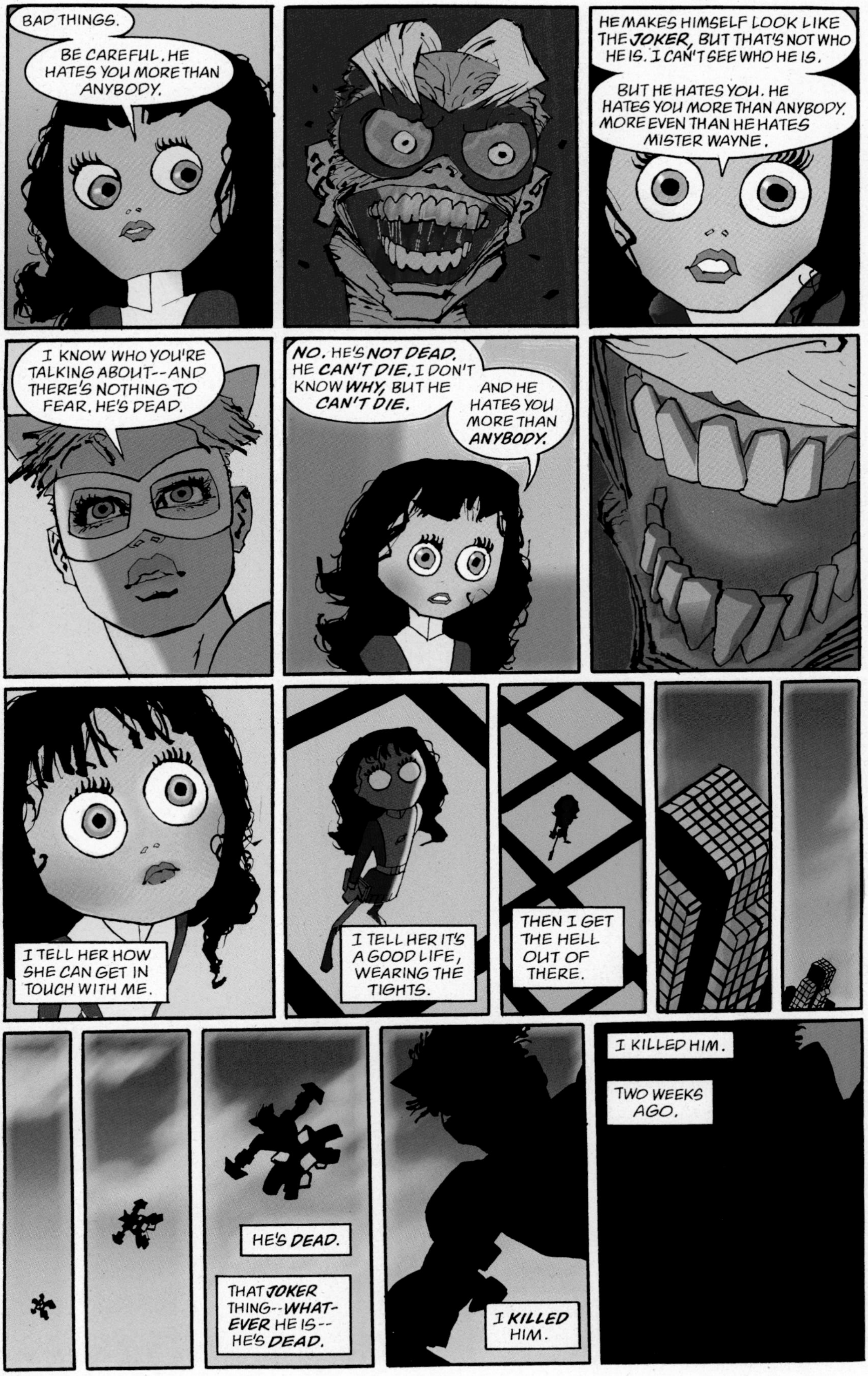

BAD THINGS.
BE CAREFUL. HE HATES YOU MORE THAN ANYBODY.
HE MAKES HIMSELF LOOK LIKE THE JOKER, BUT THAT'S NOT WHO HE IS. I CAN'T SEE WHO HE IS.
BUT HE HATES YOU. HE HATES YOU MORE THAN ANYBODY. MORE EVEN THAN HE HATES MISTER WAYNE.
I KNOW WHO YOU'RE TALKING ABOUT--AND THERE'S NOTHING TO FEAR. HE'S DEAD.
NO. HE'S NOT DEAD. HE CAN'T DIE. I DON'T KNOW WHY, BUT HE CAN'T DIE.
AND HE HATES YOU MORE THAN ANYBODY.
I TELL HER HOW SHE CAN GET IN TOUCH WITH ME.
I TELL HER IT'S A GOOD LIFE, WEARING THE TIGHTS.
THEN I GET THE HELL OUT OF THERE.
HE'S DEAD.
THAT JOKER THING--WHATEVER HE IS--HE'S DEAD.
I KILLED HIM.
I KILLED HIM.
TWO WEEKS AGO.

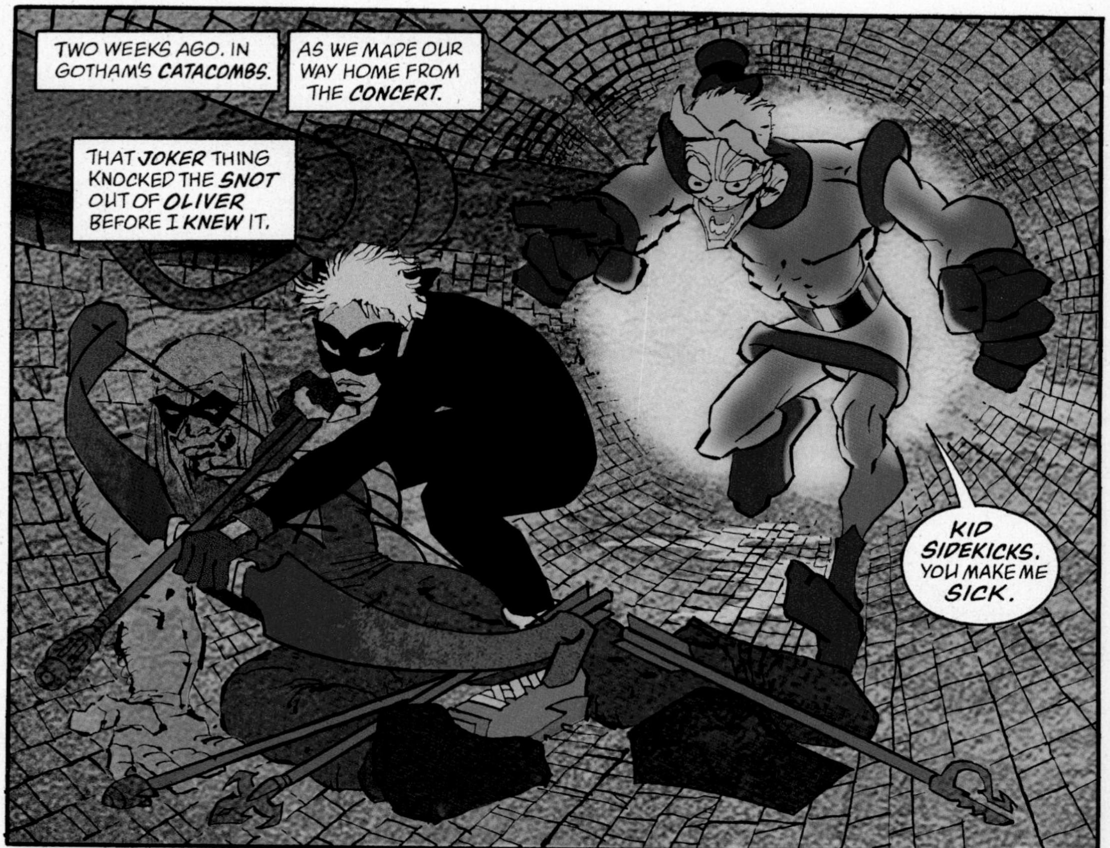
TWO WEEKS AGO. IN GOTHAM'S CATACOMBS.
AS WE MADE OUR WAY HOME FROM THE CONCERT.
THAT JOKER THING KNOCKED THE SNOT OUT OF OLIVER BEFORE I KNEW IT.
KID SIDEKICKS. YOU MAKE ME SICK.
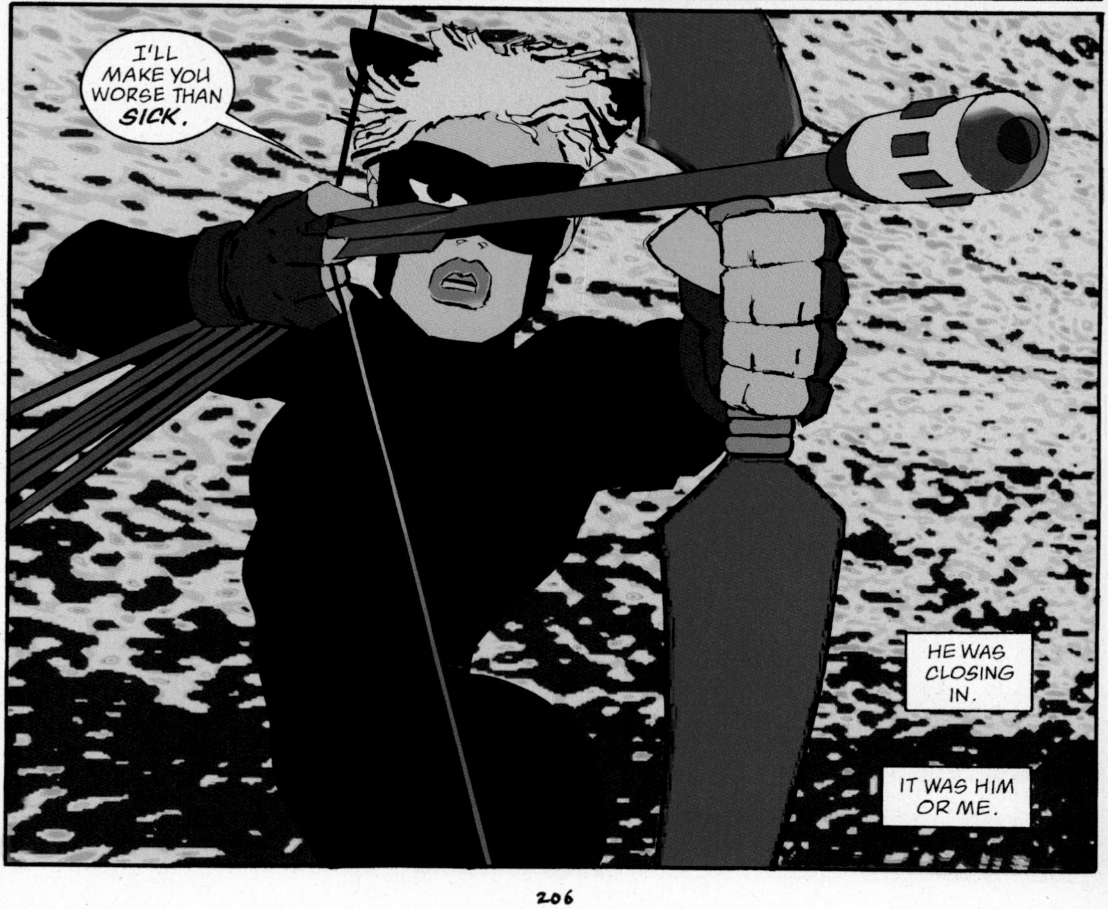
I'LL MAKE YOU WORSE THAN SICK.
HE WAS CLOSING IN.
IT WAS HIM OR ME.

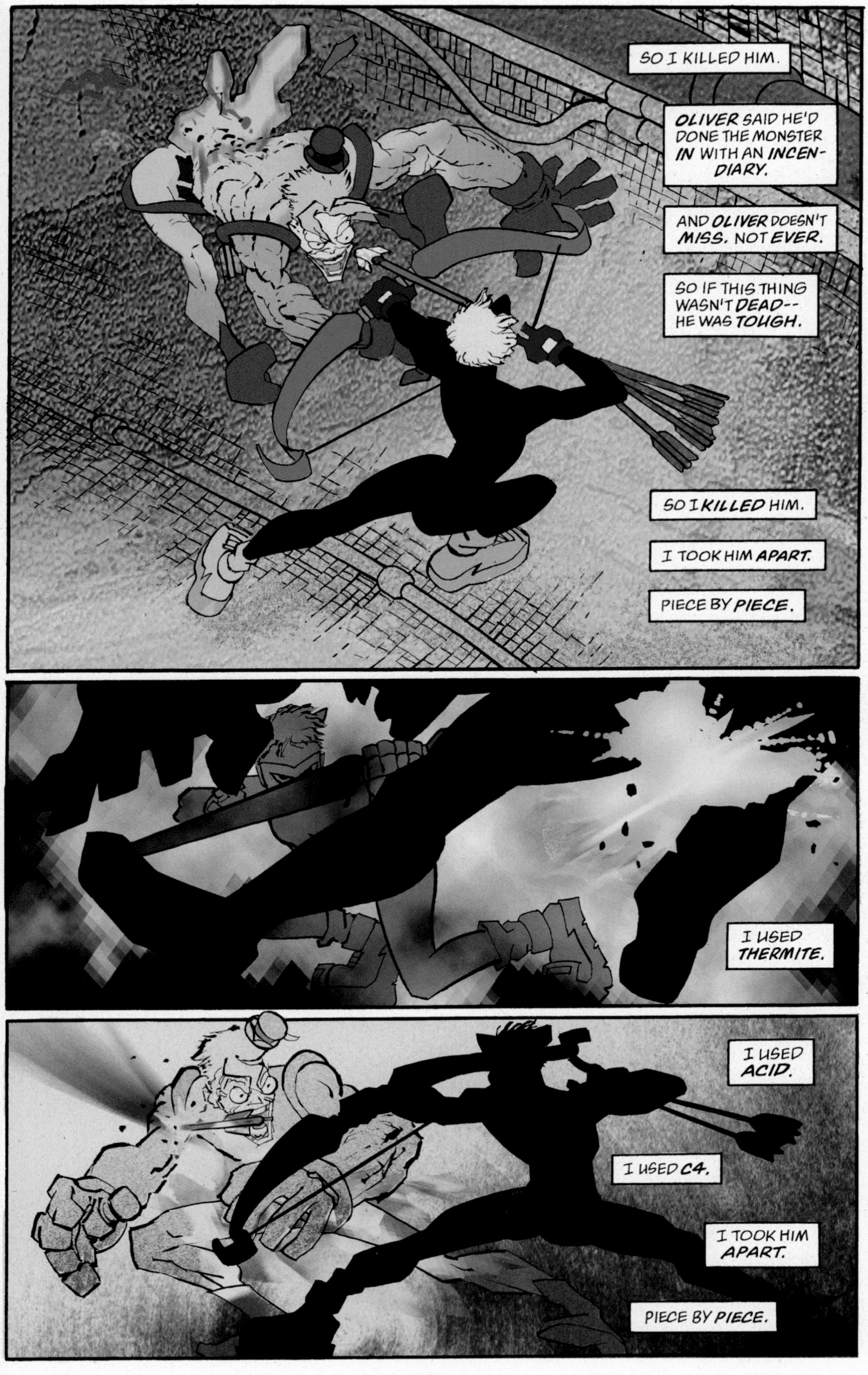
SO I KILLED HIM.
OLIVER SAID HE'D DONE THE MONSTER IN WITH AN INCEN-DIARY.
AND OLIVER DOESN'T MISS. NOT EVER.
SO IF THIS THING WASN'T DEAD-- HE WAS TOUGH.
SO I KILLED HIM.
I TOOK HIM APART.
PIECE BY PIECE.
I USED THERMITE.
I USED ACID.
I USED C4.
I TOOK HIM APART.
PIECE BY PIECE.

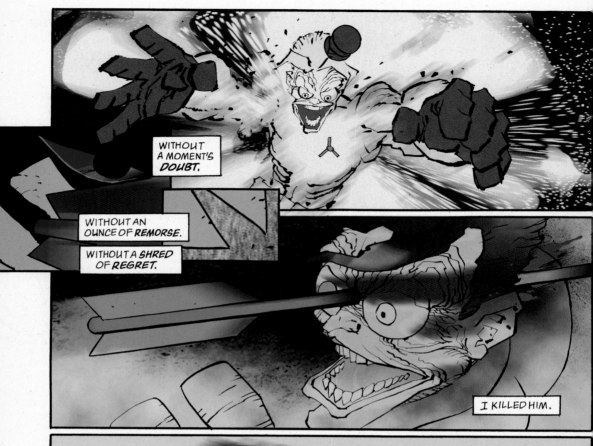

WITHOUT A MOMENT'S *DOUBT.*

WITHOUT AN OUNCE OF *REMORSE.*

WITHOUT A *SHRED* OF *REGRET.*

I KILLED HIM.

I KILLED HIM.

HE'S DEAD.

HE'S GOT TO BE DEAD.

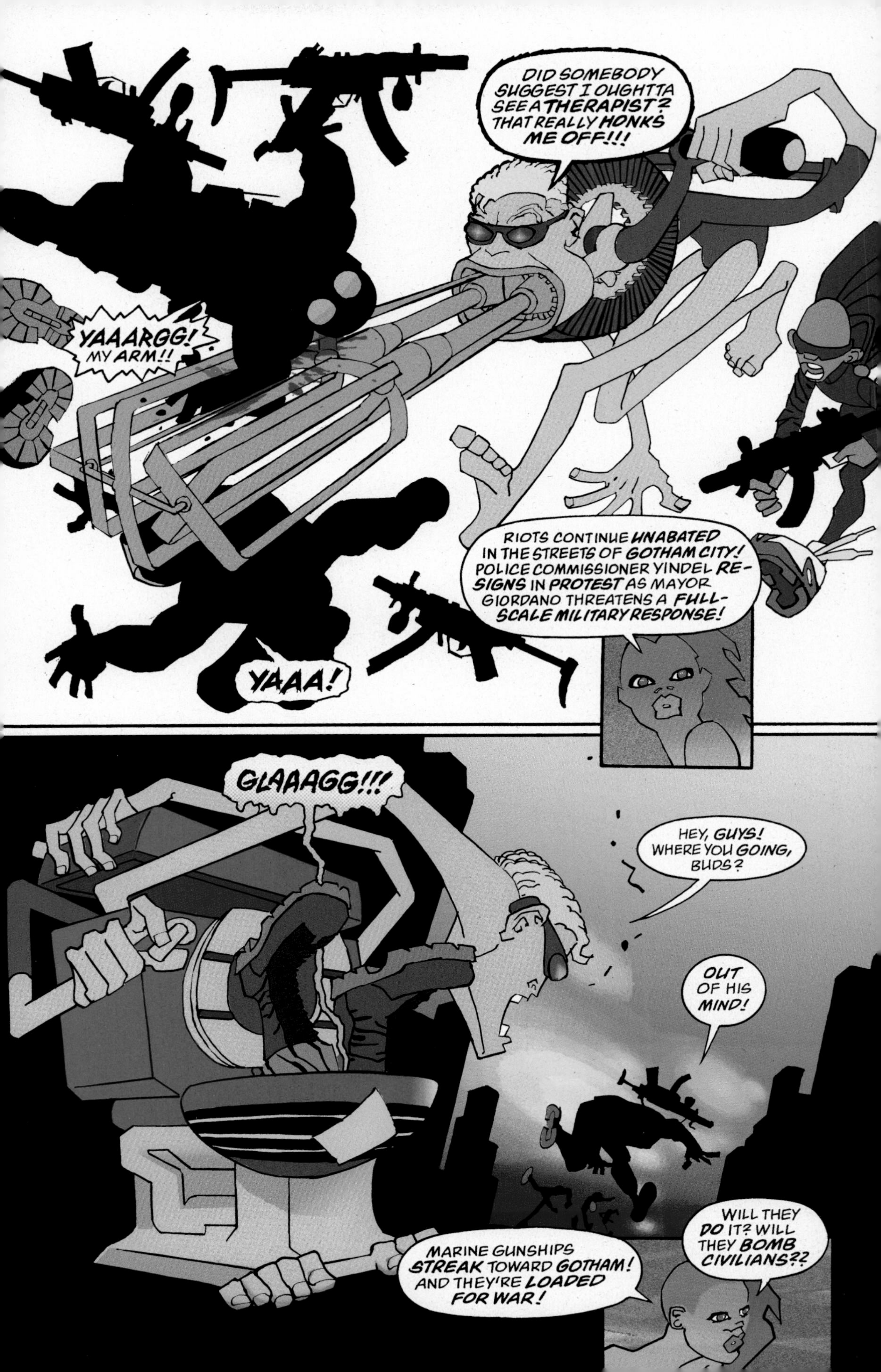

DID SOMEBODY SUGGEST I OUGHTTA SEE A THERAPIST? THAT REALLY HONKS ME OFF!!!
YAAARGG! MY ARM!!
RIOTS CONTINUE UNABATED IN THE STREETS OF GOTHAM CITY! POLICE COMMISSIONER YINDEL RESIGNS IN PROTEST AS MAYOR GIORDANO THREATENS A FULL-SCALE MILITARY RESPONSE!
YAAA!
GLAAAGG!!!
HEY, GUYS! WHERE YOU GOING, BUDS?
OUT OF HIS MIND!
MARINE GUNSHIPS STREAK TOWARD GOTHAM! AND THEY'RE LOADED FOR WAR!
WILL THEY DO IT? WILL THEY BOMB CIVILIANS??

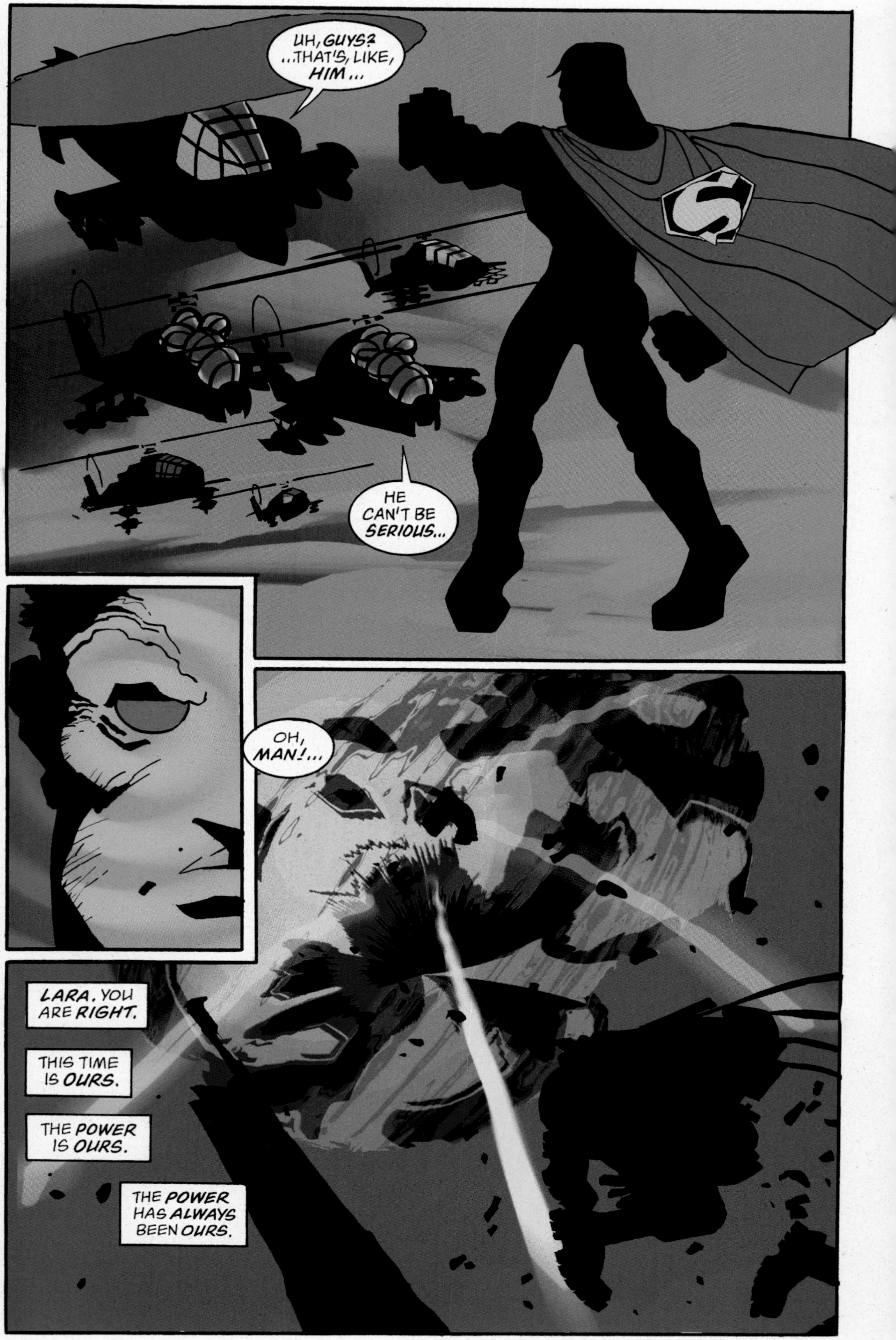
UH, GUYS? ...THAT'S, LIKE, HIM...
HE CAN'T BE SERIOUS...
OH, MAN!...
LARA. YOU ARE RIGHT.
THIS TIME IS OURS.
THE POWER IS OURS.
THE POWER HAS ALWAYS BEEN OURS.

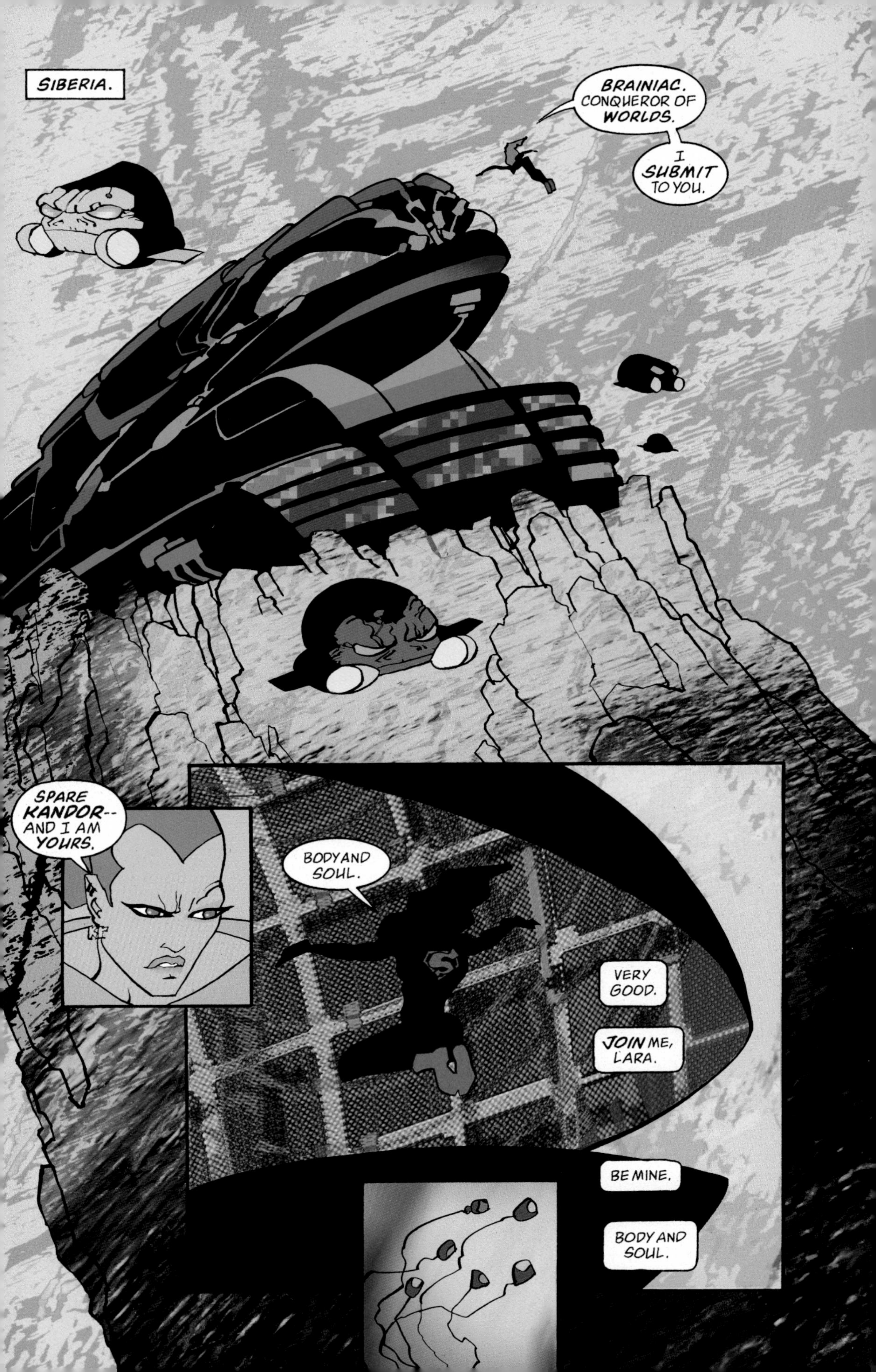
SIBERIA.
BRAINIAC. CONQUEROR OF WORLDS.
I SUBMIT TO YOU.
SPARE KANDOR-- AND I AM YOURS.
BODY AND SOUL.
VERY GOOD.
JOIN ME, LARA.
BE MINE.
BODY AND SOUL.

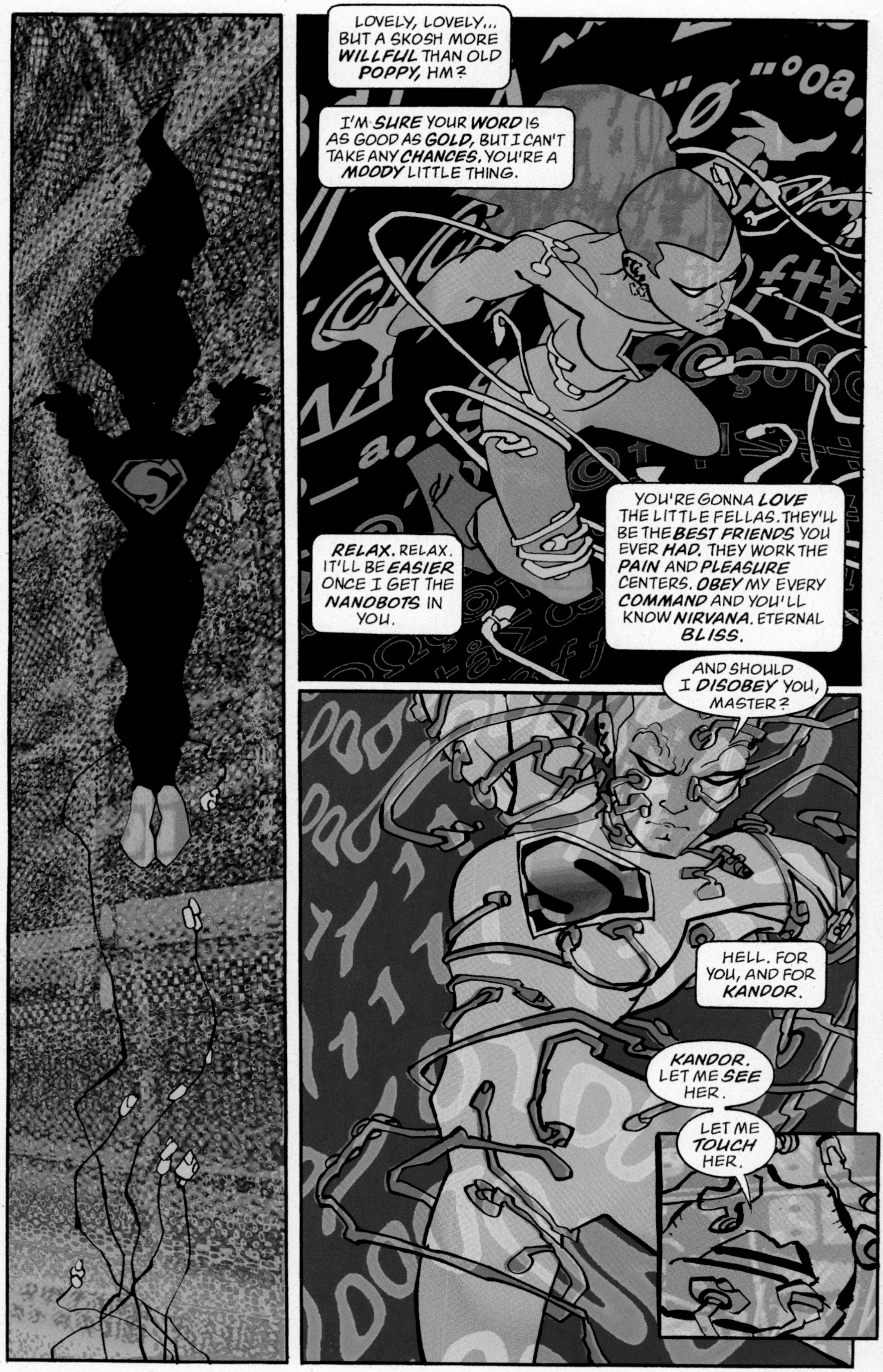
LOVELY, LOVELY... BUT A SKOSH MORE WILLFUL THAN OLD POPPY, HM?
I'M SURE YOUR WORD IS AS GOOD AS GOLD, BUT I CAN'T TAKE ANY CHANCES. YOU'RE A MOODY LITTLE THING.
RELAX. RELAX. IT'LL BE EASIER ONCE I GET THE NANOBOTS IN YOU.
YOU'RE GONNA LOVE THE LITTLE FELLAS. THEY'LL BE THE BEST FRIENDS YOU EVER HAD. THEY WORK THE PAIN AND PLEASURE CENTERS. OBEY MY EVERY COMMAND AND YOU'LL KNOW NIRVANA. ETERNAL BLISS.
AND SHOULD I DISOBEY YOU, MASTER?
HELL. FOR YOU, AND FOR KANDOR.
KANDOR. LET ME SEE HER.
LET ME TOUCH HER.

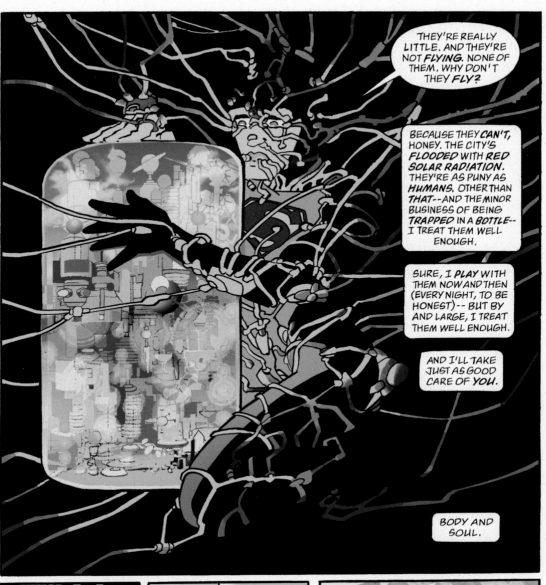

THEY'RE REALLY LITTLE. AND THEY'RE NOT *FLYING*. NONE OF THEM. WHY DON'T THEY *FLY*?

BECAUSE THEY *CAN'T*, HONEY. THE CITY'S *FLOODED* WITH *RED SOLAR RADIATION*. THEY'RE AS PUNY AS *HUMANS*. OTHER THAN *THAT*--AND THE MINOR BUSINESS OF BEING *TRAPPED* IN A *BOTTLE*--I TREAT THEM WELL ENOUGH.

SURE, I *PLAY* WITH THEM NOW AND THEN (EVERY NIGHT, TO BE HONEST)--BUT BY AND LARGE, I TREAT THEM WELL ENOUGH.

AND I'LL TAKE JUST AS GOOD CARE OF *YOU*.

BODY AND SOUL.

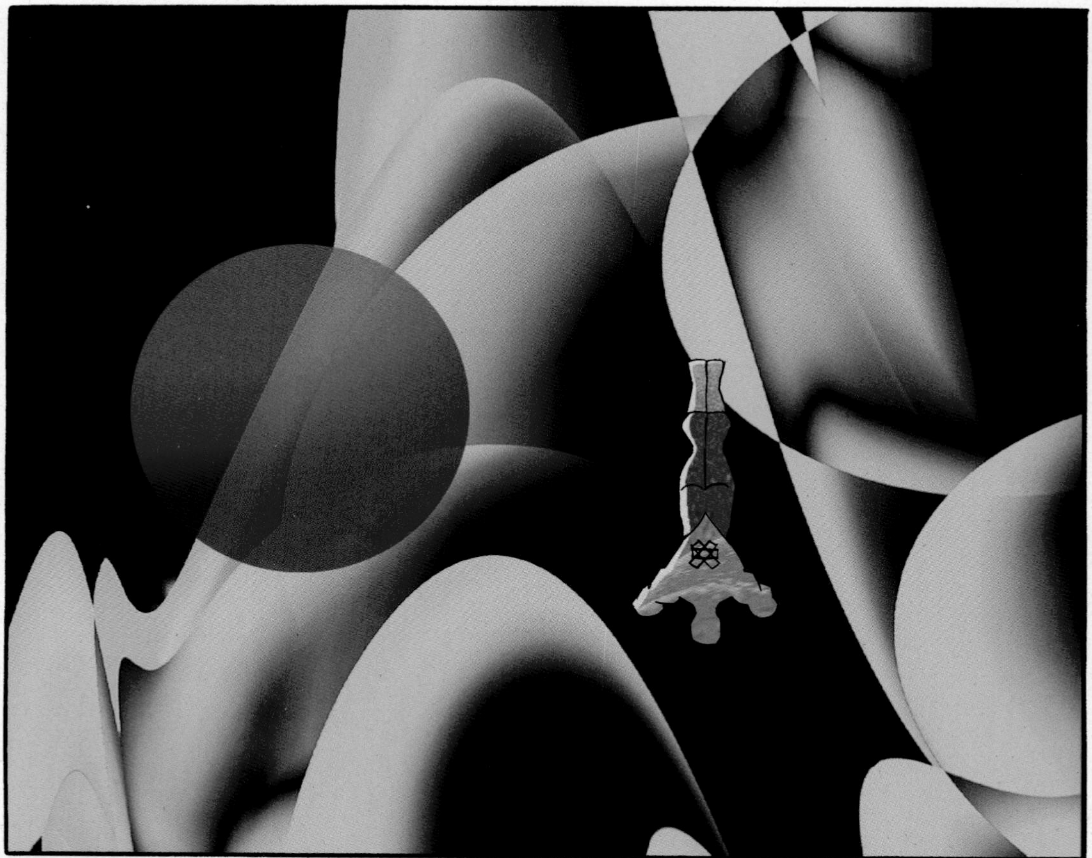

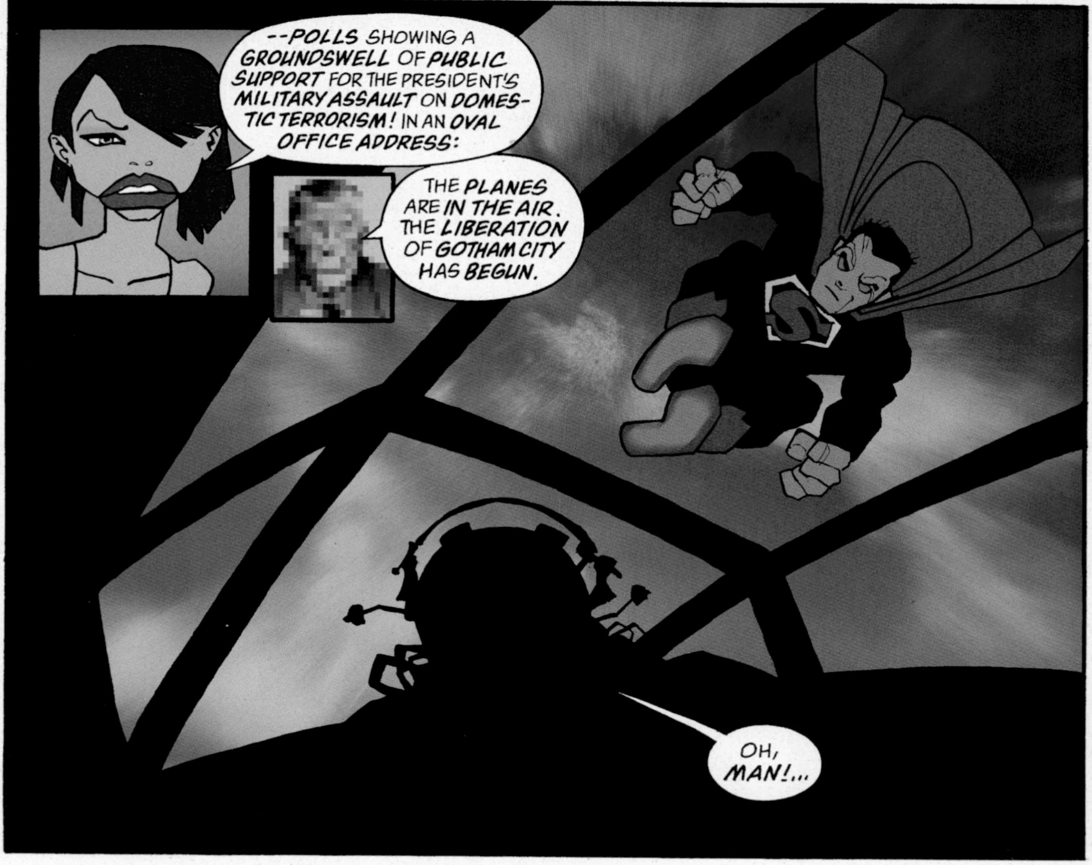
--POLLS SHOWING A GROUNDSWELL OF PUBLIC SUPPORT FOR THE PRESIDENT'S MILITARY ASSAULT ON DOMESTIC TERRORISM! IN AN OVAL OFFICE ADDRESS:
THE PLANES ARE IN THE AIR. THE LIBERATION OF GOTHAM CITY HAS BEGUN.
OH, MAN!...

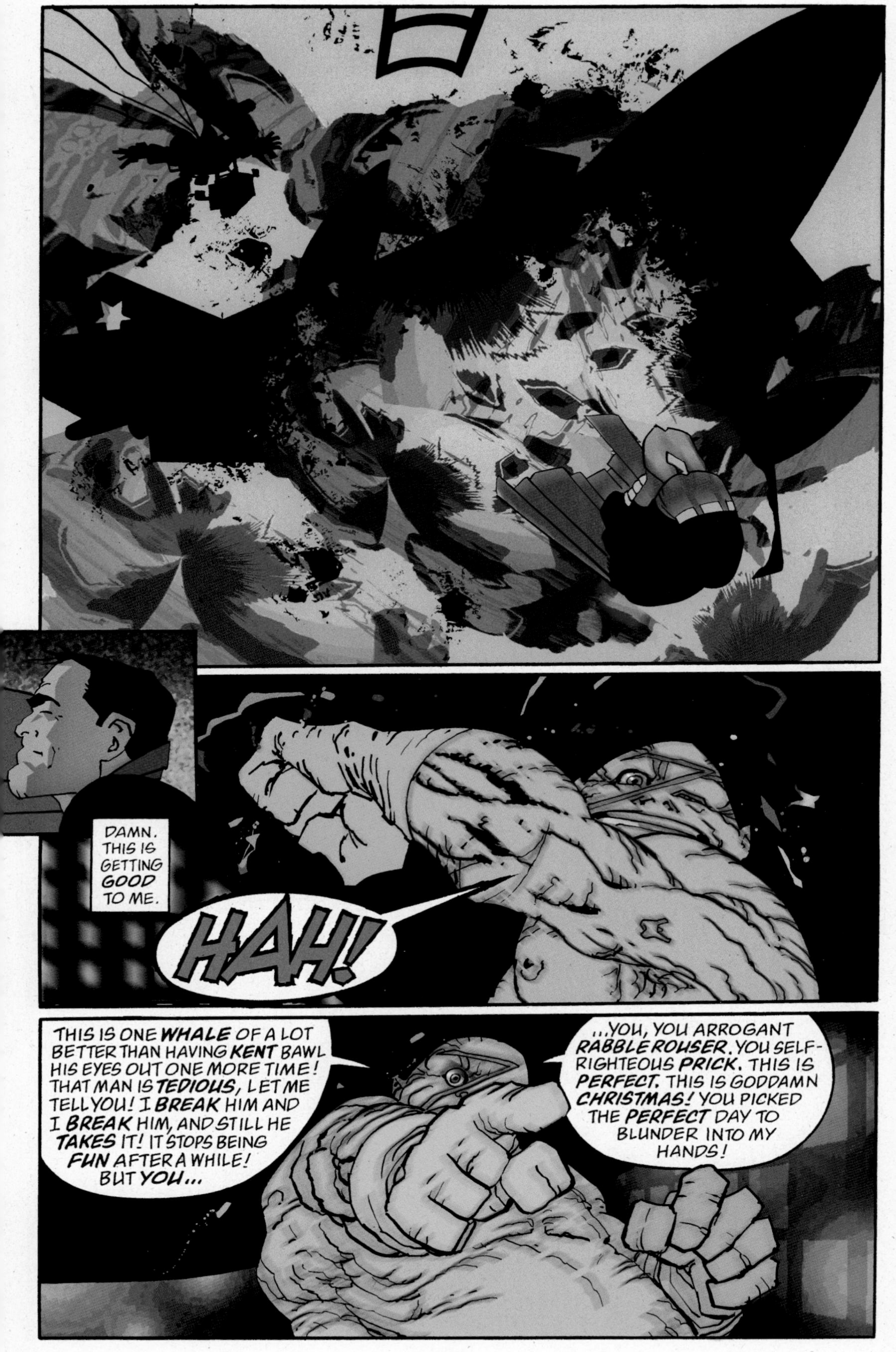

DAMN. THIS IS GETTING GOOD TO ME.
HAH!
THIS IS ONE WHALE OF A LOT BETTER THAN HAVING KENT BAWL HIS EYES OUT ONE MORE TIME! THAT MAN IS TEDIOUS, LET ME TELL YOU! I BREAK HIM AND I BREAK HIM, AND STILL HE TAKES IT! IT STOPS BEING FUN AFTER A WHILE! BUT YOU...
...YOU, YOU ARROGANT RABBLE ROUSER. YOU SELF-RIGHTEOUS PRICK. THIS IS PERFECT. THIS IS GODDAMN CHRISTMAS! YOU PICKED THE PERFECT DAY TO BLUNDER INTO MY HANDS!

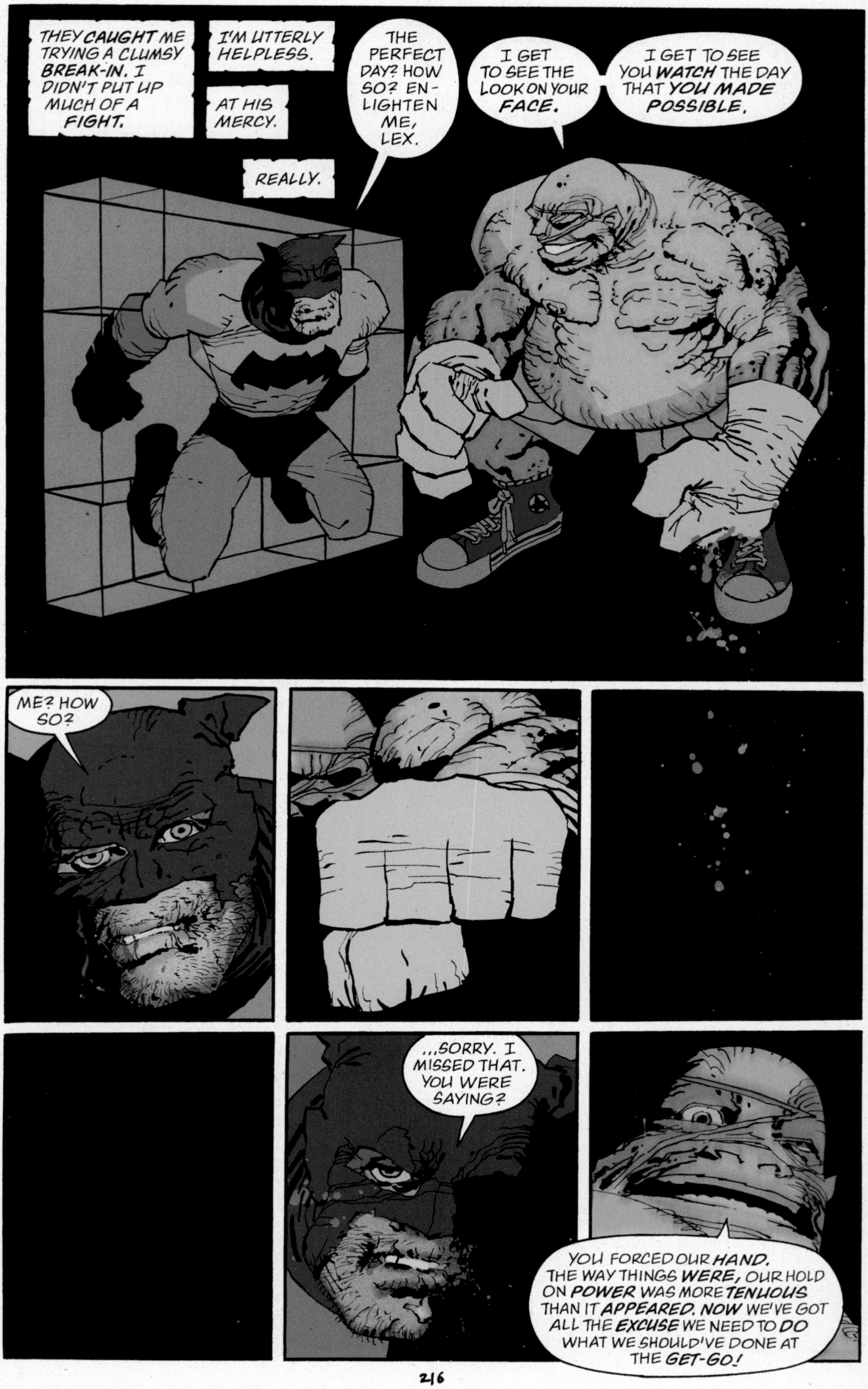
THEY CAUGHT ME TRYING A CLUMSY BREAK-IN. I DIDN'T PUT UP MUCH OF A FIGHT.
I'M UTTERLY HELPLESS.
AT HIS MERCY.
REALLY.
THE PERFECT DAY? HOW SO? EN-LIGHTEN ME, LEX.
I GET TO SEE THE LOOK ON YOUR FACE.
I GET TO SEE YOU WATCH THE DAY THAT YOU MADE POSSIBLE.
ME? HOW SO?
...SORRY. I MISSED THAT. YOU WERE SAYING?
YOU FORCED OUR HAND. THE WAY THINGS WERE, OUR HOLD ON POWER WAS MORE TENUOUS THAN IT APPEARED. NOW WE'VE GOT ALL THE EXCUSE WE NEED TO DO WHAT WE SHOULD'VE DONE AT THE GET-GO!

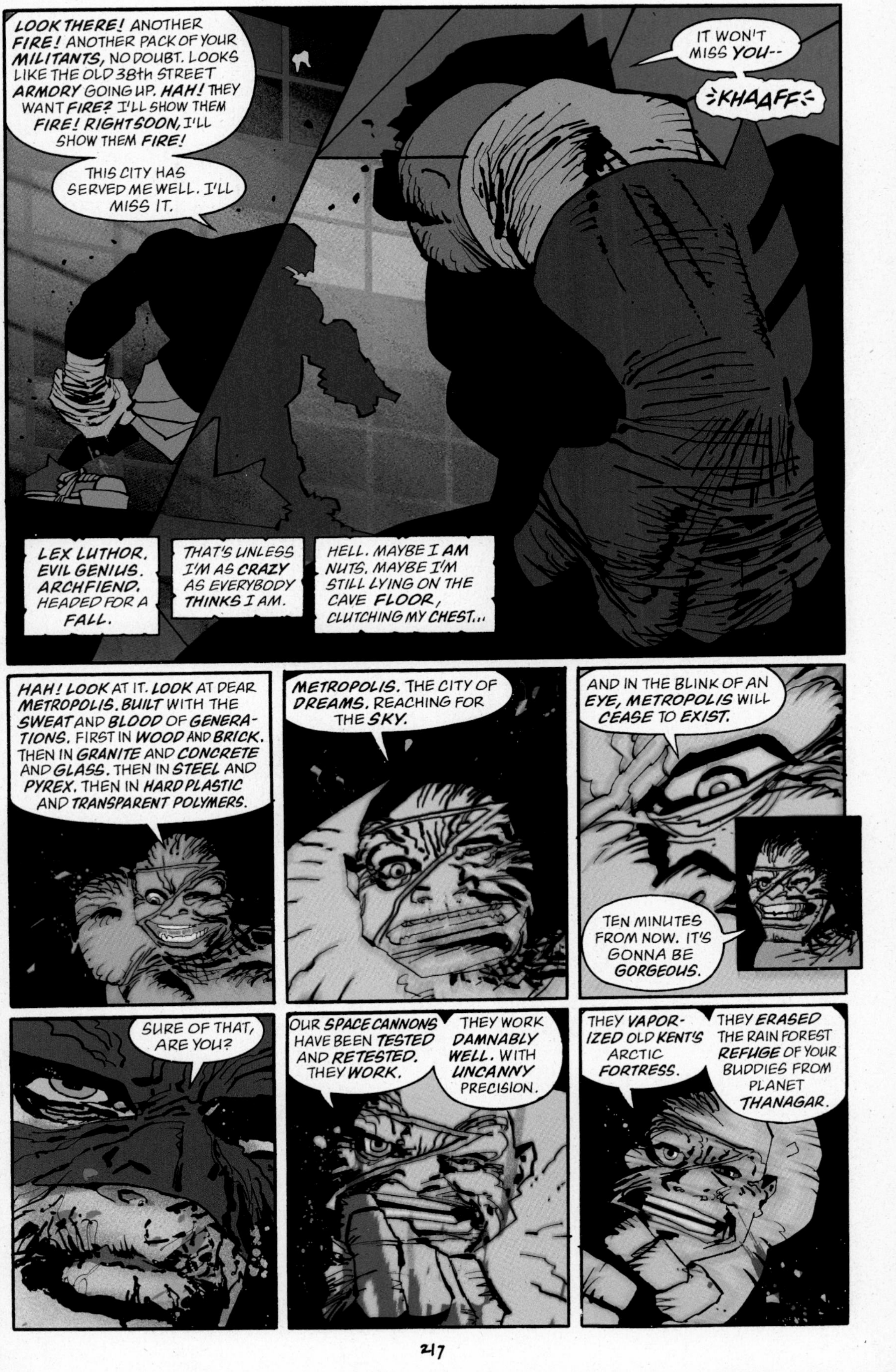
LOOK THERE! ANOTHER FIRE! ANOTHER PACK OF YOUR MILITANTS, NO DOUBT. LOOKS LIKE THE OLD 38th STREET ARMORY GOING UP. HAH! THEY WANT FIRE? I'LL SHOW THEM FIRE! RIGHT SOON, I'LL SHOW THEM FIRE!
THIS CITY HAS SERVED ME WELL. I'LL MISS IT.
IT WON'T MISS YOU--
KHAAFF
LEX LUTHOR. EVIL GENIUS. ARCHFIEND. HEADED FOR A FALL.
THAT'S UNLESS I'M AS CRAZY AS EVERYBODY THINKS I AM.
HELL. MAYBE I AM NUTS. MAYBE I'M STILL LYING ON THE CAVE FLOOR, CLUTCHING MY CHEST...
HAH! LOOK AT IT. LOOK AT DEAR METROPOLIS. BUILT WITH THE SWEAT AND BLOOD OF GENERATIONS. FIRST IN WOOD AND BRICK. THEN IN GRANITE AND CONCRETE AND GLASS. THEN IN STEEL AND PYREX. THEN IN HARD PLASTIC AND TRANSPARENT POLYMERS.
METROPOLIS. THE CITY OF DREAMS. REACHING FOR THE SKY.
AND IN THE BLINK OF AN EYE, METROPOLIS WILL CEASE TO EXIST.
TEN MINUTES FROM NOW. IT'S GONNA BE GORGEOUS.
SURE OF THAT, ARE YOU?
OUR SPACE CANNONS HAVE BEEN TESTED AND RETESTED. THEY WORK.
THEY WORK DAMNABLY WELL. WITH UNCANNY PRECISION.
THEY VAPORIZED OLD KENT'S ARCTIC FORTRESS.
THEY ERASED THE RAIN FOREST REFUGE OF YOUR BUDDIES FROM PLANET THANAGAR.

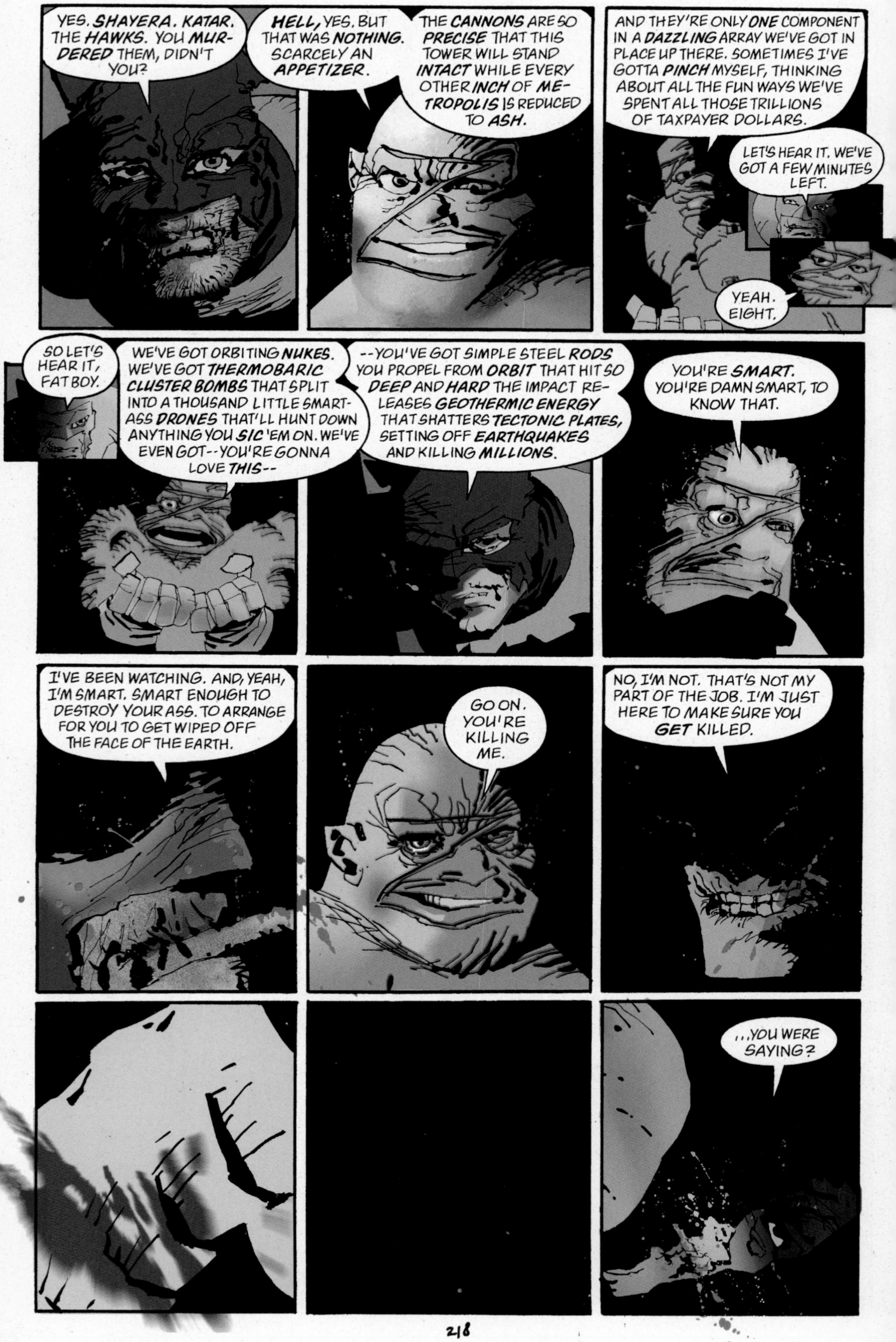
YES. SHAYERA. KATAR. THE HAWKS. YOU MURDERED THEM, DIDN'T YOU?
HELL, YES. BUT THAT WAS NOTHING. SCARCELY AN APPETIZER.
THE CANNONS ARE SO PRECISE THAT THIS TOWER WILL STAND INTACT WHILE EVERY OTHER INCH OF METROPOLIS IS REDUCED TO ASH.
AND THEY'RE ONLY ONE COMPONENT IN A DAZZLING ARRAY WE'VE GOT IN PLACE UP THERE. SOMETIMES I'VE GOTTA PINCH MYSELF, THINKING ABOUT ALL THE FUN WAYS WE'VE SPENT ALL THOSE TRILLIONS OF TAXPAYER DOLLARS.
LET'S HEAR IT. WE'VE GOT A FEW MINUTES LEFT.
YEAH. EIGHT.
SO LET'S HEAR IT, FAT BOY.
WE'VE GOT ORBITING NUKES. WE'VE GOT THERMOBARIC CLUSTER BOMBS THAT SPLIT INTO A THOUSAND LITTLE SMART-ASS DRONES THAT'LL HUNT DOWN ANYTHING YOU SIC 'EM ON. WE'VE EVEN GOT--YOU'RE GONNA LOVE THIS--
--YOU'VE GOT SIMPLE STEEL RODS YOU PROPEL FROM ORBIT THAT HIT SO DEEP AND HARD THE IMPACT RELEASES GEOTHERMIC ENERGY THAT SHATTERS TECTONIC PLATES, SETTING OFF EARTHQUAKES AND KILLING MILLIONS.
YOU'RE SMART. YOU'RE DAMN SMART, TO KNOW THAT.
I'VE BEEN WATCHING. AND, YEAH, I'M SMART. SMART ENOUGH TO DESTROY YOUR ASS. TO ARRANGE FOR YOU TO GET WIPED OFF THE FACE OF THE EARTH.
GO ON. YOU'RE KILLING ME.
NO, I'M NOT. THAT'S NOT MY PART OF THE JOB. I'M JUST HERE TO MAKE SURE YOU GET KILLED.
...YOU WERE SAYING?

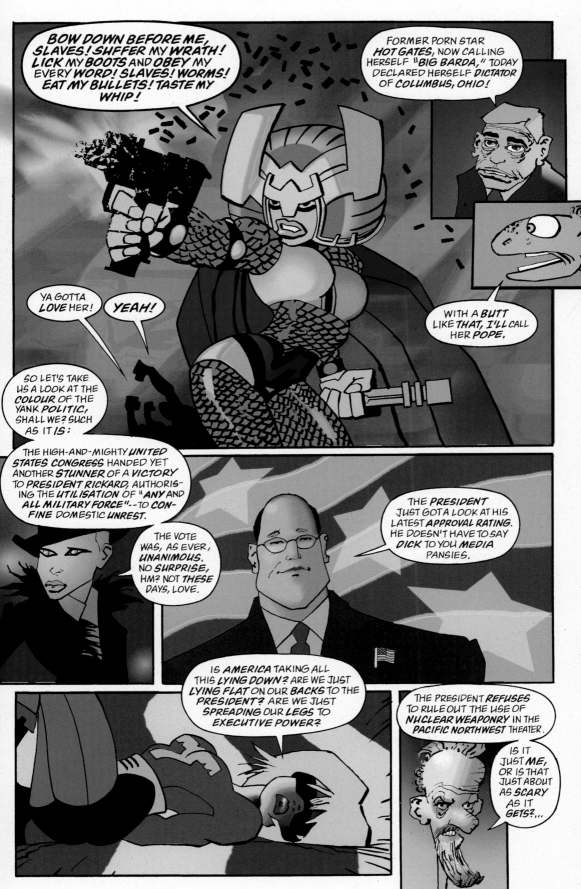

BOW DOWN BEFORE ME, SLAVES! SHFFER MY WRATH! LICK MY BOOTS AND OBEY MY EVERY WORD! SLAVES! WORMS! EAT MY BULLETS! TASTE MY WHIP!

FORMER PORN STAR HOT GATES, NOW CALLING HERSELF "BIG BARDA," TODAY DECLARED HERSELF DICTATOR OF COLUMBUS, OHIO!

YA GOTTA LOVE HER!

YEAH!

WITH A BUTT LIKE THAT, I'LL CALL HER POPE.

SO LET'S TAKE US A LOOK AT THE COLOUR OF THE YANK POLITIC, SHALL WE? SUCH AS IT IS:

THE HIGH-AND-MIGHTY UNITED STATES CONGRESS HANDED YET ANOTHER STUNNER OF A VICTORY TO PRESIDENT RICKARD, AUTHORIS-ING THE UTILISATION OF "ANY AND ALL MILITARY FORCE"--TO CON-FINE DOMESTIC UNREST.

THE VOTE WAS, AS EVER, UNANIMOUS. NO SURPRISE, HM? NOT THESE DAYS, LOVE.

THE PRESIDENT JUST GOT A LOOK AT HIS LATEST APPROVAL RATING. HE DOESN'T HAVE TO SAY DICK TO YOU MEDIA PANSIES.

IS AMERICA TAKING ALL THIS LYING DOWN? ARE WE JUST LYING FLAT ON OUR BACKS TO THE PRESIDENT? ARE WE JUST SPREADING OUR LEGS TO EXECUTIVE POWER?

THE PRESIDENT REFUSES TO RULE OUT THE USE OF NUCLEAR WEAPONRY IN THE PACIFIC NORTHWEST THEATER.

IS IT JUST ME, OR IS THAT JUST ABOUT AS SCARY AS IT GETS?...

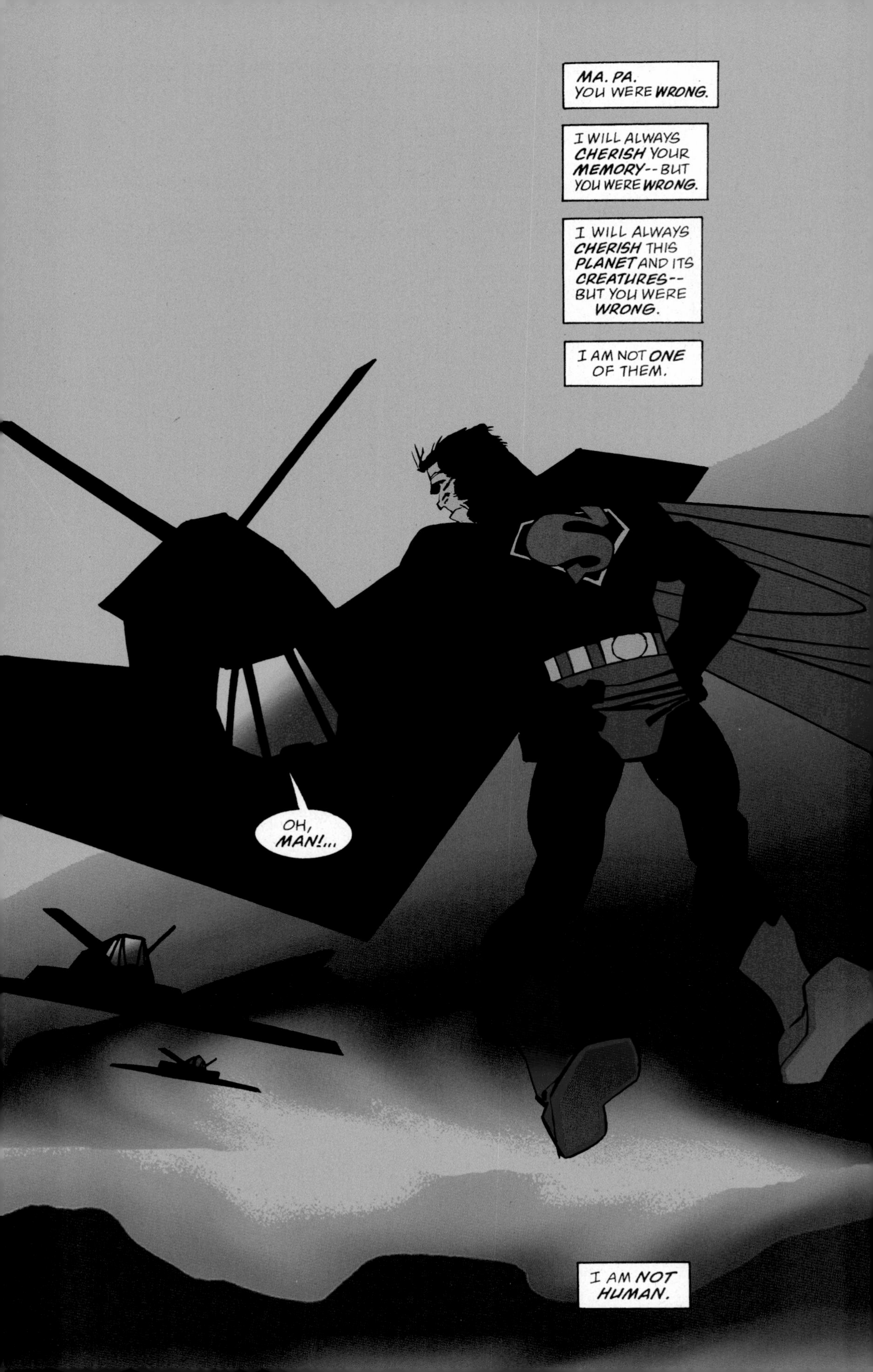
MA. PA.
YOU WERE WRONG.
I WILL ALWAYS CHERISH YOUR MEMORY-- BUT YOU WERE WRONG.
I WILL ALWAYS CHERISH THIS PLANET AND ITS CREATURES-- BUT YOU WERE WRONG.
I AM NOT ONE OF THEM.
OH, MAN!...
I AM NOT HUMAN.

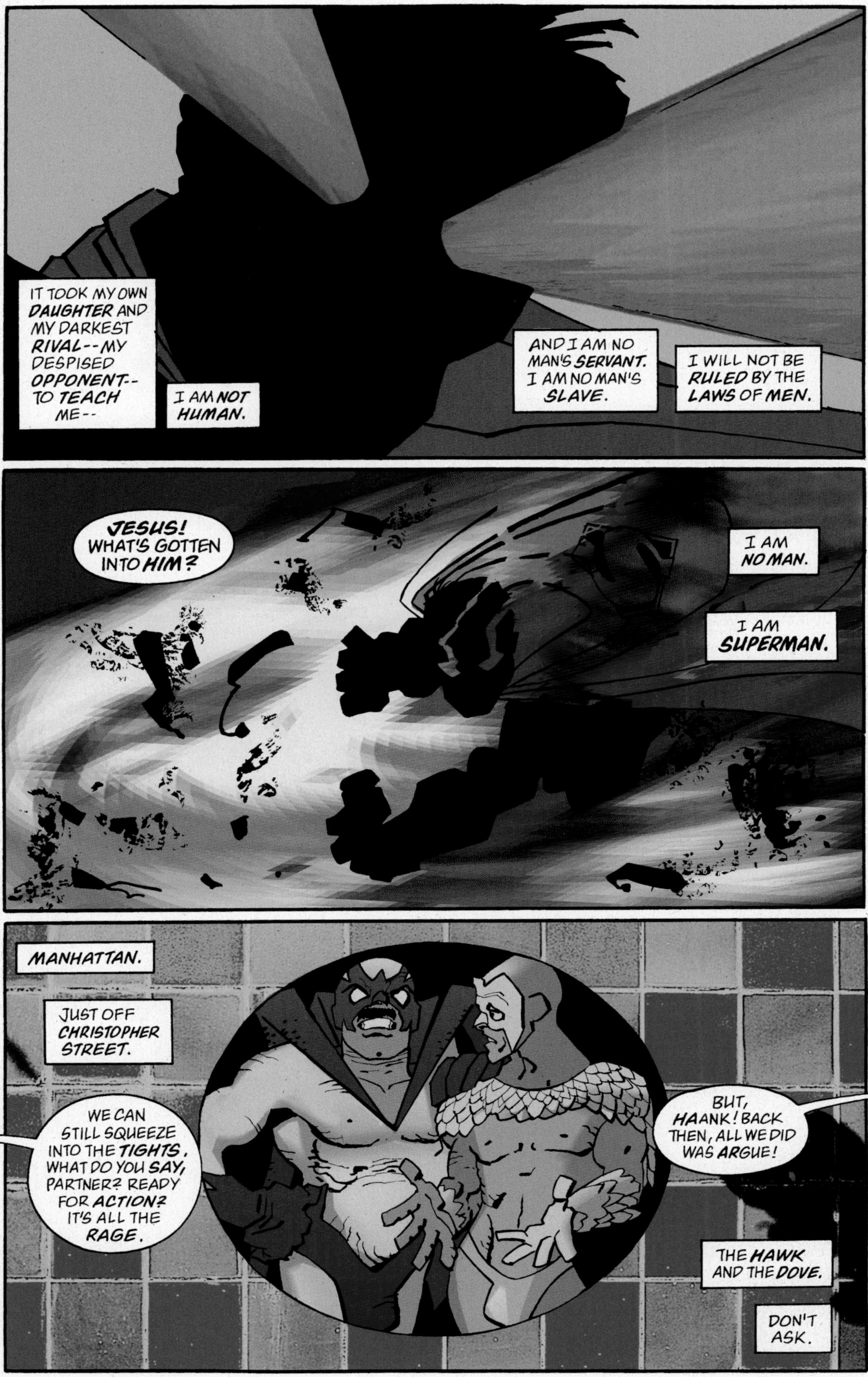
IT TOOK MY OWN DAUGHTER AND MY DARKEST RIVAL--MY DESPISED OPPONENT--TO TEACH ME--
I AM NOT HUMAN.
AND I AM NO MAN'S SERVANT. I AM NO MAN'S SLAVE.
I WILL NOT BE RULED BY THE LAWS OF MEN.
JESUS! WHAT'S GOTTEN INTO HIM?
I AM NO MAN.
I AM SUPERMAN.
MANHATTAN.
JUST OFF CHRISTOPHER STREET.
WE CAN STILL SQUEEZE INTO THE TIGHTS. WHAT DO YOU SAY, PARTNER? READY FOR ACTION? IT'S ALL THE RAGE.
BUT, HAANK! BACK THEN, ALL WE DID WAS ARGUE!
THE HAWK AND THE DOVE.
DON'T ASK.

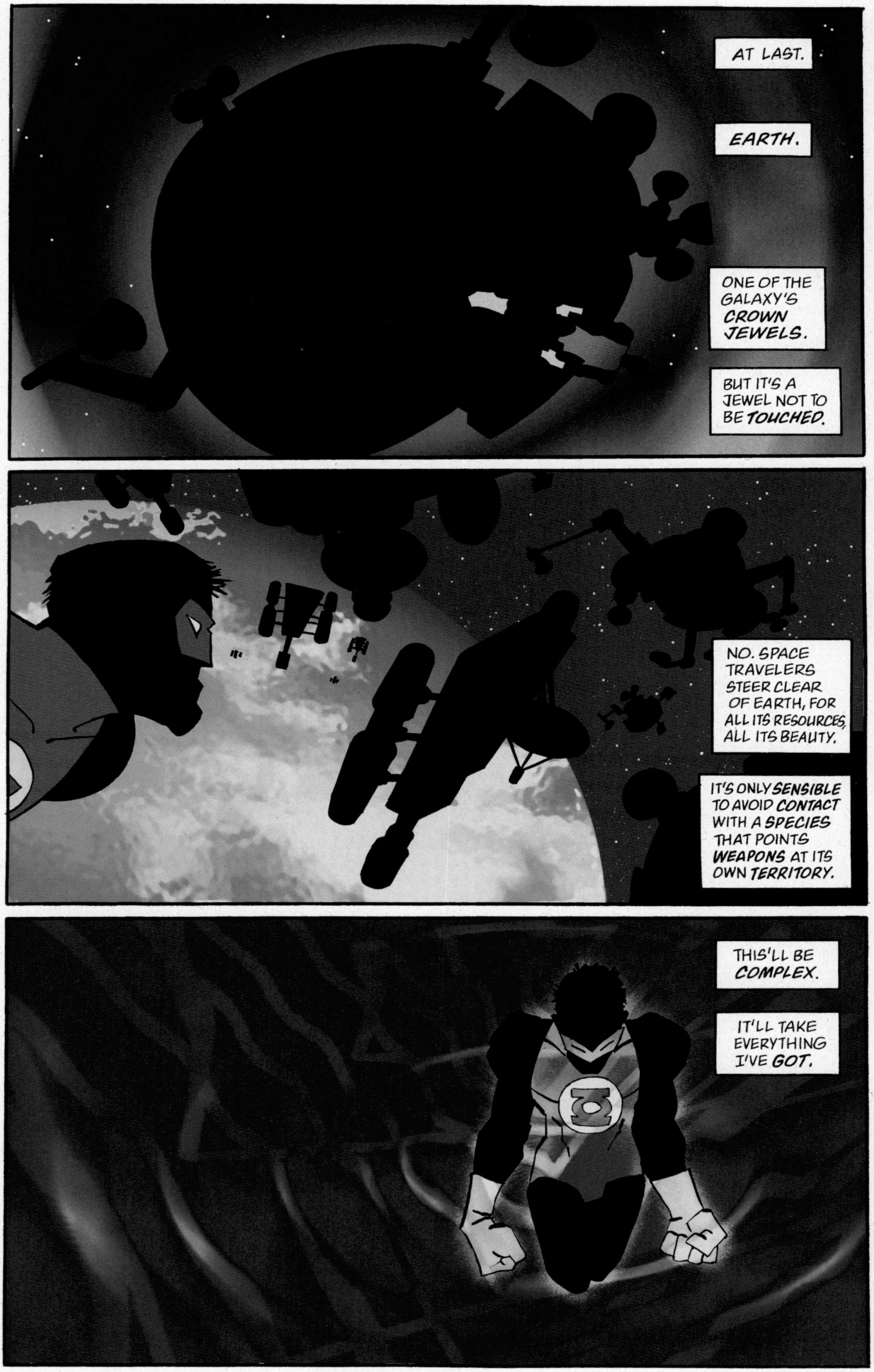
AT LAST.
EARTH.
ONE OF THE GALAXY'S CROWN JEWELS.
BUT IT'S A JEWEL NOT TO BE TOUCHED.
NO. SPACE TRAVELERS STEER CLEAR OF EARTH, FOR ALL ITS RESOURCES, ALL ITS BEAUTY.
IT'S ONLY SENSIBLE TO AVOID CONTACT WITH A SPECIES THAT POINTS WEAPONS AT ITS OWN TERRITORY.
THIS'LL BE COMPLEX.
IT'LL TAKE EVERYTHING I'VE GOT.

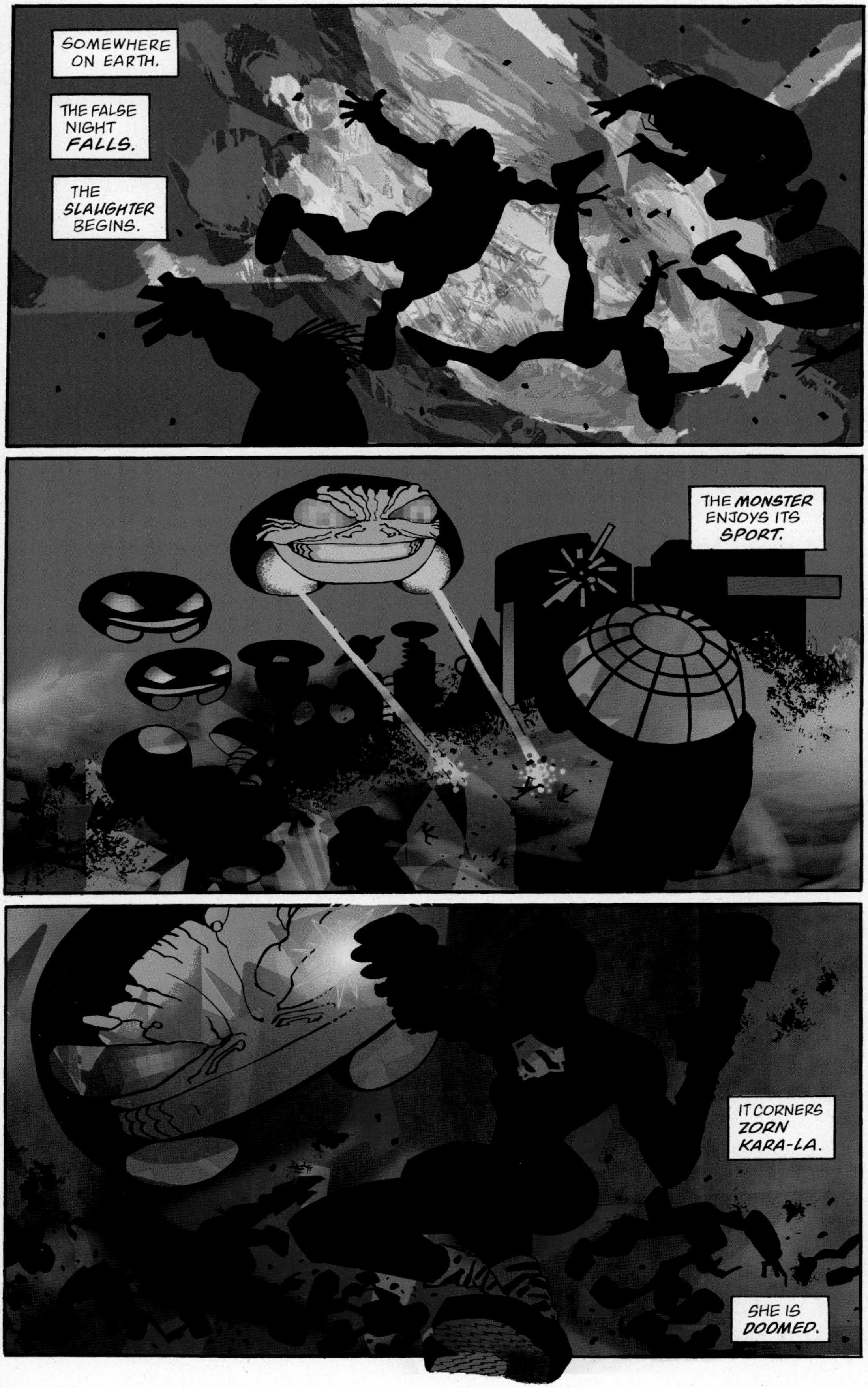
SOMEWHERE ON EARTH.
THE FALSE NIGHT FALLS.
THE SLAUGHTER BEGINS.
THE MONSTER ENJOYS ITS SPORT.
IT CORNERS ZORN KARA-LA.
SHE IS DOOMED.

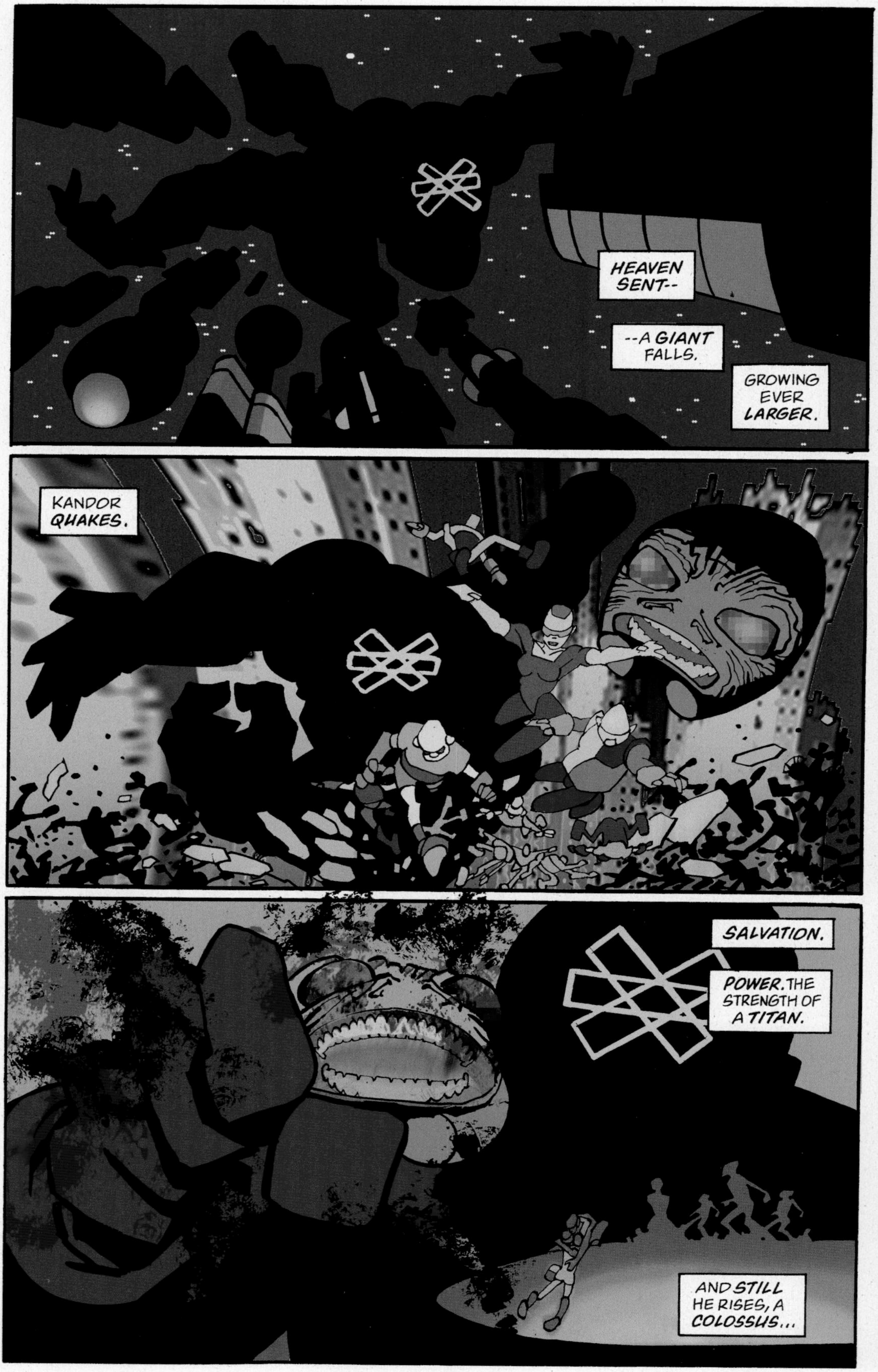
HEAVEN SENT--
--A GIANT FALLS.
GROWING EVER LARGER.
KANDOR QUAKES.
SALVATION.
POWER. THE STRENGTH OF A TITAN.
AND STILL HE RISES, A COLOSSUS...

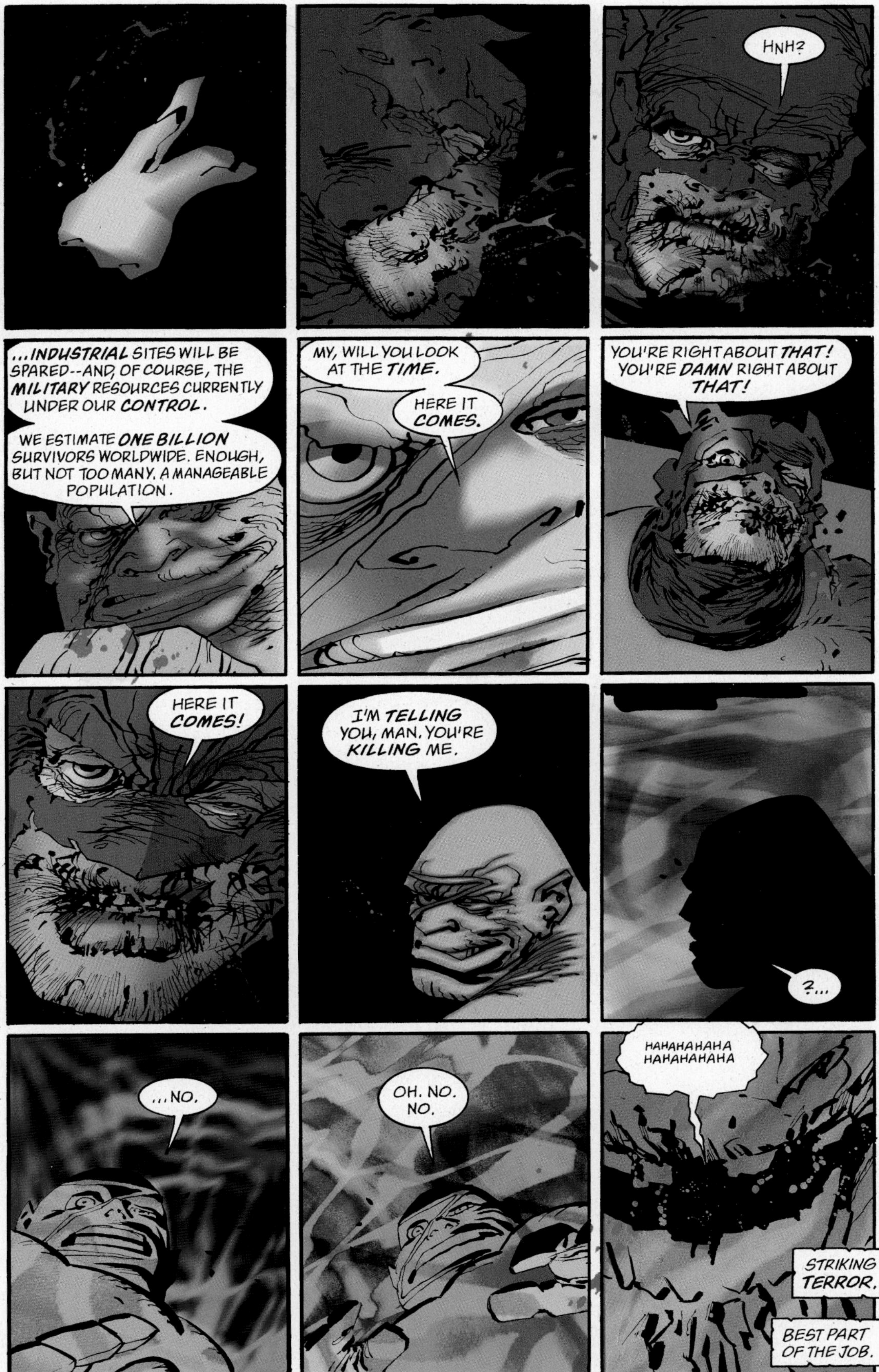
HNH?
...INDUSTRIAL SITES WILL BE SPARED--AND, OF COURSE, THE MILITARY RESOURCES CURRENTLY UNDER OUR CONTROL.
WE ESTIMATE ONE BILLION SURVIVORS WORLDWIDE. ENOUGH, BUT NOT TOO MANY. A MANAGEABLE POPULATION.
MY, WILL YOU LOOK AT THE TIME.
HERE IT COMES.
YOU'RE RIGHT ABOUT THAT! YOU'RE DAMN RIGHT ABOUT THAT!
HERE IT COMES!
I'M TELLING YOU, MAN. YOU'RE KILLING ME.
?...
...NO.
OH. NO. NO.
HAHAHAHAHA HAHAHAHAHA
STRIKING TERROR.
BEST PART OF THE JOB.

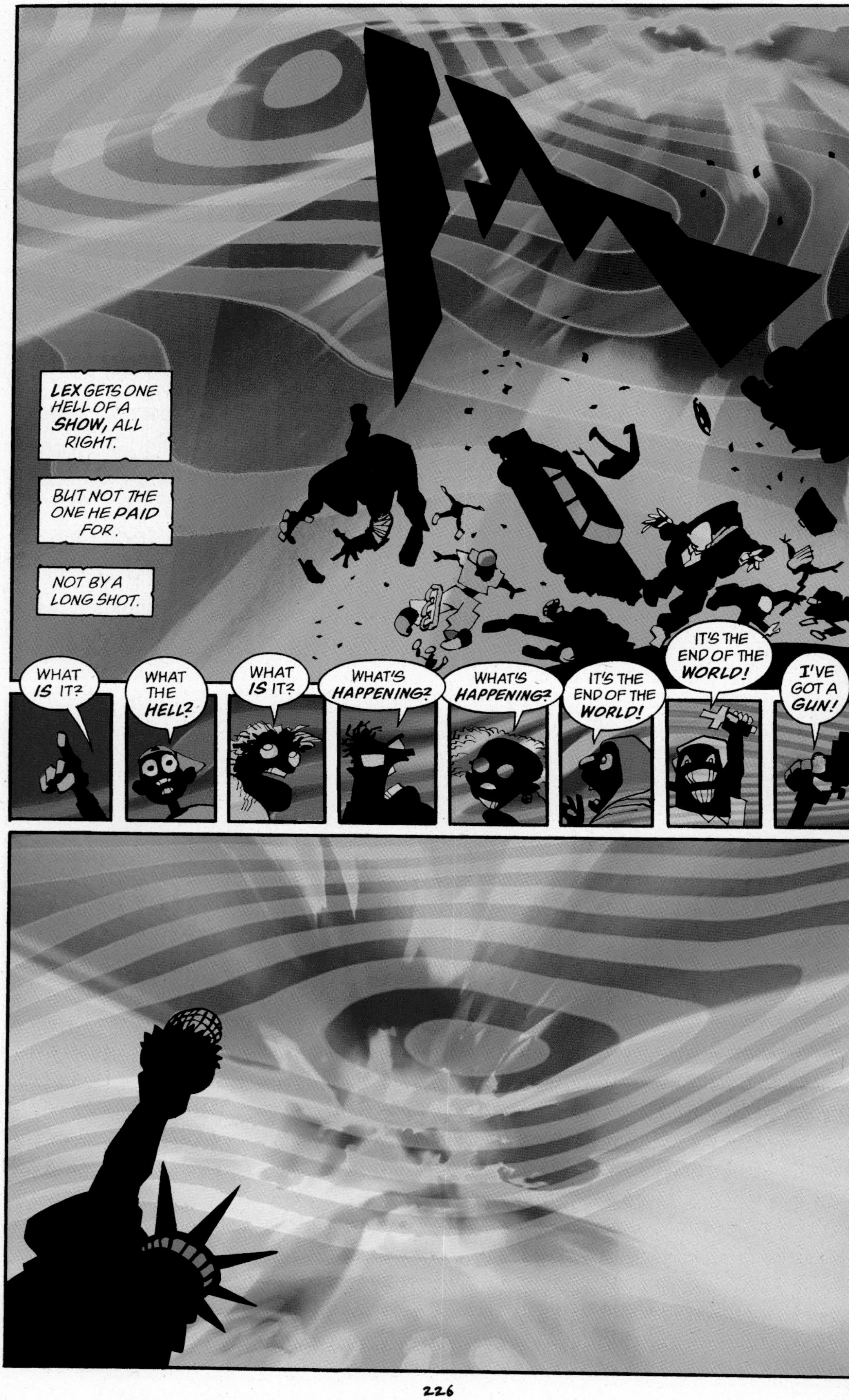
LEX GETS ONE HELL OF A SHOW, ALL RIGHT.
BUT NOT THE ONE HE PAID FOR.
NOT BY A LONG SHOT.
WHAT IS IT?
WHAT THE HELL?
WHAT IS IT?
WHAT'S HAPPENING?
WHAT'S HAPPENING?
IT'S THE END OF THE WORLD!
IT'S THE END OF THE WORLD!
I'VE GOT A GUN!

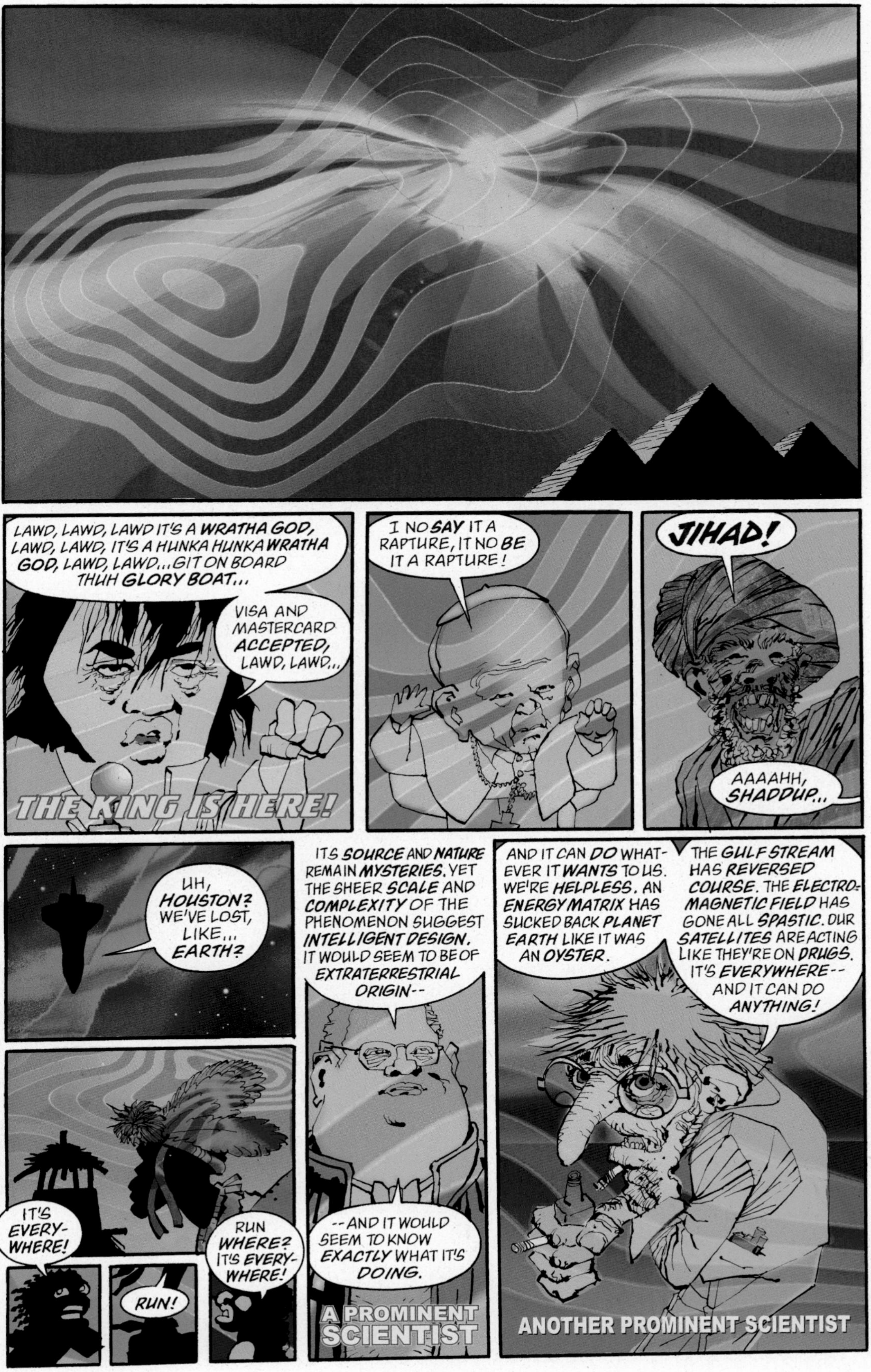
LAWD, LAWD, LAWD IT'S A WRATHA GOD, LAWD, LAWD, IT'S A HUNKA HUNKA WRATHA GOD, LAWD, LAWD... GIT ON BOARD THUH GLORY BOAT...
VISA AND MASTERCARD ACCEPTED, LAWD, LAWD...
THE KING IS HERE!
I NO SAY IT A RAPTURE, IT NO BE IT A RAPTURE!
JIHAD!
AAAAHH, SHADDUP...
UH, HOUSTON? WE'VE LOST, LIKE... EARTH?
IT'S EVERY-WHERE!
RUN!
RUN WHERE? IT'S EVERY-WHERE!
ITS SOURCE AND NATURE REMAIN MYSTERIES. YET THE SHEER SCALE AND COMPLEXITY OF THE PHENOMENON SUGGEST INTELLIGENT DESIGN. IT WOULD SEEM TO BE OF EXTRATERRESTRIAL ORIGIN--
--AND IT WOULD SEEM TO KNOW EXACTLY WHAT IT'S DOING.
A PROMINENT SCIENTIST
AND IT CAN DO WHAT-EVER IT WANTS TO US. WE'RE HELPLESS. AN ENERGY MATRIX HAS SUCKED BACK PLANET EARTH LIKE IT WAS AN OYSTER.
THE GULF STREAM HAS REVERSED COURSE. THE ELECTRO-MAGNETIC FIELD HAS GONE ALL SPASTIC. OUR SATELLITES ARE ACTING LIKE THEY'RE ON DRUGS. IT'S EVERYWHERE-- AND IT CAN DO ANYTHING!
ANOTHER PROMINENT SCIENTIST

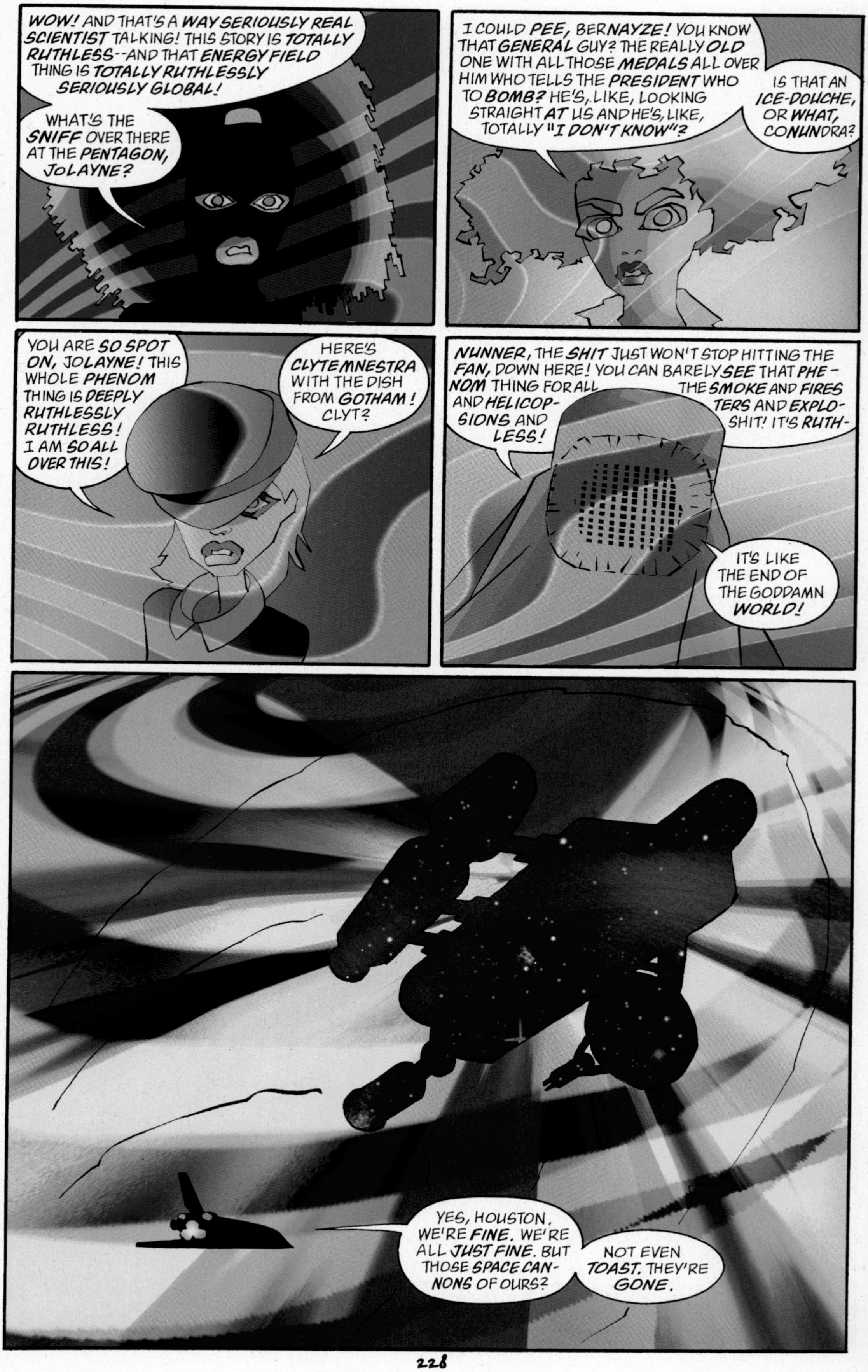
WOW! AND THAT'S A WAY SERIOUSLY REAL SCIENTIST TALKING! THIS STORY IS TOTALLY RUTHLESS--AND THAT ENERGY FIELD THING IS TOTALLY RUTHLESSLY SERIOUSLY GLOBAL!
WHAT'S THE SNIFF OVER THERE AT THE PENTAGON, JOLAYNE?
I COULD PEE, BERNAYZE! YOU KNOW THAT GENERAL GUY? THE REALLY OLD ONE WITH ALL THOSE MEDALS ALL OVER HIM WHO TELLS THE PRESIDENT WHO TO BOMB? HE'S, LIKE, LOOKING STRAIGHT AT US AND HE'S, LIKE, TOTALLY "I DON'T KNOW"?
IS THAT AN ICE-DOUCHE, OR WHAT, CONUNDRA?
YOU ARE SO SPOT ON, JOLAYNE! THIS WHOLE PHENOM THING IS DEEPLY RUTHLESSLY RUTHLESS! I AM SO ALL OVER THIS!
HERE'S CLYTEMNESTRA WITH THE DISH FROM GOTHAM! CLYT?
NUNNER, THE SHIT JUST WON'T STOP HITTING THE FAN, DOWN HERE! YOU CAN BARELY SEE THAT PHENOM THING FOR ALL THE SMOKE AND FIRES AND HELICOPTERS AND EXPLOSIONS AND SHIT! IT'S RUTHLESS!
IT'S LIKE THE END OF THE GODDAMN WORLD!
YES, HOUSTON, WE'RE FINE. WE'RE ALL JUST FINE. BUT THOSE SPACE CANNONS OF OURS?
NOT EVEN TOAST. THEY'RE GONE.

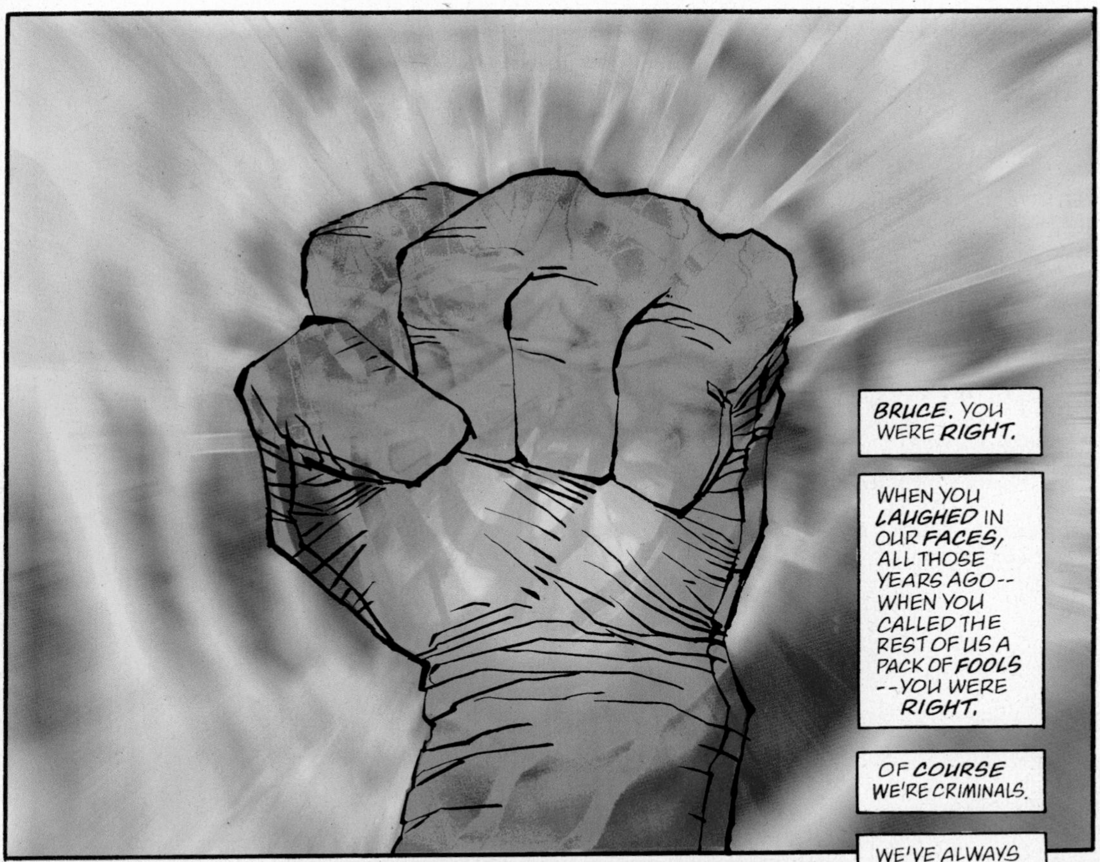
BRUCE. YOU WERE RIGHT.
WHEN YOU LAUGHED IN OUR FACES, ALL THOSE YEARS AGO-- WHEN YOU CALLED THE REST OF US A PACK OF FOOLS --YOU WERE RIGHT.
OF COURSE WE'RE CRIMINALS.

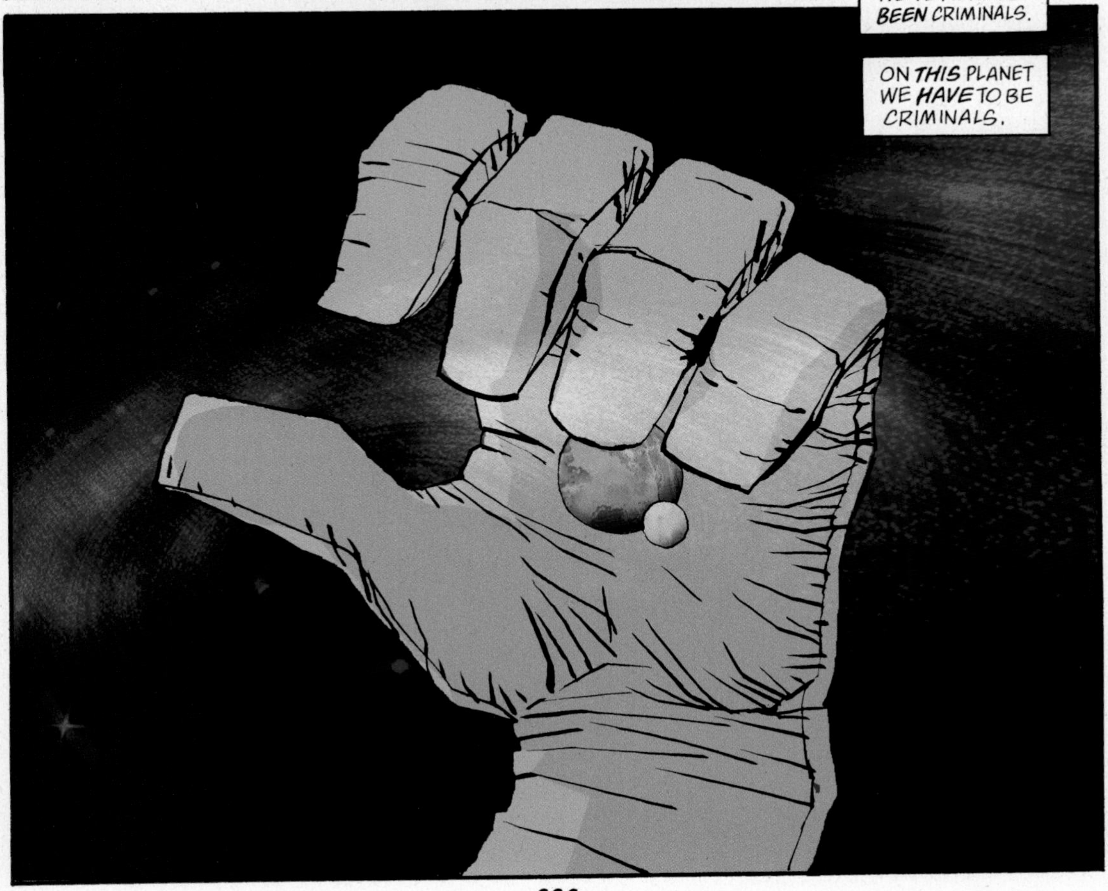
WE'VE ALWAYS BEEN CRIMINALS.
ON THIS PLANET WE HAVE TO BE CRIMINALS.

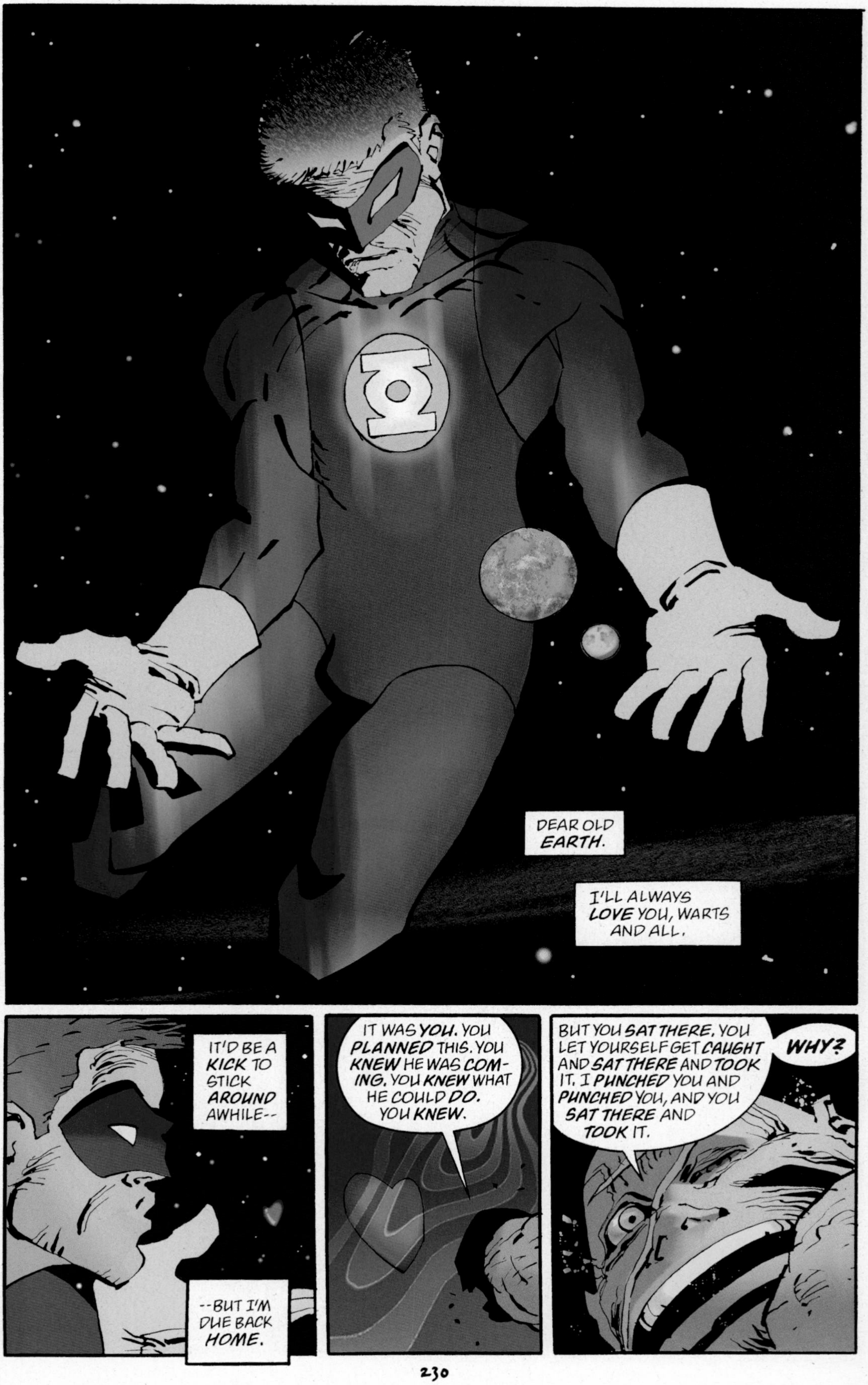
DEAR OLD EARTH.
I'LL ALWAYS LOVE YOU, WARTS AND ALL.
IT'D BE A KICK TO STICK AROUND AWHILE--
--BUT I'M DUE BACK HOME.
IT WAS YOU. YOU PLANNED THIS. YOU KNEW HE WAS COMING. YOU KNEW WHAT HE COULD DO. YOU KNEW.
BUT YOU SAT THERE, YOU LET YOURSELF GET CAUGHT AND SAT THERE AND TOOK IT. I PUNCHED YOU AND PUNCHED YOU, AND YOU SAT THERE AND TOOK IT.
WHY?

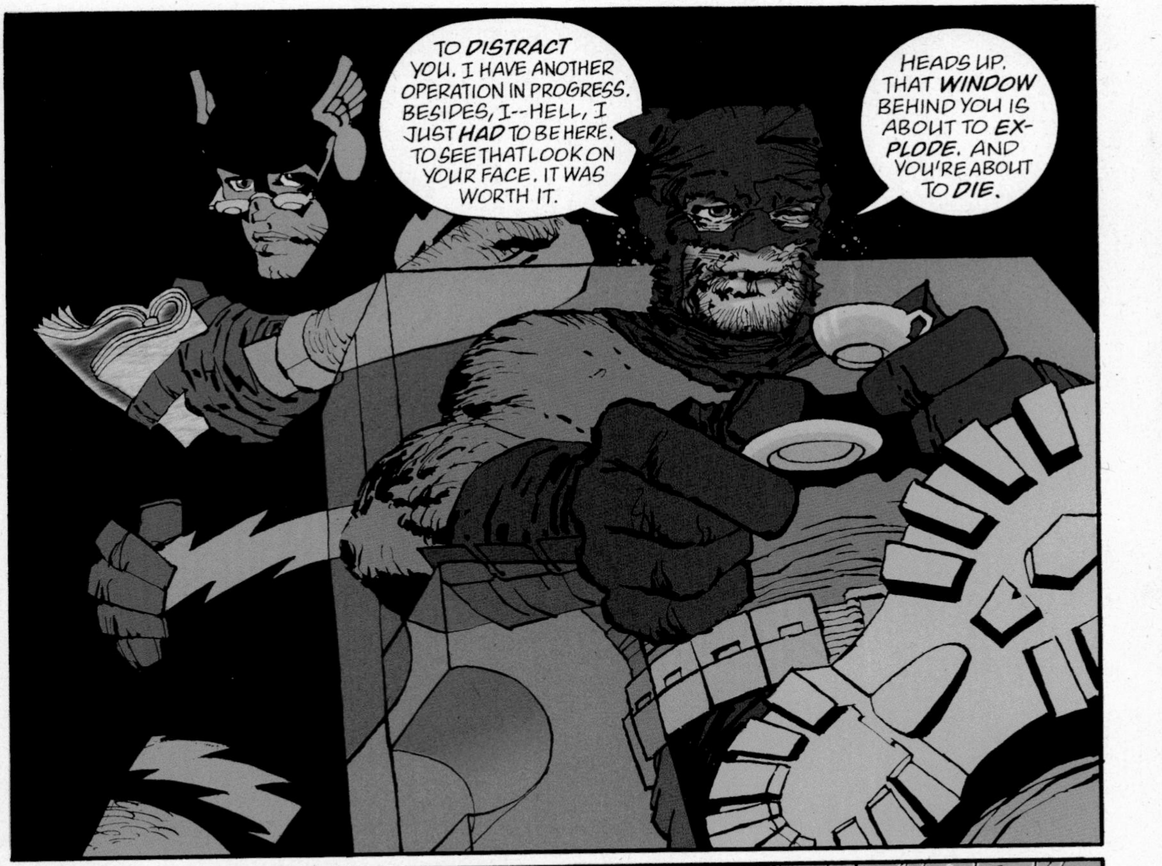
TO DISTRACT YOU. I HAVE ANOTHER OPERATION IN PROGRESS. BESIDES, I--HELL, I JUST HAD TO BE HERE. TO SEE THAT LOOK ON YOUR FACE. IT WAS WORTH IT.
HEADS UP. THAT WINDOW BEHIND YOU IS ABOUT TO EXPLODE. AND YOU'RE ABOUT TO DIE.

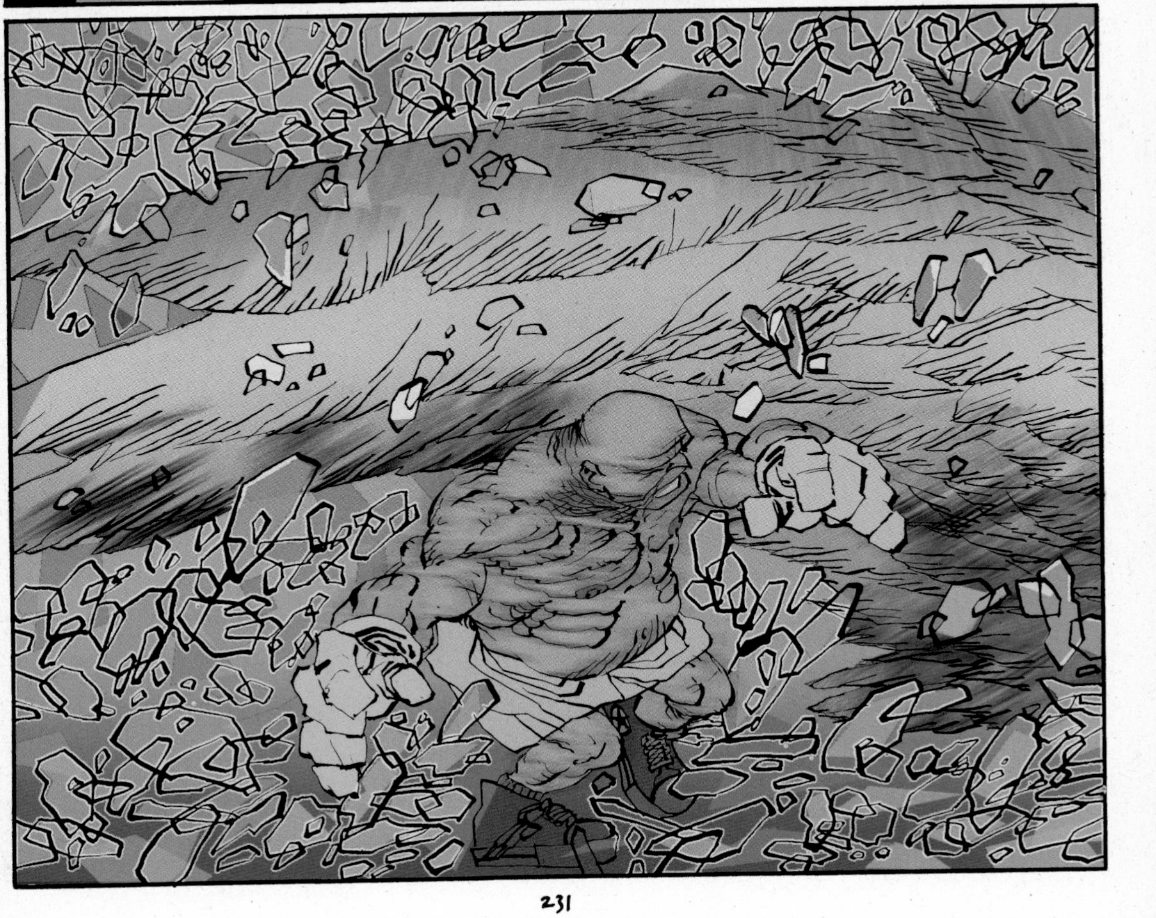

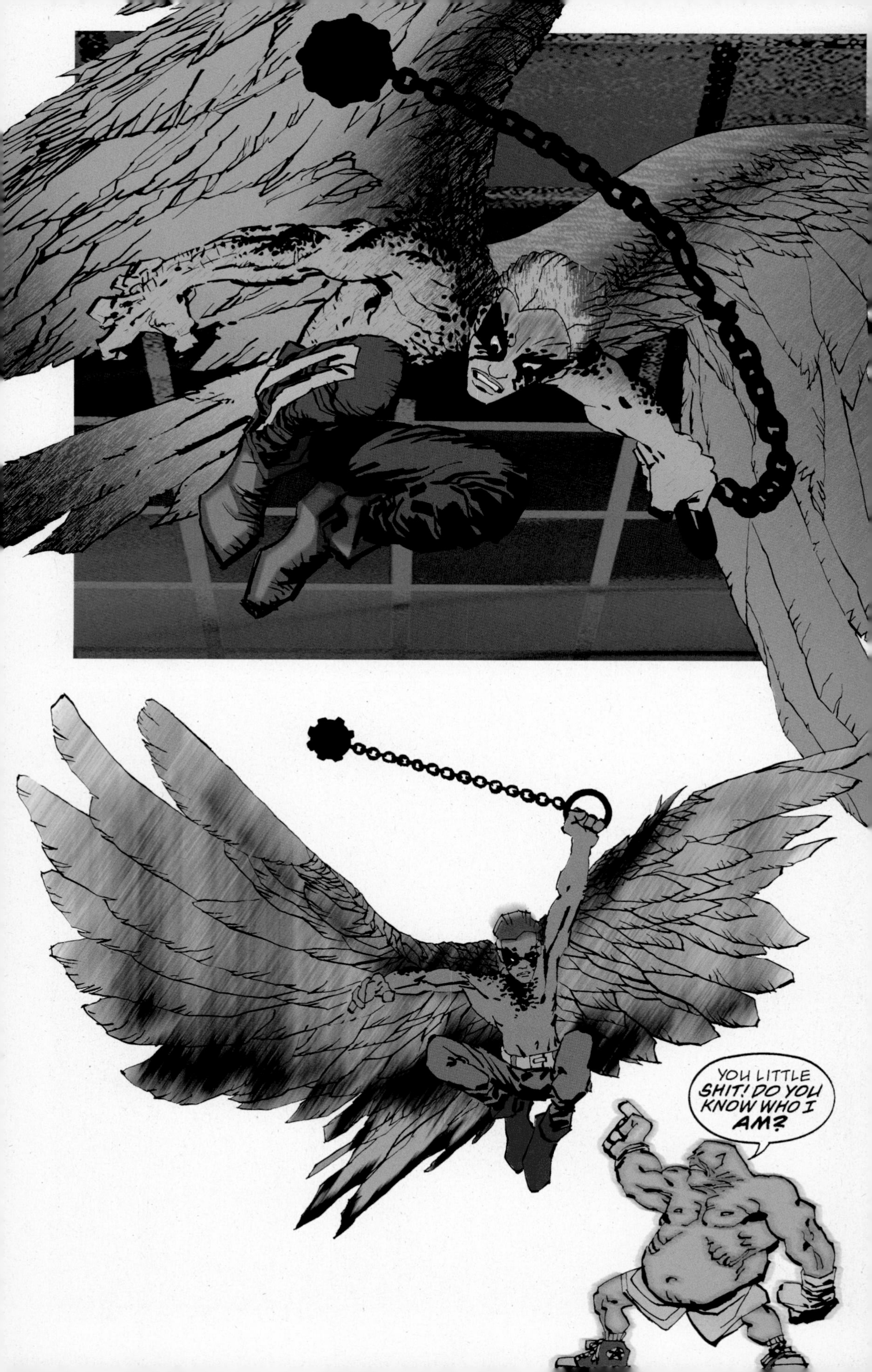
YOU LITTLE SHIT! DO YOU KNOW WHO I AM?

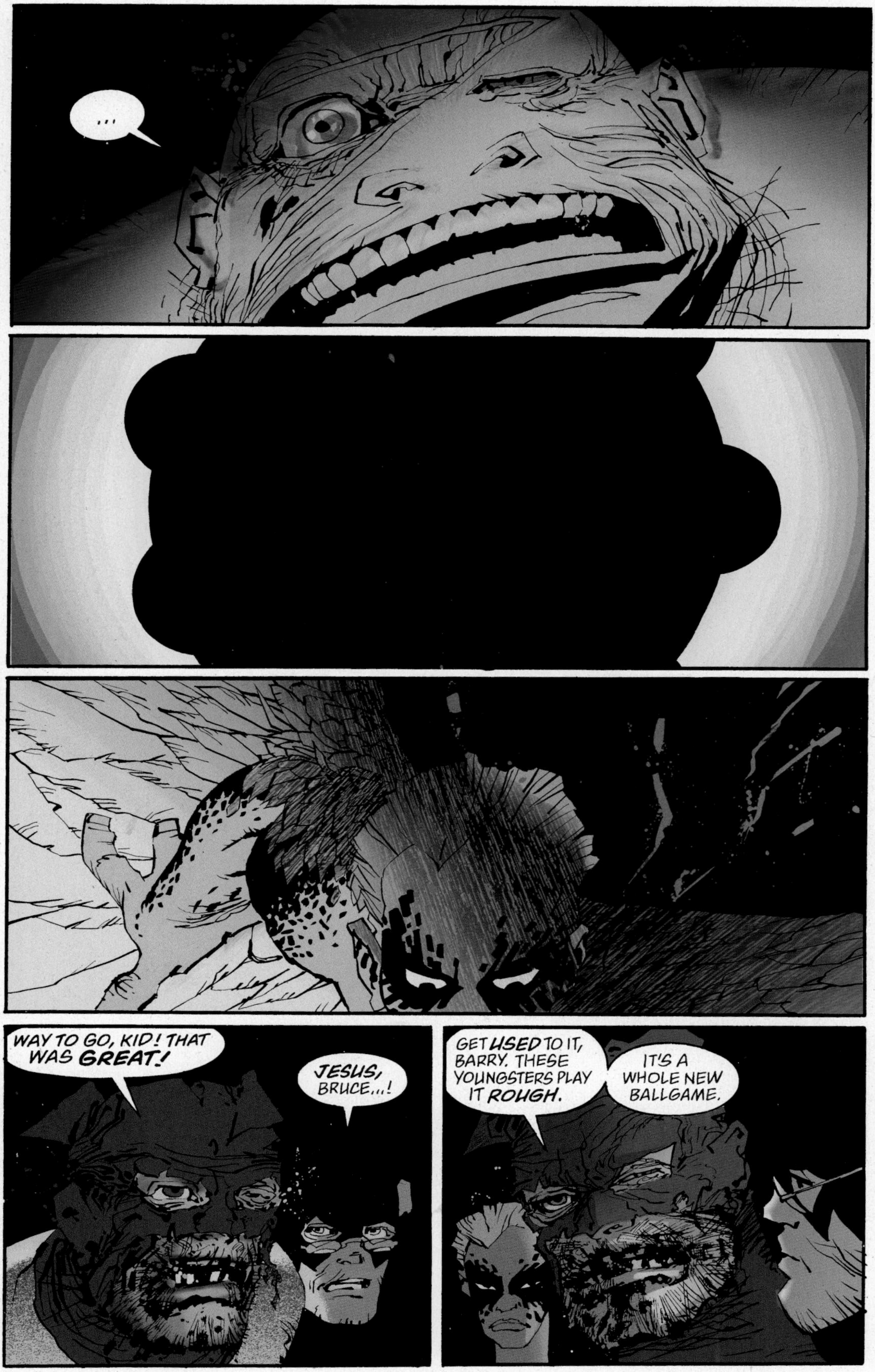
...
WAY TO GO, KID! THAT WAS GREAT!
JESUS, BRUCE...!
GET USED TO IT, BARRY. THESE YOUNGSTERS PLAY IT ROUGH.
IT'S A WHOLE NEW BALLGAME.

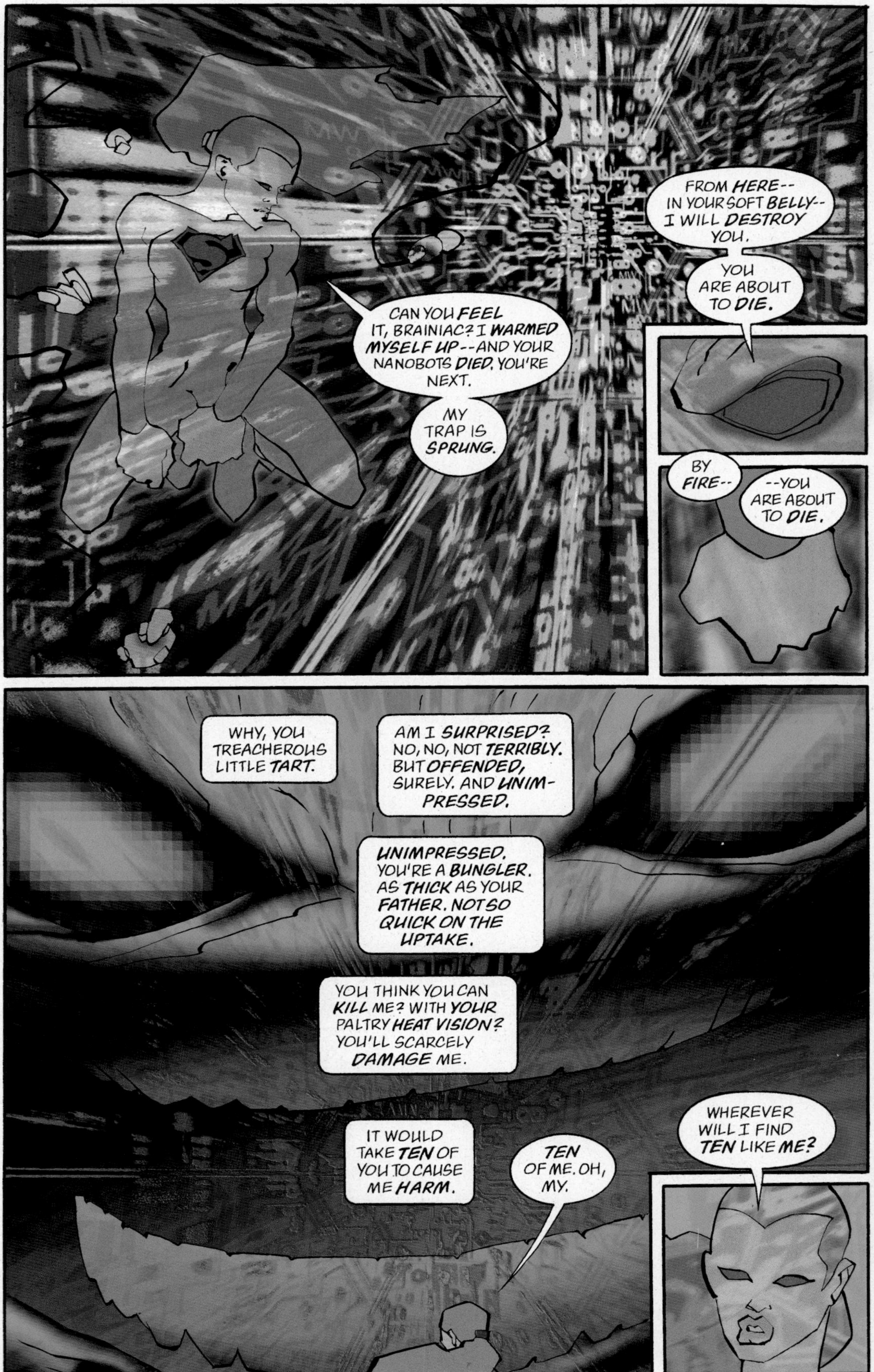
CAN YOU FEEL IT, BRAINIAC? I WARMED MYSELF UP--AND YOUR NANOBOTS DIED. YOU'RE NEXT.
MY TRAP IS SPRUNG.
FROM HERE--IN YOUR SOFT BELLY--I WILL DESTROY YOU.
YOU ARE ABOUT TO DIE.
BY FIRE--
--YOU ARE ABOUT TO DIE.
WHY, YOU TREACHEROUS LITTLE TART.
AM I SURPRISED? NO, NO, NOT TERRIBLY. BUT OFFENDED, SURELY. AND UNIM-PRESSED.
UNIMPRESSED. YOU'RE A BUNGLER. AS THICK AS YOUR FATHER. NOT SO QUICK ON THE UPTAKE.
YOU THINK YOU CAN KILL ME? WITH YOUR PALTRY HEAT VISION? YOU'LL SCARCELY DAMAGE ME.
IT WOULD TAKE TEN OF YOU TO CAUSE ME HARM.
TEN OF ME. OH, MY.
WHEREVER WILL I FIND TEN LIKE ME?

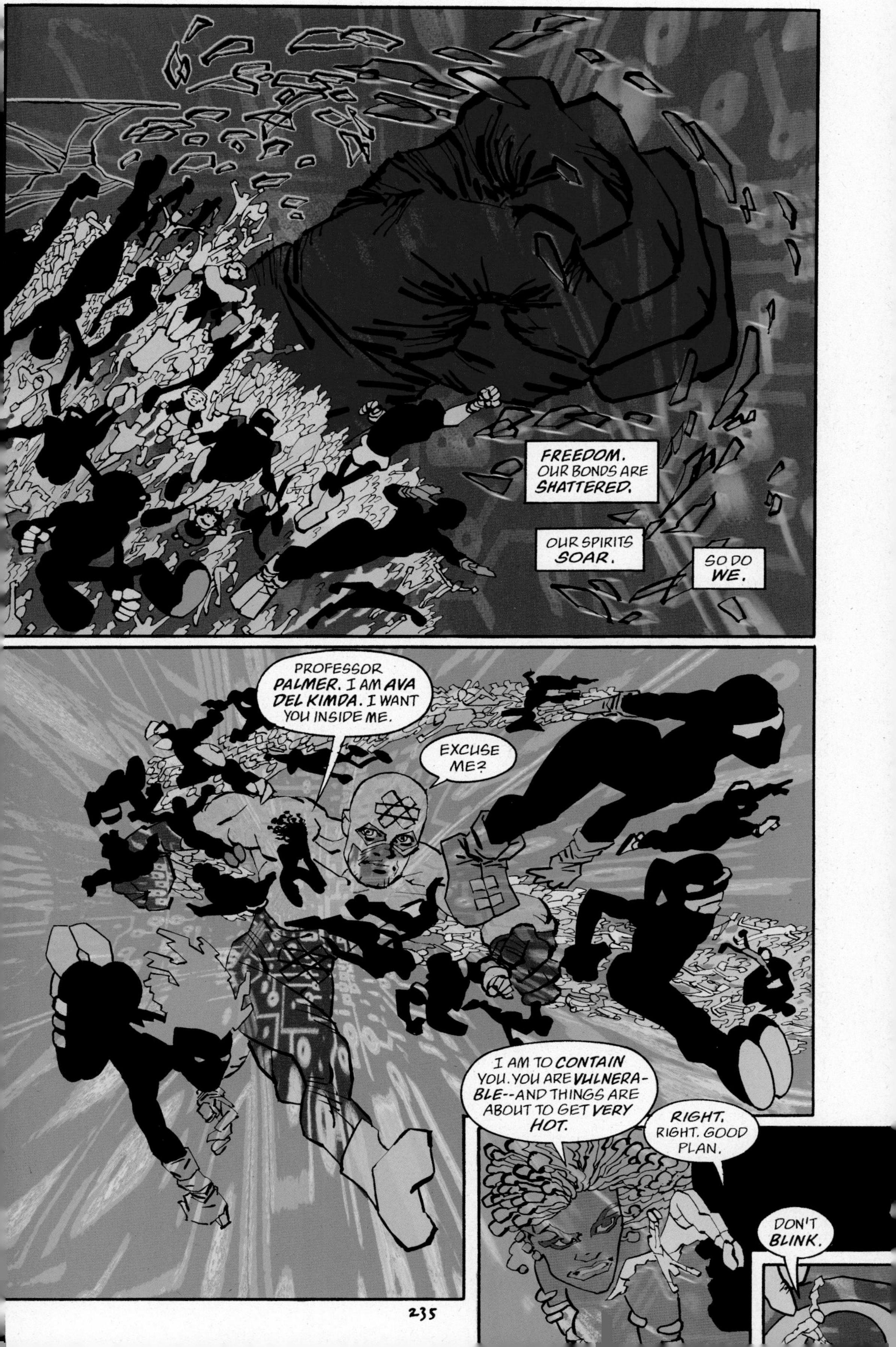
FREEDOM. OUR BONDS ARE SHATTERED.
OUR SPIRITS SOAR.
SO DO WE.
PROFESSOR PALMER. I AM AVA DEL KIMDA. I WANT YOU INSIDE ME.
EXCUSE ME?
I AM TO CONTAIN YOU. YOU ARE VULNERA-BLE--AND THINGS ARE ABOUT TO GET VERY HOT.
RIGHT. RIGHT. GOOD PLAN.
DON'T BLINK.

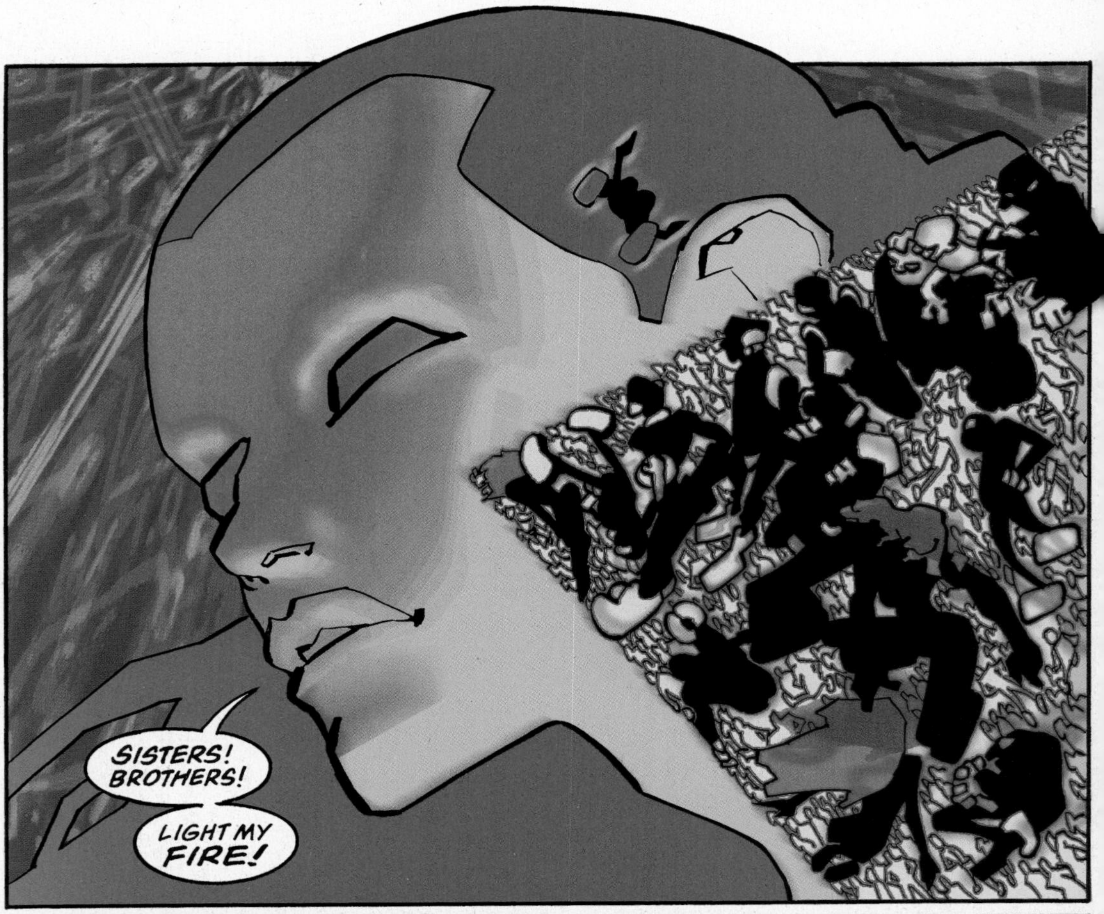
SISTERS! BROTHERS!
LIGHT MY FIRE!
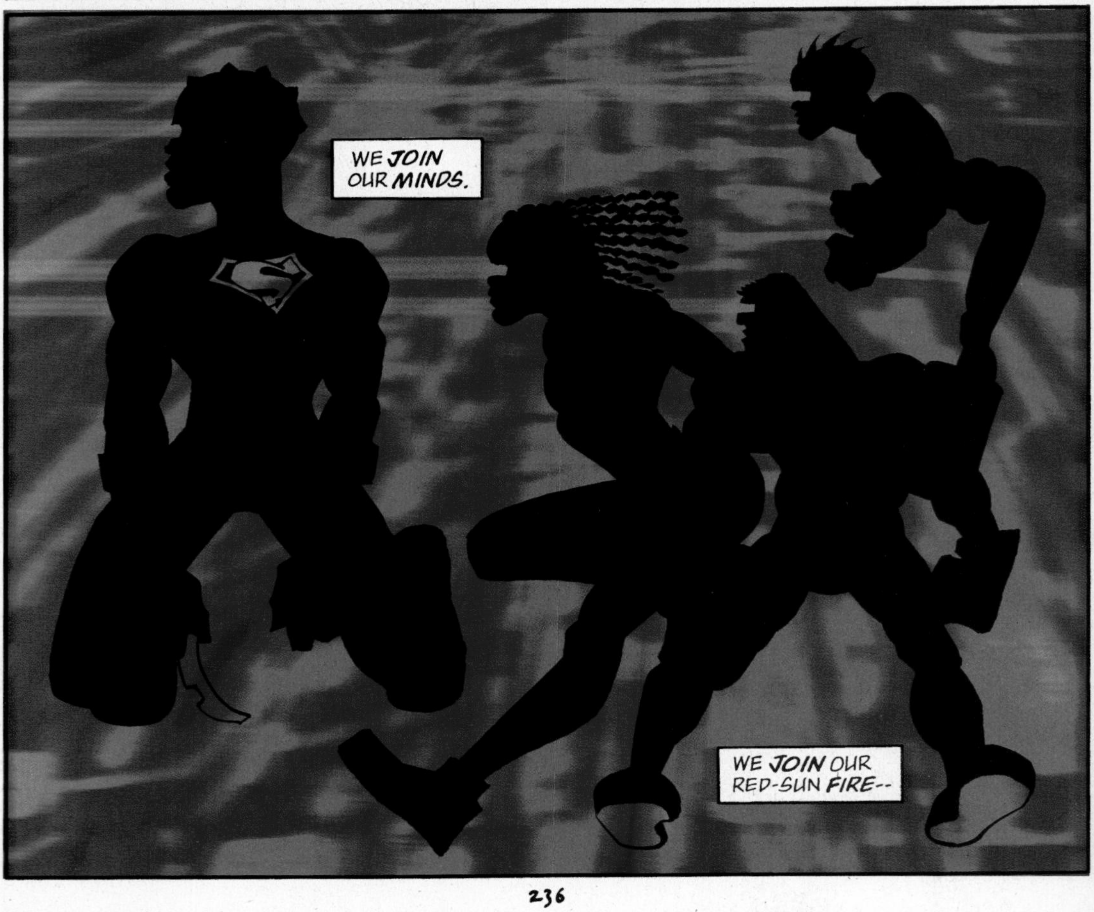
WE JOIN OUR MINDS.
WE JOIN OUR RED-SUN FIRE--

--OUR *FIRE*--
FROM ALL OUR
MILLIONS--

--WE *CHANNEL* IT
TO OUR BLESSED,
HYBRID *SISTER*--

--AND POWER-BORN,
SHE *HOLDS* IT--SHE
HARNESSES IT--

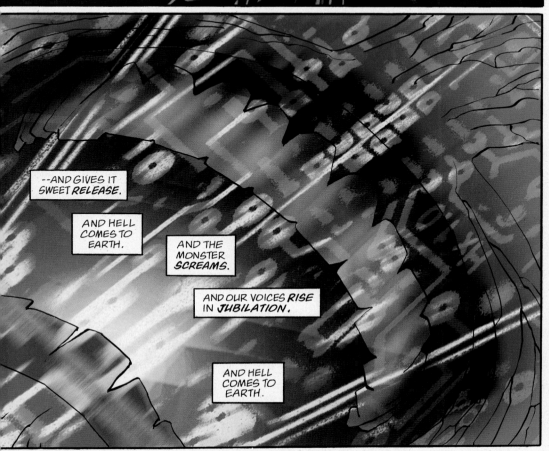

--AND GIVES IT
SWEET *RELEASE.*

AND HELL
COMES TO
EARTH.

AND THE
MONSTER
SCREAMS.

AND OUR VOICES *RISE*
IN *JUBILATION.*

AND HELL
COMES TO
EARTH.

THINGS GET VERY BAD. VERY FAST.

I'M TEN MINUTES OUT OF METROP-OLIS.

I GET A DIS-TRESS CALL.

FROM THE CAVE.

≥KHOFF≥

≥KHAKK≥

IT'S CARRIE.

BOSS, WE BEEN... WE BEEN--

≥KLAGG≥

GET OUT OF THERE. NOW.

TOO LATE. I LOVE YOU.

INSANE LAUGHTER.

AFTERBURNERS!

DAMN. THERE'S NO TIME.

NO TIME.

NNGG

I'M STILL MINUTES FROM THE CAVE.

MINUTES. TOO DAMN MANY OF THEM.

SHE'LL BE DEAD. SHE'LL BE DEAD.

DO SOMETHING. SOMETHING FAST. FAST.

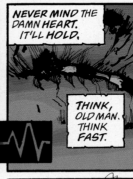

NEVER MIND THE DAMN HEART. IT'LL HOLD.

THINK, OLD MAN. THINK FAST.

YAAA

I'M GONNA DIE.

SATURN GIRL WAS RIGHT.

I CUT HIM--AND I CUT HIM--

--AND HE HEALS BACK UP.

HE CAN'T DIE.

HE CAN'T DIE.

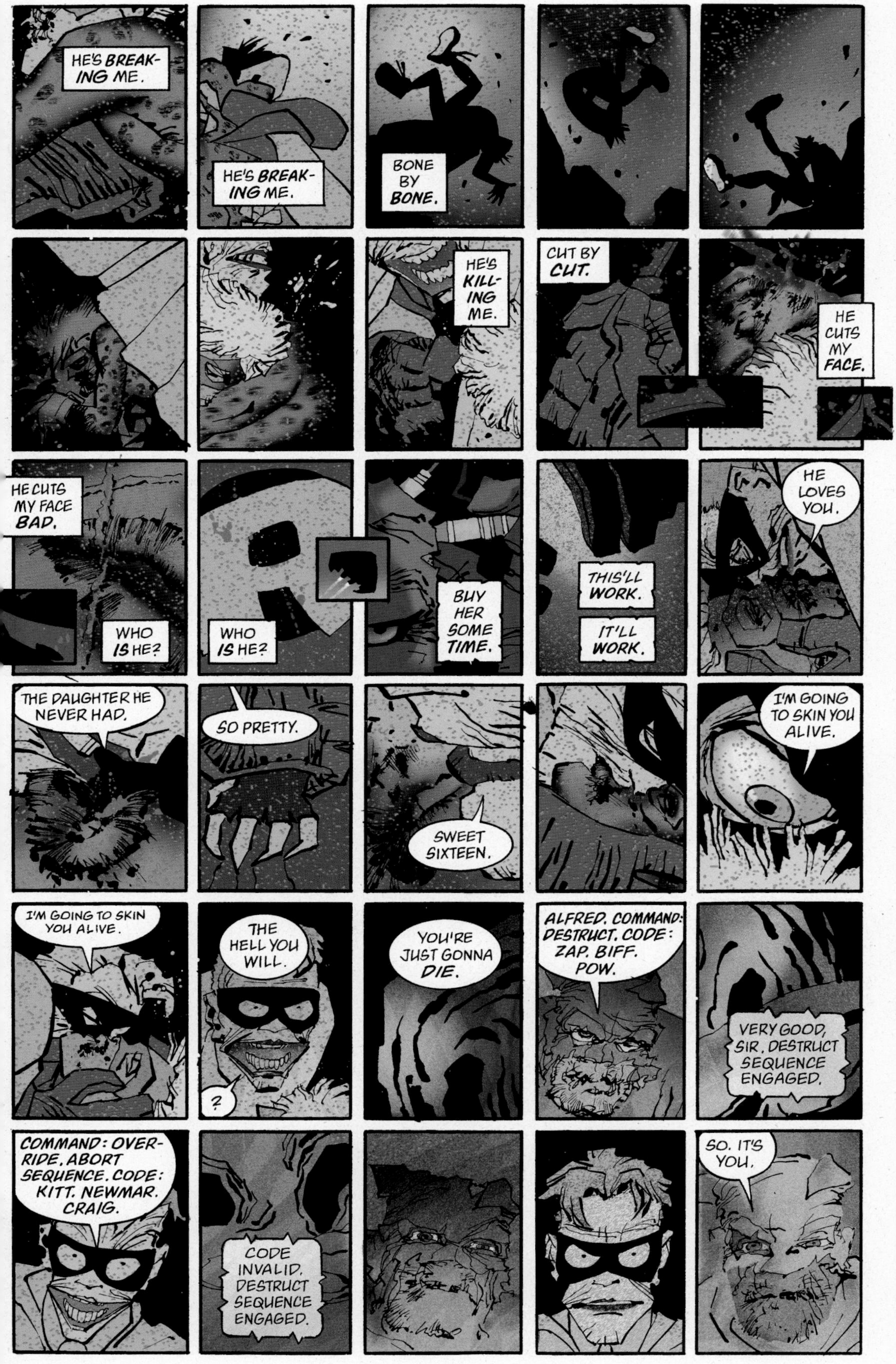
HE'S BREAKING ME.
HE'S BREAKING ME.
BONE BY BONE.
HE'S KILLING ME.
CUT BY CUT.
HE CUTS MY FACE.
HE CUTS MY FACE BAD.
WHO IS HE?
WHO IS HE?
BUY HER SOME TIME.
THIS'LL WORK.
IT'LL WORK.
HE LOVES YOU.
THE DAUGHTER HE NEVER HAD.
SO PRETTY.
SWEET SIXTEEN.
I'M GOING TO SKIN YOU ALIVE.
I'M GOING TO SKIN YOU ALIVE.
THE HELL YOU WILL.
?
YOU'RE JUST GONNA DIE.
ALFRED. COMMAND: DESTRUCT. CODE: ZAP. BIFF. POW.
VERY GOOD, SIR. DESTRUCT SEQUENCE ENGAGED.
COMMAND: OVERRIDE. ABORT SEQUENCE. CODE: KITT. NEWMAR. CRAIG.
CODE INVALID. DESTRUCT SEQUENCE ENGAGED.
SO. IT'S YOU.

I CHANGED THE *ABORT CODE* THE NIGHT I *FIRED* YOU, DICK GRAYSON.

YOU WERE ALWAYS SO DAMN *SMART.*

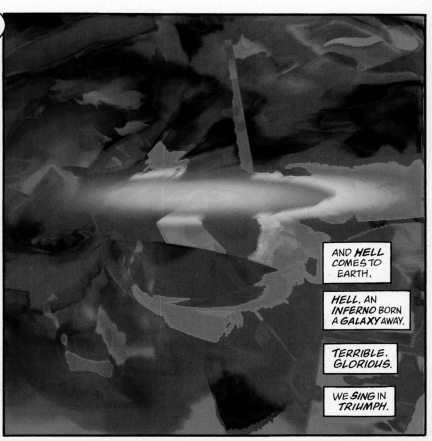

AND *HELL* COMES TO EARTH.

HELL, AN *INFERNO* BORN A *GALAXY* AWAY.

TERRIBLE. GLORIOUS.

WE *SING* IN *TRIUMPH.*

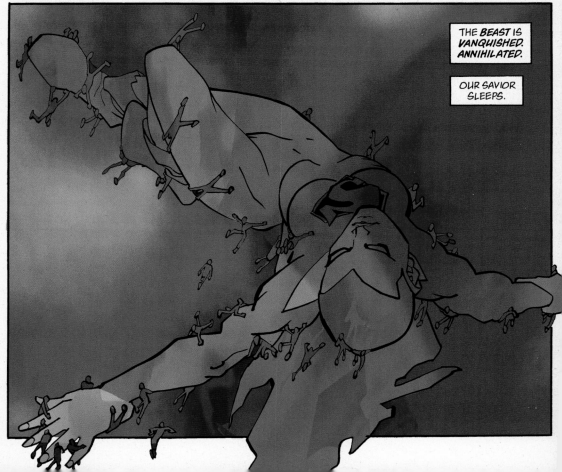

THE *BEAST* IS *VANQUISHED.* ANNIHILATED.

OUR *SAVIOR* SLEEPS.

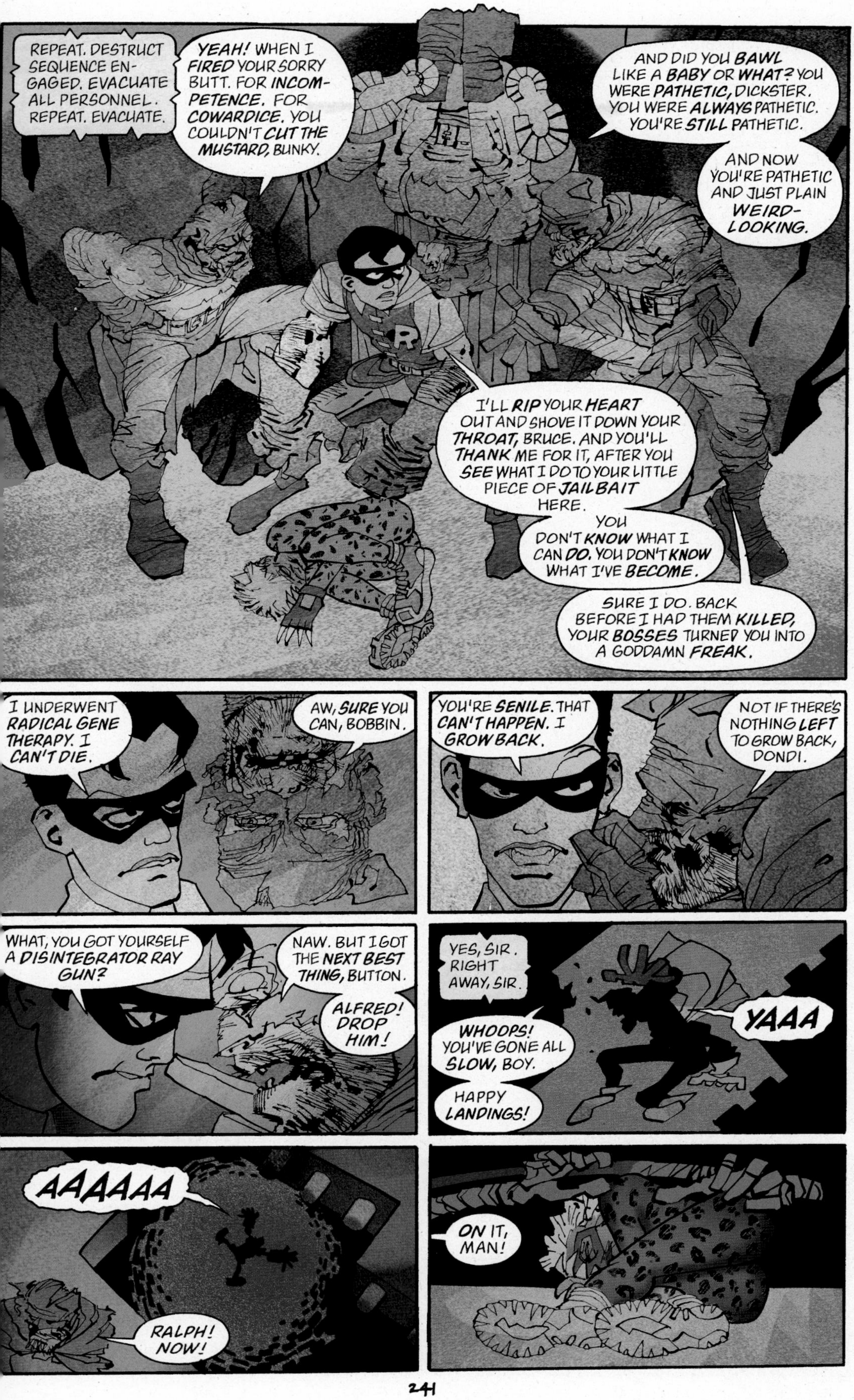
REPEAT. DESTRUCT SEQUENCE EN- GAGED. EVACUATE ALL PERSONNEL. REPEAT. EVACUATE.
YEAH! WHEN I FIRED YOUR SORRY BUTT. FOR INCOM- PETENCE. FOR COWARDICE. YOU COULDN'T CUT THE MUSTARD, BUNKY.
AND DID YOU BAWL LIKE A BABY OR WHAT? YOU WERE PATHETIC, DICKSTER. YOU WERE ALWAYS PATHETIC. YOU'RE STILL PATHETIC.
AND NOW YOU'RE PATHETIC AND JUST PLAIN WEIRD- LOOKING.
I'LL RIP YOUR HEART OUT AND SHOVE IT DOWN YOUR THROAT, BRUCE. AND YOU'LL THANK ME FOR IT, AFTER YOU SEE WHAT I DO TO YOUR LITTLE PIECE OF JAILBAIT HERE.
YOU DON'T KNOW WHAT I CAN DO. YOU DON'T KNOW WHAT I'VE BECOME.
SURE I DO. BACK BEFORE I HAD THEM KILLED, YOUR BOSSES TURNED YOU INTO A GODDAMN FREAK.
I UNDERWENT RADICAL GENE THERAPY. I CAN'T DIE.
AW, SURE YOU CAN, BOBBIN.
YOU'RE SENILE. THAT CAN'T HAPPEN. I GROW BACK.
NOT IF THERE'S NOTHING LEFT TO GROW BACK, DONDI.
WHAT, YOU GOT YOURSELF A DISINTEGRATOR RAY GUN?
NAW. BUT I GOT THE NEXT BEST THING, BUTTON.
ALFRED! DROP HIM!
YES, SIR. RIGHT AWAY, SIR.
YAAA
WHOOPS! YOU'VE GONE ALL SLOW, BOY.
HAPPY LANDINGS!
AAAAAA
RALPH! NOW!
ON IT, MAN!

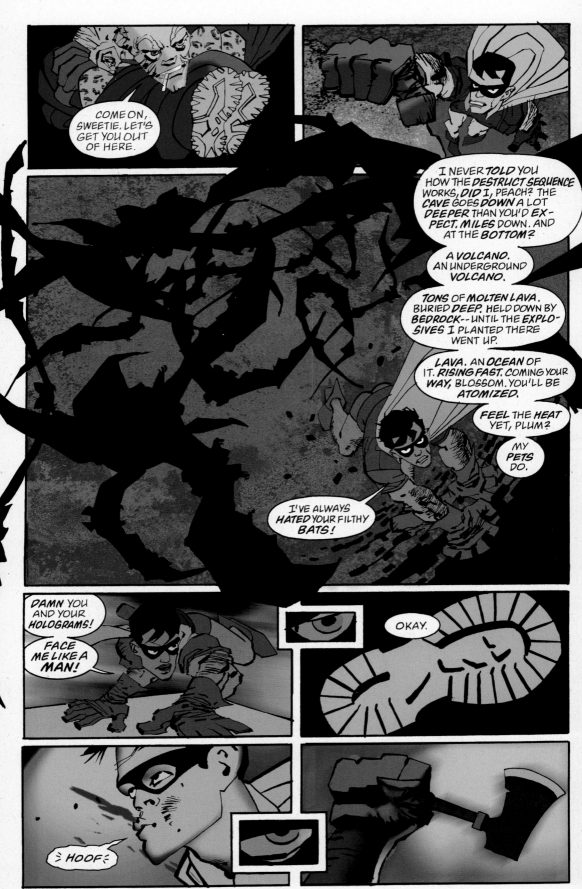

COME ON, SWEETIE. LET'S GET YOU OUT OF HERE.

I NEVER *TOLD* YOU HOW THE *DESTRUCT SEQUENCE* WORKS, *DID I*, PEACH? THE *CAVE* GOES *DOWN* A LOT *DEEPER* THAN YOU'D *EXPECT. MILES* DOWN. AND AT THE *BOTTOM?*

A VOLCANO. AN UNDERGROUND *VOLCANO.*

TONS OF *MOLTEN LAVA.* BURIED *DEEP.* HELD DOWN BY *BEDROCK*-- UNTIL THE *EXPLOSIVES* I PLANTED THERE WENT UP.

LAVA. AN *OCEAN* OF IT. *RISING FAST.* COMING YOUR WAY, BLOSSOM. YOU'LL BE *ATOMIZED.*

FEEL THE *HEAT* YET, PLUM?

MY *PETS* DO.

I'VE ALWAYS *HATED* YOUR FILTHY *BATS!*

DAMN YOU AND YOUR *HOLOGRAMS!*

FACE ME LIKE A *MAN!*

OKAY.

≶ HOOF ≶

242

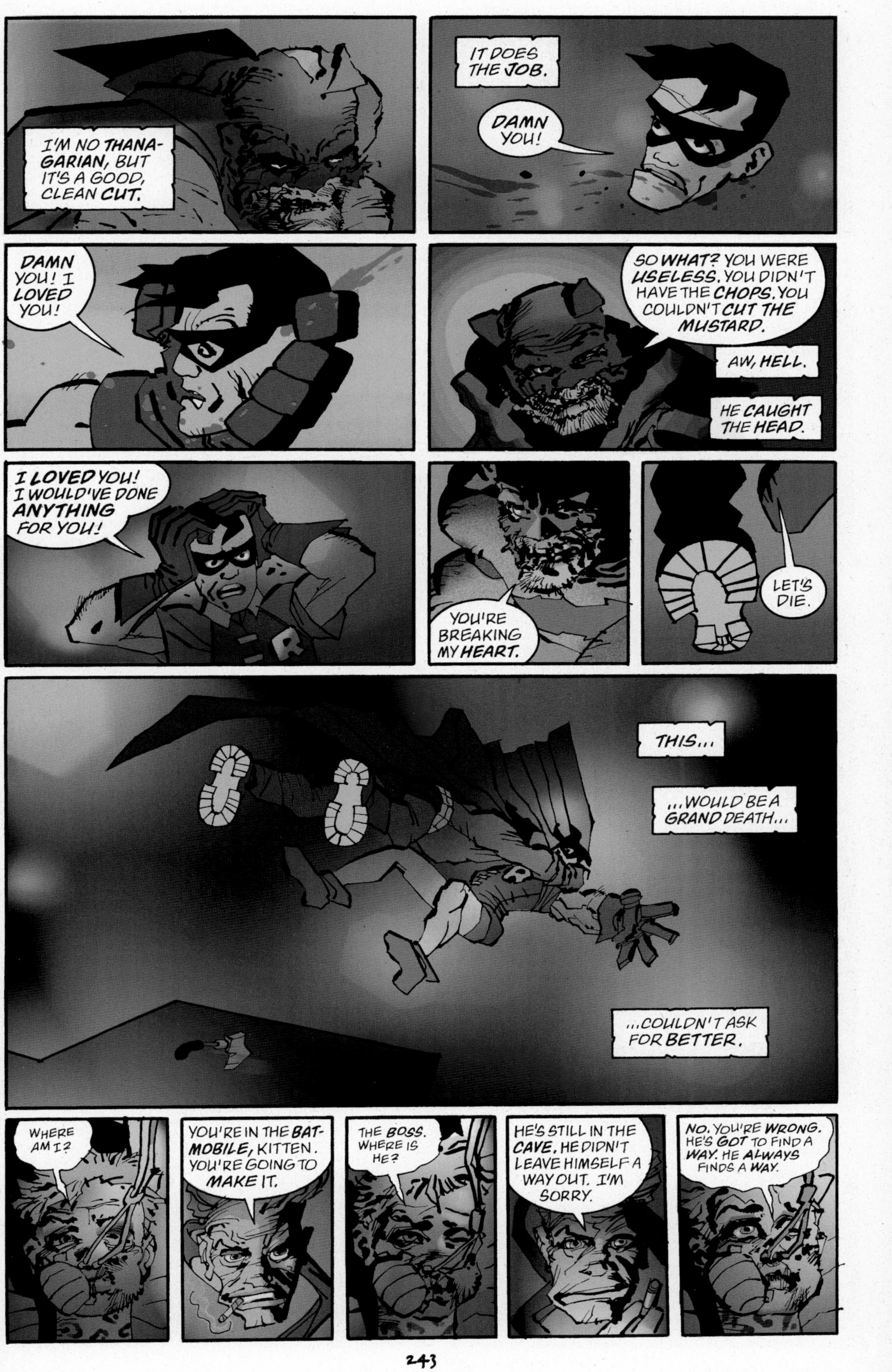

I'M NO THANAGARIAN, BUT IT'S A GOOD, CLEAN CUT.
IT DOES THE JOB.
DAMN YOU!
DAMN YOU! I LOVED YOU!
SO WHAT? YOU WERE USELESS. YOU DIDN'T HAVE THE CHOPS. YOU COULDN'T CUT THE MUSTARD.
AW, HELL.
HE CAUGHT THE HEAD.
I LOVED YOU! I WOULD'VE DONE ANYTHING FOR YOU!
YOU'RE BREAKING MY HEART.
LET'S DIE.
THIS...
...WOULD BE A GRAND DEATH...
...COULDN'T ASK FOR BETTER.
WHERE AM I?
YOU'RE IN THE BATMOBILE, KITTEN. YOU'RE GOING TO MAKE IT.
THE BOSS. WHERE IS HE?
HE'S STILL IN THE CAVE. HE DIDN'T LEAVE HIMSELF A WAY OUT. I'M SORRY.
NO. YOU'RE WRONG. HE'S GOT TO FIND A WAY. HE ALWAYS FINDS A WAY.

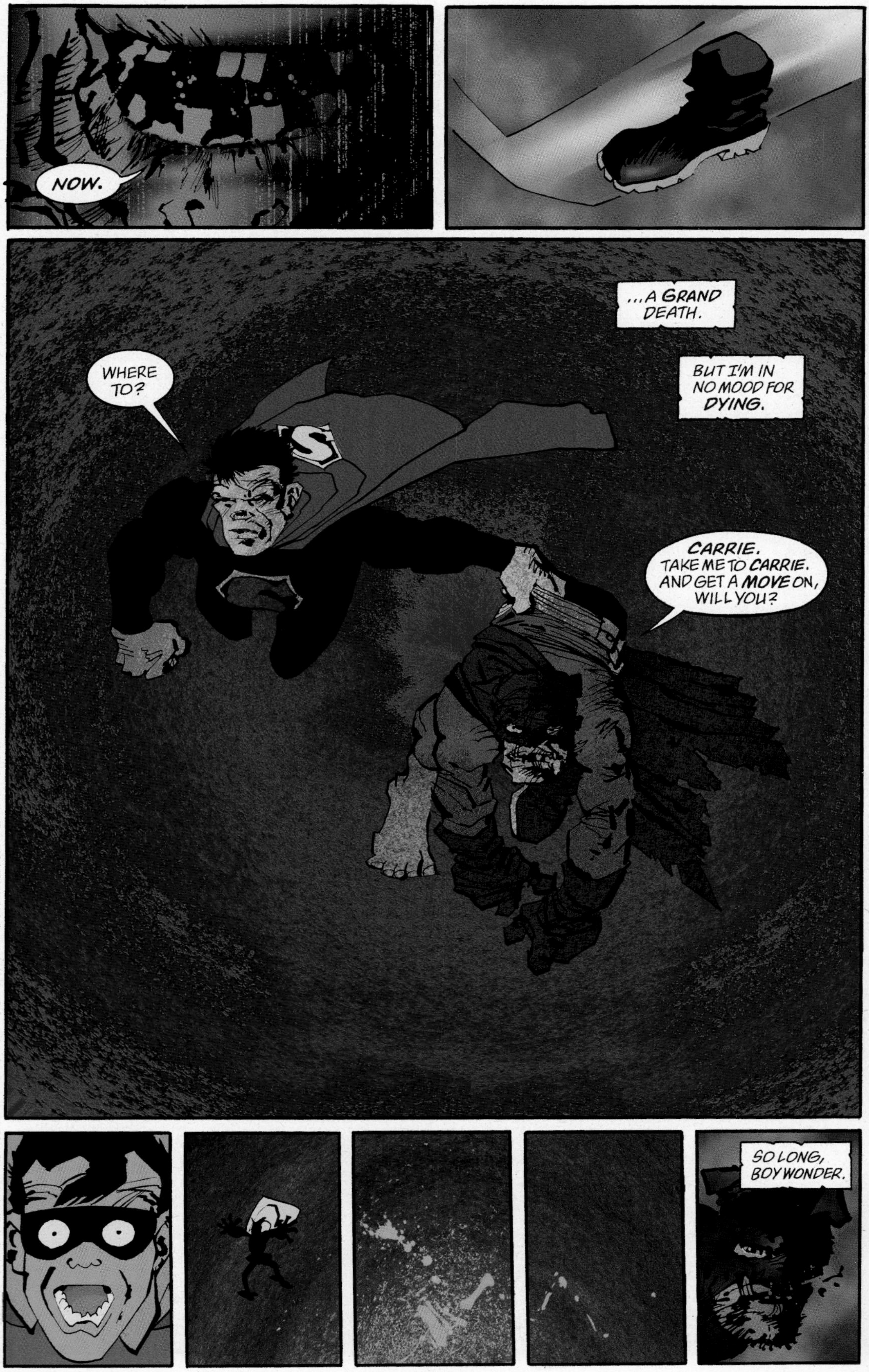
NOW.
...A GRAND DEATH.
BUT I'M IN NO MOOD FOR DYING.
WHERE TO?
CARRIE. TAKE ME TO CARRIE. AND GET A MOVE ON, WILL YOU?
SO LONG, BOY WONDER.

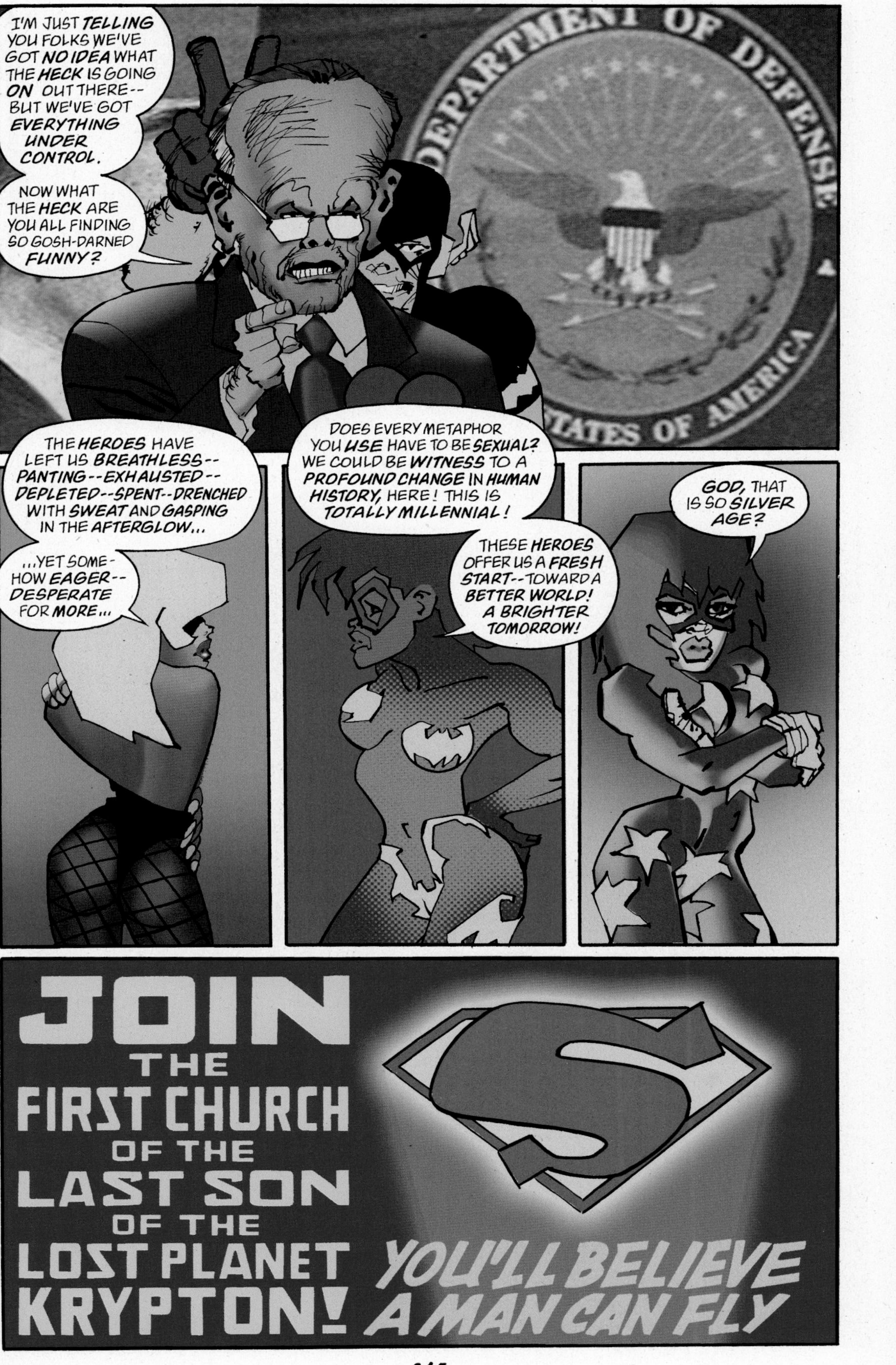
I'M JUST TELLING YOU FOLKS WE'VE GOT NO IDEA WHAT THE HECK IS GOING ON OUT THERE-- BUT WE'VE GOT EVERYTHING UNDER CONTROL.
NOW WHAT THE HECK ARE YOU ALL FINDING SO GOSH-DARNED FUNNY?
DEPARTMENT OF DEFENSE
STATES OF AMERICA
THE HEROES HAVE LEFT US BREATHLESS-- PANTING--EXHAUSTED-- DEPLETED--SPENT--DRENCHED WITH SWEAT AND GASPING IN THE AFTERGLOW...
...YET SOME-HOW EAGER-- DESPERATE FOR MORE...
DOES EVERY METAPHOR YOU USE HAVE TO BE SEXUAL? WE COULD BE WITNESS TO A PROFOUND CHANGE IN HUMAN HISTORY, HERE! THIS IS TOTALLY MILLENNIAL!
THESE HEROES OFFER US A FRESH START--TOWARD A BETTER WORLD! A BRIGHTER TOMORROW!
GOD, THAT IS SO SILVER AGE?
JOIN THE FIRST CHURCH OF THE LAST SON OF THE LOST PLANET KRYPTON!
YOU'LL BELIEVE A MAN CAN FLY

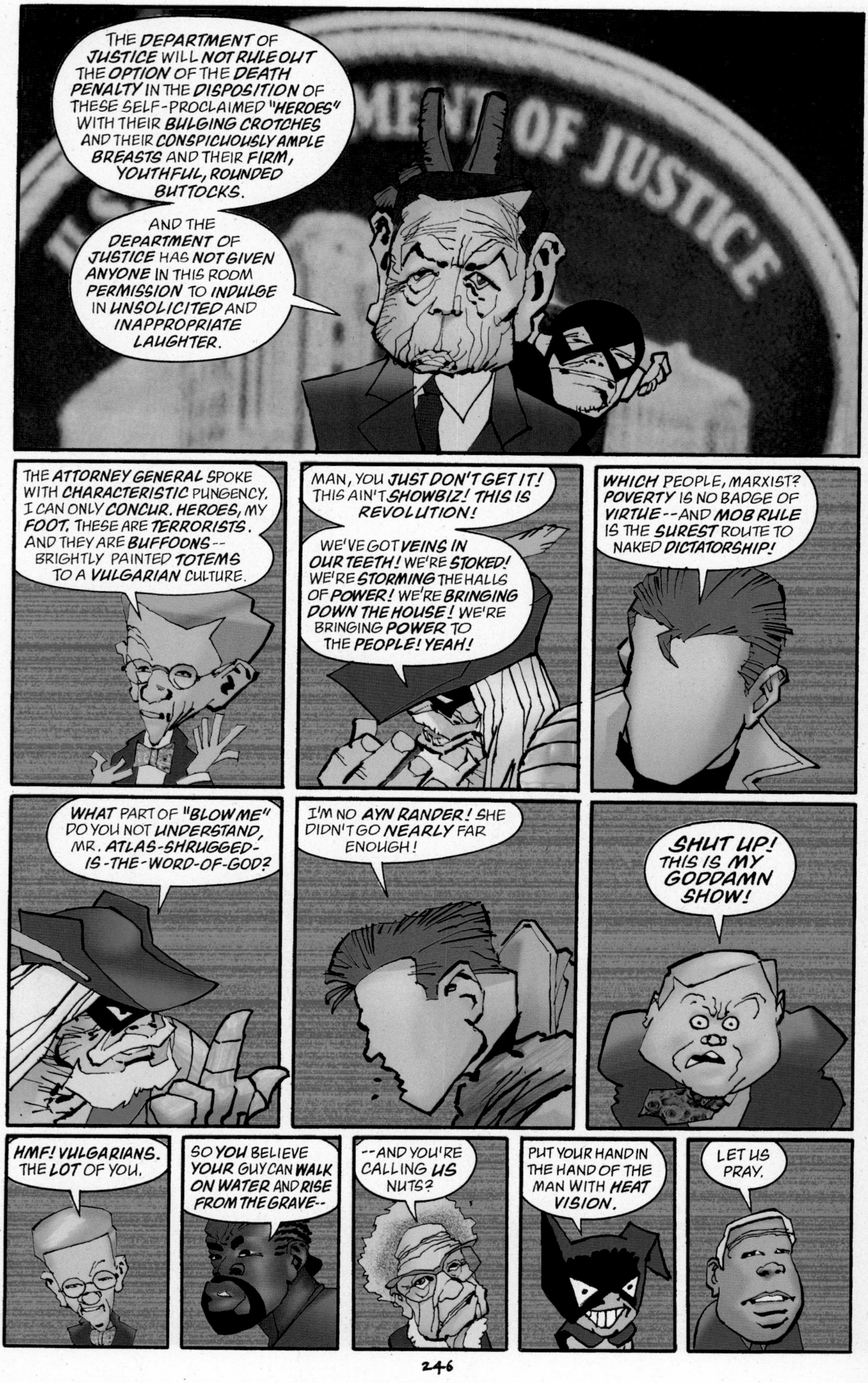
THE DEPARTMENT OF JUSTICE WILL NOT RULE OUT THE OPTION OF THE DEATH PENALTY IN THE DISPOSITION OF THESE SELF-PROCLAIMED "HEROES" WITH THEIR BULGING CROTCHES AND THEIR CONSPICUOUSLY AMPLE BREASTS AND THEIR FIRM, YOUTHFUL, ROUNDED BUTTOCKS.
AND THE DEPARTMENT OF JUSTICE HAS NOT GIVEN ANYONE IN THIS ROOM PERMISSION TO INDULGE IN UNSOLICITED AND INAPPROPRIATE LAUGHTER.
THE ATTORNEY GENERAL SPOKE WITH CHARACTERISTIC PUNGENCY. I CAN ONLY CONCUR. HEROES, MY FOOT. THESE ARE TERRORISTS. AND THEY ARE BUFFOONS-- BRIGHTLY PAINTED TOTEMS TO A VULGARIAN CULTURE.
MAN, YOU JUST DON'T GET IT! THIS AIN'T SHOWBIZ! THIS IS REVOLUTION!
WE'VE GOT VEINS IN OUR TEETH! WE'RE STOKED! WE'RE STORMING THE HALLS OF POWER! WE'RE BRINGING DOWN THE HOUSE! WE'RE BRINGING POWER TO THE PEOPLE! YEAH!
WHICH PEOPLE, MARXIST? POVERTY IS NO BADGE OF VIRTUE--AND MOB RULE IS THE SUREST ROUTE TO NAKED DICTATORSHIP!
WHAT PART OF "BLOW ME" DO YOU NOT UNDERSTAND, MR. ATLAS-SHRUGGED-IS-THE-WORD-OF-GOD?
I'M NO AYN RANDER! SHE DIDN'T GO NEARLY FAR ENOUGH!
SHUT UP! THIS IS MY GODDAMN SHOW!
HMF! VULGARIANS. THE LOT OF YOU.
SO YOU BELIEVE YOUR GUY CAN WALK ON WATER AND RISE FROM THE GRAVE--
--AND YOU'RE CALLING US NUTS?
PUT YOUR HAND IN THE HAND OF THE MAN WITH HEAT VISION.
LET US PRAY.

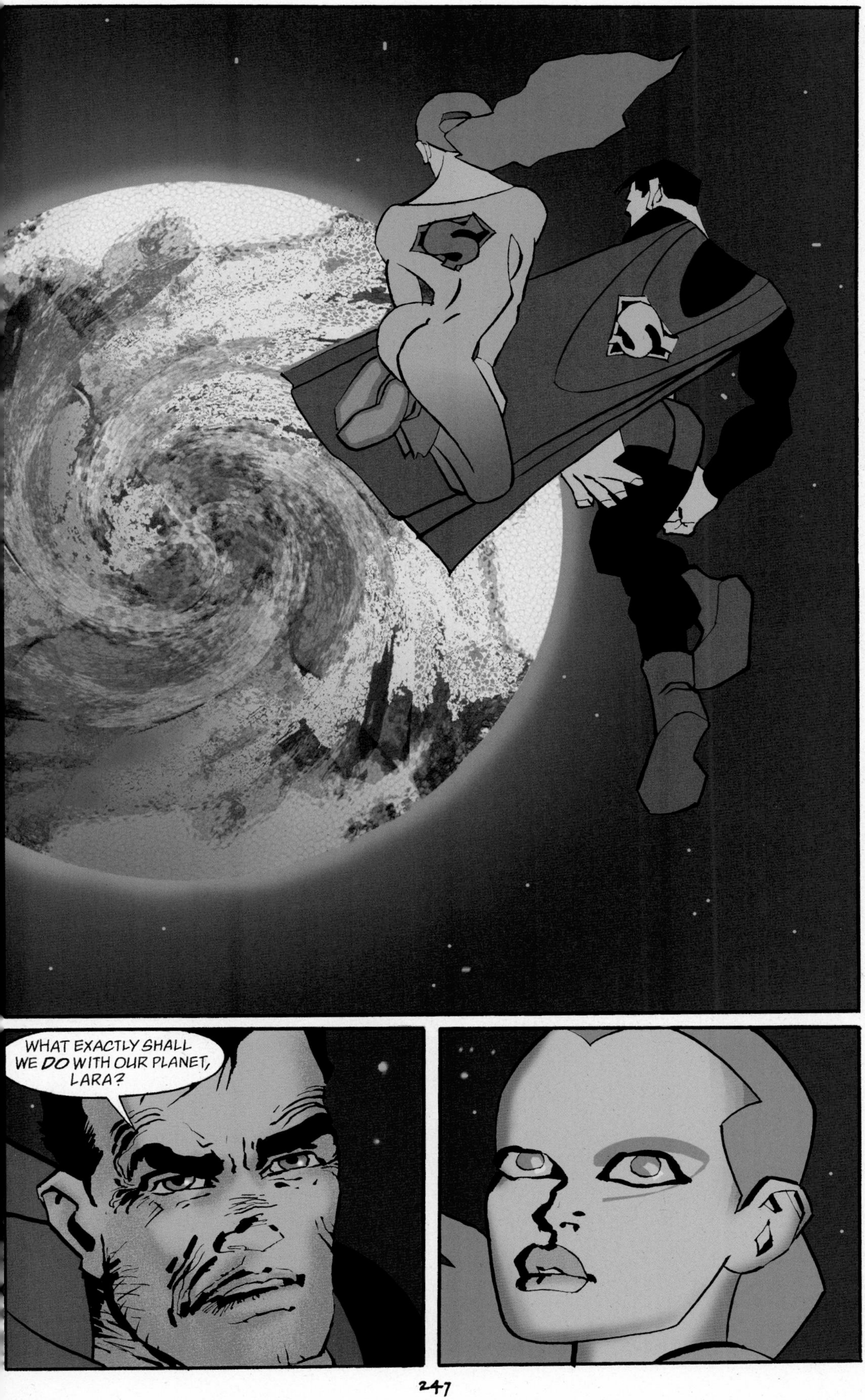
WHAT EXACTLY SHALL WE DO WITH OUR PLANET, LARA?

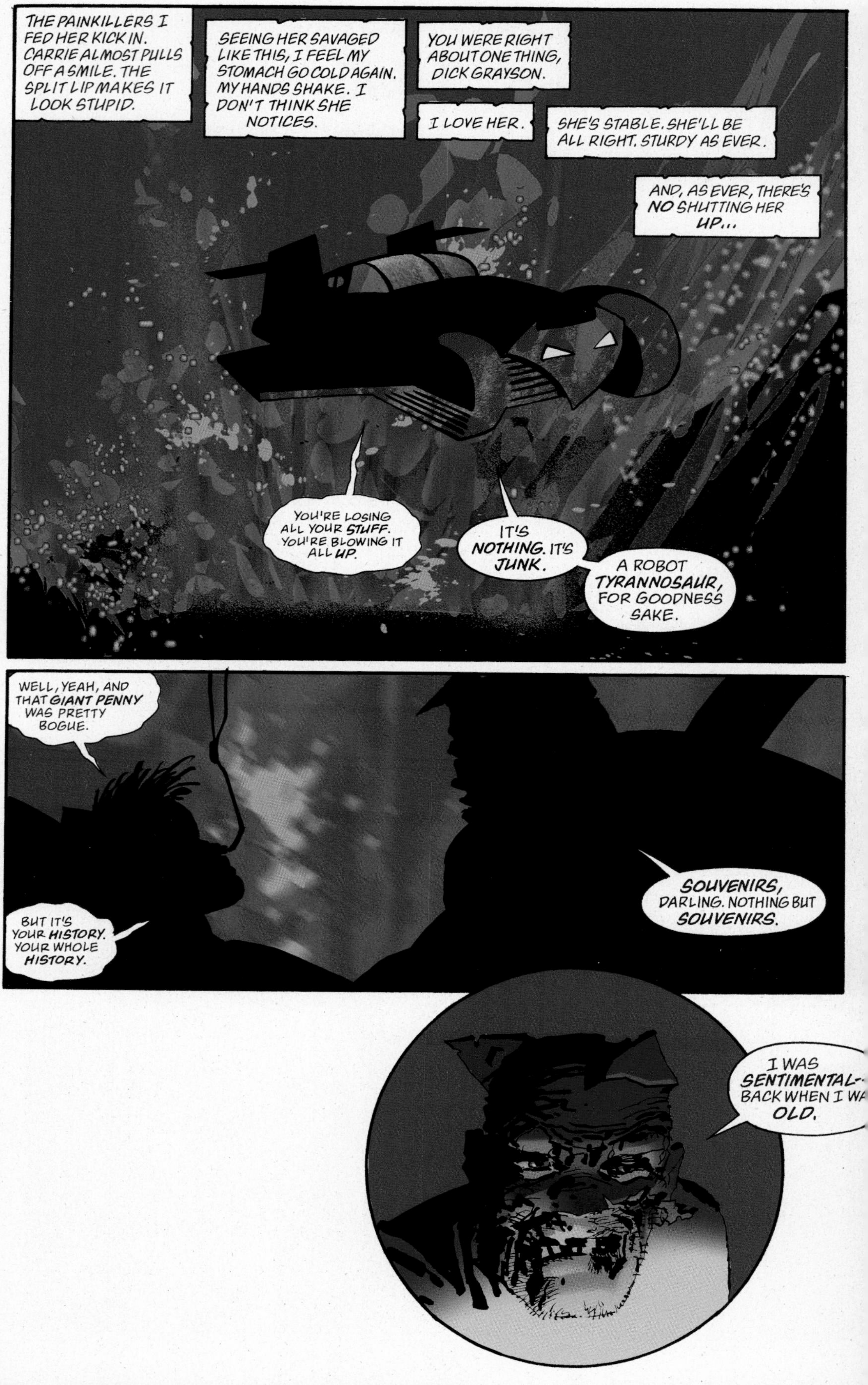
THE PAINKILLERS I FED HER KICK IN. CARRIE ALMOST PULLS OFF A SMILE. THE SPLIT LIP MAKES IT LOOK STUPID.
SEEING HER SAVAGED LIKE THIS, I FEEL MY STOMACH GO COLD AGAIN. MY HANDS SHAKE. I DON'T THINK SHE NOTICES.
YOU WERE RIGHT ABOUT ONE THING, DICK GRAYSON.
I LOVE HER.
SHE'S STABLE. SHE'LL BE ALL RIGHT. STURDY AS EVER.
AND, AS EVER, THERE'S NO SHUTTING HER UP...
YOU'RE LOSING ALL YOUR STUFF. YOU'RE BLOWING IT ALL UP.
IT'S NOTHING. IT'S JUNK.
A ROBOT TYRANNOSAUR, FOR GOODNESS SAKE.
WELL, YEAH, AND THAT GIANT PENNY WAS PRETTY BOGUE.
BUT IT'S YOUR HISTORY. YOUR WHOLE HISTORY.
SOUVENIRS, DARLING. NOTHING BUT SOUVENIRS.
I WAS SENTIMENTAL-- BACK WHEN I WA OLD.

☐ SHOT FOR COLOR
☐ SHOT FOR CODE

TITLE:
ISSUE/MONTH:

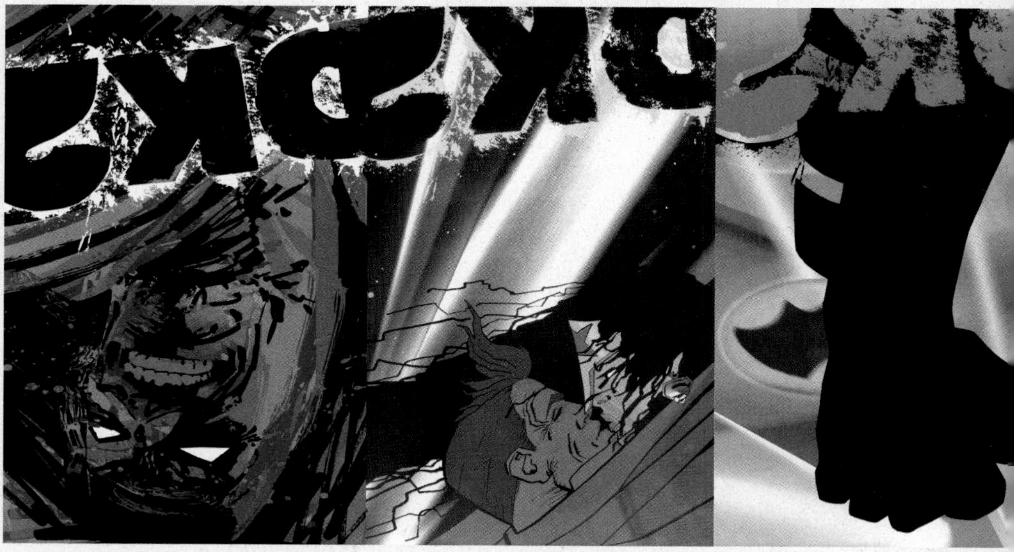
DK2

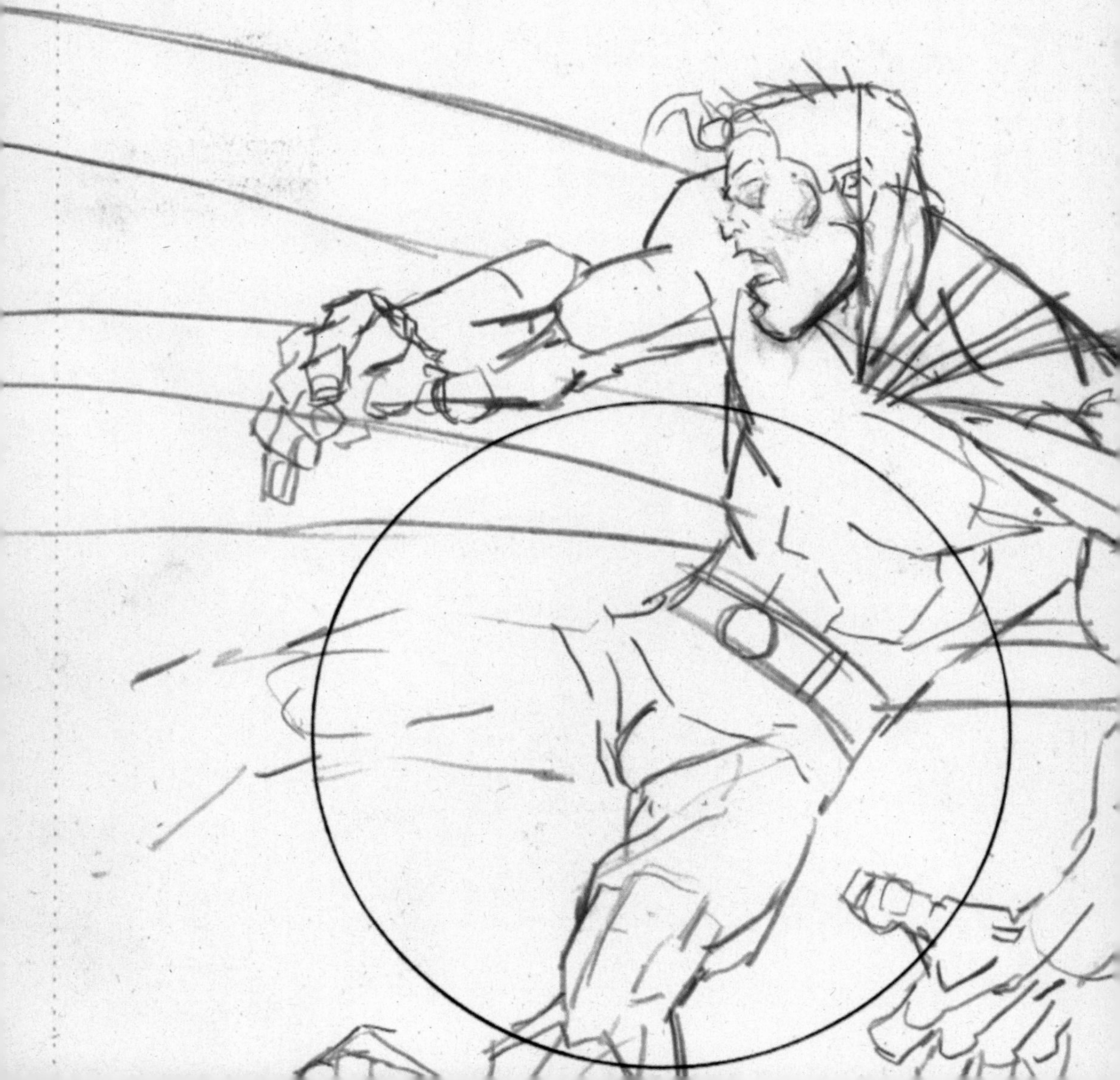

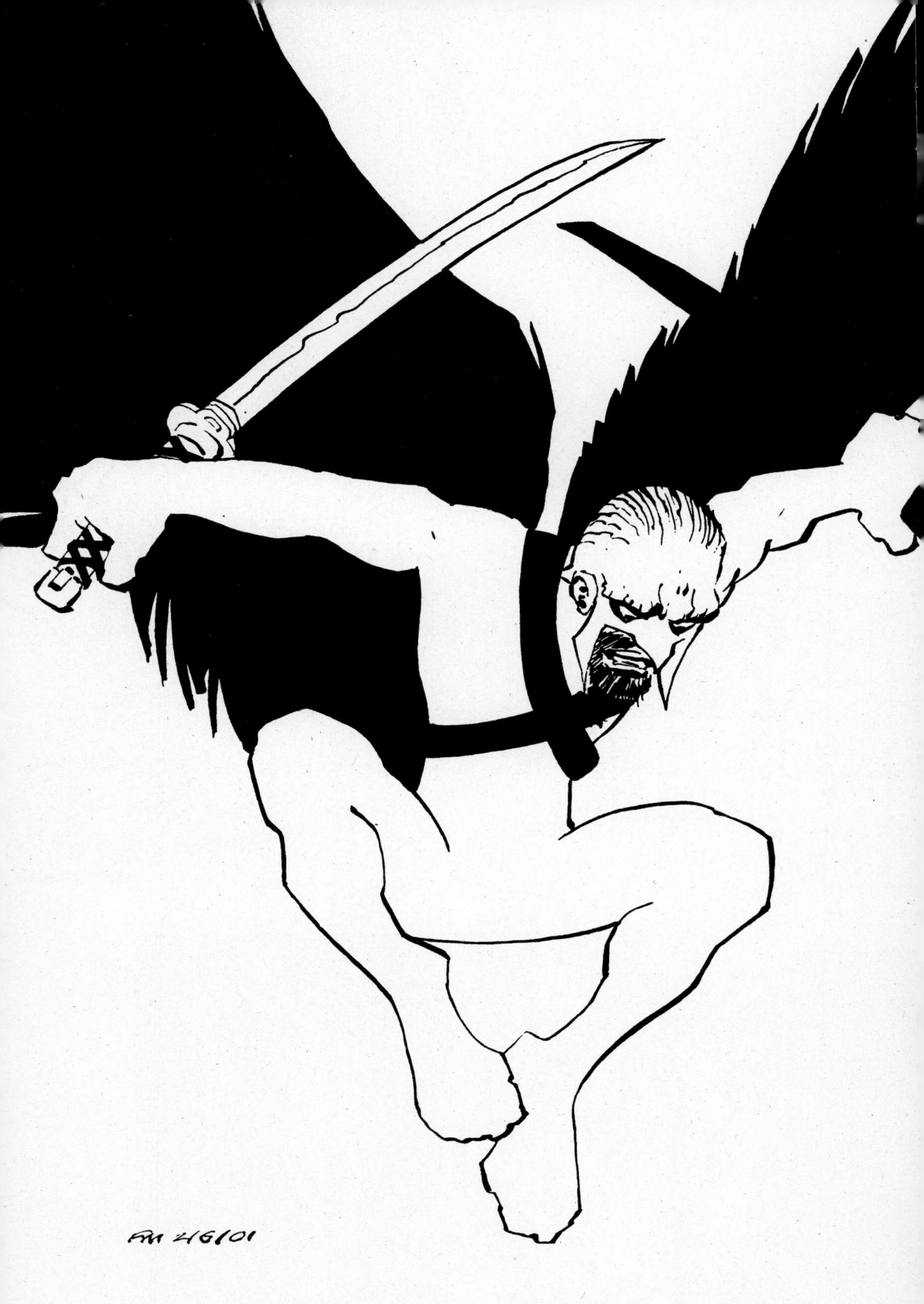
FM 4/6/01

SKETCHBOOK.

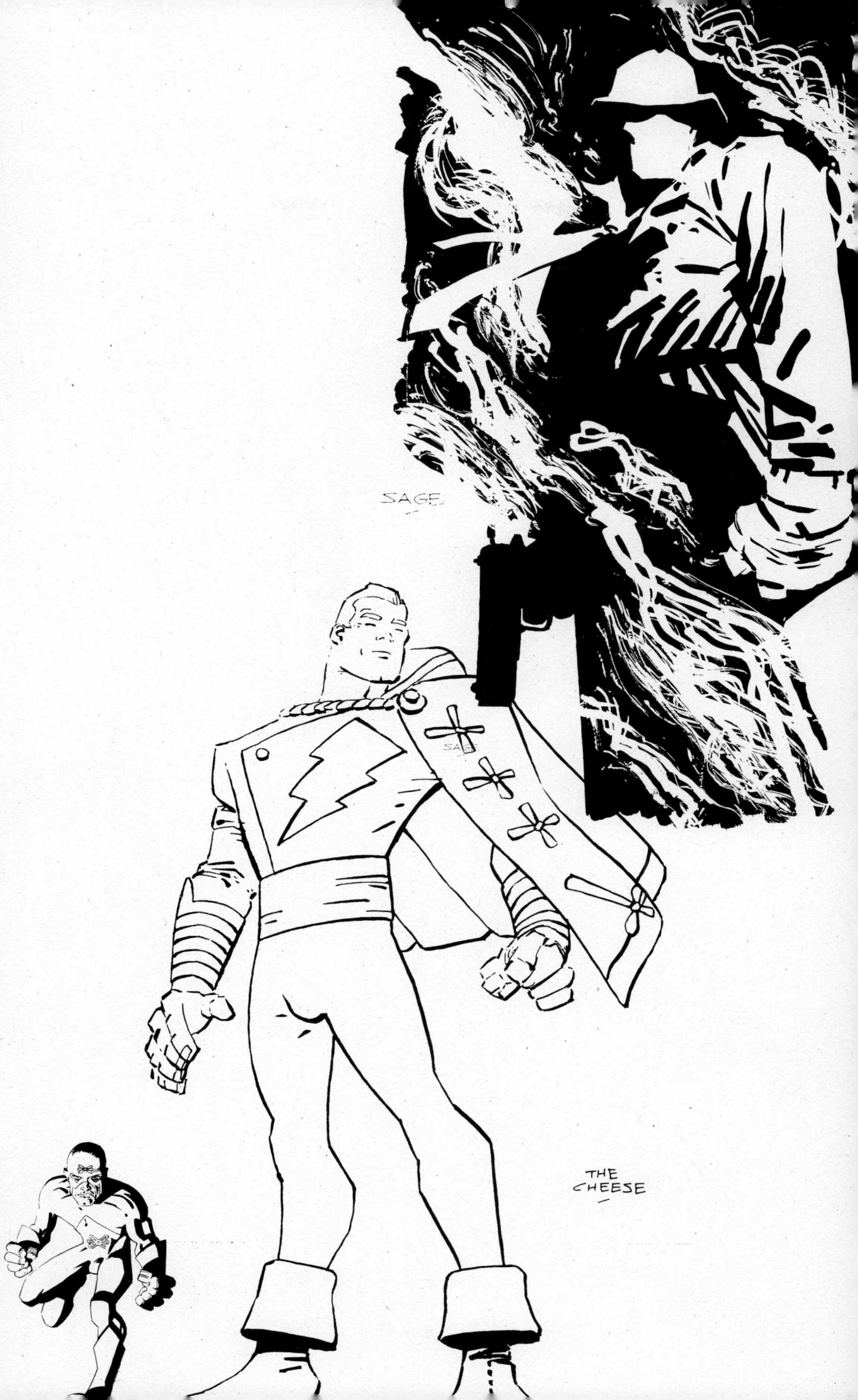
SAGE
THE CHEESE

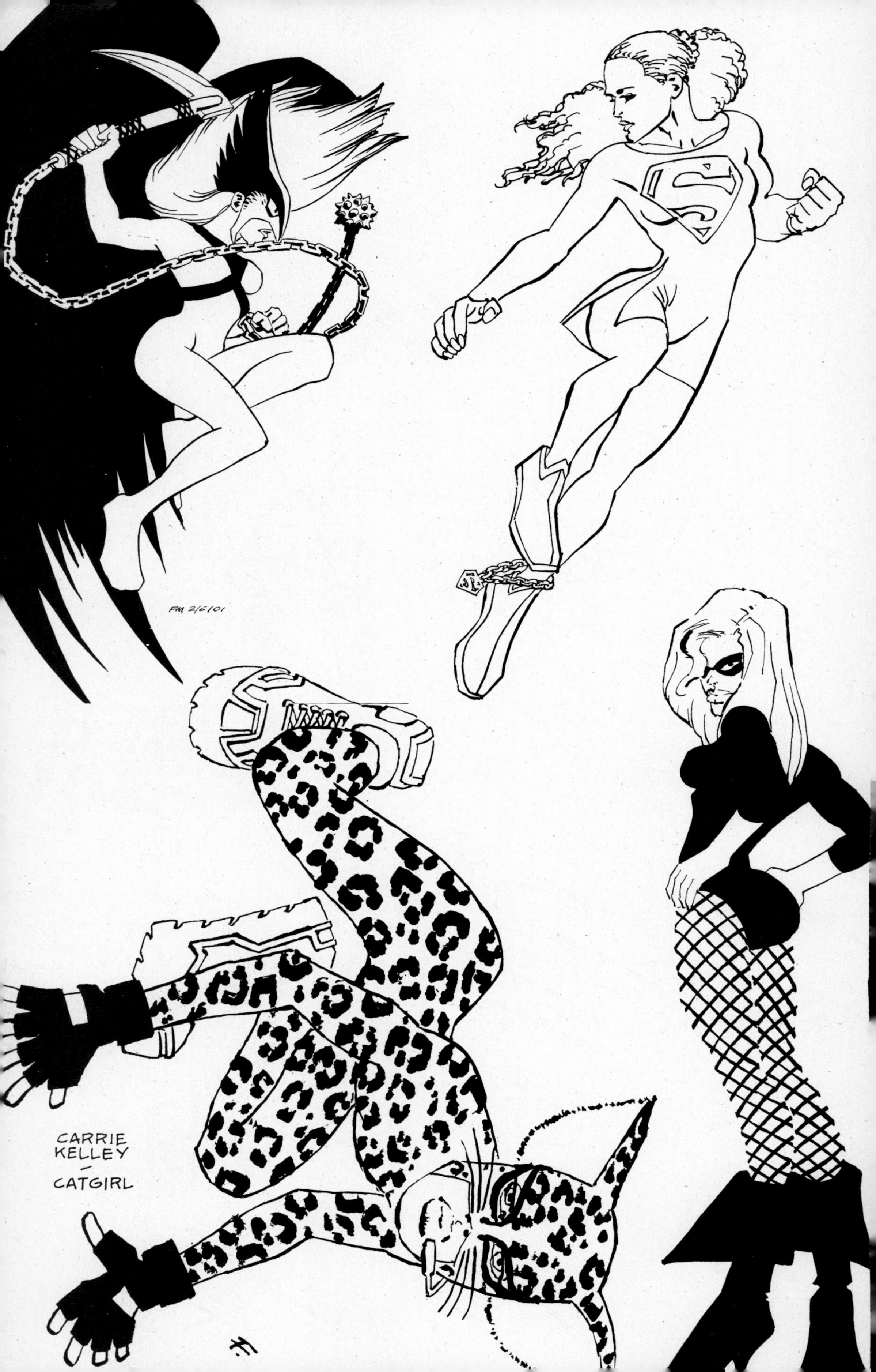
FM 2/6/01
CARRIE
KELLEY
—
CATGIRL
F.

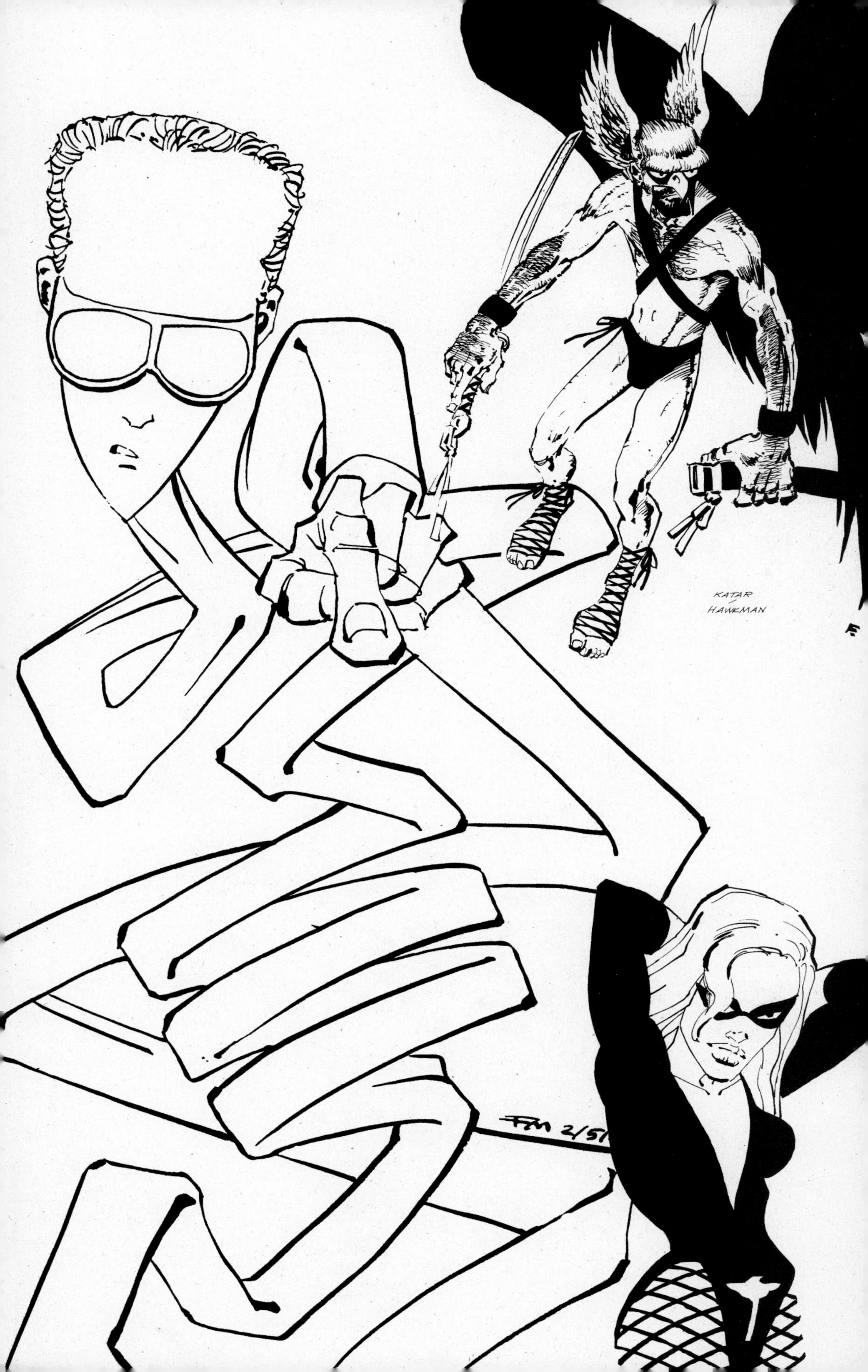
KATAR / HAWKMAN

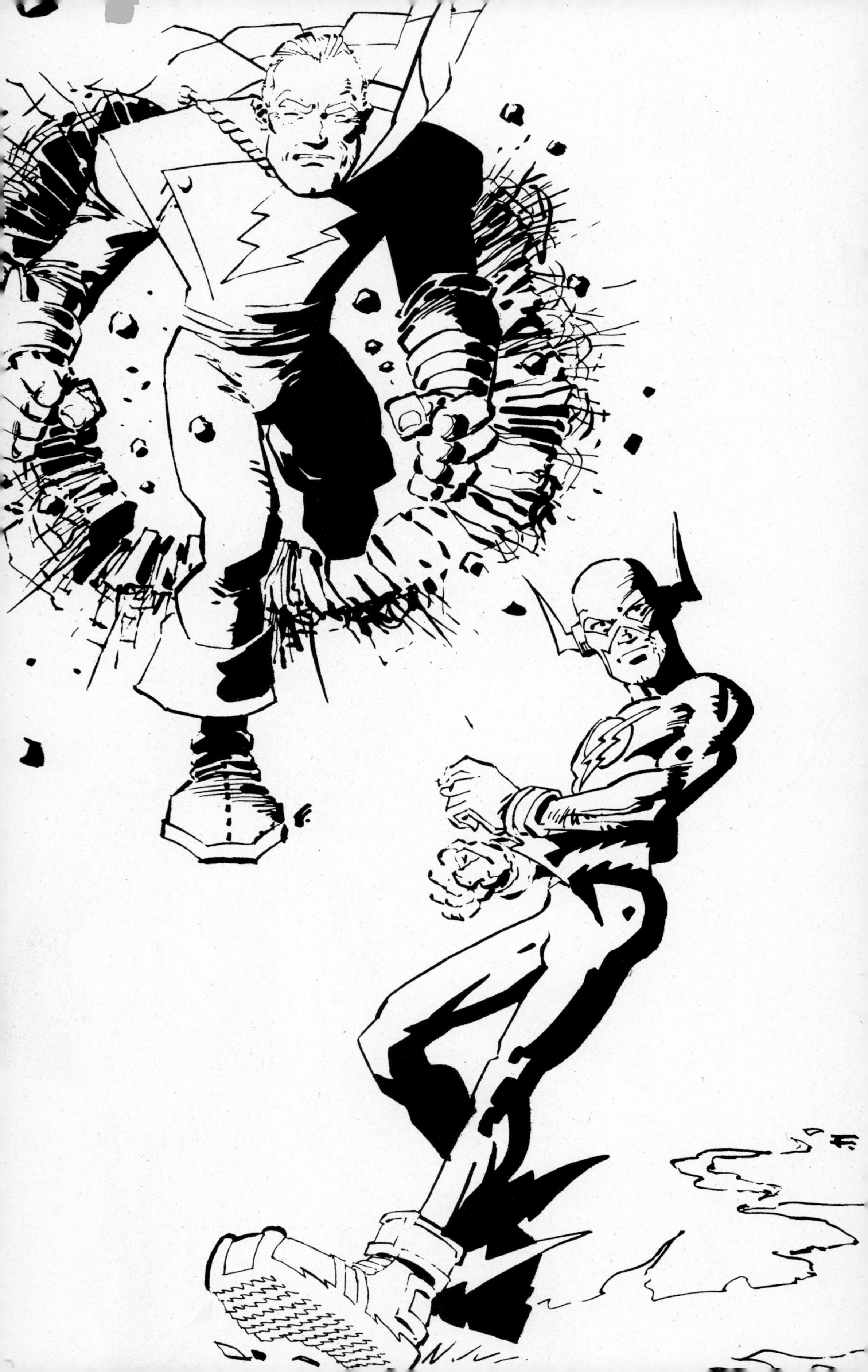

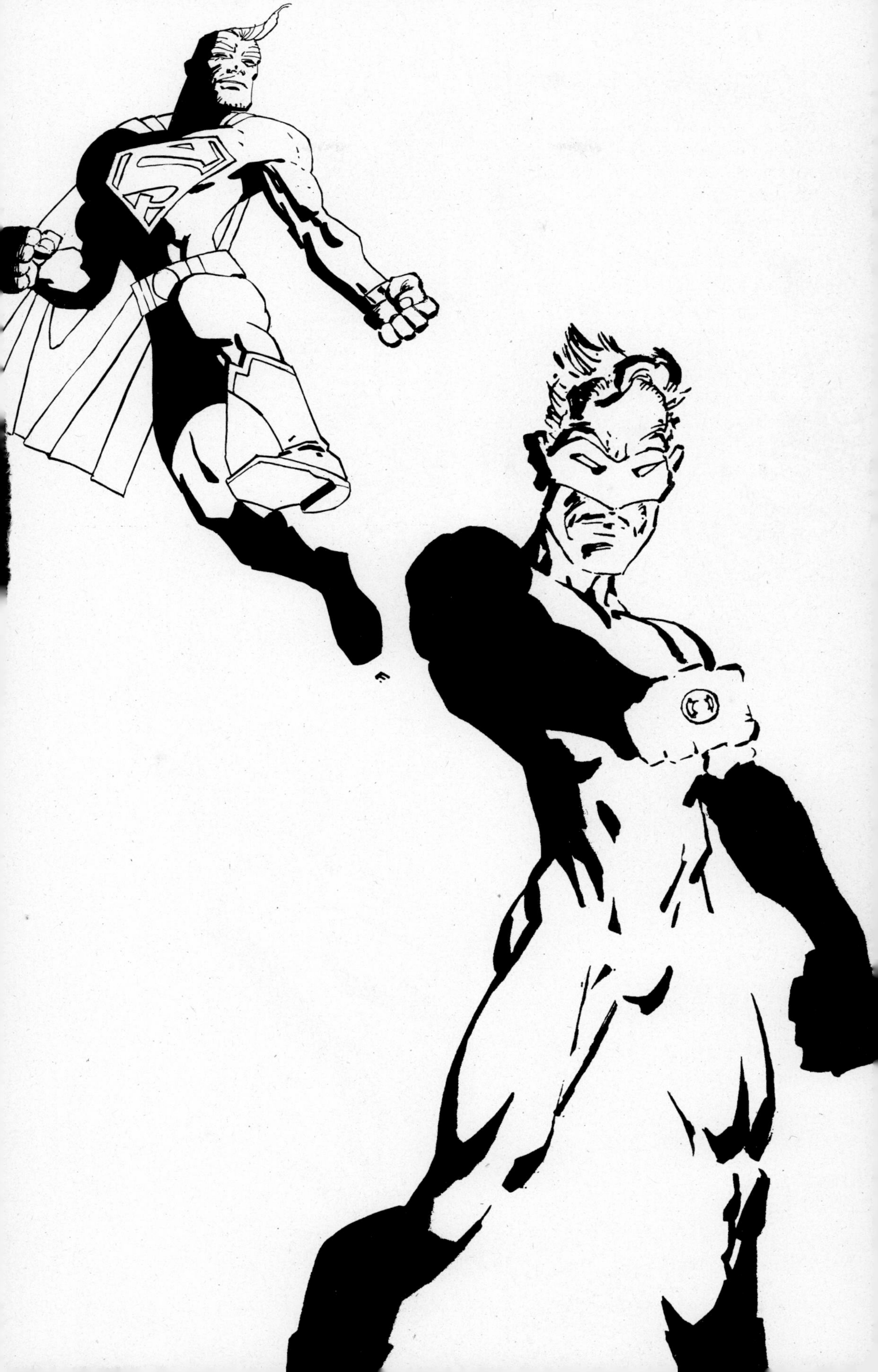

ALSO BY FRANK MILLER:

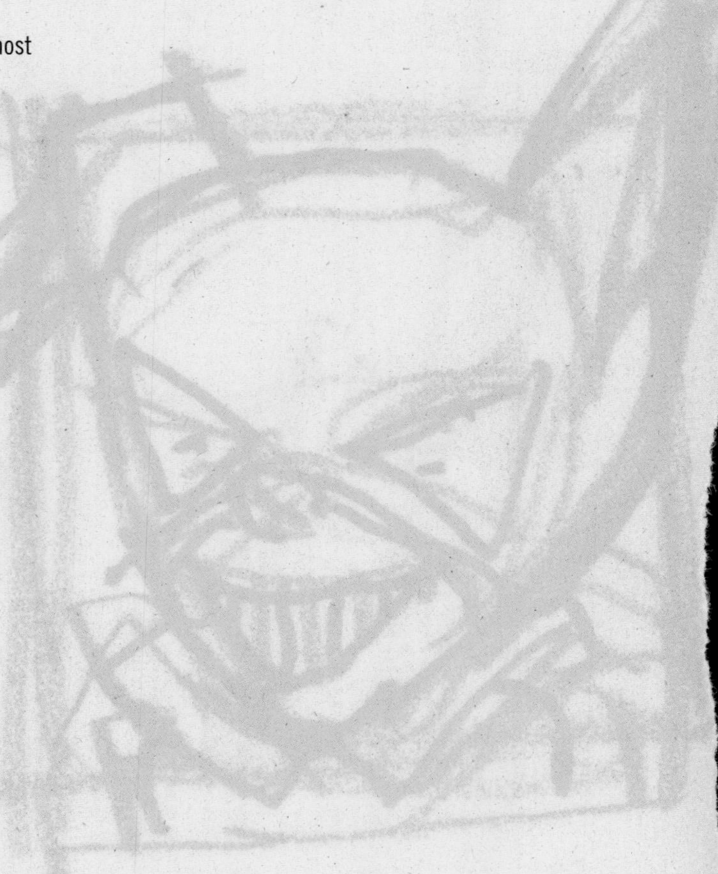

BATMAN: THE DARK KNIGHT RETURNS
(W) Miller (A) Miller/Janson/Varley
The original classic — and one of DC's most
acclaimed, groundbreaking stories — is the
tale of a tortured hero's efforts to save a city
in chaos after nearly a decade's absence.
Frank Miller's epic is storytelling perfection.

BATMAN: YEAR ONE
(W) Miller (A) Mazzucchelli (C) Lewis
Frank Miller's dramatic look at Batman's
first year of crimefighting is the master
storyteller at his finest. The origin of
Gotham City's Dark Knight, who he
is, and how he came to be
is accentuated by David
Mazzucchelli's moody,
distinctive artwork.

RONIN
(W/A) Miller (C) Varley
In this collection of Miller's classic 6-issue
miniseries (which Miller describes as a
"super-hero, science fiction, samurai
drama, urban nightmare,
gothic romance"), a 13th-century
warrior is reborn in the 21st century
to battle a demonic foe.

MORE EXCITING COLLECTIONS FROM DC COMICS!

BATMAN: ARKHAM ASYLUM
(W) G. Morrison (A) McKean

BATMAN: THE LONG HALLOWEEN
(W) Loeb (A) Sale

BIZARRO COMICS
(W/A) Various

CRISIS ON INFINITE EARTHS
(W) Wolfman (A) Pérez/Ordway/Giordano

GREEN ARROW: QUIVER
 (W) K. Smith (A) Hester/Parks

JLA: EARTH 2
(W) G. Morrison (A) Quitely

KINGDOM COME
(W) Waid (A) A. Ross

WATCHMEN
(W) A. Moore (A) Gibbons

FOR THE NEAREST COMICS SHOP CARRYING COLLECTED EDITIONS AND MONTHLY TITLES FROM DC COMICS, CALL 1-888-COMIC BOOK.